# THE COLLECTED PAPERS

OF

# JOHN BASSETT MOORE

IN SEVEN VOLUMES

## VI

NEW HAVEN

YALE UNIVERSITY PRESS

LONDON · HUMPHREY MILFORD · OXFORD UNIVERSITY PRESS

1944

# CONTENTS

## VOLUME SIX

### 1924

### 1925

### 1926

### 1927

### 1928

### 1929

# CONTENTS

# PAPERS OF JOHN BASSETT MOORE

## INTERNATIONAL LAW AND SOME CURRENT ILLUSIONS

### AND OTHER ESSAYS[1]

### INTRODUCTION

THE immediate object of the publication of the present volume, and particularly of the paper which gives to it its distinctive title, is to contribute something towards the restoration of that sanity of thinking and legal and historical perspective which the recent so-called World War has so seriously disturbed. All wars tend, in proportion to their duration, extent and intensity, to unsettle existing conditions and subvert accepted beliefs. This is one of the necessary results of that intense preoccupation with immediate exigencies which war necessarily entails.

Heretofore this disturbing influence has been distinctly perceived and taken into account in estimating the effect of war on previously established rules, but it seems to have been reserved for the present time and for certain environments to accept the view that the international law of the future is to be found in the infringement of its rules committed under the stress of war.

It is an ancient legal maxim that in the midst of arms the laws are silent—*inter arma silent leges*. In its origin, this was a maxim not of international law but of municipal law, public and private. It simply means that, under the stress of a contest by force, when men are struggling with arms in their hands for mastery, violations of law are bound to occur because the means of securing the observance of law are reduced to a minimum. When, in the early days of the civil war in the United States, the administration was charged with infringements of the Constitution, an elated Senator retorted that he approved the administration's acts in precise proportion to their violation of that fundamental law. But it was not surmised that the Constitution had perished, nor did it cease to

1. Published by The Macmillan Company, New York, 1924.

exercise a guiding and restraining power. We do not instinctively look for the exact observance of law between firing lines, where the benevolent duty to live and let live is superseded by the desperate alternative to kill or be killed. Nevertheless, it has not been supposed that, because in the din and struggle of war the laws might for a time be little heard and respected, the law as it previously stood had perished, and that the law of the future was to be found in what was most recently done in war, no matter how flagrant the disregard of prior conceptions of right, justice and humanity might be.

Grotius has been called the founder of international law. In a sense this title may not be justified, since he had his precursors. International law, or the law of nations, had been the subject of treatises before his day. But the immortal preeminence he enjoys is due to the fact that, uniting an extraordinary knowledge of the past with a prophetic vision of the future, he raised his voice in behalf of the law at a time when it seemed to be completely prostrate. When Grotius published his celebrated treatise, *De Jure Belli ac Pacis,* the Thirty Years' War was in the full tide of its destructive progress. Massacre, pillage and famine marked its course. Neither age nor sex was spared, and there was a consummate exhibition of the practical obliteration of the distinction between combatants and non-combatants. Against this brutal infatuation Grotius protested. The distinction between combatants and non-combatants is the vital principle of the modern law of war.

So say the famous General Orders No. 100, of April 24, 1863, for the government of its armies of the United States in the field, which significantly declare that, "as civilization has advanced during the last centuries, so has likewise steadily advanced, especially in war on land, the distinction between the private individual belonging to a hostile country and the hostile country itself, with its men in arms"; and that "the principle has been more and more acknowledged that the unarmed citizen is to be spared in person, property, and honor as much as the exigencies of war will admit." [1]

The preservation of this distinction was the very object and foundation of the action of the Washington Conference on the Limitation of Armament in dealing with gas warfare and submarines. In the committee report signed by General Pershing, recommending the abolition of chemical warfare, one of the two reasons given for the recommendation was the fact that

---

1. Instructions for the Government of Armies of the United States in the Field, General Orders, No. 100, April 24, 1863, War of the Rebellion, Official Records, 3d series, III, 150.

the use of poisonous gases "is fraught with the gravest danger to non-combatants and demoralizes the better instincts of humanity." [2]

No less precise is the report made to the conference by the General Board of the Navy. This report, which is signed by Admiral Rodgers as chairman of the board, adopted as its major premise the declaration that the two principles of warfare, "that unnecessary suffering in the destruction of combatants should be avoided" and "that innocent non-combatants should not be destroyed," had been "accepted by the civilized world for more than one hundred years"; and, in view of the jeopardy to which these principles were exposed by the use of various kinds of gases, the board expressed the opinion that it would be "sound policy to prohibit gas warfare in every form and against every objective." [3]

And yet there are those who tell us that, as the result of the recent war, the distinction between combatants and non-combatants has perished; or that, if it has not wholly disappeared, it must be considered as having practically succumbed, because the combatant class will in future be held to include not only those who bear arms but all who are in any way able to contribute to the national resources. This phase of thought is illustrated by a recent publisher's circular, which recommends a book on the ground that it teaches that various conditions which developed in the course of the Great War will materially modify the law of war; that one of the first that "will be modified, or even abolished, is that which distinguishes between combatants and non-combatants"; and that, in future wars, "the only non-combatants will be those who are physically unable to contribute anything to the national resources," this being, it is said, "the inevitable result of organizing a whole nation for war."

The supposed novelty of organizing a whole nation for war is dealt with in the first essay of the present volume, under the title "International Law and Some Current Illusions." On the other hand, the appalling forecast that in future wars the hard-won but long-established distinction between combatants and non-combatants will be virtually abandoned, has already been discredited by the Washington Conference, so far as the united action of governments in time of peace can do it; and in this

2. Proceedings of the Conference on the Limitation of Armament, Washington, November 12, 1921, February 6, 1922, p. 734.
3. Report of the General Board of the Navy, presented by Rear Admiral W. L. Rodgers, Chairman: Proceedings of the Conference on the Limitation of Armament, Washington, 1921–22, pp. 734–736.

respect the acts of the Washington Conference are not exceptional.

It may safely be assumed that, even among those who apprehend that the distinction between combatants and non-combatants will be abandoned, no one will be found to deny that this would, for the very reasons by which the prediction is explained, necessarily signify a reversion to conditions abhorrent to every man who cares for law, or for those elementary considerations of humanity the observance of which law is intended to assure. Indeed, so disastrous would the consequences of the concession prove to be, that its hasty sponsors may fairly be asked to reconsider the question of its legitimacy. It is hard to believe that the world is prepared to concede that, in the "next war," the first and legitimate measure of the belligerent forces will be to bomb or otherwise destroy producers of food-stuffs and other contributory classes heretofore considered as non-combatant; and yet, if the distinction between combatants and non-combatants has ceased to exist, such a measure would be legally justified and strategically correct. Napoleon said that armies move on their bellies. No one contributes more to this essential military gesture than the grower of grain; no one contributes more essentially to the national resources. This is true today and always has been true. As men must live in order to fight, their physical sustentation is obviously a primary military necessity; and, if the supply of food is a combatant activity, evidently the most dangerous fighter is the tiller of the soil. It is, however, gratifying to reflect upon the fact that there is not a single government today that is either accepting or supporting such a theory. There is, I venture to say, no government that would feel that it could espouse such a conception and face the general condemnation that would follow. Why, then, should those who profess to speak for international law foreshadow the surrender of the world to a contrary view? None render a higher or more solemn service than do those who point out infractions of the established law and warn their fellow-men of the consequences of its impairment.

While the abolition of the distinction between combatants and non-combatants, whether by its outright abandonment or by the indefinite expansion of the combatant category, would stalk the way to indiscriminate destruction of life and property, the question also has a vital relation to the conduct of commerce in time of war, especially as affecting the rights of neutrals. During and after the recent war there were many utterances betokening the belief that the world had entered into a new realm of fact as well as of imagination. Among these was the statement that there would be no more neutrals. This forecast may fairly be said to have perished with its utterance. But, even had it been verified, the question of commercial rights in time of war would hardly have disappeared unless the nations of the world had forborne, or agreed to forbear, to trade with countries at war. At the present moment there is no evidence that such a condition of things is likely to arise; and meanwhile the question of contraband of war, which forms the subject of our second chapter, will continue to be of capital importance, not only as affecting commerce, but as affecting the possibility or probability of the extension of wars to nations not originally involved in them.

The paper on international arbitration contains the substance of an address made ten years ago; but the address had not lost any of its relevancy by reason of the lapse of time. Conceivably, the conditions which it portrayed are even more serious today than they were formerly. John Stuart Mill was wont to insist that there could be no difference between theory and practice, and that, if they diverged, either the theory or the practice must be unsound. But, judging by what is said and what is done in respect of international arbitration, we perhaps might be justified in thinking either that Mill's rule has few followers, or that international arbitration forms an exception to it. Although there are few who oppose international arbitration in theory, yet the scope of its operation has by no means been so much enlarged during the past twenty years as is popularly imagined. When I stated, in 1914, that, so far as concerned the United States, the practice of arbitration was not then so far advanced as it was a hundred and twenty-four years before, I gave precise proof of the correctness of the statement. This condition has not changed.

With a view to promote the judicial settlement of international disputes, there has lately been established the Permanent Court of International Justice, whose seat, like that of the Permanent Court of Arbitration, is at The Hague. The Permanent Court of International Justice has been opened to all nations, but they are not all parties to it and contributors to its support. Among those that have not adhered is the United States. President Harding and President Coolidge have recommended our adhesion. The eventual action of the government hangs in suspense. The subject is one of general interest, without regard to the attitude of any particular government; and, with a view to the information of the public, a chapter on the constitution of the Court and the work it has done has been included in the present volume. The informative value of this chapter is greatly enhanced by the printing with it of the Court's organic Statute, together with the Rules of Procedure.

In the winter of 1922–23 an International Conference was held at The Hague for the purpose of making rules to regulate the uses of aircraft and of radio in time of war. In this conference six governments were represented: namely, the United States of America, the British Empire, France, Italy, Japan and the Netherlands. The conference consisted of a commission of jurists composed of civilian delegates of each of the designated governments, and a number of military and naval experts.

The various branches worked together in harmony and with singleness of purpose; but it is only proper to state that, if the civilians had sought to act upon the supposition that the distinction between combatants and non-combatants no longer existed, they would immediately have found themselves at hopeless variance with their military and naval advisers. No voice came from any quarter in favor of the use of aircraft for purposes of indiscriminate destruction. On the contrary, the entire work of the conference proceeded upon the unchallenged assumption that the distinction between combatants and noncombatants continued to exist, in full force and unimpaired; and, as is shown in our chapter on the subject, with which the full English text of the Commission's reasoned report is printed and made accessible, the rules that were adopted were specifically designed to assure the observance of that distinction.

While I have placed constant stress on this particular point because it is fundamental, I feel obliged to say that there are also other well-defined and heretofore unquestioned rules which the present propensity to drift in the uncharted eddies of current speculation tends to put in jeopardy. There is need all along the line of a recurrence to fundamental principles; and, when I speak of recurring to principles, I include the task of endeavoring to comprehend both the reasons on which they rest and the great facts of human experience from which they are derived. To a certain extent, a vague notion appears to prevail that the measure and test of law is to be found in the shifting sands of philosophical fancies which are subject to the inroads of each recurring tide. The law undoubtedly contains an element of speculation, but, as has been profoundly observed, the great source of law is human experience.[4] Law is supposed to incorporate, not the exaggerated or disproportionate impressions freshly created by isolated events, but the mature, condensed expression of the cumulative results of long observation of human activities and needs. As an element in legal dis-

4. Holmes, *The Common Law*, p. 1. See, also, Cardozo, *The Nature of the Judicial Process*, p. 32.

cussion, philosophy, when it parts company with this source of wisdom, is only too prone to be but the expression of moods that reflect the turbulence or the tranquillity of the time. The attempt to substitute for a rule the supposed reason of the rule should also be sparingly indulged. Thus, when writers, for example, in discussing jurisdiction over the marginal sea, speak of the "cannon-shot rule" instead of the "marine league," one cannot avoid an uncomfortable feeling that the substitution of the reason of the rule for the rule itself would unloose the world from its moorings, and substitute confusion and conflict for certainty.

The essay entitled "Law and Organization," like that on international arbitration, incorporates the substance of an address made ten years ago; but, while I have found nothing in the address to change, I have added explanations for the purpose of elucidating certain phases the definite discussion of which the circumstance and limitations of the original occasion rendered impossible. It may be superfluous to remark that the subject of organizing the world for the purpose of making and enforcing law is as difficult and perplexing as it is ambitious. Being highly speculative, it readily lends itself to the formulation of proposals. Without essaying to add to the number of those already in circulation, I have ventured to present some of the problems the existence or seriousness of which is often overlooked.

The address entitled "The Passion for Uniformity" is republished in the present volume not only because it discusses certain phases of international law, but also because it strongly emphasized, ten years ago, the importance of adopting measures to remedy the chaotic legal conditions which even then notoriously existed in the United States. The confusion continued rapidly to grow; and the increasing dissatisfaction with it eventually led to the organization at Washington, on February 23, 1923, of the American Law Institute, whose objects, as stated in the by-laws, are "to promote the clarification and simplification of the law and its better adaptation to social needs, to secure the better administration of justice, and to encourage and carry on scholarly and scientific legal work." By a gift of the Carnegie Corporation, the Institute, whose main task is usually described as that of "the restatement of the law," is assured of an income of $110,000 a year for nearly ten years. The work of the Institute has already begun, with the cooperation of men of recognized competency. So far, the reportorial work in each of the various subjects has been largely entrusted to representatives of the law schools of the country.

As a step towards the practical application of the reflections,

set forth in "The Passion for Uniformity," on the relation of
scientific studies to the development and simplification of the
law, I presented to the authorities of Columbia University, in
New York, under date of December 3, 1915, a confidential memorandum, which I had privately printed, entitled "Research
Courses in Comparative Law." I confess that I have never been
in love with the phrase "comparative law," and the thought I
had in mind would in reality have, been more fully expressed by
the word "jurisprudence." But, in view of the recent general
use of the phrase "comparative law," and of the existence of the
inclination, which more or less prevails in the United States, to
suspect that the word "jurisprudence" tends specially to raise
the hopes of those who would expound vague and ephemeral
philosophies at the expense of exact reasoning and legal erudi-
tion, I decided to sacrifice euphonious or linguistic susceptibilities on the altar of public utility.

The memorandum afterwards ceased to be confidential
through the publication of the substance of it, with expressions
of hearty concurrence, by Mr. Harlan F. Stone, then dean of
the School of Law of Columbia University, in his annual report of June 30, 1916. The proposals which the memorandum
contained have never been fully carried out; but the fact that
the recent trend in legal studies and in efforts to improve the
law has generally been in the direction which the proposals indicated, would seem to show that they were not devoid of merit.
At Columbia University, where it was hoped that the plan
might at length become completely operative, great progress
has recently been made, under the auspices of a Law Faculty
Advisory Committee, of which Mr. Frederick C. Hicks, Law
Librarian, is chairman, in building up the law library as a research library for legal scholars as well as a working library
for students. Moreover, the trustees of the University, on May
7, 1923, decided to establish the degree of *Doctor Juris,* or Doctor of Law, for the completion of studies and researches of the
same general character as those required of candidates for the
degree of Doctor of Philosophy. It has been announced that
the candidate for the doctorate in law must, in addition to having obtained a first degree in law, be in residence for one academic year or its equivalent; must pursue such work as the
Faculty prescribes, including study in "history, economics, government, in public law, legal history, or comparative jurisprudence," and must produce a printed dissertation demonstrating
his capacity for legal research and the ability to present the results in satisfactory form. He must, also, before or after submitting his dissertation, pass a general oral examination on the
subjects of his study and investigation.

In the hope that the proposals of 1915 may yet find full fruition, I have ventured to reproduce them, with such additional observations as the lapse of time has rendered necessary, under the title "Suggestions for a School of Jurisprudence."

The volume seems to be fitly concluded with the essay entitled "Relativity." This essay was prepared after the others had been sent to the printer, and without any expectation that it would be published with them. Nevertheless, after it was completed, a survey of its contents served to show that it was intimately related to the earlier discourses; that the currents of thought by which they were pervaded had to a certain extent converged and mingled in it; and that, as a result, it constituted, in a substantial sense, a useful supplement to the previous papers and an interpretation of the philosophy with which they were permeated. It was therefore included in the present collection.

I desire to make my acknowledgments to my friends Edwin M. Borchard, Joseph P. Chamberlain, and Julius Goebel, Jr., for aid on various occasions. To Dr. Goebel, however, I am specially indebted for help in gathering and sifting the statistics of earlier wars, the brief summaries, as they appear in the text, indicating little of the labor and care bestowed upon the examination and comparison of the authorities.

# I

## INTERNATIONAL LAW AND SOME CURRENT ILLUSIONS[1]

IN the Autumn of 1914, three months after the war in Europe burst upon a startled and incredulous world, I ventured, in fulfilment of an engagement of long standing, to make a public address on certain phases of international law, including the arbitration of international disputes. It soon transpired, however, that the times were not propitious for the discussion of such commonplace topics. Before I spoke, a leading citizen asked me whether I intended to announce a plan by which the war would immediately be brought to an end and peace be effectively and permanently assured. Far be it from me to suggest that such an inquiry was beyond the prerogatives of a leading citizen. When that great pioneer and empire-builder, the late James J. Hill, was asked by a representative of the press, soon after the war began, how long it would last, he is reported to have replied, "Young man, you can ask more fool questions in five minutes than I can answer in six months. The war will end when somebody gets licked." Evidently Mr. Hill did not regard his interlocutor as a leading citizen, or he would hardly have answered so brusquely. At any rate, I responded in different terms. But I feel obliged to confess that when, in all humility, I admitted that I had not brought with me any plan for the world's quick transformation, my interlocutor at once lost interest in me.

On the present occasion I hope for better fortune. The war having ended in the ordinary, human way, by the defeat of one of the parties, I count upon a patient hearing, even though I sound no grandiose strain from the nebular regions nor essay to propound a prompt panacea for the world's ills. Recently, on a railway journey, the recollections of childhood were revived by the flare, from signboards and housetops, of the undaunted commendations of certain curatives with which, by advertisement rather than by trial, I had for many years been familiar, and I could not help reflecting upon the fascination which

1. This essay incorporates, with material amplification and revision, an address made at the closing session of the Annual Convocation of the University of the State of New York, at Albany, October 19, 1923.

facile promises of benefit exercise over men's hopes and fears. Addison tells us in his time of a mountebank who cheated the country people by selling them pills which were said to be good for the earthquake. But this was, it must be allowed, a rude and primitive age: for, although it steeped itself in the ancient classics; waxed strong on Dante, Luther and Milton, on Shakespeare and Molière, on Suarez and Bodin; itself produced masterpieces in poetry and in prose, and discovered the Law of Gravitation, it knew not those speed-increasing mechanical devices which have in modern times convinced a nervous, vibrant world of its incontestable preëminence in spiritual elevation, in wisdom and reflection, and in serene self-control. In our own later, more moral, more scientific day, when the popular production and consumption even of peace plans is artificially stimulated, we have a remedy, presumptively most efficacious, advertised as "The Pill That Won the War." Such things no doubt respond to the universal longing for health and happiness, and as they have their counterparts throughout the medley of human activities, I would not dismiss them too lightly. Nevertheless, no matter in what sphere they may be found, whether in the national or the international, I am compelled to deprecate them in so far as their illusory solace tends to deaden the sense of present responsibility, and, by creating false conceptions, to divert attention from the simple, elementary truths the felt recognition of which is essential not only to future progress but to the preservation of what has been gained heretofore.

I have said that the war in Europe in 1914 burst upon a startled and incredulous world; and, if I add that this was not a strange phenomenon, I merely mean that the world then acted as it had always done before. Only by way of illustration, I may mention the incident, otherwise wholly unimportant, that when, at the end of May 1914, two months before the war began, I ventured, in my very limited sphere, publicly to set forth the existence of certain general conditions unfavorable to the preservation of peace, the knowing dispensers of soothing auguries shrewdly intimated that I was a "pessimist." The world is always reluctant to accept disagreeable realities, but, when bewildered by their apparition, it hastily proceeds to exemplify the truth of the proverb that "extremes meet," by demonstrating that even the most opposite misconceptions may have a common spring in the want or perversion of knowledge. So it was in 1914. A hundred years having elapsed since the last of the great struggles that had encompassed the globe, the public, grown unfamiliar with their history, could no longer visualize them. The prevalent impressions of war were formed upon the later and more or less contemporary conflicts, which, though often severe, were comparatively local. It is, therefore, not strange that, although Italy, Spain, the Netherlands, the Scandinavian powers and Turkey, the independent states of America, and the independent countries of the Far East, except Japan, were not among the belligerents, the new war was immediately hailed not only as the greatest, both relatively and positively, of all wars, but as being in an altogether unprecedented sense a "world war." This soon became a fixed habit of thought. But it was only a detail. Incredulity, rudely shocked, turned to credulity, and, the lessons of previous wars being generally unknown, all kinds of hasty suppositions, scudding, like the spoondrift, across the tempestuous seas, found eager and gulping recipients. Nor did propaganda, observing the symptoms, fail to contribute to the information, and, in its more amiable intervals, even to the entertainment of the public. In a state of mind which assures error against detection and falsehood against exposure, no report is too improbable, no theory too extravagant, no hypothesis too unreal for belief.

While, as the history of wars has shown, this psychopathological condition by no means readily disappears, the uncritical suppositions to which it gives rise, welded by constant repetition into the texture of current thought, strongly tend to persist. Of such suppositions, because their mischievous tendency is the greatest, I will mention only two. One is that existing conditions are wholly new; that even human motives, human interests and human ambitions have radically changed; and that, the world having broken with its past, the rules and remedies painfully wrought out by centuries of experiment have become altogether inadequate and indeed obsolete. The second is that rules are made only to be broken, and that, as they will not be observed, it is scarcely worth while to make them at all. By the combined operation of these two conceptions, one destructive and the other despondent, a general disrespect for law, and especially for international law, is created, and, as they thus constitute an evident menace to the future, I propose to examine them.

Prior to the recent great conflict, whose magnitude and momentous importance render exaggeration superfluous, the development of the laws of war, running through a number of centuries, had been in the direction of establishing and extending the following fundamental principles:

1. The observance of the distinction between combatants and non-combatants and the protection of non-combatants against injuries not incidental to military operations against combatants.

2. The protection of property not militarily used or in immediate likelihood of being so used against destruction, not, as writers sometimes seem to fancy, because of humane regard for insensate things, but because of the belief that, in the interest of humanity, war-stricken peoples should not be reduced to a condition of barbarism or savagery, but should, on the contrary, be enabled to resume the normal processes of peaceful life as soon as possible.

3. The abolition, for similar reasons, of the confiscation of private property, except so far as for special reasons it is still permitted at sea.

4. The definite assurance to states, not parties to the conflict, of the right to continue their commerce with one another, and, subject to prescribed limitations, also with the warring powers.

During and since the recent war all these principles, painfully achieved through centuries of conflict, have to a great extent been questioned. This has been done on the supposition that the recent war, in its drafts on the population, the resources and the activities of the countries involved, was unlike any previous war; that, in contributing to the conduct of the war, all work, in a sense unknown before, became war work and all the inhabitants war workers, the unarmed population no less than the military forces; that the distinction between combatants and non-combatants consequently lost its meaning and ceased to be ascertainable; and that, as the recent war is to be taken as the type of future wars, the distinction between combatants and non-combatants and the rules deduced from it, having lost their validity, can no longer be respected.

I do not hesitate to declare this supposition, both in its assumptions of fact and of principle and in its implications, to be as illusory as it is dangerous.

I pronounce it dangerous, because the distinction between combatants and non-combatants is the foundation and the vital source of those limitations on the destruction of life and property with which our boasted civilization is synonymous. I pronounce it illusory, because it proceeds from a misconception not only of the nature and extent of previous wars but also of the grounds on which the unarmed population was classed as non-combatant and protected.

According to the ancient conception of war, all the inhabitants of the states at war, including women and children, were regarded, collectively and individually, as actual enemies, in the sense that they might all be legitimately slaughtered and their property captured and confiscated or destroyed. Thus, the Hebrews were, according to the veracious Record, commanded to slay the women and children of Heshbon, of Canaan, and of other nations whose lands they were commissioned to take,[2] and the Psalmist could exultingly sing: "Blessed shall he be that taketh and dasheth thy little ones against the stones." [3] The Thracians, the Macedonians, and the Romans in numerous instances put women and children to the sword without discrimination, and it is affirmed that the princes who commanded such things "were never esteemed to be of a cruel nature." "Whence it appears," remarks Grotius, how "inhumanity was turned into custom," so that it was "no wonder if old men were also killed." [4]

While citing the ancient authorities as to what was "lawful" in war, Grotius pointed out that the Latin word *licere*, signifying to be lawful, was capable of a double meaning; that it might be understood merely in the sense of an act that was not punishable; that an act might in this sense be lawful, and yet might be inexpedient, or inconsistent with the rules of piety or morality, so that he who refrained from doing it was to be commended.[5] Hence, he maintained that, even in a just war, there were acts which were unjust in themselves and were to be considered as proscribed; and, upon the authority of many passages of Scripture, and the testimony of jurists, philosophers, historians, moralists and warriors, he particularly enjoined the observance of the limitations of the right to kill, and the abstention from anything that might result in "the destruction of innocents, unless for some extraordinary reasons, and for the safety of many." Quoting, then, the censure of Livy on those whose "savage cruelty and rage reached even to harmless infants," Grotius declares that, as children are to be spared, so also are women, "unless they have committed some crime which deserves a particular punishment, or have usurped the offices of men." The same thing, he affirmed, "may be generally said of all men, whose manner of life is wholly averse to arms." Again quoting Livy to the effect that "by the laws of war, only those that are in arms, and do resist, are to be killed," he mentions, among those who are particularly spared, old men; scholars; husbandmen; merchants, comprehending under this title all sorts of mechanics and tradesmen; captives, and those who in battle demand quarter or unconditionally surrender.[6]

2. Deut. 2. 34; 20. 16.
3. Ps. 137. 9.
4. Grotius, *De Jure Belli ac Pacis*, Bk. III, chap. iv, par. 9.
5. *Idem*, Bk. III, chap. iv, § II, par. 1, 2; § XV, par. 1.
6. *Idem*, Bk. III, chap. xi, on "Moderation Concerning the Right of Killing Men in a Just War."

In the course of years the ancient and savage conception of war, against which Grotius rang out his epochal protest, was radically modified, but not because nations and their rulers then dreamed that soldiers, like chameleons, lived on light and air; that armed forces fought and continued to fight without replenishment of their ranks, equipment or supplies; and that the productive activities, financial, industrial and commercial, on land and sea, of the unarmed population, male and female, adult and minor, were not contributory and essential to the maintenance of armed conflicts. In his celebrated work on the principles of war[7] that great master of the history as well as of the conduct of war, Marshal Foch, profoundly says: "In spite of all, the fundamental truths which govern this art remain immutable, just as the principles of mechanics always govern architecture, whether the construction is of wood, of stone, of iron, or of cement." Among those truths the first is the effective and harmonious employment of all the national resources, in men, materials and money. It has always been so.

With the great increase in population that had taken place during the previous hundred years, the general employment on the Continent of the system of conscription, and the development of quicker transportation, it was inevitable that, if a general war broke out in Europe, a larger number of men would be promptly put into the field than ever before. The inevitable happened; and as the knowledge of previous wars was confined to very limited circles, some of which had little occasion to use it, the exciting total, causing complete oblivion of the element of proportion, naturally created the popular impression that national resources, in men and materials, were drawn upon as never before. The impression was essentially fallacious.

There never was a time when in great conflicts belligerents did not draw upon and co-ordinate their various resources, such as they were, in the carrying on of hostile operations. In such operations it is obvious that among the most essential elements are arms, ammunition and food—arms and ammunition with which to fight and food with which to live; and it will hardly be contended that these elementary requirements are more essential today than they were a century, ten centuries or twenty centuries ago. It is true that in former times the requirements of warfare were simpler and less varied; but so, also, were the industrial arts, including agriculture, and incomparably less productive. And yet in the eighteenth century as well as in the nineteenth there were powers, and the United States was one of them, that deemed it proper by special treaty

7. Foch, *Des Principes de la Guerre* (Paris, 1918), Preface, IX.

stipulation to pledge protection to tillers of the soil, to artisans and manufacturers, "and in general to all others whose occupations are for the common subsistence and benefit of mankind," and the payment of a reasonable price for anything that should be taken from them for the use of armed forces.

Equally instructive is a comparison of the extent and effect of the drafts made by the recent war with the extent and effect of the drafts made by previous wars on national man-power and resources. Taking, for the recent war, France and Germany, as two of the powers that suffered most, we find that in France about 7,500,000 men were mobilized. Those killed in action or dead of wounds numbered 1,028,000, the missing 299,-000—a total of 1,327,000. Of wounded, amounting to about 3,000,000, three-fourths recovered. The total loss in man-power, killed, dead from wounds, missing, and unfit for work is estimated at 2,260,000, between twenty-six and thirty per cent of the men mobilized, or nearly six per cent of the population. In Germany 11,000,000 men were mobilized. Those killed in action or dead of wounds amounted to 1,611,104, the missing to 103,000—a total of 1,714,104. The wounded numbered 4,064,000, and, if the French proportion of recoveries be taken, the total loss in man-power would be twenty-five per cent of the men mobilized, or between four and five per cent of the population. No account is here taken of the probably higher ratio of deaths among the non-combatant population of Germany, due to shortage and impoverishment of food during or since the war, resulting from the Allied war measures.

Turning to ancient wars, it is estimated that, in the first Persian war, a fourth of the male citizen-population of Athens capable of bearing arms, and more than a half of that of Sparta, were actually engaged in hostilities; that, in the second Persian war, although the number of soldiers was greater, substantially the same proportions prevailed; but that, in the Peloponnesian war, in which the distinctive Athenian civilization practically succumbed, the proportions were even greater. During the wars against Hannibal, thirty per cent of the male citizen-population of Rome capable of bearing arms, or more than ten per cent of the total population, were kept under arms, while the total number lost exceeded those proportions of the population as it stood when the struggle began.

When the Thirty Years' War, which gradually embroiled the continent of Europe, opened in 1618, the population of the old German Empire was between 16 and 17 millions; in 1648, when it closed, the population was about 4,000,000. In order to approach this appalling destruction of life in Germany alone, due to war and its attendant devastation, famine and pestilence, we must take the total of all the belligerents in the recent war, while the proportion of human loss is not five per cent but seventy-five. By 1648 the population of the Palatinate had dwindled from 500,000 to 48,000, or ninety per cent. The economic destruction was correspondent. Occasionally the shock was quick. In Saxony it has been reckoned that within two years (1631–32) 934,000 perished. In Württemberg, between 1634 and 1641, the shrinkage was more than eighty per cent. In Bavaria, in 1645, as the result of repeated hostile incursions, the universal desolation was such that, according to a contemporary letter, even large landowners, so far as they were spared, could not find bread, but were reduced to live on dogs and cats and other victuals then considered unnatural.

In the wars of the Spanish Succession from 1700 to 1713, the losses of the belligerents, among whom were Austria, England, France, Holland and Spain, were enormous in their totality as well as in their proportions. The population of France is computed to have fallen from 19,000,000 to between 16,000,000 and 17,000,000, or nearly fourteen per cent. Levasseur speaks of the war and the famine which it engendered as having ruined the kingdom and decimated the inhabitants; and allowing, as he says, for the possible exaggerations of a feeling heart, he quotes the celebrated letter of Fénelon, who in 1709 admonished the King that the cultivation of the fields was almost abandoned, that town and country were depopulated, that trades no longer supported the workers, that all commerce was destroyed, that France as a whole was only a great hospital, desolated and without provisions, and that his Majesty, instead of taxing for the war what little the people had left, should give them alms and feed them. These conditions were approached in some of the other countries, although willful devastation and the slaughter of garrisons were not practiced as in the Thirty Years' War.

In the Seven Years' War (1756–63), so momentous in its worldwide consequences, the general drain upon the belligerents, among whom figure Austria, England, France, Prussia, Portugal, Russia and Spain, was less heavy; but Prussia is estimated to have lost, simply in killed and dead of wounds, more than six per cent of her population.

Into the varied details and shifting coalitions of the wars growing out of the French Revolution (1792–1802) and of the Napoleonic wars (1803–15), it is impracticable now to enter; but a study of their impressive totals and proportions of destruction of life and property, of expansion of debts and repudiation, of the inflation and collapse of currencies, of annihilated commerce and industry and of economic loss and disaster, may be commended to those who have not reached the exalted stage of resenting inquiry and spurning instruction. In the brief but culminating Russian campaign, in 1812, in spite of the previous twenty lugubrious and exhausting years, more than a million men confronted one another in battle. Of these more than a half perished. It is said that, with the coming of age in 1813 of the young men born during the wars growing out of the French Revolution, the average height of the men of France began to show a notable decrease, and that this decrease continued through the succeeding period of nearly twenty-five years in which there came of age the men born during the long titanic struggle whose convulsive end indelibly marks the year 1815.

Nor was the recent conflict in a distinctive and novel sense a "world war." The effects of steam and electricity in enabling wars to be extensively carried on are popularly misconceived and overestimated. The inferior means of transportation and communication, by land and by sea, did not prevent the countries of former times from warring with one another all over the globe. Although they reached their objectives more slowly, they gained them none the less surely; and empires were lost and won by the European powers in conflicts which they fought face to face, not only in Europe but also in America, in Africa and in Asia. It was in the Seven Years' War that England, displacing France, laid the foundations of her empire in India, and established her supremacy in North America and at sea. The wars growing out of the Revolution in France and the Napoleonic Wars involved in their sweep not a part but all of Europe and eventually the United States, and determined or shaped the fate of vast colonial possessions in all quarters of the world.

It is evident that, if we are now to abandon the distinction between combatants and non-combatants, and, reverting to primitive conceptions, to kill unarmed men and women as war workers and obliterate the youth of the land as war sproutage, the lapse into savagery cannot be justified on the ground that it was formerly imagined that war did not lay under contribution all national activities and resources. The founders of international law were not moved by such an infatuation. They were actuated by nobler and more rational sentiments. Profoundly learned and not at all visionary, they were the leaders of a moral revolt, the apostles of a new creed. Not only were they interpreters of the growing conviction that extirpatory methods were as impracticable and wasteful as they were brutal and brutalizing, but they were the spokesmen of a loftier conception of the destiny and rights of man and of a more humane spirit. It was just because they knew the universal drain of war and its reactionary tendencies, that they sought to limit its toll and to reform and regulate its practices.

In order to accomplish this intelligent purpose, the great expositors of international law, regarding civilization as essentially cumulative, and knowing that greed and avarice as well as hate may beget violence and thrive upon it, deemed it to be indispensable not only to limit the taking of life, but also to restrict the destruction and confiscation of property, and to assure to the world's commerce a legitimate and definite freedom. The seeds did not fall upon stony ground.

Of the restriction of the capture and confiscation of private property on land, an early reverberation may be heard in the Peace of the Pyrenees between France and Spain in 1659, of which the twenty-second article significantly declares: "All goods and merchandise arrested in either of the kingdoms, upon the subjects of the said Lords and Kings, at the time of the Declaration of War, shall be uprightly and *bona fide* restored to the owners."

In the United States, towards the end of the next century, this rule of uprightness, although assailed, was again vindicated. During the Revolutionary War certain States had passed acts by which it was provided not only that debts due to British creditors should be paid into the local treasury, but also that such payment should bar any future action for their recovery. Debts, it may be superfluous to remark, are merely one form of property; and when the acts, which were essentially confiscatory, came into question during the peace negotiations at Paris, John Adams ended the discussion by bluntly declaring, in the presence of the British plenipotentiaries, that he was "not in favor of cheating anybody." An article was then inserted in the treaty to assure to creditors their appropriate judicial remedies. But, as federal courts were lacking, and the State courts deemed themselves bound by the local laws, the article proved to be ineffectual; and in order to give it vitality, there was later incorporated in the Constitution of the United States the clause declaring treaties to be the supreme law of the land, binding on the judges in every State, notwithstanding anything in the constitution or laws of any State to the contrary. Under this clause the Supreme Court of the United States held the confiscatory statutes to be invalid,[8] but with little benefit to the creditors. Owing to lapse of time, and to intervening deaths, financial failures and loss of proofs, the judicial remedy against the debtors had become practically worthless; and, under a treaty signed on January 8, 1802, the

8. *Ware* v. *Hylton* (1796), 3 Dallas, 199.

United States paid to Great Britain the sum of £600,000, or $3,000,000, with which to compensate the creditors for their losses.

This final result may not have been uninfluenced by the memorable and successful defence of the rule of uprightness in the United States in another instance.

In the treaty with Great Britain of 1794, of which John Jay, then Chief Justice of the United States, was the American negotiator, there was the following stipulation:

Article X. Neither the debts due from individuals of one nation to individuals of the other, nor shares, nor monies, which they may have in the public funds, or in the public or private banks, shall ever in any event of war or national differences be sequestered or confiscated, it being unjust and impolitic that debts and engagements contracted and made by individuals, having confidence in each other and in their respective Governments, should ever be destroyed or impaired by national authority on account of national differences and discontents.

Of the broad and vital principle from which this article was derived no exposition could be more eloquent or more profound than that which was made by Alexander Hamilton, who, in opening his discussion of the subject, said:

In my opinion this article is nothing more than an affirmance of the modern law and usage of civilized nations, and is valuable as a check upon a measure which, if it could ever take place, would disgrace the government of the country, and injure its true interests. The general proposition of writers on the laws of nations is, that all enemy's property, wherever found, is liable to seizure and confiscation; but reason pronounces that this is with the exception of all such property as exists *in the faith of the laws of your own country;* such are the several kinds of property which are protected by this article. And though in remote periods the exception may not have been duly observed, yet the spirit of commerce, diffusing more just ideas, has been giving strength to it for a century past, and a negative usage among nations, according with the opinions of modern writers, authorizes the considering the exception as established. If there have been deviations from that usage in the actual war of Europe, they form no just objection to this reasoning: for this war has violated, in different instances, most of the most sacred laws of nations.[9]

Recurring later to the subject, Hamilton said:

The right of holding or having property in a country always implies a duty on the part of its government to protect that property, and to secure to the owner the full enjoyment of it. Whenever, therefore, a government grants permission to foreigners to acquire property within its territories, or to bring and deposit it there, it tacitly promises protection and security. . . . Property, as it exists in

9. *Works of Alexander Hamilton* (Lodge ed.), V, 160.

civilized society, if not a creature of, is, at least, regulated and defined by the laws. . . . An extraordinary discretion to resume or take away the thing, without any personal fault of the proprietor, is inconsistent with the notion of property. . . . It is neither natural nor equitable to consider him as subject to be deprived of it for a cause foreign to himself; still less for one which may depend on the volition or pleasure, even of the very government to whose protection it has been confided; for the proposition which affirms the right to confiscate or sequester does not distinguish between offensive or defensive war; between a war of ambition on the part of the power which exercises the right, or a war of self-preservation against the assaults of another.

The property of a foreigner placed in another country, by permission of its laws, may justly be regarded as a deposit, of which the society is the trustee. How can it be reconciled with the idea of a trust, to take the property from its owner, when he has personally given no cause for the deprivation? . . . There is no parity between the case of persons and goods of enemies found in our own country and that of the persons and goods of enemies found elsewhere. In the former there is a reliance upon our hospitality and justice; there is an express or implied safe conduct; the individuals and their property are in the custody of our faith; they have no power to resist our will; they can lawfully make no defense against our violence; they are deemed to owe a temporary allegiance; and for endeavoring resistance would be punished as criminals, a character inconsistent with that of an enemy. To make them a prey is, therefore, to infringe every rule of generosity and equity; it is to add cowardice to treachery. . . . Moreover, the property of the foreigner within our country may be regarded as having paid a valuable consideration for its protection and exemption from forfeiture; that which is brought in, commonly enriches the revenue by a duty of entry. All that is within our territory, whether acquired there or brought there, is liable to contributions to the treasury, in common with other similar property. Does there not result an obligation to protect that which contributes to the expense of its protection? Will justice sanction, upon the breaking out of a war, the confiscation of a property which, during peace, serves to augment the resources and nourish the prosperity of a state? . . . Reason, left to its own lights, would answer all these questions in one way, and severely condemn the molestation, on account of a national contest, as well of the property as of the person of a foreigner found in our country, under the license and guaranty of the laws of previous amity.[10]

The Jay treaty was duly ratified.

But, in time of war, no principle is ever safe against attack; and, twenty years later, when the second war with Great Britain occurred, an attempt was made to confiscate, through the courts, British private property found on land at the outbreak of hostilities. There was no specific confiscatory statute,

10. *Idem,* pp. 412–418.

but it was claimed that the act of Congress, declaring the existence of a state of war, sufficed to render the property confiscable. The attempt failed. No confiscatory law was ever passed. The decision of the Supreme Court, defeating the attempted confiscation, was delivered by the Chief Justice, John Marshall, who, in the course of his opinion, said that, while war gave to the sovereign "full right to take the persons and confiscate the property of the enemy wherever found," yet the "mitigations of this rigid rule, which the humane and wise policy of modern times" had "introduced into practice," would "more or less affect the exercise" of the right; and that, although this practice could not "impair the right itself," yet it was "not believed that modern usage would sanction the seizure of the goods of an enemy on land, which were acquired in peace in course of trade." Such a proceeding, said Marshall, was "rare, and would be deemed a harsh exercise of the rights of war"; so much so, indeed, that the "modern usage" could not be disregarded by the sovereign "without obloquy." Declaring, therefore, that the "modern rule" was "totally incompatible with the idea that war does of itself vest the property in the belligerent government," he held that the declaration of war did not authorize the confiscation.[11]

Some years ago I had occasion to comment on Marshall's intimation that the "modern usage," although it would "more or less affect the exercise" of the ancient right, could not "impair the right itself." [12] The distinction between the effect of usage on rights and on the exercise of rights may be of doubtful value. But, however this may be, the intimation was only a dictum; and the great Chief Justice twenty years later discarded it, when, in the decision of another celebrated case, he declared:

It is very unusual, even in cases of conquest, for the conqueror to do more than displace the sovereign and assume dominion over the country. The modern usage of nations, which has become law, would be violated; that sense of justice and of right which is felt and acknowledged by the whole civilized world would be outraged, if private property should be generally confiscated, and private rights annulled.[13]

11. *United States* v. *Brown* (1814), 8 Cranch, 110.
12. John Marshall: An address delivered before the Delaware Bar on February 4, 1901, on the celebration of the hundredth anniversary of Marshall's assumption of the office of Chief Justice. This address was printed in the *Political Science Quarterly*, XVI (September, 1901), 393–411, and an extract from it bearing on the present question may be found in Moore, *Digest of International Law*, VII, 312, 313.
13. *United States* v. *Percheman* (1833), 7 Peters, 51, 86. In an action in England under the Legal Proceedings against Enemies Act, 1915, the question arose as to whether a German partner in an English company, engaged in a manufacturing business, in England, was entitled (1) to a

When John Quincy Adams, as Secretary of State, affirmed that, "by the usages of modern war the private property of an enemy is protected from seizure and confiscation as such," he avowed a belief not more tenaciously held by himself than by many illustrious predecessors and successors. It is therefore not strange that the non-confiscatory principle pervades the treaties of the United States, which provide that on the outbreak of war citizens or merchants of the enemy may have six months, nine months, a year, or such time as they may require, in which to arrange their affairs and withdraw their property or effects,[14] and, almost as often, that they may remain and continue to trade as long as they behave peaceably, their property and effects meanwhile being exempt from seizure or sequestration.[15] There have indeed been Presidents such as Pierce, McKinley and Roosevelt, and Secretaries of State such as Adams, Marcy, Fish and Hay, who have proposed that even enemy private property at sea be exempt from capture; and such an exemption actually was incorporated in the treaty

share of the profits made since the dissolution of the partnership by war, or (2) to interest on his share in the partnership assets, or (3) only to the value of his share in the partnership as of August 4, 1914, the date of the beginning of the war. The House of Lords, January 25, 1918, unanimously held that the German partner was entitled to a share of the profits, so far as attributable to the use of his share of the capital. The Lord Chancellor, Lord Finlay, said: "It is not the law of this country that the property of enemy subjects is confiscated. Until the restoration of peace the enemy can, of course, make no claim to have it delivered up to him, but when peace is restored he is considered to be entitled to his property with any fruits it may have borne in the meantime." Said Viscount Haldane: "The law of this country does not in general confiscate the property of an enemy. He cannot claim to receive it during war, but his right to his property is not extinguished; it is merely suspended." Lord Dunedin concurred. So, also, Lord Atkinson, who declared that the opposite view was one "which not even the most rabid patriotism can justify." Lord Parmoor remarked that the right of confiscation of enemy property on land in favor of the Crown had "long since been disused." (Hugh Stevenson & Sons, Ltd., Appellants; and Aktiengesellschaft für Cartonnagen-Industrie, Respondents (1918), A.C. 239.)

14. Bolivia, 1858, Art. 28; Costa Rica, 1851, Art. 11; Dominican Republic, 1867, Art. 1; Ecuador, 1839, Art. 26; Haiti, 1864, Art. 3; Honduras, 1864, Art. 11; Italy, 1871, Art. 21; Morocco, 1836, Art. 24; New Granada (Colombia), 1846, Art. 27; Nicaragua, 1867, Art. 11; Paraguay, 1859, Art. 13; Peru, 1887, Art. 27; Prussia, 1799, Art. 23; 1828, Art. 12; Salvador, 1870, Art. 27; Spain, 1795, Art. 13, which also provides that indemnity shall be made for any injury meanwhile done to them; Sweden, 1783, Art. 22, containing a similar stipulation; Tunis, 1797, Art. 23.

15. Argentine Confederation, 1853, Art. 12; Bolivia, 1858, Arts. 28, 29; Colombia, 1846, Arts. 27, 28; Costa Rica, 1851, Art. 11; Ecuador, 1839, Arts. 26, 27; Haiti, 1864, Arts. 3, 4; Honduras, 1864, Art. 11; Italy, 1871, Art. 21; Nicaragua, 1867, Art. 11; Paraguay, 1859, Art. 13; Peru, 1887, Arts. 27, 28; Salvador, 1870, Art. 27.

with Italy of February 26, 1871, when Grant was President, Fish being Secretary of State.[16]

It would be an idle task minutely to analyze the language of the foregoing treaties in order to ascertain whether some particular confiscation might be enacted without flagrant violation of their precise terms. St. Paul's well-known proverb, that "the letter killeth but the spirit giveth life," [17] is equally expressed in the legal maxim *qui haeret in litera haeret in cortice,* meaning that "he who considers merely the letter of an instrument goes but skin-deep into its meaning." [18] No doubt their phraseology may in some instances have been specially designed, like the terms of criminal statutes, to prevent the repetition of particular odious acts. But, without regard to the words employed and their literal interpretation, there can be no doubt that they were understood to emanate from the general rule against confiscation, which it was not supposed that the contracting parties would seek in any respect to infringe. Even by Magna Carta the pre-war property of enemies, though they were not themselves personally present, was not, simply as enemy property, subject to confiscation by the Crown.[19]

Not long after the outbreak of the recent war, the belligerent governments, one after another, proceeded to assume control of, or, as was generally said, to "intern" enemy private property found within their jurisdiction. Individuals and property are "interned" to prevent them from doing harm. In the present instance, the avowed object of taking control of the property was for the time being to prevent its use in the enemy interest, either directly, or as a basis for credits or otherwise. Upwards of six months after entering the war, the government of the United States, under certain provisions of the "Trading with the Enemy Act," which had just then been passed, embarked on a similar course. This was not, nor did it purport to be, an exercise by Congress of its constitutional power "to make rules concerning captures on land and water." The word "capture" is in law a technical term, denoting the hostile seizure of places, persons or things. Men in arms are "captured," but a non-combatant is seized or arrested. A defended city, if taken, is said to be "captured"; if undefended, it is "occupied." Property is said to be "captured," only when seized, in a hostile sense, under claim of forfeiture or confiscation. These distinctions are very elementary. The idea of pro-

16. Art. 12.
17. II Cor. 3. 6.
18. Broom's *Legal Maxims* (8th ed.), p. 533, citing Coke's Littleton, 283 b.
19. F. E. Farrer, "The Forfeiture of Enemy Private Pre-War Property" *Law Quarterly Review,* XXXVII (1921), 218, 337, 353, 356.

visionally holding enemy property in custody in order to prevent its use in the enemy interest is by no means new. In England, it is at least as old as Magna Carta. No one understood the act of Congress to contemplate a hostile seizure. The very terms of the act preclude such an interpretation. It merely authorized the provisional holding of the property in custody, and appropriately styled the official, who was to perform this function, the Alien Property Custodian.

In the original statute the function of the alien property custodian was defined as that of a trustee. Subsequently, however, there came a special revelation, marvelously brilliant but perhaps not divinely inspired, of the staggering discovery that the foreign traders and manufacturers whose property had been taken over had made their investments in the United States not from ordinary motives of profit but in pursuance of a hostile design, so stealthily pursued that it had never before been detected or even suspected, but so deadly in its effects that the American traders and manufacturers were eventually to be engulfed in their own homes and the alien plotters left in grinning possession of the ground. Under the spell engendered by this agitating apparition, and its patriotic call to a retributive but profitable war on the malefactors' property, substantial departures were made from the principle of trusteeship.

The Preacher has told us that the thing that hath been shall be, that what is done shall be done again, and that "there is no new thing under the sun." [20] So it is in the present instance. Hamilton, in his denunciation of the principle of confiscation, did not overlook those who, as he said, "then defended the confiscation or sequestration of debts as our best means of retaliation and coercion, as our most powerful, sometimes as our only means, of defense"; and, pursuing his protest, he declared:

But so degrading an idea will be rejected with disdain, by every man who feels a true and well-informed national pride; by every man who recollects and glories, that in a state of still greater immaturity, we achieved independence without the aid of this dishonorable expedient; that even in a revolutionary war, a war of liberty against usurpation, our national councils were too magnanimous to be provoked or tempted to depart so widely from the path of rectitude; by every man, in fine, who, though careful not to exaggerate, for rash and extravagant projects, can nevertheless fairly estimate the real resources of the country, for meeting dangers which prudence cannot avert.[21]

Such a man would, said Hamilton, look for the security of the country "in the courage and constancy of a free, brave, and

20. Eccles. 1. 9.
21. *Works of Alexander Hamilton* (Lodge ed.), V, 408–409.

virtuous people—in the riches of a fertile soil—an extended and progressive industry—in the wisdom and energy of a well-constituted and well-administered government—in the resources of a solid, if well-supported, national credit—in the armies, which, if requisite would be raised—in the means of maritime annoyance, which if necessary, could be organized, and with which we could inflict deep wounds on the commerce of a hostile nation"; and would "indulge an animating consciousness, that, while our situation is not such as to justify our courting imprudent enterprises, neither is it such as to oblige us, in any event, to stoop to dishonorable means of security, or to substitute a crooked and piratical policy, for the manly energies of fair and open war." [22]

In the main, the momentous question as to what shall be done with the enemy private property taken over by the United States in the recent war is yet to be determined; and, with more than $3,000,000,000 of the world's supply of gold in the coffers of the Federal Reserve System, and continuously tolerated additions to the more than $11,000,000,000 of tax-exempt securities already in private hands, the United States is hardly in a position to put forth the plea of financial stress to excuse or palliate the retention of what it seized.

The subject has also another aspect. During the past ten years the investments abroad of citizens of the United States have enormously increased, and the process has only begun. Considering the question, therefore, purely as one of selfish calculation, I venture to think it directly contrary to the interests of the United States to resuscitate the doctrine that enemy private property found in a country on the outbreak of war may be confiscated. Such a doctrine might even create a temptation.

But there is yet another and higher reason. The United States has an honorable past as well as an expedient future to consider.

Of all the illusions a people can cherish, the most extravagant and illogical is the supposition that, along with the progressive degradation of its standards of conduct, there is to go a progressive increase in respect for law and morality. Again may we remark that "there is no new thing under the sun." The world never will be rid of the problem of preserving its elementary virtues. Three hundred years ago Grotius declared that, as he who violated the laws of his country for the sake of some present advantage to himself, "sapped the foundation of his own perpetual interest, and at the same time that of his posterity," so the people that "violated the laws of nature

22. *Idem*, p. 409.

and nations" broke down "the bulwarks of its future happiness and tranquillity."

No less pertinent is the confession of Alexander Hamilton, made a century-and-a-quarter ago, that, serious as the evil of war had appeared to him to be, yet the manner in which it might be carried on was in his eyes "still more formidable." It was, said Hamilton, "to be feared that, in the fermentation of certain wild opinions, those wise, just, and temperate maxims, which will forever constitute the true security and felicity of a state, would be overruled," and that, one violation of justice succeeding another, measures would be adopted which even might "aggravate and embitter the ordinary calamities of foreign war." [23]

Among the questions affecting freedom to trade in time of war that of contraband was easily the most important, and it still retains that character. While trade between opposing belligerents generally is prohibited, trade between belligerents and third countries, called neutrals, continues uninterrupted, subject to certain restrictions, one of which forbids a neutral to carry to a belligerent country, or to its military or naval forces, articles called contraband of war. Obviously, if the list of such articles might be extended at will, all trade with belligerents could be cut off. So, also, if inferences of hostile destination were freely admitted, might trade between countries at peace.

In treating of this subject, Grotius divided articles into three categories, the first embracing articles primarily useful for war, such as arms and ammunition, which, when bound to a belligerent country, were always contraband; the second, articles of double use, which, as they might or might not be employed for war, might, even though directly bound to a belligerent country, be captured as contraband only if there were proof that they were actually intended for military use; the third, articles not at all useful for war, and therefore never contraband. The center of conflict has been the second category, including foodstuffs. Late in the last century the articles in the first category came to be designated as "absolutely" contraband, and those in the second as "conditionally" contraband, and still later but less felicitously as "absolute contraband" and "conditional contraband," the phrase "conditional contraband" having apparently encouraged the erroneous supposition that the articles were, merely upon the strength of their destination to the belligerent country, to be considered as contraband until the contrary was proved. Nothing could be more groundless or more contrary to established law.

23. *Idem*, p. 406.

During the recent war there were exigent belligerent measures which in effect merged the second category in the first. These measures were defended on the ground that the "circumstances" of the war were "so peculiar" that "for all practical purposes the distinction between the two classes of contraband" had "ceased to have value"; that "so large a proportion of the inhabitants of the enemy country" were "taking part in the war, directly or indirectly, that no real distinction" could be drawn "between the armed forces and the civilian population"; that "similarly" the enemy government had "taken control, by a series of decrees and orders, of practically all the articles in the list of conditional contraband, so that they are now available for government use"; and that "so long as these exceptional conditions" continued, "belligerent rights in regard to the two kinds of contraband" were the same and the "treatment of them must be identical."

Probably under the influence of these arguments, and without full appreciation of the implication, which they seem to have been anxiously designed to convey, that the measures were to be regarded as highly emergent and altogether exceptional, it has lately been intimated that the distinction, defended and maintained through æons of almost forgotten time, between articles absolutely and articles conditionally contraband, has been shown by the recent war to be unsound and should no longer be preserved.[24] One writer has indeed gone so far as to assert that the distinction "dates from the time when armies were very small, and compromised only a very small fraction of the belligerent countries," [25] a statement that would have astonished Grotius, and that must equally astonish those who are familiar with the history, either legal or military, of the wars growing out of the French Revolution and the Napoleonic Wars. For reasons such as these it has been suggested, but not, I believe, by any government, that the category of "conditional contraband" should now be evacuated and decently interred, and its contents included in the absolute list. The suggestion is startling, since its acceptance would at once render illicit practically all trade with countries at war, and put in jeopardy much of the trade even between countries not at war.

But we must not permit ourselves to be betrayed by illusions of novelty. We do our ancestors grave injustice if we think they admitted that a belligerent might capture at sea and confiscate all commodities destined to his enemy which perchance might be used for a military purpose, but believed that belligerent

24. Hyde, *International Law* (1922), II, par. 813, pp. 626–629.
25. Oppenheim, *International Law* (3d ed., 1921, by Roxburgh), p. 549.

governments then could not or did not appropriate within their own jurisdiction whatever they needed for war. Our ancestors were not so hopelessly senseless. They were, on the contrary, consciously engaged in a conflict, which has not ceased, between belligerent claims to stop trade and neutral claims to carry it on. Neutrals denied the right of belligerents to capture and confiscate anything but articles primarily useful for war. So far as concerned foodstuffs, the defenders of neutral rights, while fully aware that armies must and did eat, maintained that the non-combatant mouths always vastly outnumbered the combatant, so that the preponderant consumption of food was ordinarily not hostile. They carried their point, with the single concession, the narrowness of which was mutually and perfectly understood, that foodstuffs should become contraband if, when seized, they were destined for distinctively military use. This conclusion was perhaps never better stated than by Lord Salisbury when, in January, 1900, during the Boer war, he said: "Foodstuffs with a hostile destination, can be considered contraband of war only if they are supplies for the enemy's forces. It is not sufficient that they are capable of being so used; it must be shown that this was in fact their destination at the time of the seizure."

But, by way of last-ditch argument, we are assured that the whole face of things has been changed by steam railways, which our ancestors lacked. This argument, however, can be applied only to our more or less remote ancestors. It cannot be invoked against Lord Salisbury, who, although somewhat of a recluse, must have known of the existence of steam railways in 1900. Their development in England began three-quarters of a century before, and they had long gridironed the British Isles as well as other countries. Nor is this anachronistic element the only weakness in the argument. Steam railways, like other recent means of quick locomotion, although they have facilitated transportation, did not create it. Even today innumerable caravans still traverse the desert, and "argosies with portly sail" were not wanting in earlier times to "overpeer the petty trafficker." Again, we find that all things are relative. Nor is the nutritious and sustaining quality of food diminished by its delivery even by ox-cart.

In reality, no phase that has recently arisen was previously unknown or unconsidered. For example, by an order in council of June 8, 1793, British cruisers, Great Britain being then at war with France, were authorized to stop all vessels laden with cargo of grain, flour or meal, bound to a French port, and to send them to a British port, in order that the cargo might be purchased for the government or released on security for its sale in a friendly country. France, then encompassed by a great European coalition, had adopted conscription; the crops were short and a famine was threatened, and the government was making every effort to import provisions. It was indeed declared to be notorious that the grain trade in France was in the hands of the executive council; and it was argued that the situation, being "quite new in its kind," could not be judged by the principles and rules made for previous wars.

It was in this sense that the British Minister in the United States, in communicating to the government the text of the order in council, officially jusified it. By the law of nations, so he declared, all provisions were "to be considered as contraband" and "liable to confiscation," where the depriving an enemy of them was "one of the means intended to be employed for reducing him to reasonable terms of peace." The actual condition of France was, he said, notoriously such as to lead the powers in their joint operations to employ this mode of "distressing her," and the reasoning by which it was justified, while applicable "to *all* cases of this sort," was "certainly much more applicable to the *present* case, in which the distress results from the unusual mode of war employed by the enemy himself, in having armed almost the whole laboring class of the French nation, for the purpose of *commencing* and supporting hostilities against all the governments of Europe." But this reasoning was, so the minister further stated, "most of all applicable to the circumstances of a trade which is now in a great measure entirely carried on by the actually ruling party of France itself, and which is therefore no longer to be regarded as a mercantile speculation of individuals, but as an immediate operation of the very persons who have declared war, and are now carrying it on against Great Britain." He pointed out, however, that his government, while it might have confiscated the cargoes as contraband, was not availing itself of that right, but was paying for them.

Jefferson, as Secretary of State, on the other hand, defining the position of the United States, maintained that "reason and usage" had "established that, when two nations go to war, those who choose to live in peace retain their natural right to pursue their agriculture, manufactures, and other ordinary vocations," and "to carry the produce of their industry, for exchange, to all nations, belligerent or neutral, as usual," subject to the restriction "of not furnishing to either party implements merely of war," commonly known as contraband, nor taking "anything whatever to a place blockaded." Grain, flour and meal, said Jefferson, were "not of the class of contraband" and consequently "articles of free commerce." He continued: "A culture which, like that of the soil, gives employment to such a proportion of mankind, could never be suspended by the whole earth, or interrupted for them, whenever any two nations should think proper to go to war. The state of war, then, existing between Great Britain and France, furnishes no legitimate right either to interrupt the agriculture of the United States, or the peaceable exchange of its products with all nations. . . . If any nation whatever has a right to shut up, to our produce, all the ports of the earth except her own, and those of her friends, she may shut up these also, and so confine us within our limits. No nation can subscribe to such pretensions."

In this position Jefferson was supported by his great contemporary and political antagonist, Alexander Hamilton, who declared it to be "our interest to narrow upon all occasions as much as possible the list of contraband." [26]

The order in council was afterwards modified, and full compensation for any losses occasioned by the seizures under it was obtained through the mixed commission under Article VII of the Jay treaty of 1794.

As has already been intimated, the distinction between what in very recent years has, in phraseology not altogether happy, been styled "conditional contraband," and articles absolutely contraband, never rested on logic, in the sense that it was imagined that "conditional contraband," which includes foodstuffs, was not of military value, potentially of even capital military value, to belligerents. Without undertaking to cover a wider range, one may readily find during the past three hundred years numerous situations in which the question of food supply in war was of capital importance; and yet, as has heretofore been observed, no one ever imagined that foodstuffs imported into a belligerent country could not be immediately consumed, or that the government could not or would not take for military use whatever it might need, whether imported or of domestic origin. The long-accepted rule, so clearly and forcibly reaffirmed by Lord Salisbury in 1900, that foodstuffs bound to a belligerent country could be treated as contraband only if it were shown that they were, at the time of their seizure, actually destined for the military forces, never was capable of reconciliation with a fancied belligerent right to seize whatever might possibly be useful to the enemy for purposes of war. A distinguished judge has lately quoted from a great legal oracle the classic statement that "the life of the law has not

26. *Works of Alexander Hamilton* (Lodge ed.), V, 168–169.

been logic; it has been experience." [27] Had the rule been accepted on the supposition that it could be reconciled with the right of a belligerent to seize as contraband whatever might be militarily useful to his enemy, it would have made a laughing stock of logic. In truth, the rule represented and has continued to represent a compromise between two claims, either of which, if carried to its logical conclusion, would have destroyed the other, being in this particular like most other legal rules. But it further represented and still represents the advance painfully made, through centuries of struggle, toward greater freedom of commerce in time of war.

In 1795, in the earlier stages of the wars growing out of the French Revolution, Alexander Hamilton had occasion to comment upon the argument that confiscatory practices were to be attempted, or even imitated, because the prevailing war afforded examples of them. The titanic conflict then raging was to endure yet twenty years, and with reference to its effect on established principles, Hamilton, speaking with the vision of a seer, declared:

The present war of Europe is of so extraordinary a complexion, and has been conducted, in all respects, upon such extraordinary principles, that it may truly be regarded as an exception to all general rules, as a precedent for nothing. It is rather a beacon, warning mankind to shun the pernicious examples which it sets, than a model inviting to imitation. The human passions, on all sides, appear to have been wrought up to a pitch of frenzy, which has set reason, justice, and humanity at defiance.[28]

Is the recent great war to differ in its effects from previous great wars, in that extraordinary measures which hard-pressed belligerents, as the struggle grew more intense, adopted generally on the professed ground of retaliation, are to be considered as having changed the established law, and as having created in its stead a system essentially based on the concession of belligerent pretensions? Is there reason to believe that the recent war will differ in this respect from the wars growing out of the French Revolution and the Napoleonic Wars, whose decrees and orders in council were regarded twenty years later only as the passing expedients of a contest desperately waged? Is it more likely now than it was a hundred or two hundred years ago that nations will find their general and continuing interests to be in accord with what they did in an exceptional exigency?

In reflecting upon the answer to be made to these inquiries,

27. Benjamin N. Cardozo, *The Nature of the Judicial Process* (Yale University Press, 1922), p. 33.
28. *Works of Alexander Hamilton* (Lodge ed.), V, 439.

it is pertinent to consider the report, signed by the late Sir John Macdonell, on behalf of the British Maritime Law Committee, August 1, 1919, on the laws of naval warfare. In this report, made even less than a year after the conclusion of the Armistice, we find the distinction between absolute and "conditional" contraband preserved, with a right of "interception and requisition," conditioned upon payment of the value of the merchandise to the owner, substituted for the right of capture, which it is proposed shall be wholly renounced. This is, in effect, in different phraseology, the so-called right of preëmption asserted in 1794, and previously, in mitigation of, or as a substitute for, the claim of belligerent capture which neutrals so firmly opposed; and it is needless to point out how incomparably more favorable it is, in principle and in practice, to freedom of commerce than the suggestion that a belligerent should "enjoy the right" to "intercept and condemn all articles capable of assisting the enemy," on the mere proof that they were "destined by land or by sea to the domain of the enemy." It is superfluous to point out that the concession to belligerents of a right to "seize and condemn" all articles "capable of assisting the enemy" would mean the virtual end of the right to trade with countries at war; for, by the very terminology of the subject, every article of commerce in the "conditional" list, which embraces the great bulk of articles not distinctively military, is an article "capable of assisting the enemy." Is any government today proposing to go to such a length either in claim or in concession?

No less pertinent to these inquiries is the comment made by the late Sir Erle Richards, Chichele Professor of International Law at Oxford, who, but for his untimely death, would have been one of the representatives of his government on the recent Commission of Jurists at The Hague, by which rules of warfare for Aircraft and Radio were drawn up and adopted. The last paper he published was on the subject of contraband. After examining the practices and contentions of the various governments during the war, he concluded his review with this circumspect but significant statement:

This final observation remains. The new conditions which have brought into being these new developments of international law have been the outcome of a world's war: that is, of a contest in which all the most powerful nations were engaged on the one side or the other, and in which, therefore, the force of neutral opinion was reduced to the lowest point. And, by reason of the fortunes of war and the geographical position of their enemies on the continent, it happened that the question of supplies by sea to the Central Powers assumed an importance beyond normal expectation. It may well be thought that the law of contraband as it stands today will be found appropriate to deal with neutral trade in other less extensive wars, if unhappily other wars there be. And if that be so, the argument for change loses proportionately in force.[29]

The continued existence of the distinction between articles absolutely and articles conditionally contraband is specifically recognized in the report of the Commission of Jurists on rules for Aircraft and Radio, signed at The Hague on February 19, 1923, by the representatives of the United States of America, the British Empire, France, Italy, Japan and The Netherlands.[30]

We often hear the raucous taunt that international law no longer exists, and if the rules of international law were paradoxically to be sought in its infringements, this taunt would not be wholly groundless. Great circumspection should therefore be exercised before conceding that old and established distinctions have either succumbed to change or permanently fallen before the expedients hazarded by belligerents in a conflict desperately waged. Let us rather ponder the following well-considered judicial utterance, in an international case:

A law may be established and become international, that is to say binding upon all nations, by the agreement of such nations to be bound thereby, although it may be impossible to enforce obedience thereto by any given nation party to the agreement. The resistance of a nation to a law to which it has agreed does not derogate from the authority of the law because that resistance cannot, perhaps, be overcome. Such resistance merely makes the resisting nation a breaker of the law to which it has given its adherence, but it leaves the law, to the establishment of which the resisting nation was a party, still subsisting. Could it be successfully contended that because any given person or body of persons possessed for the time being power to resist an established municipal law such law had no existence? The answer to such a contention would be that the law still existed, though it might not for the time being be possible to enforce obedience to it.[31]

But there are those who exhort us to discard the halfway measures, the feeble expedients, of the past, by which the peaceful propensities of peoples have been tricked and thwarted. Recalling the picturesque Rooseveltian ejaculation "Utopia or Hell," but drastically discounting the significant truth that the world has always had the second alternative but never the first, the harbingers of a new dispensation of nature, rather than of doctrine, tell us that we should no longer waste

29. *The British Year Book of International Law* (1922–23), p. 16.
30. General Report, Art. 60, *infra*, p. 221.
31. Judgment of Acting Chief Justice Sir Henry Berkeley, Case of the *Prometheus* (1906), Supreme Court of Hongkong, 2 Hongkong Law Reports, 207, 225.

time on international law, which is said to legalize war as well as to lack a sanction; on the reaffirmation and improvement of rules, which, it is ruefully remarked, surely will be broken; or on international courts, whose judgments, it is depreciatingly observed, cannot or will not be enforced; but that we must forthwith create a sanction, and, declaring war to be outlawed, be done with it.

To this lofty aspiration every benevolent mind must respond. But the predicament is not new. It is as old as man. That Grotius comprehended it and deliberately made his choice, is clearly shown by his comment upon lovers of peace in his own time who condemned all bearing of arms as unlawful and upon those who regard all war and all things done in it as lawful.

But [says Grotius] this very endeavor of inclining too much to the opposite extreme is so far from doing good, that it often does hurt, because, when it is readily discovered that men urge some things too far, we are apt to slight their authority in other matters, which are perhaps more reasonable. A cure therefore is to be applied to both classes, as well to prevent believing that nothing is lawful as that all things are lawful.[32]

Well may we profit by this admonition. For, verily, if, while we await the capitulation of war to a declaration of its illegality, we spurn the present opportunity to work with all our might for the preservation and advancement of that system of law which, recording from age to age the slow progress of humanity, has established the distinction between combatants and non-combatants, enjoined the humane treatment of captives, limited the destruction and confiscation of property, enlarged the bounds of commercial freedom, and furnished the rules of decision by which international courts have in countless cases determined grave disputes and stilled the voice of strife, we shall only draw upon our generation the bitter fate portrayed by Milton in the solemn lines:

"Alas! from what high hope to what relapse
Unlooked for we are fallen."

Nor is it true in any reproachful sense that international law has legalized war. Grotius, in a celebrated passage, states that he was impelled to write his treatise because he "observed throughout the Christian world a licentiousness in regard to war, which even barbarous nations ought to be ashamed of," and "a running to arms upon very frivolous or rather no occasions," after which, the war once begun, there "remained no longer any reverence for right, either Divine or Human, just as if from that time on men were authorized and firmly resolved to commit all manner of crimes without restraint."

32. *Rights of War and Peace* (London, 1738), p. xxv.

Grotius, surveying the history of man, sought to ameliorate the evils of an institution which he could not destroy. Time has vindicated his fruitful choice. His successors have been guided by his example.

Those who, censuring international law for the recurrence of international wars and the excesses by which they are attended, would stake their fate on sanctions and outlawries, seem wholly to overlook the constant recurrence of civil wars, to whose appalling total during the last century the United States contributed a conflict of the first magnitude. I have often remarked that international wars will cease when civil wars end. Within the state there is legal organization and sanction beyond anything yet proposed in the international sphere, while the very phrase "civil" implies that the war is outlawed. Nevertheless, when obliged to characterize the conflict then raging in the United States, the Supreme Court said: "Insurrection against a government may or may not culminate in an organized rebellion, but a civil war always begins by insurrection against the lawful authority of the government. A civil war is never solemnly declared; it becomes such by its accidents —the number, power, and organization of the persons who originate and carry it on." Those in insurrection, said the Court, "claim to be in arms to establish their liberty and independence, in order to become a sovereign state, while the sovereign party treats them as insurgents and rebels, who owe allegiance, and who should be punished with death for their treason." But, continued the Court, "the laws of war, as established among nations, have their foundation in reason, and all tend to mitigate the cruelties and misery produced by the scourge of war. Hence the parties to a civil war usually concede to each other belligerent rights. They exchange prisoners, and adopt the other courtesies and rules common to public or national wars." And the Court then adopted from Vattel, renowned for his learning and humanity, this profoundly illuminating passage:

The common laws of war—those maxims of humanity, moderation, and honor—ought to be observed by both parties in every civil war. Should the sovereign conceive he has a right to hang up his prisoners as rebels, the opposite party will make reprisals; . . . should he burn and ravage, they will follow his example; the war will become cruel, horrible, and every day more destructive to the nation.[33]

Reared in the aftermath of the fraternal struggle which the rules of international law were thus invoked to mitigate, I early received the impression, which the study of history as as well as experience in affairs has deepened, that, if we would

33. The Prize Cases, 2 Black, 635, 666, 667.

keep men and nations at peace, we must remove the causes of their discontent, elevate their moral sentiments, inculcate a spirit of justice and toleration, and compose and settle their differences. Tell me not that this is an idle effort. The time is rich in opportunities, and every opportunity is a summons to duty.

The speculative inquiry whether and to what extent it may be possible to create an international sanction, pales into insignificance beside the imminent and crucial question how we would use the sanction if we had it. This question cannot wait. We grope for an answer, day by day, in the darkness and confusion which invariably result from a great war, the disaster and disruption which it produces and the blinding hatreds which it engenders. But the faith of Grotius and Vattel is not dead. Shall we revive it and bear it on? And shall we, as faithful apostles, resolve not simply to recover the ground that has been yielded but also to make a farther advance? The present, the future turns upon our response; and may we, in this fateful hour, deserve the encomium, bestowed on a great ruler, that he was the irreconcilable enemy, and perpetual conqueror, not of any nation or man, but of injustice.

# II

## CONTRABAND OF WAR[1]

THE word contraband (Italian, *contrabbando;* Spanish, *contrabando*) signifies something prohibited—a trade carried on, or an article imported or dealt in, in violation of some inhibition. Thus, smuggled goods are often spoken of as contraband.

The term contraband of war denotes commodities which it is unlawful to carry to the country, or to the military or naval forces, of a belligerent. By a "belligerent" is meant one of the parties to a war. Often the word "enemy" is used instead of "belligerent." Writers constantly speak of an "enemy" or "enemy's" country, an "enemy" ship, or "enemy" goods, meaning thereby merely that the country, or the ship, or the merchandise, is that of a party to a war, that is to say, of a

1. Address delivered before the American Philosophical Society, at Philadelphia, February 2, 1912. Reprinted from the *Proceedings*, Vol. LI (1912).

belligerent government or of one of its citizens. Sometimes the word "hostile" is used instead of "enemy."

When war breaks out between two countries, the carrying on of trade by the inhabitants of the one country with those of the other becomes unlawful; but the same general interruption does not extend to the commercial intercourse between the parties to the war and third parties, called neutrals. The intercourse between the belligerents and neutrals continues. This continuance is regarded not as a favor granted by the belligerents but as a right belonging to neutrals. As between the belligerents, neither is required to grant to the other any privilege in respect of trade. On the contrary, they endeavor to subdue each other by all permissible means. This is their acknowledged right. But the rest of the world, composed of neutral powers, having no part in the quarrel and perhaps little concern in the issue, also has its rights. Its interests and convenience are not to be wholly subordinated and sacrificed to the exigencies of the one or the other of the belligerents, each of whom, while desirous to preserve its own trade, would of course be glad to cut off altogether that of its enemy; and it is therefore acknowledged to be the right of neutrals to continue their commerce with the belligerents, subject only to the restrictions imposed by the law of contraband and of blockade.

In proceeding to the discussion of the subject of contraband, it is proper to advert to the confusion which seems so widely to prevail as to the legal position of the prohibited trade. The statement is frequently made that the trade in contraband of war is lawful, even though this broad affirmation be immediately followed by the admission that the trade is carried on subject to the risk of capture and confiscation of the goods, and of the detention, loss of freight and perhaps even the confiscation of the ship. This admission should alone suffice to put us on our guard. Merchandise is not confiscated, voyages are not broken up, ships are not condemned, for acts that are innocent; these severe and destructive inflictions are penalties imposed for acts that are unlawful. The confusion so often exhibited on this subject is due to the neglect of certain simple but fundamental truths. These are:

1. That, as between nations, and particularly in matters of neutrality, the standard of what is lawful and what is unlawful is furnished by international law and not by municipal law, so that, if the statutes or other measures which a nation adopts for the performance of its neutral duties fall short of that standard, it exposes itself to complaints, to reprisals, or to claims for damages which may be prosecuted by any of the methods which international law prescribes for the enforce-

ment of international claims. Of this fundamental truth there are many examples, among which may be mentioned the settlement of the *Alabama* claims, which formed the subject of the award of the Geneva Tribunal in 1872.

2. That, as between the acts which neutral governments and their citizens are by international law forbidden to commit and the acts which neutral governments are obliged to prevent their citizens from committing, there is a clear distinction.

Municipal law is supposed to prohibit not all the unneutral acts which international law forbids, but only that part of them which neutral governments are bound to repress; the prevention and punishment of the rest, by means of visit and search on the high seas and the seizure and condemnation of the offending property, being left to the belligerents themselves as the parties primarily or preponderantly interested. The fact that there are various kinds of unneutral acts, such as the supplying of contraband of war to a belligerent, which neutral governments are not obliged to prohibit and punish by their municipal law, merely signifies that the interests of neutrals as well as of belligerents have been taken into account, and that there are limits to the burdens which neutral governments have been required to assume and to the exertions which they are required to make.

We may therefore say that, by international law, acts that are unneutral, in the sense of being unlawful, are, from the point of view of their prevention and punishment, divided into two classes, (1) those which neutral governments are bound to prevent and punish, and (2) those which neutral governments are not bound to prevent and punish, the prevention and punishment of the latter being left to the belligerents themselves.

Obviously, the answer to the question whether an act is lawful or unlawful depends not upon the circumstance that the right or the duty to punish it is committed to one agency or to another, but upon the fact that it is or is not punishable. The proof that it is unlawful is found in the fact that its commission is penalized. All acts for the commission of which international law prescribes a penalty are in the sense of that law unlawful. Should a neutral government itself supply contraband of war to a belligerent it would clearly depart from its position of neutrality and become a participant in the war. A neutral government is not permitted to perform any unneutral act whatsoever. The private citizen undertakes the business at his own risk, and against this risk his government cannot assure him protection without making itself a party to his unneutral act and doing that which is unlawful.

These propositions are abundantly established by authority. Maritime states, says Heffter, have adopted,

in a common and reciprocal interest, the rule that belligerents have the right to restrict the freedom of neutral commerce so far as concerns contraband of war, and to punish violations of the law in that regard. . . . This right has never been seriously denied to belligerents.[2]

Says Kent:

The principal restriction which the law of nations imposes on the trade of neutrals is the prohibition to furnish the belligerent parties with warlike stores and other articles which are directly auxiliary to warlike purposes.[3]

Says Woolsey:

If the neutral [government] should send powder or balls, cannon or rifles, this would be a direct encouragement of the war, and so a departure from the neutral position. . . . Now, the same wrong is committed when a private trader, without the privity of his government, furnishes the means of war to either of the warring parties. It may be made a question whether such conduct on the part of the private citizen ought not to be prevented by his government, even as enlistments for foreign armies on neutral soil are made penal. But it is difficult for a government to watch narrowly the operations of trade, and it is annoying for the innocent trader. Moreover, the neutral ought not to be subjected by the quarrels of others to additional care and expense. Hence by the practice of nations he is passive in regard to violations of the rules concerning contraband, blockade, and the like, and leaves the police of the sea and the punishing or reprisal power in the hands of those who are most interested, the limits being fixed for the punishment by common usage or law. . . . It is admitted that the act of carrying to the enemy articles directly useful in war is a wrong, for which the injured party may punish the neutral taken in the act.[4]

Says Manning:

The right of belligerents to prevent neutrals from carrying to an enemy articles that may serve him in the direct prosecution of his hostile purposes has been acknowledged by all authorities, and is obvious to plain reason. . . . The non-recognition of this right . . . would place it in the power of neutrals to interfere directly in the issue of wars—those who, by definition, are not parties in the contest thus receiving a power to injure a belligerent, which even if direct enemies they would not possess.[5]

Says Creasy:

A belligerent has by international law a right to seize at sea, and to appropriate or destroy, articles, to whomsoever they may belong,

2. Heffter, *Droit International* (Bergson ed. by Geffcken, 1883), p. 384.
3. Kent, *International Law* (2d ed. by Abdy), p. 330.
4. Woolsey, *International Law*, §§ 178, 179.
5. Manning, *Law of Nations* (Amos ed.), 352.

which are calculated to aid the belligerent's enemy in the war, and which are being conveyed by sea to that enemy's territory.[6]

Says Holland:

The neutral power is under no obligation to prevent its subjects from engaging in the running of blockades, in shipping or carrying contraband, or in carrying troops or dispatches from one of the belligerents; but, on the other hand, neutral subjects so engaged can expect no protection from their own government against such customary penalties as may be imposed upon their conduct by the belligerent who is aggrieved by it.[7]

The fact that the supplying of contraband of war is considered as a participation in the hostilities is shown not only by the authority of writers, but also by numerous state papers.

Washington, in his famous neutrality proclamation of April 22, 1793, countersigned by Jefferson, as Secretary of State, announced

that whosoever of the citizens of the United States shall render himself liable to punishment or forfeiture under the law of nations, by committing, aiding, or abetting hostilities against any of the said powers, or by carrying to any of them those articles which are deemed contraband by the modern usage of nations, will not receive the protection of the United States against such punishment or forfeiture.[8]

Jefferson, in his subsequent note to the British minister, May 15, 1793, observes that in the case of contraband the law of nations is satisfied with the "external penalty" pronounced in the President's proclamation.[9]

President Grant, in the proclamation issued by him August 22, 1870, during the Franco-German war, declares, in the most precise terms:

While all persons may lawfully, and without restriction, by reason of the aforesaid state of war, manufacture and sell within the United States arms and munitions of war, and other articles ordinarily known as "contraband of war," yet they can not carry such articles upon the high seas for the use or service of either belligerent, . . . without incurring the risk of hostile capture and the penalties denounced by the law of nations in that behalf. And I do hereby give notice that all citizens of the United States, and others who may claim the protection of this Government who may misconduct themselves in the premises, will do so at their peril, and that they can in no wise obtain any protection from the Government of the United States against the consequences of their misconduct.[10]

6. Creasy, *First Platform of International Law*, p. 604.
7. Holland, *Studies in International Law*, pp. 124–125. See, also, Moore, *Digest of International Law*, VII, 972–973.
8. *American State Papers, Foreign Relations*, I, 140.
9. Moore, *Digest of International Law*, VII, 955.
10. *Idem*, p. 751.

In the neutrality proclamations, issued during the war between the United States and Spain, the following provisions are found, in which the furnishing of arms and munitions of war to either party to the conflict is expressly treated as an act of unneutrality.

The Brazilian government, by a circular of April 29, 1898, declared to be "absolutely prohibited" the "exportation of material of war from the ports of Brazil to those of either of the belligerent powers, under the Brazilian flag or that of any other nation." [11]

The King of Denmark issued April 29, 1898, a proclamation prohibiting Danish subjects "to transport contraband of war for any of the belligerent powers." [12]

Great Britain's proclamation of April 23, 1898, warned British subjects against doing any act "in derogation of their duty as subjects of a neutral power," or "in violation or contravention of the law of nations," among which was enumerated the carrying of "arms, ammunition, military stores or materials"; and declared that "all persons so offending, together with their ships and goods, will rightfully incur and be justly liable to hostile capture, and to the penalties denounced by the law of nations." [13]

The governor of Curaçao, acting under instructions of the minister of the colonies of the Netherlands, issued a decree prohibiting "the exportation of arms, ammunition, or other war materials to the belligerents." [14]

Portugal, while stating, in Article IV of her neutrality decree of April 29, 1898, that "all articles of lawful commerce" belonging to subjects of the belligerent powers might be carried under the Portuguese flag, and that such articles belonging to Portuguese subjects might be carried under the flag of either belligerent, yet declared: "Articles that may be considered as contraband of war are expressly excluded from the provisions of this article." [15]

Were further proof needed of the unneutral and noxious character of contraband trade, it might be found in the doctrine of infection, under which innocent cargo is condemned when associated with contraband merchandise of the same proprietor, and the transportation penalized by loss of freight and expenses, and, under various circumstances, by confiscation of the ship.

11. *Proclamations and Decrees during the War with Spain*, p. 13.
12. *Idem*, p. 22.
13. *Idem*, p. 35.
14. *Idem*, p. 27.
15. *Idem*, p. 61. See, also, the proclamation of the taotai of Shanghai, *idem*, p. 20, and the instructions of the Haitian Government, *idem*, p. 39.

Bearing in mind that the subject which we are considering is one of universal interest, directly affecting the world's trade and involving the imposition of heavy pecuniary penalties upon individuals, one ventures little in saying that among present-day questions of maritime law, touching intercourse between belligerents and neutrals, the most important is that of contraband. This may be affirmed in spite of the fact that, partly because of the lack of great maritime wars in recent times, its gravity may not at the moment be generally or popularly appreciated.[16] The question of blockade, although it once assumed immense proportions, to a great extent lost its importance when the principle was established that blockades in order to be legally valid must be effective, that is to say, maintained by a force sufficient to prevent access to the blockaded port or at least to render such access dangerous. Since the definite and universal acceptance of this principle, by which neutral commerce was relieved of the hazards to which it was formerly exposed from measures generically designated by the odious name of "paper blockades," the conflict between belligerent right and neutral right has been carried on chiefly in the domain of contraband, to which it may be said that all the legal uncertainties that formerly attended the subject of blockade have been transferred, with many additions and aggravations.

In order to demonstrate the paramount importance of the question of contraband, it is unnecessary to do more than point out that, if the claim of capture on this ground be not properly limited, the two great safeguards of neutral rights established after generations of conflict become utterly worthless. I refer to the rule that free ships make free goods and the rule that blockades must be effectively maintained.

First, let us consider the rule that free ships make free goods. By what has been called the common law of the sea, the goods of an enemy were subject to capture and confiscation without regard to the character of the ship in which they were borne. The enforcement of this rule necessarily involved the capture and bringing in of neutral vessels whose cargoes were alleged to be composed even in small part of the goods of a belligerent. The breaking up of voyages in this manner, with all the resultant losses, entailed so much hardship that, as early as the seventeenth century, there sprang up an agitation for the exemption of neutral vessels from molestation for carrying goods which happened to belong to a citizen of a belligerent country. Such an exemption gradually came to be embodied in

16. Its gravity again became apparent soon after the outbreak of the war in Europe in 1914.

treaties; and when on February 28, 1780, the Empress Catherine of Russia issued her celebrated manifesto, which formed the basis of the Armed Neutrality, she announced this rule:

2. Goods belonging to the subjects of the said nations at war are, with the exception of contraband articles, free [from capture] on board neutral vessels.

This definite enunciation of the rule that free ships make free goods was incorporated in the Declaration of Paris of 1856 in the following terms:

2. The neutral flag covers the enemy's goods, with the exception of contraband of war.

The United States, Spain and Mexico (Mexico acting under the direct influence of the United States) did not adhere to the Declaration of Paris, because it undertook to abolish privateering; but the United States and Spain expressly accepted the rule that free ships make free goods, and this was proclaimed by the United States in 1898 as a principle of international law and was so accepted by Spain in the war between the two countries in that year. Moreover, Spain has since adhered to the Declaration of Paris in its entirety.[17] But, note the exception to the rule. Enemy's goods are exempt from capture under the neutral flag, "with the exception of contraband of war." In other words, the operation of this rule and the protection intended to be afforded by it are wholly dependent upon the definition of contraband. Make the list of contraband long enough, and the rule becomes a farce.

Secondly, take the law of blockade. At one time fictitious blockades were the bane of neutral commerce. In the twelve years that followed the breach of the Peace of Amiens—the days of the so-called Napoleonic wars—millions upon millions of neutral property were unlawfully confiscated for the alleged violation of or attempt to violate blockades which existed only on paper.

The declaration of the Empress Catherine above referred to contained the following rule:

4. To determine what constitutes a blockaded port, this denomination is confined to those the entrance into which is manifestly rendered dangerous in consequence of the dispositions made by the attacking power with ships stationed sufficiently near.

The Declaration of Paris of 1856 provided:

4. Blockades, in order to be binding, must be effective; that is to say, maintained by a force sufficient really to prevent access to the coast of the enemy.

The world accepted this principle with joyful unanimity. We

17. June 18, 1908.

may, however, pertinently inquire, What is it worth, if the definition of contraband be not properly limited? The answer is not difficult. If the definition of contraband be so extended as to embrace in some form, positively or conditionally, practically all articles of commerce, the question of blockade ceases to be important. The security intended to be afforded to the neutral, by requiring the belligerent to make his blockade effective, becomes a mockery; the belligerent is practically relieved of the burden of maintaining blockades, for, instead of keeping his ships at certains points and hampering his offensive use of them, he can roam the seas at will and seize all articles destined to any belligerent port under the claim of contraband.

Let us consider the significance of the question of contraband in yet another relation. It is creditable to our humanity that proposals having a benevolent sound usually evoke a prompt and generous response, but it sometimes happens that the substance upon examination turns out to be less benevolent than the sound. We have lately heard much of the proposed immunity of private property at sea from capture. The United States is said to have advocated such a measure at both Hague Conferences. What has happened is actually this: Some of our earlier statesmen, notably Franklin, did in reality advocate a very wide exemption not only of property but also of persons, on land as well as on the sea, from the operations of war; and their example was followed by some of their successors. In 1857 the government of the United States, being embarrassed by its refusal to accede to the Declaration of Paris on account of the clause abolishing privateering, offered to adhere on condition that the powers go farther and exempt private property at sea from capture; but this offer was expressly subject to the exceptions of contraband and blockade. In 1907 Mr. Choate, on behalf of the Delegation of the United States, submitted to the second Peace Conferences at The Hague the following resolution:

The private property of all citizens or subjects of the signatory powers, with the exception of contraband of war, shall be exempt from capture or seizure on the sea by the armed vessels or by the military forces of any of the said signatory powers. But nothing herein contained shall extend exemption from seizure to vessels and their cargoes which may attempt to enter a port blockaded by the naval forces of any of the said powers.

What therefore the United States since 1850 has proposed is, not that private property at sea shall be exempt from capture, but that it shall be so exempt, subject to the exceptions of contraband and blockade. The proposal, as thus qualified, no doubt had a substantial character in 1857, since the government of the United States at that day still recalled the limitations upon contraband for which it had traditionally contended. The case was the same when, by the treaty of commerce between the United States and Italy of February 26, 1871, it was actually agreed (Art. XII) that, in the event of war between the two countries, the private property of their citizens and subjects should be exempt from capture on the high seas or elsewhere, subject to the exceptions of contraband and blockade; for the treaty then proceeded (Art. XV) precisely to limit the scope of contraband, confining it to arms and munitions of war, and declaring that those articles "and no others" should be comprehended under that denomination.[18] But at The Hague, in 1907, the importance of the exceptions was greatly enhanced by the separate presentation on the part of the United States of an extremely vague and sweeping proposition on contraband of war, in which provisions appear, no doubt for the first time in American diplomacy, in the category of absolute as well as in that of conditional contraband.[19] Taking into consideration the objects of war, opinions will necessarily differ as to the merits and value of a proposal to exempt enemy ships and enemy goods as such from capture, while leaving in force the law of blockade and of contraband, without any precise definition or limitation of the latter. Such a proposal holds out no advantage to neutrals, but offers to belligerents the favor of placing them on the same footing as neutrals commercially. And even the extent of this favor would depend upon the definition and scope of contraband. Is there not, indeed, a certain incongruity in exempting from capture such an obviously important auxiliary to military and naval operations as the ships of an enemy, while subjecting to seizure and confiscation the agricultural products of a neutral?

The question of contraband may now be considered in its historical and experimental aspects. It is unnecessary for this purpose to enter minutely into the origin of the subject. It suffices to say that in the sixteenth and the early part of the seventeenth century, the law of contraband and of blockade both being unsettled, belligerents often assumed the right to capture all neutral ships and merchandise bound to an enemy's port, thus in effect denying the existence of any right of neutral trade as opposed to belligerent exigencies. The neutral, if he differed with the belligerent as to the necessity of the inhibition or the propriety of the capture, would resort to reprisals. The

18. Note *A, infra*, p. 61
19. Note *B, infra*, p. 62

conflicts that resulted and the constant interruptions of trade, rendering it impossible to carry on international commerce without risk of ruinous losses, induced governments in the latter half of the seventeenth century to concert a decided change in practice.

Grotius, in his *De Jure Belli ac Pacis* (1625), perhaps recording the transition in thought, divided articles, with reference to the question of contraband, into three classes, (1) those that were of use only in war, (2) those that were of no use in war, but served only for pleasure, and (3) those that were useful both in war and in peace (i.e., things of double use, *ancipitis usus*), as money, provisions, ships and their appurtenances. The first he held to be prohibited; the second, to be free. As to the third, the circumstances of the war must, he said, be considered; and if the belligerent could not protect himself unless he intercepted it, necessity would give him the right to intercept it, "but under the obligation of restitution, except there be cause to the contrary." As an example of "cause to the contrary," he instanced the case of the supplying of a besieged town or a blockaded port, when a surrender or a peace was daily expected.[20]

By a treaty between France and the Hanse Towns, signed at Paris, May 10, 1655, contraband was confined to munitions of war, and it was expressly declared that wheat and grains of all sorts, vegetables and other things serving to sustain life, might be carried to the enemy, provided that they were not transported to towns and places actually under attack and were taken voluntarily and not under compulsion of the enemy, in which case they might be seized and retained on paying their just value.

November 7, 1659, there was concluded between France and Spain the famous Treaty of the Pyrenees. Articles XII and XIII dealt with the subject of contraband, including therein only such things as were distinctly of warlike character, and excluding therefrom wheat, corn and other grains, pulse, oils, wines, salt, and generally all things useful to sustain life, unless destined to towns and places "besieged, blocked up, or surrounded." [21]

The Dutch agreed to these categories in 1662, and were soon followed by Great Britain, in treaties made with the United Provinces and Spain in 1667, and with France in 1677.

In 1713 came the Peace of Utrecht. By the treaties concluded between France and the other powers on that occasion, the

20. Grotius, *De Jure Belli ac Pacis*, Bk. III, chap. i, pars. 1–3.
21. Note *C*, *infra*, p. 62

subject of contraband was definitely regulated on the most advanced lines. For example, in the treaty of commerce with Great Britain signed April 11 (1713), while contraband was limited to certain enumerated articles of warlike character, the non-contraband list, which embraced wheat, barley and other grains, pulse, tobacco, spices, salt and smoked fish, cheese and butter, beer, oils, wines, sugars, salt, "and in general all provisions which serve for the nourishment of mankind and the sustenance of life," was extended to many other articles, all of which were declared to be free except when transported to places "besieged, blocked up round about, or invested." [22]

Similar stipulations were incorporated in the British-French commercial treaty signed at Versailles, September 26, 1786.

In the manifesto of the Empress Catherine of Russia of 1780, which formed, as heretofore stated, the basis of the Armed Neutrality, it was declared that her Imperial Majesty adhered to Articles X and XI of her treaty of commerce with Great Britain, and extended their provisions to all the nations at war. This treaty was concluded June 20, 1766. With the "single exception" of certain enumerated articles, which were "accounted ammunition or military stores," it was agreed that the subjects of the one party might transport "all sorts of commodities" to places belonging to the enemy of the other that were not "actually blocked up, or besieged, as well by sea as by land." [23]

Such was the condition of things when the wars growing out of the French Revolution began. The enthusiastic devotion of the French on the one hand to the principles which they had espoused, and the frenzied resistance of monarchical governments on the other hand to what they regarded as an anarchical propagandism threatening thrones everywhere by force of example if not by force of arms, imparted to these struggles a peculiarly intense and lawless character. Three months after the war between France and Great Britain was declared, the National Convention, May 9, 1793, there being a scarcity of food in France, adopted a decree authorizing the seizure of vessels laden wholly or in part with provisions, which, if found to be neutral property, were to be paid for at the price which they would have fetched at the port of destination, together with an allowance for freight and for the vessel's detention. This was a claim not of contraband but of preemption. Nevertheless, the United States protested against it, and it was not uniformly enforced against American vessels. Great Britain on the other hand, wishing not only to supply her own

22. Note *D, infra*, p. 63
23. Note *E, infra*, p. 63

wants but to increase the pressure on France, advanced a claim compounded of contraband and preemption. By an order in council of June 8, 1793, which was communicated to the Admiralty on the 28th of the same month, the commanders of British ships of war and privateers were authorized to seize all vessels laden wholly or in part with corn (i.e., cereals generally, as wheat, barley, rye and oats, but more especially wheat), flour, or meal, bound to any port in France, or any port occupied by the armies of France, in order that such provisions might be purchased on behalf of the government, with an allowance to the vessel for freight, or in order that the master might be required to give security to dispose of such cargo in a country in amity with Great Britain. The British government assumed to justify this order on the ground that by the law of nations, as laid down by the most modern writers, and particularly by Vattel, all provisions were to be considered as contraband, and as such liable to confiscation, where the depriving an enemy of them was one of the means intended to be employed for reducing him to reasonable terms of peace; and that the actual situation of France rendered this reasoning peculiarly applicable, not only because the scarcity there was caused by the unusual measure of arming almost the whole laboring class of the nation, but also because the trade was to be regarded, not as a mercantile speculation of individuals, but as an immediate operation of the very persons who had declared war and were carrying it on against Great Britain. On these considerations, said the British government, the powers at war would have been perfectly justifiable if they had considered all provisions as contraband and had directed them as such to be brought in for confiscation, but they had only sought to prevent the French from being supplied with corn, omitting all mention of other provisions, and even in respect of corn, instead of confiscating the cargoes, had secured to the proprietors, if neutral, a full indemnity for any loss they might sustain.

The United States, on the other hand, declared that the position that provisions were contraband in the case where the depriving an enemy of them was one of the means intended to be employed for reducing him to reasonable terms of peace, or in any case but that of a place actually blockaded, was entirely new; that reason and usage had established that, when two nations went to war, those who chose to live in peace retained their natural right to pursue their agriculture, manufactures, and other ordinary vocations, and to carry the produce of their industry, for exchange, to all nations, belligerent or neutral, except that they must not furnish implements of war to the belligerents or send anything to a blockaded place. Implements of war destined to a belligerent were treated as contraband, and were subject to seizure and confiscation. Corn, flour, and meal were not, said the United States, of the class of contraband, and consequently remained articles of free commerce. The state of war between Great Britain and France furnished neither belligerent with the right to interrupt the agriculture of the United States, or the peaceable exchange of its produce with all nations. Such an act of interference tended directly to draw the United States from the state of peace in which they wished to remain. If the United States permitted corn to be sent to Great Britain and her friends, and refused it to France, such an act of partiality might lead to war with the latter power. If they withheld supplies of provisions from France, they should in like manner be bound to withhold them from her enemies also, and thus to close to themselves all the ports of Europe where corn was in demand, or else make themselves a party to the war. This was a dilemma into which no pretext for forcing the United States could be found. Great Britain might, indeed, feel the desire of starving an enemy nation; but she could have no right to do it at the cost of the United States, or to make the latter the instrument of it.[24]

Such was the position maintained by the United States; and when John Jay was sent on a special mission to England in 1794 to negotiate a settlement of differences, the first topic discussed in his instructions was that of the vexations inflicted on commerce under orders in council. By the treaty which he signed on November 19, 1794, a precise enumeration was made (Art. XVIII) of the things which were admitted to be contraband, and it was stipulated that when cases arose in which "provisions and other articles not generally contraband" might, according to the existing law of nations, be regarded as becoming such, they should not, even though seized on that ground, be confiscated, but should be paid for at their full value, together with a reasonable mercantile profit, freight and demurrage.[25] Nor was this all. A mixed commission was established under the treaty (Art. VII) to adjudicate complaints on account of seizures. The British authorities, where they made compensation for cargoes of provisions, adopted as a basis the invoice price plus a mercantile profit of ten per cent. The claimants contended that this was inadequate. The commission allowed the net value of the cargo at its port of destination

---

24. For a full narrative of this incident and the text of the orders in council, see Moore, *History and Digest of International Arbitrations*, I, 299–306.

25. Note *F, infra*, p. 64

at the time at which it probably would have arrived there, had it not been seized. The awards of the commission in the case of captured vessels laden with provisions and bound to France are estimated to have amounted to £720,000, or approximately $3,500,000.[26]

The position successfully maintained by the United States in the case of Great Britain was altogether in accord with that which was reciprocally acted upon in its relations with other powers. The commercial treaty with France of 1778—the first treaty concluded by the United States—substantially incorporated the Utrecht clause on the subject of contraband,[27] as also did the later convention of 1800. A similar stipulation may be found in the treaty with Sweden of 1783, and in that with Spain of 1795. In the treaties of 1785 and 1799 the United States and Prussia went so far as to agree that even arms and munitions of war, when seized as contraband, should not be confiscated, but that the captor should pay for them if he converted them to his own use, or pay damages if he merely detained them.[28] In the treaty between the United States and Colombia of 1824 a clause on contraband was inserted which furnished the model followed by the United States with practical uniformity in its subsequent treaties.[29] It is substantially reproduced in the contraband articles of the treaty with Italy of 1871. It may also be found in identical or nearly identical terms in the treaties between the United States and the following powers: Central America, 1825; Brazil, 1828; Mexico, 1831; Chile, 1832; Peru-Bolivia, 1836; Venezuela, 1836 and 1860; Ecuador, 1839; New Granada, 1846; Salvador, 1850 and 1870; Peru, 1851 and 1870; Two Sicilies, 1855; Bolivia, 1858; Haiti, 1864; Dominican Republic, 1867.

During the war with Spain, in 1898, the subject of contraband was dealt with by the United States in General Orders No. 492, which specified certain articles as "absolutely contraband" and others as "conditionally contraband." The former included arms and munitions of war and machinery for their manufacture, saltpeter, military accoutrements and equipments, and horses. The "conditionally contraband" were: Coal, when destined for a naval station, a port of call, or a ship or ships of the enemy; materials for the construction of railways or telegraphs, and money, when such materials or money are destined for the enemy's forces; provisions, when destined for an enemy's ship or ships, or for a place that is besieged.

26. Moore, *op. cit.*, I, pp. 343–344.
27. Note *G, infra*, p. 65
28. Note *H, infra*, pp. 66–67
29. Note *I, infra*, p. 67

In the early stages of the Boer war a question arose between the United States and Great Britain as to the seizure of various articles shipped at New York, some of them on regular monthly orders, by American merchants and manufacturers on the vessels *Beatrice, Maria,* and *Mashona,* which were seized by British cruisers while on the way to Delagoa Bay. These articles consisted chiefly of flour, canned meats, and other foodstuffs, but also embraced lumber, hardware, and various miscellaneous articles, as well as quantities of lubricating oil, which were consigned partly to the Netherlands South African Railway, in the Transvaal, and partly to the Lourenço Marques Railway, a Portuguese concern. It was at first supposed that the seizures were made on the ground of contraband, and with reference to this possibility the government of the United States, on January 2, 1900, declared that it could not recognize their validity "under any belligerent right of capture of provisions and other goods shipped by American citizens in ordinary course of trade to a neutral port." It soon transpired, however, that the *Beatrice* and *Mashona,* which were British ships, and the *Maria,* which, though a Dutch ship, was at first supposed to be British, were arrested for violating a municipal regulation forbidding British subjects to trade with the enemy, the alleged offense consisting in the transportation of goods destined to the enemy's territory. The seizure of the cargoes was declared to be only incidental to the seizure of the ships. As to certain articles, however (particularly the oil consigned to the Netherlands South African Railway in the Transvaal), an allegation of enemy's property was made; but no question of contraband was raised, and it was eventually agreed that the United States consul-general at Cape Town should arrange with Sir Alfred Milner, the British high commissioner, for the release or purchase by the British government of any American-owned goods, which, if purchased, were to be paid for at the price they would have brought at the port of destination at the time they would have arrived there in case the voyage had not been interrupted. In the course of the correspondence, Lord Salisbury thus defined the position of the British government on the question of contraband:

Foodstuffs, with a hostile destination, can be considered contraband of war only if they are supplies for the enemy's forces. It is not sufficient that they are capable of being so used; it must be shown that this was in fact their destination at the time of the seizure.

This statement by Lord Salisbury was in harmony with what is laid down in Holland's Manual of Naval Prize Law, issued by the British Admiralty in 1888. In this Manual conditional contraband embraces provisions and liquors fit for consumption of army or navy; money; telegraphic materials, such as wire, porous cups, platina, sulphuric acid, and zinc; materials for railway construction, as iron bars and sleepers; coals, hay, horses, rosin, tallow, and timber. But these articles, it is stated, "are contraband only in case it may be presumed that they are intended to be used for the purposes of war," and "this presumption arises when such hostile destination of the vessel is either the enemy's fleet at sea, or a hostile port used exclusively or mainly for naval or military equipment."

On the outbreak of the war with Japan, the Russian government, in March, 1904, published instructions to its naval commanders which forbade the conveyance of contraband "to Japan or to Japanese armed forces," and denounced as contraband "foodstuffs," including all kinds of grain, fish, fish products of various kinds, beans, bean oil, and oil cakes. The British government protesting expressed "great concern" that "rice and provisions" should be treated as unconditionally contraband, this being regarded "as inconsistent with the law and practice of nations." The British government, it was declared, did not contest "that, in particular circumstances, provisions may acquire a contraband character, as for instance, if they should be consigned direct to the army or fleet of a belligerent, or to a port where such fleet may be lying"; but it could not admit "that if such provisions were consigned to the port of a belligerent (even though it should be a port of naval equipment) they should therefore be necessarily regarded as contraband of war." The true test appeared to be "whether there are circumstances relating to any particular cargo to show it that it is destined for military or naval use."

The United States was obliged to deal with the same question in the case of the steamer *Arabia,* whose cargo, composed of railway material and flour, destined to Japanese ports and consigned to various commercial houses there, was condemned by the Russian prize court at Vladivostok as contraband, on the strength of its destination. The United States protested against this judgment as involving a "disregard of the settled law of nations." The United States declared that it was "vital to the legitimate maritime commerce of neutral states" that there should be "no relaxation" of the distinctions with regard to contraband; that there was and could be "no middle ground"; that "the criterion of warlike usefulness and destination" had "been adopted by the common consent of civilized nations, after centuries of struggle in which each belligerent made indiscriminate warfare upon all commerce of all neutral states with the people of the other belligerent, and which led to reprisals as the mildest available remedy"; that, while articles such as arms and ammunition, self-evidently of warlike use, were contraband if destined to enemy territory, yet articles such as coal, cotton, and provisions, which, though ordinarily innocent, were capable of warlike use, were "not subject to capture and confiscation unless shown by evidence to be actually destined for the military or naval forces of a belligerent"; that "this substantive principle of the law of nations" could "not be overridden by a technical rule of the prize court that the owners of the captured cargo must prove that no part of it" might reach the enemy forces; and that, such proof being "of an impossible nature," its exaction would render neutral commerce impossible and result in the condemnation of the innocent with the guilty. In conclusion the ambassador of the United States at St. Petersburg was instructed to express "the deep regret and grave concern" with which his government had received the unqualified communication of the decision of the prize court, and was directed to "make earnest protest against it" and to say that his government regretted "its complete inability to recognize the principle of that decision and still less to acquiesce in it as a policy."

In consequence of the British and American protests the Russian government appointed a commission to consider the question of contraband, and on October 22, 1904, announced that, while horses and beasts of burden would continue to be treated as contraband of war, yet various other articles, including rice and foodstuffs, would be considered as contraband if destined for a belligerent government, its administration, army, navy, fortresses, naval ports, or purveyors, but not if "addressed to private individuals."

Since the war between Russia and Japan, the subject of contraband has been dealt with in the Declaration of London, signed February 26, 1909, by representatives of Germany, the United States, Austria-Hungary, Spain, France, Great Britain, Italy, Japan, The Netherlands, and Russia, with the object of laying down rules of maritime law, embracing blockade, contraband, unneutral service, destruction of neutral prizes, and various other subjects, for the government of the International Prize Court which Germany and Great Britain proposed to the Second Peace Conference at The Hague, and for which provision was made by the convention signed on October 18, 1907. As the House of Lords has lately rejected a bill, which had passed the Commons, to carry this convention into effect, the fate of the Declaration must, so far as Great Britain is concerned, be regarded as at least doubtful. It has been fiercely assailed in England, but has been ably defended by eminent persons, among whom Westlake may be particularly mentioned, who, although they naturally do not pronounce it perfect, consider that its adoption would on the whole be advantageous. Into this general question it is beyond my province now to enter, my subject being simply contraband.[30]

The Declaration (Art. 24), following the Grotian classification, divides articles into (1) "absolute contraband," (2) "conditional contraband," and (3) altogether non-contraband. The second category—the conditionally contraband—includes fourteen general heads, namely, foodstuffs; forage and grain, suitable for feeding animals; clothing, fabrics for clothing, and boots and shoes, suitable for use in war; gold and silver in coin or bullion, and paper money; vehicles of all kinds available for use in war, and their component parts; vessels, craft, and boats of all kinds,[31] floating docks, parts of docks and their component parts; railway material, both fixed and rolling-stock, and materials for telegraphs, wireless telegraphs, and telephones; balloons and flying machines and their distinctive component parts, together with accessories and articles recognizable as intended for use in connection with balloons and flying machines; fuel, and lubricants; powder and explosives not specially prepared for use in war; barbed wire and implements for fixing and cutting it; horseshoes and shoeing materials; harness and saddlery; field glasses, telescopes, chronometers, and all kinds of nautical instruments. And to this list belligerents are (Art. 25) allowed to add by declarations notified to other powers.

For all contraband the Declaration preserves (Art. 39) the penalty of condemnation; and it provides (Art. 33) that "conditional contraband" shall be liable to capture if "destined for the use of the armed forces or of a government department of the enemy state, unless in this latter case the circumstances show that the articles cannot in fact be used for the purposes of the war in progress." As to proof of destination, the provisions of the Declaration are two-fold. The doctrine of continuous

30. The ratifications were not afterwards exchanged, and the Declaration did not become operative. But, as it has been used more or less as a starting point in subsequent discussions, an understanding of its terms is essential.

31. This provision that vessels, craft and boats shown to be intended for belligerent use may be seized and confiscated as contraband evidently is not intended to alter or modify the law according to which the fitting out, arming, or equipping in neutral jurisdiction of a vessel to cruise or carry on war against one of the belligerents constitutes, not a mere transaction in contraband, but the setting on foot of a hostile expedition, which the neutral is bound to use due diligence to prevent.

voyage, though declared to be applicable to absolute contraband, is not applied to conditional, so that cargoes of the latter are not put in jeopardy when sent to a neutral port. This certainly creates an important safeguard. A hostile destination is, on the other hand, presumed (Art. 34) "if the consignment is addressed to enemy authorities, or to a merchant, established in the enemy country, and when it is well known that this merchant supplies articles and material of this kind to the enemy," or "is destined to a fortified place of the enemy, or to another place serving as a base for the armed forces of the enemy." These grounds of inference are so vague and general that they would seem to justify in almost any case the presumption that the cargo, if bound to an enemy port, was "destined for the use of the armed forces or of a government department of the enemy state." Any merchant established in the enemy country, who deals in the things described, will sell them to the government; and if it becomes public that he does so, it will be "well known" that he supplies them. Again, practically every important port is a "fortified place"; and yet the existence of fortifications would usually bear no relation whatever to the eventual use of provisions and various other articles mentioned. Nor can it be denied that, with well-kept highways, almost any place may serve as a "base" for supplying the armed forces of the enemy. And of what interest or advantage is it to a belligerent to prevent the enemy from obtaining supplies from a "base," from a "fortified place," or from a merchant "well known" to deal with him, in his own country, if he is permitted freely to obtain them from other places and persons, and especially, as countries having land boundaries can for the most part easily do, through a neutral port? No doubt the advantage of such prevention may readily become greater, if the enemy be, like Great Britain or Japan, an insular country.

The attempt to establish an international prize court constitutes one of the most remarkable advances ever proposed towards the founding of an international jurisdiction, and the effort made in the Declaration of London to furnish a universal law is a step in the right direction. The able framers of the Declaration may be assumed to have made the best compromise that was at the time obtainable. But the question of contraband remains unsolved; and it will so remain either until, by an inconceivable relapse into primitive sixteenth-century conditions, all commerce with belligerents is forbidden, or until innocent articles of universal use, such as provisions, which, even when consumed by military men, are consumed by them as human beings rather than as soldiers, are, in conformity with the traditional contention of the United States, put beyond reach of capture on loose and interested surmises.[32]

While seizures of articles commonly classed as conditional contraband have inflicted upon neutrals enormous losses, the effect of such seizures upon the fortunes of the belligerents has by no means been so appreciable as it is often hastily assumed to have been. Lawless, unrestrained and successful as were the depredations on neutral commerce during the wars following the French Revolution, not only did the struggle persist through more than twenty years, but its end was scarcely hastened by the spoliations, which indeed seem rather to have supplied the means of its prolongation. The reduction of the South, during the American Civil War, was sensibly accelerated by the cutting off of its commerce, but this result was achieved chiefly by means of blockade.

At the Second Peace Conference at The Hague, in 1907, the British government, with a view to diminish the difficulties which neutral commerce encounters in case of war, proposed that the powers should enter into an agreement to abandon the principle of contraband altogether, and to confine the right of visit to the ascertainment of the merchant vessel's neutral character. Such a measure was justified on the ground that, while it had in spite of all efforts been found to be impossible to prevent belligerents from obtaining the munitions which they needed, the attempt to do so had, by reason of the increase in the tonnage of ships, the carrying of mixed cargoes, the lack of any single destination of ship or cargo, the multiplication of the number of articles used in war, and the development of railways and other means of transportation by land, become more and more futile on the part of belligerents and more and more injurious to neutrals. The circumstance that the radical proposal of Great Britain, although it was not eventually adopted by the Conference, received the support of twenty-six of the powers represented therein, while only five voted against it,[33] alone suffices to demonstrate the existence of a general

32. The comment and forecast thus made in 1912 were remarkably verified in and after August, 1914, when, although the Declaration of London had not become legally operative, attempts were made to apply it, in whole or in part, provisionally as a *modus vivendi*.

33. For: Argentine Republic, Austria-Hungary, Belgium, Brazil, Bulgaria, Chile, China, Cuba, Denmark, Dominican Republic, Great Britain, Greece, Italy, Mexico, Netherlands, Norway, Paraguay, Peru, Persia, Portugal, Salvador, Servia, Siam, Spain, Sweden, Switzerland—26.

Against: France, Germany, Montenegro, Russia, United States—5.

Abstaining: Japan, Panama, Rumania, Turkey—4.

See *Deuxième Conférence de la Paix, Actes et Documents*, I, 259; III, 881, 890.

conviction that the present state of things is altogether unsatisfactory.

Recalling the treaties between Prussia and the United States of 1785 and 1799 for the virtual abolition of contraband, it is curious to find the United States and Germany acting together as two of the five powers that voted against its abolition in 1907; but, although the United States voted against the British proposal, it is gratifying to note that Admiral Sperry, on behalf of the United States delegation, after the British proposal had failed to secure the unanimous approval of the conference, maintained the historic American position that the right of capture should be confined to articles agreed to be absolutely contraband. In this relation it may be observed that the Institute of International Law, in 1896, after much deliberation, voted that the category of conditional contraband should be abolished, by exempting from capture the articles it includes; the belligerent, however, to have the right, at his pleasure and subject to an equitable indemnity, to sequester or to preempt, when on their way to an enemy port, articles serving equally for war and for peace.[34] Rather than allow existing conditions to continue, it might be advisable to add to the present duties of neutrals the obligation to prohibit the exportation of arms and munitions of war to belligerents, it being agreed that commerce in all other articles should be free. Under the more efficient administrative methods now in vogue, the enforcement of a measure of this kind probably would not prove to be so difficult as it was once supposed to be. Several examples of such a prohibition have already been given.[35] By a joint resolution of the Congress of the United States of April 22, 1898, passed at the opening of the war with Spain, the President was "authorized, in his discretion and with such limitations and exceptions as shall seem to him expedient, to prohibit the export of coal or other material used in war from any seaport of the United States until otherwise ordered" by himself or by Congress. Not only was this law enforced during the war with Spain,[36] but the President, by a proclamation of October 14, 1905, prohibited, without limitation or exception, till it should be otherwise ordered, the export of arms and munitions of war to the Dominican Republic. This prohibition, as the proclamation recites, was established for what appeared to the President to be "good and sufficient reasons." It was not founded upon any legal obligation. The fact that the American

34. *Annuaire de l'Institut de Droit International*, XV (1896), 231. See Westlake's comments, *International Law* (1st ed.), II, 249.
35. *Supra*, pp. 43, 44
36. Moore, *Digest of International Law*, VII, 194.

supervision of the Dominican customs administration had then in effect begun furnished a special justification for preventing acts that tended to disturb the public peace of the island. Nevertheless, the interest of the United States in the collection of the Dominican customs can hardly be considered as more important than its interest in the adjustment and preservation of the rights of neutral commerce in time of war. It is not, however, my purpose to intimate that the adoption of further measures to assure the right to trade in articles classed as "conditional contraband," should await the adoption of further restrictions upon trade in absolute contraband.[37]

# APPENDIX

## NOTE *A*

*Treaty of Commerce between the United States and Italy,*
February 26, 1871, Articles XII and XV

Art. XII. The high contracting parties agree that, in the unfortunate event of a war between them, the private property of their respective citizens and subjects, with the exception of contraband of war, shall be exempt from capture or seizure, on the high seas or elsewhere, by the armed vessels or by the military forces of either party; it being understood that this exemption shall not extend to vessels and their cargoes which may attempt to enter a port blockaded by the naval forces of either party.

Art. XV. The liberty of navigation and commerce secured to neutrals by the stipulations of this treaty shall extend to all kinds of merchandise, excepting those only which are distinguished by the name of contraband of war. And, in order to remove all causes of doubt and misunderstanding upon this subject, the contracting parties expressly agree and declare that the following articles, and no others, shall be considered as comprehended under this denomination:

1. Cannons, mortars, howitzers, swivels, blunderbusses, muskets, fusees, rifles, carbines, pistols, pikes, swords, sabers, lances, spears,

---

37. The late Earl Loreburn, in his volume *Capture at Sea*, published in London in 1913, said: "I believe it might be wise on our [Great Britain's] part, to agree that every neutral state should be bound to use the means at its disposal for preventing the export of war material in the same way as it is now obliged to prevent the departure of a vessel intending to take part in hostilities. . . . If, however, it were impossible to procure a general consent to the abolition at all events of conditional contraband, it might be possible in the last resort, as part of a comprehensive reform of maritime law, to secure the exemption of food and numerous other classes of goods which, though they may possibly be useful for military purposes, are not largely so used, and in regard to other such things to substitute a right of preemption for a right of confiscation." Pp. 128–130.

halberds, bombs, grenades, powder, matches, balls, and all other things belonging to, and expressly manufactured for, the use of these arms.

2. Infantry belts, implements of war and defensive weapons, clothes cut or made up in a military form and for a military use.

3. Cavalry belts, war saddles and holsters.

4. And generally all kinds of arms and instruments of iron, steel, brass, and copper, or of any other materials manufactured, prepared, and formed expressly to make war by sea or land.

## Note *B*

### *Proposition (translated) of the Delegation of the United States at The Hague Conference of 1907 on Contraband of War*

1. Absolute contraband shall consist of arms, munitions of war, provisions, and articles employed solely for a military purpose or for military establishments.

2. Conditional contraband shall consist of provisions, materials and articles which are employed for the double purpose of peace and of war, but which by reason of their nature or special qualities, of their quantity, or by their nature, quality and quantity are suitable and necessary for a military purpose, and which are destined for the use of the armed forces or the military establishments of the enemy.

3. The list of articles and of provisions which shall be included in each of the aforesaid classes must be duly published and notified to neutral governments, or to their diplomatic agents, by the belligerents, and no article shall be seized or confiscated under the head of conditional contraband as to which such advice has not been given. [*Deuxième Conférence de la Paix, Actes et Documents,* III, 1160.]

## Note *C*

### *Treaty of the Pyrenees,* November 7, 1759

XII. By . . . Contraband-Goods, are only understood all sorts of Fire-arms, and all things belonging to them; as Cannons, Muskets, Mortar-pieces, Petards, Bombs, Granadoes, Saucidges, Pitch'd-circles, Carriages, Forks, Bandaliers, Gunpowder, Cords, Saltpeter, Bullets, Pikes, Swords, Casks, Head-pieces, Cuirasses, Halberts, Javelins, Horses, Saddles for Horses, Holsters for Pistols, Belts, or any other warlike Furnitures.

XIII. In that kind of Contraband-Goods, shall not be comprehended Wheat, Corn, or other Grains, Pulse, Oils, Wines, Salt, nor generally anything belonging to the nourishment and sustentation of Life; but they shall remain free, as all other Merchandizes and Commoditys, not comprehended in the foregoing Article: And the transportation of them shall be free, even to Places in enmity with the Crown of Spain, except Portugal, as aforesaid, and the Towns and Places besieged, block'd up, or surrounded. [Treaty of the Pyrenees, concluded between France and Spain, November 7, 1659: I, 45–46, of *A General Collection of Treatys, Declarations of War, Mani-*

*festos, and Other Publick Papers, Relating to Peace and War,* 2d ed. London, 1732.]

## NOTE *D*

*Treaty of Commerce between Great Britain and France,* Signed at Utrecht, March 31–April 11, 1713, Arts. XIX, XX

Art. XIX.   Under this name of contraband, or prohibited goods, shall be comprehended arms, great guns, bombs, with their fusees and other things belonging to them; fire-balls, gunpowder, match, cannon-ball, pikes, swords, lances, spears, halberds, mortars, petards, granadoes, saltpetre, muskets, musket-ball, helmets, head-pieces, breast-plates, coats of mail, and the like kinds of arms, proper for arming soldiers, musket-rests, belts, horses with their furniture, and all other warlike instruments whatever.

Art. XX.   These merchandizes which follow shall not be reckoned among prohibited goods, that is to say, all sorts of clothes, and all other manufactures woven of any wool, flax, silk, cotton, or any other materials whatever; all kinds of clothes and wearing apparel, together with the species whereof they are used to be made; gold and silver, as well coined as uncoined, tin, iron, lead, copper, brass, coals; as also wheat and barley, and any other kind of corn, and pulse; tobacco, and likewise all manner of spices, salted and smoked flesh, salted fish, cheese and butter, beer, oils, wines, sugars, and all sorts of salt, and, in general, all provisions which serve for the nourishment of mankind, and the sustenance of life. Furthermore, all kinds of cotton, hemp, flax, tar, pitch, ropes, cables, sails, sailcloths, anchors, and any parts of anchors; also shipmasts, planks, boards and beams of what trees soever; and all other things proper either for building or repairing ships; and all other goods whatever, which have not been worked into the form of any instrument, or thing prepared for war, by land or by sea, shall not be reputed contraband, much less such as have been already wrought and made up for any other use; all which shall wholly be reckoned among free goods, as likewise all other merchandizes and things which are not comprehended, and particularly mentioned in the preceding article, so that they may be transported, and carried in the freest manner by the subjects of both confederates, even to places belonging to an enemy, such towns or places being only excepted, as are at that time besieged, blocked up round about, or invested. [Jenkinson, *Treaties*, II, 51.]

## NOTE *E*

*Treaty of Commerce and Navigation between Great Britain and Russia,* June 20, 1766, Arts. X and XI, referred to in the third article of the declaration of the Empress Catherine of February 28, 1780

X. Permission shall be granted to the subjects of the two contracting parties to go, come, and trade freely with those states, with which one or other of the parties shall at that time, or at any future period, be engaged in war, provided they do not carry military stores to the enemy. From this permission, however, are excepted places actually blocked up, or besieged, as well by sea as by land; but at all other times, and with the single exception of military stores, the above-said subjects may transport to these places all sorts of commodities, as well as passengers without the least impediment. With regard to the searching of merchant ships, men of war and privateers shall behave as favourably as the reason of the war, at that time existing, can possibly permit towards the most friendly powers that shall remain neuter; observing, as far as may be, the principles and maxims of the law of nations, that are generally acknowledged.

XI. All cannon, mortars, muskets, pistols, bombs, grenades, bullets, balls, fusees, flint-stones, matches, powder, saltpetre, sulphur, breast-plates, pikes, swords, belts, cartouch-bags, saddles, and bridles, beyond the quantity that may be necessary for the use of the ship, or beyond what every man serving on board the ship, and every passenger, ought to have, shall be accounted ammunition or military stores; and, if found, shall be confiscated, according to law, as contraband goods or prohibited commodities; but neither the ships nor passengers, nor the other commodities found at the same time, shall be detained or hindered to prosecute their voyage. [Chalmers, I, 7.]

NOTE *F*

*Treaty between the United States and Great Britain,* November 19, 1794, Art. XVIII

Art. XVIII. In order to regulate what is in future to be esteemed contraband of war, it is agreed that under the said denomination shall be comprised all arms and implements serving for the purposes of war, by land or sea, such as cannon, muskets, mortars, petards, bombs, grenades, carcasses, saucisses, carriages for cannon, musket-rests, bandoliers, gunpowder, match, saltpetre, ball, pikes, swords, head-pieces, cuirasses, halberts, lances, javelins, horse-furniture, holsters, belts, and generally all other implements of war, as also timber for ship-building, tar or rosin, copper in sheets, sails, hemp, and cordage, and generally whatever may serve directly to the equipment of vessels, unwrought iron and fir planks only excepted; and all the above articles are hereby declared to be just objects of confiscation whenever they are attempted to be carried to an enemy.

And whereas the difficulty of agreeing on the precise cases in which alone provisions and other articles not generally contraband may be regarded as such, renders it expedient to provide against the inconveniences and misunderstandings which might thence arise: It is further agreed that whenever any such articles so becoming contraband, according to the existing laws of nations, shall for that reason be seized, the same shall not be confiscated, but the owners thereof shall be speedily and completely indemnified; and the captors, or, in their default, the Government under whose authority they act, shall pay to the masters or owners of such vessels the full value of all such articles, with a reasonable mercantile profit thereon, together with the freight, and also the demurrage incident to such detention.

And whereas it frequently happens that vessels sail for a port or place belonging to an enemy without knowing that the same is either besieged, blockaded or invested, it is agreed that every vessel so circumstanced may be turned away from such port or place; but she shall not be detained, nor her cargo, if not contraband, be confiscated, unless after notice she shall again attempt to enter, but she shall be permitted to go to any other port or place she may think proper; nor shall any vessel or goods of either party that may have entered into such port or place before the same was besieged, blockaded, or invested by the other, and be found therein after the reduction or surrender of such place, be liable to confiscation, but shall be restored to the owners or proprietors thereof.

NOTE *G*

*Treaty of Commerce between the United States and France*, February 6, 1778, Arts. XXIII, XXIV

Art. XXIII. It shall be lawful for all and singular the subjects of the Most Christian King, and the citizens, people, and inhabitants of the said United States, to sail with their ships with all manner of liberty and security, no distinction being made who are the proprietors of the merchandizes laden thereon, from any port to the places of those who now are or hereafter shall be at enmity with the Most Christian King or the United States. It shall likewise be lawful for the subjects and inhabitants aforesaid to sail with the ships and merchandizes aforementioned, and to trade with the same liberty and security from the places, ports, and havens of those who are enemies of both or either party, without any opposition or disturbance whatsoever, not only directly from the places of the enemy aforementioned to neutral places, but also from one place belonging to an enemy to another place belonging to an enemy, whether they be under the jurisdiction of the same Prince or under several. And it is hereby stipulated that free ships shall also give a freedom to goods, and that everything shall be deemed to be free and exempt which shall be found on board the ships belonging to the subjects of either of the confederates, although the whole lading or any part thereof should appertain to the enemies of either, contraband goods being always excepted. It is also agreed in like manner that the same liberty be extended to persons who are on board a free ship, with this effect, that although they be enemies to both or either party, they are not to be taken out of that free ship, unless they are soldiers and in actual service of the enemies.

Art. XXIV. This liberty of navigation and commerce shall extend to all kinds of merchandizes, excepting those only which are distinguished by the name of contraband; and under this name of contraband or prohibited goods shall be comprehended arms, great guns, bombs with the fuzes, and other things belonging to them, cannonball, gunpowder, match, pikes, swords, lances, spears, halberds, mortars, petards, granades, saltpetre, muskets, musket-ball, bucklers, helmets, breast-plates, coats of mail, and the like kinds of arms proper for arming soldiers, musket-rests, belts, horses with their furniture, and all other warlike instruments whatever. These merchandizes which follow shall not be reckoned among contraband or prohibited goods; that is to say, all sorts of cloths, and all other manufactures woven of any wool, flax, silk, cotton or any other materials whatever; all kinds of wearing apparel, together with the species whereof they are used to be made; gold and silver, as well coined as uncoined, tin, iron, latten, copper, brass, coals; as also wheat and barley, and any other kind of corn and pulse; tobacco, and likewise all manner of spices; salted and smoked flesh, salted fish, cheese and butter, beer, oils, wines, sugars, and all sorts of salts; and in general all provisions which serve for the nourishment of mankind and the sustenance of life; furthermore, all kinds of cotton, hemp, flax, tar, pitch, ropes, cables, sails, sail-cloths, anchors and any parts of anchors, also ships' masts, planks, boards and beams of what trees soever; and all other things proper either for building or repairing ships, and all other goods whatever which have not been worked into the form of any instrument or thing prepared for war by land or by sea, shall not be reputed contraband, much less such as have been already wrought and made up for any other use; all which shall be wholly reckoned among free goods; as likewise all other merchandizes and things which are not comprehended and particularly mentioned in the foregoing enumeration of contraband goods; so that they may be transported and carried in the freest manner by the subjects of both confederates, even to places belonging to an enemy, such towns or places being only excepted as are at that time besieged, blocked up, or invested.

NOTE *H*

*Treaty between the United States and Prussia,* September 10, 1785 (signed on the part of the United States by Franklin, Jefferson, and Adams), Art. XIII

Art. XIII. And in the same case of one of the contracting parties being engaged in war with any other Power, to prevent all the difficulties and misunderstandings that usually arise respecting the merchandize heretofore called contraband, such as arms, ammunition, and military stores of every kind, no such articles carried in the vessels, or by the subjects or citizens of one of the parties to the enemies of the other, shall be deemed contraband, so as to induce confiscation or condemnation and a loss of property to individuals. Nevertheless, it shall be lawful to stop such vessels and articles, and to detain them for such length of time as the captors may think necessary to prevent the inconvenience or damage that might ensue from their proceeding, paying, however, a reasonable compensation for the loss such arrest shall occasion to the proprietors: And it shall further be allowed to use in the service of the captors the whole or any part of the military stores so detained, paying the owners the full value of the same, to be ascertained by the current price at the place of its destination. But in the case supposed, of a vessel stopped for articles heretofore deemed contraband, if the master of the vessel stopped will deliver out the goods supposed to be of contraband nature, he shall be admitted to do it, and the vessel shall not in that case be carried into any port, nor further detained, but shall be allowed to proceed on her voyage.

*Treaty between the United States and Prussia,* July 11, 1799 (signed on the part of the United States by John Quincy Adams), Art. XIII

Art. XIII. And in the same case of one of the contracting parties being engaged in war with any other Power, to prevent all the difficulties and misunderstandings that usually arise respecting merchandise of contraband, such as arms, ammunition, and military stores of every kind, no such articles carried in the vessels, or by the subjects or citizens of either party, to the enemies of the other, shall be deemed contraband, so as to induce confiscation or condemnation and a loss of property to individuals. Nevertheless, it shall be lawful to stop such vessels and articles, and to detain them for such length of time as the captors may think necessary to prevent the inconvenience or damage that might ensue from their proceeding, paying, however, a reasonable compensation for the loss such arrest shall occasion to the proprietors; and it shall further be allowed to use in the service of the captors the whole or any part of the military stores so detained, paying the owners the full value of the same, to be ascertained by the current price at the place of its destination. But in the case supposed of a vessel stopped for articles of contraband, if the master of the vessel stopped will deliver out the goods supposed to be of contraband nature, he shall be admitted to do it, and the vessel shall not in that case be carried into any port, nor further detained, but shall be allowed to proceed on her voyage.

All cannons, mortars, fire-arms, pistols, bombs, grenades, bullets, balls, muskets, flints, matches, powder, saltpetre, sulphur, cuirasses, pikes, swords, belts, cartouch boxes, saddles and bridles, beyond the quantity necessary for the use of the ship, or beyond that which every man serving on board the vessel, or passenger, ought to have; and in general whatever is comprised under the denomination of arms and military stores, of what description soever, shall be deemed objects of contraband.

## NOTE *I*

*Treaty between the United States and Colombia,* October 3, 1824, Arts. XIV, XV

Art. XIV. This liberty of navigation and commerce shall extend to all kinds of merchandises, excepting those only which are distinguished by the name of contraband; and under this name of contraband or prohibited goods shall be comprehended—

First.—Cannons, mortars, howitzers, swivels, blunderbusses, muskets, fusees, rifles, carbines, pistols, pikes, swords, sabres, lances, spears, halberds and grenades, bombs, powder, matches, balls, and all other things belonging to the use of these arms;

Secondly.—Bucklers, helmets, breast-plates, coats of mail, infantry belts, and clothes made up in the form and for a military use;

Thirdly.—Cavalry belts and horses with their furniture;

Fourthly.—And generally all kinds of arms and instruments of iron, steel, brass and copper, or of any other materials manufactured, prepared and formed expressly to make war by sea or land.

Art. XV. All other merchandises and things not comprehended in the articles of contraband explicitly enumerated and classified as above, shall be held and considered as free, and subjects of free and lawful commerce, so that they may be carried and transported in the freest manner by both the contracting parties, even to places belonging to an enemy, excepting only those places which are at that time besieged or blocked up; and, to avoid all doubt in this particular, it is declared that those places only are besieged or blockaded which are actually attacked by a belligerent force capable of preventing the entry of the neutral.

# III

# INTERNATIONAL ARBITRATION:

## A SURVEY OF THE PRESENT SITUATION[1]

IN assembling for the Twentieth Annual Meeting of the Lake Mohonk Conference on International Arbitration, it is appropriate to survey existing conditions, in order that we may take our bearings.

If we were to compare the international situation of the present moment with that which existed in the Spring of 1895, when this Conference first met, there would be little to justify a feeling of hopefulness. It is true that the international situation was not at that time by any means clear. Great Britain's controversy with the Boers was beginning to loom on the horizon; the second insurrection, which ended in the intervention of the United States, had just broken out in Cuba; and the combustibles which a few months later produced the explosion over the Venezuelan boundary were with an occasional pre-

1. An address delivered in opening, as presiding officer, the twentieth Annual Meeting of the Lake Mohonk Conference on International Arbitration, May 27, 1914. It is this address, delivered two months before the outbreak of the war in Europe, that was deemed, by serene and deprecatory forecasters of the day, to be "pessimistic." (See *supra*, p. 13.) Apart from the establishment of the Permanent Court of International Justice (*infra*, p. 79), the situation as described in the address, except in the few and relatively unimportant particulars indicated in the footnotes, remains unchanged and unimproved.

monitory report actively accumulating. On the other hand, the process of arbitration had then lately been applied or was in course of application to certain important matters. In February, 1895, the President of the United States handed down his award in the dispute between Argentina and Brazil in regard to the title to the Misiones territory. Within the preceding two years the tribunal at Paris had rendered its judgment on the Bering Sea dispute. At that moment it could not be foreseen that arbitration would be employed for the adjustment of the Venezuelan boundary, for, as has been intimated, the controversy had not then reached its acute stage. But we now know that arbitration was in the end successfully invoked, and that this was followed by the conclusion of a remarkable general treaty of arbitration between the United States and Great Britain, which barely failed to secure the necessary two-thirds vote of approval in the United States Senate.

What the immediate future may now hold in store in the way of actual arbitration it is not possible to predict; but the cases that have occurred during the past two years have not been in any respect notable. They have for the most part related to simple pecuniary questions. Perhaps the most important of them is that which is now pending before the Permanent Court of Arbitration at The Hague, between Portugal on the one side, and France, Great Britain and Spain on the other, in relation to claims against Portugal growing out of the seizure of the property of religious orders in that country by the Portuguese government on the proclamation of the Republic. For the purpose of rendering a judgment on these claims a tribunal of three persons has been established at The Hague, from the list of the Permanent Court, the president of this tribunal being the Honorable Elihu Root.[2]

On the other hand, the past two years have been marked by armed contests of exceptional destructiveness. In the Balkan Peninsula the allied powers, after their victorious contest with Turkey, quarreled among themselves and engaged in a conflict which involved a greater loss of life and was characterized by even greater ferocity than the preceding collision with their common adversary. The stories of what took place during the war between the allies are still the subject of investigation; and there is only too much reason to apprehend that the end of hostilities in that quarter of the globe is not yet in sight. In other parts of the world there have been civil conflicts, the

2. The arbitral agreement was concluded July 31, 1913; the award, because of the supervention of the war, was not rendered until September 2–4, 1920.

most considerable of which is that which is still going on in Mexico.

These lamentable events merely illustrate the course of human history. Human progress never pursues a uniformly forward course. Judged by particular junctures every century furnishes occasions when the outlook of good causes is discouraging if not almost hopeless. At such times it is necessary to rise above present conditions in order to take heart for the future.

During the twenty years since this Conference came into existence there can be no doubt that the cause of international co-operation, which is vitally connected with the cause of international justice and peace, has made striking advances. Of these advances the most remarkable is found in the two Hague Conferences of 1899 and 1907, by the former of which was established the Permanent Court of Arbitration at The Hague.

Expressing my individual opinion, I do not hesitate to say that the Convention for the Pacific Settlement of International Disputes, which was signed at The Hague, July 29, 1899, is the highest achievement of the past twenty years in the direction of an arrangement for the peaceful adjustment of international controversies. This convention, as is well known, provides not only for arbitration but also for mediation and for international courts of inquiry. The numerous treaties since concluded for the purpose of making arbitration obligatory in certain cases do not, in my opinion, represent a general advance, and certainly do not represent an advance on the part of the United States. As this question is not devoid of practical importance, I will venture to give a brief explanation of my precise meaning.

The Hague Convention, although it does not in terms make arbitration obligatory in any case, excepts nothing from the scope of arbitration, thus leaving the parties free to apply the process to any and every question for the solution of which they may see fit to employ it, without discouraging in advance its application to any class of questions or furnishing a ready means of avoiding the resort to it. The numerous treaties since concluded for the purpose of rendering arbitration obligatory are based for the most part on the treaty between France and Great Britain which was signed October 14, 1903. The first article of this treaty reads as follows:

Differences which may arise of a legal nature, or relating to the interpretation of treaties existing between the two Contracting Parties, and which it may not have been possible to settle by diplomacy, shall be referred to the Permanent Court of Arbitration established at The Hague by the Convention of the 29th of July, 1899, provided, nevertheless, that they do not affect the vital interests, the independence, or the honor of the two Contracting States, and do not concern the interests of third Parties.

On reading this article the first thing that strikes one is the fact that the most important part of it is that which specifies the exceptions. The only obligation which the article imposes is the arbitration of differences "of a legal nature or relating to the interpretation of treaties"; and it is from this restricted obligation that questions affecting the "vital interests," the "independence" or the "honor" of the contracting parties, or concerning the "interests" of third powers, are excepted. So far as the United States and Great Britain are concerned, the clause therefore ran far behind their actual practice, for they had on numerous occasions submitted to arbitration questions which had been considered as affecting the "honor" of the two parties. This was particularly true of the Geneva Arbitration relating to the Alabama Claims, the arbitration of which, when first proposed by the United States, was declined on the express ground that the controversy affected the "honor" of Her Majesty's government.

Nevertheless, the government of the United States, no doubt urged thereto by those who vaguely desired to advance the cause of international peace, signed treaties with various powers in the precise terms of the British-French agreement of October 14, 1903. These treaties, which were seven in number, were submitted to the United States Senate on January 6, 1905. Following the terms of the British-French agreement, they provided that the contracting parties should, in each individual case, before appealing to the Permanent Court of Arbitration, conclude a "special agreement" defining the matter in dispute, the scope of the arbitrators' powers and the procedure to be followed. The Committee on Foreign Relations reported the treaties to the Senate with an amendment by which the word "treaty" was substituted for the word "agreement," so as to require the advice and consent of the Senate to be given in each and every case. The effect of this amendment was to require a new treaty to be made in each instance before any question whatsoever could be submitted to arbitration. In a letter to the chairman of the Committee on Foreign Relations President Roosevelt, Mr. Hay being then Secretary of State, gave notice that, if the amendment should be adopted, he would regard it as substantially nullifying his proposal and would refrain from endeavoring to secure the exchange of the ratifications of the amended treaties. The amendment, however, was adopted by the Senate, and when, on February 13, 1905, the treaties as thus amended reached the President, he caused the Secretary of State to publish a statement to the effect that they would not in their altered form be presented to the countries with which they had been negotiated. But in 1908, the pressure to do something having been renewed, the treaties were again taken up, and President Roosevelt, Mr. Root being then Secretary of State, accepted the amendment, with the result that the "special agreement," which must precede any actual resort to arbitration, can now be made only "by and with the advice and consent of the Senate."

The result of this action is that, so far as the United States is concerned, it is now in actual practice more difficult to secure international arbitration than it was in the early days of our independence. Although this statement may occasion some surprise, its absolute correctness may easily be demonstrated.

Prior to 1908 it was the practice of the United States to arbitrate pecuniary claims against foreign governments without concluding a formal treaty. As an example of this procedure I may refer to the agreement between the United States and Spain, effected by an exchange of notes on February 11–12, 1871, under which all claims of citizens of the United States against the government of Spain, for wrongs and injuries committed against their persons and property by the Spanish authorities in Cuba since the beginning of the insurrection in 1868, were submitted to a mixed commission composed of two arbitrators and an umpire. These claims involved questions of great international importance, including the validity of decrees of the Spanish government and of legal proceedings against both persons and property in Cuba. Indeed, questions analogous to those involved in the celebrated case of the "Virginius," which had brought the two countries to the very verge of war, eventually came before the commission, as well as many delicate questions of nationality or citizenship. The commission remained in existence more than ten years, and the claims presented to it amounted to more than $30,000,000, exclusive of interest. The awards amounted to nearly $1,300,000.

The first case submitted to the Permanent Court of Arbitration at The Hague under the convention of 1899—the well-known claim preferred by the United States against Mexico on behalf of the Pious Fund of the Californias—was submitted under a simple executive agreement. Other examples might readily be given; but it suffices to say that, where the settlement embraced claims against the foreign government alone and not against the United States, twenty-seven of our international arbitrations up to 1908 were held under simple executive agreements as against nineteen under treaties. The former method is now forbidden in proceedings under the treaties of 1908.

Again, it was formerly the practice of the United States to make general claims treaties or conventions, for the submission of all claims of the one government against the other arising during a certain number of years—perhaps as many as thirty or forty years—to a mixed commission, without discrimination and without specification of any particular claims.

Since 1908 what do we witness? We have now an international commission between the United States and Great Britain, called the American and British Claims Arbitration.[3] By a convention between the United States and Great Britain concluded February 8, 1853, it was agreed that "all claims" on the part of citizens of the United States against the British Government, and "all claims" on the part of British subjects against the United States, which had arisen since the signature of the treaty of peace of December 24, 1814, commonly called the Treaty of Ghent, should be referred to a mixed commission. This convention was duly carried into effect with great satisfaction to both governments. But when, in 1910, the agreement under which the present tribunal is sitting was concluded, it was found to be necessary to specify and to submit to the Senate each particular case that was proposed for arbitration; and negotiations are understood to be now under way for a second schedule, after the conclusion of which it is not improbable that various outstanding claims will still remain unsettled.

It has been stated, and probably is a fact, that there was opposition to a general claims convention with Great Britain in 1910 because bond claims against some of the States of the United States perhaps might be presented to the commission. But it may be observed that claims were presented to the commission under the general claims convention of 1853 growing out of the non-payment of the bonds of Florida and of Texas, and were disposed of by the decision of the umpire, who disallowed the claims. The same thing took place in respect of claims on account of the Confederate debt which were presented to the United States and British claims commission under Article 12 of the Treaty of Washington of May 8, 1871.

I have referred to the Anglo-American convention of 1853; but it would have been permissible to revert even to an earlier time for proof of the previous existence of a more liberal practice than that which now prevails. We may go back to 1794,

3. This commission is still in existence; its proceedings were suspended during the war.

and find in Article 7 of the Jay Treaty of that year a provision for the reference to a mixed commission of all complaints made by citizens of the United States for loss and damage by reason of irregular or illegal captures or condemnations of vessels or other property under color of authority of his Britannic Majesty, and of all complaints of British subjects on account of loss and damage suffered by reason of the failure of the United States to enforce neutrality within its jurisdiction. Here there was no specification or limitation, the two governments being evidently anxious to remove every cause of controversy by a sweeping arbitral settlement. It is a fact, perhaps not generally appreciated, that the British government paid to citizens of the United States, under Article 7 of the treaty of 1794, upwards of $10,000,000, while a considerable sum was paid by the United States to British subjects. As we are somewhat prone to boast of leading the van in the cause of peace, it may be worth our while to consider whether we should not gain a position far in advance of that which we now hold if we were to recur to the practice we followed a hundred and twenty years ago.

With a view to remove the limitations imposed by existing treaties and set an example of confidence in amicable processes, there were concluded at Washington on August 3, 1911, two remarkable agreements, between the United States on the one part, and France and Great Britain, respectively, on the other. These agreements are commonly known as the Taft-Knox treaties. By their terms (Art. 1) all future differences between the contracting parties, which it had not been possible to adjust by diplomacy, involving a "claim of right" made by one party against the other and "justiciable in their nature by reason of being susceptible of decision by the application of the principles of law or equity," were to be submitted to arbitration. In each case there was to be a "special agreement," which, so far as the United States was concerned, was to be submitted to the Senate, while the British government on its part reserved the right, before concluding a special agreement in any matter affecting the interests of a self-governing dominion, to obtain the concurrence of such dominion. The contracting parties also engaged (Art. 2) to institute, as occasion might arise, a Joint High Commission of Inquiry, to which any controversy might be referred for investigation, including any controversy as to whether a difference was "justiciable" in the sense of the treaty; and it was further stipulated (Art. 3) that, if all or all but one of the members of the Commission should report that the difference was of that character, it should be referred to arbitration.

These treaties were submitted to the Senate, by which they were amended in three particulars. In the first place, it was made absolutely certain that a "special agreement," requiring the advice and consent of the Senate, must be made in each case of arbitration. Secondly, the clause requiring the submission to the Joint High Commission of Inquiry of the question whether a difference was arbitrable and making its affirmative response in a certain event final, was stricken out. The third amendment consisted of the following proviso:

*Provided,* That the Senate advises and consents to the ratification of the said treaty with the understanding, to be made part of such ratification, that the treaty does not authorize the submission to arbitration of any question which affects the admission of aliens into the United States, or the admission of aliens to the educational institutions of the several States, or the territorial integrity of the several States or of the United States, or concerning the question of the alleged indebtedness or monied obligation of any State of the United States, or any question which depends upon or involves the maintenance of the traditional attitude of the United States concerning American questions, commonly described as the Monroe Doctrine, or other purely governmental policy.

On the strength of these amendments the treaties were abandoned.

During the past twelve months[4] the government of the United States has been actively engaged in an effort to bring about agreements with the powers of the world for the pacific adjustment of international disputes by means of international commissions of investigation. A year ago a paper, which has since been published under the title of "President Wilson's Peace Proposal," but which is popularly known as Mr. Bryan's "Peace Plan," was handed to members of the Diplomatic Corps in Washington. By this paper it was proposed that all questions in dispute, which diplomacy should fail to adjust, should be submitted to an international commission, pending whose investigation and report war should not be declared nor hostilities begun. This proposal was supplemented by a memorandum of the Secretary of State, Mr. Bryan, in which it was suggested that the proposed international commission, which was also to have the power to act on its own initiative, should be composed of five members, each government to choose two, one of whom should not be its own citizen, and the fifth to be agreed upon by the two governments. A year was suggested as the time to be allowed for the investigation and report. It was further stated that the United States was prepared to consider the question of maintaining the status quo as to

4. 1913–14.

military and naval preparations during the period of investigation; and it was tentatively suggested that, pending such period, there should be no change in the military and naval programme of either party, unless danger from a third power should compel a change, in which case a confidential written statement of the fact by the party menaced was to release both parties from the obligation.

Salvador, by a treaty signed on August 7, 1913, accepted the plan in its entirety. A similar step was taken by Guatemala and Panama on September 20, by Honduras on November 3, and by Nicaragua on December 17, 1913. Treaties omitting the clause as to military and naval programmes were concluded with the Netherlands December 18, 1913; and with Bolivia January 22, with Switzerland and Costa Rica February 13, with Denmark April 17, and with Italy May 5, 1914. Treaties were also concluded with Portugal and Persia February 4, with the Dominican Republic February 17, and with Venezuela March 21, 1914. The form of the treaty with the Dominican Republic is exceptional in that it combines the stipulations of the arbitration treaties of 1908 with the provisions of the "peace plan," except the clause as to military and naval programmes.

In all, fifteen treaties based upon the "peace plan" have been signed. It is understood that none of the agreements thus described has been submitted to the Senate, so that their fate cannot as yet be foretold; but it may be remarked that, with the exception of a very small number of all-inclusive treaties of arbitration, they represent an advance beyond previous arrangements, in that they propose to submit to investigation all questions in dispute, of every nature whatsoever, which diplomacy may fail to adjust. Although they have been widely denounced as "all-inclusive arbitration treaties," they in fact do not bind the parties to arbitrate, but expressly reserve to them entire freedom of action after the report of the commission shall have been submitted. The underlying thought is three-fold: (1) That they furnish an honorable means of suspending controversy; (2) that the suspension of controversy will tranquillize the minds of the disputants; and (3) that the report of the commission of investigation probably will point the way to a fair and equitable adjustment.[5]

5. Down to January 18, 1924, treaties based on the Bryan plan, 1913, looking to the advancement of the cause of general peace, have been concluded, ratified and proclaimed between the United States and the following countries: Argentine Republic, Bolivia, Brazil, Chile, China, Costa Rica, Denmark, Dominican Republic, Ecuador, France, Guatemala,

It has sometimes been argued that the making of treaties for the preservation of peace is an idle task, because, in spite of all agreements to the contrary, wars will occur. This argument is obviously fallacious. Remedies for ills are not discarded merely because they do not always prove to be efficacious. Circumstances no doubt may arise in which international agreements for the employment of pacific methods may, either by reason of defects in their terms or by reason of conditions, fail to be useful. But of the practical value of such agreements, we have frequent illustrations. On two notable and recent occasions the existence of The Hague Convention for the Peaceful Settlement of International Disputes, which I do not hesitate to pronounce one of the wisest treaties ever made, has served to facilitate the prevention or the arrest of hostilities. The first occasion was that of the Dogger Bank incident, when the organization of a court of inquiry under the convention, with the addition of a limited arbitral power, relieved a dangerous tension between Great Britain and Russia and resulted in a final and satisfactory settlement. The other illustration is now before us. Prior to The Hague convention, the tender of good offices or mediation without prior solicitation or consultation was usually regarded as an intrusive act, savoring of unjustifiable interference. By that convention (Art. 3) it was declared that "powers, strangers to the dispute, have the right to offer good offices or mediation, even during the course of hostilities," and that the exercise of this right could never be regarded by the parties to the conflict "as an unfriendly act." This stipulation paved the way for the tender of good offices or mediation made a month ago by the diplomatic representatives of Brazil, Argentina and Chile, at Washington, after hostilities were begun at Vera Cruz. The offer was accepted by the immediate parties to the conflict, with the result that an armistice between them was brought about. The pending mediation of the so-called A B C powers is a remarkable event in the history of international relations in the Western Hemisphere. It has been hailed as the beginning of a new Pan-American diplomacy; and it may at any rate be regarded as the most striking development yet witnessed of the Pan-American movement which was formally inaugurated by the first International American Conference, at Washington, in 1889–90.

The present survey would be incomplete without a further reference to the Peace Conferences at The Hague. From present indications it is not probable that the Third Conference

Great Britain, Greece, Honduras, Italy, The Netherlands, Nicaragua, Norway, Panama, Paraguay, Persia, Peru, Portugal, Russia, Salvador, Spain, Sweden, Switzerland, Uruguay, and Venezuela.

will meet before 1916. The time that elapsed between the first and the second conference was eight years, and it was recommended by the second conference that the third should be convened after a similar interval; but the conditions growing out of the war over Tripoli and the wars in the Balkan Peninsula, to say nothing of the Moroccan and other international complications, caused delays in the taking of the necessary preparatory steps. In this situation, the government of the United States, on the 31st of January last, sent out a circular in which it was proposed that, with a view to the holding of the conference in 1915, the work of preparation should be committed to the Administrative Council of the Permanent Court of Arbitration at The Hague—a body composed of the diplomatic representatives of the treaty powers at The Hague and therefore already in existence. Although this proposal was favorably entertained by a number of governments, the prevalent opinion of the larger powers, so far as it has been disclosed, indicates that the holding of the Third Conference before 1916 is not thought to be practicable.[6]

After twenty years of fruitful aid and encouragement to the cause of peace and good-will, the Lake Mohonk Conference on International Arbitration today faces the future with confidence and with hope. Mindful of the fact that injustice, whether real or fancied, produces discontent, and that the causes and effects of injustice are often exaggerated by popular excitement, we may not be justified in expecting the immediate and final ushering in of the reign of universal peace. Perhaps it may be unreasonable to expect that international wars will cease before civil wars end. In the one case as in the other, the maintenance of continuously peaceful conditions will depend upon the general improvement of political and social relations. And to the accomplishment of this end all well-disposed men and women may work together in the inspiring belief that in the affairs of the world enlightened public opinion plays a constantly larger and more decisive part.

6. It may be superfluous to mention the fact that the Third Conference has not been held.

# IV

## THE PERMANENT COURT OF INTERNATIONAL JUSTICE[1]

IN order to estimate the precise significance of the addition of the Permanent Court of International Justice to the previously existing agencies for the peaceful settlement of international differences, it is necessary to know something not only of its constitution, rules and personnel, but also of its antecedents.

The amicable methods of settling international disputes are negotiation, good offices, mediation, and arbitration. Negotiation, which represents the ordinary process of diplomacy, we have always with us. Good offices and mediation, although essentially diplomatic, involve the interposition of a common friend and adviser, who, if he only uses "good offices," may even serve merely as a channel of communication, but who, if he acts as a "mediator," is supposed to give his counsel to the parties and to propose terms of settlement. On the other hand, arbitration is and always has been considered in international law as a judicial process. While the mediator recommends, it is the function of the arbitrator to decide. The term arbitration has been applied to the judicial process in international relations because, in the absence of a tribunal with a fixed personnel, it remained for the parties in each case to choose the judges who were to decide the dispute.

The determination of international controversies by arbitration runs back to a very early time. It was extensively practiced among the Greeks, with much definiteness and precision, and with an intelligent understanding of its essentially judicial character. Its employment naturally increased with the continuance of a state of peace. With the recurrence of wars and the incidental suspension of peaceful processes, the practice of arbitration would temporarily disappear. During the sixteenth and seventeenth centuries, because of the warlike

1. This chapter incorporates, with revision and supplemental matter, an address delivered before the Law Alumni of Columbia University, New York, in May, 1922. The address was printed under the title "The Organization of the Permanent Court of International Justice" in the *Columbia Law Review*, Vol. XXII, No. 6 (June, 1922); and in *International Conciliation*, No. 186 (1923).

conditions which so persistently prevailed, we find only slight traces of it. Its effective resuscitation in comparatively recent times may be said to have begun with the treaty between Great Britain and the United States of November 19, 1794, called in the United States the Jay Treaty, which provided for three distinct arbitrations, one of which may be rated among the most important ever held. During the nineteenth century the resort to international arbitration became more frequent. Especially was this the case after the settlement of the grave controversy between the United States and Great Britain, growing out of the so-called Alabama Claims, by the tribunal at Geneva in 1872. An indication of the progress of this general movement may be seen in the adoption, by the Congress of the United States, in 1890, of a concurrent resolution requesting the President to invite, as fit occasions might arise, negotiations with any government with which the United States had diplomatic relations, to the end that any differences or disputes between the two governments which could not be adjusted by diplomacy might be referred to arbitration and peaceably adjusted by that means.

The increase in the practice of arbitrating individual differences naturally gave rise to efforts to bring about the conclusion of general treaties of arbitration between particular countries, and from this it was only a natural step to the attempt to form a wider association and to establish a permanent tribunal.

This advance was reflected in the instructions given by Mr. Hay, as Secretary of State, on April 18, 1899, to the delegates of the United States to the first Peace Conference at The Hague. Referring to the eighth article of the programme, which related to "the wider extension of good offices, mediation and arbitration," Mr. Hay said:

Nothing can secure for human government and for the authority of law which it represents so deep a respect and so firm a loyalty as the spectacle of sovereign and independent States, whose duty it is to prescribe the rules of justice and impose penalties upon the lawless, bowing with reverence before the august supremacy of those principles of right which give to law its eternal foundation.

Accompanying these instructions there was a plan for a permanent international tribunal.

The conference bore fruit. The desire for a permanent tribunal was not confined to the United States; and on July 29, 1899, there was concluded at The Hague the treaty officially styled the "Convention for the Pacific Settlement of International Disputes." This convention, which was renewed in 1907 and is still in force, constitutes the highest achievement of the nineteenth century towards the creation of a permanent system for the peaceful disposition of international controversies. It represented an advance in three distinct particulars, in that it (1) enjoined and regulated the employment of mediation, (2) provided for the appointment, when occasion should arise, of international commissions of inquiry to investigate and report upon controverted facts, and (3) established the constitution and procedure of the tribunal called the "Permanent Court of Arbitration," whose seat is at The Hague. It was stipulated that this tribunal should be "accessible at all times and operating." It is also to be observed that the convention expressly declared that the object of international arbitration, which the tribunal was to administer, was "the settlement of differences between states by judges of their own choice, and on the basis of respect for law."

Of the Permanent Court of Arbitration I have naught to say but in commendation. The Permanent Court of International Justice, whose seat is also at The Hague, does not supersede it, but is, as its charter expressly declares, "in addition" to the older tribunal. But the Permanent Court of Arbitration is not a court in the ordinary sense. Under its conventional constitution, each signatory power may appoint four persons, who are called members of the court. They are appointed for six years, and may be reappointed. There are now upwards of one hundred and twenty of them, but they do not constitute an actual tribunal for the trial of cases. They form, on the contrary, a panel, or eligible list, from which, when a case is submitted, arbitrators, usually not exceeding five in number, are specially chosen to hear and determine the controversy. A majority of the judges of the Permanent Court of International Justice are, I may here remark, also members of the older tribunal.

The Permanent Court of Arbitration, although its establishment was widely acclaimed as a millennial augury, failed to satisfy the aspirations which many had indulged. In so saying I do not refer to those who were disappointed by the early demonstration of its inability to prevent the recurrence of war. Such a test is not exacted by those who keep within the sphere of realities; and its imposition would logically require the condemnation of all existing human institutions, legislative, executive and judicial. We do not refuse to diminish or to mitigate the ills of life because they cannot be abolished. Nor do I refer to those who were disappointed because a compulsory, or obligatory, jurisdiction was not created; for, while the principle of obligatory jurisdiction is not to be deprecated, it is an ideal towards the realization of which the little so far attained scarcely offsets the errors committed in its name.[2] The Convention for the Pacific Settlement of International Disputes, although it does not in terms make arbitration obligatory in any case, excepts nothing from the scope of arbitration, thus leaving the parties free to apply the process to any and every question for the solution of which they may see fit to employ it, without discouraging in advance, by means of sweeping exceptions, its application to any class of questions or furnishing a ready excuse for avoiding the resort to it.

But the Permanent Court of Arbitration also failed to meet the expectations of many persons because it was not a court in the ordinary sense, definitely organized for the hearing and determination of international questions. It was urged that an actual trial court, with a fixed personnel, would afford greater certainty and continuity in the application of legal principles and contribute more to their systematic development.

This view was definitely expressed by Mr. Root, as Secretary of State, in his instructions of May 31, 1907, to the delegates of the United States to the Second Peace Conference at The Hague, in the following terms:

It should be your effort to bring about in the Second Conference a development of The Hague Tribunal into a permanent tribunal composed of judges who are judicial officers and nothing else, who are paid adequate salaries, who have no other occupation, and who will devote their entire time to the trial and decision of international causes by judicial methods and under a sense of judicial responsibility. These judges should be so selected from the different countries that the different systems of law and procedure and the principal languages shall be fairly represented. The court should be of such dignity, consideration and rank that the best and ablest jurists will accept appointment to it and that the whole world will have absolute confidence in its judgments.

A plan supported by the United States, and containing a number of the fundamental characteristics of the Permanent Court of International Justice, was discussed by the Second Peace Conference; but it failed of adoption because of inability to agree on a method for the selection of the judges. The Conference, however, adopted the following recommendation:

The Conference recommends to the signatory Powers the adoption of the project hereto annexed, of a convention for the establishment of a Court of Arbitral Justice and its putting into effect as soon as an accord shall be reached upon the choice of the judges and the constitution of the Court.

During the peace negotiations at Paris in 1919, and particu-

2. See *supra*, pp. 70–74.

larly while the terms of the Covenant of the League of Nations were under consideration, a telegram was sent from the Bar Association of the City of New York recommending the incorporation of a provision for a Permanent Court of International Justice. Whether the insertion of a provision on that subject was or was not due to this telegram I am unable to say, but the statement has repeatedly been made that it was after the receipt of the telegram that the provision looking to the creation of such a court was inserted.

By Article 13 of the Covenant the members of the League agree that, whenever any dispute shall arise between them which they "recognize to be suitable for submission to arbitration and which cannot be satisfactorily settled by diplomacy," they will "submit the whole subject-matter to arbitration." The article then designates, as among the disputes "generally suitable" for arbitration, those concerning (1) the interpretation of a treaty, (2) any question of international law, (3) the existence of any fact which, if established, would constitute a breach of an international obligation, or (4) the nature or extent of the reparation to be made for the breach of an international obligation. Such disputes, it is provided, may be tried by a court agreed on by the parties or stipulated in any convention between them.

The provision looking to the creation of a new and permanent court is contained in Article 14, reading thus:

The Council shall formulate and submit to the members of the League for adoption plans for the establishment of a permanent court of international justice. The Court shall be competent to hear and determine any dispute of an international character which the parties thereto submit to it. The Court may also give an advisory opinion upon any dispute or question referred to it by the Council or by the Assembly.

For the purpose of carrying out this mandate, the Council appointed an international committee, known as the Advisory Committee of Jurists, one of whose members was Mr. Elihu Root. This committee sat at The Hague in June and July, 1920, and formulated a plan by which, as it was reported to the Council, the Court was, as between members of the League, to have, without any special convention or agreement, jurisdiction of cases of a "legal nature" falling within the four categories above enumerated, as well as of the interpretation of sentences passed by the Court itself; and by which, in the event of a dispute as to whether a case came within any of the specified categories, such dispute was to be settled by the decision of the Court. In the Council, however, objection was made to this clause on the ground that it in effect substituted the decision of the Court for the free choice which under the Covenant the parties had between laying their dispute before that Court, or before another international tribunal, or before the Council. In the end this objection was sustained; and by the Statute for the establishment of the Permanent Court, as approved by the Assembly of the League of Nations on December 13, 1920, it is provided[3] that the jurisdiction of the Court "comprises all cases which the parties refer to it and all matters specially provided for in treaties and conventions in force." But the advocates of a broader, more definite and more exacting obligation were not wholly defeated; since the Statute further provides[4] that any Power, either when signing or ratifying the Protocol to which the Statute is annexed, or at a later moment, may declare that it recognizes as obligatory, *ipso facto* and without any special agreement, as regards any other Power accepting the same obligation, the jurisdiction of the Court in all or any of the four legal categories above enumerated; that such declaration may be made unconditionally, or on condition of reciprocity, or for a certain time; and that any dispute as to whether the Court has jurisdiction shall be determined by the Court itself. This declaration is made by accepting the "Optional Clause" attached to the Protocol.

The entire plan reported by the Advisory Committee was, before its submission to the Assembly, considered by the Council at sessions held at San Sebastian and at Brussels. In the Assembly, where it was referred to a committee composed of representatives of all the members of the League, it was first examined by a sub-committee of jurists. It was then passed upon by the full committee. In all these stages amendments were made, some of which, like that relating to obligatory jurisdiction, were substantial and important. The main structure was, however, retained; and the Court, as constituted, accordingly consists of fifteen "members," composed of eleven judges, called "ordinary judges," and four deputy-judges. By express provision of the Statute (Art. 25), the eleven judges constitute the "full Court" for active purposes. In case they cannot all be present, deputies are to sit as judges in place of the absentees; but, if eleven judges are not available, nine may constitute a quorum.

The full Court is required to sit, except where it is expressly provided otherwise. But the Statute does so expressly provide in three classes of cases:

1. In cases under the Labor Clauses of the Treaty of Ver-

3. Art. 36, *infra*, p. 122
4. Art. 36, *infra*, p. 122

sailles (Part XIII) and of the other Peace Treaties, the Court is required to appoint every three years a special chamber of five judges, by which, instead of by the full Court, the case is, if the parties so demand, to be heard and determined. In all labor cases, whether determined by the full Court or by the special chamber, the judges are to be assisted by four technical assessors, who sit in an advisory capacity but do not vote.

2. In cases relating to transit and communications, particularly under Part XII (Ports, Waterways and Railways) of the Treaty of Versailles, and the corresponding parts of the other peace treaties, provision is made for the appointment of a similar special chamber, working under similar conditions and with similar procedure.

These special chambers may, with the consent of the parties to the dispute, sit elsewhere than at The Hague.

3. The Court is to form annually a chamber of three judges, who may, at the request of the disputants, hear and determine cases by summary procedure.

The difficulty regarding the election of judges was overcome by a provision, suggested by Mr. Root, that they should be chosen by the concurrent vote of the Council and the Assembly, acting separately, from a list of candidates nominated by the various national groups of members of the Permanent Court of Arbitration. It resulted that, although the United States group presented no names, there were eighty-nine nominees. Four of these declined to be considered as candidates. The election began on September 14, 1921, and was completed within three days.

The eleven judges thus elected were, in the order of their birth, as follows:

Viscount Robert Bannatyne Finlay (July 11, 1842), Great Britain; B. C. J. Loder (September 13, 1849), Holland; Ruy Barbosa (November 5, 1849), Brazil; D. J. Nyholm (June 21, 1858), Denmark; Charles André Weiss (September 30, 1858), France; J. B. Moore (December 3, 1860), United States; Antonio Sanchez de Bustamante (April 13, 1865), Cuba; Rafael Altamira (February 10, 1866), Spain; Yorozu Oda (July 4, 1868), Japan; Dionisio Anzilotti (February 20, 1869), Italy; Max Huber (December 28, 1874), Switzerland. Mr. Ruy Barbosa died in February, 1923; and Mr. Epitacio Pessoa, of Brazil, was, in the following September, chosen as his successor. The United States group in the Permanent Court of Arbitration joined in his nomination. The four deputies, whose precise dates of birth I do not happen to have at hand, are, in the order of age, as follows: Michailo Yovanovitch, Serb-Croat-

Slovene State; F. V. N. Beichmann, Norway; Demetre Negulesco, Roumania; Chung-Hui Wang, China.

Lord Finlay, although the oldest member of the Court, might,
if judged by his vigor and the alertness of his faculties, be
regarded as still in the prime of life. He holds at the bar of his
own country the highest rank. From 1900 to 1905 he was
Attorney General, while from 1915 to 1919 he was Lord Chancellor. He is also a member of the Permanent Court of Arbitration, before which, in 1910, he represented his government in
the celebrated case of the North Atlantic Fisheries, which was
then finally determined.

Mr. Loder, besides having sat in the supreme court of the
Netherlands, has been active in various international bodies,
being one of the founders of the International Maritime Committee, in 1896, and a participant in the international conferences on maritime law at Brussels in 1905, 1909 and 1910.
He was a delegate to the conference held at Paris in March,
1919, to discuss the plan of a League of Nations; was president of the Conference of Neutrals held at The Hague in 1920
for the purpose of drawing up a plan for the Permanent Court
of International Justice, and was a member of the Advisory
Committee of Jurists, by which the first draft of the actual
plan was drawn up.

Mr. Ruy Barbosa was one of the most eminent of Brazilian
lawyers and statesmen. He was Minister of Finance and Vice-
President of the Provisional Government when the transition
took place in Brazil from a monarchy to a republic, and was
one of the principal authors of the plan of a constitution for the
republic presented to the constituent assembly. He was one
of the most active members of the second Peace Conference at
The Hague in 1907. His successor, Mr. Epitacio Pessoa, was
lately President of Brazil, and was formerly a judge of the
Supreme Court of that country.

Mr. Nyholm, who is an honorary member of the Council of
State of Denmark, and a member of the Permanent Court of
Arbitration, had since 1897 been a member of the International
Mixed Court at Cairo, of which he had been Vice-President
since 1916.

Mr. Weiss, who is a member of the Institute of France, is
jurisconsult to the Ministry of Foreign Affairs, and a member
of the Permanent Court of Arbitration. He is professor of
private international law at the University of Paris, and is a
distinguished writer on that subject. He has also been president of the *Institut de Droit International*.

Mr. de Bustamante, who was educated for the bar at
Havana and at Madrid, was, almost at the beginning of his

professional career, appointed to the chair of international law at the University of Havana, which he still holds. He also is a member of the Permanent Court of Arbitration. Eminent as a practitioner, he is dean of the Havana bar. He has held with distinction various public positions, and is the author of numerous legal works of recognized value.

Mr. Altamira, who is a member of the senate of Spain, is professor of the history of political and civil institutions of America at the University of Madrid. He is a member of the Spanish Royal Academy of Moral and Political Sciences, a corresponding member of the Institute of France, and president of the Ibero-American Institute of Comparative Law. He was a member of the Advisory Committee of Jurists.

Mr. Oda is professor of international law at the University of Kyoto, of which he is also rector. He is a member of the Academy of Japan, and is the author of numerous works on the usages, manners and laws of China and Formosa, where he spent many years.

Mr. Anzilotti is professor of international law at the University of Rome, is jurisconsult to the Italian Ministry of Foreign Affairs, and is an author and editor of high repute. He is a member of the Institute of International Law and of various other scientific societies. He is a member of the Permanent Court of Arbitration.

Mr. Huber is honorary professor of international law and of public law at the University of Zurich, and is jurisconsult to the Swiss Government in matters of foreign affairs. He was a delegate to the second Peace Conference at The Hague in 1907, and also to the Peace Conference at Paris in 1919. He is an author of eminence, and a man of exceptional learning and intelligence.

Mr. Yovanovitch, the eldest of the four deputy-judges, is president of the Court of Cassation of Servia, and was formerly minister of justice of that country. He is an authority on the history of Slav law, and is the author of numerous legal works.

Mr. Beichmann is president of the court of appeals of Trondhjem, Norway, is vice-president of the *Institut de Droit International,* and is a member of the Permanent Court of Arbitration. He has lately served as president of an arbitral commission dealing with certain matters in Morocco.

Mr. Negulesco has been a professor at the University of Bucharest since 1901, and is the author of numerous legal works. He represents Roumania in the League of Nations, and was a member of the committee of the Assembly which revised the draft of the Statute as prepared by the Advisory Committee of Jurists.

The fourth deputy-judge, Mr. Wang, after completing his academic course at Yale University, studied law in England and later in Germany. On the formation of the provisional government of China, at Nanking, he became minister of foreign affairs. He was afterwards minister of justice in the first republican cabinet, and was president of the committee on the codification of the laws of China. He is also known among students of jurisprudence by his admirable translation into English of the German civil code.

For a sketch of himself, the writer would refer to *Who's Who*.

The explanation of how a citizen of the United States, although the United States is not a member of the League of Nations, came to be chosen as a judge of the Court, is found in the fact that the judges are not elected and that they do not sit as citizens or representatives of any particular country. As far as human nature will permit, they are expected to decide impartially between all countries, without favor or antipathy to any. To this end the Statute provides that the Court "shall be composed of a body of independent judges, elected regardless of their nationality." On the other hand, the election of more than one judge of any particular nationality is forbidden. The only personal conditions prescribed are (1) that the members shall be of "high moral character," and (2) that they shall have "the qualifications required in their respective countries" for "the highest judicial offices," or be "jurisconsults of recognized competence in international law." But the Statute also admonishes the electors that the Court as a whole should "represent the main forms of civilization and the principal legal systems of the world." In view of this provision, it is not strange that the bar of the United States was not passed over.

The circumstance that a judge may happen to be of the same nationality as one of the parties to a suit does not disqualify him from sitting. This question was very fully considered in the formulation of the Statute, with the result that the conclusion was reached that, in order to assure the full and equal representation of national points of view, if there should be a citizen of one of the parties sitting as a judge, the other party should be permitted to choose a judge of its own nationality. In the special chambers for labor and transit cases, consisting of only five judges, the judge so chosen is to take the place of one of the other judges, in order that the number may not be increased;[5] but, in the case of the full Court, the judges chosen on account of their nationality are added, and the

5. Statute, Arts. 26, 27; Rules, Art. 15, *infra*, pp. 119, 120, 128.

number of judges may then exceed eleven.[6] The provisions for
national representation do not apply to the chamber for summary procedure.[7]

The members of the Court are elected for nine years, and may
be reelected; but, where a person is chosen to fill a vacancy, he
holds office only for the remainder of the unexpired term. It
thus results that there must be an election of the whole Court
every nine years. While this part of the plan may be regarded
as an element of instability, it was deliberately adopted after
full consideration.

The compensation of the members of the Court is regulated
by the Statute, and is expressed in Dutch florins. The judges
each receive an annual salary of 15,000 florins, which, at the
normal rate of exchange, is equivalent to $6,030. The presi-
dent of the Court, who is required to live at The Hague, receives in addition a flat special allowance of 45,000 florins. The
additional pay of the other judges, apart from the refund of
traveling expenses and an allowance of 50 florins a day for
living expenses while at The Hague, depends on service, and
is in the form of a duty-allowance, which is fixed at 100 florins
a day, except in the case of the vice-president, who receives
150 florins a day. The duty-allowance is limited, however, to
a maximum of 20,000 florins a year in the case of the judges,
and of 30,000 florins in the case of the vice-president. The
maximum can thus be attained only if the sittings of the Court
during the year amount to 200 days. If the Court sits longer,
there is no further pay. A very substantial reason for these
financial provisions will be seen in the fact that the judges are
not permitted to exercise "any political or administrative
function," or to "act as agent, counsel or advocate in any case
of an international nature." These inhibitions are applicable
to deputy-judges only when they are actually sitting and as
regards cases in which they sit. Consequently, the deputy-
judges are not provided with salaries, but, if called on for
service, are to receive, in addition to their traveling expenses
and the allowance of 50 florins a day for living expenses at The
Hague, a duty-allowance of 150 florins a day, which is limited
to a maximum of 30,000 florins in any one year.

The Court must, by the terms of the Statute,[8] hold in each
year at least one session, which, unless the rules of the Court
otherwise provide, must begin on the 15th of June, and must
continue until the cases on the list are disposed of. The Presi-

6. Statute, Art. 31; Rules, Art. 4, *infra*, pp. 121, 126.
7. Rules, Art. 15, par. 2, *infra*, p. 128.
8. Art. 23, *infra*, p. 119

dent, however, may summon an extraordinary session whenever necessary.

Each member of the Court is required, before taking up his duties, to make a solemn declaration in open court that he will exercise his powers impartially and conscientiously. The members, when engaged in the business of the Court, enjoy diplomatic privileges and immunities.

The statement was widely published that the members of the Court, when engaged in the discharge of their duties, were to wear black velvet robes, lined with black silk and with collars trimmed with ermine, and also black velvet birettas, but the only robe that they have worn, or are to wear, is one of black silk, with black velvet facing, which can hardly be distinguished from the academic gown commonly worn in the United States. It differs little from the robes worn by the justices of the Supreme Court of the United States or of the higher courts in the State of New York. When we consider the divergent views that prevail in different countries as to what dress is proper on ceremonial occasions, we may be justified in thinking that, in the case of an international body, a plain and uniform dress may tend both to simplicity and to the avoidance of shocks to regional conceptions of propriety. Perhaps we have all known persons who, while avowedly opposed to any kind of official dress, saw no inconsistency in wearing, on every available occasion, all the orders and decorations of which they may have been the recipients, and who would feel no sense of impropriety in appearing during the day in a "full-dress" costume regarded in the United States and in certain other countries as being exclusively appropriate to the evening. There are countries classed as very democratic in which such dress is expected on formal occasions, without regard to the hour. The robe adopted by the Permanent Court is to be worn only on the bench. On other occasions the judges are to wear what they may individually deem to be appropriate.

The official languages of the Court are French and English, but the Court may, at the request of the parties, authorize another language to be used. The Court has permitted individual counsel to address it in a language other than English or French. The parties are to be represented by agents and, as in the case of ordinary courts, may have the assistance of counsel or advocates. Proceedings are both written and oral. This applies to the testimony of witnesses. Hearings are to be public, unless the Court shall otherwise decide, or unless the parties demand that the public be not admitted. Minutes must be kept of all hearings.

All questions are to be decided by a majority of the judges

present at the hearing, and in the event of an even division, the president or his deputy is to have a casting vote.

Every judgment is required to state the reasons on which it is based and to contain the names of the judges who have taken part in it. If the judgment is not unanimous, dissenting judges are entitled to deliver separate opinions. Judgments must be read in open court, after due notice to the agents of the parties. If the meaning or scope of the judgment is disputed, the Court, on the request of any party, is to construe it. Applications for revision may be made only on the ground of the discovery of some decisive fact which, when the judgment was rendered, was unknown to the Court and also to the party claiming revision. But no application is allowed if the want of knowledge was due to negligence. The Court frames its own rules of procedure, both regular and summary.

The Court first met on January 30, 1922. The meeting was called for purposes of organization. There were present nine judges and two deputy-judges, the two deputies, Messrs. Yovanovitch and Beichmann, having been called by the Secretariat-General of the League of Nations, in the order apparently indicated by the Statute, to take places of two judges, Messrs. Ruy Barbosa and de Bustamante, who were absent for reasons of health and climate. But as the session was only preliminary, and no statutory list[9] laying down the order in which the deputies should be called had been prepared, the Court, by a majority vote, decided to invite the two remaining deputies, Messrs. Negulesco and Wang, to attend. Mr. Negulesco duly appeared, but Mr. Wang, who was not in Europe, was unable to be present.

The first business transacted was the election of officers. Mr. Loder, who resides at The Hague, was elected president of the Court, and Mr. Weiss vice-president. Mr. A. Hammarskjöld, of Sweden, who had been deeply interested and usefully active in the establishment of the Court, was chosen as registrar or clerk. The formal opening took place at the Peace Palace on Wednesday, February 15th, in the presence of a distinguished assemblage, including the Queen and other members of the Dutch government, and representatives of other governments and of the League of Nations.

After the formal opening, the Court proceeded to the formulation of rules of procedure, which were finally adopted on the 24th of March. Among the questions to which the performance of this task gave rise, none was more debated than that as to the extent to which the records of the Court should be open to inspection or should be kept secret. This question was raised

9. Statute, Art. 15, *infra*, p. 118.

by Art. 62 of the Statute,[10] which authorizes a government to ask permission to intervene as a third party, if it considers that it has an interest of a legal nature which may be affected by the decision in the case. In order that a government may know whether it has such an interest in the litigation, it must know what the litigation comprehends, and to this an acquaintance with the contents of the documents evidently would be helpful and might be essential. The question proved, however, to be very difficult of solution, the view being strongly urged that an apprehension that third Powers, and especially the larger Powers, might abuse their privileges, would deter governments from coming to the Court. In the end a rule was adopted, under which the Court, or, if it is not sitting, the president, may, after hearing the parties, order the registrar to permit the inspection of the cases and counter-cases.[11] Much comment had been made upon the fact that none of the great Powers has accepted the obligatory principle of jurisdiction. Perhaps it may be hoped that the right of intervention given by the Statute may prove to be a means of inducing governments, be they great or small, to come before the Court, thus showing their confidence in it and enlarging its opportunities to perform a service for the world.

Another question very fully discussed was that of the giving of advisory opinions. The Statute, as adopted by the Assembly of the League, does not directly mention advisory opinions; but the Court, after careful consideration, reached the conclusion that there were certain clauses of the Statute which by implication incorporated the provision in Article 14 of the Covenant on that subject. It was therefore decided that, while the Court would not be justified in taking the position that it would not in any case give an advisory opinion, it remained with the Court to determine whether it would in a particular case, considering the nature of the question submitted, give such an opinion. The rules adopted by the Court[12] are based on this view. They assimilate the process as far as possible to a judicial proceeding, and exclude any supposition that advisory opinions may be rendered in a diplomatic sense and without publicity.

One of the most serious questions, and in some respects the most serious, which the Court was required to determine at the preliminary session was that of the position and functions of the deputy-judges. At one time there appeared to be much support for the view that the deputy-judges were, as "members" of the Court, essential participants in all functions not

10. *Infra*, p. 125
11. Rule 38, *infra*, p. 132.
12. Arts. 71–74, *infra*, pp. 137–138.

strictly judicial, such as the election of officers, the making of rules, and the giving of advisory opinions. These "non-judicial" functions were, it was urged, to be performed by all the "members" of the Court in "general assembly."

The examination of the antecedents disclosed the fact that this contention was related to a conception of the Court which was fully considered in the formulation of the Statute. It appeared that there were at the outset two views as to what the functions of the "supplementary" or "deputy" judges should be. According to one view, the deputy-judges were to act only as substitutes for absent judges. This view prevailed. The other view was bound up with a conception of the Court that failed. According to this conception, all the judges were to reside at the seat of the Court. They were also to receive liberal salaries, in order that they might give up all other occupations. The deputy-judges were to be subject to the same conditions, and were to receive the same salaries. Their continuous presence at The Hague would, it was argued, be highly desirable, if not necessary, in order that they might "saturate" themselves with the spirit of international justice evolved by the Court," and, as "young judges," designed to recruit its working force, be in training for its work. As against this conception, it was argued that it would be contrary to common sense to give the same rate of pay to those who did the actual work and to those who came simply to learn, and that it would also create "an impossible situation for the regular judges to be continually surrounded by student judges, even when considering their judgments." In the adoption of the Statute, the conception of the Court as a body continuously resident at The Hague completely disappeared, and the difference between the ordinary judges and the deputy-judges was clearly marked. This was done not only by the decision to pay the deputy-judges only a duty-allowance, but also by permitting them to act as counsel in any international case in which they are not "called upon to exercise their functions on the Court," as well as to exercise "political or administrative" functions "except when performing their duties on the Court." [13]

In interpreting the provision of the Statute forbidding the judges to act as counsel "in any case of an international nature," or to exercise "any political or administrative function," the Court held that the political function exercised by Viscount Finlay as a member of the House of Lords, and by Mr. Altamira as a senator, did not fall within this inhibition, the Court interpreting the phrase "political or administrative" as denoting a function in the exercise of which the holder is sub-

13. Statute, Arts. 16, 17, *infra*, p. 118.

ject to the direction and control of government, and is thus deprived of independence of judgment and of action. The fact that the deputy-judges are required to withdraw from or to suspend the exercise of such functions only when actually performing their duties on the Court clearly demonstrates that their active participation in the work of the Court was to be only occasional. In consideration of this fact, their ordinary activities, whether professional or governmental, were circumscribed as little as possible.

The only case in which under the Rules all the members, both the judges and the deputies, are to be summoned is in the application of Article 18 of the Statute, which provides that "a member of the Court cannot be dismissed unless, in the unanimous opinion of the other members, he has ceased to fulfil the required conditions." This article was held to apply to deputy-judges as well as to judges, since, unless it was so interpreted, no provision was made for the removal of the former. The Rules therefore provide (Art. 6) that, where Article 18 of the Statute is invoked, "the president, or if necessary the vice-president, shall convene the judges and deputy-judges." The member affected is to be allowed to furnish explanations, and, when he has done so, the question of his removal is to be discussed and a vote taken, the member in question not being present. In accordance with the provisions of the Statute, the notification to the Secretary-General of the League of Nations of the unanimous opinion that the member has ceased to fulfil the required conditions makes the place vacant.

Article 38 of the Statute provides that the Court, in rendering its decisions, shall apply (1) "international conventions, whether general or particular, establishing rules expressly recognized by the contesting States," (2) "international custom, as evidence of a general practice accepted as law," (3) "the general principles of law recognized by civilized nations," and (4), "subject to the provisions of Article 59, judicial decisions and the teachings of the most highly qualified publicists of the various nations, as subsidiary means for the determination of rules of law."

These clauses perhaps may be regarded as merely embodying the rules laid down in elementary treatises for the ascertainment of international laws and the decision of international questions. But, as it has sometimes been suggested, in more or less popular discussions, that the fourth clause prevents the Court from giving to its decisions any weight as precedents and from contributing in that way to the establishment of legal principles, a brief comment on the subject may not be super-fluous.

By the fourth clause, the use of "judical decisions" and the teachings of publicists as "subsidiary means" for determining rules of law is qualified by Article 59 of the Statute. The pre-ceding articles prescribe the manner and form in which judg-ments of the Court shall be rendered, and Article 59 then declares: "The decision of the Court has no binding force except between the parties and in respect of that particular case." Is not this essentially true of all judicial decisions? They bind only the parties, and, strictly speaking, bind them only as regards the particular case. Articles 62 and 63 of the Statute,[14] however, provide for the intervention, as a third party, of any State which considers "that it has an interest of a legal nature which may be affected by the decision in the case," and, where the interpretation of a treaty is concerned, of any party to the treaty who was not a party to the case. The fact is, moreover, to be observed that a certain weight is given to judicial decisions, and a certain law-establishing force, whether the principle of *stare decisis* be or be not accepted as an obligatory rule. Students of jurisprudence know that the difference is not so great as is commonly supposed.

Article 38 of the Statute ends with the provision that its prescription of rules of decision "shall not prejudice the power of the Court to decide a case *ex aequo et bono,* if the parties agree thereto." It has been suggested that this pro-vision may empower the Court to exercise extra-judicial func-tions. It has, on the other hand, been surmised that, as a decision by a judicial magistrate *ex aequo et bono* is not in-herently either extra-judicial or non-judicial, the design may have been merely to assure the ordinary application of legal rules. As there is no precise and all-inclusive general agree-ment as to what are in a strict sense rules of law, and as there often is room, in the domain of private as well as of public law, for wide differences of opinion as to whether judges may not have been influenced in a decision by considerations of what they conceived to be just and good, it may be admitted that the precise meaning and effect of the clause remain to be deter-mined by the Court. Meanwhile, there probably is little ground for the apprehension, which has sometimes been expressed, that a disappointed litigant might find in the clause a colorable excuse for declining to abide by an adverse judgment, by alleg-ing that the Court had decided the case *ex aequo et bono* with-out obtaining the parties' consent.

14. *Infra,* p. 125.

Since the preliminary session, which lasted from January 30 to March 24, 1922, the Court has held two regular and two special sessions, and has rendered eight advisory opinions and one judgment.[15] All the advisory opinions have been given on questions submitted by or through the Council of the League; and all have been fully reasoned and cast in the simple, narrative form. The same form was employed in the judgment.

The first advisory opinion was given upon the question whether the workers' delegate for the Netherlands at the third session of the International Labor Conference was nominated in accordance with the provisions of paragraph 3 of Article 389 of the Treaty of Versailles. Notice of the request for this opinion was, in conformity with the rules,[16] given to members of the League, to other States mentioned in the Annex to the Covenant and to various international organizations. It was also communicated to Germany and Hungary. Finally, the Court decided to hear at a public sitting the representatives of any government or of any international organization which should, within a fixed period, have expressed a desire to be so heard. As a result, the Court received a number of documents from governments and international organizations, and heard oral arguments on behalf of the British and Dutch governments and of the International Labor Office and two other international organizations. On July 31, 1922, the Court rendered an opinion answering the question in the affirmative. The opinion was unanimous.

The second advisory opinion was rendered on the question whether the competence of the International Labor Organization, created under Park XIII of the Treaty of Versailles, extends to "international regulation of the conditions of labor of persons employed in agriculture." This question was raised before the Council of the League by France. The same procedure was followed as in the preceding case; and oral arguments were heard on behalf of the British, French, Hungarian and Portuguese governments, and of the International Labor Office, the International Agricultural Commission and the International Federation of Trades Unions. The Court on August 12, 1922, answered the question in the affirmative. The French judge and the Rumanian deputy-judge, who was taking the place of an absent judge, availing themselves of their right un-

15. The first regular session began on June 15, and ended on August 12, 1922; the second began on June 15, and ended on September 15, 1923. The first special session began on January 8, and ended on February 6, 1923; the second began on November 12, and ended on December 6, 1923.
16. Rules of Court, Art. 73, *infra*, p. 137.

der the Rules, announced that they were unable to concur in the opinion.

On the same day the Court rendered its third advisory opinion, on the question, submitted on motion of the French government, whether the "examination of proposals for the organization and development of methods of agricultural production, and of other questions of a like character, fall within the competence of the International Labor Organization?"

After the usual procedure, and the consideration of the documentary proofs and oral arguments, the Court gave a negative answer; but, owing to the form in which the question was put, the Court was unable to conclude its recitals with a simple negative. Although the organization and development of the means of production were not committed to the Organization, it might be, said the Court, that in some cases the improvement of the condition of the workers might increase the amount of the production. Such increase obviously might result from the development of vocational and technical education, while the limitation of the hours of work and other measures for the benefit of the workers might diminish or increase the amount produced. So, for instance, said the Court, protection against sickness, disease and injury arising out of employment might involve the consideration of methods and processes of production, such as the use of white phosphorus, and of white lead, both of which had been dealt with as subjects within the scope of international regulation as affecting the conditions of labor. On the other hand, said the Court, "the consideration of methods of organizing and developing production from the economic point of view is in itself alien to the sphere of activity marked out for the International Labor Organization by Part XIII of the Treaty." Broadly speaking, explained the Court, any effect which the performance by the Organization of its functions under the Treaty might have on production was "only incidental"; yet, the Organization could not be "excluded from dealing with the matters specifically committed to it by the Treaty" on the ground that this might "involve in some aspects the consideration of the means or methods of production, or of the effects which the proposed measures would have upon production." And in conclusion, the Court said:

The question now put to the Court, after mentioning proposals for the organization and development of methods of agricultural production, goes on to inquire whether the consideration "of other questions of a like character" falls within the competence of the International Labor Organization.

The words used imply that the "other questions" are to be questions essentially of the same nature for the present purpose as that of the organization and development of means of production; but such "other questions" are not specified, and the Court does not undertake to say what they may be.

It follows from what has been said that the Court understands the questions to be whether the consideration of the means of production in itself, and apart from the specific points in respect of which powers are conferred upon the International Labor Organization by the Treaty, falls within the competence of that Organization.

This question, for the reasons above stated, the Court answers in the negative.

The opinion of the Court was unanimous.

The fourth advisory opinion was rendered at a special session, called for January 8, 1923, upon the question whether the "dispute between France and Great Britain as to the Nationality Decrees issued in Tunis and Morocco (French zone) on November 8, 1921, and their application to British subjects, the French government having refused to submit the legal questions involved to arbitration," "is or is not by international law solely a matter of domestic jurisdiction (Art. 15), paragraph 8, of the Covenant)."

This question was transmitted to the Court in conformity with an agreement between the British and French governments, under which, if the Court should hold that the question was not solely a matter of domestic jurisdiction, the "whole dispute" was to be "referred to arbitration or judicial settlement" under conditions later to be arranged between the two governments. It is evident that, by virtue of this agreement, the proceeding, although in the form of a request for an advisory opinion, was in effect the submission of a preliminary point for final decision. It was thus in the nature of a strictly judicial proceeding, ending in a judgment. In this respect the case was not unprecedented. The so-called Commission of Inquiry in the Dogger Bank incident possessed arbitral powers, and its report was in effect an award.

Paragraph 8, Article 15, of the Covenant, relating to matters before the Council, provides that if the dispute between the parties "is claimed by one of them, and is found by the Council, to arise out of a matter which by international law is solely within the domestic jurisdiction of that party, the Council shall so report and shall make no recommendation as to its settlement." The French equivalent for the phrase "solely within the domestic jurisdiction" is *"la compétence exclusive."* Cases and counter-cases and supplementary documents were presented by the British and French governments; and oral arguments were made before the Court by the Rt. Hon. Sir

Douglas Hogg, Attorney-General of Great Britain, assisted by
the Rt. Hon. Sir Ernest Pollock, and on the part of France by
M. Mérillon, Procureur Général, and by M. de Lapradelle.

The decrees in controversy related to persons born not on
the territory of France herself, but on the territory of the
French protectorate of Tunis and of the French zone in Morocco. Questions were thus raised as to the extent of the powers of a protecting state, first under the treaties between the
protecting state and the protected state establishing the protectorate, and secondly under the treaties or agreements under which the protectorates were recognized by other powers.
On these subjects various international treaties and agreements were invoked, and in the interpretation of them an appeal was made to principles of international law. In one part of
its argument the French government contended that the public powers exercised by the protecting state, taken in conjunction with the legal sovereignty of the protected state, constituted full sovereignty equivalent to that upon which international relations are based, and that therefore the protecting
state and the protected state might, by virtue of an agreement
between them, define and exercise in conjunction, within
the protected territory, the whole extent of the powers
which international law recognizes as belonging to sovereign states within the limits of their national territory. This
argument was applied to the particular case because, both in
Tunis and in Morocco, similar decrees were made on the same
day both by the protecting and by the protected government.
This contention was disputed by the British government, which
claimed that it would in any event be necessary to have recourse to international law in order to decide what value such
an agreement between the protecting and protected state
might have as regarded other states and their rights.

The Court on February 7, 1923, rendered an opinion holding that, as the dispute in question involved both the interpretation of treaties and the ascertainment and application of
principles of international law, it was not by international law
solely a matter of domestic jurisdiction. The opinion of the
Court was unanimous; and the two governments, instead of
proceeding to the litigation of the merits, subsequently effected
an arrangement of the dispute by direct negotiation.

The fifth advisory opinion was rendered in response to a
request submitting to the Court the following question:

Do Articles 10 and 11 of the Treaty of Peace between Finland and
Russia, signed at Dorpat on October 14, 1920, and the annexed Declaration of the Russian Delegation regarding the autonomy of East-

ern Carelia, constitute engagements of an international character which place Russia under an obligation to Finland as to the carrying out of the provisions contained therein?

Eastern Carelia, it may be remarked, is a territory lying between the White Sea and Lake Onega on the east and Finland on the west. Finland became entirely separated from Russia in 1917; and for some time there was war between the two countries, involving boundary and other questions. Eventually Eastern Carelia remained with Russia; but the Treaty of Dorpat and what was styled the annexed Declaration contained provisions in relation to the autonomy of Eastern Carelia and to certain special rights of two of its communes, called Repola and Porajärvi, which were under Finnish protection during hostilities. Both Finland and Russia acknowledged the legal existence of the treaty, but they differed as to its interpretation and legal effect; while Finland claimed, and Russia denied, that the annexed Declaration formed part of its terms. Finland contended that Articles 10 and 11 and the Declaration constituted valid executory obligations, and that Russia has not carried them out. Russia contended that the autonomy of Eastern Carelia, mentioned in Articles 10 and 11 and in the Declaration, was a pre-existing condition of things, established by a Russian decree issued prior to the treaty; that it was understood, when the treaty was negotiated, to be an internal matter; and that the Declaration was made solely for information.

On January 14, 1922, the Council, moved by Finland, adopted a resolution intimating that it would feel satisfaction if a state in diplomatic relations with the Soviet government would lend its good offices to the parties to the dispute. The Esthonian government subsequently invited the Soviet government to submit the question to the Council "on the basis of Article 17 of the Covenant," and to cause itself to that end to be represented on the Council. The Soviet government declined this request, and the Council eventually asked the Court for an advisory opinion.

The usual procedure was followed, and a notice was sent to the Soviet government. Such a notice indeed appears to have been contemplated by the Council, since, in the resolution with which the question was transmitted, the Court was requested to give its opinion, "taking into consideration the information which the countries may equally present." On June 11, 1923, however, M. Tchitcherin, the Russian People's Commissary for Foreign Affairs, sent a telegraphic reply, refusing to take any part in the proceedings, saying that the Russian government had "absolutely repudiated the claim of the so-called League of Nations to intervene in the question of the internal situation of Carelia," and declaring that "any attempt on the part of any power to apply to Russia the article of the Covenant of the League relating to disputes between one of its Members and a non-participating State would be regarded by the Russian government as an act of hostility to the Russian State."

The Court was thus confronted with the question whether it could, as an independent judicial tribunal, undertake, under the form of giving an advisory opinion, to decide or to express its views upon the merits of an international dispute the parties to which, one of whom was not a member of the League of Nations, had not agreed to submit to the Court's jurisdiction. As a test of the Court's judicial character and precise position, the case was recognized as having a certain crucial importance; and the representative of Finland was informed that, when he came to present his argument, the Court would be glad to have at the outset his views as to its competency to give effect to the request before it.

On July 23, 1923, the Court, after full deliberation, announced the conclusion that it could not give an advisory opinion on the question before it. This conclusion the Court embodied in an opinion which, after comprehensively reviewing the antecedents, reads as follows:

There has been some discussion as to whether questions for an advisory opinion, if they relate to matters which form the subject of a pending dispute between nations [Members of the League], should be put to the Court without the consent of the parties. It is unnecessary in the present case to deal with this topic.

The opinion which the Court has been requested to give bears on an actual dispute between Finland and Russia. As Russia is not a Member of the League of Nations, the case is one under Article 17 of the Covenant. According to this article, in the event of a dispute between a Member of the League and a State which is not a Member of the League, the State not a Member of the League shall be invited to accept the obligations of membership in the League for the purposes of such dispute, and if this invitation is accepted, the provisions of Articles 12 to 16 inclusive shall be applied with such modifications as may be deemed necessary by the Council. This rule, moreover, only accepts and applies a principle which is a fundamental principle of international law, namely, the principle of the independence of States. It is well established in international law that no State can, without its consent, be compelled to submit its disputes with other States either to mediation or to arbitration, or to any other kind of pacific settlement. Such consent can be given once and for all in the form of an obligation freely undertaken, but it can, on the contrary, also be given in a special case apart from any existing obligation. The first alternative applies to the Members of the League who, having accepted the Covenant, are under the obligation resulting from the provisions of this pact dealing with the pacific settlement of international disputes. As concerns States not members of the League, the situation is quite different; they are not bound by the Covenant. The submission, therefore, of a dispute between them and a Member of the League for solution according to the methods provided for in the Covenant, could take place only by virtue of their consent. Such consent, however, has never been given by Russia. On the contrary, Russia has, on several occasions, clearly declared that it accepts no intervention by the League of Nations in the dispute with Finland. The refusals which Russia had already opposed to the steps suggested by the Council have been renewed upon the receipt by it of the notification of the request for an advisory opinion. The Court therefore finds it impossible to give its opinion on a dispute of this kind.

It appears to the Court that there are other cogent reasons which render it very inexpedient that the Court should attempt to deal with the present question. The question whether Finland and Russia contracted on the terms of the Declaration as to the nature of the autonomy of Eastern Carelia is really one of fact. To answer it would involve the duty of ascertaining what evidence might throw light upon the contentions which have been put forward on this subject by Finland and Russia respectively, and of securing the attendance of such witnesses as might be necessary. The Court would, of course, be at a very great disadvantage in such an enquiry, owing to the fact that Russia refuses to take part in it. It appears now to be very doubtful whether there would be available to the Court materials sufficient to enable it to arrive at any judicial conclusion upon the question of fact: What did the parties agree to? The Court does not say that there is an absolute rule that the request for an advisory opinion may not involve some enquiry as to facts, but, under ordinary circumstances, it is certainly expedient that the facts upon which the opinion of the Court is desired should not be in controversy, and it should not be left to the Court itself to ascertain what they are.

The Court is aware of the fact that it is not requested to decide a dispute, but to give an advisory opinion. This circumstance, however, does not essentially modify the above considerations. The question put to the Court is not one of abstract law, but concerns directly the main point of the controversy between Finland and Russia, and can only be decided by an investigation into the facts underlying the case. Answering the question would be substantially equivalent to deciding the dispute between the parties. The Court, being a Court of Justice, cannot, even in giving advisory opinions, depart from the essential rules guiding their activity as a Court.

It is with regret that the Court, the Russian Government having refused their concurrence, finds itself unable to pursue the investigation which, as the terms of the Council's Resolution had foreshadowed, would require the consent and cooperation of both parties. There are also the other considerations already adverted to in this opinion, which point to the same conclusion.

The Court cannot regret that the question has been put, as all must now realize that the Council has spared no pains in exploring every avenue which might possibly lead to some solution with a view to settling a dispute between two nations.

This opinion was rendered by a vote of seven to four.[17] It has been textually quoted, because both the conclusion arrived at and the reasoning by which it was reached refute the forecasts and should dispel the apprehensions of those who have reiterated that the Court would, as the creation or creature of the League, enforce the League's organic law, the Covenant, above all other law, without regard to the rights under international law of nations not members of the League. The Court has in fact done just the contrary. While expressly holding, on the one hand, that the Covenant does not give rights to the League as against non-member States, because "they are not bound by the Covenant," the Court has upheld the rights of such States under international law. At the same time the Court has given effect to the provisions of the Covenant as between member-States, just as all courts, national and international, recognize and enforce between contracting States the reciprocal obligations they assume by specific agreement.

This has not come to pass by chance. It is obvious that the point at which the Court most directly touches the work of the League is in the giving of advisory opinions, and it therefore is not strange that the Court has from the beginning shown its consciousness of the fact that it was just at this point that its independence might, if at all, be popularly brought into question, and that its freedom from influence should be clear and unmistakable.

At the twenty-eighth meeting of the Court on March 10, 1922, while the subject of rules in relation to advisory opinions was under discussion, the suggestion was made by a member of the Court that the Council should, in the interest of the peace of the world, have the right in emergent cases to ask the Court for confidential advice. "This view," so the minutes run, "was opposed by Lord Finlay and Mr. Moore, who considered that the taking of a secret decision by the Court was incompatible with the Statute, and that the practice of giving opinions which were not made public would be a death blow to the

17. The majority consisted of Judges Loder (President of the Court, The Netherlands), Lord Finlay (Great Britain), Moore (United States), Oda (Japan), Anzilotti (Italy), Huber (Switzerland); and Deputy-Judge Wang (China).

The minority consisted of Judges Weiss (Vice-President of the Court, France), Nyholm (Denmark), de Bustamante (Cuba), and Altamira (Spain), who expressed their dissent in the simple declaration that they were "unable to share the views of the majority of the Court as to the impossibility of giving an advisory opinion on the Eastern Carelian question."

Court as a judicial body." After further discussion, the opinion thus declared was approved by the Court by a vote of eleven to one, and this decision was fully carried out in the Court's final action. Under the head of "Advisory Procedure" the rules provide that the questions upon which advisory opinions are sought shall be laid before the Court by means of a written request; that this request "shall contain an exact statement of the question upon which an opinion is required, and shall be accompanied by all documents likely to throw light upon the question"; that the Registrar shall forthwith give notice of the request, not only to the Members of the League and the States mentioned in the Annex to the Covenant, but also "to any international organizations which are likely to be able to furnish information on the question"; that the opinions shall be given after deliberation by the full Court, and that the opinions of dissenting judges may, at their request, be attached to the opinion of the Court; and that the opinions and the requests in response to which they are given shall be printed and published.[18] Finally, it may be observed that the Court reserved to itself the right to consider what its action should be on each particular request and to refuse to reply to a question as submitted should there be ground for such refusal.[19]

These decisions, by which judicial methods are applied to the rendering of advisory opinions, have been fully carried out. The Court has not thought it feasible to fill a dual rôle, acting at one moment as a judicial body rendering judgments on international differences, and at the next moment as a board of counselors giving private and *ex parte* advice on such matters. Indeed, an auditor or spectator would detect no difference between a proceeding for a judgment and a proceeding for an advisory opinion. Moreover, the Court has in all its proceedings shown an appreciation of the fact that the very breath of its life is the public confidence, and that this confidence could not exist if it should fail to observe in its conduct that openness by which the conduct of courts is supposed to be characterized. The Court has carried this principle to the point of publishing even the full minutes of the private discussions at the preliminary session at which its rules were adopted.[20] All its opinions and decisions have been read from the printed text on the day of their delivery, and the proofs and arguments have also been printed and published.

18. Rules of Court, *infra*, p. 138.
19. *Acts and Documents Concerning the Organization of the Court* (Leyden, A. W. Sijthoff's Publishing Company, 1922), pp. 160, 161, 383, 472. 637 pages, quarto.
20. *Ibid.*

In pursuing this course, the Court has had no reason to doubt that it was only fulfilling the high trust confided to it by those who provided for its establishment. Among the addresses delivered at its formal opening on February 15, 1922, none was more pronounced in its affirmation of the judicial character and entire independence of the Court than that which was made by Sir Eric Drummond, Secretary-General of the League, who, in the course of his remarks, said:

The definite establishment of the Court completes the organization of the League as laid down under the Covenant. It is clearly the greatest and will, I believe, be the most important creative act of the League. At last an international judicial body is established which is entirely free from all political control and entirely unfettered as to its decisions by political bodies. Although it derives its authority from the League, its judgments are in no way subject to advice or revision by the Council or by the Assembly. The relation between the Court and the League is similar to that which exists between the Courts and the Government in England, and elsewhere. The judges are appointed by the State, but the State cannot remove them. There can be no dictation or interference by the Government with Courts. Indeed, the Courts can give decisions on what the State itself has done, though ultimately the authority of the Courts derives from that very Government.[21]

The fact that the expenses of the Court are defrayed with funds supplied from the treasury of the League of Nations is in no wise incompatible with the Court's independence. Courts are not self-supporting, but they maintain their independence in spite of the fact that provision for their financial needs must be made by legislation in the enactment of which they take no part. The circumstance that the courts in the United States depend on legislative grants does not deter them from exercising freely even the inferential power to declare acts of the legislature to be unconstitutional and invalid.

Following its disposition of the Eastern Carelian question, the Court proceeded to hear the very intricate case of the German settlers in Poland, which forms the subject of its sixth advisory opinion. This case relates to the rights, in regard to holdings of land, of so-called settlers of German nationality, domiciled in German territory that passed to Poland, who have acquired, particularly by virtue of Article 91 of the Versailles Treaty, Polish nationality. These settlers occupied their lands under one or the other of two kinds of contract, called *Rentengutsverträge* and *Pachtverträge*. By the *Rentengutsverträge* the lands were made over to the settlers in perpetuity against payment of a fixed rental, subject to a right of with-

21. *Idem*, p. 320.

drawal and of repurchase on the part of the state on certain conditions stated in the contract: by the *Pachtverträge* the lands were leased to the settlers for a term of years. Both kinds of contract were made under laws passed by Prussia, the first of which, dated April 26, 1886, was entitled "A law concerning the promotion of German settlement in the Provinces of West Prussia and Posen." Money was placed at the disposal of the Prussian government "for the purpose of strengthening, by means of settling German peasants and workmen, the German element in the provinces of West Prussia and Posen against efforts to Polonize the provinces." With the money thus provided, lands were purchased by the Prussian state and delivered to the settlers. No question was raised as to holdings under *Rentengutsverträge,* where the contracts were made prior to the Armistice of November 11, 1918, unless *Auflassung* had not taken place before that date, *auflassung* being the reciprocal act by which, under German law, the vesting of legal ownership (*Eigentum*), as distinguished from rights under a lease, is consummated. In the case of *Rentengutsverträge,* where *Auflassung* had not occurred before November 11, 1918, as well as in the case of *Pachtverträge,* the Polish government contended that it was the legitimate owner of the lands under Article 256 of the Treaty of Versailles and might lawfully cancel the contracts and remove the settlers from their holdings.

Numerous and complex questions, both of public law and of private law, were involved in the case. The general points on which the opinion of the Court was requested were whether the matters fell within the competence of the League of Nations under the Treaty of Versailles, and whether, if this question should be answered in the affirmative, the measures adopted by the Polish government were in conformity with its international obligations. The Court, in an opinion rendered on September 10, 1923, answered the first question in the affirmative and the second in the negative.

The opinion was unanimous.

The seventh advisory opinion rendered by the Court related to the interpretation and application of the Polish Minorities Treaty, this being one of the so-called Minorities Treaties which were made for the purpose of protecting racial, religious or linguistic minorities in Austrian, German, Hungarian, or Russian territories transferred to other sovereignty by the treaties of peace. The case grew out of complaints made to the League by former German nationals domiciled in Polish territory formerly belonging to Germany. Poland denied the legal competency of the League to deal with the matter, and also questioned the interpretation put by the League on paragraph

1 of Article 4 of the Polish Minorities Treaty, which reads:

Poland admits and declares to be Polish nationals *ipso facto* and without the requirement of any formality persons of German, Austrian, Hungarian or Russian nationality who were born on the said territory of parents habitually resident there, even if at the date of the coming into force of the present treaty they are not themselves habitually resident there.

Poland, while contending that a person must be a Polish national in order to fall within the protection of the treaty, claimed that the persons described in paragraph 1 of Article 4 should not be considered as Polish nationals if their parents were not habitually resident in the territory both on the date when the children were born and on January 10, 1920, when the treaty came into force. The Court, in an opinion rendered on September 15, 1923, held that the position of the complainants fell within the competence of the League under the Minorities Treaty, and that paragraph 1 of Article 4 referred "only to the habitual residence of parents at the date of the birth of the persons concerned."

The opinion of the Court was unanimous; but Lord Finlay, while concurring in the conclusions arrived at in regard to both questions, added some observations of his own on the question of the competence of the League in the matter.

The eighth advisory opinion, which related to a boundary dispute between Poland and Czechoslovakia, was rendered on December 6, 1923, at a special session that began on the 12th of the preceding month.

From the time of the establishment of those republics, disputes had arisen between them as to the districts of Teschen, Orava, and Spisz or Jaworzina. By the treaty of peace of Saint Germain with Austria and Trianon with Hungary, the principal Allied and Associated Powers undertook the duty of fixing the frontiers; and on September 27, 1919, the Supreme Council decided that the allocation of the three districts should be determined by a plebiscite. The plebiscite did not take place. On the contrary, the Polish and Czechoslovak governments, by a declaration made at the Spa Conference on July 10, 1920, agreed to accept a settlement by the principal Allied and Associated Powers. Pursuant to this agreement, the Supreme Council on July 11, 1920, instructed the Conference of Ambassadors to divide the three territories; and on July 28, 1920, the Conference rendered a decision and set up a delimitation commission, with duly defined powers, to carry it out. Poland, however, claimed that the line indicated in the decision was, as regarded the district of Spisz, contrary to the principles of justice and equity, and formulated proposals for its modification.

These proposals were transmitted by the delimitation commission to the President of the Conference of Ambassadors, which on December 2, 1921, took a decision. This decision, as Czechoslovakia maintained, in effect finally confirmed the frontier indicated in the previous decision; but Poland contended that the decision did not exclude the possibility of modifying the line as she desired. Attempts were then made to fix the line by agreement between the parties; but, these attempts having failed, the question came yet again before the Conference of Ambassadors. Further efforts did not succeed either in adjusting the dispute or in allaying popular feeling.

Under these circumstances the Conference of Ambassadors, acting under paragraph 2 of Article 11 of the Covenant, which declares it to be "the friendly right of each Member of the League to bring to the attention of the Assembly or of the Council (of the League) any circumstance whatever affecting international relations which threatens to disturb international peace or the good understanding between nations upon which peace depends," requested the Council to propose a solution of the dispute. As a first step the Council invited the governments to make statements of their cases. This each of the governments did; and the Council, after considering the statements, submitted to the Permanent Court of International Justice the following question:

Is the question of the delimitation of the frontier between Poland and Czechoslovakia still open, and, if so, to what extent; or should it be considered as already settled by a definitive decision (subject to the customary procedure of marking boundaries locally, with any modifications of detail which that procedure may entail)?

By paragraph 2, Article 2, of the decision of the Conference of Ambassadors of July 28, 1920, creating the delimitation commission, it was provided that the decisions of the commission, for which the vote of a majority was sufficient, should be binding on the parties concerned; but, by paragraph 3, the commission was "empowered to propose to the Conference" "any modifications" which it might "consider justified by reason of the interests of individuals or of communities in the neighborhood of the frontier line and having regard to special local circumstances."

The Court, after hearing arguments and examining the voluminous documents submitted to it, held that the question of the delimitation of the frontier had been settled by the decision of July 28, 1920, and that this decision was definitive; but that it

must be applied in its entirety, and that consequently that portion of the frontier in the region of Spisz topographically described therein remains subject (apart from the modifications of detail which the customary procedure of marking boundaries locally may entail) to the modifications provided for in paragraph 3 of Article 2 of the same decision.

The opinion of the Court was unanimous.

On August 17, 1923, the Court, at its second regular session, delivered a judgment in what is known as the case of the steamship *Wimbledon,* which involved questions relating to the use of the Kiel Canal.

Article 380 of the Treaty of Peace of Versailles stipulates: "The Kiel Canal and its approaches shall be maintained free and open to the vessels of commerce and war of all nations at peace with Germany on terms of entire equality."

On the morning of March 21, 1921, the *Wimbledon,* a British ship, under charter to a French company and laden with war material consigned to the Polish Military Mission at Danzig, arrived at the entrance to the Kiel Canal on her way to Danzig. The German authorities refused to permit her to enter the canal or to pass through it; and, when the French ambassador at Berlin protested against her exclusion as a violation of Article 380 of the Versailles Treaty, reaffirmed their refusal on the ground that the cargo was destined to Poland, then declared to be at war with Russia, and that the German neutrality regulations forbade the transit across German territory of war material for either party. The *Wimbledon,* after awaiting for a reasonable time the issue of the controversy, completed her voyage and delivered her cargo by way of the Danish Straits.

Article 386 of the Versailles Treaty provides that, in case of "any violation" of "Articles 380 to 386," or of "disputes" as to their interpretation, "any interested power can appeal to the jurisdiction instituted for the purpose by the League of Nations." Supplementing this stipulation, Article 37 of the Statute of the Court provides that, when a treaty or convention "provides for the reference of a matter to a tribunal to be instituted by the League of Nations, the Court will be such tribunal."

On the strength of these provisions, by which a preexisting obligation to submit the difference was created, the British, French, Italian and Japanese governments, as "interested" powers, applied to the Court, in conformity with the rules, for a judgment that the action of the German authorities was wrongful and for damages, and asked that the German government be notified of the application. The Polish government subsequently intervened in the case, under Article 63 of the Statute, as a party to the treaty. The German government duly appeared, and, availing itself of its right under the Statute, named as a national judge Dr. Walther Schücking, of Berlin. In the case of the *Wimbledon* the Court therefore consisted of twelve judges.

After hearing the representatives of the interested governments, the Court held the refusal of access to the canal to have been wrongful, and awarded damages for demurrage, deviation and fuel, with interest at six per cent from the date of the judgment until its payment, which was to be effected in French francs within three months. Certain other claims were disallowed; and it was adjudged that each party should bear its own costs.

On the merits of the question, the Court found that, by virtue of the terms of Article 380, the canal had ceased to be an internal and national waterway the use of which by other states was left wholly to the discretion of the riparian state, and had become an international waterway affording under treaty guarantee easier access to the Baltic to the vessels of commerce and of war of all nations, subject to the condition that the vessels must belong to nations at peace with Germany. This condition, said the Court, clearly contemplated the case of a war to which Germany was a party, and recognized and proclaimed her right to defend herself against her enemies; but the prohibition of the passage through the canal of contraband destined to a belligerent in a war to which Germany was not a party was, the Court on the other hand affirmed, contrary to the terms of the treaty and was not required by the international law of neutrality. In support of this opinion the Court cited the cases of the Suez and Panama canals, and, after reviewing the acts and practice relating to those waterways, and observing that their passage by belligerent men-of-war and by ships carrying contraband had not been regarded as compromising the neutrality of the territorial sovereign, declared that these precedents invalidated the argument that Germany's duties as a neutral would have been violated by the passage of the *Wimbledon*. The precedents in question were, said the Court, "merely illustrations of the general opinion according to which when an artificial waterway connecting two open seas has been permanently dedicated to the use of the whole world, such waterway is assimilated to natural straits in the sense that even the passage of a belligerent man-of-war does not compromise the neutrality of the sovereign state under whose jurisdiction the waters in question lie."

From this judgment, in which nine judges concurred, three judges—the Swiss, Italian and German—filed each a reasoned dissent.

This completes the review of the Court's work up to the present time. Under the Statute the decision is rendered in each case both in French and in English, but the Court designates which text shall be considered as authoritative. In four advisory opinions, including the first one, the French is thus designated, and in four the English; but they have not strictly alternated. In the case of the *Wimbledon,* it is the French.

On May 17, 1922, the Council, acting under Article 35 of the Statute, passed a resolution laying down the conditions under which the Court should be open to States not members of the League or mentioned in the Annex to the Covenant. The Court had recommended that this be done. The resolution merely requires the filing with the Court of a declaration accepting its jurisdiction in accordance with the Covenant, Statute and Rules, and promising to carry out its decisions and not to resort to war against states complying with them. The declaration may be either particular, embracing a particular dispute; or general, embracing all or a particular class of disputes. The resolution, however, provides that declarant's acceptance of compulsory jurisdiction under Article 36 of the Statute shall not, without a special convention, be reciprocally binding on members of the League and States mentioned in the Annex to the Covenant which have signed or may in future sign the "optional clause." This reservation probably may be explained by the consideration that such members and states, whether they had or had not already signed the "optional clause," might be willing to accept compulsory jurisdiction as between themselves, but might be unwilling to assume the same obligation towards yet other and unknown states. It may have been thought that, while such a reservation was requisite in the case of states that had already signed the optional clause, it would avoid an obstacle to its further acceptance.

While the Court is thus open to all nations as litigants, full acceptance of the Court and full participation in its support and work are affected by adhesion to the Protocol of Signature of December 16, 1920, attached to the resolution of the Assembly by which the Statute of the Court was approved. Prior to October, 1923, this protocol had been ratified by thirty-five states, all Members of the League.[22] Eight Member-States had

---

22. Albania, Australia, Austria, Belgium, Brazil, British Empire, Bulgaria, Canada, China, Cuba, Czechoslovakia, Denmark, Esthonia, Finland, France, Greece, Haiti, India, Italy, Japan, Jugo-Slavia (Kingdom of the Serbs, Croats and Slovenes), Lithuania, Norway, Netherlands, New Zealand, Poland, Portugal, Roumania, Siam, South Africa, Spain, Sweden, Switzerland, Uruguay, Venezuela.

not as yet ratified the protocol.[23] Sixteen states had adopted and put into force the "optional clause." [24]

On February 24, 1923, President Harding, in a special message, asked the Senate to give its advice and consent to the adhesion of the United States to the protocol accepting the Statute of the Court, but not to the "optional clause" for compulsory jurisdiction; subject, however, to certain conditions which were set out in a report by Mr. Hughes as Secretary of State.

In this report Mr. Hughes, while adverting to the vast importance of provisions for the peaceful settlement of international controversies and to the time-honored policy of the United States in promoting such settlements, observed that none of the provisions of the Statute impaired the independence of the Court and that none of them made it difficult for the United States, without becoming a member of the League, to give its support to the Court, except the provision relating to the election of judges. He stated that the practical advantage of the existing system of electing judges by a majority vote of the Council and of the Assembly acting separately was quite manifest, and that this arrangement had solved the difficulty previously appearing to be almost insuperable "of providing an electoral system conserving the interests of the powers, both great and small." This system he thought it would be impracticable to disturb; but "the United States must," said Mr. Hughes, "in becoming formally a party to the Court have a voice in future elections of judges." Remarking then that the members of the Council and Assembly, in electing the judges of the Court, "do not act under the Covenant," but "under the Statute of the Court and in the capacity of electors performing duties defined by the Statute," he declared that it would be reasonable and practicable for the United States, in adhering to the protocol and accepting the Statute, to make it a condition that the government should be permitted, through representatives designated for the purpose, to participate on an equality with Members of the League in all future proceedings for the election of members of the Court, or for filling vacancies. This is incorporated in the conditions approved by President Harding which read as follows:

I. That such adhesion shall not be taken to involve any legal relation on the part of the United States to the League of Nations or the

23. Argentina, Bolivia, Chile, Costa Rica, Colombia, Panama, Paraguay, Salvador.
24. Austria, Brazil, Bulgaria, China, Denmark, Esthonia, Finland, Haiti, Lithuania, Netherlands, Norway, Portugal, Sweden, Switzerland, Uruguay. In addition, Latvia had accepted the Optional Clause, subject to approval by her ratifying body.

assumption of any obligations by the United States under the covenant of the League of Nations constituting Part I of the treaty of Versailles.

II. That the United States shall be permitted to participate through representatives designated for the purpose and upon an equality with the other States members, respectively, of the council and assembly of the League of Nations in any and all proceedings of either the council or the assembly for the election of judges or deputy judges of the Permanent Court of International Justice, or for the filling of vacancies.

III. That the United States will pay a fair share of the expenses of the court as determined and appropriated from time to time by the Congress of the United States.

IV. That the statute for the Permanent Court of International Justice adjoined to the protocol shall not be amended without the consent of the United States.

On March 2, 1923, President Harding communicated to the Senate, with his "most hearty approval," a reply by Mr. Hughes to certain questions concerning which Senator Lodge had asked for information for the Committee on Foreign Relations. The first of these was whether the President was in favor of an agreement to obligate all the governments which had accepted the Protocol of Signature to accept also the "optional clause" relating to compulsory jurisdiction. Interpreting this question as meaning whether the President was in favor of undertaking to negotiate such an agreement, Mr. Hughes answered it in the negative, for the reason that, unless the attitude of the Senate as repeatedly defined since 1897 [25] had changed, it would be futile to attempt to negotiate such an agreement. For the same reason a negative answer was made to the inquiry whether the President deemed it advisable to communicate with other powers to ascertain whether they would be willing to enter into such an agreement. It was further stated in response to the rest of the inquiries that it was not the purpose of the administration to have the United States recognize, as a binding obligation, Part XIII of the Treaty of Versailles relating to labor, and that the administration was not advised that any state that had so far ratified the Protocol of Signature had made any reservation.

President Coolidge, in his annual message of December 6, 1923, recommended the acceptance of the Court by the United States, in the following terms:

## FOREIGN AFFAIRS

For us peace reigns everywhere. We desire to perpetuate it always by granting full justice to others and requiring of others full justice to ourselves.

25. *Supra*, pp. 71–75.

Our country has one cardinal principle to maintain in its foreign policy. It is an American principle. It must be an American policy. We attend to our own affairs, conserve our own strength, and protect the interests of our own citizens; but we recognize thoroughly our obligation to help others, reserving to the decision of our own judgment the time, the place, and the method. We realize the common bond of humanity. We know the inescapable law of service.

Our country has definitely refused to adopt and ratify the covenant of the League of Nations. We have not felt warranted in assuming the responsibilities which its members have assumed. I am not proposing any change in this policy; neither is the Senate. The incident, so far as we are concerned, is closed. The League exists as a foreign agency. We hope it will be helpful. But the United States sees no reason to limit its own freedom and independence of action by joining it. We shall do well to recognize this basic fact in all national affairs and govern ourselves accordingly.

## WORLD COURT

Our foreign policy has always been guided by two principles. The one is the avoidance of permanent political alliances which would sacrifice our proper independence. The other is the peaceful settlement of controversies between nations. By example and by treaty we have advocated arbitration. For nearly 25 years we have been a member of The Hague Tribunal, and have long sought the creation of a permanent World Court of Justice. I am in full accord with both of these policies. I favor the establishment of such a court intended to include the whole world. That is, and has long been, an American policy.

Pending before the Senate is a proposal that this Government give its support to the Permanent Court of International Justice, which is a new and somewhat different plan. This is not a partisan question. It should not assume an artificial importance. The court is merely a convenient instrument of adjustment to which we could go, but to which we could not be brought. It should be discussed with entire candor, not by a political but by a judicial method, without pressure and without prejudice. Partisanship has no place in our foreign relations. As I wish to see a court established, and as the proposal presents the only practical plan on which many nations have ever agreed, though it may not meet every desire, I therefore commend it to the favorable consideration of the Senate, with the proposed reservations clearly indicating our refusal to adhere to the League of Nations.

As the Court is now open to all nations, it is proper, without regard to the formal adhesion of any particular power, to make one further observation. As submission to the jurisdiction of the Court, except as regards the powers that have accepted a limited obligation, is wholly voluntary, it follows that the amount of the business which may come before the Court depends upon the will and inclination of the world's governments. Reference has often been made—and I confess that

I have myself made it—to the small amount of business that came before the Supreme Court of the United States in the beginning and to the vast increase that came later; but it must be admitted that this is not necessarily a sure basis of forecast. As the jurisdiction of the Supreme Court is chiefly appellate, it would have been indeed strange if at the outset numerous cases had appeared on the docket; but, as submission to the court's jurisdiction, under the Constitution and laws of the United States, by no means depended upon the agreement of parties, it was morally certain that, with the growth of the business of the new federal courts, the business of the Supreme Court would increase. The Permanent Court of International Justice is not an appellate tribunal. It is a court of original jurisdiction, and, constituted as it is, it depends for its business upon the desire and the will of nations, which alone can be parties to cases before it,[26] to submit their differences to judicial determination. Hence, no effort should be omitted to cultivate a public sentiment that will induce governments, instead of resorting to violence, to come before the tribunal which has now been established, which is continuously organized and always open to them, and submit their controversies to its final and peaceful decision.

## APPENDIX I

*RESOLUTION concerning the establishment of a Permanent Court of International Justice passed by the Assembly of the League of Nations, Geneva, December 13, 1920.*

1. The Assembly unanimously declares its approval of the draft Statute of the Permanent Court of International Justice—as amended by the Assembly—which was prepared by the Council under Article 14 of the Covenant and submitted to the Assembly for its approval.
2. In view of the special wording of Article 14, the Statute of the Court shall be submitted within the shortest possible time to the Members of the League of Nations for adoption in the form of a protocol duly ratified and declaring their recognition of this Statute. It shall be the duty of the Council to submit the Statute to the Members.
3. As soon as this protocol has been ratified by the majority of the Members of the League, the Statute of the Court shall come into force and the Court shall be called upon to sit in conformity with the said Statute in all disputes between the Members of States which have ratified, as well as between the other States, to which the Court is open under Article 35, paragraph 2, of the said Statute.
4. The said protocol shall likewise remain open for signature by the States mentioned in the Annex to the Covenant.

26. Statute, Art. 34.

STATUTE OF THE COURT

*Protocol of Signature of the Statute for the Permanent Court of International Justice Provided for by Article 14 of the Covenant of the League of Nations, with the Text of this Statute*

PROTOCOL OF SIGNATURE

The Members of the League of Nations, through the undersigned, duly authorized, declare their acceptance of the adjoined Statute of the Permanent Court of International Justice, which was approved by a unanimous vote of the Assembly of the League on the 13th December, 1920, at Geneva.

Consequently, they hereby declare that they accept the jurisdiction of the Court in accordance with the terms and subject to the conditions of the above-mentioned Statute.

The present Protocol, which has been drawn up in accordance with the decision taken by the Assembly of the League of Nations on the 13th December, 1920, is subject to ratification. Each Power shall send its ratification to the Secretary-General of the League of Nations; the latter shall take the necessary steps to notify such ratification to the other signatory Powers. The ratification shall be deposited in the archives of the Secretariat of the League of Nations.

The said Protocol shall remain open for signature by the Members of the League of Nations and by the States mentioned in the Annex to the Covenant of the League.

The Statute of the Court shall come into force as provided in the above-mentioned decision.

Executed at Geneva, in a single copy, the French and English texts of which shall both be authentic.

16th December, 1920.

OPTIONAL CLAUSE

The undersigned, being duly authorized thereto, further declare, on behalf of their Government, that from this date, they accept as compulsory *ipso facto* and without special Convention, the jurisdiction of the Court in conformity with Article 36, paragraph 2, of the Statute of the Court, under the following conditions:

STATUTE

Article 1. A Permanent Court of International Justice is hereby established, in accordance with Article 14 of the Covenant of the League of Nations. This Court shall be in addition to the Court of Arbitration organized by the Conventions of The Hague of 1899 and 1907, and to the special Tribunals of Arbitration to which States are always at liberty to submit their disputes for settlement.

CHAPTER I

*Organization of the Court*

Art. 2. The Permanent Court of International Justice shall be composed of a body of independent judges, elected regardless of their nationality from amongst persons of high moral character, who possess the qualifications required in their respective countries for appointment to the highest judicial offices, or are jurisconsults of recognized competence in international law.

Art. 3. The Court shall consist of fifteen members: eleven judges and four deputy-judges. The number of judges and deputy-judges may hereafter be increased by the Assembly, upon the proposal of the Council of the League of Nations, to a total of fifteen judges and six deputy-judges.

Art. 4. The members of the Court shall be elected by the Assembly and by the Council from a list of persons nominated by the national groups in the Court of Arbitration, in accordance with the following provisions:

In the case of Members of the League of Nations not represented in the Permanent Court of Arbitration, the lists of candidates shall be drawn up by national groups appointed for this purpose by their Governments under the same conditions as those prescribed for members of the Permanent Court of Arbitration by Article 44 of the Convention of The Hague of 1907 for the pacific settlement of international disputes.

Art. 5. At least three months before the date of the election, the Secretary-General of the League of Nations shall address a written request to the Members of the Court of Arbitration belonging to the States mentioned in the Annex to the Covenant or to the States which join the League subsequently, and to the persons appointed under paragraph 2 of Article 4, inviting them to undertake, within a given time, by national groups, the nomination of persons in a position to accept the duties of a member of the Court.

No group may nominate more than four persons, not more than two of whom shall be of their own nationality. In no case must the number of candidates nominated be more than double the number of seats to be filled.

Art. 6. Before making these nominations, each national group is recommended to consult its Highest Court of Justice, its Legal Faculties and Schools of Law, and its National Academies and national sections of International Academies devoted to the study of Law.

Art. 7. The Secretary-General of the League of Nations shall prepare a list in alphabetical order of all the persons thus nominated. Save as provided in Article 12, paragraph 2, these shall be the only persons eligible for appointment.

The Secretary-General shall submit this list to the Assembly and to the Council.

Art. 8. The Assembly and the Council shall proceed independently of one another to elect, firstly the judges, then the deputy-judges.

Art. 9. At every election, the electors shall bear in mind that not only should all the persons appointed as members of the Court possess the qualifications required, but the whole body also should represent the main forms of civilization and the principal legal systems of the world.

Art. 10. Those candidates who obtain an absolute majority of votes in the Assembly and in the Council shall be considered as elected.

In the event of more than one national of the same Member of the League being elected by the votes of both the Assembly and the Council, the eldest of these only shall be considered as elected.

Art. 11. If, after the first meeting held for the purpose of the election, one or more seats remain to be filled, a second and, if necessary, a third meeting shall take place.

Art. 12. If, after the third meeting, one or more seats still remain unfilled, a joint conference consisting of six members, three appointed by the Assembly and three by the Council, may be formed, at any time, at the request of either the Assembly or the Council, for the purpose of choosing one name for each seat still vacant, to submit to the Assembly and the Council for their respective acceptance.

If the Conference is unanimously agreed upon any person who fulfils the required conditions, he may be included in its list, even though he was not included in the list of nominations referred to in Articles 4 and 5.

If the joint conference is satisfied that it will not be successful in procuring an election, those members of the Court who have already been appointed shall, within a period to be fixed by the Council, proceed to fill the vacant seats by selection from amongst those candidates who have obtained votes either in the Assembly or in the Council.

In the event of an equality of votes amongst the judges, the eldest judge shall have a casting vote.

Art. 13. The members of the Court shall be elected for nine years. They may be re-elected.

They shall continue to discharge their duties until their places have been filled. Though replaced, they shall finish any cases which they may have begun.

Art. 14. Vacancies which may occur shall be filled by the same method as that laid down for the first election. A member of the Court elected to replace a member whose period of appointment had not expired will hold the appointment for the remainder of his predecessor's term.

Art. 15. Deputy-judges shall be called upon to sit in the order laid down in a list.

This list shall be prepared by the Court and shall have regard firstly to priority of election and secondly to age.

Art. 16. The ordinary Members of the Court may not exercise any political or administrative function. This provision does not apply to the Deputy-Judges except when performing their duties on the Court.

Any doubt on this point is settled by the decision of the Court.

Art. 17. No Member of the Court can act as agent, counsel or advocate in any case of an international nature. This provision only applies to the deputy-judges as regards cases in which they are called upon to exercise their functions on the Court.

No Member may participate in the decision of any case in which he has previously taken an active part, as agent, counsel or advocate for one of the contesting parties, or as a Member of a national or international Court, or of a commission of enquiry, or in any other capacity.

Any doubt on this point is settled by the decision of the Court.

Art. 18. A member of the Court cannot be dismissed unless, in the unanimous opinion of the other members, he has ceased to fulfill the required conditions.

Formal notification thereof shall be made to the Secretary-General of the League of Nations, by the Registrar.

This notification makes the place vacant.

Art. 19. The members of the Court, when engaged on the business of the Court, shall enjoy diplomatic privileges and immunities.

Art. 20. Every member of the Court shall, before taking up his duties, make a solemn declaration in the open Court that he will exercise his powers impartially and conscientiously.

Art. 21. The Court shall elect its President and Vice-President for three years; they may be re-elected.

It shall appoint its Registrar.

The duties of Registrar of the Court shall not be deemed incompatible with those of Secretary-General of the Permanent Court of Arbitration.

Art. 22. The seat of the Court shall be established at The Hague.

The President and Registrar shall reside at the seat of the Court.

Art. 23. A session of the Court shall be held every year.

Unless otherwise provided by rules of Court, this session shall begin on the 15th of June, and shall continue for so long as may be deemed necessary to finish the cases on the list.

The President may summon an extraordinary session of the Court whenever necessary.

Art. 24. If, for some special reason, a member of the Court considers that he should not take part in the decision of a particular case, he shall so inform the President.

If the President considers that for some special reason one of the members of the Court should not sit on a particular case, he shall give him notice accordingly.

If in any such case the member of the Court and the President disagree, the matter shall be settled by the decision of the Court.

Art. 25. The full Court shall sit except when it is expressly provided otherwise.

If eleven judges cannot be present, the number shall be made up by calling on deputy-judges to sit.

If, however, eleven judges are not available, a quorum of nine judges shall suffice to constitute the Court.

Art. 26. Labour cases, particularly cases referred to in Part XIII (Labour) of the Treaty of Versailles and the corresponding portions of the other Treaties of Peace, shall be heard and determined by the Court under the following conditions:

The Court will appoint every three years a special chamber of five judges, selected so far as possible with due regard to the provisions of Article 9. In addition, two judges shall be selected for the purpose of replacing a judge who finds it impossible to sit. If the parties so demand, cases will be heard and determined by this chamber. In the absence of any such demand, the Court will sit with the number of judges provided for in Article 25. On all occasions the judges will be assisted by four technical assessors sitting with them, but without the right to vote, and chosen with a view to ensuring a just representation of the competing interests.

If there is a national of one only of the parties sitting as a judge in the chamber referred to in the preceding paragraph, the President will invite one of the other judges to retire in favour of a judge chosen by the other party in accordance with Article 31.

The technical assessors shall be chosen for each particular case in accordance with the rules of procedure under Article 30 from a list of "Assessors for Labour cases" composed of two persons nominated by each Member of the League of Nations and an equivalent number nominated by the Governing Body of the Labour Office. The Governing Body will nominate, as to one-half, representatives of the workers, and as to one-half, representatives of employers from the list referred to in Article 412 of the Treaty of Versailles and the corresponding Articles of the other Treaties of Peace.

In Labour cases the International Labour Office shall be at liberty to furnish the Court with all relevant information, and for this purpose the Director of that Office shall receive copies of all the written proceedings.

Art. 27. Cases relating to transit and communications, particularly cases referred to in Part XII (Ports, Waterways and Railways) of the Treaty of Versailles and the corresponding portions of the other Treaties of Peace shall be heard and determined by the Court under the following conditions:

The Court will appoint every three years a special chamber of five judges, selected so far as possible with due regard to the provisions of Article 9. In addition, two judges shall be selected for the purpose of replacing a judge who finds it impossible to sit. If the parties so demand, cases will be heard and determined by this chamber. In the absence of any such demand, the Court will sit with the number of judges provided for in Article 25. When desired by the parties or decided by the Court, the judges will be assisted by four technical assessors sitting with them, but without the right to vote.

If there is a national of one only of the parties sitting as a judge in the chamber referred to in the preceding paragraph, the President will invite one of the other judges to retire in favour of a judge chosen by the other party in accordance with Article 31.

The technical assessors shall be chosen for each particular case in accordance with rules of procedure under Article 30 from a list of "Assessors for Transit and Communications cases" composed of two persons nominated by each Member of the League of Nations.

Art. 28. The special chambers provided for in Articles 26 and 27 may, with the consent of the parties to the dispute, sit elsewhere than at The Hague.

Art. 29. With a view to the speedy despatch of business, the Court shall form annually a chamber composed of three judges who, at the request of the contesting parties, may hear and determine cases by summary procedure.

Art. 30. The Court shall frame rules for regulating its procedure. In particular, it shall lay down rules for summary procedure.

Art. 31. Judges of the nationality of each contesting party shall retain their right to sit in the case before the Court.

If the Court includes upon the Bench a judge of the nationality of one of the parties only, the other party may select from among the deputy-judges a judge of its nationality, if there be one. If there should not be one, the party may choose a judge, preferably from among those persons who have been nominated as candidates as provided in Articles 4 and 5.

If the Court includes upon the Bench no judge of the nationality of the contesting parties, each of these may proceed to select or choose a judge as provided in the preceding paragraph.

Should there be several parties in the same interest, they shall, for the purpose of the preceding provisions, be reckoned as one party only. Any doubt upon this point is settled by the decision of the Court.

Judges selected or chosen as laid down in paragraphs 2 and 3 of this Article shall fulfill the conditions required by Articles 2, 16, 17, 20, 24 of this Statute. They shall take part in the decision on an equal footing with their colleagues.

Art. 32. The judges shall receive an annual indemnity to be determined by the Assembly of the League of Nations upon the proposal of the Council. This indemnity must not be decreased during the period of a judge's appointment.

The President shall receive a special grant for his period of office, to be fixed in the same way.

The Vice-President, judges and deputy-judges shall receive a grant for the actual performance of their duties, to be fixed in the same way.

Travelling expenses incurred in the performance of their duties shall be refunded to judges and deputy-judges who do not reside at the seat of the Court.

Grants due to judges selected or chosen as provided in Article 31 shall be determined in the same way.

The salary of the Registrar shall be decided by the Council upon the proposal of the Court.

The Assembly of the League of Nations shall lay down, on the proposal of the Council, a special regulation fixing the conditions under which retiring pensions may be given to the personnel of the Court.

Art. 33. The expenses of the Court shall be borne by the League of Nations, in such a manner as shall be decided by the Assembly upon the proposal of the Council.

## CHAPTER II

### *Competence of the Court*

Art. 34. Only States or Members of the League of Nations can be parties in cases before the Court.

Art. 35. The Court shall be open to the Members of the League and also to States mentioned in the Annex to the Covenant.

The conditions under which the Court shall be open to other States shall, subject to the special provisions contained in treaties in force, be laid down by the Council, but in no case shall such provisions place the parties in a position of inequality before the Court.

When a State which is not a Member of the League of Nations is a party to a dispute, the Court will fix the amount which that party is to contribute towards the expenses of the Court.

Art. 36. The jurisdiction of the Court comprises all cases which the parties refer to it and all matters specially provided for in Treaties and Conventions in force.

The Members of the League of Nations and the States mentioned in the Annex to the Covenant may, either when signing or ratifying the protocol to which the present Statute is adjoined, or at a later moment, declare that they recognize as compulsory *ipso facto* and without special agreement, in relation to any other Member or State accepting the same obligation, the jurisdiction of the Court in all or any of the classes of legal disputes concerning:

(*a*)  The interpretation of a Treaty;

(*b*)  Any question of International Law;

(*c*)  The existence of any fact which, if established, would constitute a breach of an international obligation;

(*d*)  The nature or extent of the reparation to be made for the breach of an international obligation.

The declaration referred to above may be made unconditionally or on condition of reciprocity on the part of several or certain Members or States, or for a certain time.

In the event of a dispute as to whether the Court has jurisdiction, the matter shall be settled by the decision of the Court.

Art. 37. When a treaty or convention in force provides for the reference of a matter to a tribunal to be instituted by the League of Nations, the Court will be such tribunal.

Art. 38. The Court shall apply:

1. International conventions, whether general or particular, establishing rules expressly recognized by the contesting States;

2. International custom, as evidence of a general practice accepted as law;

3. The general principles of law recognized by civilized nations;

4. Subject to the provisions of Article 59, judicial decisions and the teachings of the most highly qualified publicists of the various nations, as subsidiary means for the determination of rules of law.

This provision shall not prejudice the power of the Court to **decide a case** *ex æquo et bono,* **if the parties agree thereto.**

## CHAPTER III

*Procedure*

Art. 39. The official languages of the Court shall be French and English. If the parties agree that the case shall be conducted in French, the judgment will be delivered in French. If the parties agree that the case shall be conducted in English, the judgment will be delivered in English.

In the absence of an agreement as to which language shall be employed, each party may, in the pleadings, use the language which it prefers; the decision of the Court will be given in French and English. In this case the Court will at the same time determine which of the two texts shall be considered as authoritative.

The Court may, at the request of the parties, authorize a language other than French or English to be used.

Art. 40. Cases are brought before the Court, as the case may be, either by the notification of the special agreement, or by a written application addressed to the Registrar. In either case the subject of the dispute and the contesting parties must be indicated.

The Registrar shall forthwith communicate the application to all concerned.

He shall also notify the Members of the League of Nations through the Secretary-General.

Art. 41. The Court shall have the power to indicate, if it considers that circumstances so require, any provisional measures which ought to be taken to reserve the respective rights of either party.

Pending the final decision, notice of the measures suggested shall forthwith be given to the parties and the Council.

Art. 42. The parties shall be represented by Agents.

They may have the assistance of Counsel or Advocates before the Court.

Art. 43. The procedure shall consist of two parts: written and oral.

The written proceedings shall consist of the communication to the judges and to the parties of cases, counter-cases and, if necessary, replies; also all papers and documents in support.

These communications shall be made through the Registrar, in the order and within the time fixed by the Court.

A certified copy of every document produced by one party shall be communicated to the other party.

The oral proceedings shall consist of the hearing by the Court of witnesses, experts, agents, counsel and advocates.

Art. 44. For the service of all notices upon persons other than the agents, counsel and advocates, the Court shall apply direct to the Government of the State upon whose territory the notice has to be served.

The same provision shall apply whenever steps are to be taken to procure evidence on the spot.

Art. 45. The hearing shall be under the control of the President or, in his absence, of the Vice-President; if both are absent, the senior judge shall preside.

Art. 46. The hearing in Court shall be public, unless the Court shall decide otherwise, or unless the parties demand that the public be not admitted.

Art. 47. Minutes shall be made at each hearing, and signed by the Registrar and the President.

These minutes shall be the only authentic record.

Art. 48. The Court shall make orders for the conduct of the case, shall decide the form and time in which each party must conclude its arguments, and make all arrangements connected with the taking of evidence.

Art. 49. The Court may, even before the hearing begins, call upon the agents to produce any document, or to supply any explanations. Formal note shall be taken of any refusal.

Art. 50. The Court may, at any time, entrust any individual, body, bureau, commission, or other organization that it may select, with the task of carrying out an enquiry or giving an expert opinion.

Art. 51. During the hearing, any relevant questions are to be put to the witnesses and experts under the conditions laid down by the Court in the rules of procedure referred to in Article 30.

Art. 52. After the Court has received the proofs and evidence within the time specified for the purpose, it may refuse to accept any further oral or written evidence that one party may desire to present unless the other side consents.

Art. 53. Whenever one of the parties shall not appear before the Court, or shall fail to defend his case, the other party may call upon the Court to decide in favour of his claim.

The Court must, before doing so, satisfy itself, not only that it has jurisdiction in accordance with Article 36 and 37, but also that the claim is well founded in fact and law.

Art. 54. When, subject to the control of the Court, the agents, advocates and counsel have completed their presentation of the case, the President shall declare the hearing closed.

The Court shall withdraw to consider the judgment.

The deliberations of the Court shall take place in private and remain secret.

Art. 55. All questions shall be decided by a majority of the judges present at the hearing.

In the event of an equality of votes, the President or his deputy shall have a casting vote.

Art. 56. The judgment shall state the reasons on which it is based.

It shall contain the names of the judges who have taken part in the decision.

Art. 57. If the judgment does not represent in whole or in part ⎯nimous opinion of the judges, dissenting judges are entitled ⎯ separate opinion.

⎯e judgment shall be signed by the President and by ⎯ shall be read in open Court, due notice having ⎯nts.

Art. 59. The decision of the Court has no binding force except between the parties and in respect of that particular case.

Art. 60. The Judgment is final and without appeal. In the event of dispute as to the meaning or scope of the judgment, the Court shall construe it upon the request of any party.

Art. 61. An application for revision of a judgment can be made only when it is based upon the discovery of some fact of such a nature as to be a decisive factor, which fact was, when the judgment was given, unknown to the Court and also to the party claiming revision, always provided that such ignorance was not due to negligence.

The proceedings for revision will be opened by a judgment of the Court expressly recording the existence of the new fact, recognizing that it has such a character as to lay the case open to revision, and declaring the application admissible on this ground.

The Court may require previous compliance with the terms of the judgment before it admits proceedings in revision.

The application for revision must be made at latest within six months of the discovery of the new fact.

No application for revision may be made after the lapse of ten years from the date of the sentence.

Art. 62. Should a State consider that it has an interest of a legal nature which may be affected by the decision in the case, it may submit a request to the Court to be permitted to intervene as a third party.

It will be for the Court to decide upon this request.

Art. 63. Whenever the construction of a convention to which States other than those concerned in the case are parties is in question, the Registrar shall notify all such States forthwith.

Every State so notified has the right to intervene in the proceedings: but if it uses this right, the construction given by the judgment will be equally binding upon it.

Art. 64. Unless otherwise decided by the Court, each party shall bear its own costs.

# APPENDIX II

### RULES OF COURT

### *Preamble*

The Court,
By virtue of Article 30 of its Statute,
Adopts the present Rules:

## CHAPTER I.  *The Court*

### HEADING 1.—*Constitution of the Court*

### SECTION A.  *Judges and Assessors*

Article 1. Subject to the provisions of Article 14 of the Statute, the term of office of judges and deputy-judges shall commence on January 1st of the year following their election.

Art. 2. Judges and deputy-judges elected at an earlier session of the Assembly and of the Council of the League of Nations shall take precedence respectively over judges and deputy-judges elected at a subsequent session. Judges and deputy-judges elected during the same session shall take precedence according to age. Judges shall take precedence over deputy-judges.

National judges chosen from outside the Court, under the terms of Article 31 of the Statute, shall take precedence after deputy-judges in order of age.

The list of deputy-judges shall be prepared in accordance with these principles.

The Vice-President shall take his seat on the right of the President. The other Members of the Court shall take their seats to the right and left of the President in the order laid down above.

Art. 3. Deputy-judges whose presence is necessary shall be summoned in the order laid down in the list referred to in the preceding Article, that is to say, each of them will be summoned in rotation throughout the list.

Should a deputy-judge be so far from the seat of the Court that, in the opinion of the President, a summons would not reach him in sufficient time, the deputy-judge next on the list shall be summoned; nevertheless, the judge to whom the summons should have been addressed shall be called upon, if possible, on the next occasion that the presence of a deputy-judge is required.

A deputy-judge who has begun a case shall be summoned again, if necessary out of his turn, in order to continue to sit in the case until it is finished.

Should a deputy-judge be summoned to take his seat in a particular case as a national judge, under the terms of Article 31 of the Statute, such summons shall not be regarded as coming within the terms of the present Article.

Art. 4. In cases in which one or more parties are entitled to choose a judge *ad hoc* of their nationality, the full Court may sit with a number of judges exceeding eleven.

When the Court has satisfied itself, in accordance with Article 31 of the Statute, that there are several parties in the same interest and that none of them has a judge of its nationality upon the bench, the Court shall invite them, within a period to be fixed by the Court, to select by common agreement a deputy-judge of the nationality of one of the parties, should there be one; or, should there not be one, a judge chosen in accordance with the principles of the above-mentioned Article.

Should the parties have failed to notify the Court of their selection or choice when the time limit expires, they shall be regarded as having renounced the right conferred upon them by Article 31.

Art. 5. Before entering upon his duties, each member of the Court or judge summoned to complete the Court, under the terms of Article 31 of the Statute, shall make the following solemn declaration in accordance with Article 20 of the Statute:

"I solemnly declare that I will exercise all my powers and duties as a judge honourably and faithfully, impartially and conscientiously."

A special public sitting of the Court may, if necessary, be convened for this purpose.

At the public inaugural sitting held after a new election of the whole Court the required declaration shall be made first by the President, secondly by the Vice-President, and then by the remaining judges in the order laid down in Article 2.

Art. 6. For the purpose of applying Article 18 of the Statute, the President, or if necessary the Vice-President, shall convene the judges and deputy-judges. The member affected shall be allowed to furnish explanations. When he has done so the question shall be discussed and a vote shall be taken, the member in question not being present. If the members present are unanimously agreed, the Registrar shall issue the notification prescribed in the above-mentioned Article.

Art. 7. The President shall take steps to obtain all information which might be helpful to the Court in selecting technical assessors in each case. With regard to the questions referred to in Article 26 of the Statute, he shall, in particular, consult the Governing Body of the International Labour Office.

The assessors shall be appointed by an absolute majority of votes, either by the Court or by the special Chamber which has to deal with the case in question.

Art. 8. Assessors shall make the following solemn declaration at the first sitting of the Court at which they are present:

"I solemnly declare that I will exercise my duties and powers as an assessor honourably and faithfully, impartially and conscientiously, and that I will scrupulously observe all the provisions of the Statute and of the Rules of Court."

## SECTION B. *The Presidency*

Art. 9. The election of the President and Vice-President shall take place at the end of the ordinary session immediately before the normal termination of the period of office of the retiring President and Vice-President.

After a new election of the whole Court, the election of the President and Vice-President shall take place at the commencement of the following session. The President and Vice-President elected in these circumstances shall take up their duties on the day of their election. They shall remain in office until the end of the second year after the year of their election.

Should the President or the Vice-President cease to belong to the Court before the expiration of their normal term of office, an election shall be held for the purpose of appointing a substitute for the unexpired portion of their term of office. If necessary, an extraordinary session of the Court may be convened for this purpose.

The elections referred to in the present Article shall take place by secret ballot. The candidate obtaining an absolute majority of votes shall be declared elected.

Art. 10. The President shall direct the work and administration of the Court; he shall preside at the meetings of the full Court.

Art. 11. The Vice-President shall take the place of the President, should the latter be unable to be present, or, should he cease to hold office, until the new President has been appointed by the Court.

Art. 12. The President shall reside within a radius of ten kilometers from the Peace Palace at The Hague.

The main annual vacation of the President shall not exceed three months.

Art. 13. After a new election of the whole Court and until such time as the President and Vice-President have been elected, the judge who takes precedence according to the order laid down in Article 2, shall perform the duties of President.

The same principle shall be applied should both the President and the Vice-President be unable to be present, or should both appointments be vacant at the same time.

### SECTION C.   *The Chambers*

Art. 14. The members of the Chambers constituted by virtue of Article 26, 27 and 29 of the Statute shall be appointed at a meeting of the full Court by an absolute majority of votes, regard being had for the purposes of this selection to any preference expressed by the judges, so far as the provisions of Article 9 of the Statute permit.

The substitutes mentioned in Articles 26 and 27 of the Statute shall be appointed in the same manner. Two judges shall also be chosen to replace any member of the Chamber of summary procedure who may be unable to sit.

The election shall take place at the end of the ordinary session of the Court, and the period of appointment of the members elected shall commence on January 1st of the following year.

Nevertheless, after a new election of the whole Court the election shall take place at the beginning of the following session. The period of appointment shall commence on the date of election and shall terminate, in the case of the Chamber referred to in Article 29 of the Statute, at the end of the same year, and in the case of the Chambers referred to in Articles 26 and 27 of the Statute, at the end of the second year after the year of election.

The Presidents of the Chambers shall be appointed at a sitting of the full Court. Nevertheless, the President of the Court shall, *ex officio,* preside over any Chamber of which he may be elected a member; similarly, the Vice-President of the Court shall, *ex officio,* preside over any Chamber of which he may be elected a member, provided that the President is not also a member.

Art. 15. The special Chambers for labour cases and for communications and transit cases may not sit with a greater number than five judges.

Except as provided in the second paragraph of the preceding Article, the composition of the Chamber for summary procedure may not be altered.

Art. 16. Deputy-judges shall not be summoned to complete the special Chambers or the Chamber for summary procedure, unless sufficient judges are not available to complete the number required.

SECTION D.  *The Registry*

Art. 17. The Court shall select its Registrar from amongst candidates proposed by members of the Court.

The election shall be by secret ballot and by a majority of votes. In the event of an equality of votes, the President shall have a casting vote.

The Registrar shall be elected for a term of seven years commencing on January 1st of the year following that in which the election takes place. He may be re-elected.

Should the Registrar cease to hold his office before the expiration of the term above-mentioned, an election shall be held for the purpose of appointing a successor.

Art. 18. Before taking up his duties, the Registrar shall make the following declaration at a meeting of the full Court:

"I solemnly declare that I will perform the duties conferred upon me as Registrar of the Permanent Court of International Justice in all loyalty, discretion and good conscience."

The other members of the Registry shall make a similar declaration before the President, the Registrar being present.

Art. 19. The Registrar shall reside within a radius of ten kilometres from the Peace Palace at The Hague.

The main annual vacation of the Registrar shall not exceed two months.

Art. 20. The staff of the Registry shall be appointed by the Court on proposals submitted by the Registrar.

Art. 21. The Regulations for the Staff of the Registry shall be adopted by the President on the proposal of the Registrar, subject to subsequent approval by the Court.

Art. 22. The Court shall determine or modify the organization of the Registry upon proposals submitted by the Registrar. On the proposal of the Registrar, the President shall appoint the member of the Registry who is to act for the Registrar in his absence or, in the event of his ceasing to hold his office, until a successor has been appointed.

Art. 23. The registers kept in the archives shall be so arranged as to give particulars with regard to the following points amongst others:

1. For each case or question, all documents pertaining to it and all action taken with regard to it in chronological order; all such documents shall bear the same file number and shall be numbered consecutively within the file;

2. All decisions of the Court in chronological order, with references to the respective files;

3. All advisory opinions given by the Court in chronological order, with references to the respective files;

4. All notifications and similar communications sent out by the Court, with references to the respective files.

Indexes kept in the archives shall comprise:

1. A card index of names with necessary references;

2. A card index of subject matter with like references.

Art. 24. During hours to be fixed by the President the Registrar shall receive any documents and reply to any enquiries, subject to the provisions of Article 38 of the present Rules and to the observance of professional secrecy.

Art. 25. The Registrar shall be the channel for all communications to and from the Court.

The Registrar shall ensure that the date of despatch and receipt of all communications and notifications may readily be verified. Communications and notifications sent by post shall be registered. Communications addressed to the official representatives or to the agents of the parties shall be considered as having been addressed to the parties themselves. The date of receipt shall be noted on all documents received by the Registrar, and a receipt bearing this date and the number under which the document has been registered shall be given to the sender, if a request to that effect be made.

Art. 26. The Registrar shall be responsible for the archives, the accounts and all administrative work. He shall have the custody of the seals and stamps of the Court. He shall himself be present at all meetings of the full Court and either he, or a person appointed to represent him with the approval of the Court, shall be present at all sittings of the various Chambers; he shall be responsible for drawing up the minutes of the meetings.

He shall further undertake all duties which may be laid upon him by the present Rules.

The duties of the Registry shall be set forth in detail in a List of Instructions to be submitted by the Registrar to the President for his approval.

### HEADING 2.—*Working of the Court*

Art. 27. In the year following a new election of the whole Court the ordinary annual session shall commence on the fifteenth of January.

If the day fixed for the opening of a session is regarded as a holiday at the place where the Court is sitting, the session shall be opened on the working day following.

Art. 28. The list of cases shall be prepared and kept up to date by the Registrar under the responsibility of the President. The list for each session shall contain all questions submitted to the Court for an advisory opinion and all cases in regard to which the written proceedings are concluded, in the order in which the documents submitting each question or case have been received by the Registrar. If in the course of a session, a question is submitted to the Court or the written proceedings in regard to any case are concluded, the Court shall decide whether such question or case shall be added to the list for that session.

The Registrar shall prepare and keep up to date extracts from the above list showing the cases to be dealt with by the respective Chambers.

The Registrar shall also prepare and keep a list of cases for revision.

Art. 29. During the sessions the dates and hours of sittings shall be fixed by the President.

Art. 30. If at any sitting of the full Court it is impossible to obtain the prescribed quorum, the Court shall adjourn until the quorum is obtained.

Art. 31. The Court shall sit in private to deliberate upon the decision of any case or on the reply to any question submitted to it.

During the deliberation referred to in the preceding paragraph, only persons authorized to take part in the deliberation and the Registrar shall be present. No other person shall be admitted except by virtue of a special decision taken by the Court, having regard to exceptional circumstances.

Every member of the Court who is present at the deliberation shall state his opinion together with the reasons on which it is based.

The decision of the Court shall be based upon the conclusions adopted after final discussion by a majority of the members.

Any member of the Court may request that a question which is to be voted upon shall be drawn up in precise terms in both the official languages and distributed to the Court. A request to this effect shall be complied with.

CHAPTER II.  *Procedure*

HEADING 1.—*Contentious Procedure*

SECTION A.  *General Provisions*

Art. 32. The rules contained under this heading shall in no way preclude the adoption by the Court of such other rules as may be jointly proposed by the parties concerned, due regard being paid to the particular circumstances of each case.

Art. 33. The Court shall fix time limits in each case by assigning a definite date for the completion of the various acts of procedure, having regard as far as possible to any agreement between the parties.

The Court may extend time limits which it has fixed. It may likewise decide in certain circumstances that any proceeding taken after the expiration of a time limit shall be considered as valid.

If the Court is not sitting the powers conferred upon it by this article shall be exercised by the President, subject to any subsequent decision of the Court.

Art. 34. All documents of the written proceedings submitted to the Court shall be accompanied by not less than thirty printed copies certified correct. The President may order additional copies to be supplied.

SECTION B.  *Procedure before the Court and before the*
*Special Chambers (Articles 26 and 27 of the Statute)*
*I. Institution of Proceedings*

Art. 35. When a case is brought before the Court by means of a
special agreement, the latter, or the document notifying the Court of
the agreement, shall mention the addresses selected at the seat of
the Court to which notices and communications intended for the
respective parties are to be sent.

In all other cases in which the Court has jurisdiction, the application shall include, in addition to an indication of the subject of
the dispute and the names of the parties concerned, a succinct statement of facts, an indication of the claim and the address selected at
the seat of the Court to which notices and communications are to be
sent.

Should proceedings be instituted by means of an application, the
first document sent in reply thereto shall mention the address
selected at the seat of the Court to which subsequent notices and
communications in regard to the case are to be sent.

Should the notice of a special agreement, or the application, contain a request that the case be referred to one of the special Chambers mentioned in Articles 26 or 27 of the Statute, such request
shall be complied with, provided that the parties are in agreement.

Similarly, a request to the effect that technical assessors be
attached to the Court, in accordance with Article 27 of the Statute,
or that the case be referred to the Chamber for summary procedure
shall also be granted; compliance with the latter request is, however,
subject to the condition that the case does not refer to any of the
questions indicated in Articles 26 and 27 of the Statute.

Art. 36. The Registrar shall forthwith communicate to all members of the Court special agreements or applications which have been
notified to him.

## II. *Written Proceedings*

Art. 37. Should the parties agree that the proceedings shall be
conducted in French or in English, the documents constituting the
written procedure shall be submitted only in the language adopted
by the parties.

In the absence of an agreement with regard to the language to be
employed, documents shall be submitted in French or in English.

Should the use of a language other than French or English be
authorized, a translation into French or into English shall be attached to the original of each document submitted.

The Registrar shall not be bound to make translations of documents submitted in accordance with the above rules.

In the case of voluminous documents the Court, or the President
if the Court is not sitting, may, at the request of the party concerned, sanction the submission of translations of portions of
documents only.

Art. 38. The Court, or the President, if the Court is not sitting,
may, after hearing the parties, order the Registrar to hold the

cases and counter-cases of each suit at the disposal of the Government of any State which is entitled to appear before the Court.

Art. 39. In cases in which proceedings have been instituted by means of a special agreement, the following documents may be presented in the order stated below, provided that no agreement to the contrary has been concluded between the parties:

a case, submitted by each party within the same limit of time;
a counter-case, submitted by each party within the same limit of time;
a reply, submitted by each party within the same limit of time.

When proceedings are instituted by means of an application, failing any agreement to the contrary between the parties, the documents shall be presented in the order stated below:

the case by the applicant;
the counter-case by the respondent;
the reply by the applicant;
the rejoinder by the respondent.

Art. 40. Cases shall contain:

1. a statement of the facts on which the claim is based;
2. a statement of law;
3. a statement of conclusions;
4. a list of the documents in support; these documents shall be attached to the case.

Counter-cases shall contain:

1. the affirmation or contestation of the facts stated in the case;
2. a statement of additional facts, if any;
3. a statement of law;
4. conclusions based on the facts stated; these conclusions may include counter-claims, in so far as the latter come within the jurisdiction of the Court;
5. a list of the documents in support; these documents shall be attached to the counter-case.

Art. 41. Upon the termination of the written proceedings the President shall fix a date for the commencement of the oral proceedings.

Art. 42. The Registrar shall forward to each of the members of the Court a copy of all documents in the case as he receives them.

### III. Oral Proceedings

Art. 43. In the case of a public sitting, the Registrar shall publish in the Press all necessary information as to the date and hour fixed.

Art. 44. The Registrar shall arrange for the interpretation from French into English and from English into French of all statements, questions and answers which the Court may direct to be so interpreted.

Whenever a language other than French or English is employed, either under the terms of the third paragraph of Article 39 of the Statute or in a particular instance, the necessary arrangements for translation into one of the two official languages shall be made by the party concerned. In the case of witnesses or experts who appear at the instance of the Court, these arrangements shall be made by the Registrar.

Art. 45. The Court shall determine in each case whether the representatives of the parties shall address the Court before or after the production of the evidence; the parties shall, however, retain the right to comment on the evidence given.

Art. 46. The order in which the agents, advocates or counsel, shall be called upon to speak shall be determined by the Court, failing an agreement between the parties on the subject.

Art. 47. In sufficient time before the opening of the oral proceedings, each party shall inform the Court and the other parties of all evidence which it intends to produce, together with the names, Christian names, description and residence of witnesses whom it desires to be heard.

It shall further give a general indication of the point or points to which the evidence is to refer.

Art. 48. The Court may, subject to the provisions of Article 44 of the Statute, invite the parties to call witnesses, or may call for the production of any other evidence on points of fact in regard to which the parties are not in agreement.

Art. 49. The Court, or the President should the Court not be sitting, shall, at the request of one of the parties or on its own initiative, take the necessary steps for the examination of witnesses out of Court.

Art. 50. Each witness shall make the following solemn declaration before giving his evidence in Court:

"I solemnly declare upon my honour and conscience that I will speak the truth, the whole truth and nothing but the truth."

Art. 51. Witnesses shall be examined by the representatives of the parties under the control of the President. Questions may be put to them by the President and afterwards by the judges.

Art. 52. The indemnities of witnesses who appear at the instance of the Court shall be paid out of the funds of the Court.

Art. 53. Any report or record of an enquiry carried out at the request of the Court, under the terms of Article 50 of the Statute, and reports furnished to the Court by experts, in accordance with the same Article, shall be forthwith communicated to the parties.

Art. 54. A record shall be made of the evidence taken. The portion containing the evidence of each witness shall be read over to him and approved by him.

As regards the remainder of the oral proceedings, the Court shall decide in each case whether verbatim records of all or certain portions of them shall be prepared for its own use.

Art. 55. The minutes mentioned in Article 47 of the Statute shall in particular include:

1. the names of the judges;
2. the names of the agents, advocates and counsel;
3. the names, Christian names, description and residence of witnesses heard;
4. a specification of other evidence produced;
5. any declarations made by the parties;
6. all decisions taken by the Court during the hearing.

Art. 56. Before the oral proceedings are concluded each party may present his bill of costs.

### IV. Interim Protection

Art. 57. When the Court is not sitting, any measures for the preservation in the meantime of the respective rights of the parties shall be indicated by the President.

Any refusal by the parties to conform to the suggestions of the Court or of the President, with regard to such measures, shall be placed in record.

### V. Intervention

Art. 58. An application for permission to intervene, under the terms of Article 62 of the Statute, must be communicated to the Registrar at latest before the commencement of the oral proceedings.

Nevertheless, the Court may, in exceptional circumstances, consider an application submitted at a later stage.

Art. 59. The application referred to in the preceding Article shall contain:

1. a specification of the case in which the applicant desires to intervene;
2. a statement of law and of fact justifying intervention;
3. a list of the documents in support of the application; these documents shall be attached.

Such application shall be immediately communicated to the parties, who shall send to the Registrar any observations which they may desire to make within a period to be fixed by the Court, or by the President, should the Court not be sitting.

Art. 60. Any State desiring to intervene, under the terms of Article 63 of the Statute, shall inform the Registrar in writing at latest before the commencement of the oral proceedings.

The Court, or the President if the Court is not sitting, shall take the necessary steps to enable the intervening State to inspect the documents in the case, in so far as they relate to the interpretation of the convention in question, and to submit its observations thereon to the Court.

### VI. Agreement

Art. 61. If the parties conclude an agreement regarding the settlement of the dispute and give written notice of such agreement to the Court before the close of the proceedings, the Court shall officially record the conclusion of the agreement.

Should the parties by mutual agreement notify the Court in writing that they intend to break off proceedings, the Court shall officially record the fact and proceedings shall be terminated.

## VII. Judgment

Art. 62. The judgment shall contain:

1. the date on which it is pronounced;
2. the names of the judges participating;
3. the names and style of the parties;
4. the names of the agents of the parties;
5. the conclusions of the parties;
6. the matters of fact;
7. the reasons in point of law;
8. the operative provisions of the judgment;
9. the decision, if any, referred to in Article 64 of the Statute.

The opinions of judges who dissent from the judgment, shall be attached thereto should they express a desire to that effect.

Art. 63. After having been read in open Court the text of the judgment shall forthwith be communicated to all parties concerned and to the Secretary-General of the League of Nations.

Art. 64. The judgment shall be regarded as taking effect on the day on which it is read in Open Court, in accordance with Article 58 of the Statute.

Art. 65. A collection of the judgments of the Court shall be printed and published under the responsibility of the Registrar.

## VIII. Revision

Art. 66. Application for revision shall be made in the same form as the application mentioned in Article 40 of the Statute.

It shall contain:

1. the reference to the judgment impeached;
2. the fact on which the application is based;
3. a list of the documents in support; these documents shall be attached.

It shall be the duty of the Registrar to give immediate notice of an application for revision to the other parties concerned. The lattter may submit observations within a time limit to be fixed by the Court, or by the President should the Court not be sitting.

If the judgment impeached was pronounced by the full Court, the application for revision shall also be dealt with by the full Court. If the judgment impeached was pronounced by one of the Chambers mentioned in Articles 26, 27 or 29 of the Statute, the application for revision shall be dealt with by the same Chamber. The provisions of Article 13 of the Statute shall apply in all cases.

If the Court, under the third paragraph of Article 61 of the Statute, makes a special order rendering the admission of the application conditional upon previous compliance with the terms of the judgment impeached, this condition shall be immediately communicated to the applicant by the Registrar, and proceedings in revision shall be stayed pending receipt by the Registrar of proof of previous compliance with the original judgment and until such proof shall have been accepted by the Court.

## Section C. *Summary Procedure*

Art. 67. Except as provided under the present section the rules for procedure before the full Court shall apply to summary procedure.

Art. 68. Upon receipt by the Registrar of the document instituting proceedings in a case which, by virtue of an agreement between the parties, is to be dealt with by summary procedure, the President shall convene as soon as possible the Chamber referred to in Article 29 of the Statute.

Art. 69. The proceedings are opened by the presentation of a case by each party. These cases shall be communicated by the Registrar to the members of the Chamber and to the opposing party.

The cases shall contain reference to all evidence which the parties may desire to produce.

Should the Chamber consider that the cases do not furnish adequate information, it may, in the absence of an agreement to the contrary between the parties, institute oral proceedings. It shall fix a date for the commencement of the oral proceedings.

At the hearing, the Chamber shall call upon the parties to supply oral explanations. It may sanction the production of any evidence mentioned in the cases.

If it is desired that witnesses or experts whose names are mentioned in the case should be heard, such witnesses or experts must be available to appear before the Chamber when required.

Art. 70. The judgment is the judgment of the Court rendered in the Chamber of summary procedure. It shall be read at a public sitting of the Chamber.

## Heading 2.—*Advisory Procedure*

Art. 71. Advisory opinions shall be given after deliberation by the full Court.

The opinions of dissenting judges may, at their request, be attached to the opinion of the Court.

Art. 72. Questions upon which the advisory opinion of the Court is asked shall be laid before the Court by means of a written request, signed either by the President of the Assembly or the President of the Council of the League of Nations, or by the Secretary-General of the League under instructions from the Assembly or the Council.

The request shall contain an exact statement of the question upon which an opinion is required, and shall be accompanied by all documents likely to throw light upon the question.

Art. 73. The Registrar shall forthwith give notice of the request for an advisory opinion to the members of the Court, and to the Members of the League of Nations, through the Secretary-General of the League, and to the States mentioned in the Annex to the Covenant.

Notice of such request shall also be given to any international organizations which are likely to be able to furnish information on the question.

Art. 74. Any advisory opinion which may be given by the Court and the request in response to which it was given, shall be printed and published in a special collection for which the Registrar shall be responsible.

### HEADING 3.—*Errors*

Art. 75. The Court, or the President if the Court is not sitting, shall be entitled to correct an error in any order, judgment or opinion, arising from a slip or accidental omission.

Done at The Hague, the twenty-fourth day of March, one thousand nine hundred and twenty-two.

(*s.*) LODER,
*President.*

(*s.*) A. HAMMARSKJÖLD,
*Registrar.*

### RESOLUTION CONCERNING THE SALARIES OF THE MEMBERS OF THE PERMANENT COURT OF INTERNATIONAL JUSTICE

*Passed by the Assembly of the League of Nations, Geneva, December 18, 1920*

The Assembly of the League of Nations, in conformity with the provisions of Article 32 of the Statute, fixes the salaries and allowances of members of the Permanent Court of International Justice as follows:

President:                                          Dutch florins.
    Annual salary ........................ 15,000
    Special allowance .................... 45,000
        Total ............................ 60,000

Vice-President:
    Annual salary ........................ 15,000
    Duty-allowance (200×150) ............. 30,000 (maximum)
        Total ............................ 45,000

Ordinary Judges:
    Annual salary ........................ 15,000
    Duty-allowance (200×100) ............. 20,000 (maximum)
        Total ............................ 35,000

Deputy-Judges:
    Duty-allowance (200×150) ............. 30,000 (maximum)

Duty allowances are payable from the day of departure until the return of the beneficiary.

An additional allowance of 50 florins per day is assigned for each day of actual presence at The Hague to the Vice-President and to the ordinary and deputy-judges.

Allowances and salaries are free of all tax.

## APPENDIX III

### RESOLUTION OPENING THE COURT TO ALL NATIONS [27]

The Council of the League of Nations, in virtue of the powers conferred upon it by Article 35, paragraph 2, of the Statute of the Permanent Court of International Justice, and subject to the provisions of that Article,

*Resolves:*

1. The Permanent Court of International Justice shall be open to a State which is not a Member of the League of Nations or mentioned in the Annex to the Covenant of the League, upon the following condition, namely: that such State shall previously have deposited with the Registrar of the Court a declaration by which it accepts the jurisdiction of the Court, in accordance with the Covenant of the League of Nations and with the terms and subject to the conditions of the Statute and Rules of Procedure of the Court, and undertakes to carry out in full good faith the decision or decisions of the Court and not to resort to war against a State complying therewith.

2. Such declaration may be either particular or general.

A particular declaration is one accepting the jurisdiction of the Court in respect only of a particular dispute or disputes which have already arisen.

A general declaration is one accepting the jurisdiction generally in respect of all disputes, or of a particular class or classes of disputes which have already arisen or which may arise in the future.

A State in making such a declaration may accept the jurisdiction of the Court as compulsory, *ipso facto,* and without special convention, in conformity with Article 36 of the Statute of the Court; but such acceptance may not, without special convention, be relied upon vis-à-vis Members of the League of Nations or States mentioned in the Annex to the Covenant which have signed or may hereafter sign the "optional clause" provided for by the additional Protocol of December 16th, 1920.

3. The original declarations made under the terms of this Resolution shall be kept in the custody of the Registrar of the Court. Certified true copies thereof shall be transmitted, in accordance with the practice of the Court, to all Members of the League of Nations and States mentioned in the Annex to the Covenant, and to such

27. The text of this Resolution was reconsidered by the Council on May 17, 1922. The Resolution is given here in the form in which it was finally approved on that date.

other States as the Court may determine, and to the Secretary-General of the League of Nations.

4. The Council of the League of Nations reserves the right to rescind or amend this Resolution by a Resolution which shall be communicated to the Court; and on the receipt of such communication by the Registrar of the Court, and to the extent determined by the new Resolution, existing declarations shall cease to be effective except in regard to disputes which are already before the Court.

5. All questions as to the validity or the effect of a declaration made under the terms of this Resolution shall be decided by the Court.

# V

# RULES OF WARFARE: AIRCRAFT AND RADIO

## HAGUE CONFERENCE, 1922–23[1]

As in the process of particular pleas between private men, all things ought to be ordered by rules of civil laws; so in the proceedings of the war nothing ought to be done against the law of nations, or the law of honor. Lord Bacon, 1592: *Works* (London, 1740), IV, 342.

FROM December 11, 1922, until February 19, 1923, there was held at the Peace Palace, at The Hague, an international conference, composed of a Commission of Jurists and their Military and Naval Advisers, for the purpose of formulating a code of rules for the regulation of the use of aircraft and of radio in time of war.[1] The parties to this con-

1. The personnel of the conference was as follows:

American Delegation—Members of the Commission: The Honorable John Bassett Moore, Ambassador Extraordinary, Judge of the Permanent Court of International Justice; The Honorable Albert Henry Washburn, Envoy Extraordinary and Minister Plenipotentiary of the United States at Vienna. Advisers: Rear-Admiral William Ledyard Rodgers, Naval Adviser; Brigadier-General William H. Johnston, Military Adviser; Captain Samuel W. Bryant, Naval Adviser (Radio); Colonel Frederick M. Brown, Military Adviser; Colonel George S. Gibbs, Military Adviser (Radio); Commander Forde A. Todd, Naval Adviser; Lieutenant-Commander Newton H. White, Naval Adviser (Aviation); Major William C. Sherman, Military Adviser (Aviation); Lieutenant Frederic W. Neilson, Naval Adviser (Aviation) and Aide to Admiral Rodgers; Mr. George R. Merrell, Jr., Third Secretary of Legation, Secretary to the Delegation.

British Delegation—Members of the Commission: The Right Honorable Sir Rennell Rodd, G.C.B., G.C.M.G., G.C.V.O.; Sir Cecil Hurst,

ference were the United States of America, the British Empire, France, Italy, Japan, and The Netherlands. Its origin is to be sought in the convocation and the acts of the international conference on the Limitation of Armament which sat at Washington from November 12, 1921, until February 6, 1922.

K.C.B., K.C. Advisers: Mr. Alexander Flint, C.B., Principal Assistant Secretary of the Admiralty, Naval Adviser; Captain John C. Hamilton, R.N., Deputy Director of Plans at the Admiralty, Naval Adviser; Colonel W. K. Venning, C.M.G., M.C., Military Adviser; Lieutenant-Colonel S. J. Lowe, D.S.O., O.B.E., Military Adviser; Air Commodore C. L. Lambe, C.B., C.M.G., D.S.O., Military Adviser (Aviation); Major F. W. Home, Military Adviser (Radio); Mr. J. M. Spaight, O.B.E., Assistant Secretary of the Air Ministry, Air Adviser; Mr. F. E. F. Adam, First Secretary, Foreign Office, Secretary to the Delegation.

French Delegation—Members of the Commission: M. de Lapradelle, Professor of the Faculty of Law at the University of Paris, Legal Adviser of the Ministry of Foreign Affairs; M. Basdevant, Professor of the Faculty of Law at the University of Paris, Legal Adviser of the Ministry of Foreign Affairs. Advisers: General Ferrié, Military Adviser (Radio); Colonel Faure, Military Adviser (Aviation); Lieutenant-Colonel Plée, of the Army Staff, Military Adviser; Captain Revault, of the Naval Staff, Naval Adviser; Commander Noel, Naval Adviser (Radio); Commander Sire, Naval Adviser (Aviation); M. Robert Siegfried, First Secretary of Embassy, Secretary to the Delegation.

Italian Delegation—Members of the Commission: His Excellency M. Vittorio Rolandi Ricci, Senator, Former Ambassador. Advisers: Colonel Riccardo Moizo, Military Adviser (Aviation); M. Arrigo Cavaglieri, Professor of International Law, Adviser; Major (Air Force) Carlo Graziani, Military Adviser (Aviation); Major Giuseppe Raineri-Biscia, Naval Adviser; Count Vittorio Negri, Chargé d'Affaires at The Hague, Adviser; Count Alberto Barbarich, Secretary.

Japanese Delegation—Members of the Commission: His Excellency Baron Matsui, Ambassador Extraordinary and Plenipotentiary; His Excellency M. Matsuda, Minister Plenipotentiary. Advisers: Brigadier-General Shizuma, Military Adviser; Rear-Admiral Kiyokawa, Naval Adviser; M. Sugimura, Secretary and Legal Adviser to the Foreign Office, Legal Adviser; M. Ito, Chargé d'Affaires at The Hague, Legal Adviser; M. Fujita, Councillor to the War Department, Legal Adviser; Commander Wada, Assistant Naval Adviser; Major Sonobe, Assistant Military Adviser; Lieutenant-Commander Sato, Assistant Naval Adviser; M. Yenomoto, Councillor to the Naval Department, Legal Adviser; M. Katagiri, Secretary; M. Sato, Secretary; M. Matsumoto, Secretary.

Netherlands Delegation—Members of the Commission: Professor A. A. H. Struycken, Member of the Council of State, and of the Permanent Court of Arbitration; Jonkheer W. J. M. Van Eysinga, Professor of International Law at the University of Leyden. Advisers: Lieutenant-General (retired list) H. L. Van Oordt, Military Adviser; Rear-Admiral (retired list) H. G. Surie, Naval Adviser; Captain C. Aronstein, Naval Adviser (Radio); Captain F. A. Van Heyst (Air Force), Assistant Military Adviser; Lieutenant H. J. Bueninck, Assistant Naval Adviser; M. E. N. Van Kleffens, Assistant Director of the Legal Section, at the Ministry of Foreign Affairs, Secretary.

Secretariat: Professor J. P. A. François, Head of Department at the Ministry of Foreign Affairs, Secretary-General; M. E. E. Menten, LL.D., Assistant Secretary-General.

On August 11, 1921, the Secretary of State of the United States, in the name of the President, extended to the governments of Great Britain, France, Italy and Japan an invitation to take part in a conference on the subject of the limitation of armament, in connection with which Pacific and Far Eastern questions should also be discussed. The government of China, because of its obvious and primary interests, was at the same time invited to participate in the discussion of questions relating to the Pacific and the Far East; and later, on October 4, 1921, the governments of Belgium, The Netherlands and Portugal, in view of their interests in the same quarter, were also invited to take part in the discussion of Pacific and Far Eastern questions.

In the invitation extended to France, Great Britain, Italy and Japan on August 11, 1921, it was stated that, in connection with the subject of the limitation of armament, it might "also be found advisable to formulate proposals by which in the interest of humanity the use of new agencies of warfare may be suitably controlled."

The Washington conference did in fact undertake to consider such proposals, but, by reason of the variety and complexity of the questions relating to the limitation of armament and to the Pacific and the Far East, the conference was able to deal with those proposals only to a limited extent.

On February 6, 1922, a treaty was concluded between the United States, the British Empire, France, Italy and Japan agreeing to prohibit, as between themselves, the use of submarines as commerce destroyers, as well as the use in war of asphyxiating, poisonous, or other gases, and all analogous liquids, materials or devices. The contracting parties further engaged to invite other nations to adhere to these prohibitions to the end that they might be universally accepted as a part of international law. This is as far as the conference found it possible to go in the treatment of new agencies of warfare.

Proposals were presented to the conference in regard to the use of aircraft and in regard to the regulation of radio in time of war, but, although these proposals were to some extent considered and discussed both in committees and in plenary sessions of the conference, it was found to be impracticable adequately to examine them and still less to give them effect.[2]

Under these circumstances the United States of America, the British Empire, France, Italy, and Japan, the governments which had been dealing with the subject of the limitation of armament and which had then agreed upon the terms of a treaty

2. See, particularly, *Conference on the Limitation of Armament*, pp. 800–810.

for the limitation of their naval armaments, adopted a resolution by which they engaged to constitute a commission, composed of not more than two representatives of each of the contracting powers, to consider (1) whether existing rules of international law adequately covered "new methods of attack or defense resulting from the introduction or development, since The Hague Conference of 1907, of new agencies of warfare"; and, if they did not, (2) "what changes in the existing rules" ought in consequence to be adopted as a part of the laws of nations.

It was provided that the Commission might have the assistance and advice of experts in international law and in land, naval and aerial warfare, and that it should report its conclusions to each of the powers represented in its membership, which were then to confer as to the acceptance of the report and as to the course to be followed to secure the consideration of its recommendations by other powers.

This was known as Resolution No. 1. At the same time another resolution, known as Resolution No. 2, was adopted, by which it was declared that the powers, in agreeing to the appointment of the Commission, did not intend that it should review or report upon the rules or declarations relating to submarines or the use of noxious gases and chemicals, which had already been adopted in the Washington conference.

By subsequent correspondence between the parties to these resolutions it was definitely agreed that the work of the Commission should be substantially confined to the two subjects of aircraft and radio. In explanation of this limitation, it has been stated that other recent agencies, such as tanks, were considered merely as inventions extending or intensifying the operations of well-known methods of attack and offence, while aviation and radio seemed to be on a somewhat different footing.[3]

The Commission held thirty plenary sessions, the first of which was formally opened by His Excellency Jonkheer H. A. Van Karnebeek who, as Minister of Foreign Affairs of The Netherlands, attended and made on behalf of his government an address of welcome. This formal opening was immediately succeeded by a business meeting at which the delegate of the United States was named as president of the Commission.

The Commission, when it first assembled, was composed of ten members, each of the six governments being represented by two delegates except the United States and Italy, which had only one each. On December 23rd, however, Mr. Moore, the delegate of the United States, the scope of whose duties had

3. Rear Admiral William L. Rodgers, U. S. N., *The American Journal of International Law*, XVII, No. 4 (October, 1923), 629.

been enlarged by his election as president of the Commission, suggested that the United States appoint an additional delegate; and the President named for the post Mr. Washburn, Envoy Extraordinary and Minister Plenipotentiary at Vienna. Mr. Washburn reached The Hague on January 10, 1923, and immediately entered upon the discharge of his duties. He attended the meetings of the Subcommittee on Radio; and for a time the demands upon him were exceptionally heavy by reason of a special session of the Permanent Court of International Justice, whose meetings Mr. Moore was obliged to attend. Mr. Washburn later served as the United States member of the Drafting Committee (*Comité de Rédaction*), which supervised the final text of the codes of rules and drew up the General Report.[4]

The expert advisers not only were present at all the plenary meetings of the Commission, but they also performed services on or in connection with committees and subcommittees throughout the conference.

The spirit and purpose with which the conference was convoked, and in which its task was performed, was well stated by Jonkheer Van Karnebeek in his address of welcome, in the course of which he said:

It is evident that this work is necessary. Nevertheless, at this period in the world's history, so soon after the great war, some sceptics may feel inclined to doubt the usefulness of your work; others, who will accept none but ideal and final solutions of the existing difficulties, may hesitate to acknowledge its importance. They are wrong. In the midst of the passions which agitate mankind, law is irresistibly moving forward throughout history and extending its empire in every direction. To doubt of its usefulness and of its power to educate the human mind means to despair of progress and not to believe in the promptings of the international conscience. Whatever future may lie in store for us, the work you are undertaking, Gentlemen, is necessary; it is a striking realisation of the wish that the work for the development of International Law shall be resumed.

In his response Mr. Moore, speaking in a similar vein, said:

No explanation is needed of the fact that the parties to the Resolution, under which the Commission of Jurists has been constituted, subsequently extended to the government of the Netherlands an invitation, which that government has graciously accepted, to be represented in the membership of the Commission. Not only as the representatives of the nation on whose hospitable soil we are to hold our sessions, but also as representatives of the land of Grotius and of Bynkershoek, a land immemorably associated with the origin,

4. For the text of the General Report, see *infra*, p. 160.

development and improvement of the modern system of international law, it is a pleasure and an inspiration to be assured of the collaboration and aid of the members from the Netherlands in the performance of the responsible task with which the Commission is charged.

The importance of this task will not be gainsaid. It is true that the Commission is not, in a proper sense, to be considered as a diplomatic body by which international agreements are to be formally concluded. Its function is rather that of a committee by which certain subjects are to be examined in order that definite conclusions may be arrived at and reported. In its constitution and its comparatively limited membership, the Commission is well designed for the accomplishment of this purpose. But the fact that its task is essentially preliminary does not detract from the importance and gravity of its work.

During the past eight years we have constantly been hearing, and we still hear, the despairing declaration that international law no longer exists; while the affirmation that we can ever again be justified in speaking of such a thing as the laws of war is received with a gesture of incredulity.

Such manifestations serve only to indicate the existence of a general distemper which has not yet entirely passed away. But, faith and hope will again revive. The sense of law and of the need of law will again reassert itself. Standing today in the Peace Palace at The Hague, which symbolizes the attainment of peace through the administration of the law between nations and its application to the settlement of their disputes, and recalling the work of the two Hague Conferences of 1899 and 1907, whose acts we are in some measure to reconsider and to supplement, I deem it to be inconceivable that a generation accustomed to boast that it is the heir of all the ages, in the foremost files of time, should consciously relinquish the conception that all human affairs, in war as well as in peace, must be regulated by law, and abandon itself to the desperate conclusion that the sense of self-restraint, which is the consummate product and the essence of civilization, has finally succumbed to the passion for unregulated and indiscriminate violence.

To a counsel of despair so repugnant to the teachings of history and so recreant to the ideals and achievements of the past, the constitution of the present Commission, with a view so to regulate the use of new agencies of warfare as to keep their employment within the bounds of permissible violence set by international law, is the appropriate answer.

The regulation of the use of radio in time of war was not altogether a new question.[5] Several international conventions already contained provisions on the subject, but the ever-increasing development of this means of communication rendered it necessary that the whole matter should be reconsidered; and this was deemed to be the more important in view of the

5. See General Report, *infra*, p. 162.

fact that several of the existing international conventions had not been ratified by all the Powers.

As an eminent naval authority has elsewhere explained,[6] the principal service of radio in war is the provision of news and information. Aviation also observes, obtaining news and information, and it sometimes transmits the latter. Radio transmits news; and both aviation and radio fight, each after its own fashion, to protect its own function and to deny to the enemy the exercise of similar activities. In view of the vital importance in war of accurate information, for offensive as well as defensive purposes, the radio rules deal with the transmission of despatches, including the current news of the world, which has no reference to the war, for the use either of belligerents or of neutrals; and they deal in this respect chiefly with neutral states and the ships flying their flag.

According to the same eminent authority,[7] an aircraft is to be considered, not as a weapon, but rather as a vehicle, possessing two characteristic qualities which distinguish it from all other vehicles, these being (1) the highest speed of travel known to man, and (2) the ability to rise in the air. These qualities make it necessary to provide that it shall not be used, by those directing and controlling it, to do things "which are not in accordance with the general spirit of existing rules of warfare." Its main uses are (1) to collect news for strategic or for technical purposes; (2) to fight other aircraft seeking to interfere with its own observation and reconnoitering, and to attack the enemy's information or reconnoitering branches of the air service; and (3) to direct attack on surface targets, be they personnel or material, by bombs, machine guns, torpedoes, and other weapons.

At the first business meeting of the Commission, comprehensive proposals, which had been informally distributed in advance, in English and in French, were formally presented on the part of the United States both on aircraft and on radio. Proposals on aircraft were then presented by the British delegation. The American proposals on aircraft contained eight chapters or sections, embracing forty-two articles. The British proposals, which also bore the traces of study and reflection, were divided into six chapters or sections, embracing thirty-six articles. In the British draft, which was somewhat longer than the American, there was a tendency to fulness of detail, and in numerous articles there were cross-references to other articles, while, in the framing of the American draft, an effort

6. Rodgers, *op. cit.*, pp. 637–638.
7. *Idem*, p. 634.

had been made to render each article complete in itself. The American draft on radio, which was the only draft presented, contained nine articles.

During the first ten days of the conference, the discussions and decisions of the Commission, which was then dealing with aircraft, were directly based on the American and British drafts on that subject, the consecutive provisions of the American draft being accepted as the order of business. But, as all the delegations, except those of the United States and Japan, could readily reach their homes, the Commission at its eleventh plenary session on December 21, 1922, adjourned for the Christmas and New Year's holidays; and in so doing the Commission, with a view to expedite its business, constituted, on the suggestion of the president, two subcommittees to deal respectively with aircraft and with radio. On each subcommittee each delegation was directly represented by only one member, who might be either a delegate or an expert adviser; but the delegates were entitled at all times to be present and to take part in the discussions; and the members of the subcommittees, whether delegates or expert advisers, were accompanied by experts. The Subcommittee on Aircraft met on January 8, 1923, electing as its chairman Sir Cecil Hurst, second British delegate. The Subcommittee on Radio, which met on January 16, elected as its chairman General Ferrié, French military adviser on that subject.

Under the terms of reference, the Subcommittee on Aircraft took over all draft proposals which had not already been adopted, and, on the basis of such proposals, endeavored to frame a single draft for the consideration of the Commission on its reassembling. As the discussion of radio by the Commission had not begun, the subcommittee on that subject was merely instructed to examine and report upon the proposals which had then been presented.

The date originally set for the resumption of the plenary sessions of the Commission was January 22, 1923; but, in order to afford the subcommittees, and particularly that on aircraft, whose work was especially complex and onerous, an opportunity to complete their reports, this date was twice postponed. The suspension, however, of the sittings of the Commission as a body was nominal rather than real. Although the subcommittees could only make recommendations, which the Commission itself was wholly free to accept or to reject, their proceedings resembled informal conferences of the Commission, divided into appropriate sections for the expeditious examination of the two subjects under consideration. The plenary sessions of the Commission were resumed on February 2, 1923.

The codes of rules adopted by the Commission are incorporated and explained in its General Report.[8] In most instances the review thus made appears to be adequate; but supplementary observations are desirable on the subject of aerial bombardment, of visit and search of merchant vessels by aircraft, and of aerial blockade.

A proposal to prohibit the launching of projectiles or explosives from balloons found a place on the programme of the first Peace Conference at The Hague, in 1899. The aeroplane had not then been invented and, although numerous attempts had been made to construct a machine in the nature of a balloon having self-propelling and self-directing power, the general conception of an aircraft continued to be that of a device essentially at the mercy of the winds and of limited and uncertain offensive value in war. Under these circumstances the conference unanimously adopted, with little or no opposition, a resolution absolutely forbidding for a term of five years the employment of "balloons or other similar means not yet known for launching projectiles or explosives."

The five years' limitation was inserted at the instance of Captain Crozier, of the United States delegation, who, sagaciously reckoning with the developments which might soon occur, reminded the conference that it was proposing to prohibit forever the use of arms of which it had no experience. Captain Crozier argued that if, by means of some new invention, balloons could be used at the critical point of a battlefield and at the critical point of the conflict, with such certainty and concentration that they would determine the victory, their employment would be entirely compatible with the humane objects which the conference had in view. But, in view of the fact that the balloon, as the conference knew it, was not dirigible, had small carrying capacity, and could launch only on indeterminate points, more or less at hazard, non-decisive quantities of explosives which fell as the useless hail on combatants and on non-combatants, he thought it proper to forbid its use temporarily.

Three years before the assembling of the Second Hague Conference, in 1907, the prohibition expired and the subject again became open to regulation.

Meanwhile, the development of aircraft had been such as to bring their use in war more definitely within the realm of practical consideration, and, although the absolute prohibition was renewed until the end of the next Hague Conference, whenever that might be, the agreement was signed by a smaller number

8. *Infra*, p. 160

of powers than any other act of the conference. This circumstance has often been ascribed to the arrival at The Hague, while the conference was sitting, of Santos Dumont in his flying machine.

When the war broke out in Europe in August, 1914, the prohibition became a dead letter. Not only had the aeroplane and other aircraft been so developed as to be capable of effective use in war, but the prohibitory agreement, like the rest of The Hague conventions relating to warfare, contained a clause to the effect that it should not be regarded as being in force in a war to which a nonsignatory power was a party. This alone sufficed immediately to nullify the prohibition.

From the beginning of the sessions of the Commission of Jurists, it was generally felt that perhaps the severest test of the possibility of a general agreement would be found in the efforts of the Commission to regulate the subject of bombardment from the air. Both the American and the British proposals contained articles on this subject; and it is not to be assumed that they fundamentally differed. The essence of the British proposal was the phrase "military objective," but no attempt was made to explain or define it. In the American draft the phrase "military objective" or "military target" was not used, but the draft undertook specifically to designate the objects which might or might not be bombarded. The British delegation set great store by the phrase "military objective" as having a limitative effect, while the delegation of the United States thought that the phrase left too much to the discretion of the individual commander. The American draft also expressly prohibited aerial bombardment for the purpose of enforcing either contributions or requisitions.

Informal conference between members of the various delegations disclosed the greatest diversity of views as to what might be found to be practicable in dealing with the subject. It was, however, generally admitted that the fact of being "defended," which exposes cities and towns to bombardment by land forces, was altogether inappropriate and insufficient as a test of liability to bombardment by air forces. When a city or town by reason of its being "defended" is subject to bombardment by land forces, the bombardment may be general, and thus the exception made in favor of hospitals, monuments of art, and other privileged buildings often proves to be ineffective in practice. Aircraft, on the other hand, have, so it is argued, the faculty of attacking directly distinctive military objectives, without generally bombarding the city, town or community in which such objectives are situated. Nevertheless, such objectives may often be so situated that a bombardment directly aimed at them could not be conducted without danger to the lives of the civilian or non-combatant population, as well as to property not used for military purposes. Such was the complex problem with which the Commission was to deal.

In the original American proposal a distinction was drawn between cities, towns, villages, dwellings or buildings within the "combat area" and those not within such area, the term "combat area" signifying the area of active hostile operations between the land forces of the belligerents. Within such area the non-combatant population, except so far as it might be prepared to take the chances of war, would not ordinarily be found, but would have departed voluntarily or have been removed by the military authorities. Within such an area all buildings, except those specially privileged, would be subject to occupation and use by the combatant forces in furtherance of their operations, and would be correspondingly subject to attack. Outside that area, the bombardment by aircraft of cities, towns, villages, dwellings or buildings was to be prohibited; but the bombardment of enemy forces, lines of communication and transportation, military or naval establishments, depots of arms or war material, and workshops, plants and factories used for the manufacture of war material, wherever situated, was not prohibited.

Informal consultations made it evident that neither the original American proposal nor the original British proposal would be accepted by the Commission. Moreover, it is probable that both delegations, and it is certain that the American delegation, became convinced that neither proposal should be adopted without revision and modification in the direction of greater definiteness and precision.

The problems involved in the question of aerial bombardment were subjected to prolonged and critical examination by the Subcommittee on Aircraft, but the subcommittee was unable to agree upon the text of an article to be reported to the Commission. The position in which the question was then left was summed up in the subcommittee's report as follows:

No agreement has been reached in the sub-committee as to the text of any article to submit to the Full Commission prescribing the legitimate objects of aerial bombardment. Failure to reach a unanimous agreement on this subject must not, however, obscure the fact that in very large measure the views entertained by the members of the sub-committee are unanimous. No delegation is in favour of adopting rules which would authorize the repetition of the bombardments from the air of great masses of civilian population, as such, without any attempt to attack particular objects of which the destruction would bring some distinct military advantage to the belligerent. The delegations differed as to the path by which they would attain their object, and as to the terms in which they would express the rule, more than as to the principle which should be laid down.

It should, however, be stated that the Netherlands and Japanese Delegations were in favour of the utmost restriction possible and advocated a general prohibition of aerial bombardment of towns and villages outside the immediate area of military operations, whatever the nature of the object to be attacked.

The Italian Delegation also was in favour of differentiating between the extent to which bombardments should be permissible in the immediate vicinity of the operations of the land forces and outside that area. . . .

As no text submitted to the sub-committee obtained a majority of votes, it was decided merely to explain to the Full Commission the course of the discussions and the texts proposed, leaving to the Full Commission the task of finding a solution.

It will be seen from an examination of the texts set out above, that they all admit in some form that enemy forces, military works, lines of military communication, military or naval establishments, depots of arms or ammunition (or war material) may properly be bombarded. Indeed unanimous votes in favour of this principle were passed. These votes should afford the Full Commission a useful basis for further examination of the general question.

Briefly stated, what proved to be so difficult was the determination of the conditions under which the bombardment of objects, intrinsically liable to attack, was to be forbidden, when they were found in centers of population.

When the subject came before the Commission for final action at its twenty-second plenary session on Monday, February 12, the consideration of the matter was substantially reduced to two drafts, one of which was presented by the American delegation and the other by the Italian.[9]

9. The American draft was as follows:
"Aerial Bombardment: Revised American
Proposal, Article . . . . . .

"1. Aerial bombardment is legitimate only when directed at a military objective, that is to say, an object of which the destruction or injury would constitute a distinct military advantage to the belligerent. It may be directed only at military forces, vessels of war, military works, military establishments, or depots of arms or war material; at factories constituting important and well-known centres engaged in the manufacture of arms, ammunition, or distinctively military equipment, or at lines of communication or transportation used for military purposes. It must not involve the indiscriminate bombardment of the civilian population, but must be directed solely at military objects as herein designated.

"2. The bombardment of military forces in cities, towns, or villages is prohibited, unless the military concentration therein is sufficiently important to justify such bombardment, having regard to the danger thus caused to the civilian population.

"3. A belligerent state is liable to pay compensation for injuries to

A previous comparison of these two drafts had convinced the American delegation that there was little or no substantial difference between them. The chief difference in the specification of military objectives was that "railway stations" were included in the Italian enumeration; and the Italian delegation very readily agreed to omit this item. Strangely enough, although "railway stations" have so generally been included in lists of conjectural military objectives, a moment's reflection must suffice to convince one that a railway station as such bears no more relation to the effective use of a railway line by military forces than does a Cook's tourist agency or a railway ticket office in any part of a city or town, or in the country. Ordinarily a railway station as such possesses no military value whatever and its use is distinctively non-military in war as well as in peace.

In paragraph 3 of the Italian draft the original United States conception of a combat area was incorporated. This is shown

person or to property caused by the violation by any of its officers or forces of the provisions of this Article."

The Italian draft was as follows:

"Bombardment: Italian Proposal.

"1. Aerial bombardment is only legitimate when it is directed exclusively at the following objectives: (a) Enemy military forces, (b) barracks and military works, (c) vessels of war, (d) military arsenals, land and naval, (e) depots of arms and munitions, (f) railway stations, (g) lines of military communications and transport, (h) workshops and plant effectively and directly employed in the manufacture and immediate production of arms, munitions and means of transport.

"2. The bombardment of towns, villages and civil habitations of any kind outside the immediate neighborhood of the operations of land forces and naval or military bases, is absolutely prohibited.

"In cases where the objectives which are liable to bombardment in accordance with the provisions of paragraph 1 above are in proximity to towns, villages or civil habitations of any kind, bombardment of such objectives can only be carried out on condition that no hurt is suffered by the civilian population.

"In the event of absolute observance of this condition being impossible the aircraft must abstain from bombardment.

"3. In the immediate neighborhood of the operations of land forces and of naval or military bases, in view of the fact that the civil population will have had to be removed by its government or put in a place of safety from the risks of aerial warfare, the bombardment of towns, villages and civil habitations of any kind shall be legitimate provided that there exists a reasonably justifiable presumption of sufficiently important military concentrations.

"4. In case of any infraction of the prohibitions contained in this article a belligerent state shall be responsible and may be obliged to pay an indemnity.

"5. Commanders of aircraft who have committed a breach of the provisions of the present article may be brought to trial personally as having committed acts of perfidy."

not only by the phrase "immediate neighborhood of the operations of land forces," but also by the recital of the fact that the civil population would have been removed by its government or put in a place of safety. But, even in these circumstances it was provided that the bombardment of towns, villages, civil habitations of any kind should be legitimate only if there existed a reasonably justifiable presumption of sufficiently important military concentrations. This test of military concentration was also incorporated in the American draft, in which it was taken from the revised proposal which had been presented to the Subcommittee on Aircraft by the British delegation.

Before the meeting of the Commission on Monday, February 12, the American delegation had prepared a condensation of the Italian proposal; and, after the Commission met, the American delegation readily assented to a suggestion that it combine its own revised proposal with the condensed Italian proposal.

On presenting the matter to the full Commission for its final action, Mr. Moore made, for himself and for the American delegation, the following statement:

In approaching the final consideration of this subject, the Commission no doubt is deeply conscious of the fact that it has reached a critical stage in its proceedings.

Among the elementary principles which the development of modern rules of warfare, running through several centuries, has been designed to establish and confirm, the principle most fundamental in character, the observance of which the detailed regulations have largely been designed to assure, is the distinction between combatants and non-combatants, and the protection of non-combatants against injuries not incidental to military operations against combatants.

The Commission has already adopted rules intended to assure the protection of buildings used for various purposes and particularly of monuments of art. The protection of the lives of non-combatants, including women and children, would seem to demand consideration at least equal to that shown for inanimate objects.

Not only does the preservation of the distinction between combatants and non-combatants, especially as affected by aerial bombardment, loom larger in the public mind than any other question before the Commission, but it occupied a similar position in the proceedings of the Washington Conference, whose work the present Commission was appointed to continue and to complete.

The sense in which the Commission is expected to find a solution is shown not only by the discussions in the Washington Conference, but also by the very terms of the original invitation to that Conference, which specified as one of its objects the formulation of 'proposals by which in the interest of humanity the use of new agencies of warfare may be suitably controlled.'

In the acts of the Washington Conference, and particularly in those restricting the use of submarines and prohibiting the use of poisonous gases, there is no room for doubt that the great purpose by which the conference was inspired and controlled was the preservation of the fundamental principle to which I have just referred.

The Commission is now face to face with the question of preserving this great principle, for the benefit of the present generation and of future generations.

I have made these remarks with a view to concentrate the thoughts of all the members of the Commission, including myself, upon the vital relation of the subject to the success or the failure of our conference. All the members of the Commission no doubt are animated with a common purpose; but the various proposals which have been presented disclose certain divergencies in matters of detail, which it is necessary to adjust and to reconcile. I can not believe that the accomplishment of this task will prove to be impossible, and I am confident that we shall all earnestly work together in order to reach with one unanimous voice the great goal, the attainment of which is so much to be desired. The moral effect of such a result will be incalculable.

These were the only formal remarks made during the session. They were followed by nearly five hours of earnest, anxious conference and consultation, in which the members of the delegations and their expert advisers took part. At length at 7.45 P.M. a vote was quickly taken, and the text, which now forms Article 24 of the rules relating to aerial warfare, was unanimously adopted.[10]

The capital points in this article are, (1) that aerial bombardment is legitimate only when directed at a military objective; (2) that it is legitimate only when it is "directed exclusively at such an objective"; (3) that such objectives are specifically enumerated and defined; (4) that the bombardment of cities, towns, villages, dwellings or buildings not within the combat area is prohibited; (5) that, where a military objective is so situated that it cannot be bombarded without the indiscriminate bombarding of the civilian population, it cannot be bombarded at all; (6) that even in the combat area the bombardment of cities, towns, villages, dwellings is legitimate only if there exists a reasonable presumption that the military concentration is sufficiently important to justify such bombardment, having regard to the danger thus caused to the civilian population, and (7) that a belligerent state is liable to pay compensation for injuries to person or to property caused by the violation of the rules.

The fact is further to be borne in mind that the article by which aerial bombardment is thus restricted is in addition to

10. *Infra*, p. 187

other articles by which it is forbidden to employ aerial bombardment, either (1) for the purpose of terrorizing the civilian population, of destroying or damaging private property not of a military character, or of injuring non-combatants, or (2) for the purpose of enforcing compliance with requisitions in kind or the payment of contributions in money.

Furthermore, provision is also made by Article 25 for the protection of certain classes of privileged buildings, and by Article 26 for the more efficient protection of important historic monuments. In order to assure the preservation of such monuments there are to be established about them zones of protection, which are to be internationally notified and recognized and which are to be free from attack provided they are not militarily used.

Among the numerous and varied questions with which the Commission undertook to deal, the only one for the regulation of which it was unable to agree upon a rule was that of visit and search of merchant vessels by aircraft. Proposals on the subject were presented by the British as well as by the American delegation; but the American delegation, in the light of what the discussions developed, soon became convinced that both proposals were defective, and that, without stricter and more specific regulation and control, aircraft might inflict on life and property at sea calamities fully as startling as those that had resulted in the recent war from the employment of submarines.

In insisting upon the separate regulation of visit and search by aircraft, without regard to what might be conceded to surface ships or even to submarines, the American delegation merely adhered to the decision taken at the Washington Conference, on the suggestion of the United States.

On January 5, 1922, when the resolution to restrict the exercise of visit and search by submarines and to prohibit their use as commerce destroyers was before the Washington Conference, Lord Lee, one of the delegates from Great Britain, remarking that, if it was impossible for a submarine to make provision for the safety of the passengers and crews of merchant vessels, it was yet more clearly impossible for an aircraft to do so, proposed that the words "or aircraft" be inserted in the resolution, so as to make its restrictive and prohibitive provisions apply to aircraft and to submarines alike.

The Chairman, Mr. Hughes, Secretary of State of the United States, adverting to the fact that there was a special subcommittee on aircraft, expressed the hope that "the matter of aircraft, which presented difficulties of its own, would be reserved for a separate discussion." It was, he declared, "impossible to forecast the result of a discussion regarding the use of aircraft." There might, he said, be questions pertaining to aircraft of a different sort from those pertaining to submarines; and he greatly feared that, if the question of aircraft was brought into the discussion of the question of submarines, "it would be very difficult to reach a solution of either question." He therefore proposed that the discussion be continued on the resolution as it stood.

This course was taken.[11]

The American delegation at The Hague also bore in mind the findings contained in the report made to the Washington Conference by the Aeronautical Subcommittee on December 21, 1921, on the visit and search by aircraft of (1) another aircraft, (2) a surface ship, and (3) a submarine. As regards the second topic—the visit and search of surface ships—the report, after describing the normal practice of cruisers, including the sending of an officer aboard in order to ascertain whether there is cause for capture, and the sending of a prize crew aboard if a case for capture is established, found that, if aircraft observed regular methods, they could exercise visit and search "only under favorable conditions," but that, if "the right of diverting merchant vessels, without boarding them," were "legally established," aircraft could exercise it "up to the limit of their range of action from their land or floating base." Such range of action may fairly be considered as extending to a distance of at least two hundred-and-fifty miles. As regarded the right under certain conditions to sink a prize after due provision has been made for the safety of the crew, the report, while not intimating that such provision could ordinarily be made by the aircraft itself, stated that, "in favorable weather, and when it is easy to reach a friendly or neutral port, a crew may be compelled to abandon their ship and the ship may be fired upon and sunk by the aircraft." The contemplation of aircraft thus ranging the seas and issuing to unvisited and unsearched vessels orders enforcible by bombing the ship or by firing upon the persons aboard, can scarcely be indulged without grave apprehensions. It was the possibilities thus suggested that led Mr. Struycken, first delegate from The Netherlands, to declare, both in subcommittee and in plenary session, that such a method of warfare might readily mean the terrorizing of the seas.

From first to last the American delegation consistently declined to enter into the interpretation of the provisions of the

11. *Conference on the Limitation of Armament.* Senate Document No. 126, 67th Congress, 2d Sess., pp. 365–366; Report, in English and French, pp. 688–690.

Washington treaty relating to submarines. This did not, however, prevent the disclosure, among other things, of the fact that the treaty was interpreted by the British delegation and perhaps by the Italian not only as permitting the deviation of a merchant vessel from its course for the completion of a search which a preliminary visit and search on the spot had seemed reasonably to justify, but also as permitting deviation without any preliminary visit and search or boarding whatsoever. The disclosure of this interpretation, which was elicited by inquiries of the Netherlands delegation, immediately rendered impossible the adoption by the Commission of the terms of Article I of the Washington treaty on submarines, without some additional safeguard, as an appropriate and adequate regulation for aircraft. The effort of the American delegation to obtain a separate and independent regulation was thus doubly justified.

Had the American delegation, in view of the divergence of opinions as to the right, or the extent of the right, even of surface craft to deviate merchantmen without search, been willing to concur in a mere enunciation of the principle that aircraft should have, as regarded the exercise of visit and search, the same rights as surface vessels, without attempting to say what those right were, a majority vote might have been obtained for such a resolution. This would have been a compromise, and compromise is said to be of the essence of statesmanship. But there are two kinds of compromise. One kind is that in which there is a meeting of minds, resulting in an agreement. This is a wholesome and salutary process. The other kind is that in which there is no meeting of minds, but the divergence is veneered with a deft formula, cloaking a disagreement. This process is but a breeder of future quarrels.

While the Commission failed to agree upon a specific regulation of visit and search by aircraft, the discussions were of great value in disclosing the positions of the various governments and in eliciting and elucidating their respective views in detail. Towards the end of the conference an intimation was occasionally heard to the effect that, if a concerted effort had been made at the outset to secure an absolute prohibition for a limited term, the attempt might have been successful. But, however this may be, none of the governments, with the exception perhaps of that of the Netherlands and possibly of that of Japan, entered upon the work of the Commission with thoughts of such a solution. Nor was it suggested that aircraft might not be employed in visit and search as scouts in connection with surface ships.

Clause "(i)," Article 53, of the rules on aircraft, relates to

aerial blockade.[12] There was no similar clause in either the
original American or the original British draft, although the
British draft contained certain clauses the subsequent modification of which was said to have induced that delegation to
desire a special provision in regard to blockade. Clause "(i)"
was inserted in Article 53 by the Subcommittee on Aircraft,
and when the article as thus amended was brought before the
Commission, an objection to the clause by the Netherlands
delegation led to the appointment of a committee of experts to
report on the question. A report was prepared, but because
of lack of time had not been circulated when Article 53 came
up for final action. A hurried examination of the report resulted in a divergence of opinions as to what conclusions the
experts had intended to express, but the clause was adopted by
five votes to one. The vote of the Netherlands delegation was
the only one recorded against it, but the American delegation
voted in the affirmative only *ad referendum,* explaining that in
its opinion the subject had not been sufficiently considered and
that the delegation was not to be understood as giving to the
clause its individual approval.

No term in the whole range of maritime law has been the
subject of greater abuse than that of "blockade"; and, as it
was not contended that aircraft could in their present stage
of development maintain a blockade in the same sense as surface ships can do, there was evident reason to apprehend that
the anticipatory application to their activities of the term
blockade would inject into the law an additional element of
uncertainty and confusion capable of vast extension. Under the
other provisions of the rules a considerable measure of power
is conceded to belligerents in regard to the control of the movements of aircraft in the neighborhood of their military operations or military forces. This measure of control would evidently be helpful to a surface force maintaining a blockade,
and to a land force maintaining a siege. Whether it is desirable
to go further is a question for mature consideration.

The General Report contains no recommendation as to the
steps to be taken to make the rules effective. The American
delegation presented an outline of a convention to be recommended for that purpose; but the Commission went no farther
than to express the belief that, if the rules were brought into
force, they should be reexamined after a relatively brief period
in order to see whether any revision of them was necessary.
The sketch of a convention presented by the American delegation, while stipulating that the rules should remain in force

12. *Infra,* p. 217.

until July 1, 1933, provided that a conference might previously be called for their revision, but that they should continue in force so long as no desire for their revision was manifested.

The American delegation deliberately refrained from incorporating in its proposal the clause found in The Hague conventions, to the effect that they shall not be binding in a war the parties to which are not all parties to the convention. The destructive effect of such a stipulation was immediately demonstrated on the outbreak of the war of 1914. It has indeed been argued that in applying the clause the participation in the war of a relatively unimportant non-contracting power should be disregarded; but the legal foundation of this view is as little apparent as is the rule by which it is to be definitely applied. On the other hand, in the absence of such a clause, the contracting parties, instead of treating their agreement as having immediately ceased to be binding, probably would offer it to a non-contracting belligerent as a *modus vivendi;* and if the offer were declined, they would still be at liberty to consider the relation of the non-contracting belligerent to the war as affecting their relations with one another under a treaty which had not automatically ceased to operate.

The deprecatory comment often is heard that it is idle to make rules of warfare because they are always broken and cannot be enforced. This sapient skepticism, which is often related to a gruesome and unreasoning credulity, does not reflect the attitude of men of arms. Just as the mythical "man who broke the bank at Monte Carlo" is celebrated in song and in story, and the criminal activities of a few fill even in time of peace the columns of the daily press to the exclusion of the unexciting labors of the millions who keep the law, so, in time of war, all kinds of agitating reports, including the widely disseminated stories of atrocities, readily pre-occupy the public mind. A distinguished naval officer has lately said[13] that "during all wars there are always some cases of illegal action and brutality in the forces of all the nations engaged," but "perhaps in not much greater proportion than in certain strata of civil life"; and that, "if the war is of considerable duration and intensity, the relatively few cases of atrocities are multiplied by the inevitable popular hatred until a general belief is created that all members of the enemy's forces are just plain beasts." The essential truth of these statements will be readily recognized by those who are familiar with the contemporary literature of wars.

The point of view of the combatant forces has been ably set

13. Rear Admiral William S. Sims, U. S. N., *The Fortnightly Review* (July, 1923), p. 174.

forth by another distinguished naval officer,[14] who has recently stated that those forces "desire the limitation of the exercise of belligerent power in humanitarian interest because they themselves as individuals share the views of the general public as to avoidance of the infliction of suffering having no influence on the outcome of the war." But he declares that combatants "have two reasons for such limitations additional to those governing the general public," and that these reasons are, first, that "combatants themselves are the first to feel the horrors of war," and secondly, that "both in victory and in defeat cruelty and license towards individuals and wanton damage and destruction of property tend to destruction of discipline and make the national forces less efficient instruments in the execution of the national will." He is undoubtedly also sustained by the general testimony of military men in his further statement that the impressment of humane principles upon the mass of men under arms and their education in such principles during peace renders the military forces more efficient, while it aids the accomplishment of the popular desire for the amelioration of the sufferings of war.

We should not think highly of one who, because civil crimes persist, should either affirm that criminal law does not exist or propose that it be abandoned. War crimes, too, will persist; but, as has been well observed, "the laws of war must also persist." [15]

## GENERAL REPORT [16]

The Conference on the Limitation of Armament at Washington adopted at its sixth Plenary Session on February 4, 1922,

14. Rodgers, *op. cit.*, p. 633.

15. Elbridge Colby, Captain of Infantry, U. S. Army, "War Crimes and Their Punishment," *Minnesota Law Review* (December, 1923), pp. 40, 46.

16. In the *American Journal of International Law*, XVII, No. 4 (October, 1923), Official Documents, pp. 242–260, under the title "General Report of the Commission of Jurists at The Hague," there may be found the rules adopted by the Commission, but nothing of the report is given beyond the brief introduction to the text of the rules relating to radio. In a footnote it is stated that this "general report" is "printed from text supplied by the Department of State"; but this evidently refers to what was prepared for the daily press, which would hardly have space for the entire text of the report. The report has long ceased to be a confidential document. The entire French text was published in the *Rivista di Diritto Internazionale* (Anno XV, Series III, Vol. II, 1923), at Rome, January–April, 1923; and both the commentary and the rules have been discussed, in Europe and in the United States, in the public press. An excellent summary and review, by J. W. Garner, may be found in *The American Journal of International Law*, XVIII, No. 1 (January, 1924), 56. It will be observed that, in the report, the rules are printed in italics. The commentary precedes the rule, as an introduction to it.

a resolution for the appointment of a Commission representing the United States of America, the British Empire, France, Italy and Japan to consider the following questions:

(a) *Do existing rules of international law adequately cover new methods of attack or defense resulting from the introduction or development, since The Hague Conference of 1907, of new agencies of warfare?*

(b) *If not so, what changes in the existing rules ought to be adopted in consequence thereof as a part of the law of nations?*

The Commission was to report its conclusions to each of the Powers represented in its membership.

The resolution also provided that those Powers should thereupon confer as to the acceptance of the report and the course to be followed to secure the consideration of its recommendations by the other civilized powers.

By a second resolution adopted at the same session it was agreed to exclude from the Jurisdiction of the Commission the rules or declarations relating to submarines and to the use of noxious gases and chemicals already adopted by the Powers in the said Conference.

With the unanimous concurrence of the Powers mentioned in the first of the above resolutions an invitation to participate in the work of the Commission was extended to and accepted by the Netherlands Government. It was also agreed that the program of the Commission should be limited to the preparation of rules relating to aerial warfare, and to rules relating to the use of radio in time of war.

The United States Government proposed that the Commission should meet on December 11, 1922, at The Hague, and the representatives of the six Powers mentioned above assembled on that date in the Palace of Peace. At the second meeting of the Commission the Honorable John Bassett Moore, First Delegate of the United States, was elected President of the Commission.

The Commission has prepared a set of rules for the control of radio in time of war which are contained in Part I of this Report, and a set of rules for aerial warfare which are contained in Part II of this Report.

The Commission desires to add that it believes that if these sets of rules are approved and brought into force, it will be found expedient to make provision for their reëxamination after a relatively brief term of years to see whether any revision is necessary.

PART I

### RULES FOR THE CONTROL OF RADIO IN TIME OF WAR

The regulation of the use of radio in time of war is not a new question. Several international conventions already contain provisions on the subject, but the ever-increasing development of this means of communication has rendered it necessary that the whole matter should be reconsidered, with the object of completing and co-ordinating existing texts. This is the more important in view of the fact that several of the existing international conventions have not been ratified by all the Powers.

The articles of the existing conventions which deal directly or indirectly with radio telegraphy in time of war are as follows:

The Land War Neutrality Convention (No. V of 1907) [17] prohibits in Article 3 the erecting of radio stations by belligerents on neutral territory and also the use by belligerents of any radio station established on neutral territory before the war for purely military purposes and not previously opened for the service of public messages. Article 5 obliges the neutral Power not to allow any such proceeding by a belligerent.

Under Article 8 a neutral Power is not bound to forbid or restrict the employment on behalf of belligerents of radio stations belonging to it or to companies or private individuals.

Under Article 9 the neutral Power must apply to the belligerents impartially the measures taken by it under Article 8 and must enforce them on private owners of radio stations.

Article 8 of the Convention for the Adaptation of the Geneva Convention to Maritime Warfare (No. X of 1907) provides that the presence of a radio installation on board a hospital ship does not of itself justify the withdrawal of the protection to which a hospital ship is entitled so long as she does not commit acts harmful to the enemy.

Under the Convention concerning Neutral Rights and Duties in Maritime Warfare (No. XIII of 1907) [18] belligerents are forbidden, as part of the general prohibition of the use of neutral ports and waters as a base of naval operations, to erect radio stations therein, and under Article 25 a neutral Power is bound to exercise such supervision as the means at its disposal permit to prevent any violation of this provision.

17. Convention respecting the Rights and Duties of Neutral Powers and Persons in War on Land.
18. Convention respecting the Rights and Duties of Neutral Powers in Maritime War.

The unratified Declaration of London of 1909, which was signed [19] by the Powers represented in the Naval Conference as embodying rules which corresponded in substance with the generally recognized principles of international law, specified in Articles 45 and 46 certain acts in which the use of radio telegraphy might play an important part as acts of unneutral service. Under Article 45 a neutral vessel was to be liable to condemnation if she was on a voyage specially undertaken with a view to the transmission of intelligence in the interest of the enemy. Under Article 46 a neutral vessel was to be condemned and receive the same treatment as would be applicable to an enemy merchant vessel if she took a direct part in hostilities or was at the time exclusively devoted to the transmission of intelligence in the interest of the enemy. It should be borne in mind that by Article 16 of the Rules for Aerial Warfare an aircraft is deemed to be engaged in hostilities if in the interests of the enemy she transmits intelligence in the course of her flight.

The following provisions have a bearing on the question of the control of radio in time of war, though the Conventions relate principally to radio in time of peace. These provisions are Articles 8, 9 and 17 of the International Radio Telegraphic Convention of London of 1912. Of these provisions Article 8 stipulates that the working of radio telegraph stations shall be organized as far as possible in such a manner as not to disturb the service of other radio stations. Article 9 deals with the priority and prompt treatment of calls of distress. Article 17 renders applicable to radio telegraphy certain provisions of the International Telegraphic Convention of St. Petersburg of 1875. Among the provisions of the Convention of 1875 made applicable to radio telegraphy is Article 7, under which the High Contracting Parties reserve to themselves the right to stop the transmission of any private telegram which appears to be dangerous to the security of the State or contrary to the laws of the country, to public order or to decency. Under Article 8, each Government reserves to itself the power to interrupt, either totally or partially, the system of the international telegraphs for an indefinite period if it thinks necessary, provided that it immediately advises each of the other contracting Governments.

Regard has also been given to the terms of the Convention for the safety of life at sea, London, 1914.

With regard to the radio telegraphy conventions applicable in time of peace, it should be remembered that these have not

19. February 26, 1909.

been revised since 1912 and that it is not unlikely that a conference may before long be summoned for the purpose of effecting such revision.

The work of the Commission in framing the following rules for the control of radio in time of war has been facilitated by the preparation and submission to the Commission on behalf of the American Delegation of a draft code of rules. This draft has been used as the basis of its work by the Commission.

The first article which has been adopted cannot be appreciated without reference to Article 8 of the Radio Telegraphic Convention of 1912. This latter article enunciates the broad principle that the operation of radio stations must be organized as far as possible in such a manner as not to disturb the service of other stations of the kind. The object of Article 1 is to demonstrate that this principle is equally to prevail in time of war. Needless to say, it is not to apply as between radio stations of opposing belligerents. In the same way as in time of peace the general principle cannot be applied absolutely, so also in time of war it can only be observed "as far as possible."

## Article 1

*In time of war the working of radio stations shall continue to be organized, as far as possible, in such manner as not to disturb the services of other radio stations. This provision does not apply as between the radio stations of opposing belligerents.*

Article 17 of the Radio Telegraphic Convention of 1912 enables States to regulate or prohibit the use of radio stations within their jurisdiction by rendering applicable to radio telegraphy certain provisions of the International Telegraphic Convention of 1875. In particular it is Articles 7 and 8 of that Convention which enable such measures of control or prohibition to be taken. The object of Article 2 is to make it clear that such rights subsist equally in time of war.

## Article 2

*Belligerent and neutral Powers may regulate or prohibit the operation of radio stations within their jurisdiction.*

The next article is really only an adaptation of Articles 3 and 5 of the Land Warfare Neutrality Convention (No. V of 1907). Article 3 (*b*) of that Convention only prohibits the use of any radio telegraphic installations established by belligerents before the war on the territory of a neutral Power for purely military purposes. The object of Article 3 as now adopted is to prohibit any erection or operation by a belligerent Power or its agents of radio stations within neutral territory.

The wording shows that the responsibility of the neutral State is affected as well as that of the belligerent State in the case in question. The words "personnes à son service" in the French text are employed in the same sense as the word "agents" in the English text.

It should be understood that neutral Governments are bound to use the means at their disposal to prevent the acts which the article is designed to stop. This implies that they will be responsible in any serious case of negligence.

### Article 3

*The erection or operation by a belligerent Power or its agents of radio stations within neutral jurisdiction constitutes a violation of neutrality on the part of such belligerent as well as on the part of the neutral Power which permits the erection or operation of such stations.*

Article 4 covers the same ground, so far as concerns radio, as that provided for in Articles 8 and 9 of Convention V of 1907 mentioned above; but while Article 8 stipulates that a neutral Power is not bound to forbid or restrict the use of wireless installations by a belligerent, and Article 9 relates to the restrictive or preventive measures taken by a neutral Power for this purpose, measures which must be applied impartially to the belligerents, Article 4 imposes on neutral Powers the duty of preventing the transmission by radio of any information destined for a belligerent concerning military forces or military operations.

This article is a compromise. On one side one Delegation pointed out that the 1907 system had stood the test during the war when neutral Governments had taken under Article 9 of the 1907 Convention restrictive or preventive measures which were quite satisfactory. On the other side it was pointed out that those measures had been taken precisely for the purpose of complying with the obligation imposed by neutrality, and that it would be well to define this obligation so as to help and protect neutral Powers in preventing the violation of their neutrality and thereby reducing the probability of their becoming involved in the war. Agreement was reached on the basis of a text indicating exactly the character of the messages prohibited, viz., messages concerning military forces and military operations. It is understood that the prohibition would not cover the repetition of news which has already become public.

The phrase "destined for a belligerent" covers all cases where the information is intended to reach the belligerent, and not merely messages which are addressed to the belligerent.

It has been agreed that the article does not render necessary the institution of a censorship in every neutral country in every war. The character of the war and the situation of the neutral country may render such measures unnecessary. It goes without saying that neutral Governments are bound to use the means at their disposal to prevent the transmission of the information in question.

The second paragraph merely reproduces the first paragraph of Article 9 of the Convention of 1907.

### Article 4

*A neutral Power is not called upon to restrict or prohibit the use of radio stations which are located within its jurisdiction, except so far as may be necessary to prevent the transmission of information destined for a belligerent concerning military forces or military operations and except as prescribed by Article 5.*

*All restrictive or prohibitive measures taken by a neutral Power shall be applied impartially by it to the belligerents.*

The legislation of a large number of Powers, for instance that of the Powers represented in the Commission, already provides for the prohibition of the use of radio installations on board vessels within their jurisdiction. In harmony with Articles 5 and 25 of the Convention concerning the Rights and Duties of Neutral Powers in Maritime Warfare (No. XIII of 1907), Article 5 enacts the continuance of this régime in time of war and makes it obligatory for all mobile radio stations.

### Article 5

*Belligerent mobile radio stations are bound within the jurisdiction of a neutral State to abstain from all use of their radio apparatus. Neutral Governments are bound to employ the means at their disposal to prevent such use.*

The transmission of military intelligence for the benefit of a belligerent constitutes an active participation in hostilities and therefore merchant vessels or private aircraft have no right to commit such an act. If they do so they must be content to lose the immunity which their non-combatant status should confer.

The vessel or aircraft concerned renders itself liable to be fired upon at the moment when the act is committed and is also liable to capture. In case of capture the vessel or aircraft will, if the facts be established, be dealt with in the prize court on the same footing as an enemy merchant vessel or enemy private aircraft. Members of the crew and passengers, if implicated, are to be regarded as committing an act in violation of the laws of war. A neutral vessel or aircraft which has been fired upon without adequate justification will be entitled to address a demand for compensation to the competent authorities. Jurisdiction over such claims might with advantage be conferred upon the prize court.

The second paragraph of the article places neutral merchant vessels or neutral aircraft when on or over the high seas in a position which corresponds to that laid down by Article 4 for radio stations in neutral territory. Such radio stations on land must not transmit information destined for a belligerent concerning military forces or military operations and the neutral Power must see to it that this rule is observed. Mobile radio stations when on or over the high seas are not subject to the control of the neutral government to the same extent as radio stations on land, and consequently the rule laid down in this article does not impose any obligations on the neutral government. The neutral mobile radio stations themselves will, however, be subject to the same measure of prohibition as the radio stations in neutral territory. They must not transmit information of the nature specified which is destined for the belligerent.

The distinction between the acts dealt with in the first and second paragraphs is that in the first and graver case it is assumed that the merchant vessel or aircraft will have been acting in connivance with the enemy. In flagrant cases, as for instance where the vessel or aircraft is found transmitting intelligence as to the movement or strength of military forces to an enemy in order to enable the latter to shape his movements accordingly, such connivance would be presumed.

The phrase "destined for a belligerent" has the same meaning as in Article 4. As in the case of Article 4, it is understood that the prohibition would not cover the repetition of news which has already become public.

The collection by the belligerent of the necessary proofs to establish his case against an aircraft or a vessel may take time. The examination of the message logs of many other vessels or aircraft may be necessary before responsibility can be fixed upon the particular vessel or aircraft which transmitted the incriminating message. It is therefore not possible to limit the right of capture to the duration of the voyage or flight during which the message was sent. How long the liability to capture should subsist was a more difficult point to determine. Agreement was ultimately reached on a basis of one year.

It is realized that the risk of capture during this period will be a great prejudice to neutrals, but on the other hand the injury done to the belligerent by the transmission by radio of improper messages may under modern conditions of warfare be irreparable, and therefore the sanctions attached to the rule must be serious. The neutral will, however, not be gravely inconvenienced by the measures necessary to protect himself against any violation of the rule.

In the case of all aircraft and of merchant vessels which are not carrying passengers, no great injury will result from the prohibition of radio messages other than those which are authorized by Article 9, and in the case of merchant vessels carrying passengers, there can be no insuperable difficulty in the institution on board the merchant vessel, if it is thought necessary, of the same measures as the neutral State may institute on land to protect itself under Article 3.

Paragraph 3 is limited to neutral vessels and aircraft because enemy vessels and aircraft are liable to capture at any time by reason of their enemy status.

It goes without saying that as capture is a belligerent right it cannot be exercised except in time of war, and therefore if the war terminates before the expiration of the time limit, the liability to capture is at an end.

The Netherlands Delegation has made a reserve on the subject of this article. It feels that the difficulties of obtaining satisfactory proofs against a neutral vessel or aircraft in the prize court will be so great in these cases that provision should be made for the international review of prize court decisions under this article. In its opinion the Permanent Court of International Justice would be the most appropriate tribunal for this purpose.

## Article 6

*1. The transmission by radio by a vessel or an aircraft, whether enemy or neutral, when on or over the high seas of military intelligence for the immediate use of a belligerent is to be deemed a hostile act and will render the vessel or aircraft liable to be fired upon.*

*2. A neutral vessel or neutral aircraft which transmits when on or over the high seas information destined for a belligerent concerning military operations or military forces shall be liable to capture. The Prize Court may condemn the vessel or aircraft if it considers that the circumstances justify condemnation.*

*3. Liability to capture of a neutral vessel or aircraft on account of the acts referred to in paragraphs (1) and (2) is not extinguished by the conclusion of the voyage or flight on which the vessel or aircraft was engaged at the time, but shall subsist for a period of one year after the act complained of.*

Apart from the question of the acquisition by the enemy of information, the use of radio installations by merchant vessels or aircraft may very well be a source of great embarrassment to the commander of a belligerent force. Not merely may it be essential to him to keep secret the strength of his forces or the operations in which they are engaged, but it may be necessary to ensure that there should be no interference with his communications. Further provisions are, therefore, required to complete the protection afforded to belligerents by Article 6.

For this purpose power is given to a belligerent commander to warn off neutral vessels and neutral aircraft and to oblige them to alter their course so that they will not approach the scene of the operations of the armed forces.

A second right given to a belligerent commander is to impose on neutral vessels and aircraft a period of silence in the use of their transmitting apparatus when in the immediate vicinity of the forces under his command. No matter what technical measures may be taken by neutral mobile stations in accordance with the provisions of Article 1, their messages, if made at a short distance from the receiving apparatus of belligerent forces, might interfere with the working of such apparatus, and such interference might prevent the hearing of messages to or from the commanding officer or the other units under his command.

To avoid undue hardship to neutrals, the faculty conferred upon the belligerent commander is limited to the duration of the operations in which he is engaged at the time. The article presupposes the actual presence of naval or aerial forces engaged in operations, and that the measures will not be applicable to widely extended zones or to zones in which no military action is taking place.

It is also understood that the change of course provided for in the first paragraph of the article must not prevent a ship or an aircraft from continuing its voyage and from reaching its port of destination.

The article is confined in terms to neutral vessels and aircraft because the belligerent commanding officer requires no special provision to protect himself against the operations of enemy vessels and enemy aircraft.

It will be noted that the terms in which the article is drafted as well as those employed in Articles 6 and 8 would cover neutral public vessels or aircraft. This does not imply any intention to encroach upon the rights of neutral States. It is assumed that no such neutral public vessels or aircraft would attempt to interfere in any such manner with the naval or aerial operations conducted by the forces of a State engaged in war.

### Article 7

*In case a belligerent commanding officer considers that the success of the operation in which he is engaged may be prejudiced by the presence of vessels or aircraft equipped with radio installations in the immediate vicinity of his armed forces or by the use of such installations therein, he may order neutral vessels or neutral aircraft on or over the high seas:*

*1. To alter their course to such an extent as will be necessary to prevent their approaching the armed forces operating under his command; or*

*2. Not to make use of their radio transmitting apparatus while in the immediate vicinity of such forces.*

*A neutral vessel or neutral aircraft, which does not conform to such direction of which it has had notice, exposes itself to the risk of being fired upon. It will also be liable to capture, and may be condemned if the Prize Court considers that the circumstances justify condemnation.*

Article 8 was intended to avoid, as far as possible, the eventuality of one of the belligerents being able to find on board a neutral mobile radio station any texts of radio messages transmitted from the radio stations of the belligerents and not destined for such neutral mobile station.

Such radio messages might possess military importance, and the neutral would thus involuntarily assist one of the belligerents by furnishing him with the means of becoming acquainted with such radio messages.

The seizure of the texts, entailing as it will the removal from the official log of the pages on which the operator enters the messages transmitted and received, together with an indication of the hour of such transmission and reception, has appeared to the Commission to be a sufficient penalty in view of the fact that such a proceeding would attract the attention of the administration to which the mobile station belongs, and would show that the responsible persons in the service of that station had not obeyed the provisions of the present article.

Provision is only made for the mere removal by the belligerent of the relevant pages.

The origin of the radio messages received is shown by the indications at the beginning of the message or in the call-sign. Military stations use the indications entered in the register of the International Bureau at Berne, or else secret indications which do not appear in that official register. No written record should therefore be preserved of radio-telegrams which are preceded either by the indications of a belligerent military station or by an unknown indication.

It is to be noted that the text of this article does not exclude the application of sanctions directed against unneutral service, if it is proved that the breach of the provisions in question was committed with an intention of rendering unneutral service.

### Article 8

*Neutral mobile radio stations shall refrain from keeping any record of radio messages received from belligerent military radio stations, unless such messages are addressed to themselves.*

*Violation of this rule will justify the removal by the belligerent of the records of such intercepted messages.*

In the first paragraph of Article 9 the Commission was anxious to indicate that belligerents who heard signals or messages of distress must, when deciding whether or no they would respond to such signals, take into account both their duties to humanity and their military duties.

The second paragraph is inspired solely by sentiments of humanity with a view to saving human life at sea. The text specifies clearly that every mobile station finding itself in danger or perceiving an immediate danger for other mobile stations will have the right, however it may be affected by other provisions of these rules, to transmit messages in order to ask for help or to signal the danger for navigation which it has perceived. By the words "messages which are indispensable to the safety of navigation," should be understood only such messages as are immediately necessary for preventing the collision, stranding or loss of ships or aircraft.

### Article 9

*Belligerents are under obligation to comply with the provisions of international conventions in regard to distress signals and distress messages so far as their military operations permit.*

*Nothing in these rules shall be understood to relieve a belligerent from such obligation or to prohibit the transmission of distress signals, distress messages and messages which are indispensable to the safety of navigation.*

Article 10 is inserted to prevent the employment of signals and messages of distress as ruses of war. It is justified by considerations of honour and humanity. Persons who violate the rule may be punished.

### Article 10

*The perversion of radio distress signals and distress messages prescribed by international conventions to other than their normal and legitimate purposes constitutes a violation of the laws of war and renders the perpetrator personally responsible under international law.*

The purpose of Article 11 is to show clearly that the question whether an act which involves a breach of these rules constitutes also an act of espionage cannot be answered except by reference to the rules of international law which determine what acts amount to espionage.

### Article 11

*Acts not otherwise constituting espionage are not espionage by reason of their involving violation of these rules.*

The purpose of Article 12 is to define clearly the position of the radio operator so far as regards personal liability to punishment. The operator works in his cabin where he executes the orders of those above him. Consequently it is right that he should incur no personal responsibility merely because he has executed orders which he has received in the discharge of his duties as radio operator. Liability to punishment for acts which contravene rules such as Articles 9 or 10 falls on those who have given the orders for such acts.

### Article 12

*Radio operators incur no personal responsibility from the mere fact of carrying out the orders which they receive in the performance of their duties as operators.*

It has not been thought necessary to insert in the rules an article defining the word "radio-station" or "station radio-télégraphique." The phrase is used in both texts as covering radio-telegraphic stations, radio-telephonic stations, radio-goniometric stations and generally all stations which use Hertzian waves transmitted through air, water or earth.

The Japanese Delegation submitted to the Commission the following proposal:

"The belligerent may take such measures as to render inoperative the coastal radio stations in enemy jurisdiction, irrespective of their owners."

After examining and discussing this proposal, the Commission came to the conclusion that it was not necessary to insert a special article referring to the subject. It was of opinion that the texts of other international conventions or the usages of war covered the question in all its practical aspects and gave the right to take the measures contemplated in the Japanese proposal.

The Land Warfare Regulations and the Naval Bombardment Convention, 1907 (No. IX of 1907), permit the bombardment of coastal radio stations by land or naval forces. Article 24 of the rules for aerial warfare enables similar measures to be taken by the air forces against radio stations used for military purposes. Furthermore, Article 53 of the Land Warfare Regulations authorizes the seizure by a belligerent in occupation of enemy territory of coastal radio stations, even if such stations belong to private individuals.

An interesting proposal was submitted by the Italian Delegation for protecting the radio-telegraphic communications of combatant forces by the establishment around them of a kind of "zone of silence." The Commission agreed that this idea was already implied in the text of Article 7, and that it was consequently not necessary to express it in a special article.

## PART II

### RULES OF AERIAL WARFARE

In the preparation of the code of rules of aerial warfare the Commission worked on the basis of a draft submitted by the American Delegation. A similar draft, covering in general the same ground, was submitted by the British Delegation. In the discussion of the various articles adopted by the Commission the provisions contained in each of these drafts were taken into consideration, as well as amendments and proposals submitted by other Delegations.

## CHAPTER I

### APPLICABILITY: CLASSIFICATION AND MARKS

No attempt has been made to formulate a definition of the term "aircraft," nor to enumerate the various categories of machines which are covered by the term. A statement of the broad principle that the rules adopted apply to all types of aircraft has been thought sufficient, and Article 1 has been framed for this purpose.

## Article 1

*The rules of aerial warfare apply to all aircraft, whether lighter or heavier than air, irrespective of whether they are, or are not, capable of floating on the water.*

For states which are parties to the Air Navigation Convention of 1919, aircraft are divided by Article 30 into two classes, State aircraft and private aircraft, State aircraft being subdivided into military aircraft and aircraft exclusively employed in State service, such as posts, customs or police. The article also provides, however, that State aircraft, other than military, customs and police aircraft, are to be treated as private aircraft, and subject as such to all the provisions of that Convention. For practical purposes, therefore, States which are parties to the Convention of 1919 divide aircraft in time of peace into three categories:

(a) Military aircraft;
(b) State aircraft employed for customs and police purposes;
(c) Private aircraft and such State aircraft as are employed for purposes other than those enumerated in (b).

The Convention of 1919 has not yet become by any means universal, but it would be so inconvenient for States, which are parties to it, to come under different rules in time of war, that account has been taken of the provisions of the Convention when framing the articles adopted by the Commission.

It has also been necessary to take into account the fact that Italy has entrusted the supervision of the customs service to the military forces, a fact which has prevented the adoption of exactly the same language as that employed in Article 30 of the Convention of 1919. When read in conjunction, however, with Article 5 below, it will be found that the classification adopted by the code of rules of aerial warfare corresponds very nearly with that prescribed in Article 30 of the Convention mentioned above.

## Article 2

*The following shall be deemed to be public aircraft:*
*(a) Military aircraft;*
*(b) Non-military aircraft exclusively employed in the public service.*
*All other aircraft shall be deemed to be private aircraft.*

A clear distinction must be made between aircraft which form part of the combatant forces in time of war and those which do not. Each class must be easily recognizable; this is essential if the immunities to which non-combatant aircraft are entitled are to be respected. Article 3 has been framed with this object.

### Article 3

*A military aircraft shall bear an external mark indicating its nationality and military character.*

Public non-military aircraft are not in command of persons commissioned or enlisted in the fighting forces; consequently there must be evidence on board the aircraft of the service in which they are engaged. Such evidence is afforded by their papers. It will be seen by reference to Article 51 below that aircraft of this class may be visited for the purpose of the verification of their papers.

### Article 4

*A public non-military aircraft employed for customs or police purposes shall carry papers evidencing the fact that it is exclusively employed in the public service. Such an aircraft shall bear an external mark indicating its nationality and its public non-military character.*

Article 5 has been adopted for the purpose of regulating the position of state-owned aircraft employed in the postal service, or for commercial purposes. Such aircraft will be engaged in international traffic which should properly subject them to the same measures of control as those to which private aircraft are subject. They should also bear the same marks.

In terms the article applies to all public non-military aircraft other than those employed for customs or police purposes, following in this respect the language adopted in the last paragraph of Article 30 of the Air Navigation Convention of 1919. It is in connection with aircraft employed in the postal service or for commercial purposes that it will find its chief application.

Objection has been expressed to this article by the Netherlands Delegation on the ground that its effect will be to subject state-owned aircraft to capture and to the jurisdiction of belligerent prize courts.

### Article 5

*Public non-military aircraft other than those employed for customs or police purposes shall in time of war bear the same*

*external marks, and for the purposes of these rules shall be
treated on the same footing, as private aircraft.*

Private aircraft must in time of war bear marks to indicate
their nationality and character and to enable the aircraft to
be identified. It would be inconvenient that the marks to be
borne in war time should differ from those borne in time of
peace. For peace time the marks which a private aircraft is to
bear are prescribed in the Air Navigation Convention of 1919.
This Convention, however, is not universal in character and
account must be taken of the position of States which are not
parties to it. Nevertheless all States, whether parties to the
Convention or not, will before long have enacted legislation as
to the marks which aircraft of their nationality are to bear.
The Commission has therefore felt that it will be sufficient to
lay down as the rule for time of war that aircraft must bear
the marks which are prescribed by the legislation in force in
their own country. Foreign Powers, whether belligerent or
neutral, are not concerned with the enforcement of that legislation as such; that is a matter for the municipal courts of the
country concerned. The object of the articles is to afford to
belligerent and neutral authorities a guide as to the marks
which a private aircraft must bear.

### Article 6

*Aircraft not comprised in Articles 3 and 4 and deemed to
be private aircraft shall carry such papers and bear such external marks as are required by the rules in force in their own
country. These marks must indicate their nationality and character.*

Great abuses might prevail if the external marks affixed
to an aircraft could be altered while the machine was in flight.
It is also necessary that the marks should be clearly visible.
The principles adopted in Article 7 are in harmony with the
provisions of the Air Navigation Convention of 1919.

### Article 7

*The external marks required by the above articles shall be
so affixed that they cannot be altered in flight. They shall be
as large as is practicable and shall be visible from above,
from below and from each side.*

Each State chooses for itself the marks which its aircraft
are to bear. The marks chosen for private aircraft in time
of peace by States which are parties to the Air Navigation
Convention of 1919, are set out in that Convention, and are
generally known. It is equally important that the marks for

public aircraft, whether military or non-military, should be equally well known and also the marks chosen for private aircraft possessing the nationality of a State, which is not a party to the said Convention. Notification to all other Powers is, therefore, provided for of the marks prescribed by the rules in force in each State.

Necessity may arise for a change in the marks adopted by each State. When that happens the change must be notified. If the change is made in time of peace, there can be no difficulty in notifying it before it is brought into force.

In time of war changes must be notified as soon as possible and at latest when they are communicated by the State concerned to its own fighting forces. It will be important to a State, which changes the marks on its military aircraft in time of war, to notify the change as quickly as possible to its own forces, as otherwise the aircraft might run the risk of being shot down by their own side. For this reason no anxiety need be felt that there will be any attempt to evade compliance with the rule.

Regret has been expressed in some quarters that any change should be allowed in time of war of the marks adopted by a particular State. The practical reasons, however, in favor of allowing such modifications are overwhelming. The marks adopted by different countries for their military machines are in some cases not very dissimilar, and if war broke out between two countries whose military machines bore marks which were not readily distinguishable, it would be essential that a modification should be made.

### Article 8

*The external marks, prescribed by the rules in force in each State, shall be notified promptly to all other Powers.*

*Modifications adopted in time of peace of the rules prescribing external marks shall be notified to all other Powers before they are brought into force.*

*Modifications of such rules adopted at the outbreak of war or during hostilities shall be notified by each Power as soon as possible to all other Powers and at latest when they are communicated to its own fighting forces.*

Article 9 is founded upon a proposal first submitted by the Japanese Delegation; an American proposal to the same effect was submitted at a later stage. The subject of the article is one of some difficulty and one which has in times past been fruitful of discussions and disagreements in connection with warships, the Powers not having been able to agree whether the act of sovereignty involved in the commissioning of a war-ship might properly be exercised on the high seas (see the preamble to Convention VII of 1907).

The proposal received the support of a majority of the delegations only, the French Delegation being unable to accept it.

### Article 9

*A belligerent non-military aircraft, whether public or private, may be converted into a military aircraft, provided that the conversion is effected within the jurisdiction of the belligerent State to which the aircraft belongs and not on the high seas.*

The proposal submitted by the Japanese Delegation would also have prevented the conversion of military aircraft into private aircraft except within the jurisdiction of the belligerent State concerned. The majority of the members of the Commission were of opinion that an article on this subject was not required. It does not seem likely that such conversion would be effected upon the high seas except for the purpose of enabling an aircraft, not otherwise entitled to do so, to enter neutral territory. There would be many practical difficulties in the way of any such conversion: not only would identity marks have to be affixed which would depend on the registration in the home State, but a civilian crew would have to be obtained and various certificates would be required, all of which should be dated. If the marks and papers belonging to some other aircraft were used, the marks and papers would be false. A fraud would have been practiced on the neutral State. Even if the proceeding were authorized by the belligerent State concerned, so that it would be valid under its own law, the marks would still be false marks so far as concerned the neutral State, and if it became aware of the fraud committed, it would be justified in disregarding the conversion.

Article 10 adopts for time of war a principle which has already been adopted for private aircraft in time of peace by Article 8 of the Air Navigation Convention of 1919.

### Article 10

*No aircraft may possess more than one nationality.*

### CHAPTER II

#### GENERAL PRINCIPLES

Article 11 embodies the general principle that outside the jurisdiction of any State, i.e., in the air space over the high seas, all aircraft have full freedom of passage. Provisions embodied in other articles which restrict the liberty of individual aircraft are to be regarded as exceptions to this general principle.

## Article 11

*Outside the jurisdiction of any State, belligerent or neutral, all aircraft shall have full freedom of passage through the air and of alighting.*

In time of peace many States are subject to treaty obligations requiring them to allow aircraft of other States to circulate in the air space above their territory. In time of war a State must possess greater freedom of action. Article 12 therefore recognizes the liberty of each State to enact such rules on this subject as it may deem necessary.

## Article 12

*In time of war any State, whether belligerent or neutral, may forbid or regulate the entrance, movement or sojourn of aircraft within its jurisdiction.*

### Knowledge of the Existence of the War

Among the provisions contained in the original American draft was an article to the following effect:

"The liability of an aircraft for violation of the laws of war is contingent upon her actual or constructive knowledge of the existence of the war."

The discussions upon this article led the American Delegation to withdraw the proposal.

Knowledge of the existence of a state of war was frequently in the past an important element in deciding cases instituted in prize courts for the condemnation of a ship or goods. Sailing ships were often at sea in old days for months without touching at any port, and under such conditions it was easy for a vessel to be unaware of the outbreak of war. The question diminished in importance when steamships tended to replace sailing ships, and diminished still more in importance when wireless telegraphy was invented and fitted to sea-going ships.

With aircraft the case is different; the velocity of their flight and the small supplies of fuel which they can carry will render it unusual for a flight to exceed 12 hours in length. Cases are therefore not likely to arise in which there can be any doubt of the actual knowledge of the existence of a state of war, or in which constructive knowledge has to be relied on. Furthermore, all aircraft of important size are likely to be fitted with a wireless installation.

The Declaration of London, framed in 1909, contained provisions on this subject (see Articles 43 and 45), and it was then found necessary to deal with the matter in greater detail than is attempted in the above American proposal. Until experience shows that it is necessary to frame a rule on this subject for aircraft, it seems more prudent to leave the matter to rest on the basis of the general rules of international law.

So far as concerns neutral Powers, the Convention on the Opening of Hostilities (No. III of 1907) lays down that the existence of a state of war must be notified to neutral Powers, and that they are subject to no obligations arising therefrom until the receipt of such notification. They cannot, however, rely on the absence of any such notification, if it can be established that they were actually aware of the existence of the state of war. This provision seems adequate and satisfactory.

## CHAPTER III

### BELLIGERENTS

The use of privateers in naval warfare was abolished by the Declaration of Paris, 1856. Belligerent rights at sea can now only be exercised by units under the direct authority, immediate control and responsibility of the State. This same principle should apply to aerial warfare. Belligerent rights should therefore only be exercised by military aircraft.

### Article 13

*Military aircraft are alone entitled to exercise belligerent rights.*

Operations of war involve the responsibility of the State. Units of the fighting forces must, therefore, be under the direct control of persons responsible to the State. For the same reason the crew must be exclusively military in order that they may be subject to military discipline.

### Article 14

*A military aircraft shall be under the command of a person duly commissioned or enlisted in the military service of the State; the crew must be exclusively military.*

Combatant members of the armed land forces must, if they are not in uniform, wear at least a distinctive emblem. So long as the officers or crew of a military aircraft are on board the aircraft there is no risk of any doubt as to their combatant status, but if they are forced to land they may become separated from the machine. In that event it is necessary for their own protection that their combatant status should be easily recognized.

### Article 15

*Members of the crew of a military aircraft shall wear a fixed distinctive emblem of such character as to be recognizable at a distance in case they become separated from their aircraft.*

The next article indicates the aircraft which may engage in hostilities, and forbids private aircraft from being armed when they are outside the jurisdiction of their own country.

The immunities which a belligerent is bound to respect in a non-combatant impose upon the non-combatant a corresponding obligation not to take part in hostilities. This principle applies equally to aerial warfare. If a distinction is to be drawn between military and other aircraft, the distinction must be observed on both sides, and non-military aircraft must not attempt to engage in hostilities in any form.

To give full effect to this principle, a non-military aircraft must be debarred from transmitting, during flight, military intelligence for the benefit of a belligerent. This rule will be seen to be natural and logical if the peculiar characteristics of aircraft are borne in mind. It is as scouts and observers that one of their principal uses is found in time of war. If non-military aircraft were to be allowed to act in this capacity, injury of very serious consequence might be done to the opposing belligerent. If exposed to such risk, no belligerent could agree to respect the immunities which a non-combatant aircraft should enjoy, and the only way to ensure such respect is to recognize that the transmission of military intelligence for the benefit of a belligerent is a participation in hostilities, which would constitute a violation of the laws of war and would be dealt with accordingly.

The rule as framed has been restricted within the narrowest limits compatible with military safety. It is limited to transmission of intelligence during flight. When the flight has been completed, the individual concerned will be within the jurisdiction of some State, and there the control of the transmission of information will be subject to the regulations of that State. It will not be affected by the provisions of this article.

The mounting of arms in time of war may be construed as *prima facie* evidence of an intention to take part in hostilities. It is true that of recent years certain States found it necessary to arm merchant ships in self-protection, but the conditions of air warfare are so different that it has not been thought necessary to allow for such a proceeding on the part of aircraft. A gun would not be an adequate protection to an aircraft against illegal attack, as the first warning the aircraft might have of any such attack would be an act which might involve its destruction.

On the other hand, to permit private aircraft to be armed would facilitate acts of perfidy on the part of an opposing belligerent; an aircraft masquerading under false marks might suddenly open fire, and the risk of this would be sufficient to render it dangerous for an honest belligerent to respect the immunities of private aircraft to the extent which he would wish.

The interests of private aircraft are from every point of view better served by the adoption of a rule against the arming of private aircraft in time of war.

The article as framed does not extend to aircraft within the jurisdiction of their own State. Such an extension would be an unreasonable interference with the domestic jurisdiction of the State concerned.

The rule against aircraft being armed is limited to private aircraft. Public non-military aircraft engaged in customs or police work may find it necessary to carry arms because the fulfilment of their functions renders it essential for them to be able to apply coercion in case of need. In their case, the carriage of arms would raise no presumption of an intention to take part in hostilities, but they are subject just as much as private aircraft to the provisions of the first two paragraphs of the article.

## Article 16

*No aircraft other than a belligerent military aircraft shall engage in hostilities in any form.*

*The term "hostilities" includes the transmission during flight of military intelligence for the immediate use of a belligerent.*

*No private aircraft, when outside the jurisdiction of its own country, shall be armed in time of war.*

The provisions of the Geneva Convention have been applied to maritime warfare by the Convention signed at The Hague in 1907 (Convention X of 1907). It will probably be found desirable to extend them in due course to warfare in the air and to negotiate a special convention for this purpose. Pending the conclusion of any such convention, a rule has been adopted stating broadly that these conventions apply to aerial warfare. Flying ambulances should enjoy the privileges and immunities conferred by the Geneva Convention upon mobile medical units or sanitary formations. The work of such flying ambulances must of course be carried out subject to similar conditions of belligerent control as those laid down in the Conventions of 1906 and 1907, and they must devote themselves to the task of succoring all wounded impartially in accordance with the principles embodied in these Conventions. When the new special convention referred to above is concluded, the opportunity will no doubt be taken to extend to flying ambulances the exemption from dues already conferred by treaty upon hospital ships which enter a foreign port.

### Article 17

*The principles laid down in the Geneva Convention, 1906, and the Convention for the adaptation of the said Convention to Maritime War (No. X of 1907) shall apply to aerial warfare and to flying ambulances, as well as to the control over flying ambulances exercised by a belligerent commanding officer.*

*In order to enjoy the protection and privileges allowed to mobile medical units by the Geneva Convention, 1906, flying ambulances must bear the distinctive emblem of the Red Cross in addition to the usual distinguishing marks.*

### CHAPTER IV

#### HOSTILITIES

Article 18 is intended to clear up a doubt which arose during the recent war. The use of tracer bullets against aircraft was a general practice in all the contending armies. In the absence of a hard surface on which the bullet will strike, an airman cannot tell whether or not his aim is correct. These bullets were used for the purpose of enabling the airman to correct his aim, as the trail of vapor which they leave behind indicates to him the exact line of fire. In one case, however, combatant airmen were arrested and put on trial on the ground that the use of these bullets constituted a breach of the existing rules of war laid down by treaty.

The use of incendiary bullets is also necessary as a means of attack against lighter-than-air craft, as it is by setting fire to the gas contained by these aircraft that they can most easily be destroyed.

In the form in which the proposal was first brought forward

its provisions were limited to a stipulation that the use of tracer bullets against aircraft generally, was not prohibited.

Various criticisms were, however, made about the proposed text, chiefly founded on the impracticability for an airman while in flight to change the ammunition which he is using in the machine gun in his aircraft. He cannot employ different bullets in accordance with the target at which he is aiming, one sort of ammunition for other aircraft and another sort for land forces by whom he may be attacked.

The Commission, therefore, came to the conclusion that the most satisfactory solution of the problem would be to state specifically that the use of tracer, incendiary or explosive projectiles by or against aircraft is not prohibited.

### Article 18

*The use of tracer, incendiary or explosive projectiles by or against aircraft is not prohibited.*

*This provision applies equally to States which are parties to the Declaration of St. Petersburg, 1868, and to those which are not.*

In order that there may be no doubt that the use of false external marks is not a legitimate ruse, it has been specifically prohibited. By later provisions in the rules, the use of false external marks is made a ground for capture and condemnation of a neutral aircraft.

What are here referred to are false marks of nationality or character, the marks which are dealt with in Chapter I of these rules. The article would not apply to mere squadron badges or other emblems which are only of interest to one particular belligerent force.

### Article 19

*The use of false external marks is forbidden.*

Another mode of injuring the enemy, which it has seemed desirable to prohibit, is that of firing at airmen escaping from a disabled aircraft.

### Article 20

*When an aircraft has been disabled, the occupants when endeavoring to escape by means of a parachute must not be attacked in the course of their descent.*

Incidents took place in the recent war which showed the desirability of having a distinct rule on the question whether the dropping of leaflets for propaganda purposes was a legitimate means of warfare. Attempts were made by one belligerent to impose heavy penalties on airmen who were forced to descend within his lines after engaging in this work.

Article 21 has been framed to meet this case. It is not limited to dropping leaflets, as aircraft can disseminate propaganda by other means, such, for instance, as emitting trails of smoke in the form of words in the sky.

What is legalized by the article is the use of aircraft for distributing propaganda. It does not follow that propaganda of all kinds is thereby validated. Incitements to murder or assassination will, for instance, still be considered illegitimate forms of propaganda.

### Article 21

*The use of aircraft for the purpose of disseminating propaganda shall not be treated as an illegitimate means of warfare.*

*Members of the crews of such aircraft must not be deprived of their rights as prisoners of war on the charge that they have committed such an act.*

### Bombardment

The subject of bombardment by aircraft is one of the most difficult to deal with in framing any code of rules for aerial warfare.

The experiences of the recent war have left in the mind of the world at large a lively horror of the havoc which can be wrought by the indiscriminate launching of bombs and projectiles on the non-combatant populations of towns and cities. The conscience of mankind revolts against this form of making war in places outside the actual theater of military operations, and the feeling is universal that limitations must be imposed.

On the other hand, it is equally clear that the aircraft is a potent engine of war, and no State which realizes the possibility that it may itself be attacked, and the use to which its adversary may put his air forces can take the risk of fettering its own liberty of action to an extent which would restrict it from attacking its enemy where that adversary may legitimately be attacked with effect. It is useless, therefore, to enact prohibitions unless there is an equally clear understanding of what constitute legitimate objects of attack, and it is precisely in this respect that agreement was difficult to reach.

Before passing to a consideration of the articles which have been agreed, mention must be made of the Declaration prohibiting the Discharge of Projectiles and Explosives from Balloons, signed at The Hague in 1907. Three of the States represented on the Commission[20] are parties to that Declaration; the other three are not. Under the terms of this Declaration the Contracting Powers agree to prohibit the discharge of projectiles and explosives from balloons *or by other new methods of a similar nature*. Its terms are, therefore, wide enough to cover bombardment by aircraft. On the other hand, the scope of the Declaration is very limited; in duration it is to last only until the close of the Third Peace Conference, a conference which was to have been summoned for 1914 or 1915, and its application is confined to a war between contracting States without the participation of a non-contracting State.

The existence of this Declaration can afford no solution of the problems arising out of the question of bombardment from the air, even for the States which are parties to it.

The number of parties is so small that, even if the Declaration were renewed, no confidence could ever be felt that when a war broke out it would apply. A general agreement, therefore, on the subject of bombardment from the air is much to be desired. For the States which are parties to it, however, the Declaration exists and it is well that the legal situation should be clearly understood.

As between the parties it will continue in force and will operate in the event of a war between them, unless by mutual agreement its terms are modified, or an understanding reached that it shall be regarded as replaced by some new conventional stipulation; but it will in any case cease to operate at the moment when a Third Peace Conference concludes its labours, or if any State which is not a party to the Declaration intervenes in the war as a belligerent.

No difficulty was found in reaching an agreement that there are certain purposes for which aerial bombardment is inadmissible.

Article 22 has been formulated with this object.

## Article 22

*Aerial bombardment for the purpose of terrorizing the civilian population, of destroying or damaging private property not of military character, or of injuring non-combatants is prohibited.*

The Naval Bombardment Convention of 1907 (No. IX) allows bombardment for enforcing payment of requisitions for supplies necessary for the immediate use of the naval forces (Article 3), but not for enforcing payment of money contributions (Article 4).

20. United States of America, Great Britain and The Netherlands.

For aerial warfare it has been decided to adopt the more stringent rule of the Land Warfare Regulations.

### Article 23

*Aerial bombardment for the purpose of enforcing compliance with requisitions in kind or payment of contributions in money is prohibited.*

Agreement on the following article specifying the objects which may legitimately be bombarded from the air was not reached without prolonged discussion. Numerous proposals were put forward by the various delegations before unanimity was ultimately attained. The text of these proposals will be found in the minutes. In particular, mention may be made of an Italian proposal of February 8, on which the text ultimately adopted was in great part founded. Regret was expressed by some delegations that a more far-reaching prohibition did not meet with unanimous acceptance.

The terms of the article are so clear that no explanation of the provisions is necessary, but it may be well to state that in the phrase in paragraph 2, "military establishments or depots," the word "depots" is intended to cover all collections of supplies for military use which have passed into the possession of the military authorities and are ready for delivery to the forces. "Distinctively military supplies" in the succeeding phrase is intended to cover those which by their nature show that they are certainly manufactured for military purposes.

If the code of rules of aerial warfare should eventually be annexed to a convention, paragraph 5 of the article would find a more appropriate place in the convention.

It will be noticed that for aerial bombardment the test adopted in Article 25 of the Land Warfare Regulations, that of the town, etc., being defended, is abandoned. The nature of the objective or the use to which it is being put now becomes the test.

### Article 24

*(1) Aerial bombardment is legitimate only when directed at a military objective, that is to say, an object of which the destruction or injury would constitute a distinct military advantage to the belligerent.*

*(2) Such bombardment is legitimate only when directed exclusively at the following objectives: military forces; military works; military establishments or depots; factories constituting important and well-known centers engaged in the manufacture of arms, ammunition or distinctively military*

*supplies; lines of communication or transportation used for military purposes.*

*(3) The bombardment of cities, towns, villages, dwellings or buildings not in the immediate neighborhood of the operations of land forces is prohibited. In cases where the objectives specified in paragraph 2 are so situated, that they cannot be bombarded without the indiscriminate bombardment of the civilian population, the aircraft must abstain from bombardment.*

*(4) In the immediate neighborhood of the operations of land forces, the bombardment of cities, towns, villages, dwellings or buildings is legitimate provided that there exists a reasonable presumption that the military concentration is sufficiently important to justify such bombardment, having regard to the danger thus caused to the civilian population.*

*(5) A belligerent State is liable to pay compensation for injuries to person or to property caused by the violation by any of its officers or forces of the provisions of this article.*

Both in land warfare and in maritime warfare the principle has been adopted that certain special classes of buildings must be spared so far as possible in case of bombardment; for the former, by Article 27 of the Land Warfare Regulations, for the latter by Article 5 of the Naval Bombardment Convention of 1907 (No. IX). A similar provision, largely based on that in the Naval Bombardment Convention, has been adopted as Article 25. By day, these privileged buildings must be marked in a way which will make them visible to aircraft; the marks agreed on being those laid down in the Geneva Convention and in the Naval Bombardment Convention; the use of such marks is made obligatory so as to correspond with the duty placed on the adversary of sparing such buildings. By night, however, the use of lights to make the special signs visible is optional, because experience has shown that such lights may serve as guides to night-flying aircraft and may thereby be of service to the enemy.

## Article 25

*In bombardment by aircraft, all necessary steps must be taken by the commander to spare as far as possible buildings dedicated to public worship, art, science, or charitable purposes, historic monuments, hospital ships, hospitals and other places where the sick and wounded are collected, provided such buildings, objects or places are not at the time used for military purposes. Such buildings, objects and places must by day*

*be indicated by marks visible to aircraft. The use of marks to
indicate other buildings, objects or places than those specified
above is to be deemed an act of perfidy. The marks used as
aforesaid shall be in the case of buildings protected under the
Geneva Convention the red cross on a white ground, and in the
case of other protected buildings a large rectangular panel
divided diagonally into two pointed triangular portions, one
black and the other white.*

*A belligerent who desires to secure by night the protection
for the hospitals and other privileged buildings above mentioned must take the necessary measures to render the special
signs referred to sufficiently visible.*

A proposal was submitted by the Italian Delegation for the
purpose of securing better protection from aerial bombardment for important historic monuments. During the recent
war it was not found that the articles in the Land Warfare
Regulations and the Naval Bombardment Convention were
sufficient to prevent historic monuments from being bombarded. An unscrupulous opponent can always allege that they
are being used for military purposes and ignore the written
agreements accordingly. There is also the possibility that in
the attack on some object which is a legitimate subject for
bombardment, a historic monument in the immediate vicinity
may be injured.

The Italian proposal comprised two new features, the creation of a zone round each historic monument within which the
State was to be debarred from committing any act which constituted a use of the area for military purposes, and a system
of inspection under neutral auspices to ensure that the undertaking was carried out, both as regards the monument itself
and the zone. By this means any pretext for the bombardment
would be removed, and the risk of unintentional injury would
be minimized.

The proposal received the sympathetic consideration of all
the Delegations, and it was accordingly remitted to an expert
committee for more detailed consideration. Article 26 has
been prepared in the light of their report.

The Italian proposal comprised not only historic but also
artistic monuments. It has seemed better to omit the word
"artistic" for fear lest a divergence should appear to be created
between the new article and Article 25, the language of which
is modelled on Article 27 of the Land Warfare Regulations
and Article 5 of the Naval Bombardment Convention (No. IX
of 1907). The words "historic monument" in this article are
used in a broad sense. They cover all monuments which by

reason of their great artistic value are historic today or will become historic in the future.

It should be clearly understood that adoption of the system is only permissive. If a State prefers to trust only to Article 25 to secure protection of its monuments, there is no obligation upon it to notify them to other Powers in peace time and to establish the surrounding zones which are not to be used for military purposes.

The notification must be made through the diplomatic channel. It will then be open to any State receiving the notification, if it thinks it necessary to do so, to question within a reasonable time the propriety of regarding a particular place as an historic monument. If no question is raised with regard to the monuments notified, other States will be regarded as having accepted the demand for the protection of such monuments from bombardment, and the immunity will then rest on the basis of agreement. For the same reason the notification once made must not be withdrawn after the outbreak of hostilities.

Considerable hesitation was expressed in accepting the provision that notification must be made in time of peace. It was urged that the system proposed was a new procedure, that particular monuments might be forgotten, and that more elasticity should be allowed. On the other hand, it was urged that the essence of the scheme was to get agreement as to the immunity of these monuments, and that unless notification in time of war was excluded, it was not likely that any would be notified in time of peace.

The effect of allowing a 500-meter zone to be drawn round each monument may well be that in certain special cases, as for instance Venice or Florence, which are particularly rich in ancient and historic monuments, a large portion of the city would be comprised within the protected zones. The zones round each monument will overlap and so create a continuous area. The subsequent provisions will, however, ensure that there is a complete absence of military use of any portion of the area so protected.

It was agreed that if the belligerents did not for military reasons place the signs indicated in the article, enemy aviators had no right by reason merely of their absence to bombard the zone in question, if it had been duly determined and notified.

In their report, the experts stated that they considered that the marks designed to indicate the zones of protection round monuments should differ in design from those prescribed by

Article 25 for the historic monuments themselves. The Commission took note of this recommendation.

The prohibition against the use of the zone surrounding the monument must be very strictly interpreted. There must be a complete cessation of the use of any place, including, for instance, factories and railway lines, with a military purpose in view.

The special committee of inspection provided for by the article will be constituted by the State which has taken advantage of the article. There would not seem to be any need to establish the committee until the outbreak of war. As these special arrangements will have been made in order to secure full protection for its historic monuments, the State will be bound to afford to this committee the fullest opportunity for making the investigations they may think necessary.

## Article 26

*The following special rules are adopted for the purpose of enabling States to obtain more efficient protection for important historic monuments situated within their territory, provided, that they are willing to refrain from the use of such monuments and a surrounding zone for military purposes, and to accept a special régime for their inspection.*

*(1) A State shall be entitled, if it sees fit, to establish a zone of protection round such monuments situated in its territory. Such zones shall in time of war enjoy immunity from bombardment.*

*(2) The monuments round which a zone is to be established shall be notified to other Powers in peace time through the diplomatic channel; the notification shall also indicate the limits of the zones. The notification may not be withdrawn in time of war.*

*(3) The zone of protection may include, in addition to the area actually occupied by the monument or group of monuments, an outer zone, not exceeding 500 meters in width, measured from the circumference of the said area.*

*(4) Marks clearly visible from aircraft either by day or by night will be employed for the purpose of ensuring the identification by belligerent airmen of the limits of the zones.*

*(5) The marks on the monuments themselves will be those defined in Article 25. The marks employed for indicating the surrounding zones will be fixed by each State adopting the provisions of this article, and will be notified to other Powers at the same time as the monuments and zones are notified.*

*(6) Any abusive use of the marks indicating the zones re-*

*ferred to in paragraph 5 will be regarded as an act of perfidy.*

*(7) A State adopting the provisions of this article must abstain from using the monument and the surrounding zone for military purposes, or for the benefit in any way whatever of its military organization, or from committing within such monument or zone any act with a military purpose in view.*

*(8) An inspection committee consisting of three neutral representatives accredited to the State adopting the provisions of this article, or their delegates, shall be appointed for the purpose of ensuring that no violation is committed of the provisions of paragraph 7. One of the members of the committee of inspection shall be the representative (or his delegate) of the State to which has been entrusted the interests of the opposing belligerent.*

## Espionage

The articles dealing with espionage follow closely the precedent of the Land Warfare Regulations.

Article 27 is a verbal adaptation of the first paragraph of Article 29 of the Regulations, so phrased as to limit it to acts committed while in the air.

Consideration has been given to the question whether there was any need to add to the provision instances of actions which were not to be deemed acts of espionage, such as those which are given at the end of Article 29 in the Regulations, and it was suggested that Article 29 [21] of the American draft might appropriately be introduced in this manner. It was decided that this was unnecessary. The article submitted by the American Delegation was intended to ensure that reconnaissance work openly done behind the enemy lines by aircraft should not be treated as spying. It is not thought likely that any belligerent would attempt to treat it as such.

## Article 27

*Any person on board a belligerent or neutral aircraft is to be deemed a spy only if acting clandestinely or on false pretences he obtains or seeks to obtain, while in the air, information within belligerent jurisdiction or in the zone of operations of a belligerent with the intention of communicating it to the hostile party.*

Acts of espionage by members of the crew of an aircraft or by persons who have been carried in an aircraft may well be

21. "Acts of the personnel of correctly marked enemy aircraft, public or private, done or performed while in the air, are not to be deemed espionage."

committed after they have left the aircraft. They will in that case be subject to the Land Warfare Regulations.

## Article 28

*Acts of espionage committed after leaving the aircraft by members of the crew of an aircraft or by passengers transported by it are subject to the provisions of the Land Warfare Regulations.*

Two rules have been adopted in land warfare with respect to espionage which should apply equally to aerial warfare. These are that a spy cannot be punished without previous trial, and that a member of an army who commits an act of espionage and succeeds in rejoining the army cannot, if he is subsequently captured, be made responsible for the previous act of espionage. He is entitled to be treated as a prisoner of war.

## Article 29

*Punishment of the acts of espionage referred to in Articles 27 and 28 is subject to Articles 30 and 31 of the Land Warfare Regulations.*

## CHAPTER V

### MILITARY AUTHORITY OVER ENEMY AND NEUTRAL AIRCRAFT AND PERSONS ON BOARD

The rapidity of its flight would enable an aircraft to embarrass the operations of land or sea forces, or even operations in the air, to an extent which might prove most inconvenient or even disastrous to a belligerent commander. To protect belligerents from improper intrusions of this kind, it is necessary to authorize belligerent commanders to warn off the intruders, and, if the warning is disregarded, to compel their retirement by opening fire.

It is easy to see that undue hardship might be occasioned to neutrals if advantage were taken of the faculty so conferred on belligerent commanding officers and attempts were made to exclude for long or indefinite periods all neutrals from stipulated areas or to prevent communication between different countries through the air over the high seas. The present provision only authorizes a commanding officer to warn off aircraft during the duration of the operations in which he is engaged at the time. The right of neutral aircraft to circulate in the airspace over the high seas is emphasized by the provisions of Article 11, which provides that "outside the jurisdiction of any State, belligerent or neutral, all aircraft shall have full freedom of passage through the air and of alighting."

Article 30 is confined in terms to neutral aircraft, because enemy aircraft are in any event exposed to the risk of capture, and in the vicinity of military operations are subjected to more drastic treatment than that provided by this article.

It will be noticed that the terms of the article are general in character and would comprise even neutral public or military aircraft. It goes without saying that the article is not intended to imply any encroachment on the rights of neutral States. It is assumed that no neutral public or military aircraft would depart so widely from the practice of States as to attempt to interfere with or intrude upon the operations of a belligerent State.

### Article 30

*In case a belligerent commanding officer considers that the presence of aircraft is likely to prejudice the success of the operations in which he is engaged at the moment, he may prohibit the passing of neutral aircraft in the immediate vicinity of his forces or may oblige them to follow a particular route. A neutral aircraft which does not conform to such directions, of which it has had notice issued by the belligerent commanding officer, may be fired upon.*

The power to requisition aircraft in occupied enemy territory is recognized in Article 53 of the Land Warfare Regulations. The text of Article 53 is not specific as to whether it includes neutral property, and though in practice it is regarded as doing so, it has been thought well to adopt a special rule in harmony with Article 53. It is not unreasonable that neutral owners of property should receive payment for their property at once, as they are not concerned with the peace which will be ultimately concluded.

### Article 31

*In accordance with the principles of Article 53 of the Land Warfare Regulations, neutral private aircraft found upon entry in the enemy's jurisdiction by a belligerent occupying force may be requisitioned, subject to the payment of full compensation.*

Property of the enemy State, which may be used for operations of war, is always liable to confiscation if it falls into the hands of the opposing belligerent. It is natural, therefore, that public aircraft of the enemy should be so treated.

Article 17 will create an exception in favour of flying ambulances as they will be protected by Article 6 of the Geneva Convention, but this exception will be subject to the principle laid down in Article 7 of the same Convention that the protection accorded to mobile medical units ceases if they are made use of to commit acts harmful to the enemy.

### Article 32

*Enemy public aircraft, other than those treated on the same footing as private aircraft, shall be subject to confiscation without prize proceedings.*

Non-military aircraft of belligerent nationality, whether public or private, should not in general be exposed to the risk of instant destruction, but should be given the opportunity to land. If they are flying in the jurisdiction of their own State and enemy military aircraft approach, they should, for their own protection, make the nearest available landing. Failure to do so exposes them to the risk of being fired upon.

### Article 33

*Belligerent non-military aircraft, whether public or private, flying within the jurisdiction of their own State, are liable to be fired upon unless they make the nearest available landing on the approach of enemy military aircraft.*

The preceding article has dealt with the case of belligerent non-military aircraft flying in the jurisdiction of their own State. Article 34 deals with the same category of aircraft in certain other circumstances. If such aircraft are in the immediate vicinity of the territory of the enemy State, or in the immediate vicinity of its military operations by land or sea, they run the risk of being fired upon. They are, of course, liable to capture by reason of their enemy status, but in an area where it is probable that military operations will be in progress, or in any place where they are actually in progress, non-combatant aircraft of belligerent nationality can only proceed at their own risk. By their mere presence they expose themselves to the risk of being fired upon.

### Article 34

*Belligerent non-military aircraft, whether public or private, are liable to be fired upon, if they fly (1) within the jurisdiction of the enemy, or (2) in the immediate vicinity thereof and outside the jurisdiction of their own State, or (3) in the immediate vicinity of the military operations of the enemy by land or sea.*

The principle has already been recognized in Article 30 that a belligerent commanding officer may warn off neutral aircraft from the immediate vicinity of his military operations. If they fail to comply with such a warning, they run the risk of being fired upon. Article 35 deals with neutral aircraft which may be flying within the jurisdiction of a belligerent country at a moment when military aircraft of the opposing belligerent approach. If warned of the approach of such military aircraft, it is their duty to make a landing; otherwise they might hamper the movements of the combatants and expose themselves to the risk of being fired upon. They are not, however, exposed to the risk of capture and condemnation as are neutral aircraft failing to comply with directions issued by a belligerent commander under Article 30.

### Article 35

*Neutral aircraft flying within the jurisdiction of a belligerent, and warned of the approach of military aircraft of the opposing belligerent, must make the nearest available landing. Failure to do so exposes them to the risk of being fired upon.*

Article 36 regulates the position of members of the crew and of passengers of an enemy aircraft which falls into the hands of a belligerent.

If the aircraft is a military aircraft, the crew will consist of members of the military forces and will of course be made prisoners of war. Any passengers will share the same fate, because in time of war a belligerent State would not be using its military aircraft for carrying non-combatant individuals unless their journey was a matter of importance to the State. Combatant passengers would naturally be made prisoners of war.

In the case of public non-military aircraft, the same principle applies. It is true that the members of the crew may not be members of the military forces, but they constitute part of the State organization. As to passengers, they would not be carried on such aircraft, except for government purposes. There is, however, one important exception. A state-owned passenger-carrying aircraft line is not by any means an unlikely development and, if such should be instituted, there would be no reason to apply this principle to all the passengers on such aircraft. They should only be made prisoners of war if in the service of the enemy, or enemy nationals fit for military service.

As regards private aircraft, it must be remembered that the crew will consist of trained men, constituting a reserve upon

which the belligerent can draw in case of need. If they are of
enemy nationality, or in the service of the enemy, there is good
reason to hold them as prisoners of war. If they are neutrals
not in the service of the enemy, they are by their service on
board an enemy aircraft releasing other men for military purposes. If they are to be given their release, the belligerent
should be entitled to protect himself in the future against such
indirect assistance by exacting an undertaking from each individual against his serving in an enemy aircraft during the
remainder of the war. Such an undertaking corresponds to that
provided for in the second paragraph of Article 5 of the Convention concerning restrictions on the right of capture in
maritime war (No. XI of 1907). It was adopted there only for
the officers of a merchant vessel, because the officers are the
highly trained men. In the case of aircraft, it is reasonable to
extend it to all the members of the crew.

What is said in the report on Article 37 dealing with the
crew and passengers of neutral private aircraft as to temporary delay in effecting the release in certain cases and as to
members of the crew or passengers who have rendered special
services to the belligerent being made prisoners of war, applies
also in the case of the crew and passengers of an enemy aircraft.

## Article 36

*When an enemy military aircraft falls into the hands of a
belligerent, the members of the crew and the passengers, if
any, may be made prisoners of war.*

*The same rule applies to the members of the crew and the
passengers, if any, of an enemy public non-military aircraft,
except that in the case of public non-military aircraft devoted
exclusively to the transport of passengers, the passengers will
be entitled to be released unless they are in the service of the
enemy, or are enemy nationals fit for military service.*

*If an enemy private aircraft falls into the hands of a bellig-
erent, members of the crew who are enemy nationals or who
are neutral nationals in the service of the enemy, may be made
prisoners of war. Neutral members of the crew, who are not
in the service of the enemy, are entitled to be released if they
sign a written undertaking not to serve in any enemy aircraft
while hostilities last. Passengers are entitled to be released
unless they are in the service of the enemy or are enemy nationals fit for military service, in which cases they may be made
prisoners of war.*

*Release may in any case be delayed if the military interests of the belligerent so require.*

*The belligerent may hold as prisoners of war any member of the crew or any passenger whose service in a flight at the close of which he has been captured has been of special and active assistance to the enemy.*

*The names of individuals released after giving a written undertaking in accordance with the third paragraph of this article will be notified to the opposing belligerent, who must not knowingly employ them in violation of their undertaking.*

When circumstances have arisen which have led to the detention of a neutral private aircraft by a belligerent, the question will arise of the treatment to be meted out to the crew and to the passengers, if any, of such aircraft. In general, the crew of an aircraft will be very expert individuals, whose services would be of great value to a belligerent. If they are of enemy nationality or in the service of the enemy, or engaged in a violation of neutrality, there is good reason for detaining them as prisoners of war. If not, they should be released unconditionally.

Passengers who are in the service of the enemy or who are enemy nationals fit for military service may likewise be detained.

Immediate release of persons who cannot be made prisoners of war may not in all cases be feasible. The fact that military exigencies may necessitate a temporary delay in according release does not prejudice the right to such release in due course.

The peculiar characteristics of aircraft may enable members of the crew or passengers in a neutral aircraft in time of war to render services of special importance to a belligerent. Where such services have been rendered in the course of the flight in which such persons were captured, the individuals may be made prisoners of war, whatever their nationality.

The rules adopted on this subject are in conformity with the practice of the recent war, but they have not secured unanimous assent. The Netherlands Delegation has felt unable to accept them for two reasons, viz., firstly, that they constitute an extension of the accepted rules of international law, and secondly, because of the absence of any provision to the effect that where the detention of the aircraft has taken place in circumstances which are subsequently made the subject of prize court proceedings, and the capture is held to be invalid, the crew and passengers of the aircraft should be released unconditionally.

### Article 37

*Members of the crew of a neutral aircraft which has been detained by a belligerent shall be released unconditionally, if they are neutral nationals and not in the service of the enemy. If they are enemy nationals or in the service of the enemy, they may be made prisoners of war.*

*Passengers are entitled to be released unless they are in the service of the enemy or are enemy nationals fit for military service, in which cases they may be made prisoners of war.*

*Release may in any case be delayed if the military interests of the belligerent so require.*

*The belligerent may hold as prisoners of war any member of the crew or any passenger whose service in a flight at the close of which he has been captured has been of special and active assistance to the enemy.*

The phrase "prisoner of war" in its narrower sense is applied to the combatant and non-combatant members of the armed forces of the belligerent (see Article 3 of the Land Warfare Regulations). It is used in Articles 36 and 37 in a broader sense and is applied to passengers or members of the crew of neutral and enemy aircraft who may not be members of the belligerent armed forces at all. To avoid any risk of doubt as to the treatment to which such persons are entitled, Article 38 lays down that their treatment shall not be less favourable than that to which members of the armed forces are entitled.

### Article 38

*Where under the provisions of Articles 36 and 37 it is provided that members of the crew or passengers may be made prisoners of war, it is to be understood that, if they are not members of the armed forces, they shall be entitled to treatment not less favourable than that accorded to prisoners of war.*

### CHAPTER VI

### BELLIGERENT DUTIES TOWARDS NEUTRAL STATES AND NEUTRAL DUTIES TOWARDS BELLIGERENT STATES

To avoid any suggestion that it is on the neutral government alone that the obligation is incumbent to secure respect for its neutrality, Article 39 provides that belligerent aircraft are under obligation to respect the rights of neutral Powers and to abstain from acts within neutral jurisdiction which it is the neutral's duty to prevent.

It will be noticed that the article is not limited to military aircraft; in fact the second phrase will apply only to belligerent aircraft of other categories, as it is they alone which may remain at liberty within neutral jurisdiction. All aircraft, however, including military, are bound to respect the rights of neutral Powers.

## Article 39

*Belligerent aircraft are bound to respect the rights of neutral Powers and to abstain within the jurisdiction of a neutral State from the commission of any act which it is the duty of that State to prevent.*

The principle that belligerent military aircraft should not be allowed to enter or circulate in neutral jurisdiction met with ready acceptance. It is in conformity with the rule adopted by the European States during the recent war.

The immunities and privileges which Article 17 confers on flying ambulances will enable the neutral State to admit them to its jurisdiction, if it sees fit.

## Article 40

*Belligerent military aircraft are forbidden to enter the jurisdiction of a neutral State.*

The customary rules of international law authorize the admission of belligerent warships to neutral ports and waters. There is no obligation upon neutral States to admit warships belonging to belligerent States, but it is not in general refused. The admission of belligerent military aircraft, however, is prohibited by Article 40, and account must therefore be taken of the fact that it has now become the practice for warships to have a certain number of aircraft assigned to them and that these aircraft usually rest on board the warship. While they remain on board the warship they form part of it, and should be regarded as such from the point of view of the regulations issued by the neutral States. They will therefore be allowed to enter the neutral jurisdiction on the same footing as the warship on board which they rest, but they must remain on board the warship and must not commit any act which the warship is not allowed to commit.

## Article 41

*Aircraft on board vessels of war, including aircraft-carriers, shall be regarded as part of such vessels.*

The principle is well established in land warfare that combatant forces of a belligerent must not penetrate within neutral jurisdiction. If they do, they are beyond the reach of their enemy: they have entered what is to them an asylum, and consequently, if after their visit to neutral territory they were allowed to re-enter hostilities, they would be making use of neutral territory to the detriment of their adversary.

From this principle arises a duty, which is incumbent on all neutral States, to do what they can to prevent combatant forces from entering their jurisdiction, and to intern those which do. These principles are recognized and adopted for aerial warfare by Article 42. The obligation to intern covers also aircraft which were within the neutral jurisdiction at the outbreak of hostilities.

Where aircraft and their personnel are in distress and seek shelter in neutral territory, knowing that their fate will be internment, or where the entry is due to the fact that the aircraft has lost its bearings or experienced engine trouble or run out of fuel, the neutral State is under no obligation to exclude them; it is in fact morally bound to admit them. This is due to the principle that those who are in distress must be succored. The prohibition in the article is aimed at those who enter in violation of the rights of the neutral State.

The prohibition on entry into neutral jurisdiction leads naturally to the further obligation incumbent upon neutral States to enforce compliance with the rule. It is beyond the power of any neutral State to ensure that no belligerent military aircraft will ever violate its neutrality; its obligation is limited to the employment of the means at its disposal, conforming in this respect to the phraseology employed in the Convention dealing with the Rights and Duties of Neutral Powers in Maritime War (No. XIII of 1907).

The provision in the article is limited to military aircraft because it is only in respect of such craft that the prohibition on entry is absolute. Under Article 12 the admission of private or public non-military aircraft is within the discretion of the neutral State. Where such aircraft penetrate within neutral jurisdiction in violation of the measures prescribed by the neutral Power, they will be subject to such penalties as the neutral Power may enact; these may or may not include internment. Recognition of this fact has enabled the Commission to omit a provision which figured as Article 11 in the American draft:

"A neutral government may intern any aircraft of belligerent nationality not conforming to its regulations."

The obligation on the part of the neutral Power to intern covers not only the aircraft, but its equipment and contents. The obligation is not affected by the circumstance which led to the military aircraft coming within the jurisdiction. It applies whether the belligerent aircraft entered neutral jurisdiction, voluntarily or involuntarily, and whatever the cause. It is an obligation owed to the opposing belligerent and is based upon the fact that the aircraft has come into an area where it is not subject to attack by its opponent.

The only exceptions to the obligation to intern an aircraft are those arising under Articles 17 and 41. The first relates to flying ambulances. Under the second, an aircraft on board a warship is deemed to be part of her, and therefore will follow the fate of that warship if she enters neutral ports or waters. If she enters under circumstances which render her immune from internment, such aircraft will likewise escape internment.

The obligation to intern belligerent military aircraft entering neutral jurisdiction entails also the obligation to intern the personnel. These will in general be combatant members of the belligerent fighting forces, but experience has already shown that in time of war military aeroplanes are employed for transporting passengers. As it may safely be assumed that in time of war a passenger would not be carried on a belligerent military aircraft unless his journey was a matter of importance to the government, it seems reasonable also to comprise such passengers in the category of persons to be interned.

## Article 42

*A neutral government must use the means at its disposal to prevent the entry within its jurisdiction of belligerent military aircraft and to compel them to alight if they have entered such jurisdiction.*

*A neutral government shall use the means at its disposal to intern any belligerent military aircraft which is within its jurisdiction after having alighted for any reason whatsoever, together with its crew and the passengers, if any.*

Under Article 15 of the Convention for the adaptation of the principles of the Geneva Convention to Maritime War (No. X of 1907), the shipwrecked, wounded or sick members of the crew of a belligerent warship, who are brought into a neutral port, must be interned. The same rule is applied by Article 43 to the personnel of a disabled belligerent military aircraft, when the men are brought in on board a military aircraft. It goes without saying that such individuals could not be brought in and landed at a neutral port without the consent of the neutral authorities.

## Article 43

*The personnel of a disabled belligerent military aircraft rescued outside neutral waters and brought into the jurisdiction of a neutral State by a neutral military aircraft and there landed shall be interned.*

The principle is well established in international law that in time of war a government, which remains neutral, must not itself supply to a belligerent government arms or war material. For aerial warfare effect is given to this principle by the following article:

## Article 44

*The supply in any manner, directly or indirectly, by a neutral government to a belligerent Power of aircraft, parts of aircraft, or material, supplies or munitions required for aircraft is forbidden.*

No obligation rests on a neutral State to prevent the purchase by a belligerent government of articles of contraband from persons within the neutral jurisdiction. The purchase of contraband under such conditions constitutes a commercial transaction which the neutral government is under no obligation to prevent, although the opposing belligerent may take such means as international law authorizes to intercept the delivery of the articles to his enemy. This principle has already been embodied in Article 7 of the Convention concerning the rights and duties of neutral Powers in land war (Convention V of 1907) and in Article 7 of the corresponding convention for maritime war (Convention XIII of 1907). To apply it to aerial warfare, the following article has been adopted:

## Article 45

*Subject to the provisions of Article 46, a neutral Power is not bound to prevent the export or transit on behalf of a belligerent of aircraft, parts of aircraft, or material, supplies or munitions for aircraft.*

An exception to the principle that a neutral State is under no obligation to prevent the export of arms and war material, is found in the accepted rule of international law that neutral territory must not be utilized as a base of operations by a belligerent government, and that the neutral State must therefore prevent the fitting out or departure from its jurisdiction of any hostile expedition intended to operate on behalf of one belligerent against the other. Such an expedition might consist of a single aeroplane, if manned and equipped in a manner which would enable it to take part in hostilities, or carrying or accompanied by the necessary elements of such equipment. Consequently, its departure under circumstances which would constitute the despatch of a hostile expedition, must be prevented by the neutral government.

It is easy to see that it is aircraft which have flown out of the neutral jurisdiction, which are most likely to engage in hostilities in some form before delivery to the belligerent purchaser in the belligerent State, and it is in these cases that the neutral government must take special precautions. All risk will be avoided if the aircraft, despatched to the order of a belligerent Power, does not come within the neighborhood of the operations of the opposing belligerent. The neutral State should therefore prescribe the route which the aircraft is to follow. This alone, however, will not be sufficient. The aircraft might ignore the instructions it receives. Guarantees for compliance must therefore be exacted. It will be for the neutral State to determine the guarantees which it thinks necessary, but they must be effective guarantees, such, for instance, as insisting on the aircraft carrying a representative of the government to see that the route indicated is followed.

To meet these requirements, the following article has been adopted:

## Article 46

*A neutral government is bound to use the means at its disposal:*

*(1) to prevent the departure from its jurisdiction of an aircraft in a condition to make a hostile attack against a belligerent Power, or carrying or accompanied by appliances or materials the mounting or utilization of which would enable it to make a hostile attack, if there is reason to believe that such aircraft is destined for use against a belligerent Power;*

*(2) to prevent the departure of an aircraft the crew of which includes any member of the combatant forces of a belligerent Power;*

*(3) to prevent work upon an aircraft designed to prepare it to depart in contravention of the purposes of this article.*

*On the departure by air of any aircraft despatched by persons or companies in neutral jurisdiction to the order of a belligerent Power, the neutral government must prescribe for such aircraft a route avoiding the neighborhood of the military operations of the opposing belligerent, and must exact whatever guarantees may be required to ensure that the aircraft follows the route prescribed.*

The height to which aircraft can ascend would enable them to be used for observation purposes from a spot within neutral jurisdiction, i.e., within the airspace above neutral territory or territorial waters, if hostilities were in progress close to the frontier between two States. Such proceedings might be extremely harmful to belligerent interests, and if the observations were made on behalf of one of the belligerents and for the purpose of supplying him with information, would amount to an improper use of neutral territory. To meet this contingency, the following provision has been adopted:

### Article 47

*A neutral State is bound to take such steps as the means at its disposal permit to prevent within its jurisdiction aerial observation of the movements, operations or defences of one belligerent, with the intention of informing the other belligerent.*

The prohibition of aerial observation within neutral territory on belligerent account must apply equally to the case of aircraft on board belligerent warships when in neutral waters. To avoid all misconception on this point, the following paragraph has been added:

*This provision applies equally to a belligerent military aircraft on board a vessel of war.*

The measures which a neutral government may be obliged to take to compel respect for its rights may entail the use of force; fire may have to be opened on foreign aircraft, even military aircraft of another State. Following the analogy of Article 10 of Convention V of 1907 (Rights and Duties of Neutral Powers in Land War) and Article 26 of Convention XIII (Rights and Duties of Neutral Powers in Maritime War), it has been thought well to declare that the measures, even of force, taken by a neutral Power for this purpose cannot be regarded as acts of war. Still less could they be regarded as unfriendly acts, seeing that they are taken in specific exercise of rights conferred or recognized by treaty.

It may be well to add that the neutral government will not be responsible for any injury or damage done to the aircraft or other object.

### Article 48

*The action of a neutral Power in using force or other means at its disposal in the exercise of its rights or duties under these rules cannot be regarded as a hostile act.*

## CHAPTER VII

### VISIT AND SEARCH, CAPTURE AND CONDEMNATION

Both the American and British drafts when first submitted to the Commission provided for the use of aircraft in exercising against enemy commerce the belligerent rights which international law has sanctioned. This principle has not met with unanimous acceptance; the Netherlands Delegation has not felt able to accept it. The standpoint adopted by this Delegation is that the custom and practice of international law is limited to a right on the part of belligerent warships to capture after certain formalities merchant vessels employed in the carriage of such commerce. No justification exists for the extension of those rights to an aircraft, which is a new engine of war entirely different in character from a warship and unable to exercise over merchant vessels or private aircraft a control similar to that exercised by a warship over merchant vessels. Consequently there is no reason to confer on a military aircraft the right to make captures as if it were a warship, and no reason to subject commerce to capture when carried in an aircraft. In developing international law the tendency should be in the direction of conferring greater, not less, immunity on private property.

For these reasons the Netherlands Delegation has not accepted the rules contained in Chapter VII and its participation in the discussion of individual rules has been subject to the general reserves made with regard to the whole chapter.

The majority of the delegations have not felt able to reject the principle that the aircraft should be allowed to exercise the belligerent right of visit and search, followed by capture where necessary, for the repression of enemy commerce carried in an aircraft in cases where such action is permissible. This principle is embodied in Article 49, of which the text is as follows:

### Article 49

*Private aircraft are liable to visit and search and to capture by belligerent military aircraft.*

No article on the subject of the exercise by belligerent military aircraft of the right of visit and search of merchant vessels has secured the votes of a majority of the delegations, and therefore no article on the subject is included in the code of rules. Nevertheless all the delegations are impressed with the necessity of surrounding with proper safeguards the use of aircraft against merchant vessels. Otherwise excesses analogous to those which took place during the recent war might be reproduced in future wars.

The reason why no agreed text has been adopted by the Commission is due to divergence of view as to what action an aircraft should be permitted to take against a merchant vessel.

The aircraft in use today are light and fragile things. Except in favourable circumstances they would not be able to alight on the water and send a man on board a merchant vessel at the spot where the merchant vessel is first encountered *(visite sur place)*. To make the right of visit and search by an aircraft effective it would usually be necessary to direct the merchant vessel to come to some convenient locality where the aircraft can alight and send men on board for the purpose. This would imply a right on the part of the belligerent military aircraft to compel the merchant vessel to deviate from her course before it was in possession of any proofs derived from an examination of the ship herself and her papers that there were circumstances of suspicion which justified such interference with neutral trade. If the deviation which the merchant vessel was obliged to make was prolonged, as might be the case if the aircraft was operating far from land, the losses and inconvenience imposed on neutral shipping would be very heavy.

Is or is not a warship entitled to oblige a merchant vessel to deviate from her course for the purpose of enabling the right of visit and search to be carried out? Would an aircraft be exercising its rights in conformity with the rules to which surface warships are subject if it obliged a merchant vessel to deviate from her course in this way? Even if a warship is entitled on occasion to oblige a merchant vessel to deviate from her course before visiting her, can a similar right be recognized for military aircraft without opening the door to very great abuses?

These are the questions upon which the views entertained by the delegations differed appreciably, and indicate the reasons why it was not found possible to devise any text on which all parties could agree.

The French Delegation declared that aircraft must conform to the rules to which surface warships are subject.

The French Delegation proposed the following text:

"Aircraft are forbidden to operate against merchant vessels, whether surface or submarine, without conforming to the rules to which surface warships are subject."

In view of the differences of opinion manifested in regard

to the above questions, the Delegation regarded this formula as the only one which was likely to receive the support of a majority of the Commission.

The American Delegation considered that a merchant vessel should be boarded when she is encountered, but maintained that, even if a departure from this rule might in exceptional circumstances be permitted in visit and search by surface ships, a similar concession to aircraft, with their limited means of boarding, would readily have the effect of converting the exception into the rule. They stated that they were not advised of anything in the record of the Washington Conference showing an intention to authorize surface ships or submarines to divert merchant vessels, without boarding them, to a port for examination; but that, were the case otherwise, the Washington Conference had decided that the subject of aircraft, which presented difficulties of its own and which might involve questions different from those pertaining even to submarines, should be dealt with separately; and that to permit aircraft, with their rapidity and range of flight, to control and direct by orders enforceable by bombing, and without visit and search, the movement of merchant vessels on the high seas would, in their opinion, give rise to an inadmissible situation.

The American Delegation, therefore, proposed the following text:

Aircraft are forbidden to visit and search surface or subsurface vessels without conforming in all respects to the rules to which surface vessels authorized to conduct visit and search are subject.

In view of the irregularities to which the use of aircraft against merchant vessels might give rise, it is declared that aircraft cannot divert a merchant vessel from its course without first boarding it; that in no event may an aircraft destroy a merchant vessel unless the crew and passengers of such vessel have first been placed in safety; and that if an aircraft cannot capture a merchant vessel in conformity with these rules it must desist from attack and from seizure and permit such vessel to proceed unmolested.

The British Delegation maintained that the problem connected with visit and search of merchant vessels by aircraft was analogous to that of the exercise of such rights by submarines, and that the most satisfactory solution of the problem would be to apply *mutatis mutandis* the wording of Article 1 of the Treaty signed at Washington on February 6, 1922, for the protection of the lives of neutrals and non-combatants at sea in time of war.

This Delegation maintained that by using the language of that treaty as proposed, the question of the right to oblige a merchant vessel to deviate to a reasonable extent would be solved because the wording adopted at Washington had been modified so as to admit this right. The British Delegates proposed the following text:

The use of aircraft against merchant vessels must be regulated by the following provisions, which, being in conformity with the rules adopted by civilized nations for the protection of the lives of neutrals and non-combatants at sea in time of war, are to be deemed an established part of international law:

A merchant vessel must be ordered to submit to visit and search to determine its character before it can be seized.

A merchant vessel must not be attacked unless it refuses to submit to visit and search after warning or to proceed as directed after seizure.

A merchant vessel must not be destroyed unless the crew and passengers have first been placed in safety.

Belligerent aircraft are not under any circumstances exempt from the universal rules above stated; and if an aircraft cannot capture a merchant vessel in conformity with these rules, the existing law of nations requires it to desist from attack and from seizure and to permit the merchant vessel to proceed unmolested.

The Japanese view was based on the practical difficulty in the way of exercise of the right of visit and search by aircraft. Visit and search is a necessary preliminary to capture, and unless an aircraft is physically capable of carrying it out, the recognition of the right of military aircraft to conduct operations against merchant vessels may lead to a recurrence of the excesses practiced against enemy and neutral merchant vessels in the submarine campaign initiated during the recent war. Therefore, the Japanese Delegation preferred not to recognize the right at all. But, in the end, as the amended American text[22] removed the greater part of their fear of possible abuse, they expressed readiness to accept it, and suggested at the same time that the text had better be completed by the addition of the last sentence of the British text.

The Italian Delegation accepted the British point of view; it maintained that diversion of merchant vessels by surface warships was recognized and that the wording of the Washington Treaty should be repeated. To prevent any abusive exercise of the right by aircraft, the Italian Delegation proposed to add the following sentences to the paragraphs of the Washington Treaty as set out in the British text.

After the first paragraph add:

Visit must in general be carried out where the merchant vessel is first encountered. Nevertheless, in cases where it may be impossible to alight and there is at the same time good ground for suspicion,

22. See Minute 105 (Minutes of the Commission, p. 98).

the aircraft may order the merchant vessel to deviate to a suitable locality, reasonably accessible, where she may be visited. If no good cause for this action is shown, the belligerent State must pay compensation for the loss caused by the order to deviate.

After the third paragraph add:

If the merchant vessel is in the territorial waters of the enemy State and not on the high seas, she may be destroyed after previous notice has been given to the persons on board to put themselves in a place of safety and reasonable time has been given them for so doing.

The Italian Delegation also intimated that for the sake of arriving at an agreement, it would vote in favour of the French text given above. In accepting it, however, it declared:

(1) That in the existing practice of maritime war the majority of European Powers admitted that if visit on the spot where the merchant vessel was encountered was impossible, surface warships are entitled to oblige merchant vessels to deviate to a suitable spot where the visit can take place;

(2) That even if it is not desired to rest on the maritime practice indicated above, the Italian Delegation must maintain the right of belligerent aircraft to exercise the right of visit in accordance with the texts of the amendments proposed.

The Netherlands Delegation accepted the American proposal as the one which limited most narrowly the exercise of belligerent rights by aircraft.

When put to the vote the American proposal was supported by the Japanese and Netherlands Delegations and opposed by the British, French and Italian. The French proposal was opposed by the American, British, Japanese and Netherlands Delegations. The British and Italian Delegations explained that they could only support it if it was amplified in the way indicated in the British and Italian amendments.

Although all the Delegations concurred in the expression of a desire to adopt such rules as would assure the observance of the dictates of humanity as regards the protection of the lives of neutrals and non-combatants, the Commission, by reason of a divergence of views as to the method by which this result would best be attained, was unable to agree upon an article dealing with the exercise of belligerent rights by aircraft against merchant vessels.

The code of rules proposed by the Commission therefore leaves the matter open for future regulation.

While aircraft are in flight in the air, the operation of visit and search cannot be effected so long as aircraft retain their present form. Article 49 therefore necessitates the recognition of a right on the part of belligerent military aircraft to order non-military aircraft to alight in order that the right of visit and search may be exercised. They must not only be ordered to alight, but they must be allowed to proceed to a suitable locality for the purpose. It would be a hardship to the neutral if he was obliged to make a long journey for this purpose, and the locality must, therefore, not only be suitable, but must be reasonably accessible—that is, reasonably convenient of access. A more precise definition than this can scarcely be given; what is reasonably convenient of access is a question of fact to be determined in each case in the light of the special circumstances which may be present. If no place can be found which is reasonably convenient of access, the aircraft should be allowed to continue its flight.

As is the case with merchant vessels, a refusal to comply with such belligerent directions will expose the aircraft to the use of force for the purpose of insisting on compliance. Just as the belligerent right has received universal acceptance in maritime war, so is the principle admitted that the neutral vessel is under a duty to submit to it and if in consequence of her failure to do so, she is damaged or sunk, she has no right to complain, seeing that she has failed to comply with an obligation imposed upon her by the law of nations. This principle does not, however, entitle a belligerent to apply force unnecessarily. His measures of coercion must be limited to what is reasonably required to secure the fulfilment of his object.

It is for this reason that a warship always fires a shot across the bows of a vessel before attempting to hit the vessel herself, and, even when obliged to fire at the vessel herself, must still take all measures within her power to rescue the crew and passengers. Recognition of a similar right on the part of aircraft to apply force must be conditioned by the obligation on the part of the aircraft not to apply force to a greater extent than is necessary. It would be so easy for the aircraft to take measures which might at once entail the destruction of the aircraft and the loss of life of everybody therein that it is essential to recognize the principle that force must only be employed to the extent which is reasonably necessary.

### Article 50

*Belligerent military aircraft have the right to order public non-military and private aircraft to alight in or proceed for visit and search to a suitable locality reasonably accessible.*

*Refusal, after warning, to obey such orders to alight or to proceed to such a locality for examination exposes an aircraft to the risk of being fired upon.*

The next article deals with the position of a neutral public non-military aircraft. The future of commercial aviation may involve the establishment of state-owned lines of aircraft for commercial purposes. The principle has already been recognized that such aircraft must be treated upon the same footing as private aircraft. Their subjection to the exercise of the right of visit and search and capture must, therefore, be assured. Where public non-military aircraft are not used for commercial purposes, the general rule must apply according to which a belligerent warship can only visit the public vessels of a friendly Power so far as may be necessary for the purpose of ascertaining their character, i.e., by the verification of their papers.

### Article 51

*Neutral public non-military aircraft, other than those which are to be treated as private aircraft, are subject only to visit for the purpose of the verification of their papers.*

Article 52 applies to aircraft in time of war the principle which already obtains in the case of merchant vessels, namely, that an enemy merchant vessel is liable to capture in all circumstances.

### Article 52

*Enemy private aircraft are liable to capture in all circumstances.*

The next article deals with the grounds upon which a neutral private aircraft may be captured.

(a) The first is where it resists the legitimate exercise of belligerent rights. This is in harmony with Article 63 of the Declaration of London. As first submitted to the Commission, the text included the words "or flees." On due consideration, however, these words were omitted. The reasons for this omission cannot be stated better than is done in the report on Article 63 of the Declaration of London, prepared by M. Renault:

If the vessel is stopped, and it is shown that it was only in order to escape the inconvenience of being searched that recourse was had to flight, and that beyond this she had done nothing contrary to neutrality, she will not be punished for her attempt at flight. If, on the other hand, it is established that the vessel has contraband on board, or that she has in some way or other failed to comply with her duty as a neutral, she will suffer the consequences of her infraction of neutrality, but in this case, as in the last, she will not undergo any punishment for her attempt at flight. Expression was given to the contrary view, namely, that a ship should be punished for an obvious attempt at flight as much as for forcible resistance. It was suggested that the prospect of having the escaping vessel condemned as good prize would influence the captain of the cruiser to do his best to spare her. But in the end this view did not prevail.

(b) The second ground for capture is that of the failure of a neutral aircraft to comply with directions given by a belligerent commanding officer enjoining the withdrawal of neutral aircraft from the immediate vicinity of his military operations. By the terms of Article 30, a neutral aircraft disregarding such a prohibition is exposed to the risk of being fired upon. It might well be thought that such risk would involve a sufficient deterrent without rendering non-compliance a ground of capture. The reason why capture has been added is due to the peculiar circumstances of warfare in the air. The right to oblige aircraft to avoid the scene of military operations would only be made use of in cases where it was a matter of importance to the belligerent to ensure their absence, and consequently where effective measures must be taken to secure compliance. If a neutral private aircraft is to be fired upon for this purpose, it is desirable to render it as little likely as possible that it shall be fired upon in a way that will involve its destruction. If the airman knows that the aircraft, when forced to alight, may be made the subject of capture, he is less tempted to secure observance of the rule by firing in a way which will involve the destruction of the aircraft.

(c) The third ground for capture is where the aircraft is engaged in unneutral service. This phrase "unneutral service" formed the subject of careful consideration in the Naval Conference of London in 1908 and 1909, at the time when the Declaration of London was framed. The meaning attached to the term by the Commission in the preparation of the present text is that used in Articles 45 and 46 of that Declaration, the intention being to render those articles applicable in the case of similar action on the part of aircraft. For instance, it will cover an act amounting to taking a direct part in hostilities, such as that mentioned in the second paragraph of Article 16. The Commission would also refer to that portion of the Report on the Declaration of London which deals with unneutral service (Articles 45 and 46) as they are in entire concurrence with it.

(d) The fourth ground for capture is that a neutral private aircraft is armed in violation of Article 16, which stipulates that outside its own jurisdiction a private aircraft must not be armed. The carriage of arms by a private aircraft under such circumstances gives rise to a well-founded suspicion of an intention to take part in hostilities in volation of the laws of war.

(*e*) The fifth ground for capture is that an aircraft has no marks or is bearing false marks in violation of Article 19.

(*f*) The sixth ground for capture is the absence or irregularity of the papers of the aircraft. This rule is in accordance with that which prevails in maritime warfare. The papers which must be carried are indicated with greater precision in Article 54.

(*g*) The seventh ground for capture is that of an aircraft being found manifestly out of the proper line of its flight as indicated by its papers and where no sufficient reason is found for its presence in that locality. The importance of this rule from the point of view of aerial warfare is due to the ease with which aircraft can be used for reconnaissance work, even though they may be masquerading as neutral aircraft engaged in innocent occupations. It may well be that in any particular case the aircraft will be able to establish the innocence of its presence. It may have been blown out of its course; it may have been compelled to make a deviation to secure supplies; it may even have intentionally deviated for the purpose of avoiding an area in which it considered that military operations were possible. It is, therefore, to the interest of both parties—the belligerent and the neutral—that ample opportunity for enquiry should be given to the belligerent before exercising his right of capture. It will only be where the results of such investigations show that there is good cause for suspicion that the aircraft was engaged in some improper operations that capture will be resorted to.

(*h*) The eighth ground for capture is where the neutral private aircraft carries, or itself constitutes, contraband of war. This sub-head is framed upon the basis that the term "contraband of war" will bear the same meaning as it has in maritime warfare.

(*i*) The ninth ground for capture is that the aircraft is engaged in a breach of blockade. "Blockade" is here used in the same sense in which it is employed in Chapter 1 of the Declaration of London, that is to say, an operation of war for the purpose of preventing by the use of warships ingress or egress of commerce to or from a defined portion of the enemy's coast. It has no reference to a blockade enforced without the use of warships, nor does it cover military investments of particular localities on land. These operations, which may be termed "aerial blockade," were the subject of special examination by the experts attached to the various Delegations who framed a special report on the subject for consideration by the Full Commission. The conditions contemplated in this sub-head are those of warships enforcing a blockade at sea with aircraft acting in cooperation with them. As the primary elements of the blockade will, therefore, be maritime, the recognized principles applicable to such blockade, as for instance that it must be effective (Declaration of Paris, Article 4), and that it must be duly notified and its precise limits fixed, will also apply. This is intended to be shown by the use of the words "breach of blockade duly established and effectively maintained" in the text of the sub-head.

It is too early yet to indicate with precision the extent to which the cooperation of aircraft in the maintenance of blockade at sea may be possible; experience alone can show. Nevertheless it is necessary to indicate the sense in which the Commission has used the word "effective." As pointed out in the Declaration of London, the effectiveness of a blockade is a question of fact. The word "effective" is intended to ensure that it must be maintained by a force sufficient really to prevent access to the enemy coast-line. The prize court may for instance have to consider what proportion of surface vessels can escape the watchfulness of the blockading squadrons without endangering the effectiveness of the blockade; this is a question which the prize court alone can determine. In the same way, this question may have to be considered where aircraft are cooperating in the maintenance of a blockade.

The invention of the aircraft cannot impose upon a belligerent who desires to institute a blockade the obligation to employ aircraft in cooperation with his naval forces. If he does not do so, the effectiveness of the blockade would not be affected by failure to stop aircraft passing through. It is only where the belligerent endeavours to render his blockade effective in the air space above the sea as well as on the surface itself that captures of aircraft will be made and that any question of the effectiveness of the blockade in the air could arise.

The facility with which an aircraft, desirous of entering the blockaded area, could evade the blockade by passing outside the geographical limits of the blockade, has not escaped the attention of the Commission. This practical question may affect the extent to which belligerents will resort to blockade in future, but it does not affect the fact that where a blockade has been established and an aircraft attempts to pass through into the blockaded area within the limits of the blockade, it should be liable to capture.

The Netherlands Delegation proposed to suppress (*i*) on the ground that air blockade could not be effectively maintained, basing its opinion on its interpretation of the experts' report on the subject.

The British, French, Italian and Japanese Delegations voted for its maintenance. The American Delegation voted for its maintenance *ad referendum.*

(*k*) The tenth ground for capture is that the private aircraft has been transferred from belligerent to neutral nationality with a view to escaping the disadvantages which enemy status confers upon aircraft. This sub-head has been inserted in order that so far as possible the rules applicable to maritime warfare should apply to warfare in the air.

The sub-head as adopted does not embody the detailed provisions of the Declaration of London (Articles 55 and 56) because those articles constituted a compromise between two competing principles and have not stood the test of experience.

The sub-heads enumerated above comprise those which the Commission has considered sufficient to justify capture. Experience may show that other cases will arise in which capture may be necessary, as great development may yet occur in the science of aviation.

The article concludes with a proviso that the act which constitutes the ground of capture must have occurred in the course of the flight in which the neutral aircraft came into belligerent hands. This proviso would not, of course, apply to the case of transfer from belligerent to neutral nationality.

Account must also be taken of the special case provided for in Article 6 of the rules for the control of radio in time of war under which merchant vessels or aircraft transmitting intelligence may in certain circumstances be liable to capture for a period of one year from the commission of the act complained of.

## Article 53

A neutral private aircraft is liable to capture if it:
(a) resists the legitimate exercise of belligerent rights;
(b) violates a prohibition of which it has had notice issued by a belligerent commanding officer under Article 30;
(c) is engaged in unneutral service;
(d) is armed in time of war when outside the jurisdiction of its own country;
(e) has no external marks or uses false marks;
(f) has no papers or insufficient or irregular papers;
(g) is manifestly out of the line between the point of departure and the point of destination indicated in its

*papers and, after such enquiries as the belligerent may deem necessary, no good cause is shown for the deviation. The aircraft, together with its crew and passengers, if any, may be detained by the belligerent, pending such enquiries;*

(h)  *carries, or itself constitutes, contraband of war;*

(i)  *is engaged in breach of a blockade duly established and effectively maintained;*

(k)  *has been transferred from belligerent to neutral nationality at a date and in circumstances indicating an intention of evading the consequences to which an enemy aircraft, as such, is exposed.*

*Provided that in each case, except (k), the ground for capture shall be an act carried out in the flight in which the neutral aircraft came into belligerent hands, i.e., since it left its point of departure and before it reached its point of destination.*

By custom and tradition practical uniformity has arisen as to the papers which a merchant vessel is expected to carry. There is no serious divergence between the legislation now in force in civilized countries. No practical inconvenience, therefore, arises in the application of the established rule of maritime war, that a vessel is liable to capture if it has no papers or if the papers are irregular. Similar uniformity would no doubt in time arise in connection with aircraft, particularly if the Air Navigation Convention of 1919 becomes universal. It has, however, been thought prudent to indicate in a special article the facts which the papers found on board an aircraft must indicate if its papers are to be held sufficient. Under Article 6 the papers to be borne by an aircraft are those prescribed by the laws of its own State. The forms, names and number of such papers are therefore a matter to be determined by each State except so far as it may already be bound by treaty stipulations. Article 54 prescribes the points that must be established by such papers, that is to say, it ensures that the papers shall give the belligerent information on the points which it is important for him to know. They must show the nationality of the aircraft, the names and nationality of the crew and the passengers, the points of departure and destination of the flight, particulars of the cargo, and must include the necessary logs. The legislation in force in each State must be sufficient to satisfy this rule if it desires that its aircraft shall escape trouble in time of war. It is not thought that this article will involve any inconvenience, as legislation which would not prescribe at least as much as the above on the subject of aircraft is unlikely to be enacted by any State.

## Article 54

*The papers of a private aircraft will be regarded as insuffi-
cient or irregular if they do not establish the nationality of the
aircraft and indicate the names and nationality of the crew and
passengers, the points of departure and destination of the
flight, together with particulars of the cargo and the conditions
under which it is transported. The logs must also be included.*

The practice has now become universal for belligerent States
to institute a prize court in which proceedings will take place
for adjudicating on all cases of capture of ships or goods effected in maritime war. It is in the interest of neutrals that this
system has been developed. If aircraft are to be allowed to
exercise the belligerent right of capture, it is only proper that
the same protection should be accorded to neutrals as in the
case of captures effected by warships.

This view has readily obtained unanimous assent, and is
embodied in Article 55.

## Article 55

*Capture of an aircraft or of goods on board an aircraft shall
be made the subject of prize proceedings, in order that any
neutral claim may be duly heard and determined.*

The provisions of Articles 52 and 53 deal only with the
grounds for capture. They do not prescribe the rule which is
to be applied by the prize court. Reflection has led the Commission to the view that, save in certain exceptional cases
where aircraft will have been captured for reasons peculiar to
aerial warfare, the decisions of the prize courts in adjudicating on captures effected by aircraft, should proceed on the same
principles as those which obtain in captures by warships. If
the jurisdiction of the prize courts is to apply in aerial warfare
as well as in maritime warfare, it is convenient that the rules
applied should be the same in both cases. It would be impossible
to frame an exact code, at the present stage, of the rules which
prize courts apply, nor indeed would it be within the competence of this Commission to do so as far as concerns maritime
warfare. It would certainly lead to divergence between rules
applied in the case of aerial captures and those applied in the
case of maritime captures. The simplest solution has therefore
been found in the adoption of the principle that the prize
court should apply the same rules in both cases.

The special cases which have to be provided for are those
where an aircraft has no marks or has used false marks, or
has been found armed in time of war outside the jurisdiction
of its own country, and also in the case where a neutral air-

craft has violated the rule that it must not infringe the directions of the belligerent commanding officer to keep away from the immediate vicinity of his military operations. In these cases it is agreed that the aircraft should be liable to condemnation.

### Article 56

*A private aircraft captured upon the ground that it has no external marks or is using false marks, or that it is armed in time of war outside the jurisdiction of its own country, is liable to condemnation.*

*A neutral private aircraft captured upon the ground that it has disregarded the direction of a belligerent commanding officer under Article 30 is liable to condemnation, unless it can justify its presence within the prohibited zone.*

*In all other cases, the prize court in adjudicating upon any case of capture of an aircraft or its cargo, or of postal correspondence on board an aircraft, shall apply the same rules as would be applied to a merchant vessel or its cargo or to postal correspondence on board a merchant vessel.*

The destruction of neutral merchant vessels first came into prominence as a belligerent practice at the time of the Russo-Japanese War. It was not without difficulty that an agreement was reached between the Powers as to the extent to which the practice should be recognized in maritime war. In the case of enemy vessels, the practice has always been recognized as legitimate, subject to the overriding principle that the persons on board must be placed in safety and the papers of the vessel must be secured. This principle has been adapted to aerial warfare by Article 57, of which the text is as follows:

### Article 57

*Private aircraft which are found upon visit and search to be enemy aircraft may be destroyed if the belligerent commanding officer finds it necessary to do so, provided that all persons on board have first been placed in safety and all the papers of the aircraft have been preserved.*

The articles dealing with the destruction of neutral aircraft are largely based upon the provisions of the Declaration of London, but the language used is of a more restrictive character, so as to reduce the possibilities of an abuse of the practice, as happened in the late war. Destruction is limited to cases where an aircraft is captured in circumstances which show that it would be liable to condemnation on the ground of unneutral service, or on the ground that it has no marks or bears false marks. Apart from these cases, destruction can only be

justified by the existence of grave military emergencies which
would not justify the officer in command in releasing the aircraft. In all cases, destruction must be justified by the circumstance that sending the aircraft in for adjudication would be
impossible, or would imperil the safety of the belligerent aircraft or the success of the operations in which it is engaged.

## Article 58

*Private aircraft which are found upon visit and search to be
neutral aircraft liable to condemnation upon the ground of unneutral service, or upon the ground that they have no external
marks or are bearing false marks, may be destroyed, if sending them in for adjudication would be impossible or would
imperil the safety of the belligerent aircraft or the success of
the operations in which it is engaged. Apart from the cases
mentioned above, a neutral private aircraft must not be destroyed except in the gravest military emergency, which would
not justify the officer in command in releasing it or sending it
in for adjudication.*

The safeguards designed to ensure full protection for neutral
interests in the case of any such destruction are embodied in
Article 59. The persons on board must be placed in safety. The
papers must be secured in order that they may be available in
the forthcoming prize court proceedings. The captor must then
bring the case before the prize court and must establish, firstly,
the need for destruction, and secondly, when that is established,
the validity of the capture. Failure to establish the first point
will expose him to the risk of paying compensation to all the
parties interested in the aircraft and its cargo. Failure to establish the second will place him in the same position in which
he would be if the aircraft had not been destroyed, and he had
been ordered to make restitution of the aircraft or cargo improperly captured.

## Article 59

*Before a neutral private aircraft is destroyed, all persons
on board must be placed in safety, and all the papers of the aircraft must be preserved.*

*A captor who has destroyed a neutral private aircraft must
bring the capture before the prize court, and must first establish that he was justified in destroying it under Article 58. If
he fails to do this, parties interested in the aircraft or its cargo
are entitled to compensation. If the capture is held to be invalid,
though the act of destruction is held to have been justifiable,*

*compensation must be paid to the parties interested in place of the restitution to which they would have been entitled.*

The special case of the destruction of contraband on board an aircraft, apart from the destruction of the aircraft itself, is dealt with in Article 60, which proceeds on lines similar to Article 54 of the Declaration of London. After the contraband has been destroyed, the aircraft will be allowed to continue its flight. Similar provision is made for the protection of neutral interests as under the preceding articles.

The article as adopted is limited to absolute contraband, but three Delegations considered that the word "absolute" should be deleted, and that the article should extend to all forms of contraband, as in Article 54 of the Declaration of London.

### Article 60

*Where a neutral private aircraft is captured on the ground that it is carrying contraband, the captor may demand the surrender of any absolute contraband on board, or may proceed to the destruction of such absolute contraband, if sending in the aircraft for adjudication is impossible or would imperil the safety of the belligerent aircraft or the success of the operations in which it is engaged. After entering in the log book of the aircraft the delivery or destruction of the goods, and securing, in original or copy, the relevant papers of the aircraft, the captor must allow the neutral aircraft to continue its flight.*

*The provisions of the second paragraph of Article 59 will apply where absolute contraband on board a neutral private aircraft is handed over or destroyed.*

### Chapter VIII

#### DEFINITIONS

In some countries, the word "military" is not generally employed in a sense which includes "naval." To remove any ambiguity on this point a special article has been adopted.

### Article 61

*The term "military" throughout these rules is to be read as referring to all branches of the forces, i.e., the land forces, the naval forces and the air forces.*

Article 62 is intended to remove all risk of doubt as to whether aircraft personnel should, in matters not covered by these rules or by conventions as to the application of which there can be no doubt, be governed by the Land Warfare Regulations or by the unwritten rules governing maritime war. The rules to be applied are those contained in the Land Warfare Regulations. Regard must be had to the last paragraphs of the Convention to which the Land Warfare Regulations are attached, that cases not provided for are not intended, for want of a written prohibition, to be left to the arbitrary judgment of military commanders. In all such cases the population and belligerents are to remain under the protection of the rule of the principles of the law of nations, as they result from the usages established between civilized nations, from the laws of humanity and the requirements of the public conscience.

The French Delegation expressed the opinion that the terms of Article 62 were hardly adequate to cover a subject so complex.

## Article 62

*Except so far as special rules are here laid down and except also so far as the provisions of Chapter VII of these Rules or international conventions indicate that maritime law and procedure are applicable, aircraft personnel engaged in hostilities come under the laws of war and neutrality applicable to land troops in virtue of the custom and practice of international law and of the various declarations and conventions to which the States concerned are parties.*

## Jurisdiction

The British draft code contained an article (No. 9) stipulating that for the purpose of the proposed rules, territory over which a Power exercises a protectorate or a mandate, and also protected States, should be assimilated to the national territory of that Power. The Japanese Delegation drew attention to the necessity of providing also for the case of leased territories if any such article were adopted. Throughout the articles adopted the word "jurisdiction" is used. The Commission has considered the question whether it is necessary to add a definition of the word "jurisdiction" and has come to the conclusion that it would be better not to do so. The area within which each State is responsible is well understood; no difficulty of this sort arises in practice; and no inconvenience has been caused by the absence of any such definition from Convention No. XIII, of 1907, in which the word "jurisdiction" is used in a manner very similar to that in which it is used in the present rules.

## Marginal Territorial Air Belt

An interesting proposal was made by the Italian Delegation that along the coast of every State the national jurisdiction in the air space should for aerial purposes extend to ten miles. The proposal did not comprise any extension of territorial waters generally, a matter which would have been outside the reference to the Commission under the terms of the Washington Resolution.

Detailed consideration of the proposal led the majority of the delegations to think that the suggestion is not practicable.

It seems inevitable that great confusion would follow from any rule which laid down a different width for the territorial air space from that recognized for territorial waters, more particularly in the case of neutral countries for whose benefit and protection the proposal is put forward. As an example it is only necessary to take Article 42, which obliges a neutral State to endeavor to compel a belligerent military aircraft entering its jurisdiction to alight. If the aircraft entered the jurisdiction from over the high seas, it would do so at ten miles from the coast, and if in compliance with neutral orders it forthwith alighted on the water, it would then be outside the neutral jurisdiction, and the neutral State could not intern the aircraft.

On principle it would seem that the jurisdiction in the air space should be appurtenant to the territorial jurisdiction enjoyed beneath it, and that in the absence of a territorial jurisdiction beneath, there is no sound basis for jurisdiction in the air.

Furthermore, it is felt that the obligation to enforce respect for neutral rights throughout a ten-mile belt would impose an increased burden on neutral Powers without adequate compensating advantages. Even with this wider belt it would still be easy for airmen fighting in the air to lose their bearings in the heat of the combat, and to encroach inadvertently on neutral jurisdiction. Lastly, the greater the distance from the coast, the more difficult it is for the position of an aircraft to be determined with precision and the more frequent, therefore, will disputes become between belligerent and neutral States as to violation by the former's aircraft of the latter's jurisdiction.

With a view to meeting these criticisms the Italian Delegation recast the proposal in a different shape, and suggested that in time of war a State, whether neutral or belligerent, should be authorized, if it so desired and if it notified other Powers accordingly at the beginning of the war, to extend its jurisdiction over the marginal air belt to a distance of ten miles at any given places along its coast. In this form the proposal would have placed no burden upon neutrals, because they would not have made use of it unless they considered it to their advantage. The anomalies of the divergent widths of the marginal air belt and the marginal belt of sea would have remained.

After due consideration of the proposal, the majority of the Delegations felt unable to accept the proposal even in its amended form.

The Italian Delegation made the following statement:

(1) It does not think it desirable to resume in Plenary Commission the discussion of a question which has on several occasions been considered in all the necessary detail during the meetings of the Sub-Committee;

(2) nevertheless, although the majority of the Delegations have already put forward views opposed to its proposal, it continues to believe in the importance of that proposal and in the necessity for its adoption and insertion in an international convention;

(3) from the point of view both of belligerent and of neutral States, there are reasons of the highest juridical and technical importance which make it indispensable to allow each State the power of including in its jurisdiction the atmospheric space to a distance of ten miles from its coast;

(4) the difficulties resulting from the difference between the width of the marginal air belt and the width of national territorial waters would not seem to be so serious as to render the Italian proposal unacceptable in practice;

(5) in any case, there is no juridical obstacle to the fixing of the same width of space for the marginal air belt as for territorial waters, the Italian Delegation being of opinion that international law, as generally recognized, contains no rule prohibiting a State from extending its territorial waters to a distance of ten sea-miles from its coasts;

(6) in conclusion, it urges that a question of such paramount importance should be re-opened and placed upon the agenda of a conference in the near future.

### COMPENSATION AND DISPUTES.

The Netherlands Delegation submitted the following proposal:

The belligerent Party who, intentionally, or through negligence, violates the provisions of the present rules is liable to pay compensation in case damage is caused as a result of such violation. Such Party will be responsible for all acts committed by members of his armed forces.

If any dispute should arise on the subject which is not otherwise settled, such dispute shall be submitted for settlement to the Permanent Court of Arbitration, in conformity with Convention I of 1907, or to the Permanent Court of International Justice, in respect of such States as have accepted as compulsory *ipso facto* its jurisdiction.

The Commission approving the principle of indemnity decided to incorporate the proposal in its general report, so as to bring it to the attention of the governments.

### VIOLATION OF THE RULES.

No provision is made in the articles adopted as to the penalties to which persons violating the rules are to be subject. Some of the provisions in the drafts laid before the Commission stated that persons violating the article in question were to be punishable with death, or were to be treated as war criminals. No such stipulation figures in the Land Warfare Regulations and it has seemed better to omit it. Its absence will not in any way prejudice the imposition of punishment on persons who are guilty of breaches of the laws of aerial warfare.

*Done at The Hague, the nineteenth day of February, 1923.*

UNITED STATES OF AMERICA:

JOHN BASSETT MOORE.          ALBERT HENRY WASHBURN.

BRITISH EMPIRE:

RENNELL RODD.          CECIL J. B. HURST.

FRANCE:

A. DE LAPRADELLE.          BASDEVANT.

ITALY:

V. ROLANDI RICCI.

JAPAN:

K. MATSUI.          M. MATSUDA.

NETHERLANDS:

A. STRUYCKEN.          VAN EYSINGA.

*The Secretary General,*
J. P. A. FRANÇOIS.

## LAW AND ORGANIZATION[1]

WEBSTER, as a prelude to his reply to Hayne, asked for the reading of the resolution before the Senate, in order that the minds of his hearers might be led back to the original and perhaps forgotten subject of the debate. Today we may well imitate his example, by recurring to fundamental principles. For five months we have stood in the presence of one of the most appalling wars in history, appalling not only because of its magnitude and destructiveness but also because of its frustration of hopes widely cherished that the progress of civilization had rendered an armed conflict between the leading powers of the world morally impossible. As a result we have since the outbreak of the great conflict been tossing about on the stormy sea of controversy, distrustful of our charts and guides, and assailed on every hand with cries of doubt and despair. We have been told that there is no such thing as international law; that, even if its existence be admitted, it is at most nothing but what superior force for the time being ordains; that international understandings, even when embodied in treaties, are practically worthless, being obligatory only so long as they may be conceived to subserve the interests or necessities of the moment; that the only security for the observance of international rules, general or conventional, is force, and that in force we must in the last analysis find our sole reliance.

Thoughts such as these, to which distrustful minds have been known to give expression even in time of peace, are the natural product of times like those through which we are now passing. Students of law are familiar with the maxim, bequeathed to us by Cicero, that in the midst of arms the laws are silent—*inter arma silent leges*. This maxim primarily refers to municipal rather than to international law, but it may be applied to either. Its meaning and scope may easily be misconceived. It signifies in effect that, when a contest by force

1. Presidential address at the eleventh annual meeting of the American Political Science Association, at Chicago, in December, 1914. Reprinted from *The American Political Science Review*, Vol. IX, No. 1 (February, 1915).

prevails, the ordinary rules and methods of administration become inadequate and give way to measures dictated by public necessity. The system by which the ordinary administration is superseded is called martial law. Under this system the ordinary guarantees of individual liberty are suspended; but, although this is the case, we should stray far from the truth if we were to accept in a literal or popular sense the statement that martial law is "the will of the general who commands the army." The true meaning of this phrase was expounded by the Duke of Wellington, the great commander who uttered it. The general in command, although he possessed supreme power, was, said the Duke of Wellington, "bound to lay down distinctly the rules and regulations and limits according to which his will was to be carried out." The Duke declared that he had in another country carried on martial law, and in so doing "had governed a large proportion of the population of the country by his own will." But then, he asked, what did he do? and his answer was, "he declared that the country should be governed according to its own national laws, and he carried into execution that will. He governed the country strictly by the laws of the country; and he governed it with such moderation, he must say, that political servants and judges who at first had fled or had been expelled, afterwards consented to act under his direction. The judges sat in the courts of law, conducting their judicial business and administering the law under his direction." [2]

It is thus evident that when, in discussing martial law, we refer to the "will" of the commanding general, we refer to regulated and not to arbitrary action, so that even in the theatre of war, where the military commander is supreme, the idea of law does not disappear.

The idea of law is in reality the very foundation of the entire theory of military occupation. The obedience which the inhabitants of the occupied territory owe to the military commander is merely an expression of this principle. While the inhabitants owe obedience, it is equally true that the military commander is on the other hand bound to render them protection, and is not permitted to treat them altogether as enemies so long as they observe the rules and regulations established for their government. Such is the principle laid down by writers on international law and by military commanders who have respected the established rules of international intercourse.

2. Speech of the Duke of Wellington, Debate on Affairs in Ceylon, House of Lords, April 1, 1851. Hansard, 3d series, CXV, 880.

But it may be asked, what is international law? What is its essential nature; and, particularly, what is its position as compared with municipal law, and what is its sanction?

It may at the outset be admitted that a vast deal of time has been wasted in controversy over the question whether international law is law at all. These controversies, if minutely examined, will usually be found to have proceeded from one of two causes, namely, either (1) that the disputants have approached the subject from the point of view of preconceived definitions which were incapable of reconciliation, or (2) that, if they have agreed upon a definition, they have differed as to its application.

Probably no definition ever had a more pronounced effect on legal thinking than had the definition of law, given by Austin in his work on *Jurisprudence,* upon the legal mind of England and the United States. According to Austin, "a law, in the literal and proper sense of the word," is "a rule laid down for the guidance of an intelligent being by an intelligent being having power over him." This definition, according to its author, embraced "laws set by God to men" and "law as set by men to men." Of the latter, some were "established by political superiors acting as such," and constituted "positive law"—the appropriate matter of jurisprudence. "Closely analogous to human laws," but "improperly termed laws," were, he declared, "rules set and enforced merely by the opinion of an intermediate body of men," such as "the law of honor," or the "laws of fashion." Rules of this species constituted, he said, much of what was commonly termed "International Law"; and he placed them all in the category, not of law, but of "positive morality." Among the essentials of a law properly so called, he specified a "command" and a "sanction," the latter being the evil which would probably be incurred in case a command should be disobeyed.

Without commenting upon a terminology that smacks of the medieval *jure divino* conception of law as the product of superior power rather than of delegated authority, a moment's reflection suffices to show that Austin's so-called definition is at most merely a description of municipal law, and even for that purpose is not sufficiently comprehensive, since it would, for instance, exclude a large part of constitutional law, much of which, like a considerable part of international law, is not enforced by courts by means of specific penalties. Nor would it be difficult to show that it is in its conceptions historically faulty. Sir Henry Maine, in his volume on *International Law,* dismisses Austin's criticisms on that system as "very interesting and quite innocuous," and rather scouts the supposition "that Austin had intended to diminish, and had succeeded in diminishing, the dignity or imperative force of international law." I am altogether unable to accept this cheerful view. I think it may easily be shown that at one time Austin's relegation of international law to the sphere of morality had a pronounced effect even upon legal decisions in England, as in the case of the *Franconia*.[3]

Acting upon the assumption that Austin's description of municipal law was to be received as the ultimate test by which the admission of rules of conduct to the category of "law" was to be determined, writers have now and then made vain attempts to bring international law within his definition, and in order to prove that such inclusion was possible, have invoked the principle that international law is "a part of the law of the land." This principle has, as is well known, been enunciated and applied in a number of cases by the English courts, though with less precision and confidence since Austin's day than before. In the decisions of the American courts it may, I think, be said fortunately to have escaped an eclipse. But, even if we were to assume that it had nowhere been questioned, it must be admitted that the principle that the "law of nations," or international law, is a part of the law of the land, does not go to the root of the difficulty. Even though a court may accept the doctrine in good faith, its interpretation of international law may, by reason of national bias or local influence, prove to be contrary to the general sense; or, still worse, the court may be compelled by legislative direction to apply a rule flagrantly inconsistent with what is generally understood to be the accepted principle. In such a contingency, the question necessarily arises as to what is to be done to secure the application and enforcement of that principle.

It is just here that we disclose the practical difference between international law and municipal law. Speaking comprehensively, we may say that a law is an obligatory rule of action. In the course of history, men, acting in various ways and through varied forms, have worked out and have come to accept certain rules for the government of their conduct. In a general sense all such rules may be called laws; but with a view to preserve that freedom of action which is essential to self-development, it has been deemed expedient to give to only a part of such rules the force of positive obligation. The observance of the rest of them is left to the choice of the individ-

---

3. *Queen* v. *Keyn* (1876), 13 Cox C. C. 403; 2 Ex. Div. 63.

ual, who may be deterred from disregarding them by a good disposition, or by an apprehension of self-injury or of moral censure.

To the rules lying within the sphere in which observance is deemed to be essential to the general welfare and is therefore admitted to be obligatory, we give the name of law. These rules we undertake by one means or another to enforce, and measures are adopted for the purpose of making their observance compulsory.

For this reason, the world has come to regard the rules governing the intercourse of nations as constituting a system of law, for the maintenance of which even the use of coercion is justified, and this system is, as students know, much older than is popularly supposed. Phillipson, in his recent work entitled *The International Law and Custom of Ancient Greece and Rome*, has given a comprehensive and systematic survey of the international practices of those great commonwealths, with a special view to demonstrate "their respective acceptance of and insistence on juridical principles, and their application of a regularized procedure and legal methods to international relationships." The popular supposition that international law, as we now know it, originated with Grotius, whose great work *De Jure Belli ac Pacis* was published in 1625, is due to the circumstances that his treatise was exceptionally clear, comprehensive and systematic, and for that reason formed a landmark in the development of the science; but if one will take the trouble, as few now do, to examine the pages of Grotius, it will be found not only that he drew his inspiration and his opinions largely from earlier times and writers, but also that some of his fundamental doctrines are now quite obsolete. Sir John Macdonell, indeed, in his introductory note to Phillipson's work, declares that the

system of international law in the ancient world [is] in some respects much more akin to that of today than international law as it was in the time of Grotius. In the number and variety of autonomous states [says Sir John]; in the many different forms of their constitutions; in the existence of autonomous democratic states; in the conception of the state itself, wholly different from the feudal or patrimonial conception; in the number and variety of dependent communities, in the existence of federations; in the unstable balance of power; in the relations of the mother countries to autonomous colonies; in the multitude of treaties dealing with many subjects besides peace and war; in the developed use of arbitration, as a mode of settling differences; in the practice as to passports—in these and many other matters there is more likeness between the international law in ancient Greece and that of today than there is between the latter and international law as described in *De Jure Belli ac Pacis.*

In the development of international law, we find that the same forces have operated and to a certain extent the same methods have prevailed as in municipal law. Till a comparatively recent day international law developed chiefly through the gradual evolution of opinion and practice; and, just as in the case of municipal law, the prevailing opinion and practice would from time to time be embodied in some notable declaration or decision, which would be received as the authoritative formulation of accepted usage. The gradual evolution of international law was exemplified with the utmost precision and force by the Supreme Court of the United States in the case of the Spanish fishing smacks, in 1900.[4] The particular point decided was that coast fishing vessels, unarmed and honestly pursuing the peaceful calling of catching and bringing in fresh fish, were exempt from capture in time of war. In opposition to this view there was cited by counsel an opinion of Lord Stowell to the effect that the exemption was "a rule of comity only, and not of legal decision." The Supreme Court, however, declared that the period of a hundred years that had elapsed since Lord Stowell's opinion was uttered was "amply sufficient to have enabled what originally may have rested in custom or comity, courtesy or concession, to grow, by the general assent of civilized nations, into a settled rule of international law."

But, just as, in the case of municipal law, the statutory element has increased at the expense of the customary, so, in international law, there has been an increasing tendency to introduce modifications and improvements by acts in their nature legislative. A great advance towards assuring the free navigation of international streams of water was made by the Vienna Congress Treaty of June 9, 1815, by which the contracting parties agreed that rivers which separated or traversed two or more states should, along their whole navigable course, be, in respect of commerce, entirely free to everyone, subject only to regulations of police. This principle, although applied primarily to the Rhine, was expressly extended to the Neckar, the Mayne, the Moselle, the Meuse, and the Scheldt. With a limitation of the right of free navigation in some instances to the citizens or subjects of the riparian powers, similar stipulations may be found in treaties relating to the rivers and canals of the ancient kingdom of Poland; to the Elbe, Po, Pruth, Douro, Danube, and other rivers in Europe;

4. The *Paquete Habana* (1900), 175 U. S., 677.

and to the rivers Amazon, Paraguay, Uruguay, St. Lawrence, Yukon, Porcupine, and Stikine, in America.

By the same Congress, an important contribution to international law was made in the form of rules to regulate the rank and precedence of diplomatic agents. These rules, slightly modified by the Congress of Aix-la-Chapelle of 1818, were accepted by all the powers which then composed the international circle, and resulted in the regulation of a subject which had constantly given rise to disputes.

Yet more remarkable as an act of legislative aspect was the Declaration on Maritime Law, made by the Congress of Paris of 1856. This Declaration embraced four rules:

1. Privateering is and remains abolished.

2. A neutral flag covers an enemy's goods, with the exception of contraband of war.

3. Neutral goods, with the exception of contraband of war, are not liable to capture under the enemy's flag.

4. Blockades, in order to be binding, must be effective, that is to say, maintained by a force sufficient really to prevent access to the coast of the enemy.

The fourth rule may be considered as merely declaratory of international law, and so also may the third rule. But by the first two rules it was proposed to give the character and force of law to principles which had previously been obligatory only when they were made so by treaty; and to this end the signatories announced their purpose to invite the adhesion of other powers with a view "to establish a uniform rule." The powers invited to adhere embraced practically all those within the sphere of international law; and, with the exception of the United States, Spain and Mexico, they accepted the Declaration in its entirety. Spain gave her adhesion several years ago, but the United States has not as yet done so. Their original objection to adhering was based upon the naked inhibition of privateering, an objection which would have lost much of its force if it had been foreseen that merchant vessels might be incorporated into the navy without violating either the letter or the spirit of the Declaration. All the powers, however, approved the second rule, that free ships make free goods, and it has since been regarded as a principle of international law. It was expressly so proclaimed both by the United States and by Spain at the outbreak of the war between them in 1898.

Since 1860 numerous attempts have been made, by means of international conferences, to legislate on the mode of conducting warfare. The Geneva Convention of 1864, for the amelioration of the condition of the wounded in armies in the field, commonly called the Red Cross convention, is known to all. It was revised in 1906. The observance of its provisions is considered a test of civilization. Agreements such as the Declaration of St. Petersburg of 1868, which was framed by an international military commission, have been made as to the nature of the weapons that may be used in war, and as to the treatment of prisoners of war. Nor should we omit to mention the projected Declaration concerning the Laws of War on Land, formulated by the Brussels Conference of 1874. Although the powers represented in the conference afterwards failed to make the declaration binding, it forms the basis of the "Manual" of the Institute of International Law of 1880, of the plan adopted by the Spanish-Portuguese-Latin-American Military Congress at Madrid in 1892, and also of The Hague Convention relating to the Laws and Usages of War on Land. Unfortunately, it cannot be said that the Hague conventions relating to the conduct of war on land and sea have, as to the conflict now in progress in Europe, the force of international compacts. Each of the conventions contains a clause to the effect that its provisions "do not apply except between contracting parties, and then only if all the belligerents are parties to the conventions." Servia, one of the belligerents in the pending war, has not ratified any of the conventions; and yet other belligerents have not ratified some of them. The rules they lay down are therefore binding upon the belligerents only so far as they are declaratory of existing international law.

But, let us assume that international rules of conduct, founded either on usage or on treaties, are disregarded. What then is to be done? It is just here, as I have intimated, that we find the practical difference between international law and municipal law, and this difference relates to organization.

Before proceeding to discuss the subject of organization, I desire to comment upon certain impressions, which I conceive to be erroneous, in regard to international law and its observance. It is often hastily assumed (1) that the rules of international law are, as contrasted with the rules of municipal law, exceedingly indeterminate, and (2) that, even when they are ascertainable, they are little heeded. Both these assumptions are for the most part unfounded. The fact cannot be denied that there exists in the sphere of international law a considerable amount of uncertainty as to what the law actually is; but, that such uncertainty is not unknown in the domain of municipal law is amply demonstrated by the ever-accelerating accumulation of judicial decisions and the diverse, discordant, conflicting views which they so often exhibit. Even our legislative enactments do not uniformly afford relief. It took, for instance, nearly twenty years, with the aid of our judicial authorities, to ascertain the meaning of the so-called Sherman Law, and when the Supreme Court at length applied to it "the rule of reason," there were those who felt so little regard for the wisdom of Congress as to assert that the object and intent of the statute had been defeated. And even yet its bearing upon some of our most important companies remains to be determined.

At the present moment there are important forms of contract, of almost world-wide use, the sense of whose eventual interpretation by the courts on capital points is a matter of pure conjecture, not because of any difficulty as to facts or even as to the application of principles to facts, but because of absolute uncertainty as to the rules of municipal law. How can one predict what the decision of a common law court will be on a point of law not before precisely determined, when the court may "on full consideration" overturn a previously established rule, as happened, for instance, when it was held that insurance on enemy property was illegal and void?

In respect of actual observance, I venture to say that international law is on the whole as well observed as municipal law. Perhaps one would not go too far in saying that it is better observed, at any rate in time of peace. In time of war, when a contest by force exists, it is needless to repeat that the application of law, whether municipal or international, becomes more or less uncertain, and that, as turmoil and excitement grow, the uncertainty increases. In time of peace, however, the regard which nations are accustomed to feel for their reputation and dignity strongly influences them, perhaps quite as much as does the dread of retaliation, to respect the rules by which their intercourse is confessedly regulated. If one would only reflect upon the smallness of the number of international claims that arise in times of internal and external peace, he would not be disposed to question the correctness of this statement. It is in seasons of disturbance, domestic or international, that complaints and claims chiefly spring up.

Assuming, however, that international law has been disregarded, where is a remedy to be sought? If municipal law is violated, we apply to the administrative officials, or to the courts, as a means of securing redress. We appeal, in other words, to constituted authorities, who are empowered to do justice; and, if law is lacking, we may go to the legislature to supply the defect, at least for the future. In other words, we have within the state an organization for the enforcement of justice according to law.

In the international sphere, under similar conditions, we proceed in the first instance amicably, through diplomatic officials, who are the constituted authorities for this purpose. We negotiate and, in case an agreement should not be reached, we may accept the good offices or the mediation of a third power; or we may submit the question to judicial settlement, by means of arbitration. These are all amicable modes of redress, which international organization in its present state provides. If they do not succeed, it is laid down that we may try inamicable methods, ranging all the way from retorsion or retaliation, embargo, commercial non-intercourse, severance of diplomatic relations, and display of force, to reprisals, which are acts of war, and to war itself, which is in its physical aspect merely general reprisals. Nevertheless, if actual force be employed, there is always the danger of forcible resistance, ending in war; and in that event we may have the incongruous result that the aggressor, without submitting to the examination of any tribunal the justice of his cause, may, in the exercise of the "rights of war," conquer or destroy the injured power which he has by his own wrong driven to become his adversary.

This principle, which I conceive to be the capital defect of international law at the present day, is perhaps to be explained as a survival of the superstitions that preserved in municipal law for so many centuries the process of trial by battle. However this may be, it is flagrantly at variance with all conceptions of human right, and can be effectually got rid of only through further organization. It is in this respect, as I have intimated, that international law differs from municipal law —not in its essence or its obligation, but in the method of its declaration and administration. Within the state we have an organization for the making, declaration and enforcement of law, whereas, as between nations, we are obliged to a great extent to rely upon their voluntary concurrence or co-operation. In other words, we lack in the international sphere that organization which gives to the administration of law within the state a certain security. This defect it is the business of nations to supply by forming among themselves an appropriate organization.

The essential features of such an organization would be somewhat as follows:

1. It would set law above violence: (1) By providing suitable and efficacious means and agencies for the enforcement of law; and (2) by making the use of force illegal, except (a) in support of a duly ascertained legal right, or (b) in self-defense.

The first effect of such an organization would be to give an additional sanction to the principle of the equality of independent states before the law. "No principle of general law," said

Chief Justice Marshall, "is more universally acknowledged than the perfect equality of nations. Russia and Geneva have equal rights." [5] "Power or weakness," said the great Swiss publicist, Vattel, "does not in this respect produce any difference." And, incidentally, in proportion as this principle was maintained, the monstrous supposition that power is the measure of right would tend to disappear, and the claims of predatory conquest would become less and less capable of realization.

2. It would provide a more efficient means than now exists for the making and declaration of law.

We have adverted to the development of international law through the gradual evolution of opinion and practice, and also to attempts made during the past hundred years to establish rules by acts in their nature legislative. The chief obstacle to the efficacy of the second method is the requirement of unanimity. In the declaration of law on the strength of usage, it has never been supposed to be necessary to show that each particular nation had affirmatively adopted it. It appearing that the usage is general, all nations that profess to be law-governed are assumed at least tacitly to have accepted it. But, when we come to legislation, each nation must, it is held, give its assent, in order that it may be bound. Undoubtedly it would be going too far in the present state of things to propose a mere majority rule. But it is altogether desirable that a rule should be adopted whereby it may no longer be possible for a single state to stand in the way of international legislation. The adoption of such a rule could not be regarded as impairing in a proper sense the principle of the equality of nations. Nations have responsibilities as well as rights.

3. It would provide more fully than has heretofore been done for the investigation and determination of disputes by means of tribunals, possessing advisory or judicial powers, as the case might be.

The neglect of such processes has been the great defect of the European Concert. I am not among the number of those who hold towards that organization an attitude wholly accusatory. Its efforts have no doubt in the main been sincerely directed to the preservation of peace. But, its proceedings would often have been less open to suspicion and would have tended to produce more lasting results, if considerations of fact and of law had played a larger part in its deliberations.

Such I conceive to be the essentials of an organization which would place international law on substantially the same footing as municipal law, as regards its making, declaration and

5. The *Antelope*, 10 Wheaton, 66, 122.

enforcement. But, the fact is not to be lost sight of that, in the present state of human development, there is no absolute security for the uninterrupted maintenance of law, national or international, or for the continuous preservation of peace. We are often told that in the last analysis the ultimate sanction of law is "public opinion," by which is meant, we may assume, not so much the intelligent conclusions reached by processes of reasoning, as the general state of mind which, frequently dominated by sentiment, determines the attitude of a people or of the world. Logically speaking, whether the popular attitude be dictated by reason or by sentiment, forcible opposition to law has no excuse where universal suffrage practically prevails; for, if the predominant opinion is admitted rightfully to control, then, where ballots have been substituted for bayonets, forcible opposition to law and its administration would seem to be without justification. Nevertheless, we know that the United States has not wholly escaped the civil calamities to which other nations, in which the suffrage was less extended, have now and then been subject. This fact may be ascribed (1) to the circumstance that there is a large part of human activities, especially of a competitive kind, not yet brought within the sphere of legal regulation, and (2) to the propensity of men acting in the mass to attain their ends by violence. At the moment the United States, with its immense extent of territory and its diversified population, presents the spectacle of long-continued internal peace with a standing military force that would barely form the nucleus of an army sufficient for any serious emergency, but it would be rash to assume that this apparent immunity from the danger of domestic strife is permanent. Conditions resembling war sometimes locally arise, and the same thing is true of the British empire and of other well-ordered countries.

Occasional disturbances such as these should by no means lessen our estimate of the importance of organization for the maintenance of law, either international or internal. They should, on the contrary, serve to emphasize not only the necessity of organization, but also the importance of extending its scope and increasing its efficiency. Meanwhile, they also indicate the futility of relying upon any particular device as an all-sufficient means of preserving peace and order. Experience has demonstrated that, even within comparatively small areas, local conditions must be consulted, in order that the administration of law may not produce discomfort and discontent; and, as long as discontent and ambition continue to play in the affairs of the world a conspicuous part, so long will it be necessary to be prepared either to satisfy or to resist them.

Postscript, January 31, 1924.—On re-reading the foregoing address after the lapse of ten years I find nothing of substance to change, but I will add something in explanation of the concluding part, which was brief and necessarily vague and fragmentary.

When I referred to an international organization for the purpose of making and enforcing international law, I obviously had in mind an association embracing all the nations of the world; and by this I meant an open association of which all the nations of the world would be members, and in which membership would not be dependent upon selection determined by the favor of certain powers or combinations of powers. For this reason, while I suggested that the rule of absolute unanimity eventually might to some extent be dispensed with, I emphasized the legal equality of independent states as the very foundation of any plan that might be devised.

Within the past ten years we seem to have witnessed the revival in certain cases of the supposition that a state may suffer an impairment of its essential rights as an independent political entity through the refusal or omission of various other powers to recognize its government. As this idea widely prevailed in earlier times, its recrudescence after a century of suspended animation should not excite our special wonder; but it tends to give an undue importance to the question of formal recognition. A perception of this fact is shown by what was recently done in the case of the International Union of the American States. By the constitution of this Union, its governing board was composed of the diplomatic representatives of those states accredited to the government of the United States. In consequence, if the government of a particular country was not recognized by the United States, it ceased to have a representative on the governing board. In order to remedy this incongruity, it was provided by the Fifth International American Conference at Santiago, Chile, in 1923, that, if an American republic should not for any reason have a diplomatic representative accredited to the United States, it might appoint a special representative on the governing board. Nevertheless, in the acts of the board, the principle of unanimity is preserved.

An example of equality of state representation, joined with majority rule, is furnished by the constitution of the United States Senate. This is the one provision of the Constitution of the United States which is practically placed beyond the reach of change, since the Constitution provides that no State shall be deprived of its equal representation in the Senate without its consent. The equality of representation of the States in the

Senate of the United States has often produced a sense of inconvenience, especially among those who are impatient of any delay in the enactment of whatever legislation they may conceive to be desirable. But the stipulation for equality was the price originally paid for the Union, and we may not go too far in saying that it continues to be the price paid for its preservation. How long the Union, with its vast extent and varied interests, could survive if its government were committed to the ten most populous States, containing an actual majority of the entire population, it would be a waste of time to attempt to conjecture.

If this be true of States not sovereign, whose inhabitants all have a common national allegiance, a fatal weakness necessarily would inhere in any scheme to endow a few of the larger nations, whether known as Great Powers or by a title less patronizing, with power to make law for all the rest and to enforce it upon them. Forty years ago a well-known writer, pronouncing "the old doctrine of the absolute equality of all independent States before the law" to be "dead," declared that there should be "put in its place the new doctrine that the Great Powers have by modern International Law a primacy among their fellows, which bids fair to develop into a central authority for the settlement of all disputes between the nations of Europe." [6] This proposal, compounded of dogma and prophecy, has been sadly discredited; for, unfortunately, the Great Powers have failed to exhibit such harmony of views and of action as would justify the concession to them of so high a prerogative.

When we consider the association of nations, whether for the purpose of making law and securing its observance, or for the purpose of assuring the preservation of peace, we must bear in mind that wars are precipitated by psychological conditions, sometimes stimulated by ambition, but are in the main produced by rivalries, by misunderstandings, by injuries and oppressions, real or fancied, and by a sense of resentment. The causes that operate to produce international wars likewise operate to produce civil wars, which, during the century intervening between the Napoleonic wars and the recent great war, were perhaps more frequent than international wars and claimed as many victims.

Another problem, obviously fundamental, is that of the real attitude of human beings towards war. In order to appreciate the seriousness of this question, it is not necessary to accept in its full extent the mechanistic view of war, so vividly por-

6. T. J. Lawrence, *The Primacy of the Great Powers: Essays on Some Disputed Questions in Modern International Law* (2d ed. London, 1885).

trayed by Dr. Crile.[7] History and the manifestations of daily life amply attest the reality of the problem; and yet no subject is shrouded in greater uncertainty or more persistently evaded. Nor is the evasion always conscious. On the contrary, it frequently tends to recall the Temanite's scornful inquiry whether a wise man should "fill his belly with the east wind" and "reason with unprofitable talk." The familiar slogan, "the war to end war," has been constantly invoked even by pacifists, perchance to stimulate or to excuse their militant activities; but of all illusions it is the vainest. The circumstance that the motto "peace through victory" has been much used by advocates of peace cannot obscure the fact that it altogether postpones the end to the attainment of the means, and that this is, in the particular instance, very human. Even the assumption which each nation, after the manner of each individual, is wont to indulge, that its own desires are more pacific than those of others, betrays a marked skepticism as to the world's peaceful proclivities. That the people of the United States, who are by no means military in their habits, believe themselves to be peculiarly addicted to peace, is proverbial; but when, some years ago, a great popular leader, distinguished as a man of action, declared that he knew his fellow-countrymen and that they would fight at the drop of the hat, it is not recorded that the throng to whom he spoke manifested displeasure. Perhaps they politely accepted the imputation as a compliment addressed to them individually. But the persistent popular interest not only in war but in all forms of conflict is a factor that cannot be overlooked. While bull-fighting still exemplifies the Ephesian form of diversion, heavyweight contests no less betoken the survival of the gladiatorial instinct; nor would multitudes of men and women gloat over the mimic bloodshed of the stage, unless, in spite of their tears and their moans, they found a fascination in it. Such things should not be blinked, since they admonish us that, if we would have peace in our own time, whether at home or abroad, no process by which differences may be settled and passions composed is to be neglected.

Yet another serious problem is that of the part which force possibly may play in the preservation of international peace. This part is easily overestimated. The supposition that preponderant force, because it may end a war, can be relied upon to insure peace involves more than one vaulting assumption. One of these is that men in the mass, constituting a great nation, can be controlled with the same promptitude and effective-

7. Dr. George W. Crile, *A Mechanistic View of War and Peace* (New York, 1916).

ness with which an individual, charged with a violation of law, can be arrested in the street and brought to justice. The futility of such a supposition is remarkably demonstrated by what took place in Europe during the twenty-five years that succeeded the French Revolution. In 1793 France, then threatened with a shortage of food, was confronted with practically a united Europe, with the world's greatest maritime power at the head of the coalition. And yet, with the exception of the brief respite following the peace of Amiens, the war continued twenty-two years, and in the end France emerged from the conflict with her boundaries scarcely diminished. This example is not incapable of repetition.

Another such assumption is the supposition, quite unfounded in human experience, that a people, laboring under a sense of grievance, will be deterred by a disparity of numbers and of force from incurring the hazards of a conflict. All history teaches the contrary. On this point the lessons furnished by America are peculiarly impressive. The patriots of 1776 took a desperate chance, and won; the leaders in the movement for secession took a chance apparently less desperate, and lost.

One of the gravest dangers to which any association of nations is exposed is the tendency of the members to divide into groups and to form balances of power based on particular interests and sympathies which are thus made paramount to the general interest. Judged by various public utterances during the past few years an impression seems more or less to prevail that the balance of power is an artificial contrivance employed to defeat the instinct of concert among nations. The truth is just the reverse. Balance of power is the instinctive measure; concert is the artificial contrivance employed to counteract that instinct. What is called the balance of power is merely a manifestation of the primitive instinct of "self-defense," which tends to produce combinations in all human affairs, national as well as international, and which so often manifests itself in aggression. Not only was the Civil War in the United States the result of a contest over the balance of power, but the fact is notorious that certain sections of the country have, during the past generation, constantly found themselves in general relations of mutual support because of a continuing common interest in a single question.

It has sometimes been astutely suggested that a "preponderance" of power would not be a "balance" of power, but this is a very deceptive play upon words. It never has occurred to the actual designers of balances of power that there was any difference between a "balance" and a "preponderance." What they sought was a "preponderance" as big as they could make it. Nor have they ever refrained from increasing it, even after the beam was tipped in their favor. They have indeed conceived of it in the accountant's sense of a substantial surplus or reserve which might be drawn upon for working capital.

Another problem—and perhaps the most serious one—with which an association of nations for the preservation of peace must deal is that of determining the responsibility for armed conflicts which, in spite of all peaceful efforts, occur. Recent events have unfortunately tended to create the hasty impression that, when war breaks out, it will always be clear which one of the parties began it. This supposition betrays a lack both of perspective and of familiarity with the origin of wars.

Ward, in his *Law of Nations,* narrates how, in 1292, two sailors, the one Norman, the other English, quarreled in the port of Bayonne and began to fight with their fists. In the affray one stabbed the other. The fight spread to the ships of the two countries in the harbor, then to the high seas, and, continuing to grow till it involved the two governments, resulted in the war which, by the loss of Guienne, entailed upon the English and the Normans the train of hostilities which eventuated in the Hundred Years' War.

Passing over many intervening outbreaks, the uncertainties of which yet remain to be dispelled, we may recur to the situation in 1762, when Spain and France, assembling their forces on Spanish territory, demanded that Portugal join them in their war with Great Britain. They justified their action by alleging, with some show of reason, that Portugal had not observed neutrality in the war. Portugal, acting in self-defense, declared war against them, and by so doing no doubt gained an advantage. In 1793, France declared war against Great Britain; but even English historians are by no means agreed that her action in so doing was not essentially defensive. The fact is well known that France in 1870 declared war against Prussia. The conflict was precipitated by the Hohenzollern candidacy for the Spanish throne and the supposed insult to the French ambassador at Ems. France, upon the face of the record, was the aggressor. Twenty years later the world learned that the Hohenzollern candidacy was originally suggested to Spain by Bismarck, and also became acquainted with the circumstances attending the preparation of the version of the Ems incident which carried the French parliament off its feet.

On October 26, 1827, a combination of the naval forces of England, France, and Russia destroyed the Turkish fleet in the harbor of Navarino. The first actual shot appears to have been fired by the Turks, but English naval writers have candidly admitted that the Ottoman commander was not unjustified in believing that he was repelling an attack. Possibly he was; the allied fleet called it a "reconnaissance." Subsequently the Tsar declared war against the Sultan. France and England remained, as an English historian remarked, "idle spectators." But the war had momentous consequences in the affairs of the Orient, and was inspired by rivalries which have not yet ceased to exist.

President Madison, in 1812, declared that Great Britain was at war with the United States while the United States was at peace with Great Britain, and called upon Congress to redress the balance. Congress promptly responded. Ten years later, Albert Gallatin, who had been Madison's Secretary of the Treasury, discovered in the French archives documents which led him to avow the belief that, if the truth had been known, the United States would never have entered upon the course that resulted in the war. President Polk, in May, 1846, declared that war existed by the act of Mexico, and Congress accepted his declaration; but there has always been a profound difference of opinion in the United States upon the question whether this view was justified. This difference is due to the fact that the title to the territory where the first armed collision took place was in dispute. If the territory belonged to Mexico, its occupation by the United States forces was an act of invasion; if the territory belonged to Texas, the Mexican attack upon those forces was an act of aggression. The insertion in the treaty of 1848, by which the war was ended, of a stipulation to the effect that, if differences should in future arise, neither republic should resort to "reprisals, aggression, or hostility of any kind" against the other, without having maturely considered whether the difference should not be arbitrated, has not prevented the recurrence of incidents whose merits are by no means clear.

The outbreak of war between China and Japan in 1894 presents striking analogies to that between the United States and Mexico in 1846. The answer to the question whether certain initial acts, such as the sinking of the *Kowshing,* had an aggressively hostile character, depends upon the solution of disputed claims as to what was at the time the status of Korea.

The examples that have been cited suffice to demonstrate how extravagant and groundless is the assumption that nations in general could be expected to hold together in attacking a particular nation, on the mere allegation from some quarter that it had "begun" hostilities. They further serve to show that, in many instances, the only proper course would be to seek to compel both parties to suspend hostilities. In private law, we should hardly undertake to justify a policeman who made it a rule, when a fight occurred, to side with the party whom he believed to be in the right and help him kill his adversary. Such an innovation in domestic jurisprudence would be truly startling. It can hardly work satisfactorily in the international sphere.

Another question with almost infinite ramifications is that of the relation of the limitation of armaments to the preservation of peace. The Peace Conference at The Hague in 1899 was originally convoked by the Tsar solely for the consideration of that question, but it proved to be almost the only subject related to war which the Conference sedulously avoided. As some nations suddenly grow shy when the "freedom of the seas" is mentioned, so others suddenly balk when the regulation of military preparations is proposed. Nevertheless, it will not do to say that the subject lies wholly outside the realm of practical statesmanship. There have been numerous instances in which agreements, voluntary or involuntary, have been made for the prohibition or limitation of armaments of various kinds. Such prohibitions or limitations may be found in various agreements for the neutralization of territory or of waterways. The mutual prohibition, for more than a hundred years, of naval armaments on the Great Lakes, which probably accounts for the unfortified state of the land frontier, bears eloquent testimony to the tranquillizing influence of abstention from menace. The most striking example in recent times of an agreement for the limitation of armaments is that which resulted from the Washington Conference in the winter of 1921–22 for the limitation of naval armaments as between the United States of America, the British Empire, France, Italy and Japan. Perhaps it may be said that the fundamental principle in such arrangements is that of mutuality. The mere absence of armaments will not ensure peace, nor will their mere existence provoke war. On the other hand, rivalry in armaments necessarily excites apprehension, apprehension begets fear, and fear breeds hatred. In the relative adjustment of forces with a view to a fair equilibrium, many and diverse elements must be taken into account. The question cannot be solved in a day or by one stroke, nor can the creation of new "balances" or of a "preponderance" of power be regarded as a step toward its solution. In the formulation of plans for the preservation of peace, all the complicated methods which are employed for the regulation of human affairs must be reckoned with. They can no more be neglected in the external than in the internal affairs of states. There must be organization of such character and extent as to gratify the desires, reconcile the ambitions, and settle the disputes of peoples, so that their attitude toward international order and toward internal order may be substantially the same. To this end it will be necessary to rid the mind of exaggerated but old and widely prevalent notions as to the functions and mission of the state, of superstitions as to "trial by battle," of the conceptions that underlie the law of conquest, and of the delusion that one's own motives are always higher, purer, and more disinterested than those of other persons, to say nothing of the passion for uniformity that denies the right to be different. Evidently such a state can be attained only through a substantial and somewhat radical change in the mental attitude of peoples such as will lead them to think first of amicable processes rather than of war when differences arise.

VII

THE PASSION FOR UNIFORMITY[1]

IN the ancient and beautiful city of Münster, with its mediaeval arcades and gabled houses, the traveler finds his curiosity excited by the strange spectacle of three iron cages suspended from the tower of a church. If he consults his Baedeker he learns that these cages once contained the remains of three religious zealots, who, desirous to convert the inhabitants to their way of thinking, swept down upon the place with fire and sword, and committed for the good of their cause many acts such as in these gentler times we seek to discountenance by harshly calling them atrocities. For a while their ardent zeal swept all before them, but they were subsequently driven out; and when later they returned to the charge, they were captured, and, after they were duly tortured with red hot pincers and put to death, their bodies were, to speak with legal precision, severally suspended in the three iron cages, as a warning to the people against the excessive indulgence of the passion for uniformity.

The tendency thus visualized pervades all human history, and has been one of the profoundest causes of the struggles which constitute so great a part of the story of the life of man on earth. From the Scriptures we learn that the Hebrews re-

1. An address before the Society of the Alumni of the Law School of the University of Pennsylvania, April 24, 1914. Reprinted from the *University of Pennsylvania Law Review and American Law Register*, LXII, No. 7 (May, 1914), 525–544.

garded themselves as the chosen people of God. So regarding themselves, they naturally deemed it to be their duty to spread their faith by force if necessary. They looked upon other nations not only as inferiors, but as being enemies because of their inferiority. By the same process of reasoning, they deemed it to be a virtuous act to put their enemies to death, not as combatants but simply as enemies, and they therefore embraced in their destructive plan women and children, so as to prevent the propagation and growth of dissimilarity.

The attitude of the ancient Hebrews was shared in one form or another by other peoples. To the Greeks, alien peoples were barbarians. Being different from themselves, they necessarily bore the stamp of inferiority. The view of the Romans was the same, and they exhibited even more strongly than the Greeks had done the propensity to extend their power and their institutions to other lands by force. We are told that when the Thracians took Mycalessus they put to death the women and children; that so did the Macedonians when they took Thebes, and the Romans when they took Ilurgis in Spain; while Germanicus ravaged the Marsi with fire and sword and without sparing sex or age. And we are assured that some of the warriors under whom these things were done were counted as humane men.

From these highly authoritative sources, religious and political, the same ideas descend to the modern world. Grotius, whose great work, *De Jure Belli ac Pacis*, appeared at the close of the first quarter of the seventeenth century, reviewed the ancient authorities to the effect that war, when declared against a country, extended to all the people, so that the slaughter of women and infants was attended with impunity, as comprehended in the right of war. Grotius doubted whether there should be adduced in support of this right the slaying of the women and children of Heshbon, as recorded in Deuteronomy,[2] or what was done to the Canaanites and their allies, for these were, he said, "the doings of God, who has a more absolute right over man than men have over brutes"; but he quoted as unquestionably pertinent a passage which, as he declared, approached "more nearly to a testimony of the common usage of nations." This was the ninth verse of the one hundred and thirty-seventh Psalm, reading thus: "Happy shall he be that taketh and dasheth thy little ones against the stones." And to this "testimony" Grotius added that of Homer.[3]

2. Deut. 2. 34.
3. *De Jure Belli ac Pacis*, Bk. III, chap. iv, sec. 9. For Grotius's repudiation and condemnation of such conceptions and practices, see *supra*, p. 16.

Towards the end of the Middle Ages, the passion for uniformity was especially exhibited in a religious form. For many years the European world was convulsed with the struggles which are known in history as religious wars. These contests are commonly regarded as culminating in the Thirty Years' War, which involved the greater part of Europe but fell with peculiarly devastating force upon the states forming the German Empire of that day. It may be true that, as has been suggested, the element of religious faith or sentiment was not so exclusively the cause of these conflicts as writers have generally represented, and that, just as in most human affairs, there was a material element that had to be dealt with. Nevertheless, the element of faith was an active force, and gave to the contests their peculiarly stubborn, relentless character.

We commonly think of the Thirty Years' War as marking the end of religious conflicts carried on with arms, but this view is not altogether justified. Differences in religious belief, although they have during the past three hundred years seldom been the avowed cause of armed conflicts, have in many instances been highly influential in producing the state of feeling that led to hostilities. It is no doubt the blending of religious differences with those of a racial character that largely accounts for the singularly fierce and sanguinary aspect which has distinguished some of the struggles that have taken place in the Balkan Peninsula since 1910.

When we come to consider the state of the modern world, the thoughts which have just been expressed give rise to interesting reflections. The thing that chiefly distinguishes the modern world from the ancient is the study of the physical sciences, and the application of physical forces to the conveniences of life by means of inventions. Neither in art nor in literature can the modern world boast of achievements that excel the productions of the ancients. In art we still recur to the works of the ancient masters, while in literature and in oratory we can scarcely be said to have gained either in substance or in form by an increasing unfamiliarity with the language of Homer and Demosthenes, or with that of Virgil and Cicero. It is a matter of common remark that time has developed nothing in the way of political thought that may not be found in Aristotle's Politics; and this observation may be accepted as substantially true, unless, as some one has facetiously suggested, the idea of a "nation-wide presidential primary" in the United States must be placed in the category of absolute novelty! But by the discovery and application of the uses of steam and electricity, a greater facility has been attained in the conduct of the relations of peoples and states.

In the first place, all parts of the world have, as the result of improved means of transportation, been brought into closer and more constant contact; the barriers to intercourse that formerly existed have been overcome. In the second place, as the result of this new contact, there has come about a general development of resources which has rendered impossible the predominance which single nations sometimes previously enjoyed. Barely sixty years have elapsed since the Far East seemed to lie practically helpless before the onset of the West; but in that brief period a single Far Eastern nation, Japan, has, by a process of conscious and deliberate self-development, never before witnessed in the history of the world, raised itself to a position of political equality with the nations of the West; and this has been done not more by the development of political institutions than by demonstrated capacity in war.

We are thus brought face to face with the fact that a condition of things has arisen in which the indulgence on a large scale of the passion for uniformity, after the manner of the zealots at Münster, has become increasingly difficult. For centuries the mind of Europe was haunted with the spectre of universal monarchy. Repeated and long-continued efforts were put forth to make it a reality. In the end they disastrously failed; and the renewal of such an attempt at the present day is inconceivable. The general development of the world's physical resources is strengthening more and more the power of the nations to defend and preserve their independent existence. Not only is this so in Europe and in the Far East, but there are abundant proofs of the operation of the same tendency in other quarters of the globe. Notable illustrations of it may be found among the nations of America. There can be no doubt that, contrary to what is often apparently supposed, the nations of South America today are as a whole far better able to defend themselves against aggression and to maintain their independence than they were eighty years ago, or at any intervening time. Although in some of these states political conditions are still insecure, the prevalent tendency has been in the direction of order and stability, while in many of them rapid and striking advances have been made and still are making in the paths of orderly progress.

From these facts there seem to result certain necessary inferences. One is, that wars for the purpose of extermination, or for the purpose of spreading either political institutions or social and religious conceptions, must be regarded as fatuous. By keeping alive antagonisms, they strengthen and perpetuate differences, as is seen in the history of the Balkan Peninsula. Another inference which it is necessary to draw is that such wars, no matter how futile they may be, can be avoided only by the frank recognition of the fact that differences do not necessarily denote an inferiority which it is the duty of the self-assumed superior forcibly to obliterate.

The importance of accepting these inferences becomes even more apparent when we reflect upon the fact that on the whole national and racial differences do not tend to disappear. No doubt there are cases in which an amalgamation has taken or is still taking place; but even here the result is something different from what existed before. On the whole, taking history as we know it, and speaking in terms of time rather than of eternity, the indestructibility of nations and of races may be accepted as axiomatic.

Differences in social and political institutions spring from differences in disposition and in views of life. Among the qualities that tend to render life not only supportable but enjoyable, none plays a larger part than the sense of humor. In some peoples this sense is highly developed, while in others it seems to be almost wholly wanting. Not long ago, an intelligent traveler, speaking of the aboriginal element in the population of a country in which he had spent a number of years, said that he had for a long time sought to determine whether this element possessed a sense of humor. Close observation failed to discover any, till one day when he saw some natives working on the roof of a house. One of the workmen, through his awkwardness, slipped and fell to the street, and was instantly killed. This incident, the traveler said, seemed to afford to the other natives, who had retained their footing on the roof, intense amusement, and he came to the conclusion that this attitude towards human misfortune must, as the resultant of underlying forces, exert a decided influence upon the development of customs, laws and institutions.

Even before the time of Pope, who wrote—

> "For forms of government let fools contest;
> What'er is best administered is best," [4]

philosophers had animadverted upon the tendency to regard political institutions as the cause rather than the effect of differences between peoples. In reality, if there existed all over the world one form of government, the habits, customs, laws, and even the institutions, of different peoples would continue to be different. When I say that institutions would continue to be different, I mean that they would be so in essence, as tested by their working, even though they were the same in form. We have in the world today many governments which are

4. *Essay on Man*, Epistle iii, line 303.

called monarchies. Some of them are despotic; others are constitutional. Others yet are largely democratic. We have at the same time many republics. All of them are nominally constitutional, or hope to be so; but, while in some of them government is popular and free, in others it is more or less arbitrary, the real differences being due to differences in the character, disposition and development of the peoples over whom the government rules.

We observe similar differences in social institutions and laws, proceeding from similar causes. In the United States we have witnessed more and more the development of a tendency to legislate on subjects which were formerly considered to lie within the sphere of individual action. Of this tendency an example is found in the spread of prohibitory laws; that is to say, laws prohibiting the sale and consumption of intoxicating liquors. The regulation of government in the matter has now proceeded so far that in the capital of the United States the prohibition to serve liquors on Sunday extends even to clubs and precludes a member even from giving a drink to a fellow-member or to anyone else; so that, in order to avoid the chances of a violation of the law, clubs have forbidden members to keep flasks in their lockers.[5] There are other civilized and well-ordered countries in which such a measure would be impossible. Comment has often been made upon the fact that, while the Englishman and the American boast of political liberty, they will submit to a measure of governmental interference with their personal habits such as would probably produce a revolution if tried, for example, in France or in Italy. If the Englishman or the American, quietly submitting to sumptuary laws, is content to consume his spirituous beverages in some sheltered retreat, the Frenchman or the Italian prefers to sip his wine at a table in the open air, and would keenly and quickly resent any attempt on the part of the government to interfere with the enjoyment of this traditional freedom.

But, in considering the passion for uniformity, we must note a capital distinction. Like other natural forces, if wrongly directed or excessively indulged, it operates destructively; but if wisely directed and properly regulated, it may operate beneficially. Even before the Thirty Years' War, philosophers began to dream and to write of a uniform law for the regulation of international relations. More and more impressed with the demonstrated fatuity of the attempt to create uniformity by force, they conceived the necessity of recognizing the right to be different, and in order to make such recognition effective,

5. This passage serves to recall the gradual growth of the movement that later resulted in national prohibition.

adopted, as the very basis of the new system, the principle that independent nations have in the eye of the law equal rights. In time this principle worked a marvelous transformation. The affairs of nations began to be adjusted in international conferences, and the adjustments so effected were embodied in great international charters. Disorder was succeeded by system; the tendency towards strife was in a measure counterbalanced by a tendency towards federation, and eventually there resulted from this co-operative policy an effort to bring about genuine acts of international legislation, culminating in the attempts made in that direction at the Peace Conferences at The Hague in 1899 and 1907, and at the Naval Conference in London in 1909.

Meanwhile, various proposals have been made for the adoption of a general international code. Drafts of such a code have been prepared by eminent jurists. A German, Bluntschli, and an American, David Dudley Field, were pioneers in this work; and the draft prepared by the great Italian publicist, Pasquale Fiore, of which an English version is in existence, has reached a fifth edition. All these drafts, it is proper to say, represent for the most part a summary of existing law; and this remark is made in a spirit of commendation. But as yet none of them has been submitted to an international body for consideration and action.

In the Western Hemisphere a movement has been formally set on foot for an international code. By a treaty or convention adopted by the Third International American Conference at Rio de Janeiro on August 23, 1906, the American nations agreed to establish an International Commission of Jurists, consisting of one delegate from each country, to codify international law; and although discussions in previous International American Conferences, and particularly in the first one, had disclosed in the differences between the jurisprudence of the United States and that of the countries of Portuguese and Spanish origin serious obstacles to the creation of uniformity in private law, they included private, as well as public, international law in the plan. The International Commission of Jurists held its first meeting in Rio de Janeiro in the summer of 1912. By a supplementary agreement each government was permitted to send two delegates instead of one, and a number of the governments, including that of the United States, availed themselves of this privilege. Seventeen states were actually represented, and a delegate from yet another state was on his way to Rio de Janeiro when the congress adjourned.

Immediately on the assembling of the commission the question was raised as to whether codification should be effected by means of identical national laws, or by means of international conventions; whether it should be at the first moment complete, or should be gradual and progressive; in what form amendments should be made or defects supplied; whether new rules should continue to be elaborated so as to keep the code or the agreed points in harmony with the progress of nations. The discussion of these questions at once disclosed what may be regarded as fundamental differences of view. On the one hand it was proposed that the commission should proceed at once to the adoption of codes. This proposal, in view of the magnitude and difficulties of the task before the commission, would have been incomprehensible but for the fact that two eminent Brazilian jurists, Dr. Epitacio Pessôa, then a member of the Supreme Court of Brazil, and Dr. Lafayette Rodriguez Pereira, a former Minister of Justice of the republic, had respectively prepared drafts of codes of public international law and private international law for the use of the commission. On the other hand, the view was taken that it was practically impossible for the commission to proceed at once to take definitive action upon the texts of codes. In reality, the Brazilian draft codes reached the various governments to which they were sent only towards the end of 1911; and the agreement fixing the date of the assembling of the commission was signed only in January, 1912. On the eve of sailing for Brazil the United States delegates[6] were furnished with copies of the original drafts in Portuguese, together with an English translation of them; but there had scarcely been an opportunity to make a competent translation of the texts into English—for by translation I mean not the mere matching of word for word, but the conversion of the sense and idiom of the one text into the equivalent sense and idiom of the other.

It was therefore contended by various delegations, including that of the United States, that the commission should be divided into committees, to which should be assigned certain subjects for investigation and report; that the reports of these committees should be printed in all the languages represented in the commission, and should be exchanged, and that after such lapse of time as would enable this to be done, the commission should meet again to consider the adoption of texts for submission to the various governments, and perhaps for the eventual consideration of the International American Conference. This view substantially prevailed. The commission was divided into six committees, four of which were to be concerned with subjects of public international law and two with subjects

6. The present writer, and the late F. Van Dyne, sometime Assistant Solicitor of the Department of State.

of private international law. The four committees on public international law were to sit respectively at Washington, Rio de Janeiro, Santiago (Chile), and Buenos Aires. To the first committee was assigned the preparation of drafts of codes on maritime war, and the rights and duties of neutrals; to the second, the preparation of drafts on war on land, civil war, and the claims of foreigners growing out of such wars; to the third, international law in time of peace; to the fourth, the pacific settlement of international disputes and the organization of international tribunals. The two committees on private international law were to sit at Montevideo and Lima. The subjects assigned to the first committee embraced capacity, the status of aliens, domestic relations, and succession. To the second was entrusted the consideration of matters of private international law not embraced in the preceding enumeration, including the conflict of penal laws.

The commission, which held its first formal session on June 26, 1912, adjourned on the twentieth of the following month, to meet again in Rio de Janeiro in June, 1914. The date of the next meeting has since been postponed till June, 1915. Some of the committees have already made reports, but there has not yet been an opportunity for the completion of their work, and the printing and exchange of the results of their investigations.[7]

As a concession to those who desired immediate action, the commission while in session at Rio de Janeiro undertook to act upon the subject of extradition in the domain of public international law, and on the execution of foreign judgments within the domain of private international law. After comparatively brief debate, a draft on extradition was voted. But when the special committee on the execution of foreign judgments came to consider the draft prepared on that subject, it soon appeared that there existed as between the different delegates irreconcilable divergences of view. These divergences resulted from the circumstance that the members of the committee immediately found themselves dealing with questions of procedure.

During the past hundred years, and especially during the last fifty, some progress has been made in the work of embodying the rules of public international law in international agreements of world-wide operation. This is in a limited sense codification, whether we describe it by that name or not. The process, in spite of the difficulties and uncertainties that at-

7. As a result of the disorders resulting from the war, the work of the commission was suspended and virtually abandoned. Provision for its revival was made by the Fifth International American Conference at Santiago, Chile, in 1923.

tend it, and the inadequacy of the means and methods often employed, will go on. The codification of private international law is even more difficult, because it deals with private rather than with public law, and involves to a great extent the element of procedure, which, according to a well-recognized rule, is governed by local law. This rule is not artificial, but inheres in the nature of the subject. It is important always to bear in mind that the object of law is the attainment of justice; that the different forms which prevail in different countries under their various legal systems have presumptively been worked out for the accomplishment of that end, and that efficiency is more to be desired than a preconceived uniformity of methods.

In dealing with the subject of the codification of international law we may well profit by the example of the Germans in preparing the Imperial Civil Code. When the Germans took up this great task, they appointed in the first place a commission to prepare a project. This commission was appointed in 1874, and devoted thirteen years to its work, presenting its report in 1887. After three years of public discussion, the project was committed to another commission in 1890. The code received the imperial approval in 1896, but did not take effect until 1900. —twenty-six years after the appointment of the first commission. And yet, the states for which this code was adopted were not only united under a federal government, with a supreme legislature, but had similar political and legal traditions.

Passing from the sphere of international to that of municipal law, it is not extravagant to say that for the operation of the passion for uniformity, whether in its regulated and constructive or in its unregulated and destructive form, the jurisprudence of the United States presents the world's largest opportunity. Looking at the bewildering confusion in the midst of which we dwell, our first impulse should be to assume that the desire for uniformity had been lacking altogether; and yet our political history affords one of the most remarkable examples of all time of the attempt suddenly to obliterate deepseated differences by legislative fiat. Scarcely fifty years ago the people of the United States entered upon what was called the period of Reconstruction. The policy of Reconstruction was apparently founded on the supposition that the only difference between, for instance, the New England Yankee and the lately emancipated slave was the fact that the one had had an opportunity to go to school, while the other had not. In order to insure equality in this and other respects, the emancipated slaves were invested with the elective franchise, in the expectation that they would at once use it intelligently and effectively, not only for the preservation of their own political rights, but also for the good of the community as a whole. In ten years the experiment broke down, and after the lapse of a certain time, in which the passion for uniformity steadily cooled, the States of the South were permitted effectually to nullify what had been done. The pendulum swung from one extreme to the other. Whether it be true, as has been suggested, that the people of the North suffered "a certain paralysis of feeling about the whole matter, due to exhaustion," it is certain that they at length acquiesced in the result.

This incident instructs us in the necessity of examining fundamental conditions, if our lawmaking is to endure. But it in no wise teaches that diversity is in itself a blessing or that we should refrain from seeking to bring about uniformity where convenience, which is the true foundation of all law, demands it.

Three hundred years ago Sir Francis Bacon, in his Proposition touching the Compiling and Amendment of the Laws of England, declared that, owing to the state of the laws at that time, there resulted among other things (1) "that the multiplicity and length of suits is great"; (2) "that the contentious person is armed, and the honest subject wearied and oppressed," and (3) "that the ignorant lawyer shroudeth his ignorance of law, in that doubts are so frequent and many." He therefore proposed a searching examination of all public and judicial records with a view to a compilation in which the following points should be observed: That overruled and obsolete cases should be omitted; that mere repetitions should be purged away; that idle queries and uncertainties should be left out; that tautologies and impertinencies should be cut off, and that the reports that were preserved should be carefully tested by the records and rectified so far as they were defective.

If Lord Bacon were now alive and were transplanted to the United States, what would he find? Certainly, from the scientific point of view, a legal chaos buttressed with shapeless masses of digests and indexes. And still the augmentation of more or less unformed material goes on at an ever-increasing rate. In 1819 the reports of the decisions of the American courts, including the federal decisions, were embraced in one hundred and eighty volumes. Seventy years later, in 1883, the number had grown to three thousand two hundred, with an annual increase of one hundred volumes. At the end of 1913, after the lapse of only thirty years more, the total had reached eight thousand four hundred and twenty volumes, with an annual output of two hundred and fourteen; and the number of reported cases which all the volumes contain is almost beyond computation. The multiplication of statutes goes on apace.

Statutory law in the United States may now be sought in more than three thousand volumes, with an adequate annual increase.[8]

We have spoken of the annual "output" of judicial reports, and the phrase, with its thrifty flavor, is deliberately chosen; for the publication of reports is little regulated and thoroughly commercialized. With each court there is connected a pipe promptly to convey its product to the great centre of distribution; and from this centre, day by day, month by month, year by year, there is poured out, as through a great main, upon a gurgling, gasping, sputtering Bar, a turgid stream of judicial decisions. Here there is no discrimination, no estimation of merit or of importance. Cases petty and cases important, cases of national interest and cases of interest purely local, final decisions, and decisions either reversed or on the way to reversal, are, with generous impartiality, spread broadcast over the entire land.

This system is supported by the Bar, with mingled feelings of gratitude and despair; for the Bar is conscious of the fact that, while it is in a sense served by the system, it is also enslaved and debauched by it. The very multiplicity of cases, and the consequent impossibility of dealing with them scientifically, reduces practitioners to a reliance upon particular decisions rather than upon general principles; and this in turn accentuates the tendency, long ago abnormally developed, to pay undue respect to mere cases as authority. How often do counsel produce with an air of triumph the latest decision, rendered perhaps in some far-off jurisdiction by a judge whose opinions derive their weight solely from his official position! How often, too, do they cite cases in their briefs indiscriminately. Some years ago the statement was made that in a single volume of reports then lately published more than five thousand cases were cited; and although this number would seem to suffice, possibly it may since have been exceeded.

8. The assistant librarian in charge of the shelves of the library of the Association of the Bar of the City of New York made in 1914 the following table, which, although it did not purport to be absolutely accurate, was sufficiently so for purposes of comparison:

| | | |
|---|---|---|
| English Reports, total number of volumes | | 2431 |
| Present annual increase | | 16 |
| American State Reports | 7370 volumes | |
| United States Reports | 1050    " | |
| Total number of volumes | | 8420 |
| Present annual increase | | 214 |
| English Public Statutes, total number of volumes | | 160 |
| Annual increase | | 1 |
| American Statutes, total number of volumes | | 3164 |
| Present annual increase | | 32 |

From the same causes our text-books also have deteriorated. We do not have to go back very many years to find treatises that rose to the dignity of codes, in the sense that they reduced to "a definite and systematic shape" the "results obtained and sanctioned by the experience of many centuries." [9] Such treatises today are exceedingly rare, and it is becoming daily more difficult to write them, because of the insistent demand for the citation of all decided cases. In consequence the preparation of text-books has to a great extent become a mechanical incident of the publishing business, so that, with here and there a notable exception, they mainly consist of lists of cases strung upon slender propositions, and scarcely rise above the dignity of amplified indexes.

For the conditions that have been described, when and how shall there be found a remedy? The remedy will not come immediately or all at once, but we may form a conjecture as to the lines along which it will progress. In the first place, so long as we maintain the separation of jurisdictions as between the federal government and the States and as between the States themselves—a separation that may be counted upon to continue indefinitely—that which is of general interest must be carefully divided from that which is essentially local. Probably we have been too much disposed in thinking of this division to follow simply the lines of the federal Constitution, but these are by no means adequate. There are many subjects not embraced in the federal Constitution, as so far legislatively construed or developed, which are of general interest, and yet this interest may be of a kind that does not require legal uniformity. Local conditions may so vary in the several States as to make an attempt at uniformity undesirable. It may be worthy of consideration whether the subject of marriage and divorce does not as yet fall within this category, although the tendency at present is to approach it from the point of view of legal uniformity.

On the other hand there are subjects in respect of which, in spite of the fact that national legislation does not deal with them, the general convenience calls loudly for uniformity. This is particularly the case in regard to the law relating to commercial matters. For this reason, I confess I have always considered the conception of the Supreme Court of the United States in *Swift* v. *Tyson*[10] as essentially sound. Speaking through Mr. Justice Story, the court held that the thirty-fourth section of the Judiciary Act, in prescribing "the laws of the

9. Stephen, *History of the Criminal Law of England*, III, chap. xxxiv.
10. 16 Peters, 1 (1842).

several States" as rules of decision in trials at common law in the federal courts, was to be "strictly limited to local statutes and local usages" and did not extend to "contracts and other instruments of a commercial nature, the true interpretation and effect whereof are," declared the court, "to be sought not in the decisions of the local tribunals, but in the general principles and doctrines of commercial jurisprudence." And the authority of Lord Mansfield was invoked to the effect that the law respecting negotiable instruments may be affirmed to be in great measure "not the law of a single country only, but of the commercial world."

This decision has been criticized by a great Pennsylvania judge as an "unfortunate misstep," on the strength of which the courts of the United States "have persisted in the recognition of a mythical commercial law, and have professed to decide so-called commercial questions by it, in entire disregard of the law of the State where the question arose." [11] The word "mythical," as here used, evidently was intended to convey the thought that the law which the courts in this instance professed to lay down was not law in the proper sense, because it had never been prescribed by the competent sovereign power. But, however this may be, we may find in the decision of the Supreme Court a response to the desire which has manifested itself in all times and in all lands, and which has in so many countries led to the establishment, in one way or another, of a uniform civil and commercial law.

The existence of this desire, which is but an expression of human convenience, emphasizes the importance of distinguishing carefully and in essence between that which is general and that which is local. The tendency of our national legislation to occupy new fields is a matter of common remark. In numerous instances its right has been disputed; but there are spheres unquestionably belonging to it which it has not yet occupied. One of these is the legislative and judicial assurance of the treaty rights of aliens.[12] This defect in our federal statutes has been glaringly revealed on more than one occasion, and no doubt will in time be corrected, so that we may confidently stand before the world in the attitude of enforcing treaties rather than in that of paying damages for their local infraction.

11. Judge Mitchell, in *Forepaugh* v. *Delaware, Lackawanna & Western Railroad Co.*, 128 Pa., 217 (1889).
12. See the valuable monograph, *The Treaty-Making Power of the United States and the Methods of Its Enforcement as Affecting the Police Powers of the States*, by Charles H. Burr, Esq., of the Philadelphia Bar.

In the effort to ameliorate confusion and gain a rational uniformity of law, it is always necessary specially to beware of that haste and superficiality which so often characterize proposals for codification. Codification, which in a proper sense and in appropriate spheres is an ideal to be kept in view, has in reality been discredited in the United States by many of its advocates. We have even heard the so-called codes of the Roman law invoked as an argument in favor of codification, evidently without knowledge of the fact that the *Corpus Juris* is not a code in the modern sense. Persons indeed are not wanting who will upon slight provocation undertake to furnish in short order a code either for the world or for a particular country. A legal society is formed, and we should not be surprised if one of its first acts is to appoint a committee on codification, with instructions to bring in, perhaps at the next annual meeting, if not a draft of a code, at least a report as to what such a work should be. The committee, composed perchance of estimable men not known to be specially fitted for the task, takes up its burden with due solemnity, and holds a certain number of consultations, and if at the end of a year the world is not enriched with what was proposed, the failure may be ascribed to preoccupation with other matters or perhaps to a want of facility in dictation. Or, possibly the fact may have been discovered that the task is great, and that the time is not ripe for its performance. Here is indeed a question truly fundamental. When it was proposed in 1815 that a civil code should forthwith be made for Germany, Savigny objected on the ground that German legal science was not sufficiently developed to justify the undertaking; and we are assured by a profound student of political and legal history that every German jurist today admits that Savigny was right.[13]

In the United States the law is at present in a singularly shifting state. Proposals are constantly put forward for material and even radical change, not only in constitutional law but also in criminal law and in various branches of civil law, such as contracts and torts. The difficulties in dealing with such a situation are illustrated by the experience of the National Conference of Commissioners on Uniform State Laws, whose members are appointed by the governors of the various States and Territories, under local law, for the purpose of conferring upon and recommending uniform laws in matters in which uniformity seems to be practicable and desirable. The moderation as well as the earnestness of this body is much

13. Professor Munroe Smith, in the *Political Science Quarterly*, II (1887), 134 *et seq.*

to be commended, and the general interest in its work is shown by the circumstance that forty-eight States, two Territories, the District of Columbia and our insular possessions are represented in it. In the twenty-three years of its existence it has formulated ten drafts of statutes.[14] The first of these, The Negotiable Instruments Act, has been adopted in forty-six States, Territories and possessions; the second, the Warehouse Receipts Act, in thirty. In no other instance has the number of adoptants exceeded eleven. The Divorce Act has, it may be observed, been adopted in only three States. It is true that some of the later recommendations have not been long before the public, so that their fate is not yet finally determined. But it is evident that, even where the need of uniformity is generally acknowledged, the task of formulating and securing the adoption of a uniform law is always attended with great uncertainty.[15]

An encouraging sign of a tendency to furnish practical relief without awaiting the development of comprehensive schemes of uniformity may be seen in the interest lately taken in the subject of legislative drafting. The loose and unregulated way in which bills are introduced in our legislatures, National and

14. These respectively relate to negotiable instruments, warehouse receipts, bills of lading, sales of goods, certificates of stock, divorce, family desertion, the probate of foreign wills and the evasion of marriage obligations.

15. Note, January 19, 1924. By the proceedings of the thirty-third annual meeting of the National Conference, at San Francisco, August 21–27, 1923, it appears that the total number of drafts of uniform acts then made and approved by the Conference was thirty-two. Their titles, the years in which they were respectively approved, and the number of jurisdictions in which they had, sometimes with modifications, been enacted, were as follows: Acknowledgments Act (1892), 9; Acknowledgments Acts, Foreign (1914), 7; Aeronautic Act (1922), 7; Bills of Lading Act (1909), 26; Child Labor Act (1911), 4; Cold Storage Act (1914), 6; Conditional Sales Act (1918), 8; Declaratory Judgments Act (1922), 5; Desertion and Non-support Act (1910), 19; Extradition of Persons of Unsound Mind (1916), 8; Fiduciaries Act (1922), 5; Foreign Depositions Act (1920), 10; Flag Act (19117), 9; Fraudulent Conveyance Act (1918), 11; Illegitimacy Act (1922), 4; Land Registration Act (1916), 3; Limited Partnership Act (1916), 13; Marriage and Marriage License Act (1911), 2; Marriage Evasion Act (1912), 5; Negotiable Instruments Act (1896), 51; Occupational Diseases Act (1920), 0; Partnership Act (1914), 16; Proof of Statutes Act (1920), 7; Sales Act (1906), 27; Sales Act, Amendments (1922), 2; Stock Transfer Act (1909), 17; Vital Statistics Act (1920), 1; Warehouse Receipts Act (1906), 48; Warehouse Receipts Act, Amendments (1922), 3; Wills Acts, Foreign Executed (1910), 7; Wills Act, Foreign Probated (1915), 4; Workmen's Compensation Act (1914), 2.

The "jurisdictions" include the forty-eight States of the United States, and Alaska, District of Columbia, Hawaii, Philippine Islands, and Porto Rico.

See Report of the American Bar Association (1923), XLVIII, 685, 698.

State, with little or no governmental responsibility for their presentation, affords an exceptional opportunity for the services of men trained in the study of legislation and its interpretation. The same need exists in the case of the numerous commissions appointed to investigate and report upon matters which are expected to be dealt with by means of new legislation. These commissions are often largely composed of persons who are much more interested in what they conceive to be the social or moral side of public questions than in the formulation and interpretation of statutes. It would be a great gain for our legislation if provision were made by the federal government, as well as by the State governments, for expert advice and assistance in the drafting and revision of legislative measures.[16]

An interesting incident in its relation to the development of rational uniformity was the formation in New York a year ago of a Conference of Teachers of Law and Philosophy. No matter what may be the fate of this particular movement, a step was taken in the right direction; for I venture to say that reform in our legal conditions must be the work of students and philosophers rather than of politicians and practicing lawyers. Not only does association with political and forensic controversies create prepossessions, but it also absorbs one's time and attention. Should we not have in legal science, just as we have in medical science, an Institute of Research, in which men of ability and learning, profoundly interested in their work, may be enabled to devote their entire time to the study of law, on its theoretical as well as its technical side, with a view to its development and perfection? The establishment of such an institute, either independently or in connection with some university, might solve the problem of how to obtain that thorough, orderly and comprehensive disclosure of fundamental conditions which is essential to intelligent action.[17]

16. See, *infra*, p. 264.
17. See Introduction, *supra*, p. 9.

## VIII

## SUGGESTIONS FOR A SCHOOL OF JURISPRUDENCE[1]

### GROWTH OF INTEREST IN LEGAL SCIENCE

IN recent years there have been many signs of the growth in the United States of an interest in the study of law for scientific rather than purely professional purposes, with the practical object always in view of improving and simplifying legislation and rendering it more nearly uniform. When the University of Chicago was established it was proposed to found there a School of Jurisprudence, but this proposal was not carried out for reasons that did not go to the merits of the question. Nearly fifteen years ago such a project was announced at the Johns Hopkins University, but they still lack the funds to carry it out. At Harvard University important studies in comparative law have been carried on by Rosoce Pound, since 1913 Carter Professor of Jurisprudence. A fund of a hundred thousand dollars was some years ago given to the University of Pennsylvania for the establishment of legal research fellowships. There are, however, four incidents that furnish remarkably clear and distinct proof of the progress of the tendency above mentioned.

One is the creation by the American Bar Association of a Comparative Law Bureau. A second is the initiative taken by the Association of American Law Schools to secure the translation of works on foreign law and on legal philosophy. A third is the action taken by the Librarian of Congress. In his annual report for 1910–11 he said:

The Law Division of the Library of Congress is making a systematic effort to bring its collection of foreign law to a state of high efficiency. The growing interest in comparative law manifested by legislators, lawyers, and scholars has indicated the utility and stimulated the acquisition of a well-developed laboratory of comparative law, in which shall be represented the best legal literature of the important States of the world.

In pursuance of this plan, the Librarian of Congress continued to develop his collections of legal literature, and issued a guide, prepared by Edwin M. Borchard, now a Professor of

1. For an explanation of the origin of this chapter, see the introduction to the present volume, *supra*, p. 9.

Law at Yale University, to the law and legal literature of Germany. This was followed by a similar guide for Spain; and, in 1917, by a *Guide to the Law and Legal Literature of Argentina, Brazil and Chile*. As a result of these developments, students of law in increasing numbers are turning to the Library of Congress.

Fourthly, Congress made provision for a legislative reference division in the Congressional Library.

### TASK FOR SCHOLARS UNDER UNIVERSITY PATRONAGE

This work, important as it is, is merely a preliminary to the more serious task which scholars must perform. The Comparative Law Bureau of the American Bar Association has assumed to some extent this more difficult and more serious task. The most pretentious of its earlier products, a translation of the Visigothic Code, was unreservedly condemned by competent critics.[2] But there have since been published, under its auspices, translations that have been more favorably received, including those of the civil codes of Argentina and Switzerland. The Bureau also published, from 1908 to 1914, inclusive, an Annual Bulletin, containing a review, by some qualified person, of the legislation of each country for the year, with notes on important legal events and a bibliography. Since 1915 this annual summary has been continued in the American Bar Association Journal. Great credit is due to those who have unselfishly contributed to this work.

An editorial committee of the Association of American Law Schools has arranged for the translation of numerous foreign works on Continental Legal History and Modern Legal Philosophy, and for the publication of the translations. Under trying conditions, including sometimes the lack of funds, and with much general apathy on the part of the Bar, the committee has, since 1915, brought forth some creditable translations by persons of recognized competency. Among these it is not invidious to mention the translations of Huebner's History of Germanic Private Law, Kohler's Philosophy of Law, Miraglia's Comparative Legal Philosophy, Del Vecchio's Formal Bases of Law, Tourtoulon's Philosophy in the Development of Law, Fouillée and others' Modern French Legal Philosophy, the Rational Basis of Legal Institutions, and the Science of Legal Method, Select Essays by various authors.

It is obvious, however, that, if work of the highest order in Comparative Law is to be done permanently and on a large scale, it must be efficiently organized and amply supported. To

2. See Vinogradoff, *Law Quarterly Review* (London, 1911), p. 373; Munroe Smith, *Columbia Law Review*, XI (1911), 695.

this end it should be taken up by some institution which has the sagacious inclination and the resources to employ competent men to give to the work their time and continuous attention and to pursue it unremittingly and systematically. The institution entering upon and effectively pursuing such a course will, it is believed, not only gain in prestige, but will also be enabled to guide the rapidly spreading movement for the application of scientific methods to legislation.

## LEGISLATIVE DRAFTING

In the development and guidance of this movement, a highly significant and promising beginning has already been made, at Columbia University, by the Legislative Drafting Research Fund, endowed by Mr. Joseph P. Chamberlain. Under this endowment there has been conducted by Mr. Chamberlain, Mr. Middleton Beaman, Mr. Thomas I. Parkinson, and their staff a legal laboratory, with a view to the improvement of legislation. Important work has been done by the Fund on Workmen's Compensation and other labor legislation, the Navigation and Shipping Laws, Criminal Procedure, Administrative Organization, Constitutional Law, and Methods of Law Enforcement; and in the prosecution of all these tasks a thorough knowledge of foreign law has been found to be essential. In regard to Workmen's Compensation, particularly, it has been necessary to seek information abroad, the subject being new in American law. The use, in labor disputes, of advisory councils, in which employer and employee are equally represented, has been derived from the legislation and experience of other countries. The preparation of legislation amendatory of our navigation and admiralty laws has also necessarily required an accurate knowledge both of the laws of other countries and of their operation. For the fact is always to be borne in mind that a knowledge of law, such as a draftsman should possess, signifies an acquaintance not only with the text of statutes and decisions, but also with the methods and results of their administration. Superficial copying of foreign laws would be as bad as the total disregard of them. Differences in economic conditions, in administrative organization, and in systems of jurisprudence must be appreciated by trained men if an effective practical result is to be obtained.

In the spring of 1919, directly, I believe, as the result of the expert work of Mr. Beaman and other members of the Fund, and its demonstrated helpfulness in the formulation of bills, the Congress of the United States established, both in the Senate and in the House of Representatives, a legislative drafting service, Mr. Parkinson becoming chief of the Senate's service and Mr. Beaman of that of the House. The greater number of the men who have since worked in the service have had training in the bureau at Columbia University. This is a striking example of the recognition of the value of scientific methods in the development of the law, and the value of appropriately trained men in the public service.

## PLAN AND SCOPE OF RESEARCH WORK

In view of what has been stated, the time appears to be opportune for taking up the study of Comparative Law, and placing it upon a broad and firm foundation. As part of the project, there should be established, to appear with the opening of the courses, a Journal of Comparative Law, such journal to be conducted on the strictest scientific principles. The publication of such a journal is contemplated in the articles of incorporation of the Legislative Drafting Association, now carrying on its work at Columbia. It would furnish the vehicle for the communication to the world of the results of the work done, and would also be available for the publication of the results of the work of scholars elsewhere. It would also furnish the basis for an Encyclopaedia of Jurisprudence, which would be the ultimate end to be labored for. In this relation it is proper to call attention to what has already been accomplished by the Legislative Drafting Research Fund not only in the basic formulation of legislative measures, but also in the preparation of an index-digest of all the constitutions of the States of the United States, and of a review for the American Bar Association of current national and State legislation, which is expected to be done annually.

To sum up, the plan would contemplate the following things:

1. Research Courses in Comparative Law.
2. A Journal of Comparative Law.
3. An Encyclopaedia of Comparative Law.

## NATURE OF NEW COURSES

One mistake that is generally made, when the study of Comparative Law is discussed, is in proposing to convert purely professional law-school courses into jurisprudence courses. This is impracticable and undesirable. Professional courses should not be diverted from their proper ends or diluted. This principle should be accepted as fundamental and unquestionable; and, if its operation is not interfered with by injudicious artificial contrivances, it will preserve itself automatically.

The new professorial work, taking as a basis of calculation such instruction in law as is, for instance, now given at Columbia University, should embrace courses in the jurisprudence of France, Germany, Italy, Spain, and Latin-America, and perhaps of other countries; additional work in Roman Law; additional work in the Conflict of Laws; and the comparative study of American and foreign legislation. The hours of lectures should aggregate fourteen a week, three of which should be given to Roman law and three to the Conflict of Laws, the remaining eight to be divided among the other topics mentioned.

For the research courses thus proposed, four years' study should be required, and upon its completion there should be awarded a degree. The question of the form of the degree is, however, a matter of detail.

By requiring at least four years' study, it is possible that a student might in that time obtain the degree of LL.B. as well as the comparative law degree, but this could not be done by the average student. It might be possible to perhaps a fifth of the candidates for the LL.B. This computation is based upon the supposition that a fifth of the students in the Law School could do the work necessary for the LL.B. in two-and-a-half years, and that the courses for the comparative law degree would positively exact a year-and-a-half's work in addition to that now required for the LL.B. The object would be to discourage rather than to encourage the average student to take distinctive comparative law work, and this to prevent degree-hunting as well as mental distraction.

## TEACHING FORCE AND FUNDS REQUIRED

In order to carry out such a project, it would be necessary to have an ample teaching force, and ample funds for the law library.

At Columbia University, for example, it is to be observed that, in addition to what is done in Legislative Drafting, the University already has courses in Roman Law and Jurisprudence, in the Conflict of Laws, in Administrative Law, in Comparative Constitutional Law, and in International Law. In order to extend the work in the direction of Comparative Law, it would be necessary to have, as a beginning, at least two additional instructors and an editor of the Journal, who might also deliver lectures. The Journal, so far as concerns the cost of printing, probably would eventually become self-supporting, since it would attract attention in all countries in which law is seriously studied; but its financial needs would have to be provided for independently of subscriptions at the outset.

## THE PRESENT OPPORTUNITY

It is evident that the provision of the means for the carrying out of a plan of work, such as has been outlined, involves the adoption of a broad and far-reaching policy with reference to legal studies. The experience of the past twenty years not only at Columbia University but also at other American universities seems to show that the demands upon their financial resources invariably increase faster than income, no matter how rapidly the latter may be augmented. This result seems to be due not so much to improvement in instruction as to an active competition in the diversification of the wares offered to the public. This diversified sales policy has demonstrably tended to degrade the standards of production. It is not unreasonable to think that the point has been reached where the comprehensive but intensive development of particular subjects at particular institutions would be justified by results. The institution that, besides training men to be skilled legal practitioners, will afford to those, who are qualified and so inclined, the opportunity to pursue the scientific ideal, thus producing great legal scholars, will not only hold a position of preëminence in legal studies, but will also fulfil its highest obligations to society.

The confusion and uncertainties of the law, denounced by Sir Francis Bacon three hundred years ago, find in the United States at the present moment their most striking modern exemplification. We have here what I ventured to describe ten years ago, as "a legal chaos buttressed with shapeless masses of digests and indexes"; and still the unscientific multiplication of decisions and statutes goes on. Prior to the creation of the American Law Institute, in 1923, the attempts made to find a remedy were lacking in permanence, consistency and resources. But the Institute is not a teaching body, and it has a specific and perhaps temporary mission. It is interested in using the services of legal scholars rather than in educating young men. The schools must continue to train the men for such work. The carrying out of the suggestions made in this chapter would constitute an important advance in that direction, besides furnishing invaluable guides to legislative action. The danger sometimes supposed to be inherent in studies in general jurisprudence is the possible development of a tendency to subordinate the practical concerns of life, with which legislation must necessarily deal, to the pursuit of theories more or less fanciful. In the present plan, double assurance against the development of such a tendency is found in the connection of the courses (1) with the law school and its professional train-

ing and (2) with the legislative drafting work, which, being
directly concerned with the reform and improvement of law
through legislation, must be carried on in concert with men
of affairs.

A great opportunity presents itself. The work will not remain unperformed. The time is ripe for it; and much lustre
would be reflected on the institution under whose auspices it
should be carried out.

# IX

## RELATIVITY[1]

I HAVE ventured to take as the title of the present discourse
the word "relativity"; but I do not intend to encroach on
the domain of the American Philosophical Society by discussing the merits or demerits of the theory associated with
the name of Einstein. My purpose is altogether different.

I use the word "relativity" to denote the great principle of
estimation by which human transactions are to be judged. This
principle is that all things are relative, in the sense that they
are to be considered not as isolated facts but as facts having
relation to other facts, past as well as present. This is not a
mere play of words or of fancy. The principle is fundamental,
and not less practical than profound. If suspended or hampered
in its operation, the world quickly deteriorates; its restoration
to activity carries the assurance of safety and growth. In its
effects it is both conservative and constructive. It is conservative, in that it preserves what ages of struggle have painfully
won; it is constructive, in that it intelligently guides progressive effort. Its roots strike deep into the past. Even from
the remotest antiquity it derives sustentation; but the vital
essence it draws from ancient sources serves but to enrich its
efflorescence and to increase the abundance of its fruits.

Nevertheless, there are and always have been those, and
their name is legion, by whom this great principle is little
understood; and its proponents are constantly forced to defend
it. The conflict between those who would study the past for its
lessons, and those who assume that the sights and sounds of
the present suffice, is not confined to any age. Nearly two
hundred years ago Sir William Temple, surveying the contro-

1. Address delivered at the University of Pennsylvania on "University
Day," February 22, 1924.

versy then going on in England as to the relative excellence of the ancient and the modern learning, inveighed against those who would discourage scholars, in all degrees, from reading the ancient authors. This protest, so he declared, he was induced to make not only by the common interest of learning, particularly in the universities, but also by a just indignation at the insolence of the modern advocates in defaming heroes whose memory had been sacred and admired for so many ages. But, wholly apart from the tendency, which re-writers of history still so often exhibit, to defame those whose work they would undermine, there is a common propensity to regard with complacent superiority the things with which one is familiar.

At one of the meetings held twenty-three years ago to celebrate the hundredth anniversary of the assumption by John Marshall of the office of Chief Justice of the United States, a speaker took occasion to comment upon the physical changes that had taken place since Marshall's time in the conditions of everyday life. Whether this was intended by way of praise or of disparagement of what was accomplished by Marshall and his contemporaries, the speaker did not make clear, but the note of disparagement seemed rather to prevail. What the speaker was apparently most desirous to do was to convey a caution against the inadvertent overestimation of the value and importance of what was done in earlier times; and in order to impress this thought upon his hearers, he remarked upon the fact that Marshall had never seen electric light, except as nature's flashes had illuminated his Virginian hills; had never used the telegraph or the telephone, and had never even traveled on a steam railway. The inference thus was obviously to be drawn that, tried by the higher, more diversified, more exacting standards of the centennial year, 1901, Marshall would be rather out of date.

This is a very prevalent point of view. One may indeed say that it reflects the popular attitude, and when I say "popular" I do not intend to exclude all those who make a profession of learning and intelligence. But it is easy to show that, tried by the test set up by the speaker in 1901, those who have survived to the present day are very much in advance of those who lived only as late as twenty-three years ago.

If proof of this fact were required, probably we should unanimously agree on one single and sufficient demonstration, and that is the recent development and use of radio. Its efficiency in the transmission of sound for purposes of instruction and amusement is evident; but if, applying the test of relativity, we undertake to estimate its value in imparting useful knowledge, in raising ideals, in stimulating and elevating the conception of public service, and in otherwise ministering to man's spiritual needs, it is by no means clear that the quick broadcasting of sound is necessarily to have an advantage over earlier and less speedy methods. I will give a practical illustration of my meaning.

Not long ago I happened to be at a place where there was a radio apparatus actively employed for the entertainment of those who were present. In the first instance connection was successively made with two broadcasting stations in the City of New York, and in each case the result was the same. The sound that floated through the room was that of jazz and a comic song. It was then suggested that a connection be made with Pittsburgh and, after some preliminary confusion, reverberations were heard from that more distant place. Again it was jazz and a comic song. It was then proposed that a connection be made with Philadelphia. Perhaps it was expected that we should hear from that quarter, if not the thunders of the law, yet a grave and quiet discussion of the mooted question as to the precise spot on which William Penn signed the treaty with the Indians. But this did not prove to be the case. After the usual preliminary convulsion a dominant note asserted itself, and, in the language of Byron, "there was heard a sound of revelry by night"; and yet again—it was jazz and a comic song.

Far be it from me to reflect, even in the smallest measure, on the menu of radio. The particular occasion to which I have adverted happened to be the hour when men and women dance and dine and dine and dance. As the newspaper displays with type, so radio displays with sound, all forms of human activity, grave as well as gay; the solemn but diffident admonitions of the university oration as well as the flaunting enchantments of the sentimental ditty. Nor would I be understood to intimate that dance and song did not occupy a place, even a large and hilarious place, in the life of earlier and indeed of all previous generations. All I intend to convey is the thought that the development and accumulation of scientific discoveries, and of inventions that quicken locomotion and the dissemination of sound, bear no intrinsic relation to the progress of mankind in spiritual things, and that, so far as they minister to mistaken assumptions of moral or intellectual superiority, their effect may even be harmful.

The intense preoccupation of the present generation with the physical sciences has exerted a profound influence both on instruction and on the selection of subjects of instruction in our schools, and this influence has been no less visible and pronounced in our colleges and universities than elsewhere. This was natural and in a measure inevitable. None of us can be insensible to the human activities by which we are daily encompassed; nor is a mere bovine imperviousness to their effects to be commended. But it is, on the other hand, of the utmost importance to be on our guard against the impulsive, headlong rush after passing fancies, the extreme pursuit of which may, like the over-hasty movement of an army, result in the loss of essential equipment and supplies.

Some years ago, in the bazaars of the Orient, I watched the caravans as they arrived and departed; and I observed that the camels were always preceded by a donkey. My curiosity being excited by this singular form of leadership, I later investigated its origin, and found in a learned source this explanation: "An unladen ass precedes the file, for luck, some say, for guidance, say others." We thus see that the tendency to follow some kind of leadership, and to trust to it rather blindly, is more or less characteristic of all animate nature. But human beings possess in this regard a manifest advantage. Palgrave, in his narative of a journey in Arabia, tells us that the camel, though "never tame," is "not wide-awake enough to be exactly wild." This is not true of human beings. Without regard to the question how far they can be tamed, they are wide-awake enough for every purpose; but, while thus fully alert, they also fortunately possess, as a check on impulse, the power of discrimination.

The need to exercise this power is ever present; but the effort may be futile and even disastrous, if it be not informed and guided by a comprehensive acquaintance with the records of human experience. The conscious recognition of this truth is one of the reasons of the present demand for the reëxamination of recent tendencies in our colleges and universities, and particularly of the permissive substitution of modern for ancient languages, including Latin as well as Greek, and the consequent abandonment of the study of the ancient classics as a requisite for even the higher degrees.

These changes have been justified by the argument that the study of the ancient languages has lost its relative educational value, a knowledge of the physical sciences having become more important than that of the humanities, as well as by the argument that the modern languages had been neglected and that they would in future, by reason of the substitution, be more effectively taught and more generally learned. The former argument, which touches a fundamental point, will be considered farther on; the second may be disposed of somewhat briefly. Its validity may readily be tested by comparing the earlier with the later results in the case of candidates in our universities who apply for the higher degrees, such as that of doctor of philosophy. Of candidates for these degrees a knowledge of the ancient languages, or at any rate of Latin, and also of two modern languages other than the candidate's native tongue, was strictly exacted. In recent days there has been a logical tendency, conforming to the subordination or waiving of classical studies in college courses, to permit the candidate to substitute modern languages for the classical tongues. It is probable that no one having experience in such matters could be found to affirm that this subordination or waiving of the classics has resulted in a higher proficiency in the modern languages. The earlier candidate who knew Latin usually knew his French far better and his German equally well. So that, from the linguistic point of view, there has been no gain, but a net loss.

The observation of results such as these has contributed to the agitation now going on for the revival and restoration of the study of the classics. This movement may be said to be international, and the fact that it is international merely denotes that the same process of educational deterioration has been of wide extent, and that the need of its correction is recognized and felt in many lands. The other day I had the pleasure to receive from that eminent judge and jurist, Lord Finlay, formerly Lord Chancellor of Great Britain and now a member of the Permanent Court of International Justice at The Hague, a copy of an address which he delivered on the occasion of his recent installation as President of the Scottish Classical Association. In the numerous proofs which Lord Finlay adduces of the returning sense of the importance of classical studies, he cites the decree issued in France as late as May 3, 1923, restoring Latin and Greek to their former place as essentials of secondary education. This decree, which has also been noted and widely discussed in the United States, was based upon a report of the Minister of Public Instruction, M. Léon Bérard, in which he maintained the sound and enduring doctrine that the object of training in the secondary schools is to introduce the mind to fruitful methods of learning rather than to burden it with a mass of heterogeneous and unrelated facts.

But another and yet profounder reason may be given for preserving our acquaintance with the languages commonly called dead; and, when I say "commonly called dead," I speak advisedly, since the mortuary assumption is supported by the proofs only in a limited sense. The Apostle Paul, when referring to one long departed, of whose gifts God had testified, described him as one who "being dead yet speaketh." No dubious license is needed to extend this affirmation of continuing vital force to Homer and Virgil, Herodotus and Livy, Thucydides and Tacitus, Demosthenes and Cicero, Plato and Seneca, to say nothing of others whose works still furnish models for students of poetry and prose, of eloquence and logic, of history, politics and philosophy. No less evident is the persistence of Greek in the terminology of science, or the perpetuation of the speech of the Romans in the great Romance languages, of which Latin is the vital source. Nor is this all. Long after Greek had ceased to be widely spoken, Latin remained, even as in limited circles it does today, the language of ecclesiastics and scholars, thus serving both as the vehicle of expression, and as the living repository and perpetuation, of the learning of the times as well as of the ancient learning. Nor was the inexorable character of this succession altogether done away with by the advent of the Encyclopedists. Should anyone entertain a doubt on this point, let him, for instance, essay to trace the application of judicial methods to the settlement of international disputes during the past thousand years.

The educational results accomplished by the encyclopedist are severely conditioned by the nature of his task, the fundamental limitation of which may be illustrated by an anecdote, more witty than polite, told of Lord Eldon. Speaking one day of the narrowness of his early circumstances, his lordship is said to have remarked that when, at his marriage, he repeated the words "with all my worldly goods I thee endow," he had barely a crown to his name; and when Lady Eldon, who was present, amiably observed that his lordship had his "splendid talents," he is reported to have replied: "Yes, my dear; but I did not endow you with them."

So it is with the encyclopedist. No matter how profound may be his individual researches, he cannot endow the general reader with that understanding of a subject which can be gained only by the mastery of all its processes, nor has he the time and attention of his reader at command for such a purpose. Especially is this true of subjects which, although they touch the primary springs of human conduct, can, because they are technical and essentially recondite, be mastered only by recurring to the original sources.

Thus by converging streams of argument are we surely borne to the consummate conclusion that, for preserving a familiar acquaintance with the ancient languages, the profoundest reason that can be given is the fact that the study of them, in conserving our connections with the past and its inexhaustible treasures, not only induces habits of inquiry and reflection, but qualifies us intelligently to estimate the current phenomena of life, relatively and in their true perspective, as incidents in the unbroken procession of human activities, and not, in dazed and hasty fashion, as new and isolated things, without precedent in the annals of human experience.

This vital phase of the subject, so far as I am acquainted with what has been said concerning it, has never been explained with greater force or felicity than was done by President Coolidge, in the address which, while he was still Vice-President of the United States, he delivered at the annual meeting of the American Classical League at the University of Pennsylvania in July, 1921. Speaking on that occasion, President Coolidge said:

We come here today in defense of some of the great realities of life. We come to continue the guarantee of progress in the future by continuing a knowledge of progress in the past. . . . The age of science and commercialism is here. There is no sound reason for wishing it otherwise. The wise desire is not to destroy it, but to use it and direct it rather than to be used and directed by it, that it may be as it should be, not the master but the servant, that the physical forces may not prevail over the moral forces and that the rule of life may not be expediency but righteousness.

No question can be adequately comprehended without its historical background. Modern civilization dates from Greece and Rome. The world was not new in their day.

As the world was not new in the days of Greece and Rome, so it is not new in our own day. As we owe our models in art, in literature, and even in politics and government in some measure to Greece, so also do we owe a large part of our heritage of literature and law, and of experience in the forms and processes of government, to Rome.

Very recently I had occasion to reperuse the Politics of Aristotle, and I confess that I did it in an expert translation, my own knowledge of Greek, which was at one time, as things go, relatively substantial, having been impaired by a desuetude which I will not call innocuous or otherwise seek to extenuate. If there is any phase of political action not dealt with in the disquisition of Aristotle, it is a phase which, I do not hesitate to affirm, our modernists will not be able to point out. The most fundamental conceptions are there. The doctrine of the separation of governmental powers is often spoken of as a modern development, for the exposition of which few go farther back than to the celebrated treatise of Montesquieu. But it is set forth with unsurpassed comprehensiveness, clearness and force in the work of Aristotle. This is but a single illustration.

We beat the air today and demand the instant eradication of all human ills, chiefly by means of legislation, national and international. In keeping with the profound and serious character of such demands, a popular but apparently inopulent writer has lately offered a lock of a certain senatorial Sampson's hair as a prize for the best definition of a "progressive." The competition for the prize is said to be very active, but there appears to be a dominant note of common sense in the comment of a western editor who, while professing to be "avowedly progressive and proud of it," declares that he is prepared to endorse "neither extreme communism nor extreme corporationism," but prefers to "fumble along, trying to salvage some of the old finer western American qualities of courage and independence, being illogical, inconsistent, and full of fight."

No one who reflects upon current transactions and contrasts them with what was done in the earlier days of the Republic can fail to acknowledge that we cannot afford either to cut our connections with the past, or to act upon the assumption that we do not need its experience and example as a stimulus and guide. At the present moment the tendency to consider recent conditions as isolated facts is producing unfortunate effects even among those who might have been expected to apply the principle of relativity and to explore the past for the purpose of testing the validity of current impressions. As a result we often hear today that established rules, heretofore unchallenged, are no longer to be maintained, because they are inapplicable to present conditions, which are mistakenly assumed to be wholly or substantially new. By reason of the same superficial and erroneous impression, we are told that even the elementary, humane distinction between combatants and non-combatants in war has to a great extent become invalid, so that it can no longer be reckoned upon to safeguard the lives of unarmed men and women or to assure protection to property and commerce. Certainly it is high time to reëxamine the premises on which such conclusions rest, and to do it in the light of past experience and of the agonizing cost of the hard-won advance which it is now proposed incontinently to abandon.

Taking a still wider range, no matter in what direction we turn, we hear the same impressive admonition. We all are familiar with Gladstone's celebrated pronouncement that the Constitution of the United States is "the most wonderful work ever struck off at a given time by the brain and purpose of man." The President of the Constitutional Convention was George Washington, the anniversary of whose birth the University of Pennsylvania has most fitly adopted as its "University Day." In repeating the encomium that he was "first in war, first in peace, and first in the hearts of his countrymen," we have the same justification as when we recite the proverbs of the past for the instruction and improvement of the present. Nor can we too often recur to his wise words and patriotic example.

There never was a period in the history of the world in which work of a higher constructive order in politics and in government was done than in the years made illustrious by the achievements of Washington and his contemporaries. If there were among them a few to whom, as Cardinal Newman has said, the just estimate of passing events might possibly be a natural gift, yet there were others who had gained their power of just estimation through the study of what had gone before. Indeed, when one reads the records of that formative and fruitful time, nothing can impress him more than the learned effort on the part of the framers of the Constitution and its expounders to utilize all that could be derived from accessible sources concerning the experience of the past. The idea that, in throwing off one government and setting up another they were so breaking with the past as to render its teachings negligible or superfluous, never entered their sober counsels.

But the Constitution was not the only momentous document which the efforts of the time brought forth. Almost as remarkable was the Judiciary Act, under which the federal courts were set up, and by which their jurisdiction and processes were defined and regulated; a statute so sagaciously contrived that it stood for a hundred and twenty years without substantial amendment.

By such great constructive measures those who gave us independence also gave us unity. Of all national blessings this is the greatest, but, like other blessings, it is neither self-created nor self-preserved. Conceived in our own case in a broad and tolerant spirit, and not in a mere grasping after concentrated power, it was brought about through mutual concession and the considerate adjustment of conflicting interests. It was destined in time to be subjected to the arbitrament of battle; but, from the fact that it survived the ordeal, we are not to infer that it was permanently placed beyond peril or impairment. At every juncture in our national life, there will be need of the vision and the spirit to which the gift was originally due. While we must guard, on the one hand, against starving the capacity for self-government by sweeping everything into the maw of a centralized, bureaucratic organization, we must, on the other hand, equally be on our guard against the indulgence of a propensity to split up into groups or *blocs* on differences not only not fundamental but often vague and whimsical. It may be characteristic that this propensity is often most strikingly exemplified by those who go to the greatest length in demands for the extension of federal power to local objects, thus menacing the poise of the national structure. But the propensity is also anti-national because it forces government to depend from day to day on the promiscuous combination of elements that are essentially narrow and self-centered, and, in the sense of political bargaining, exacting and corrupt. In such a plight, even a constitutional and parliamentary government may, as we know, occasionally find in a dictatorship a convenient supplement. Against the indulgence of the spirit of faction, Washington never failed to warn his countrymen, by words of wisdom as well as by generous acts.

But, if the achievements of Washington and his contemporaries were remarkable in the national sphere, hardly less so were they in the international. I cannot now enter into particulars, and designate all the constructive measures, such as those relating to the recognition of governments, non-intervention in their internal affairs, and the performance of the duties of neutrality, by which the rules of international law were made more definite and secure. I will only say that the foundations were then well and surely laid of the foreign policy which the United States has in the main since pursued. Based on the principle of the independence and equality of nations, in no respect was its development more striking than in the use of mixed commissions or arbitral boards designed to assure the settlement of international disputes by the application of rules of law. By what was done in that direction, particularly under the Jay Treaty, signed and ratified while Washington was President, this legal and pacific method, which the recurrent wars in Europe had caused to fall into disuse, may be said to have been revived.

The Jay Treaty was concluded at London on November 19, 1794, the signers being Lord Grenville on the part of Great Britain, and John Jay, then Chief Justice, on the part of the United States. It provided for three international boards of arbitration. To the first was committed the ascertainment of the boundary river designated in the treaty of peace as the St. Croix. This was successfully accomplished by means of a decision which the contracting parties, in conformity with their engagement, accepted as final. By the establishment of the second board, it was intended to assure compensation to British creditors for the loss of debts which some of the States of the Confederation had undertaken to confiscate during the Revolutionary War; but, owing to certain causes, partly personal, the proceedings of this commission were suspended, and a direct settlement was effected through the payment by the United States of a round sum. Of vastly greater importance, however, was the third board, which was established under Article VII of the treaty.

By this article provision was made for the settlement of two classes of claims, one American and the other British, both of which arose during the war between Great Britain and France growing out of the French Revolution. In this war Washington had declared the United States to be neutral. The American claims were demands for compensation for loss and damage suffered by citizens of the United States by reason of British captures or condemnations of their vessels and other property. The British claims were, on the other hand, demands for compensation for loss and damage suffered by British subjects through French captures of their vessels and merchandise, made either within the jurisdiction of the United States or by vessels originally armed there. In the case of the American claims, it was contended that the British government had violated rights of neutral trade. In the case of the British claims, it was contended that the government of the United States had failed to perform its neutral duties. The contentions on both sides profoundly affected the interests both of belligerents and of neutrals.

For the purpose of settling in a legal, orderly, peaceful way these serious controversies, on which potentially hung the issues of peace and war, it was agreed to establish at London a mixed commission to consist of five persons, two of whom should be appointed by the United States and two by Great Britain, while the fifth, if not unanimously chosen by the other four, was to be drawn by lot. This plan was carried out, and the board was duly installed.

The individual distinction of the members of this tribunal would alone suffice to give it a high place in the annals of international arbitration. The commissioners chosen on the part of the United States were Christopher Gore, of Massachusetts, and William Pinkney, of Maryland. Gore, who is commemorated at Harvard University by the hall bearing his name, was one of the chief ornaments of the Boston bar, but his reputation was by no means purely local. His professional renown had spread far beyond his city and State. Of Pinkney, it may be said that his star was in the ascendant. Destined later to play a distinguished rôle in statesmanship and in diplomacy, he lived to become the pride and the acknowledged leader of the American bar. Great Britain, on the other hand, appointed as her commissioners two eminent civilians, one of whom, Sir John Nicholl, eventually succeeded Lord Stowell as Judge of the High Court of Admiralty. The other British commissioner was John Anstey, an advocate of the highest professional rank at the admiralty bar. The fifth commissioner, who was drawn by lot, was Colonel John Trumbull, of Connecticut, who later became governor of that State.

Nor was the tribunal distinguished solely by the high quality of its membership. It was rendered equally notable by the amplitude of its jurisdiction. Not only were the claims sweepingly embraced in general categories, but the powers of the commissioners in deciding upon them were unhampered by words of limitation or exception. It was thus left to the commission to pronounce on questions of a fundamental character, and this the commission did. In the first place, it asserted and exercised the power to determine for itself the limits of its jurisdiction under the terms of its constitution; and, in the second place, it entertained claims based on condemnations of property by national prize courts of the highest jurisdiction, and awarded damages where it held such condemnations to have been wrongful. The settlements effected through the commission rose to the extraordinary total for those days of ten million dollars, and the money as it became due was paid punctually and without protest. Evidently the impression then prevailed that the determination of international disputes by judicial methods could be efficacious only if the tribunals were invested with power and supported in the exercise of it.

The work of the London commission had yet another result. Among the international arbitrations so far held, that of the *Alabama* claims at Geneva in 1872 still represents the high-water mark. But it is a fact, known to the intelligent negotiators of that time, but perhaps little known today, that the germination of the Geneva arbitration may be traced to the Jay treaty and the proceedings of the London commission, which was, it is believed, the first international tribunal judicially to award pecuniary compensation for damages resulting from the alleged failure of a government to perform its duties as a neutral.

Today we are not improving upon those precedents. On the contrary, if arbitral agreements are made, there is a disposition to hedge them about with limitations and to emasculate them with exceptions, and, if the award is against us, to question its justice or even its validity. Such things may imply either a change of attitude towards the method, or a want of confidence in its administration, or, like certain popular comestibles, a blend of both. But, no matter which it may be, the explanation reflects a state of mind just now very prevalent and by no means confined to any particular subject. There is grave discontent with existing conditions. The public mind is troubled, perplexed, excited. There is a general want of confidence, and a corresponding unrest. The depression will not last. Hope will revive and confidence eventually return, but not as a result of the lowering of our standards. Many prate of service to democracy, and, in the name of this much-abused shibboleth, would seek to popularize all learning by relaxing the tests of toil and self-denial; but, if we believe in democracy and do not wish to exploit it, we should resist such proposals as the greatest disservice to democracy that could possibly be rendered. Democracy will justify the faith of its true believers only by its strivings after better and higher things.

In moving in a babel of sights and sounds the present generation is not exceptional. The predicament is characteristically human. Like the hosts on the plains of Troy, we still struggle on in the midst of ululations. Some think more than they speak, but the preponderance of those who speak more than they think is so great that the volume of sound necessarily becomes confusing. Here again we must invoke the principle of relativity, lest we permit our attention to be wholly preoccupied and our senses benumbed by the diverting clamors of the moment. From the deadening effect of such a situation we can extricate ourselves only by rising to higher altitudes, at which, as we listen to the echoes of our historic past, we can also pick up the beacons that light the ways of human progress.

Plato, in his Republic, depicts an inspiring spectacle in which mounted horsemen carry torches which they pass one to another during the race. Such ever has been, and ever will be, the sacred office of those who perpetuate the deeds and learning of the past for the benefit of the future. In the unending succession there has been committed to us, in our own time, the same exalted trust. Those who are to succeed us await in turn our testimony, our precept and example. Even now we can hear in advance their eager inquiry. We must answer: and our answer will be adjudged in the great book of posterity. Our responsibility is great, but equally great is our opportunity; and may the judgment be recorded, in proof of our fidelity and our faith, that the torches handed to ourselves were borne on with well-replenished flame to a fortunate and grateful generation.

# BOOK REVIEW

RECENT DEVELOPMENTS IN INTERNATIONAL LAW.
*By* JAMES WILFORD GARNER. Calcutta, Calcutta University
Press, 1925. Pp. x, 840.

This volume incorporates a course of lectures, substantially
as they were originally written, delivered by Dr. Garner in
November and December 1922, as Tagore Professor of Law in
the University of Calcutta for that year. His selection for that
post no doubt may in a measure be ascribed to the impression
made by his treatise entitled *International Law and the World
War,* published in 1920, in two volumes. To the reflection of
those who are accustomed to contemplate the "codification" of
international law with a lightness of heart similar to that with
which Louis Napoleon declared that he entered upon the
Franco-German war of 1870, it may be appropriate to commend Dr. Garner's prefatory remark, in the volume now under
review, that international law, like the common law of England and the United States, "has grown up slowly and gradually, largely by the process of accretion"; that the results are
"the culmination of historical and evolutionary processes,"
which can be "satisfactorily studied only by beginning with
their origins"; and that much of what has taken place since
the opening of the present century, instead of being in any
true sense of the word a "development," belongs more properly
to the domain of "interpretation" and "application," sometimes representing "retrogression rather than progress." On
the other hand, the reaching of a specific agreement, as is now
and then done, on rules concerning matters about which there
has been a divergence of opinion among states, involves, he
observes, "the work of codification in the larger sense of the
word"; and notable attempts have been made in recent years
to advance in this direction.

As regards present doctrine and practice, Dr. Garner says
that "the supremacy of international law does not exist in the
sense that national courts may disregard the law of their own
state when in their opinion it is repugnant to the prescriptions
of international law"; and, employing the terminology of certain other writers, the value of which he questions, he remarks
that, in the aspect just mentioned, international law "is still

*inter*-national and not *super*-national." Not only do I fully share Dr. Garner's doubts as to the value of this terminology, but I think it clearly betrays, on the part of its authors, a want of appreciation of certain elementary legal principles. The phrase "international law" has to a great extent superseded the title "law of nations," or, as we often find it in earlier writers, "laws of nations"; and the specific object of the substitution was to indicate that this body of law, instead of being a law *of* nations, in the sense of emanating and deriving its authority from the legislation and decrees of each nation separately and individually, was "international," or, in other words, a law *between* nations, binding them as between themselves, individually and collectively, by a superior obligation, and constituting a standard to which their municipal law must be made to conform. Of this conception there is the familiar corollary that all states within the circle of law-governed nations are conclusively presumed to have accepted that obligation and standard. This is simple and altogether intelligible. The part national courts may play in the interpretation and application of international law is another matter. National courts are not the sole nor the final interpreters of international law, nor are they the designated agencies of foreign intercourse; and if, in discharging their functions, they violate a rule of international law either freely, by reason of misunderstanding, or under compulsion, by reason of an act of national legislation, the nation is answerable through its proper organ. This is an admitted principle so constantly acted upon that the citation of examples of its observance should be superfluous.

In the course of his discussions Dr. Garner deals, among other things, with The Hague conventions, maritime warfare and the Declaration of London; with the interpretation and application of international law in recent wars, including the "world war," and with the peaceful settlement of international disputes by means of arbitration and otherwise. He devotes to the history of the development of an international court of justice an entire lecture, concluding with a comprehensive account of the Permanent Court of International Justice which was eventually opened at The Hague in 1922. In describing the so-called convention for the limitation of the use of force for the collection of contract debts (The Hague, 1907), he inadvertently speaks (pp. 70, 71) of Señor Drago as a Chilean; he was, like Calvo, an Argentine. But this is not a matter of substance. On the other hand, one naturally looks for the author's considered opinions on questions of such profound importance as the professed interpretations and applications of international law during the "world war"; and it is interesting to find here the clear and significant statement that, in respect of the treatment of the property and business enterprises of enemy aliens, "the policy of all the belligerents was severe and largely unprecedented" (p. 311). No less clear and significant is his opinion that, although none of the belligerents appears to have "intended" that the properties taken into their custody should be "confiscated outright," yet the provision of the treaties of peace (the Versailles treaty with Germany, and the treaties with Austria, Bulgaria, Hungary and Turkey) that such properties should be held for the satisfaction of claims "amounted virtually to confiscation," and that "the requirement that the enemy governments should indemnify their nationals for the losses sustained by the appropriation of their property for this purpose hardly rendered it less so" (pp. 312–313). A writer is to be commended who, thus brushing sophistry aside, candidly goes to the heart of the matter.

Reprinted from the *Yale Law Journal*, XXXV (1925), 123–125.


# HOW THE WORLD COURT OPERATES[1]

THE Court, as constituted, consists of fifteen "members," composed of eleven judges, called "ordinary judges," and four deputy-judges. By express provision of the Statute (Art. 25), the eleven judges constitute the "full Court" for active purposes. In case they cannot all be present, deputies are to sit as judges in place of the absentees; but, if eleven judges are not available, nine may constitute a quorum. The full Court is required to sit, except where it is expressly provided otherwise.

The judges are not elected and do not sit as citizens or representatives of any particular country. As far as human nature will permit, they are expected to decide impartially between all countries, without favor or antipathy to any. To this end the Statute provides that the Court "shall be composed of a body of independent judges, elected regardless of their nationality." On the other hand, the election of more than one judge of any particular nationality is forbidden.

The members of the Court are elected for nine years, and may be re-elected; but, where a person is chosen to fill a va-

1. Extracts from *International Law and Some Current Illusions and Other Essays* (New York, The Macmillan Company, 1924). Reprinted from the *Congressional Digest*, V (February, 1926), 51–52.

cancy, he holds office only for the remainder of the unexpired term. It thus results that there must be an election of the whole Court every nine years.

The compensation of the members of the Court is regulated by the Statute, and is expressed in Dutch florins. The judges each receive an annual salary of 15,000 florins, which, at the normal rate of exchange, is equivalent to $6,030. The president of the Court, who is required to live at The Hague, receives in addition a flat special allowance of 45,000 florins. The additional pay of the other judges, apart from the refund of traveling expenses and an allowance of 50 florins a day for living expenses while at The Hague, depends on service, and is in the form of a duty-allowance, which is fixed at 100 florins a day, except in the case of the vice-president, who receives 150 florins a day.

The Court must, by the terms of the Statute, hold in each year at least one session, which, unless the rules of the Court otherwise provide, must begin on the 15th of June, and must continue until the 'cases on the list are disposed of. The President, however, may summon an extraordinary session whenever necessary.

Each member of the Court is required, before taking up his duties, to make a solemn declaration in open court that he will exercise his powers impartially and conscientiously. The members, when engaged in the business of the Court, enjoy diplomatic privileges and immunities.

The members of the Court wear robes with black velvet facing, which can hardly be distinguished from the academic gown commonly worn in the United States. The robe adopted by the Permanent Court is worn only on the bench.

The official languages of the Court are French and English, but the Court may, at the request of the parties, authorize another language to be used. The parties are to be represented by agents and, as in the case of ordinary courts, may have the assistance of counsel or advocates. Proceedings are both written and oral. This applies to the testimony of witnesses. Hearings are to be public, unless the Court shall otherwise decide, or unless the parties demand that the public be not admitted. Minutes must be kept of all hearings.

All questions are to be decided by a majority of the judges present at the hearing, and in the event of an even division, the president or his deputy is to have a casting vote.

Every judgment is required to state the reasons on which it is based and to contain the names of the judges who have taken part in it. If the judgment is not unanimous, dissenting judges are entitled to deliver separate opinions. Judgments must be read in open court, after due notice to the agents of the parties. If the meaning or scope of the judgment is disputed, the Court, on the request of any party, is to construe it. Applications for revision may be made only on the ground of discovery of some decisive fact which, when the judgment was rendered, was unknown to the Court and also to the party claiming revision. But no application is allowed if the want of knowledge was due to negligence. The Court frames its own rules of procedure.

The Court, or, if it is not sitting, the president, may, after hearing the parties, order the registrar to permit the inspection of the cases and counter-cases.

Article 38 of the Statute provides that the Court, in rendering its decisions, shall apply (1) "international conventions, whether general or particular, establishing rules expressly recognized by the contesting States," (2) "international custom, as evidence of a general practice accepted as law," (3) "the general principles of law recognized by civilized nations," and (4), "subject to the provisions of Article 59, judicial decisions and the teachings of the most highly qualified publicists of the various nations, as subsidiary means for the determination of rules of law."

By the fourth clause, the use of "judicial decisions" and the teachings of publicists as "subsidiary means" for determining rules of law is qualified by Article 59 of the Statute. The preceding articles prescribe the manner and form in which judgments of the Court shall be rendered, and Article 59 then declares: "The decision of the Court has no binding force except between the parties and in respect of that particular case."

Articles 62 and 63 of the Statute, however, provide for the intervention, as a third party, of any State which considers "that it has an interest of a legal nature which may be affected by the decision in the case," and, where the interpretation of a treaty is concerned, of any party to the treaty who was not a party to the case.

The Statute, as adopted by the Assembly of the League, does not directly mention advisory opinions; but the Court, after careful consideration, reached the conclusion that there were certain clauses of the Statute which by implication incorporated the provision in Article 14 of the Covenant on that subject. It was therefore decided that, while the Court would not be justified in taking the position that it would not in any case give an advisory opinion, it remained with the Court to determine whether it would in a particular case, considering the nature of the question submitted, give such an opinion. The rules adopted by the Court are based on this view. They assimilate the process as far as possible to a judicial proceeding, and exclude any supposition that advisory opinions may be rendered in a diplomatic sense and without publicity.

All the advisory opinions have been given on questions submitted by or through the Council of the League. Under the head of "Advisory Procedure" the rules provide that the questions upon which advisory opinions are sought shall be laid before the Court by means of a written request; that this request "shall contain an exact statement of the question upon which an opinion is required, and shall be accompanied by all documents likely to throw light upon the question"; that the Registrar shall forthwith give notice of the request, not only to the Members of the League and the States mentioned in the Annex to the Covenant, but also "to any international organizations which are likely to be able to furnish information on the question"; that the opinions shall be given after deliberation by the full Court, and that the opinions of dissenting judges may, at their request, be attached to the opinion of the Court; and that the opinions and the requests in response to which they are given shall be printed and published. The Court reserved to itself the right to consider what its action should be on each particular request and to refuse to reply to a question as submitted should there be ground for such refusal.

The Court has not thought it feasible to fill a dual rôle, acting at one moment as a judicial body rendering judgments on international differences, and at the next moment as a board of counselors giving private and ex parte advice on such matters. Indeed, an auditor or spectator would detect no difference between a proceeding for a judgment and a proceeding for an advisory opinion. All its opinions and decisions have been read from the printed text on the day of their delivery, and the proofs and arguments have also been printed and published.

On May 17, 1922, the Council, acting under Article 35 of the Statute, passed a resolution laying down the conditions under which the Court should be open to States not members of the League or mentioned in the Annex to the Covenant. The Court had recommended that this be done. The resolution requires the filing with the Court of a declaration accepting its jurisdiction in accordance with the Covenant, Statute and Rules, and promising to carry out its decisions and not to resort to war against states complying with them. The declaration may be either particular, embracing a particular dispute; or general, embracing all or a particular class of disputes. The resolution, however, provides that declarant's acceptance of compulsory jurisdiction under Article 36 of the Statute shall not, without a special convention, be reciprocally binding on members of the League and States mentioned in the Annex to the Covenant which have signed or may in future sign the "optional clause."

While the Court is thus open to all nations as litigants, full acceptance of the Court and full participation in its support and work are effected by adhesion to the Protocol of Signature of December 16, 1920, attached to the resolution of the Assembly by which the Statute of the Court was approved.

## AMERICAN HISTORICAL ASSOCIATION ENDOWMENT FUND[1]

I FEEL much honored that I should have been asked to be present, and to make some remarks, on the occasion of firing the "first gun" in the effort to increase the Endowment Fund of the American Historical Association from $50,000 to $1,000,000. In a community so diversely active as the city of New York one must, unless he would sacrifice his main objectives, exercise a severe discrimination in dealing with invitations to dine, or to lunch, and to speak; and probably no one has exercised a stricter self-restraint in this particular than I have done. But, when the present occasion was mentioned to me, I did not for a moment hesitate to make an affirmative response. Among those who are giving to the movement their active support, I am glad to note, as Chairman of the Committee on Endowment, the Hon. Albert J. Beveridge, who has earned this new titular distinction by the substantial contributions which he has made, and which he is still engaged in making, to American history. No one understands better than he does the meaning of historical research, and the great importance of collecting and preserving, for present and for future use, the materials forming the sources of American history.

Having carefully read the printed statement of the American Historical Association, in which the objects of the present movement are explained, I am at a loss to see how the reasons for the creation of the proposed endowment could have been better set forth. The truth is simply stated when it is declared that the work the Association has already done has been made possible only through an immense amount of unpaid service. Probably this will never cease to be the case. Indeed, when a professedly scientific association has reached the point where

1. Notes of remarks made at a luncheon at Columbia University, Saturday, March 27, 1926.

its members will work only for pecuniary rewards, it may be said to have reached the end of its usefulness. But, it may safely be predicted that historians never will have the opportunity to take such an attitude. To the end of time they will be found repeating the prayer for their daily bread, while dedicating their time and their efforts to the service and instruction of the public; and the best that can be hoped for is that they may be enabled, by appropriate endowments, to perform the necessary tasks that lie beyond the reach of their individual and collective financial resources. Such endowments must come from private sources. As the printed statement before us declares, it is not desirable, even if it were possible, to appeal to Congress for the requisite funds. Nothing is more likely to sap the independence and undermine the integrity of a scientific body than the condition of being subsidized; and nothing could be more deplorable than to place the writing of history under governmental supervision, or to make it dependent upon governmental grant. Some time ago it was proposed that we should have an official history of the recent so-called World War. I have nothing to say in regard to the character or the competency of the persons by whom it was proposed that such a work should be written or edited; but I do undertake to say that the idea of governments causing to be prepared and published official histories of what they themselves do is inherently vicious, and should be unreservedly condemned. For governments to undertake to tell their constituents what they shall think, and then to see to it that they shall have no opportunity to change their opinions, would be to introduce a system under which the maintenance of free institutions would be impossible.

Among the subjects discussed in the prospectus of the proposed endowment is the care of the public records. The present condition of the national archives in Washington is described as "disgraceful." Here is a task in which the co-operation of the government is obviously essential. A government owes it to the people whom it represents not only to preserve its archives, but also to keep them in a condition in which they are readily available for consultation. In this relation I am glad to see that special mention has been made of the work of the late Herbert L. Osgood, in his reports on the archives of New York. Osgood was one of my original colleagues, when I came to Columbia University in 1891; but it is not merely the memory of an old and cherished association that leads me to say that he was one of the greatest historical investigators that ever lived. Not only was he indefatigable in research, but he sedulously kept himself free from all influences that might tend to bias his judgment or to warp his conclusions concerning the times of which he wrote. As a teacher he inspired, among those who were capable of appreciating him, a spirit akin to his own, and his life may be said to have been a continuous but splendid sacrifice to the highest ideals of historical work. On the other hand, there can be no doubt that the performance of his great task would have been facilitated by the existence of an endowment such as it is now proposed to obtain.

Our attention has been drawn to the need, in dealing with political and social problems in the United States, of an intelligent study of the European historical background. What is called the "European background" no doubt is of the highest importance; but a comprehensive study of the foreign relations even of the United States requires the use of the archives of American countries as well as of the archives of European countries. As an example of what may be done in this direction, I would mention the monumental work of the late Benjamin Franklin Stevens in making his collection of facsimiles of manuscripts in European archives relating to American history. Long before Stevens began his great collection, George Bancroft, in writing his history of the United States, obtained for his personal use copies of many manuscripts in foreign archives. Fortunately, Bancroft was able personally to bear the cost; but the fact is well known that Stevens had at one time embarked so much of his private fortune in his enterprise that he was glad to obtain financial aid from the United States. An endowment such as is now proposed would enable essential work of this kind to be carried on continuously and systematically.

Moreover, provision for the systematic prosecution of searches in governmental archives probably would tend to bring about a more uniformly liberal policy in permitting the use of such archives for historical purposes. Governmental practice in this particular greatly varies. I happen to have a personal familiarity, particularly derived from the preparation of my *Digest of International Law,* which was published by the government, with the records of the United States relating to foreign affairs down to the year 1905; and, speaking for that long period of our national development, to which my examination of the manuscript archives was confined, I desire to say that the public was most frankly dealt with. The liberal publication of our diplomatic correspondence by no means began with the annual publication known as the *Diplomatic Correspondence of the United States;* but it is a remarkable fact that the publication of that serial was begun in the first year of the Civil War, and that, in the course of that momentous conflict, in which the national life quivered in the balance, and our foreign relations were often of the most delicate character, the quantity of correspondence annually accompanying the President's message to Congress increased rather than diminished. There still are governments which are today making public the contents of their archives with much freedom, but this practice is by no means universal. Anyone who supposes that the policy of "open covenants openly arrived at" now prevails throughout the world, and that it is exemplified in the granting of free access to public archives, may justly be regarded as an object of compassion with whom an historical association devoted to the exposition of the truth can have no concern. Credulity is not a qualification for historical investigators.

It is most fitly proposed that the raising of the endowment now desired shall be an incident of the celebration of the sesquicentennial of the national independence of the United States in July of the present year. Certainly there cannot be a more appropriate memorial of that occasion than the establishment of an endowment intended to facilitate the intelligent study of history. Lincoln spoke of the government of the United States as having been conceived in freedom; and we have been assured that the truth shall set us free. The object of history, unless crimes are committed in its name, is, and ever must be, the ascertainment and publication of the truth. A disingenuous and misleading propaganda, calculated to produce certain impressions, may do for a servile people, but freemen must ever demand the truth. It may therefore be said that the historian performs a function essential to the perpetuity of free institutions, and he who contributes of his means to this end may be regarded as performing a patriotic service of the highest order.

# POST-WAR INTERNATIONAL LAW[1]

IN the vocabulary of prohibition in the United States the words pre-war and post-war carry certain well understood implications. As prohibition came into force as a national measure during the war, if a beverage is offered as pre-war, it is comfortably accepted as licit; but if it is supposed to be post-war, although it may not be refused, it is felt to be doubtful in quality and open to inquiry as to its legality.

1. Reprinted from the *Columbia Law Review*, Vol. XXVII, No. 4 (April, 1927).

A similar distinction more or less prevails throughout the world in regard to international law. That which is offered as pre-war is accepted, sometimes perhaps more readily than it deserves, while that which is offered as post-war is more or less suspect, especially as it is so often tendered in terms of confusion and doubt. It is for this reason that I have ventured to take the present publication[2] as a text for comments and observations transcending the ordinary limits of a book review. It conveniently lends itself to such treatment, because eight editions were published before the war, and a ninth during the war (1915), all by the author himself, while the present, or tenth, edition, published after the author's death, appears six years after the close of the war.

As I have already intimated, I do not, in taking the present work as a text, intend to treat the appearance of a new edition as an event of unusual importance, or to imply that either the late author's text, or the editor's additions to it, are specially open to criticism. On the contrary, my purpose is rather to note the effect of certain conditions, prevalent during and since the late "world war," which tend to unsettle the foundations of international law, and to confirm in the mind of the rising generation the impression, somewhat blatant during the past ten years, that after all international law is more or less of a myth. Among these conditions I would particularly mention (1) the propensity of writers, instead of bringing what was done during the late war to the impartial test of long-established principles, either to gloss over or ignore the infractions committed by their own government or group or to treat such infractions as having created the law of the future, and (2) the propensity to treat agreements made between a certain number of powers, especially if the number happens to embrace most of the Great Powers, including, as a matter of course, one's own country, as having law-making force. I would by no means intimate that such aberrations are wholly conscious or altogether new. To a great extent they proceed from natural impulses, and their development is much facilitated by lack of knowledge and the widespread habit of propaganda. Naturally, they are abnormally predominant during and after great wars. But it is much to the credit of Grotius that his epoch-making protest—*De Jure Belli ac Pacis*—was written and published in the midst of a vast international conflict; and we are justified in believing that the growth of his influence was aided by the learned self-restraint and abiding

2. T. J. Lawrence, M.A., LL.D., *A Handbook of Public International Law* (10th ed. by Percy H. Winfield, LL.D., London, Macmillan and Co., Ltd., 1925), pp. xvi, 205.

faith in fundamental principles exhibited by the worthy disciples who carried his gospel to succeeding generations.

In the preface to the eighth edition of the present work, in 1912, the author narrated the following incident:

There was (some years ago) a war far away, and we were neutral. A belligerent cruiser was engaged in some interference with our trade which the captain of a British man-of-war on the spot deemed to go beyond her rights. A young officer was hastily put into a boat, and ordered to inform the belligerent that she must desist. In the act of taking his seat he shouted that he knew nothing about the matter. Thereupon a copy of this book was thrown into his hands as he left the side of the British vessel. And his hurried studies were so effective that when he reached the belligerent, he was able to convince her commander of the unwarrantable nature of the action in question, which ceased forthwith!

This signal demonstration, first revealed by the author in 1912, of the power of sudden enlightenment, is retained by the editor in the present edition; but it does not seem to have occurred either to the author or to the editor that the young officer to whom the tutorial mission was entrusted argued from a coign of vantage not ordinarily available to an instructor in international law. No matter how clear or forcible may have been the unidentified passage with which the belligerent commander was overcome, its convincing quality may have been enhanced by the presence of a British man-of-war and the delivery to the belligerent cruiser of the explicit information that "she must desist." That the belligerent commander would have been equally moved if the passage had been read to him by the master of the merchantman with whose rights he was interfering may be doubted. But, be this as it may, it should be admitted that the passage must have been fairly definite in meaning in order to be useful as the accompaniment of a categorical demand. Can this be said of the text as a whole, and particularly of the changes or additions made during or since the "world war?"

With reference to the war and its results, we are told in the editor's preface that "the Grotian system has been vindicated at one of the bloodiest prices ever paid for any human ideal." This assertion evidently ranges the editor with those who maintain that the previously established rules of international law have not been destroyed or radically changed; but it also justifies the expectation that, in the statement of the law as it is, their survival will be definitely affirmed. Not only is this expectation usually disappointed, but there is a tendency either to deny their survival or to put it in doubt.

Numerous examples of this may be found in the treatment

of questions of maritime law. In the eighth edition (p. 119), under the head of "goods of the enemy found on board enemy vessels," the author stated that "these may be captured with the exception of mail bags, which were exempted by the Hague Conference of 1907." This is retained in the author's ninth edition (1915). In the tenth edition (pp. 123–124), the editor, under the head of "goods of the enemy found afloat," states that "among the plentiful crop of problems to which the regulation of The Hague Conference concerning mails gave rise during the war, . . . was the question whether the exemption from capture applied where the post was used for enemy propaganda inciting to incendiarism and insurrection . . ."; "that Great Britain and France countered this German practice by searching mails even on neutral vessels . . ."; that their action met "with strong protests," but that "they were morally justified in view of the fact that the Hague regulations had never contemplated abuse of the immunity in this fashion." With reference to these statements it may be remarked that the so-called Hague regulations did not of themselves have the force of law, since the XIth Convention, with which they were connected, was not in force during the war. The Hague Conventions relating to war invariably contained the following clause: "The provisions of the present convention do not apply except between contracting parties, and then only if all the belligerents are parties to the convention." By virtue of this clause they for the most part, immediately on the outbreak of the late war, automatically ceased to be binding; and the rules they laid down equally ceased to be binding except so far as they were declaratory of existing international law. This was clearly the case with the XIth Convention, which, although signed by forty states, was ratified by only twenty-four. Among the non-ratifying powers were Greece, Italy, Servia and Turkey. Russia, one of the original belligerents, never even signed it; and, in the war with Japan, disregarded it. But the signatories no doubt considered the exemption accorded to postal correspondence to be in conformity with modern practice. The subject is well summarized in J. A. Hall's *Law of Naval Warfare* (London, 1921, pp. 91–94). On the ground that Germany made use of the inviolability of the mails to smuggle contraband of small bulk but great value, such as rubber, and to communicate war information, France and Great Britain, in a joint note to neutrals of April 3, 1916, following an international discussion, eventually announced, (1) that goods sent by parcels post would enjoy no immunities, (2) that mail bags would be searched for "goods concealed in wrappers, envelopes, or letters," (3) that "real 'correspondence,' letters or despatches"

would not be captured at sea and confiscated, but would be for-
warded "so soon as their genuine character" had been established. These announcements were at least intelligible, and they
related to contraband and the communication of military information rather than to "propaganda inciting to incendiarism
and insurrection."

The eighth and ninth editions (pp. 159–160), in dealing with
the liability of private property at sea to capture, cite the Declaration of Paris of 1856, Article 2, that the neutral flag covers
enemy goods, contraband of war excepted, and Article 3, that
neutral goods, except contraband of war, are not liable to capture under the enemy flag. In the tenth edition the editor (p.
171), after stating that Germany carried on sea warfare with
such disregard of previously accepted principles that the Allies
"were compelled as a measure of reprisal to abandon" the articles just cited, adds:

How much of the Declaration now survives is problematical. It is not
adequate to meet the probabilities of future naval warfare, which are
that the list of contraband articles will be greatly extended, that destruction of sea-borne commerce will be commoner than it was before
1914, and that the "economic blockade" of an enemy by cutting off all
commercial intercourse with him will certainly be employed again.
However, the Declaration has not been expressly repudiated.

If we were to accept these statements as correct, the entire
subject of maritime law in time of war would be thrown into
doubt and confusion; but, are they justified? Wholly apart
from the exceptional character of the situation that arose during the late war, we may remark, first, that the adoption of a
measure of reprisal is generally understood not as questioning
but rather as admitting the valid existence of the rule which
is thus to be temporarily disregarded; and secondly, that, as
the Declaration does not enumerate or define contraband articles, it does not in any way prevent belligerents from extending
the list. The statement that the "economic blockade" of an enemy by "cutting off all commercial intercourse with him will
certainly be employed again," no doubt refers to the fourth
article of the Declaration, which provides that "blockades, in
order to be binding, must be effective; that is to say, maintained by a force sufficient really to prevent access to the coast
of the enemy." The attempt to cut off all commercial intercourse with the enemy was made during the Napoleonic wars,
but this was not regarded as having supplanted the pre-existing law. On the contrary, the very belligerents who had, "as a
measure of reprisal," tried that desperate expedient, afterwards made the Declaration of Paris, by which the pre-existing
law was confirmed and amplified. Why should their resort a

hundred years later, under similar pressure, to the same desperate expedient, be regarded as having destroyed the established law? Hall, in his *Law of Naval Warfare* (1921), affirms that the Declaration is still to be regarded "as the universal law on the subjects with which it deals" (p. 191). Surely the fact that it has not been "expressly repudiated" is not to be taken as proof that it has been tacitly abandoned. We may indeed well ask whether there is a single Power that is prepared to treat the rules of the Declaration of Paris, either in whole or in part, as a thing of the past. Perhaps we may go somewhat farther, and express the belief that, if war should occur between two Powers tomorrow, and either should assume that the "economic blockade" of an enemy had become an ordinary belligerent right, neutrals with adequate navies not only would resume the method of instruction so vividly described in the preface to the eighth edition of the present work but would be content with that edition and its proved effectiveness as a manual.

The present work is by no means exceptional in dealing in an uncertain way with the Declaration of London of 1909; but, for such uncertainty, there is really no foundation. Formulated by a naval conference early in 1909 for the purpose of furnishing a uniform law for the International Prize Court which was to have been set up under one of the Hague Conventions of 1907, it never became effective by the deposit of ratifications. In Great Britain the House of Lords threw out a bill which the Commons had passed to give it effect. In reality, it may be argued that the provisions of the Declaration in regard to hostile destination were such as to operate, both positively and negatively, to the disadvantage of insular countries. But, whatever may be one's opinion on these points, the Declaration as such never acquired international force, nor can such force be derived from the circumstance that the belligerents played fast and loose with it during the war.

In the eighth edition (1912) and the ninth (1915) the author (p. 148) says: "Belligerents have no right to seize, under the name of Angary, neutral merchant vessels found within the waters controlled by them, for the purpose of using such vessels in furtherance of their warlike operations. Extreme necessity may excuse such a proceeding, but even then apology and satisfaction are due." In the tenth edition (pp. 158–159) the editor introduces the foregoing statement with the phrase "it has been argued that," and adds that "in view of the occurrences during the war" the author's "argument" must be "considered doubtful." As the author stated that "extreme necessity" might "excuse" such a proceeding, although "apology and satisfaction" were due, it may be asked whether this did not afford to belligerents sufficient leeway. The author certainly did not make an "argument." His statement was direct and precise; and a careful examination of what occurred during the war will not demonstrate that he was wrong.

Previous editions and the present edition are inaccurate in saying that the Suez Canal was "neutralized by the Convention of 1888." The convention was signed subject to a general reservation by Great Britain of her "freedom of action" during the occupation of Egypt by her forces. It was this that induced the United States Senate to insist upon the amendment of the Hay-Pauncefote treaty as originally signed.

There is some excuse for the vague and uncertain statements made by the editor (pp. 157, 159) concerning the rights and duties of belligerents and neutrals as regards the uses of aircraft; but he nowhere mentions the report of the Commission of Jurists which sat at The Hague in 1922–23. This commission, composed of representatives of the United States, the British Empire, France, Italy, Japan, and the Netherlands, drew up a code to regulate the uses of aircraft and radio in time of war; and, although this code has not been incorporated in an international convention, the report contains a comprehensive discussion of the entire subject, and constitutes a prominent part of the documentary materials essential to a study of it.

A similar omission may be noted under "peace and arbitration" (pp. 142–145). The numerous general arbitration treaties made since 1900 are said to except "vital interests or national honor." In reality, the usual exception also includes "independence" and the "interests of third parties"; and all these things are excepted from an obligation which includes only differences "of a legal nature or relating to the interpretation of treaties." But no mention whatever is made of the so-called Bryan treaties, which have been so widely adopted. The report adopted at Geneva, in September, 1922, as a provisional substitute for the limitation of armaments, was essentially based on the Bryan plan.

In the discussion of pacific blockade, no mention is made by the author or by the editor of the capital case of Venezuela, in 1902, when, upon the protest of the United States against the "pacific" exclusion of the vessels of third powers, Germany, Great Britain and Italy established a warlike blockade. Nor is notice taken of the fact that the United States, in the case of the pacific blockade of Crete, in 1898, took the same position. The United States, in other words, recognizes pacific blockade as a measure affecting the rights and commerce of the parties to the controversy, but denies that it may be so extended as to exclude the vessels of third parties; and the correctness of this position appears to be generally admitted.

In dealing with the "sources" of international law, the eighth and ninth editions, while enumerating treaties, define "law making treaties" as "treaties assented to by all or nearly all civilized states, and avowedly altering or adding to the law." "The most conspicuous examples of these" are said to be "the conventions drawn up at The Hague Conferences of 1899 and 1907, and the Declaration of London." The present edition properly omits the Declaration of London, but inserts in its place the International Air Convention of 1919. The eighth and ninth editions (p. 30) say, "We may also mention the Declaration of Paris of 1856," but the tenth adds ,"though the effect of the war . . . upon it is doubtful." Finally, the tenth edition (p. 32) includes instruments like the Peace Treaty of Versailles, the Washington Treaties of 1922 for the limitation of naval armaments and other purposes, and the Geneva protocol establishing the Permanent Court of International Justice. With the single exception of the Declaration of Paris, which I have already discussed, it is believed that the law-making force attributed to these agreements is overstated and incapable of justification. That The Hague conventions have never been regarded as constituting international law for non-signatory or non-ratifying powers is clearly demonstrated by the presence, in the conventions relating to war, of the clause that their provisions do not apply except between contracting parties, and then only if all the belligerents are parties to the convention. If the treaties were considered as having made international law, this would be tantamount to a repudiation of the obligation to observe international law in time of war. I intentionally emphasize this point, because, in view of the non-observance of The Hague Conventions during the war, nothing has, in my opinion, contributed more to the prevalent haziness in regard to international law than the widespread misconception that their provisions were considered before the war as constituting a part of the existing law of nations. For this misconception a large measure of responsibility must be ascribed to writers who, in treating of subjects so vital and profound as contraband and blockade, literally incorporated the provisions of The Hague conventions and even of the Declaration of London, by wholesale and without comment, in the text of what purported to be treatises on international law. This method, besides satisfying the commercial desire for something up-to-date and in the latest fashion, dispensed from the drudgery of study and reflection those whose Cyclo-

pean eye the fame of authorship allured; but, as is now fully
apparent, it was rashly anticipatory, and, in point of law, misleading and indefensible. The warning should not be lost on
those who have since the war been clamoring for a new "law-
making" conference in which an important part of the world
might not even be represented.

A similar looseness of conception in regard to law making
may be found in connection with the subject of piracy. The
author, in various editions (e.g., the ninth, p. 67), mentioned,
as a distinguishing mark of piratical acts, that "they must be
committed by persons destitute of authorization from any recognized political community." The editor (tenth ed., p. 70)
adds: "This last requisite is unnecessary with respect to belligerent submarines which violate the ordinary rules as to
visit and search: they can be treated as pirates even if they
act under the authority of the State owning them (*post*, p.
133)." At page 133, the only authority given for this assertion is the statement that the signatories of the Washington
treaty of February 6, 1922, relating to the use of submarines
and noxious gases in warfare, "agreed to treat as pirates submarines violating" the rules governing visit and search,
"whether they act under State authorization or not." The
parties to the treaty were the United States of America, the
British Empire, France, Italy and Japan. What they did was
to insert in the treaty (Art. III) a declaration that any person violating the rules in question, whether under superior
orders or not, should be deemed to have "violated the laws of
war" and should be "liable to trial and punishment as if for
an act of piracy and may be brought to trial before the civil
or military authorities of any Power within the jurisdiction of
which he may be found." The signatories, however, did not
think that their declaration sufficed to create international
law. On the contrary, they regarded it as a proposal, and accordingly stipulated (Art. VII) that the United States should
transmit a copy of the treaty to non-signatory powers and
"invite" their "adherence thereto." As late as the present
writing, more than four years after the treaty was signed,
one of the signatories, France, has not ratified the treaty. Nor
do all the signatories appear to be fully convinced that the use
of noxious gases in war either will or should be wholly prohibited.

The author, in his eighth and ninth editions (p. 121), says
that prize courts, "though they are municipal tribunals," "purport to administer international law." In the tenth edition,
however, the editor (p. 126) adds that "the better view is
that they are not international courts, and that their deci-

sions are only municipal law, though they may be founded on international law and (where they lay down a new rule) may become the source of international law if other States adopt such rules." How this "better view" differs from the author's is not readily apparent. When the author said that prize courts were "municipal tribunals," he distinctly affirmed that they were not international courts; and, when he stated that they "purported" to administer international law, he clearly meant that their decisions were supposed to be founded on that law. That a new rule, no matter how or by whom laid down, may become international law if states adopt it as such, it is superfluous to affirm.

In the eighth and ninth editions (p. 111), it is stated that "ordinary personal property" "was confiscated till quite modern times." This was sufficiently indeterminate, but, in the present edition (p. 115) the editor adds that in the recent war all the more important belligerents, "without confiscating real or personal property, applied the doctrine of confiscation to both," and as an example states that Great Britain "created a custodian in whom enemy property might be vested, and who was to hold such property till the end of the war, and then to deal with it as the Crown should direct." What afterwards happened we are not told; but, without regard to what was eventually done, it certainly was not at the time understood that the creation of alien property custodians was an application of the "doctrine of confiscation." The taking over or interning of enemy private property in order that the enemy may not make hostile use of it during the war, and the confiscation of such property or its seizure for confiscation are two different things. The difference has always been recognized, and should not give rise to confusion.

In previous editions, as well as in the present edition (p. 99), the statement is repeated that "the question of the effect of war upon treaties is very complicated"; that it is "difficult to decide when a treaty is merely suspended by war, and when it is entirely abrogated"; that boundary conventions are said to be "unaffected," alliances "abrogated," and extradition treaties "suspended." An investigation of international practice will show that the subject is not so complicated as is here supposed. Boundary treaties are not affected by war for the simple reason that they are executed engagements, under which rights of property have vested. On the other hand, commercial treaties, extradition treaties, and other agreements requiring future acts the daily performance of which depends upon the continuance of peace, it is convenient to consider as terminated by a war between all the contracting parties. This distinction is sound in theory, and is observed in practice. Multipartite treaties, where only some of the parties go to war, require separate consideration.

In the previous editions (p. 49), and in the tenth (p. 50), we are told that it is "often said" that "all bays" more than ten miles wide at the mouth "are in law parts of the open sea, and free from the territorial authority of any power"; but that "this rule, though general, is by no means universally accepted, and that there are many exceptions to it, and several disputed cases." It would have been more helpful to say that in certain conventions, following the precedent set in that between Great Britain and France of 1839, relating to the Channel, the contracting parties agreed to treat bays less than ten miles wide at the mouth as exclusively territorial for purposes of fishing. This rule was adopted for the practical reason that, after subtracting the marine league on either side, there would remain, in a bay ten or more than ten miles wide, a free space of at least four miles within which the foreign fisherman might conduct his operations. As the foreign fisherman would, in a smaller space, be in constant danger of drifting into the ordinary marginal sea, it was deemed better to exclude him altogether from bodies of water less than ten miles wide at the mouth. But there is not the slightest foundation for saying that this has been adopted as a general rule for the determination of territorial waters for all purposes and in all cases; and the writers who have "often said" it, whoever they may be, have merely been guilty of inadvertence.

Under "exceptions to territorial jurisdiction" (eighth and ninth editions, p. 69; tenth, p. 72), we are told that when the head of a foreign state visits a country in his "official capacity," he and his suite are exempt from the local jurisdiction. As proof that the word "official" is misleading, it is only necessary to cite the leading case of *Mighell* v. *Sultan of Johore,* [1894] 1 Q. B. D., 149, in which the defendant, while living in England *incognito,* under the name of Albert Baker, was sued for breach of promise of marriage. His presence and activities were confessedly unofficial; but, the moment his character as a foreign sovereign was disclosed, he was held to be exempt from judicial process. On the other hand, there is an exaggeration of privilege in the statement (eighth and ninth editions, p. 82; tenth, p. 85) that an official diplomatic residence is "for most purposes" "under the jurisdiction of the state which the embassy represents," and may only in extreme cases "be entered by the local authorities." There is confusion here between jurisdictional exemption and jurisdictional right. Such confusion is more common than it should be. Lorimer, for instance, says that the house of an English ambassador "is English ground." [3] Such statements are contrary both to elementary principles and to adjudicated cases. The immunity which a minister and his suite enjoy proceeds from their representative character and not from the place in which they live. It exists as fully outside the official residence as within it; and non-diplomatic persons who happen to be in such a residence are fully subject to the local law, although the limited exemption of the residence from ordinary police activities may momentarily stand between them and arrest. Indeed, the privilege even of the minister and his suite is that of exemption from judicial process rather than exemption from obedience to the local law, since it is established by adjudicated cases that, if their sovereign waives their immunity, they may be tried and punished under that law.

In the eighth edition (p. 60) it is stated that a dispute arose between Great Britain and the United States as to whether the Hay-Pauncefote treaty allowed "discrimination with regard to tolls" in favor of the coastal shipping of the United States, and the tenth edition (p. 62) says that this dispute "was settled in 1914 by the repeal of the clause in the act of Congress which allowed such discrimination." There is much excuse for a want of precision in this matter, as such precision is frequently lacking in official documents. In reality, the British government admitted that the United States might by way of subsidy remit or refund the tolls on its coastwise vessels, but claimed that such vessels must under the treaty be included in the computation of the rate of tolls. The difference is substantial. The coastwise tonnage of the United States had in fact been included in making the schedule of tolls actually adopted; and while the act, under the terms of which such tonnage might have been excluded from the computation, was, upon the urgent and somewhat cryptic request of President Wilson, repealed, the repeal was accompanied with a reservation under which a right of exemption, broader than that originally authorized, is asserted.

I have but one more observation to make. In previous editions of the present work the list of European "Great Powers" included Great Britain, France, Germany, Austria-Hungary, Italy and Russia. In the tenth edition the editor, while retaining in the list (p. 18) Germany and Russia, properly omits Austria-Hungary, the Imperial-Royal government having been destroyed and its dominions partitioned; but farther on (p. 43) he remarks: "Since the war, the defeat of Germany with its consequent military and naval limitations, and the instability and degradation of government in Russia, have reduced those

3. *Institutes*, I, 249.

states at least temporarily to the rank of second-rate powers."

No one will question the diminished military and naval power of Germany and Russia; but, in the further imputation to Russia of "instability and degradation" of government since the war, there is matter for reflection. No one could believe less than does the present writer in communism either as a philosophical principle or as the practical foundation of a political or economic system. But, in spite of what has constantly been seen in publications during and since the war, he cannot help strongly deprecating the employment in professedly legal works of the tone and terminology of pamphleteering. In earlier writings on international law, a distinction was made between Christian and non-Christian powers, but it was not made with the intention of censure or offence. It was a distinction of fact, on which depended certain recognized differences in legal theory and practice. With the avowed admission of Turkey in 1856 to the advantages of the public law and system of concert of Europe, the classification began to lose its applicability, and, with the recognition of Japan by Western nations as a fully independent and coequal sovereign power, it was abandoned. The attempt, so marked during and since the war, to introduce a new classification, by imputing to nations which do not at the moment enjoy our favor a lack of "civilization," of "enlightenment," of "culture," or of other things hardly susceptible of legal definition, cannot contribute to the value or the finality of scientific discussions. In the phrase "instability and degradation," as applied to government in Russia, there is a combination of assertion and opinion. The word instability asserts a fact, the word degradation conveys an opinion. The assertion is manifestly inaccurate, since those who, because they disapprove the Soviet government in Russia, its attitude and policies, oppose its recognition, find in its stability a source of continuing, if not increasing, difficulty. Had the earlier forecasts of its instability been fulfilled, it would long since have disappeared, and the question of its recognition would have ceased to be mooted. On the other hand, the word "degradation" ordinarily carries a moral rather than a legal significance. Degradation may result from or imply a loss of honor, of position, or of esteem, or a reduced moral or intellectual condition. It is an elastic term, conveying no definitive meaning, and involving matters of individual opinion, and questions of degree, for the determination of which, taking the world as a whole, with all its governmental diversities at any particular moment, international law furnishes no rule or standard. To speak of the Soviet Government as having confiscated private property, or as refusing to recognize certain commonly accepted international obligations, is intelligible and within the range of legal discussions. The legal gravity of such statements is not enhanced by the addition of moral censures. This is perhaps fortunate, since it relieves writers on international law from the necessity of engaging in discussions that would give rise to interminable disputes without contributing to a definite legal result. Writers on international law should not be less careful than writers on municipal law to keep within the range of legal ideas and legal terminology. I say this without special reference to the present volume. If international law is to be restored to the legal position which it formerly held, or is to recover the legal reputation which it formerly enjoyed, those who essay to expound it must keep within the realm of legal conceptions.

# BOOK REVIEW

A HISTORY OF AMERICAN FOREIGN POLICY. *By* JOHN
HOLLADAY LATANÉ, *Professor of American History and
Creswell Lecturer on International Law in Johns Hopkins
University.* New York, Doubleday, Page & Company, 1927.
Pp. xiv, 725. $4.00.

The present work constitutes a comprehensive survey of
the foreign relations of the United States from the beginning
of the American Revolution down to the date of publication;
and as its author has long been known as a careful and intelligent investigator, with a tendency to form views of his own
and to express them with candor and independence, the reader
will naturally find it to be a distinctive and stimulating contribution to the literature of the subject to which it relates.

In the United States there exists, especially on the Atlantic
seaboard, a considerable number of persons, perhaps relatively
larger than in any other country, who contemplate foreign
policy as something to be cultivated for its own sake; as something distinct and perchance even divergent from domestic
policy; as a system to be conducted, on preconceived and permanent lines, with little regard to changing national moods
and shifting national interests. In reality, the supposition that,
because certain nations have a foreign policy different from
that of the United States, they pursue it in a spirit of conscious and deliberate detachment from national moods and national interests, has little support in human history; and in the
present volume abundant proof will be found that the foreign
policy of the United States, far from being an exception to the
rule, has had the flavor of the native soil and has strikingly
exemplified the course of national sentiments and national
tendencies.

At the very outset the learned author points out not only
that the keynote of the great experiment inaugurated by the
American revolution was sounded in the Jeffersonian phrase
that "governments derive their just powers from the consent
of the governed," but also that this declaration was a challenge
to substantially all governments then existing. The attempt
practically to enforce the principle of the "consent of the
governed" was but the assertion by arms of the right of revo-

lution; and the success of the effort, while it resulted in the establishment of a new government the existence of which the world could not ignore, by no means did away with the challenge. The foreign policy of the United States, as formulated by Washington and his first Secretary of State, Jefferson, and developed by their successors, with its doctrine of non-intervention and the correlative rule of neutrality, the principle of the freedom of the seas, the recognition of governments simply on the strength of their existence in point of fact, and the contest with the colonial system and its commercial restrictions, followed naturally and inevitably, just as, from the enunciation of the right to liberty and the pursuit of happiness, there eventually resulted the doctrine of voluntary expatriation.

An excellent account is given by the author of the acquisition of Louisiana and the Floridas, and of the subsequent territorial expansion of the United States; and the same thing may be said of his exposition of the Monroe Doctrine and its successive and widening developments. Only when he undertakes to interpret President Wilson's proposal that all nations "should with one accord adopt the doctrine of President Monroe as the doctrine of the world" does he appear to find the task of definition somewhat baffling. The interpretation he hazards is that the "Monroe Doctrine, stripped of its imperialistic tendencies, was to be internationalized, and the American policy of isolation, in the sense of avoiding secret alliances, was to become a fundamental principle of the new international order." President Wilson, however, spoke not of "secret" alliances but of "entangling" alliances, and declared that there could be "no entangling alliance in a concert of power." To the nations of Europe this deft assurance would have brought glad tidings of great joy, had their long practical experience in honestly endeavoring to maintain, in name and in fact, a "concert" of power, been undisturbed by clashes of interest and armed conflicts. The learned author speaks (p. 618) of President Wilson as holding in December 1918 "the moral leadership of the world," and there are other passages which strongly imply that the United States might, but for obstructionists at home, still perform that beneficent function. But, unfortunately, the indisposition to concede moral superiority to others is no less general than the disposition to claim it for one's self; and, so far as concerns the United States, the utterances of the foreign press are not at the moment encouraging.

While I have commended as a whole the author's account of the Monroe Doctrine, I can by no means concur in his virtual acceptance of Thayer's version of the episode of the blockade of Venezuelan ports by the combined forces of Germany, Great Britain and Italy, a version in which, as I did not fail to point out at the time, emotional surmises and interested personal assertions and afterthoughts were permitted to displace the unimpeachable evidence of the authentic contemporaneous official record of what actually took place. In his account of the Panama affair, the learned author of the present work properly rejects this method of proof. In reality the powers, in blockading Venezuelan ports, justified their action not on the fact that President Castro had refused to recognize the validity of their claims but on the fact that he had refused to arbitrate them. The author is quite correct in saying that the subsequent decision of the Permanent Court of Arbitration at the Hague in favor of the preferential claim of the blockading powers "was received with no small degree of criticism," but the Court, unlike its critics, was obliged to base its decision upon the facts and the law as it found them.

Towards the end of his work the learned author in due course treats of two pending controversial questions—that of the inter-allied debts and that of the recognition of the present Russian government; and, as might have been expected, he does not accept the view that the fact that his government has taken in regard to each of them a certain attitude, has placed them beyond the range of free public discussion. With regard to the debts, he believes that the present agreements have not disposed of the "real problem," and that the settlements so far made are likely to undergo radical revision; while, with regard to Russia, he holds that the refusal of recognition, after all the other nations engaged in the war have accorded it, lends color to the charge of the radicals "that ours has become the most conservative and reactionary government on earth." For these conclusions he gives his reasons.

Reprinted from *The American Historical Review*, XXXII (1927), 887–889.

# WILLIAM A. DAY

## A TRIBUTE[1]

IN the death of William A. Day, the Chairman of its Board
of Directors, not only does The Equitable Life Assurance
Society of the United States lose a great executive, but it
shares with the country the loss of an exemplar of the highest
type of citizenship. Born in the State of Delaware on June 11,
1850, he spent his adult life in the broadest sense in the public
service. Having chosen the law as his profession, he attended
the Harvard Law School, and, after graduation, settled at
Champaign, in Illinois; but his instinct for affairs was soon
manifested by his election for two successive terms to the State
legislature, in which he served on the committees on the judiciary and the judicial department, on state and municipal indebtedness, on federal relations, on railroads, and on insurance, and introduced various important measures, including
bills relating to the railways, and regulating contracts of insurance. In 1883 he was chosen as mayor of Champaign. From
1885 to 1889 he served, by appointment of President Cleveland,
as Second Auditor of the Treasury Department, at Washington. Thus, in a comparatively short time, he gained, through
the legal care of private interests, and the performance of public legislative, administrative, and judicial functions, a well-
rounded experience, which, united with ability and integrity,
marked him out for the varied activities and the great responsibilities with which he was afterward identified.

For a time Judge Day acted as special counsel to the Interstate Commerce Commission. Later, in the midst of the confused and tumultuous conditions that characterized the extraordinary expansion of business, public as well as private, at
the beginning of the present century, he was designated by
President Roosevelt as special assistant to the Attorney-
General of the United States in cases under the interstate commerce and anti-trust laws; and in 1903 his field of action was
still further enlarged by his appointment to the highly important post of Assistant to the Attorney-General, just then created by an act no doubt passed with his nomination in view.

1. Memorial address before the Board of Directors of The Equitable
Life Assurance Society of the United States, April 19, 1928.

In these several positions he took a leading part for the government in important investigations and litigations of railway affairs, the most notable being the Northern Securities case, decided by the Supreme Court [2] in March, 1904. The case was crucial not only because it involved the most powerful financial interests in the country, but also because the legal questions at issue were contentious and undetermined. On the strength of certain prior decisions, and particularly that in the Knight case,[3] to the effect that the power of Congress over commerce could not reach stock ownership in State corporations, even though their manufactured products might become the subject of interstate commerce, it was contended that two parallel and competing railways, the Great Northern and the Northern Pacific, operating under State charters, might, in spite of the anti-trust laws, be combined and placed under a single control by transferring the ownership of the stock in them to a company organized under the laws of yet another State. In behalf of those who worked out this plan there appeared in the argument before the Supreme Court the names of seven eminent attorneys; in behalf of the United States there appeared Philander C. Knox, then Attorney-General, and, on the brief with him, William A. Day, by whose examination of the witnesses the government's record had chiefly been made. The decision, far-reaching in its effects, was in favor of the government; and the circumstance that the judgment was pronounced by a bare majority of five to four does not tend to lessen our estimate of the energy and power with which the government's cause was conducted. Subsequently, in the same year, Judge Day was sent by President Roosevelt to France at the head of a mission to consummate the transfer to the United States of the rights owned or represented by the French Company in the Panama Canal. This transaction concluded, he was dispatched to Alaska to investigate complaints of oppression of the inhabitants by public officials; and on the strength of his report several persons were removed from office.

On the accession of Paul Morton to the presidency of the Equitable in 1905, Judge Day exchanged one kind of public service for another by accepting with the Society the position of Comptroller, which he held until February 28, 1907. On May 31, 1906, he also became Vice-President, and this position he retained until April 20, 1911, when, after Mr. Morton's death, he was elected President. In October, 1927, he retired from the presidency, and became Chairman of the Board of Directors.

His record as President of the Society is distinguished by

2. 193 U. S., 197.
3. *United States* v. *E. C. Knight Co.*, 156 U. S., 1.

numerous constructive developments and by an expansion probably unrivaled in the history of life insurance. Among the notable steps taken were the inauguration of group insurance; the introduction of a home purchase plan for lending money to home owners, with a provision for life insurance; a new form of retirement annuity, including a provision for disability; the adoption of a plan of salary savings insurance for employees through payroll deductions; and the construction of the new and adequate Home Office Building which the Society now occupies. But by none of his achievements did he set greater store than by the complete mutualization of the company. This work, after the approval, in February 1918, of the plan of mutualization presented by the Society under the Act of 1917, was persistently carried on until he was able, in his report for 1925, to announce that the Society, free at last from any possibility of lawful control by outside influences, had become, finally and definitely, both legally and in fact, "the great cooperative enterprise" which he and his colaborers had for so long sought to make it, and which alone could best serve its purposes. Meanwhile, the Society waxed strong and prospered. Its assets, amounting at the end of 1911 to $503,867,097, had grown at the end of 1927 to $966,825,151. The new insurance written in 1911 was $122,781,129; in 1927 it was $941,412,538; while the total outstanding insurance, amounting in 1911 to $1,375,441,460, had risen in 1927 to $5,631,834,438.

Simple in his life and quiet in his manner, Judge Day performed his duties unostentatiously and without any effort at self-advertisement; but his love of justice and his stern and unyielding sense of right burned as a consuming flame, steady and unquenchable. He loved his country and revered its institutions. His loyalty was not of that calculated kind, which is gauged by the indulgence shown to particular classes or individuals. He not only obeyed the law but gave to it his full support. On the other hand, he knew his rights, and did not hesitate firmly to maintain them by all proper and lawful means. He regarded, and properly regarded, the great company which he served as a public institution, in the management of which the public and the private interest must be identical; and, with this ideal constantly before him, he gave himself without stint to the building up of the company and the enlargement of its sphere of usefulness. Not only did his example, supplemented on occasion by stirring appeals, encourage and strengthen the Society's personnel, to whom he was an ever-present, sympathetic and vital force, but it served to inspire in the public that confidence which today eloquently attests the general recognition of the sureness of his understanding, his rare capacity for business, and the high purpose, probity and fidelity that pervaded all his actions. As his services to the Society were of incalculable benefit, so will he stand in the first rank of those who have contributed most to its growth and prosperity, and have broadened and deepened the foundations on which that growth and prosperity rest.

We recommend that, in testimony of the great respect in which our associate and friend was held, and of the loss we have suffered in his departure, this memorial be entered upon the minutes of the Board, and that an engrossed copy be sent to his family.

EUGENIUS H. OUTERBRIDGE<br>
J. H. WALBRIDGE<br>
JOHN B. MOORE

*On hearing the Memorial, the Directors, by a standing vote, adopted the following resolution:*

BE IT RESOLVED *that the Memorial upon the death of Judge Day be inscribed in full upon the minutes of the Board, and that a suitably engrossed copy thereof be prepared and sent to his family, and that as a further mark of respect this meeting stand adjourned upon the adoption of this motion.*

# EDWARD GREEN BRADFORD[1]

*May it please the Court:*

On two previous occasions has Edward Green Bradford, who for twenty-one years occupied the seat which Your Honor now so worthily holds, been the subject of an address in this Court. The first occasion was ten years ago, when he retired from the bench; the second was early in the present year, when he passed away. On both occasions the spokesman was my friend, John Percy Nields. To-day, when formal resolutions are to be presented, the fraternal kindness of the members of my original Bar has opened to me the privilege of appearing; and I desire to say that, for any shortcomings in the tribute I am to pay, I am consoled with the reflection that what has heretofore been spoken was characterized not only by abundant information, but also by a depth of understanding, a sureness of touch, and a real eloquence which, even if they could be equaled, could not be surpassed.

1. Memorial address before the United States District Court, at Wilmington, Delaware, December 3, 1928, Judge Hugh M. Morris, presiding.

From his birth until his death, the late Judge Bradford was closely identified with the State of Delaware. The son of Edward G. and Mary Alicia (Heyward) Bradford, he was born at Wilmington on March 12, 1848, and after his departure out of this life on March 30, 1928, at the age of eighty, his remains were interred in his native soil. He was prepared for college at the Military Academy conducted by the Reverend W. Murphy, and an academy kept by T. Clarkson Taylor, both at Wilmington; and on his graduation at Yale, as Bachelor of Arts, in 1868, he returned to his native city.

His career in life was then already determined upon. He was born into the legal profession. Not only was his father, to whom he was deeply attached, a distinguished lawyer, whose career was later to be crowned with a seat on this bench, but his own unerring instincts drew him in the same direction. He therefore entered his father's office as a student; and in 1870 he was admitted to the Bar.

It is just forty-five years ago to-day that, after three years spent as a student in the office of Bradford, the son, I was, on his motion, made before his father as judge, admitted as an attorney and counselor of this court. In itself this circumstance is relatively unimportant, but it has a world of meaning for me, as an incident in an association that brought me into contact with his private as well as with his professional and public life, and thus, while enabling me to appreciate him as a lawyer, a citizen and a magistrate, also led me to cherish a deep affection for him as a man.

When I entered his office, he had been at the Bar just long enough to be qualified, under the rules then existing, to receive students, and I was his first registered pupil. I had not previously known him. In reality, I acted on friendly advice given to my father by Joseph P. Comegys, then Chief Justice of the State. As I was born in the Democratic party, the Chief Justice, who deprecated the propensity of legal fledglings to try their wings in politics, thought that I should be safer from this danger in a Republican nest; but, at the same time, he laid special stress on the habitual thoroughness with which Bradford prepared his cases, and on the power of analysis, the mastery of principles, and the clearness of statement with which he argued questions before the court.

Not only was the impression thus conveyed of my future preceptor soon completely confirmed, but I found myself in association with a man of the most pronounced individuality. When I first saw him I was reminded of the statement I had read in an old book that on a certain occasion John Calvin, while visiting a place where he was known only by report, was recognized in the crowd by the piercing glance of his dark eyes. In what was said here earlier in the year, Judge Bradford's general appearance was thus described:

The image . . . that remains with me is as clear cut as any cameo. His raven locks, coal-black eyes, high cheek bones, aquiline nose, pallid face, high square shoulders, deep chest, full incisive voice, distinguished bearing and dignified mien suggested the high-bred Spanish type rather than our familiar English features.

No portrayal could be more graphic than this.

In manner and in speech he was quiet and reserved. His abilities were substantial rather than showy; and he made his way at the Bar, not by the exercise of the arts of publicity, of which he knew nothing, but, slowly and surely, by laborious and convincing demonstrations, as occasion arose, of the fact that there had appeared on the legal horizon a luminary of the first order.

When I first knew him, his practice was not large or general. Indeed, he deliberately selected it. Again and again have I known him to refuse business, such as ordinary claims for the collection of debts, in which no contested principle was at stake; but I never knew him to refuse a case, no matter how slight the promise of pecuniary reward, in which there was involved an interesting legal question. In this way he was building up a professional business in which the scientific study of the law was constantly united with its practical application. His studies were prosecuted with a painstaking exactitude, and with an effort to penetrate to the very foundations, which I have never known to be surpassed. This habit was exemplified in his study of the old Common Law forms of pleading. Most lawyers, and they are hardly to be blamed, are content to accept the current established forms without recondite inquiries. Usually the ancient forms, which served to entrap rather than to allure, are dreary enough; but Bradford insisted on treating them as living documents, and strove beneath their cumbrous and awkward phraseology to ascertain the meaning which each clause originally bore, so that he could have met the exactions of an earlier day, when it was commonly agreed that one's mastery of the art or science of pleading was the crucial test of his ability as a lawyer. Of these educational conditions I had as his pupil the full benefit, working with him, as far as I was able, in the preparation of his cases, besides reading by his prescription legal treatises, such as Sharswood's *Blackstone*, Holmes' *Kent*, Greenleaf's *Cruise on Real Property*, Leake on *Contracts*, Chitty's *Pleading*, Story's *Equity*, and Jarman on *Wills*.

Soon after I entered his office, he made his first appearance before the Supreme Court of the United States, in Ex parte Hagar,[2] a case in admiralty, in which, before the argument took place, the late Thomas F. Bayard came to be associated with him as counsel. The decision was in favor of Bradford's client. Bradford had indeed already gained a high reputation in the argument of admiralty cases; and I recall that he relished, with special keenness, the affirmation by the Circuit Court in 1882 of the decree of the District Court in the case of The Golden Grove,[3] in which counsel on the other side, who came from another and larger Bar, had blandly remarked, with a wave of the hand, that the trial below was only a "preliminary skirmish," and that the decision certainly would be reversed on appeal.

While cases such as these enhanced Bradford's reputation with the public as well as with the bar, it was only in the winter of 1882–83 that he may be said to have come into his own. I here refer to the case of Anthony Reybold, a citizen of Delaware, against the New York and Baltimore Transportation Line, a Maryland corporation. The trial began on December 29, 1882, and on January 22, 1883, the jury returned a verdict for the plaintiff in the sum of $84,334.29, which was then the largest verdict ever rendered in the State, with the exception of that given in the case of Randel against the Delaware and Chesapeake Canal Company, in the Superior Court, sitting at New Castle, in 1834. As in the earlier case, in which John M. Clayton, Charles J. Ingersoll, James Rogers, and George Read, Jr., appeared for the plaintiff, and Robert Frame, Walter Jones, and James A. Bayard for the defendant, so in the later case the trial was a great legal battle. For the defendant there appeared Thomas F. Bayard and George Gray, and for a time a well-known member of the Maryland Bar, Alexander Evans, of Elkton; but Evans was by reason of ill health later obliged to retire. The plaintiff was represented by George H. Bates, Levi C. Bird and Edward G. Bradford; but, after the first of January, Bates, who was a member, and had been elected speaker, of the House of Representatives of the State, was required to spend much of his time at Dover, so that the conduct of the plaintiff's cause fell mainly to Bird and Bradford. It was a drama worthy of the best traditions of the legal stage. Bradford was by far the youngest of the participants and in physical stature the smallest; but his association with Bird constituted an ideal combination for the conduct of a litigation in which judge and jury both figured. Each supplemented the other. Bird, although he had an extensive and varied practice, was preeminently a

2. 140 U. S., 520.
3. 13 Fed. Rep., 674, 700.

student of men. By this I do not mean that he was an anthropologist. His studies were not such as to involve him in the worldwide and heated controversies as to the origin of species. He took men as he knew them, and dealt with them as beings in action rather than as subjects of scientific conjecture. As a manager of juries I have never known his superior, and as a cross-examiner he was unexcelled. Sufficiently preoccupied with these activities, he left the presentation of the law chiefly to his associate, who, as he afterwards remarked to me, never once fell short of the emergency. I can now recall how, after an impressive legal argument by Bayard or Gray, such as they only could make, the whisper would be heard about the court room: "That's fine; that looks like the end; but wait till that little Spaniard gets on his feet."

The professional prominence into which Bradford was thus brought immediately resulted in an appreciable increase in his practice, which continued to grow until his elevation to the bench. But the proposal that he should take the place which his father had once filled with distinction, powerfully appealed to him. It appealed to him both as a matter of sentiment, and also as opening to him a career for which his whole life had been a preparation. On the strength of a petition signed by almost all the members of the Delaware Bar, President McKinley, on May 11, 1897, nominated him to the Senate of the United States as Judge of this Court. His nomination was promptly confirmed, and on May 21 he took the oath of office. It was the ordinary oath, but its terms cannot be considered ordinary in the sense of ever becoming commonplace.

You do solemnly swear [so reads the text] that you will administer justice without respect to persons, and do equal right to the poor and to the rich, and that you will faithfully and impartially discharge and perform all the duties incumbent on you . . . , according to the best of your abilities and understanding, agreeably to the Constitution and Laws of the United States; so help you God.

I venture to say that no one ever took this oath with a fuller realization of its meaning, with a deeper sense of the obligations it imposed, or with a more heartfelt and adequate resolution to keep it. It was said by Coke, the great Chief Justice, renowned alike for learning and for integrity, of a famous case momentously involving the political interests of the English Crown, that "no commandment or message" from any quarter whatsoever was sent to any of the judges to cause them to incline to one opinion or another, and that this was as it should be. Of this sentiment, which is the very foundation of the confidence which our courts fortunately enjoy, Bradford was a perfect exemplification. That considerations of rank or of power should influence his decisions was inconceivable. Nor was he in any relation of life a respecter of persons. The most contemptuous expression I ever heard him use was spoken of a man of high station, who was less scrupulous than successful.

The published record of Bradford's twenty-one years of judicial activity, which closed with his retirement on May 20, 1918, runs through a-hundred-and-sixty-five volumes of the Federal Reporter, beginning with the eighty-second volume, and ending with the two-hundred-and-forty-sixth. In this series I have noted almost two hundred of his written opinions, and have traced more than a hundred cases in the Circuit Court of Appeals in which he took part, without writing an individual opinion. His individual written opinions cover a wide range and variety of causes. The insurrection in Cuba immediately brought him into the international sphere, through the interpretation of the neutrality laws; and in this sphere he again figured prominently, in the leading case of *Tucker* v. *Alexandroff*, involving interesting questions of international law and of admiralty law. This case, in which, it may be noted, evidence from governmental sources and not before the courts below was by leave of court introduced on the final hearing, was finally disposed of by the Supreme Court on January 6, 1902[4] by a majority of five to four, in an opinion harmonizing with a minority opinion of Judge Bradford in the Circuit Court of Appeals.[5] Nor was his situation wholly changed, when, in dealing with subjects such as marine insurance, maritime liens, collisions at sea, salvage, and the rights, duties and status of seamen, he administered maritime law, which is so largely international. As a United States Judge, it goes without saying that he was called into the great and unique field of constitutional law. As a judicial magistrate, sitting in an age marked by the rapid growth of commerce and industry, questions of a commercial and industrial order came to him in great abundance; and some of his pronouncements have found their way into the text-books and become a part of the current language of the law. At one time he was brought, although only incidentally, into the epoch-making litigation, known as the Northern Securities case[6] concerning the application of the anti-trust law to railway consolidations. A striking proof of his capacity for labor, and of his singular aptitude in the discriminating application of legal rules even to the driest and most intricate mechanical details, is found in the large number of patent cases submitted to his judgment even from distant quarters. The rec-

4. 183 U. S., 424.
5. *Motherwell* v. *United States*, 107 Fed. Rep., 437, February 25, 1901.
6. 193 U. S., 197, March 14, 1904.

ognition of the ability and fairness with which he administered his criminal jurisdiction is illustrated by the circumstance that, in the only case in which the defendant appealed from his rulings and judgment, the appeal was abandoned after the affirmation by the Supreme Court, in another case, of the view of the law to which exception was taken.

As a practitioner and as a Judge, Bradford was conscious of the fact that he lived in a changing world, and that the law, in order to meet human needs, must grow with the world's growth. He was an indefatigable student of cases. With a keen sense of gratitude, I look back on the educational days and nights spent with him in the search for and discussion of precedents; and yet he never forgot that the letter killeth, but the spirit giveth life. He sought always the reason. He analyzed, arranged, systematized, and deduced an intelligent, consistent theory, imbued with the essence of legal philosophy. He was incapable of offering to the court, for its selective digestion, possibly two grains of wheat hidden in two bushels of unassorted chaff. On the contrary, if I may suddenly change the metaphor, let me say it was he who made the voyages of discovery, who sought to conquer the poles, who laid, explored and charted the course. As a lawyer, he endeavored to do this for the bench; and, as a judge, he did not leave the task wholly to the bar. Investigating exhaustively, as he did, every question brought before him, we are told that counsel were constantly surprised by finding their cases adjudicated upon reasons and authorities not suggested in the argument. But, while counsel were surprised, they were not necessarily discredited. How many could be compared with Bradford in comprehensive and minute knowledge of the law? He never ceased to be a student and to add to the store of his legal knowledge. On the other hand, in the capacity for legal reasoning I have never known his superior. His logic was unerring, and if his conclusion was at fault, it must have been because of an infirmity in the premises. The opinion heretofore expressed before this court that for combined logic and learning he stood preeminent among the district judges of his day, is fully justified. Had it been his lot to reach the Supreme Court, as I often wished might happen, he would have contributed to the endowment and prestige of that exalted tribunal a full and generous share.

Nor was Bradford's only public service the judicial. He was a member of the Delaware House of Representatives in 1881, and received the vote of his party, which was then in a minority, for the speakership. This legislative experience was distinctly advantageous to him, in withdrawing him temporarily from his seclusive pursuits and bringing him more into contact with the public. An examination of the journal of the House shows that he figured prominently in the transaction of business; and one is also struck with the large proportion of bills, many of which he introduced, disposed of on their merits, and not by a party division. The Speaker at the close congratulated the House on the spirit of harmony and good feeling that had pervaded the session, and his remark appears to have been well founded.

In 1888, Bradford was chairman of the Delaware delegation to the Republican National Convention at Chicago, the vote of the delegation being cast for Harrison. Later in the same year he was mentioned as a candidate for the United States Senate; but he refused to be considered as a competitor with Anthony Higgins, his own and his father's friend. In 1896, however, he was elected a member of the Convention by which was framed the present Constitution of Delaware. The convention assembled at Dover on December 1, 1896, and adjourned on June 4, 1897. He received the vote of his party, again in the minority, for the post of presiding officer. The journals show that he took in the proceedings of the Convention an effective and most important part. He was a member of the Committees on the Legislature and the Judiciary, and chairman of the Committee on Securing the Purity of the Ballot. He was also chairman of the Committee on Phraseology and Arrangement, by which the text of the constitution was finally revised.

In 1907 he attended, as a delegate of the Maritime Association of the United States, the conference of the International Maritime Committee, at Venice; and, actively participating in the Committee's deliberations, he was elected a vice-president of it. He was also present at the conference at Bremen in 1909. I know that he greatly enjoyed those meetings, and the instructive contacts they established with representatives of different systems of law and procedure as well as of legal education.

It has been said of Bradford that there was for him no "twilight zone between right and wrong"; that his "standards of conduct were inflexible and eternal"; that "political corruption of every form, lax social or domestic conduct and professional dishonesty, he loathed with the loathing of a moral and deeply religious nature." These words were most fitly spoken. His sense of the sacredness of domestic ties probably was intensified by his individual experience, in which an early attachment ripened into a union marked by perfect sympathy and devotion. But fidelity and sincerity were of the essence of his nature. And yet, when no question of moral rectitude was at stake, he was ever ready to consider and discuss a point of view different from his own, without showing the slightest proscriptive inclination. In our walks and talks, although divided in party allegiance, we discussed all manner of questions, political, social and religious, but no harsh word ever passed between us. He was much gratified, as I recall, with the statement, in old annals, that his lineal ancestor, William Bradford, second governor of Plymouth Colony, when entertaining a Catholic priest on Friday, took care to give him fish to eat, thus furnishing an agreeable contrast with other seventeenth-century apostles of religious liberty in the same quarter, who hanged Mary Dyer, also in his ancestral line, because after repeated banishments on pain of death for preaching Quaker doctrine, she persisted in returning for that purpose. On his mother's side he was descended from Judge Thomas B. Heyward, a signer of the Declaration of Independence. Of these things he was conscious, not in the unworthy way that begets a feeling of irresponsibility and a tendency to idleness or self-indulgence, but as incentives to the exertion of every faculty and the maintenance of the highest standards of conduct.

Of pride of opinion, Bradford was too sincere to be the victim. He would discuss questions of law with an uninformed client, and the reason he gave was twofold. The first was that, if he could make the point clear to the layman, he certainly could do so to the lawyer; the second was, that he perhaps might receive from the layman some practical suggestion that would not readily occur to the legal mind.

He was devoted to his church, and was active in its affairs, serving as a delegate to nine Triennial General Conventions, and often representing his parish in diocesan conventions; but his religion was unobtrusive, manifesting itself in conduct rather than in profession. One day, stopping over unannounced on a railway journey to see him, I waited for him in his judicial chambers and, when he appeared, found that he had been with the aged sexton of his church, to whom he was in the habit of bearing comfort and cheer in his sickness and infirmity. Of these things the world saw little, for his public and his private life were singularly separate.

As we come and go in this life, we inhale, even from the circumambient air, the germs of life and of death. This we do to a great extent unconsciously. But we also are subject, especially in our earlier years, to influences of the effects of which we are at the time and ever afterwards conscious, and for which we are always grateful. It was this feeling that led Wordsworth, standing at the grave of Burns, to think of him, in memorable lines, as one who had shown his youth—

"How Verse may build a princely throne
On humble truth."

As it is with literature, so it is with the law, to which, as the great regulator of human relations, the conception of truth is equally fundamental. Nor do literature and the law in this respect stand alone. They but share a universal human want; and, while the nature of man changes not, the world, which knows no repose, does only justice when it pays a tribute of respect and gratitude, as we do today, to one who exemplified in his life the eternal verities.

## THE LATE COUNT CHINDA[1]

### Japanese Statesman's Rare Qualities Endeared Him to Associates

To the Editor of *The New York Times:*

I cannot allow the announcement of the death of Count Chinda, Japan's Grand Chamberlain, to pass without a word of personal remembrance.

In 1913–14, when the so-called anti-Japanese land legislation in California and elsewhere was under discussion, it fell to my lot to be an official of the Department of State and in that capacity to see him at times almost daily. No one could have maintained the claims of his government more assiduously than he did, or with greater ability, dignity and poise; and I have always felt that it was in no small measure due to his untiring and sagacious efforts that the controversy, which involved elements of sentiment as well as of interest, was kept within proper bounds.

But his course in this particular matter was merely consistent with the general tenor of his conduct. High-minded, earnest and sincere, he commanded the confidence and respect of all those with whom he dealt, and he thus exerted an influence which a man less faithful and wise could not have acquired. The great distinction to which he rose in his country's service is a gratifying proof that his exceptional merits as a national representative and statesman were fully appreciated by his own government and people. We in America may also feel a justified pride in him as the graduate of an American university.

JOHN BASSETT MOORE.

New York, Jan. 17. 1929.

1. Reprinted from *The New York Times*, January 21, 1929.

# THE OFFICE OF LEGISLATIVE COUNSEL[1]

THE Office of the Legislative Counsel of the Congress of the United States, which may now be regarded as an established institution, enjoys the double distinction of having justified its creation both before and since it came into existence; for it was created by the Congress, not as an untried experiment, but as the means of assuring the continuance, in legal and permanent form, of a definite kind of aid which had demonstrated its usefulness in improving the quality of legislation.

The present age may be said to enjoy an undisputed preeminence in the making of laws. When one uses now the awesome word "law," he instinctively thinks not of the congenial rules which the habits and experience of the community conveniently evolve, but of the torrent of statutes annually poured forth, with little mercy, alike upon the just and the unjust. The inevitable result of excessive legislation is that the law constantly tends to fall into confusion, if not into chaos. The legislator of an earlier age, of whom it was then humorously said that, when questioned concerning his official activities, he always declined to hazard any conjectures in advance of the formal publication of the Sessional Laws, might today be seriously reckoned as a man of only ordinary prudence.

The law is or should be treated as a science. The Office of the Legislative Counsel, devoted in the widest sense to expert draftsmanship, is designed to represent that ideal and to arrest, as far as possible, the tendency more or less due to the pressure of circumstances, to prolixity, disorder and uncertainty in statutory enactments.

Eminent analysts of the law and its administration have with reason maintained that the law is to be found not so much in the words that appear in the text of the enactment as in the terms of the statute as interpreted and applied by the courts. Statutes are not self-interpreting, even interpretative schedules can make them so only to a certain extent. It is in respect of this fundamental, vital point that the exercise of learning and skill in draftsmanship may and often does play a part of the first importance.

1. Foreword to *The Office of the Legislative Counsel* by Frederic P. Lee. Reprinted from the *Columbia Law Review*, Vol. XXIX, No. 4 (April, 1929).

The preparation of an act of legislation may present various phases, each of which involves a distinct problem. First, there must be a definite purpose or intention; but this is not as simple as it sounds. The purpose or intention, unless it is to evaporate in a mere sentimental yearning, must be correctly expressed in apt words; and it not infrequently happens that the would-be legislator, in his expression of his purpose or intention, fails to convey it with precision and effectiveness. Secondly, the sub-ject-matter, instead of being single or simple, may be highly complicated and require the consideration, adjustment and reconciliation of numerous elements. In the third place, it is necessary to bear in mind the machinery already provided for the application and enforcement of the proposed measure and the possible necessity of prescribing administrative details. Fourthly, the new measure should be examined in connection with any previous legislation on the same subject or on similar subjects, and not merely with the text of such legislation but also with pertinent judicial and administrative interpretations.

These examples will serve to illustrate the complexity of law-making, and the need of expert criticism and advice at all stages of the process. The capital importance of such supervision was impressed upon me by an incident in my early official expe-rience. Called upon as Third Assistant Secretary of State to ascertain the rights of foreign governments under the Inter-national Copyright Act, I was informed by the author of the act, and also by the chairman of the committee by which it was originally reported, that under a certain clause, the citizens of countries that were parties to the Bern convention were as such entitled to all the privileges of the statute. After full considera-tion, however, the conclusion was reached that the clause in question could not be so interpreted, and this conclusion was approved by the President, and was afterwards sustained by the Supreme Court. This was fifteen years before the creation by the Congress of the Office of the Legislative Counsel.

I esteem it a high honor to have been one of the original trustees of the Legislative Drafting Research Fund at Colum-bia University; and I may mention, as an historical detail, the fact that there was previously created a corporation called the Legislative Drafting Association. The bulk of the endowment for the Association, however, and the work were later concen-trated in the Research Fund, the diversified activities of which have permeated many fields and contributed to improve and render more effective the efforts of other bodies and organi-zations to render public service.

# ADDRESS ON THE 70TH ANNIVERSARY OF THE EQUITABLE LIFE ASSURANCE SOCIETY[1]

IN the celebration of the seventieth Anniversary of the founding of The Equitable Life Assurance Society of the United States, there has been allotted to me the grateful part of speaking to the agency force.

To be a member of this force is to hold a position which has constantly increased in dignity and in usefulness. In the early days of life insurance in the United States, when the business was so generally regarded as a private enterprise, was little supervised, and was often conducted in a hazardous way, the activities of its agents were hampered by a prevalent doubt as to whether an investment in a policy would eventually prove to be safe and beneficial. Indeed, I distinctly recall that, when I was a boy and lived in a rural community, there was a tendency to put life insurance in the same category with the sale of lightning rods, with which an old lady was reported to have refused to have her house equipped because, as she said, the lightning came near enough in the adjacent woods, and she did not want to bring it any closer.

Only to think of the revolutionary change in the public attitude and of the marvelous growth of the business since that time! On December 31, 1928, the estimated life insurance in force in the United States was $95,000,000,000, or $787 per capita. In the succeeding eight months, in the present year, the grand total increased probably more than $5,000,000,000, thus rising to $100,000,000,000, and denoting a gathering momentum likely to fulfil the forecast, made in Washington last week, that by 1940 the total would be doubled. The present total in the United States represents the highest amount for any country in the world, not only collectively but also per capita. The next largest amount per capita is found in that great and growing neighbor of ours to the north, Canada, where on December 31, 1928, the grand total of life insurance in force was more than $5,500,000,000, the per capita being $580.

These truly remarkable figures owe their existence largely to the activities of the agency forces. The name of our Society —The Equitable Life Assurance Society of the United States—

1. Reprinted from *Agency Items*, No. 1139 of The Equitable Life Assurance Society (October 6, 1929).

was taken over from that of the then venerable English company called The Equitable Life Assurance Society of London. The English company has always operated without agents, and the cost of its new business enables us to answer an inquiry often made as to whether the American companies ought not merely to keep open offices, and to deal directly with the public rather than through intermediaries. The answer is found in the fact that new business costs the English company as much as it costs the larger American companies. In other words, the much greater rate of increase of business of the American companies so much reduces the average cost as to make the agency force practically self-supporting. But we must also consider, as an additional and still greater advantage, the extension of the benefits of life insurance to a vastly increased proportion of the population. This aspect may be strikingly illuminated by the statement that the United States and Canada, with a combined population of 140,000,000 out of a world total of 1,500,-000,000 have three-fourths of all the life insurance in the world.

We sometimes hear the question raised whether the business of life insurance is not a governmental function, and should not be exclusively conducted by the government. We are not wholly without light on this question. During the recent so-called World War, the United States, after it entered the conflict in April, 1917, established the Bureau of War-Risk Insurance. At the end of October, 1918, this Bureau had received 4,090,031 applications for $35,762,516,000 insurance. On December 31, 1927, the latest date for which I have found an available report, the total war-risk insurance in force was $3,200,000,184.70. Considering the fact that in these days a billion dollars has become a prevalent unit of value, the war-risk insurance seems to be rapidly approaching the vanishing point.

An accomplished writer has told us the story of Garibaldi and the Thousand—the force with which that ardent patriot set out to make his inestimable contribution to the unification of modern Italy. The agency force of The Equitable Life Assurance Society of the United States now embraces 10,000 men, but it is not a military force. Like Garibaldi's force, it is constructive; but its method is educational. We hear a great deal in these days about education and educational methods. We have public education and private education, religious education and secular education, military education and civil education; and perhaps it may be said that we have a great deal of education that is not educational at all—not, at any rate, in any good sense. But, even where the objective may be admitted to be praiseworthy, there often exists a diversity of views giving rise to unhappy controversies, such, for instance, as that which persists between modernists and fundamentalists.

Life insurance agents may congratulate themselves upon the fact that there are now practically no diversities of view or of sentiment as to the beneficence of the work in which they are engaged. Having long since passed out of the contracted sphere in which they originally labored, they have entered a higher and wider domain, in which, as the record of their accomplishment amply attests, they enjoy to a marked degree the public confidence. But it by no means follows that their way is easy and their burden light. There is in the human make-up an element of inertia or of perversity that often leads men not only to neglect but even to resist what is good for them. By reason of this factor, the agent, like other teachers, must exercise patience, skill and tact. And here it is proper to remark that The Equitable, recognizing these facts, has made a specialty of contributing to the training of its agents, thus helping to increase their efficiency as well as to raise the general standard of action. This it has done through its Educational Courses, its Correspondence Course, its Field Schools, and its Specialist's Course, and through Special Articles and Conventions. It may, indeed, be said that The Equitable expends more on the training of its agents than any other two or three companies, and that this is one of the reasons why it has in its agency force such an excellent body of men and women. In a recent publication, in which were listed the million dollar producers in all companies of the United States, The Equitable had more than 18% of the total, although there are 250 companies in the United States.

Of the educational work of the life insurance agent, the great objective is the spread of thrift and security. The first is a stimulus to industry and to good citizenship; the second brings solace to men, women and children in time of need. But this is not the only phase. By means of personal and repeated interviews with the agents of American Life Insurance Companies, the people of the land are learning the way to certainty of education of their children; to appropriate provision for the payment of death taxes; to the obtaining of funds for the building of homes; to the financing of public works; to the endowment of colleges and benevolent institutions; to the creation of trusts and to the provision of annuities.

I have spoken of the educational phase of the agency forces and their activities, and this brings me to the final stage of development of the system, and that is the application of the principle of co-operation. In the modern world, with its great diversity of interests, political, social, commercial and financial, the great problem has been that of avoiding the conflicts which the rivalry of individual interests so directly tends to produce. Happily, in the vast domain of life insurance, this problem has been solved by the progressive elimination of the private interest, and the cultivation and pursuit of the practice of co-operation, of which it may truly be said that, like righteousness, it exalteth a nation. Not only do our great life insurance institutions rank, as President Hoover has lately declared, with the highest forms of our national achievements, but, taking the home office and the agencies as a whole, they constitute unitary organizations carrying on, with and for the benefit of the policyholders, certainly one of the greatest, if not the greatest co-operative enterprise of modern times. In the name of The Equitable Life Assurance Society of the United States, I congratulate the agency force on the distinction with which it has performed its part in this inspiring undertaking, and renew to it the pledge of the Society's confidence, and full and cordial support.

# THE OPTIONAL CLAUSE OF THE STATUTE OF THE PERMANENT COURT OF INTERNATIONAL JUSTICE. A SYMPOSIUM

TO the protocol of signature of the constitution, technically called the "Statute," of the Permanent Court of International Justice, popularly called the "World Court," as signed at Geneva on December 16, 1920, there was annexed an "Optional Clause," by which the adhering governments were permitted to make exceptions to the Court's otherwise compulsory jurisdiction.

President Harding, in a special message to the Senate on February 24, 1923, recommended the adhesion of the United States to the Court's Statute, subject to certain specified exceptions. President Coolidge pursued a similar course.[1] The agitation of the subject was for some years continued and, in *The World Tomorrow* of October, 1929, there was a leading editorial which raised a question as to the relationship between the Court and the Briand-Kellogg treaty, popularly called the Pact of Paris, the parties to which, while renouncing war "as

1. For full information as to the constitution, personnel and proceedings of the Court during its first three years, see my volume entitled *International Law and Some Current Illusions, and Other Essays* (New York, The Macmillan Company, 1924), *supra*, pp. 79–140.

an instrument of national policy," agreed that "the settlement or solution of all disputes or conflicts" between them, no matter what their "nature or origin," should "never be sought except by pacific means." On the other hand, while the Pact neither specified any particular method of settling controversies nor required them to be settled at all, it expressly reserved the right to wage war "in self-defense," thus benevolently cloaking all wars—past, present and future; for, no matter what the origin of an armed conflict may have been, it is certain that, once begun, it becomes, with the rights and liabilities which war confers and entails, a matter of life and death for both parties. For the purpose of illustration, the editorial inquired what the situation would be in case the then pending conflict between Soviet Russia and China over the Chinese eastern railway, both being actual parties to the Pact of Paris, should result in an avowed war. By Section (c) of Article 36 of the Court's Statute a "legal" question was defined as one involving a decision as to "the existence of any fact which, if established, would constitute a breach of an international obligation"; and from this it followed that a political or an economic question became "legal" when specifically covered by a treaty, and therefore not to be settled by other than "pacific means." Such being the facts, the editorial insisted that some method of escape should be agreed upon in advance of a crisis, lest its legal value be suddenly and wholly lost.

In *The World Tomorrow* of November, 1929, there were ten responses, some short and some long, from persons to whom the editorial had been submitted for comment. The first, in the order of printing, was my own, and, as it was short, I reproduce it textually:

I assume that you consider the "optional clause" as an example of what is desirable rather than something the acceptance or rejection of which, in its precise form and its present connections, is to be taken as a test of one's attitude towards the question of arbitration. I make this remark because I think that the cause of peaceful adjustment of international disputes has suffered detriment from the disposition of many of its advocates to adopt some particular measure or method as a sort of test, and then to decry everything else. The general tenor of your editorial leads me to think that you may share this opinion, and, assuming this to be the case, I do not hesitate to say that I consider your editorial to be sound and helpful. To renounce war on the one hand, and then, on the other, to refuse to make actual, definite provision in advance for the settlement of disputes which are bound to arise presents a flagrant incongruity, and an evident want of appreciation of what always has been and always will be an essential element of the problem of preserving peace between nations as well as between individual men.

The next comment was that of Norman Thomas, who thought that the Pact would "inevitably become a monument to hypocrisy" unless the "United States and other nations" that were "in earnest" about it should "establish some sort of machinery or method for deciding what is a war of self-defense." He thought that a "war of aggression" was best defined as "a war begun by a nation which refused to submit its claim to any form of settlement."

Wickham Steed summarily disposed of the entire matter in these words:

To my mind the point is very simple. The progress of civilization now depends upon the effective ruling out of war. If war is ruled out, law must take its place. The administration of law presupposes a court. The value of a court depends upon the readiness of litigants to accept its decisions or on the power of the court to enforce its decisions. In the case of the World Court this power must necessarily be moral. Moral suasion is effective when it is practically universal. The signing of the Optional Clause of the Statute of the Hague Court is a step towards the universalisation of the recognized competence of the Court. In other words, it leads in the direction of bringing international law into the conscience of the international community and of rendering the "sanctions" of that conscience automatic. The day will come when contempt of the World Court will be looked upon as an offence that places the offender outside the pale of civilisation.

Less aeronautic was the response of John Haynes Holmes, who was unable to accept the editorial argument in favor of the Optional Clause because it seemed in effect to propose that the World Court should be empowered to decide that one of the parties to a dispute had the right to go to war "in self-defense or in vindication of the Pact." He was absolutely opposed to this. The great virtue of the Pact, as he saw it, was that it avoided precise definitions while precluding the use of war as an instrument of national policy. This was enough. Had Russia or Japan, in the Russo-Chinese crisis, obtained from the Court a finding that the Peace Pact had been violated, then war would have been on, and the world as a whole would have been behind the nation that got the Court's favorable judgment. But, as neither nation was able to get any support of its claims, public opinion held both to be acting in contempt of the Pact, and the war simmered out. While heartily in favor of settling international disputes by judicial processes, he was absolutely opposed to any device, judicial or otherwise, for establishing the legal right of a nation to take up arms.

Viscount Cecil of Chelwood thoroughly agreed with the editorial in its position that, if each country was to be the sole judge of whether it was acting in self-defense, the Pact of Paris was at an end. This difficulty was not, he thought, due to a defect in the Pact or in its interpretation, but was inevitable in dealing with international problems. No outlawry of war could take from a nation the right to defend itself against invasion or destruction; and nothing was gained by forbidding all war except self-defense, or in denouncing aggressive war as an international crime. The only way out was to leave the decision to some external tribunal; and, for cases that could not reasonably be said to depend exclusively on the interpretation of the Pact of Paris, a more nearly complete form of arbitration would have to be devised.

John Bakeless, while thinking that the point raised in the editorial was well taken, and that it might be well to "close the gap" in existing peace pacts, feared that in a time of national crisis even a plain obligation might be either circumvented or disregarded.

Jackson H. Ralston thought that the question of self-defense was "purely one of fact," and that, if self-defense became "necessary," this would itself establish a refusal to abide by the Pact, and present a case for judicial decision. The question of reparation might offer difficulties, but such questions were daily passed upon in courts of law.

Edwin Borchard, who was unable to agree with the editorial's legal analysis, found it difficult to believe that the nations would actually accept the suggested procedures for deciding whether the Kellogg Pact had been violated. In the first place, he was not so sure that anything was really gained by renouncing war "as an instrument of national policy," but reserving self-defense. If war was waged in "self-defense," as it *invariably* was, was not that an instrument or measure of national policy? If, as the editorial said, war in self-defense was not renounced, what was it then that had been renounced? In the second place, admitting that the difference between China and Russia was "legal," was it possible that either country would appeal to the World Court and assert that the Kellogg Pact had been violated? He doubted it because, even if the Court ventured to decide the question, the plaintiff country would in all probability lose the case for the reason he had already mentioned, and in this connection he referred to his comment in the January, 1929, number of the *American Journal of International Law*. In the third place, if the Court assumed jurisdiction, it would put its life in jeopardy; for, if it decided that the defendant country had violated the Kellogg Pact, this probably would cause such consternation in the Ministries of Foreign Affairs that both the Pact and the Court would be in danger. The fact that no nation had as yet been willing to leave such questions in the hands of a third party was clearly indicated by the very terms of the reservations made by all the countries in signing the Pact. Such being the facts, Mr. Borchard thought it would be better to rely on the Kellogg Pact as a basis for moral propaganda against war in any form, as reliance upon its supposed legal meaning or significance would, he feared, end in disappointment.

James W. Garner concurred in the view that the outstanding defect of the Briand-Kellogg Pact was the reservation by the parties of the right to wage "defensive" wars and the right of each to be the sole and final judge in a particular case of that question. Under the reservation each party had virtually a free hand to make war for any purpose it chose to regard as "defensive," subject solely to the limitation of public opinion. In this particular the Pact was a backward step, since the old legal theory that each state was the final judge of its obligations under international law had been definitely abandoned, and no important civilized state would any longer profess to act on such a theory. No country had, said Mr. Garner, more vigorously rejected it than the United States, which had, through its Secretaries of State, repeatedly asserted that the municipal law of a state could not be set up as the measure of its international obligations. The United States had indeed emphatically taken this position in recent controversies with Mexico and Roumania. On the other hand, the proposal to empower the Permanent Court of International Justice to decide whether a particular war was, as between the parties to it, self-defensive, or whether it violated the Pact, was logical and reasonable. Such a dispute would clearly involve the "interpretation of a treaty" and possibly also the "existence of a fact which, if established, would constitute a breach of an international obligation"—questions which the signatories of the Optional Clause of the Court's statute had recognized as falling within its compulsory jurisdiction. A stipulation requiring the submission of such controversies to a common judge, whether the Permanent Court or some other tribunal, would be a happy solution of a difficult problem and would remove from the Pact its one great defect.

The last commentator was Norman Angell, who, besides expressing general agreement with the argument that the acceptance of the Optional Clause by the signatories of the Pact would give it a legal value which otherwise it did not possess, thought the need of such a supplement was the more obvious in view of the implications of the phrase "self-defense" in the identic note of June, 1923. Should a war take place between signatories of the Kellogg Pact, it could with complete certainty be predicted that both belligerents would declare that they were waging a purely defensive war; and, being actually at war, both were likely to be completely sincere. Mr. Angell thought that Mr. Kellogg's proposal that the right of self-defense be limited to the effort "to defend national territory from attack or invasion," would, had it been adopted before the recent war, have condemned most of the Allies, including the United States, as none of them was threatened with immediate invasion when they went to war. Moreover, there was the question of how the right in defense of which the war was waged was to be established. The claim of a country to be the sole judge of its own rights necessarily involved, in international matters, the right to determine the rights of other nations, and this was something that no nation would accept or agree to. Mr. Angell thought, and very properly thought, that the whole discussion was vitiated by false analogies drawn between persons and nations. Such an analogy was not well-founded. Should an individual, attacked by a footpad or a lunatic with a knife, fail to defend himself, he would be quickly dead, but this was not the case with nations. When France invaded the Ruhr, there would have been a war if Germany had been armed. Germany did not resist because she could not, but Germany did not die. Very few individual Germans died; but, before the invaders went away, Germany had taken other means to protect her rights. The right of self-defense accorded to the individual citizen did not include the right to be his own judge. On the contrary, said Mr. Angell, there was a whole body of law defining the rights of citizens, and the whole of society within the state was organized with a view to defend the individual in the enjoyment of those rights. In the international sphere all this was lacking; nor, in the absence of a common sovereign, superior over all, had it been shown how that which was lacking could be supplied.

Not only was Mr. Angell's statement cogent and to the point, but, had he seen fit to do so, he might have gone further and commented, as I have repeatedly done, on the frequent recurrence of civil wars, in spite of the existence of highly organized and efficient national governments.

# JOSEPH STORY: REMARKS ON THE UNVEILING OF HIS BUST IN THE HALL OF FAME[1]

IT was, or should have been, easy to agree that the bust of Joseph Story should have a place among the representatives of jurisprudence in the Hall of Fame. Had his bust been omitted, it would, like the images wanting to the Roman procession, have been conspicuous by its absence.

Born at Marblehead, in Massachusetts, on September 18, 1779, Story lived in the formative period of American political and legal institutions; and from his precocious appearance on the public stage until his death, in 1845, he incessantly labored to contribute to their development. The range of his activities was extraordinary. He was admitted to the bar, at Salem, in 1801. Engaging also in politics, he entered the Massachusetts legislature in 1805; and in the same year he published his first law book, an annotated selection of pleadings in civil actions. From the Massachusetts legislature he passed to the Congress of the United States. In 1820 he was a member of the convention for the revision of the constitution of his native State.

Meanwhile, in 1811, at the unprecedentedly early age of thirty-two, Story was appointed an associate justice of the Supreme Court of the United States, and, among all those who have held that position, none has contributed more copiously or more learnedly to the jurisprudence of that exalted tribunal. His opinions in the Supreme Court fill an important part of thirty-four volumes of its reports, to say nothing of his judgments and charges in the circuit court. Moreover, from 1829 to the end of his life, as Dane Professor of Law in Harvard College, he expounded legal principles to the youth of the land. But his capacity evidently expanded with the strain put upon it; for, while performing his duties as a judge and as a teacher, he poured forth legal treatises of prodigious and varied learning, not only in the domain of private and of public law, but also in the sphere of general and international jurisprudence. In quick succession there appeared his *Commentaries on the Law of Bailments*, with illustrations from the civil and foreign law, in 1832; on the *Constitution of the United States*, in 1833; on the *Conflict of Laws, Foreign and Domestic*, the first original work of its kind in English, in 1834; on *Equity Jurispru-*

1. May 8, 1930.

*dence,* as administered in England and America, in 1836; on *Equity Pleadings,* in 1838; on the *Law of Agency,* in 1839; on the *Law of Partnerships as a Branch of Commercial and Maritime Jurisprudence,* in 1841; on the *Law of Bills of Exchange, Foreign and Domestic,* in 1843; and on the *Law of Promissory Notes,* in 1845. Of the *Equity Jurisprudence,* which is still in daily request at the law libraries, the fourteenth American edition appeared as late as 1918, while a new edition appeared in England in 1920. The *Equity Pleadings* reached a tenth American edition in 1892; the *Law of Agency* a ninth, in 1882; the *Law of Bailments* also a ninth, in 1878. The rest have run through numerous editions, the smallest number being four, in the case of the treatises on *Bills of Exchange* and *Promissory Notes.* An abridged but copiously annotated edition of his commentaries on the Constitution was published in French, at Paris, in 1843; and in Spanish, in Mexico, in 1879. His treatise on *Bills of Exchange* was published in German, at Leipzig, in 1845. In the catalogue of the Harvard Law Library of 1909, the enumeration of his writings and their various editions fills six pages.

In spite of the necessitous demand of practising lawyers for works containing citations of the latest decisions, the treatises of Story are still held in the highest esteem as legal classics, while many of them are constantly consulted and studied as repositories of learning and as models of luminous exposition of legal principles. Thus, while hardly exampled in quantity, they have, by reason of their exceptional quality, survived to justify his past renown. In this real sense the bust of Story speaks to us today as that of a living jurist.

## ADDRESS OF WELCOME AT THE LUNCHEON IN HONOR OF REAR-ADMIRAL RICHARD E. BYRD, U.S.N. RETIRED, GIVEN BY THE AMERICAN ARBITRATION ASSOCIATION AT THE HOTEL ASTOR, NEW YORK, JUNE 25, 1930, ON HIS RETURN FROM HIS ANTARCTIC EXPEDITION

Mr. Chairman, Admiral Byrd, Ladies and Gentlemen:

I cannot say, with Rienzi, that "I come not here to talk," for that is precisely what I have come here to do. But, in truth, the occasion is not one that calls for much talking, as deeds speak louder than words.

When I told a friend the other day that I was to make a speech of welcome to Admiral Byrd on behalf of the American Arbitration Association, he inquired whether the Admiral had at length done something to require the Association's services. I was glad immediately to assure him that this was not the case; that the occasion was altogether exceptional; and that, while it was the Association's specific function to bring about the adjustment of differences by methods less formal, less lengthy and less expensive than those of contentious litigation, it desired in the present instance, without appointing any board, or summoning any experts, or taking any testimony, to assure Admiral Byrd of the universal honor, respect and admiration in which he is held by the great commercial and industrial interests with which the Association is identified.

Nevertheless, I confess that I felt a certain concern lest I might merely repeat what everybody was saying until I recalled an incident of my student-days at the University of Virginia. Being somewhat under the weather, I had the good fortune to be attended by that most delightful of men, the late Dr. John Staige Davis, who, when he came to consider my diet, told me that I might have an egg for breakfast. I intimated to him that I was not wholly unfamiliar with that particular article of food at the University boarding house, and that it had become somewhat monotonous; but my views were broadened and enlightened when, with a slight lisp in his voice, he asked me to consider the fact that I had "never eaten the same egg twice." I at once admitted that this profound and comforting thought had never occurred to me before. Since Admiral Byrd's arrival a week ago, he has heard many speeches; but I would ask him to remember that, even though they may have a common flavor, he has, in reality, never heard the same speech twice.

In reflecting recently on the things that have differentiated Admiral Byrd's explorations from those of earlier days, I recalled a song, which I heard and occasionally sang in my youth, running thus:

> Were I a bird of air,
>     And had two pinions fair,
> I'd fly to thee,
>     I'd fly to thee;
> But this can never be,
>     But this can never be;
> Oh woe is me,
> Oh woe is me!

At a notable meeting of the New York Historical Society a number of years ago, William Cullen Bryant, poet and journalist, related some personal reminiscences of Genêt, who was sent as minister from France to the United States during the French Revolution, and who, after the termination of his official services, married and settled in the United States and spent the rest of his life here. In this way Bryant came to know him, and he concluded his reminiscences by sadly remarking that Genêt in his later years became demented—that he experimented with flying machines.

I have adverted to the tuneful lament of the lover and to the short-sighted comment of the poet and journalist merely as illustrations of how the folly and despair of one generation may become the wisdom and delight of another. We have now just entered upon the era of aviation; but the aeroplane is already available for the far-flung expeditions of the explorer, as well as for everyday business and social uses. We know the eventful part it has played in the vast explorations of Admiral Byrd, and, speaking from his personal experience, he has recently declared it to be difficult fully to appreciate the two ends of the earth without flying over large areas of the Arctic ocean and of the South Polar plateau.

This leads me to remark that, among the things for which Admiral Byrd commands our admiration and respect is the intelligent and comprehensive forecast with which he forms his plans and avails himself of all the means which invention and science afford for the successful prosecution of his designs. We may well hesitate to associate ourselves with those highly romantic persons who find delight in the story of magnificent failures, even when they might by the exercise of ordinary foresight have been avoided; nor are we obliged to subscribe to the common saying that nothing succeeds like success, a sentiment too often associated with the pursuit of unworthy ends by unworthy means. But surely our homage is due to those who, with adequate preparation, achieve great ends to the attainment of which preparation is essential.

Another ground on which Admiral Byrd commands our admiration and respect is the heartiness with which he accords to his associates full and unreserved credit for the aid which they have rendered him in the perilous adventures in which he has so often risked all that men commonly hold dear. When visiting Trafalgar Square, in London, in which stands the tall column surmounted with the figure of Admiral Lord Nelson I have always recalled an incident of the evening before the battle of Trafalgar. Just as the mail boat was casting off without waiting for the letters of some of the men who were slow in writing, the great Admiral ordered it to return until the last man had had an opportunity to finish perhaps his last letter to his home. That is what Admiral Byrd would under similar circumstances have done. In the fact that he attaches to him, as with hooks of steel, the comrades who, confiding in his courageous and unfaltering leadership, share his fortunes and his fate, we have another proof of those sterling and generous qualities which so eloquently attest a man's greatness.

We are brought still nearer to Admiral Byrd when we see in his acts and conduct constant manifestations of those touches of nature and of sentiment which are declared to make the whole world kin. We may stand in awe or dread of an iceberg and, at a safe distance, with the sun shining on it, may even admire it; but we never can love it. So, in our relations with our own kind, our affections are reserved for those who do good, not evil, to their fellow men; who act constructively, not destructively; who seek to advance the common lot, to ascend to heights previously unscaled, and to increase the bounds of knowledge and of aspiration.

Taking him, therefore, for what he is and for what he has done, we are proud to welcome Admiral Byrd today, not only as an American who has shed lustre on his native land, but also as one among the men of all lands and all times who have deserved and will have, enduring fame.

## WHY WE HAVE NOT SEEN THE LAST OF WAR[1]

I DO not share the widely current but hasty and shallow supposition that, as the result of improved means of communication, international wars are no more to be expected or may by certain agreements or devices be averted. They tell us that the steam railroad, the modern ocean liner, the telegraph, the telephone, radio, movies, and airplanes have brought races and nations so close together that, realizing that they cannot afford to fight, they will refrain from doing so. I do not think so. Propinquity does not always breed affection. Nor do men always count the cost before they come to blows.

We often call the last war the World War. Actually, there are others that better deserve the title. Take the Seven Years' War. That was relatively in the Dark Ages so far as transportation and communication are concerned. But the fighting more

1. The present paper is the connected text of what Mr. Moore said in the course of an interview published in the *Review of Reviews* (July, 1930), pp. 71–73. A condensed version appeared in *The Reader's Digest* (August, 1930), pp. 292–294.

nearly covered the entire globe than did that of the last conflict, which was pretty well confined to Europe. During the Seven Years' War not only did men, as it has been said, fight in Saxony for dominion in America, but the military and naval activities of the belligerents encircled the globe. At the expense of France the British established their supremacy in North America and their empire in India, while they assailed on land and sea the dominions of Spain in America and in the Pacific. Again, the wars growing out of the French revolution and the Napoleonic Wars more nearly involved all of Europe than did the late war, to say nothing of their fateful effects elsewhere. No; while modern communications seem to have made the world smaller, steam, electricity, and gasoline carry us no farther, except a few miles skyward, than did horse and sail. Modern inventions may carry us more quickly; but, in the words of the popular song, our ancestors "got there just the same."

As regards the effect of propinquity, take France and Germany. When the telegraph was invented the prediction was constantly and confidently made that nations, being brought into closer touch, would learn to love one another and to dwell together in peace and amity. But railways and telegraphs never were needed to bring France and Germany within quick and common reach. Dwelling side by side for centuries, they had daily passed and repassed their thin divisional line for purposes of peace or of war. Meanwhile, how much had they learned to understand, to appreciate and to love one another? From the close of the Napoleonic Wars until the conflict of 1870 there was a lapse of fifty-five years; from the peace of 1871 until the late war there was an armed truce of hardly forty-four years. The supposition that international good will specially characterizes the relations of neighboring peoples is as unfounded as it is common.

In Europe, as Frank H. Simonds has, in his articles in the *Review of Reviews,* so often pointed out, they put their faith in various agreements which undertake to guarantee, by force and otherwise, security as against an aggressor, while here we rely upon the comfortable assurance that our word is law in the Western Hemisphere, that we want no wars, and that it is enough to tell the world so—while the same old conflicts of interest between nations go steadily on.

The clash of views becomes apparent when the representatives of the United States and Europe meet for the purpose of devising some method of assuring world peace. As an instance, we may take the proposal of a "consultative pact" during the recent naval conference at London. It was said that, if the United States would promise to consult with the nations of

Europe when trouble loomed, France would agree to cut her naval tonnage sharply. This served to recall, as regarded reality, the story of the traveler who, when riding through the country on a wintry day, was lured to a tavern by the sign "Hot mince pie." Cold and hungry, he alighted and gave his order, but, when the pie was served, he found it frozen. Surprised and incensed, he demanded an explanation; but the waiter, with a chuckle, blandly replied: "Oh, suh, dat pie's all right. Hot mince pie is only de name of it."

So with the consultative pact, that was only the name of it. The idea that France would give up some 200,000 tons of cruisers for a mere friendly consultation with the United States is ridiculous. What she naturally wanted was "consultation" that would bring her help when, in her opinion, she was attacked.

And this brings us to another difficulty. How are you to know when a nation is "aggressively" attacked? The supposition that, when war breaks out, it will always be clear who was the "aggressor," gained great currency in the excited times when it was readily asserted and believed that the late war was premeditated, prepared for and brought on by the sole act of Germany. But this assertion has never been seriously entertained by persons intelligently familiar with the sordid diplomacy and the legislative and administrative acts of the fifteen years that preceded the war; and its incorporation in the Versailles peace treaty is now generally acknowledged to have been a mistake. In reality, it is impossible even today confidently to say who was in a real sense the aggressor in some of the greatest wars the world has known.

Often nations have simply drifted into war through what may be called a normal conflict of interests, even while their professional orators were protesting that the use of armed force between civilized peoples was no longer thinkable. When, in May, 1914, in a public address, I described international conditions as I knew them to be, I was dubbed a "pessimist"; but, as the war came two months later, I let bygones be bygones and bore my critics no ill will.

Another popular fallacy is the idea that an unwillingness to arbitrate may be accepted as a conclusive indication of the "aggressor." The beaming proponents of this theory forget the judgment of Solomon, who, as between two women, each of whom claimed to be the mother of the child, awarded it to the one who refused to have it cut in two. Nor do true owners welcome the expenses and hazards of litigation, even though they may prefer it to a contest by violence.

While this may seem to optimists and dreamers to forecast a gloomy future, the cause of peace will be conserved rather than injured by dealing with things as they actually are and ever have been. There always have been and there always will be conflicts of interest and of ambition between nations and tribes, just as there are and always have been between individual human beings. An enlightened foreign policy will, admitting this, put a nation's interests in the hands of diplomats who will frankly, but honestly and fairly, advocate and try to adjust those interests. In case diplomacy fails to bring an adjustment, we should cultivate the habit of submitting these conflicts to judicial settlement; and if, in spite of all peaceful efforts, war should nevertheless come, we should not despairingly cry out that courts and arbitral boards are worthless, and that we must have something wholly new and previously untried. On the contrary, regarding such institutions as a part of international, just as they are of national life, we should seek to strengthen them and to extend their jurisdiction. No one proposed to abolish the Supreme Court of the United States either because it failed to prevent or to end the Civil War. The prevention or ending of wars is the function of judicial courts, whether national or international, only in the sense that their primary function is the adjudication of such disputes as may be brought before them.

Sometimes I think we talk too much. We are too often like the man who, before we got into the late war, was volubly and rather incoherently discussing the European conflict at the breakfast table. When I quietly commented, "You seem to be somewhat excited this morning," he rose, sputtering, and, bringing his fist down on the table, shouted: "But I *like* to be excited!"

I am afraid the human propensity to get excited and to like excitement enters very deeply into the question of peace and war.

## A DECALOGUE FOR DIPLOMATS[1]

EVEN if you do not love your neighbor as yourself, you need not hate or misjudge him. Remember that, while justice is due to every man, even mercy, which becomes the thronéd monarch better than his crown, may sometimes not be out of place.

Do not heedlessly swish your bamboo, lest your neighbor may be provoked to swish his, to the disturbance of that tran-

1. Reprinted from the *Review of Reviews* (July, 1930), pp. 72–73.

quillity by which international relations should ever be pervaded.

Do not impute to other peoples a lack of the virtues which you yourself profess, lest the world judge you by what you do rather than by what you say. Even the assumption of exceptionally peaceful propensities may be questioned by others.

Do not covet Naboth's vineyard, and especially that which you may chance already to occupy, lest you be openly accused or secretly suspected of wishing to keep it.

With two ears to hear but only one mouth to speak, do not overtax the mouth with vocal activities, especially as it has prandial and yet other useful functions to perform. Better an hour of reflection and silence than five minutes of unprofitable talk; for God and man may be angry at thy voice, and destroy the work of thine hands.

Be not deceived by propaganda, nor swerved from duty by sudden clamors, which, though seemingly spontaneous, may perchance be premeditated, highly organized and well financed. Look beneath the surface, and remember that, as the water runs smooth where the brook is deep, so more noise may be made over an evil deed than over a good one.

Beware of purchasing, with benevolent formulas, even agreements for the limitation of armaments, especially on the grounds of economy, lest you be suddenly called to incur vast expenses for the increase of your military and naval forces. He who exacts a price naturally expects to be paid what he intended to get. The voluntary costs of peace may be computed in advance; the involuntary costs of war cannot be foreseen.

All the Lord requires of man is to do justly, to love mercy, and to walk humbly with his God. This formula sounds simple, and, if it were automatic, the question of peace and war would not exist; but, unhappily, its earthly application has constantly given rise to differences of opinion. So, while all nations profess to wish for peace, yet, as they all desire it more or less on their own terms, they often lack the will to make or to keep it. Therefore, trust not unduly to vague pacts or glowing promises as safeguards against war, no matter how well meant they may be.

As he who does not control his emotions may risk abatement as a public nuisance, so he who loves other countries better than his own is in danger of perdition. Reverence and defend your own heroes, and let others freely do the same by theirs. Muckrakers are peculiarly out of place in international life. Great deeds cannot be circumscribed by national boundaries. They constitute a common heritage, from which the minds of men everywhere may be nourished with great thoughts.

Do not betray or disparage your country's cause, or fail faithfully to defend it. Even your adversary, while he may not decline the fruits of incompetence or disloyalty, will despise the person guilty of either. On the other hand, if you cannot convince your adversary, do not try to overreach him or humiliate him, or let him overreach or humiliate you. While partial advantages thus gained are seldom profitable, remember that justice and mutual respect are the only foundations of enduring amity.

## CANDOR AND COMMON SENSE[1]

WHEN the President of this Association asked me to meet its members this evening and to make an address, he told me that I might choose my own subject—reminiscences, international law, anything that might seem to me to be appropriate; and he further intimated that I might indulge a certain informality. Taking into consideration the fact that I had for seven years been a judge, wearing the insignia of office and observing other ceremonials, he properly assumed that, instead of essaying the unnatural, uncongenial rôle of the bigwig, enshrining commonplaces and errors alike in sesquipedalian words, I should prefer to commune with my legal brethren heart to heart, in the direct and simple terms that so well befit the discussion of fundamental things.

In my preference for this course, I was confirmed by the recollection of a passage I read years ago in a volume by Dowden on Shakespeare. I chanced to see the passage in a copy of the volume which had evidently been read before by a member of that much admired and superior class of beings called the *intelligentsia,* which gracefully and vaguely floats in the upper ether. Some of the passages were heavily underscored, and among them was that to which I have referred, which reads as follows: "Shakespeare, in his tragedies, has flung himself abroad over the vast sea of the unknowable which moans around the little solid sphere of the known."

The contemplation of this highly luminous utterance served to recall a story told by Fielding in his delightful piece, *A Journey from This World to the Next.* The traveler, who was also a student of Shakespeare, had not gone far in Elysium when he came upon a group warmly disputing the proper

1. Address before the Association of the Bar of the City of New York, December 4, 1930.

interpretation of the celebrated line in *Othello,* "Put out the light, and then put out the light." Among the disputants were the celebrated English actors, Thomas Betterton and Barton Booth. According to Betterton the line was to be read just as it stood, without special emphasis on particular words. Booth contended that it should be rendered thus: "Put out the light, and then put out THE light." The traveler, joining the group, suggested that it might perhaps be: "Put out the light, and then put out THY light." Another gave the sophisticated hint: "Put out the light, and then put out THEE, light," making light to be the vocative case. Yet another, apparently surmising a possible printer's error, suggested that the last word might have been written "sight," instead of "light," and that it should be read: "Put out thy light, and then put out thy sight." But Betterton retorted that, if the text was to be disturbed, he saw no reason why a word might not be changed as well as a letter, and, instead of "put out thy light," you might read "put out thy eyes." At last it was agreed on all sides to refer the matter to the decision of Shakespeare himself, who delivered his sentiments as follows: "Faith, gentlemen, it is so long since I wrote the line, I have forgot my meaning. This I know, could I have dreamt so much nonsense would have been talked and writ about it, I would have blotted it out of my works; for I am sure, if any of these be my meaning, it doth me very little honor."

An excellent illustration of how large and learned words may tend to becloud, even to the person using them, the pith of a simple matter was given by the late Samuel Sullivan Cox, more than forty years ago, in some inimitable papers on "Legislative Humors." There was pending before the House of Representatives at Washington a measure containing a clause by which the interest on certain proposed bonds was to be exempt from taxation. This clause suggested to the mind of Judge Van Trump, of Ohio, the thought that the proposal raised a question as to the shifting and incidence of taxation, a subject with which we usually become acquainted, individually and painfully, by the incidence rather than the shifting of the burden. The bill was in charge of General Schenck, then also a member of the House from Ohio; and the learned judge therefore put to the General, in somewhat involved and technical phrases, a question the actual meaning of which was whether the exemption from taxation would follow the interest on the new bonds into other things in which it might be invested. The inquiry, as put, had an imposing sound; but General Schenck, whom James G. Blaine once described to me as one of the best rough-and-tumble debaters he had ever known, made this response: "Suppose a man has a quantity of whisky, on which there is now levied a tax, and he swaps the whisky for a horse, you do not then proceed to tax the horse as whisky." Mr. Cox, personally testifying as a member of the House, tells us that the verbose and complicated query of the dignified judge was simplified amazingly, and that the House thankfully rode the free horse and enjoyed the whisky.

Admonished by these incidents and the reflections they excited, I decided that it might be a wholesome relief to disengage our minds from obscure disputations and, dealing with things in a wider and more human way, to consider how they may strike the layman as well as the lawyer. I was further encouraged to take this course because we have been passing, during the past fifteen years, through events of a somewhat unusual and exciting nature which have tended to upset the ordinary processes of digestion and assimilation, and thus to provoke ill humor, unsettle the reason and create false and distorted views. A number of years ago, just after the country had passed through one of its periods of financial and other convulsions, a distinguished member, one of the original members, of this Association, and one of the profoundest lawyers and statesmen New York has ever produced—I refer to Samuel J. Tilden—prescribed for the public as well as for the bar a simple diet of salt meal, by which I fancy he meant plain corn-meal mush with a pinch of flavoring. It was characteristic of Tilden that he seemed never to lose his balance, and it was characteristic of his modes of thinking that the more he studied a question the clearer and plainer it became. No doubt we are, after our recent experiences, still more or less confused; but we may be sufficiently penitent to try to look at things as they are. I therefore venture to take as the title of my remarks "Candor and Common Sense," with a view to come down to earth and contemplate a few elementary things.

At the present moment we hear a great deal about law enforcement. In my early days there was a vast deal of discussion over the resumption of specie payments, which were suspended during the Civil War as the result of the issue of paper money, called greenbacks. The discussion was heated and tumultuous and continued a long while, and it was naturally attended with many heretical proposals all tending to inflation. Nor did the hurly-burly end until there arose a Secretary of the Treasury who announced that the way to resume was to resume—and did it.

To a great extent, indeed for the most part, the law is not enforced because we make no real effort to enforce it; and, because such an effort is lacking, we say that the law is unenforceable. And what do we then do? Everybody knows. We propose the enactment of some new legislation; and, if this were all, the matter would be very simple. We are all aware of the fact that the obtaining of new legislation is easy. It is so easy that the legislature often passes laws without knowing it. Many now within reach of my voice can remember how the community was once startled with the announcement that there was a legal holiday called Columbus Day, and, among those who shared the astonishment, members of the legislature by which the law was passed were conspicuous.

But in these days with our progressive and scientific tendencies, we do not content ourselves with multiplying laws; and, although all the essential facts, blazoned in the press and filmed in the movies, may be notorious, daily crying out to heaven our degradation and our shame, we must have an investigation, and for that purpose we naturally appoint a commission not only to receive the facts which enthusiasts and learned but innocent pundits are always ready spontaneously to furnish, but also to make recommendations. The stately but hazardous procession then begins.

The gathering of facts is supposed to be an easy thing, and so it is, if we are content with facts in the popular sense. But, as lawyers so well realize, there are different kinds of facts. There are important facts and unimportant facts, relevant facts and irrelevant facts, and alleged facts which are not facts at all. Moreover, in the attempt to gather real facts, we encounter the tendency on the part of many persons, instead of observing things for themselves, to see what they have been told they will see. As a traveler and dweller more or less in other countries, I have been deeply impressed with the prevalence of this infirmity. On my first visit to Italy, many years ago, I read on the steamer a well-known book of travels in which the sketch of Naples opened with the words: "I always approach Naples with a feeling of dread and awe." I entered the city on a beautiful day when the air was balmy and laden with the perfume of flowers. Everything was garlanded. I felt no sense of dread and awe. For days I explored the city, day and night. I never was molested by any evil-minded person. Even the solicitations of beggars were much rarer than I had found in many other places; and in the end I recognized the fact that those who are accustomed to give such a gloomy view of the wonderful city were merely seeing what they were told they would see, but did not in reality see at all, for the simple reason that it did not exist. What they fancied they were seeing were things that occurred in the days when King Bomba ruled, or when the novel *Doctor Antonio* was written; the evil conditions described by historians and novelists, and perpetuated in the guide-books.

When so-called facts have been accumulated in sufficient bulk, we reach the advanced and dignified stage of having what we respectfully call statistics. It is evident that statistics are, like bread and milk, a prime human necessity. We cannot do without them. But, as there is good bread and bad bread, and good milk, bad milk, and milk that is chiefly water, so, as regards statistics, it is not irreverent to quote the caution uttered by a great statistician, the late Colonel Carroll D. Wright, who remarked that, while it was true that figures would not lie, it was equally true that liars would figure.

Having compiled our statistics, we reach the stage of theoretical discussion, at which dispensers of fads and fancies claim it as their due to bear a prominent and enlightening part. And perchance we get in the end a measure which, after the legislature has bowed to superior knowledge and enacted it, we are soon anxious to repeal. Nor do such measures always come singly. They have a gregarious tendency to herd together, in groups of three or more. Meanwhile, we lament the increase of crime; and the keepers of our jails are often so inconsiderate as to ascribe flagrant manifestations of unlawful violence to the provocative tendency of some of our much vaunted laws.

In contrast with the grandiose and impotent methods to which I have just adverted, I may mention an incident that lately came to my notice. About a month ago there appeared in the press an account of the trial in London of a person who, with an apparent propensity to imitate what he saw going on abroad, decided to adopt the career of a gunman. In making his first bow to the public in that character, he shot at and wounded a policeman. A commonplace jury promptly convicted him, and an unfeeling judge, acting under a commonplace law, sentenced him to ten years' penal servitude, thus removing him from his proposed theatre of operations. The judge, evidently somewhat provincial in his notions, even went so far as to intimate that, as far as concerned himself, he did not intend to permit the importation of such forms of activity into England. It is also worthy of remark that the account of the transaction occupied scarcely more than two inches in the columns of the press. I mention this incident merely as an illustration of a way of dealing with such matters. It is not exactly our way.

Let it not be supposed that, in what I have said concerning the execution of the criminal laws, I have particularly had in mind the National Commission on the Observance and Enforcement of Law of which our eminent and honored friend, Mr. Wickersham, formerly a President of this Association, is chairman. The creation of the commission was not of their seeking. It was determined upon by a higher authority to which we all bow, the President and the Congress of the United States. The members of the commission responded to the call of duty, and this entitles them to our support and our sympathy, for we know that the path they were called to tread is thorny, and that their present predicament is perilous. The Coliseum is packed and the throng is impatient, while the lions and the leopards, the one dry and the other wet, ranged on either side of the arena, are chafing at the gratings, hungry and in ill-humor. The most we can do for our devoted public servants is to wish that, after the gratings are opened, the lions and the leopards will become so much preoccupied with each other that they will permit their proposed victims to pass out comparatively unobserved and uninjured.

At the present moment, while our gunmen go unpunished, and our Treasury officials are trying to ferret out the amounts of the individual incomes of our capitalistic princes of blackmail, divertingly known as racketeers, strenuous efforts are being made to excite the public on the subject of communism. This certainly is a most interesting development. Many years ago, I read a book by Charles Nordhoff, a great Washington newspaper correspondent, on communistic societies in the United States. We have had, in times past, many of them; some have survived, but many have perished. In their disappearance they may, in the language of an old play, be said to have died "unhonored and unhung"; but neither in their appearance nor in their disappearance did they excite our special wonder. As time has gone on our country has grown richer and richer, and the number and proportion of persons having an individual interest and stake in the maintenance of the principle of private property has steadily increased.

Let us take, for illustration, the single business of life insurance. Examining the figures as of December 31, 1929, we find (1) that the total number of holders of life insurance policies in the United States was 67,000,000, (2) that the total amount of life insurance in force, including ordinary, industrial and group insurance, was $103,146,000,000, and (3) that the total admitted assets of life insurance companies amounted to $17,600,000,000. These assets represented investments in a great diversity of securities, including railway bonds and shares, the bonds and shares of what are generically known as public utility companies, and mortgages and loans on lands and buildings in the cities as well as in the country. It is manifest that every one of the 67,000,000 policy holders has a stake in the maintenance of the right of private property.

It is also worthy of notice that the total number of farm owners in the United States, as of 1925, was 3,868,000, of whom 3,313,000 were full owners and the rest part owners; and that the total number of homes owned, not on farms, in 1920, as was shown by the census of that year, was 7,041,283.

In 1927, the number of shareholders in our corporations was estimated at 3,300,000 receiving dividends amounting to $4,300,000,000; and, according to recent estimates which are considered trustworthy, there are now between 4,500,000 and 5,000,000 shareholders, and some put the estimate as high as 16,000,000. The number of persons having a proprietary interest in unincorporated businesses must also be enormous.

In view of this wide distribution of direct personal interests in private property, it is no wonder that the United States is today reckoned the most "capitalistic" country in the world.

The most striking contrast with this condition of things is found in the attempt now going on in Russia to apply the principle of communism. No one believes less in communism than I do, or has less interest in justifying it in principle or applying it in practice. On the other hand, I am not ambitious to figure among those who ignorantly assume and rabidly declare that either the people of Russia or their political leaders have deliberately adopted the communistic system with the fell and devilish intention of raising themselves upon the ruins of the rest of the world. The lightning is, as far as I know, the only thing that can be said to come to us out of a clear sky, but even the lightning is not wholly self-created.

The Russian mind was not unprepared for communism for the simple reason that under the Czarist government, clear down to 1906, the so-called allotment land, that is, the land received by the peasants on the emancipation of 1866, as distinguished from land privately owned, was held either in communal or in family (*podvornoe*) tenure; and the proportion of private owners, including all classes, was exceedingly small. In 1892, out of a total of 11,071,100 owners of land, 10,589,900, or more than nineteen out of twenty, were peasants farming the so-called allotment land, held, as we have seen, in communal or family tenure as distinguished from private individual ownership. In 1905, according to the census of that year, the situation remained essentially unchanged, the privately owned estates and farms, including those belonging to corporations and institutions, numbering 827,500, while the estimated peasant holdings numbered upwards of 12,000,000.

At the end of 1906, Stolypin undertook to abolish the communal and family tenures and to substitute for them private individual ownership. But the authorities state that, on the eve of the revolution of 1917, approximately only one-half of the peasant holdings in European Russia had freed themselves from the previous archaic forms and had adopted more modern methods of agriculture, and that to a very great extent the private individual holdings were not sufficient to cause the owners to be greatly enamored of the new system. My authority for these statements will be found in *Russian Agriculture during the War,* a volume published this year by the Yale University Press for the Carnegie Endowment for International Peace in its series of works covering the economic phases of the late war.

Let me also commend, to those who are inclined to approach all foreign questions in a passionate spirit and to discuss them in terms of denunciation, the reading of the series of illuminating essays *Approaches to History,* written in a broad and candid spirit by a learned man of Russian lineage, my friend and former colleague, Vladimir G. Simkhovitch, and now in course of publication in the *Political Science Quarterly.* Like all wide surveys of human history, these essays serve to admonish us of the importance of studying the causes of the conditions with which we are confronted, and endeavoring, as reasonable and honest men, to understand them before we begin furiously to exhort others vicariously to gird on their armor and take up the sword.[2]

In the United States there are, as has already been shown, comparatively few who may be said to have no individual interest in maintaining the system under which we have lived and prospered, and yet there are among us today those who are suddenly affrighted by the very mention of the word communist. I do not share this feeling of alarm, and most certainly do not share it to the extent of believing that it is advisable to make new laws further to curtail freedom of thinking or suppress freedom of speech. I was born in the belief, and was taught in my childhood, that, in the free exchange of opinions and the calm discussion of issues, the truth would emerge and survive, and I still cherish that faith today.

There is, in my opinion, no better way to nourish and diffuse erroneous opinions than to persecute and advertise them; and this conviction was confirmed by a recent incident.

2. For a remarkably comprehensive, but compact, specific and detailed account of the rise and development of the existing condition of things in Russia, see *Russia's Productive System,* by Emile Burns, just published by E. P. Dutton and Co. This book has come to my notice since the present address was delivered.

Late in July last I had occasion to spend a night in the city of Poughkeepsie. The air was still and warm, and the demeanor of the inhabitants was tranquil. The police, probably feeling the heat, were little in evidence; while plain citizens, like myself, walked the streets unconscious of the need of protection. In the course of my stroll I refreshed myself at an ice-cream parlor long kept by the makers of a well-known cough drop. The place was crowded, and the occupants evidently were intent upon cooling their bodies rather than their minds.

The next morning, however, there appeared in the excellent local newspaper the announcement that some communists were enjoying a picnic in a neighboring grove, and that they were likely to be honored with the visit of a congressional committee. The local reporters then promptly visited the local district attorney, who had so little imagination as to say that he saw nothing he could do; that he had not been advised of any infraction of law, or of anything requiring unusual measures to assure the safety of the community. But the case with the communists was altogether different. Like the indolent colored waiter, who, when he heard a brass band, "quickly came to life," they rose handsomely to the occasion. It was evident that the picnic had previously been a rather dull affair; so dull indeed that the picnickers, in their drowsiness, had not even bayed the moon with their futile cries; but now, with the prospect of becoming national figures, they suddenly felt that, in the immortal words of the Marseillaise, "the day of glory had arrived." As Longfellow says, in his famous lines on Paul Revere's Ride, "you know the rest." The country has been temporarily but only tentatively saved, and we must await, perhaps not without misgivings, the possible legislative proposals that may follow.

Having taken as my subject "Candor and Common Sense," I should not live up to my title or perform what I feel to be a very solemn duty, if I were to refrain from mentioning a question of the first importance, the need of the full and intelligent discussion and understanding of which daily becomes more and more apparent. A year ago the American people were suddenly reminded of the fact that for a long while they had had no diplomatic relations with Russia, a vast country embracing an immense population with which our relations were once thought to be traditionally friendly. The immediate occasion of the jolt was the tender by our government to the Soviet government, through a third party, of advice peacefully to settle a controversy with China. When it is difficult to explain an act by ordinary considerations we are accustomed to ascribe it to idealism; but, in the present instance, it was idealism and something more. We had entered into an international agreement commonly called the Kellogg Pact, to which the Soviet government, upon the solicitation of one of our co-signers, had, with our full knowledge and acquiescence, been permitted to adhere. By this act we necessarily recognized the Soviet government; for, by the hornbooks—the very primers of the kindergartens—of international law and diplomacy, recognition may be implied as well as express, and one of the stock examples of implied recognition is the entrance into conventional relations. But, as we had refused to establish regular diplomatic relations, we offered our peaceful reminder of the mutual obligations of the Kellogg pact to our co-contractant through a third party; but the response we got was such as even peace-loving peoples do not specially relish. It breathed indeed a sense of resentment that we should presume to offer advice, through a third party, to a government to which we refused to speak directly. Our government and people did not, I believe, congratulate themselves upon the reply, but, at the same time, did not see a way to prolong an interchange of views for which a third party, in view of the turn the matter had taken, might not have been eager to continue to lend its good offices.[3]

On the other hand, we have lately been startled by an impulsive and heated outburst, on the part of certain of our own officials, over the importation into this country by some of our steel manufacturers of a cargo of Russian manganese, and a short sale by the Soviet government of some wheat on the Chicago grain exchange. It was hastily charged that the manganese was mined or delivered by convict labor, and that the wheat was "dumped" on the exchange with a view to depress the price of wheat in the United States market. An investigation promptly established the fact that the outcry was not justified; but language had been used and declarations had been made which necessarily raised the question whether our foreign relations were to be conducted constitutionally by the President and his legal agent, the Secretary of State, or chaotically by the subordinates or heads of other executive departments.

During my early service of the government of the United States, in the first administration of Grover Cleveland, there was an opinionated comptroller, who was disposed to disturb the orderly administrative procedures. Cleveland invited him to a conference; but it had not gone far when the comptroller

3. For the diplomatic exchanges, see *Current History* (January, 1930), pp. 758–763.

somewhat curtly remarked, "Mr. President, under the law my opinion is final." President Cleveland quietly replied: "Yes, Mr. Comptroller, I am aware of that; but the law vests in me the power to make and unmake comptrollers." The trouble ended.

A sound and becoming rule regarding utterances by public officials was laid down in an executive order issued on the outbreak of war between Russia and Japan in 1904, when Theodore Roosevelt was President and John Hay was Secretary of State. In this order, which was addressed to "all officials of the government, civil, military, and naval," it was declared that, while it was always "unfortunate . . . by speech or conduct to excite anger and resentment toward our nation in friendly foreign lands," it was pointed out that "in a government employee, whose official position makes him in some sense the representative of the people, the mischief of such actions is greatly increased." The order concludes with these golden words: "A strong and self-confident nation should be peculiarly careful not only of the rights but of the susceptibilities of its neighbors; and nowadays all the nations of the world are neighbors one to the other. Courtesy, moderation, and self-restraint should mark international, no less than private, intercourse." [4]

But it is not especially in respect of Russia that our recent attitude towards recognition needs examination. The question is no less urgent in the Western Hemisphere, in our relations with what we endearingly call our sister republics of America.

On October 15, 1930, the Department of State formally announced that, there being nothing in the news from Brazil to prevent the United States "from exercising the same friendly offices towards the government of Brazil which we would exercise toward any government with which we are in friendly relations," the Brazilian government had "a perfect right to buy munitions in this country"; and the Department stated, orally, in answer to questions, that, although no application had been received for arms from any party in Brazil save the government, an attempt by the rebels to buy arms here would raise a different question. The Department was further reported to have announced, orally, that a small sale of airplane parts by the War Department, through the United Airways Corporation, to the Brazilian government had already been approved.

We cannot fail at once to remark the unusual character of

4. Executive order, March 10, 1904, *Foreign Relations*, 1904, p. 185; Moore, *Digest of International Law*, VII, 868.

these statements in the following particulars: First, the association of a sale or purchase of arms either with the exercise of "friendly offices" towards governments with which we are in friendly relations, or with the right of a foreign government to buy munitions of war in the United States; and secondly, the sale of what was apparently regarded as war equipment directly or indirectly from the government stores to what was evidently a party to an armed civil conflict. As regards armed conflicts, whether international or civil, the term "friendly offices," or "good offices," has in international law and diplomacy a fixed and definite meaning, namely, the impartial employment of a government's conciliatory services between parties to a controversy for the purpose of bringing about a peaceful adjustment of it. The application of the term "friendly offices" to the sale or supply of munitions of war to one or even to both of the parties to an armed conflict has not the sanction of usage, and probably will never find its way into the dictionaries. Indeed, but for a train of antecedents to which I shall hereafter refer, it might be thought that we had suddenly drifted into a fog and lost our bearings.

The statements made at Washington on October 15 appeared in full in the newspapers of the next morning, October 16. On October 18th the press published reports telegraphed from South America on October 17, criticizing the announcement that the United States would help the federal government of Brazil, and intimating that the United States helped to bolster up or to tear down governments at its whim, or at the behest of financial interests. But such charges are easily made, and we are not concerned with them, except so far as they may be naturally provoked by our so-called policies.

On October 23 the newspapers announced that the President, acting upon the request of the Brazilian ambassador at Washington, had on the preceding day declared an embargo on the shipment of arms to the Brazilian revolutionists, and that this was done under the authority granted by Congress in 1922 to impose such embargoes in respect of Latin American countries and of China. The proclamation recited, as the grounds on which the embargo was laid, that conditions of "domestic violence" existed in "several zones of the Brazilian territory," and that the Brazilian ambassador had stated that he had "been informed that some elements in the United States, in close union with the revolutionary element against the federal government in Brazil," were "endeavoring to purchase arms and munitions in the United States to turn them against the federal government of Brazil." On the other hand, the proclamation specifically permitted the

shipment of munitions of war to the federal government
of Brazil on licenses to be issued by the Secretary of State.
The publication in the press naturally carried the comment
that this precisely followed the formal announcement of
October 15 that the United States would permit the purchase of
such munitions as an act of friendship to the Government at
Rio de Janeiro; and, as for the question whether this implied
a broad policy of supporting established governments in South
America, without regard to the special circumstances of each
case, attention was called to the fact that, when the Secretary
of State recently dealt with the question of recognizing the
revolutionary governments in Argentina, Bolivia and Chile,
he let it be known that he was considering each case as a "special case." On the same day dispatches appeared in the press
from Brazil of steady advances and numerous victories by the
insurgents, who were said to be rushing horses to the front
"to speed chase of fleeing federals."

It is further to be observed that on October 23 the Department of State, with a view to clear up the confusion that
seemed to prevail in the public mind, gave out a written
announcement particularly referring to the comment made in
some of the newspapers that the embargo on the sale of arms
and munitions to the revolutionaries in Brazil "was unprecedented." While it was admitted to be true that this was the first
occasion on which an embargo had been placed on the shipment of arms and munitions to a South American country,
it was declared to be misleading to call the action unprecedented, as it was, so the announcement said, the government's
"regular action under similar circumstances." The United
States, said the announcement, had previously placed embargoes on such shipments to Central America, Mexico, Cuba and
the Orient; but it had just happened that "a situation requiring the application of this principle" had not previously arisen
and furnished an occasion for "applying the general principle." This was clear enough, but the announcement further
stated that we were "acting according to general principles
of international law," and that those principles declared that,
when we were in friendly diplomatic relations with a government which we had recognized as the "legitimate government
of a country," that government was entitled to the "ordinary
rights of any government" to buy arms in this country; while
the people who are opposing and trying to overthrow that government and were not yet recognized as belligerents were not
entitled to that right. "It is not a matter of choice on our
part," said the announcement, "but is a practice of mankind
known as international law. We have no personal bias and are

doing nothing but attempt to carry out the law of mankind."

Most heartily may we accept the disclaimer of personal bias; but we are equally bound, as lawyers, to inquire when and where there came into existence an alleged rule of international law at variance with the neutrality statutes of the United States, with the uniform decisions of our courts, including the highest, and with the precepts of writers? In truth, is it not manifest that the Department of State found itself in the unfortunate position of being obliged to defend, as being in accordance wtih international law, that which supposedly was done in accordance with a resolution of Congress which goes outside of international law, which may be so applied as to authorize acts contrary to international law, and which had its origin in exceptional conditions the attempt to meet which gave rise to a so-called policy which, whenever applied, provokes resentment and risks disaster.

We may now state, briefly and with precision, just what the law relating to the manufacture, sale and shipment of contraband, comprising arms and munitions of war, really is. There is much confusion on this comparatively simple subject, evidently due to a want of knowledge of very elementary rules. On the outbreak of the war in Europe in 1914, President Wilson, in the performance of his legal duties under the statutes of the United States, as they then stood and still stand, issued a proclamation of neutrality. Immediately afterwards, as was reported in the public press, well-armed customs officials paced the docks in New York to prevent the shipment of any contraband of war. But, as this manifestation of law enforcement, commendable in spirit as it may have been, was not based on the law, it was soon abandoned, and the contraband purchases were duly shipped. This spectacle was not novel. I had seen similar ones on previous occasions and had done what I could to put an end to them.

The late Thomas Erskine Holland, an eminent writer whose authority will hardly be questioned even by the most uninformed, lays it down, in a remarkably condensed and lucid paper entitled "Neutral Duties in a Maritime War," that the obligations of a neutral State may be considered in three aspects or phases, namely, abstention, prevention, and acquiescence; and at the outset he correctly declares that a neutral government is "bound not to supply armed forces to a belligerent; . . . and not to sell him . . . munitions of war even when the sale takes place in the ordinary course of getting rid of superfluous or obsolete equipment." This rule is based upon the unquestionable fact that the supply of contraband to a fighting force is a direct contribution to its military resources, and, as such, is a participation in the war; and, if a government does this, it directly takes part in the war, and commits what is virtually an act of war. If it does this in behalf of one of the parties, it abandons its impartiality and in effect commits an act of armed intervention; and, if it does it for both parties, although it may be said to be impartial, it does what neither of the parties themselves can do, namely, it fights for each against the other.

But, when we come to the dealings of individuals, we enter the sphere of governmental prevention and acquiescence. We often see the statement that trading in contraband is lawful and also the statement that it is unlawful; and, when properly made and understood, they are both correct. Because of the fact that there is much dispute as to what the term contraband comprises, and of the further fact that it has, on grounds of general convenience, been deemed proper to limit the burdens to which a neutral is subject, international law has not up to the present time required neutral governments to prevent their citizens from manufacturing, selling and shipping contraband, including arms and munitions of war, in the regular course of commerce. In other words they are permitted to acquiesce in it, as most of them, including the United States, by their laws actually do; and in this sense the trade is lawful. On the other hand, international law recognizes the right of a party to a war to prevent such articles from reaching his adversary, and, if he seizes them, to confiscate them, thus inflicting on the seller, if he has not got his money, a total loss. In other words, international law, treating the trade as intrinsically unneutral and unlawful, permits the parties to the struggle to inflict the penalty, and to this the trader's government cannot object.

But, the liberty which domestic statutes, known as neutrality laws, may tolerate in private persons to deal commercially in contraband, or to commit other acts intrinsically unneutral, at their own risk, is not shared by governments. Neutrality, as we have just intimated, means impartiality and something more. It embraces abstention from any and all participation in the armed strife. Neutral governments, therefore, are not permitted themselves to perform any act in its nature unneutral, or to aid or protect their citizens in so doing. International law does not, for instance, require a neutral government to prevent the floating of loans to belligerents; but, if the government in any way promotes or aids such a loan, it abandons its neutrality. During the war between the United States and Spain, France even refused to continue or to extend to Spain the privilege enjoyed by various states of coining money in a commercial way at the French mint, deeming that this would under the circumstances be in the nature of an unneutral act.[5] While international law still permits a government to make war on its own account, or to go to the aid of one of the parties to an armed conflict, international or civil, it furnishes no middle ground on which a government can do this and still profess to be neutral or non-participant in the struggle.

From these elementary principles of international law it clearly follows that, even though a government may see fit to put an embargo on the shipment of munitions of war to a country in which it recognizes the existence of a condition of civil strife or "domestic violence," yet, if it permits the shipment to one party and forbids it to the other, it intervenes in the internal politics of the country in an essentially military sense.

The end to the war in Brazil came quickly. The journals of October 25 carried the news that the revolution had triumphed in all Brazil, that the President was a prisoner and the President-elect in hiding, and that the new régime ruled in the Brazilian capital. Side by side with this announcement there was a telegram from Mr. Morgan, our ambassador at Rio de Janeiro, who knows Brazil and Brazilians as few have done, that popular enthusiasm "was being expressed in a carnival spirit," that the offices of "late government newspapers" had been sacked and the building in one case burned; that, while red flags had been displayed, they indicated revolution and not communism, and that an army detachment had occupied the Banco do Brazil to protect it and the national funds deposited there.

A dispatch from London, carried in the newspapers of the same day, somewhat exultantly stated that the British government "expected to give prompt recognition to the victorious rebels in Brazil, as soon as it learned from the British ambassador at Rio that the new government was likely to be stable," and that "throughout the Brazilian civil war" the British government had been "scrupulously neutral."

It is not my purpose to enter into a discussion of the merits of the revolution that has taken place in Brazil. I leave that task to the Brazilians, who will be inclined to think, as we ourselves ordinarily do, that they know their own business and are entitled to conduct it as they like, so far as they do not violate the rights of other nations. Perhaps I the more readily accept this point of view because I may profess to know somewhat intimately the Brazilian people, among whom there have been and still are some of my most honored and most attached friends. Personally I did not expect the armed conflict to last

5. Moore, *Digest of International Law*, chap. xxviii, Neutrality; § 1288, *Governmental Conduct*, VII, 863–868.

long. I say this, not as a judge of the merits of the late over-turn, but as one who knows that the Brazilian people are not a ferocious or warlike people. They have been distinguished for the production of statesmen and orators, of learned lawyers, and of men of letters and poets. I vividly recall the lovely June morning in 1912 when, on my arrival at the Brazilian capital, the whole nation was ringing with a beautiful sonnet by Bilac, its own native bard, who was then recognized as the greatest poet in the Portuguese-speaking world. The swift overthrow, in 1889, of the monarchy, which was presided over by a wise and patriotic ruler, Dom Pedro II, was accomplished without effusion of blood, and the disturbances that later occurred were eventually brought to an end with little loss of life. In the constitution of the country the republic is forbidden to under-take, directly or indirectly, a war of conquest, either by itself or in alliance with any other government. Things such as these do not characterize a people addicted to war, or likely to carry on war merely for the love of it. If they err, they merely illus-trate a human propensity which we should not assume to cen-sure as perverse or exceptional in this human, emotional, and more or less shortsighted world. We might even be so charita-ble as to recall our own bloody four years' struggle on the mer-its of which, although it is now freely conceded that both par-ties believed themselves to be right, we still differ.

So far as concerns the recent civil disturbances in Brazil, we need only add that on November 8th the Department of State announced that it had instructed Ambassador Morgan to re-spond to a note, which he had received from the new govern-ment, that the United States would "be happy to continue" with it "the same friendly relations as with its predecessors." In so doing we marched in stately procession with fifteen other governments, including the Vatican, Austria, Czechoslovakia, Great Britain, Italy, Portugal, Sweden, Argentina, Bolivia, Chile, Ecuador, Mexico, Paraguay, Peru, and Uruguay.

Two days later the Prime Minister of Great Britain clinched the action of his government by a highly significant and saga-cious speech in which he used these words:

South America has gone through revolution after revolution. They are all friends of ours. It is not our business to inquire into their internal conditions, and we recognize government after government so soon as that government has shown signs that it has come to stay for a reasonable time.

When our government, abandoning the departures that have marked the past fifteen or twenty years, shall resume the use of similar language and exemplify its words by its conduct, we probably shall see less and hear less of the spectacular good-will missions to Latin America which seem to have become a permanent and necessary part of our recent policies.

Let us now consider for a moment what was and still is, for practically all the world except ourselves, the established rule, or in other words the legal principle, regarding the recognition of governments. It is clearly enunciated in an instruction which Thomas Jefferson, as Secretary of State, addressed to Gouverneur Morris, our minister to France, on March 12, 1793, in these words:

We surely can not deny to any nation that right whereon our own Government is founded—that every one may govern itself according to whatever form it pleases, and change these forms at its own will; and that it may transact its business with foreign nations through whatever organ it thinks proper, whether king, convention, assembly, committee, president, or anything else it may choose. The will of the nation is the only thing essential to be regarded.

From that time down to 1913, this was the rule by which our government was guided. It is true that, while Seward was Secretary of State, there were certain instances in which recognition was withheld because the new government was of revolutionary origin; but this was only a temporary and politic attitude suggested by our own Civil War, and it is to be classed with Seward's protests against the recognition by foreign governments of the belligerency of the Confederate States—protests in principle expressly abandoned by the United States in 1869, and not since revived.

But, on March 11, 1913, President Wilson, under whom I later had the honor to serve, enunciated, in a public statement called a "Declaration of Policy with Regard to Latin America," a novel principle. This statement, incorporated in a circular telegram, was sent the next day by Mr. Bryan, as Secretary of State, to all our diplomatic officers in Latin America; but it had already been spread broadcast through the press. The text was as follows:

DECLARATION OF POLICY WITH REGARD TO LATIN
AMERICA

DEPARTMENT OF STATE,
Washington, March 12, 1913—1 P. M.

TO THE AMERICAN DIPLOMATIC OFFICERS IN LATIN AMERICA:
In view of questions which are naturally uppermost in the public mind just now, the President issued the following statement to the public, March 11, 1913.

One of the chief objects of my administration will be to cultivate the friendship and deserve the confidence of our sister republics of

Central and South America, and to promote in every proper and honorable way the interests which are common to the peoples of the two continents. I earnestly desire the most cordial understanding and co-operation between the peoples and leaders of America and, therefore, deem it my duty to make this brief statement.

Co-operation is possible only when supported at every turn by the orderly processes of just government based upon law, not upon arbitrary or irregular force. We hold, as I am sure all thoughtful leaders of republican government everywhere hold, that just government rests always upon the consent of the governed, and that there can be no freedom without order based upon law and upon the public conscience and approval. We shall look to make these principles the basis of mutual intercourse, respect, and helpfulness between our sister republics and ourselves. We shall lend our influence of every kind to the realization of these principles in fact and practice, knowing that disorder, personal intrigues, and defiance of constitutional rights weaken and discredit government and injure none so much as the people who are unfortunate enough to have their common life and their common affairs so tainted and disturbed. We can have no sympathy with those who seek to seize the power of government to advance their own personal interests or ambition. We are the friends of peace, but we know that there can be no lasting or stable peace in such circumstances. As friends, therefore, we shall prefer those who act in the interest of peace and honor, who protect private rights, and respect the restraints of constitutional provision. Mutual respect seems to us the indispensable foundation of friendship between states, as between individuals.

The United States has nothing to seek in Central and South America except the lasting interests of the peoples of the two continents, the security of governments intended for the people and for no special group or interest, and the development of personal and trade relationships between the two continents which shall redound to the profit and advantage of both and interfere with the rights and liberties of neither.

From these principles may be read so much of the future policy of this Government as it is necessary now to forecast, and in the spirit of these principles I may, I hope, be permitted with as much confidence as earnestness to extend to the Governments of all the Republics of America the hand of genuine disinterested friendship, and to pledge my own honor and the honor of my colleagues to every enterprise of peace and amity that a fortunate future may disclose.

BRYAN.[6]

This declaration constituted a radical and subversive departure from our previous policy and practice, and also from the established practice and policy of all other governments, in the following particulars:

1. In declaring that co-operation with other governments was possible only so far as it was supported by the

6. *Foreign Relations of the United States*, 1913, p. 7.

observance in their own affairs of orderly processes free from the exercise of arbitrary or irregular force.

2. That it was our purpose to make these principles the basis of mutual intercourse, respect and helpfulness between our sister republics and ourselves.

3. That we should "lend our influence of every kind" to the realization of those principles in fact and in practice by the other governments of the hemisphere.

4. That there could be "no lasting or stable peace" between us and those who sought to seize the power of government "to advance their own personal interests or ambition."

5. That we should "prefer" in our friendships those who acted in the interest of peace and honor, and who respected the restraints of constitutional provisions.

It is to be observed that there was no intimation that we should leave it to our sister republics to determine whether they were behaving in an orderly way and respecting the restraints of their constitutions. On the contrary, there was a clear implication that we should determine this question for ourselves; and manifestly this was a logical necessity, as the question whether our own attitude should be friendly could not be left to the determination of others.

As a useful illustration of how this declaration of our superiority might have struck and in fact did strike at least some of our sister republics I may mention the circumstance that, when I had occasion, as a representative of the United States, to spend several months in 1910 in Buenos Aires, while the great journals of that progresive city published European news, particularly from France, Italy and Spain, by the column and the page, the most spacious attentions paid to the United States were an account of the attempt to assassinate Mr. Gaynor, then mayor of New York, and the story of a scandal involving one of our educational institutions. Well may we invoke the immortal lines of Robert Burns:

> "Oh wad some power the giftie gie us
> To see oursel's as others see us!
> It wad frae monie a blunder free us,
>         And foolish notion."

It is a legal maxim that hard cases make bad law. To those familiar with the conditions then existing it is superfluous to point out that the declaration of March 11, 1913, was inspired by a feeling of repugnance to the newly established government of Huerta in Mexico, which, although installed with formal observance of the provisions of the Mexican constitution, was alleged to have been brought into power by abhorrent acts and manipulation. The application of the new principle to Mexico, then and thereafter, I cannot on this occasion undertake to review. I am now concerned only with the more far-reaching consequences of the attempt since made to apply it to all the independent countries of America, and even to extend it to the rest of the world.

Upon its very face it furnishes us with no tangible or consistent rule of action whatever. It makes the question of international relations in each instance altogether problematical, not unlike the meeting of two canines, one of whom, as Burns in his "Twa Dogs" has sagely remarked, may be a mere

"ploughman's collie,
A rhyming, ranting, roaring billie,"

while the other, as his trappings show, may be "the gentleman and scholar." They sniff each other. If nothing specially offensive is detected, they may even wag their tails and briefly play with each other. If, on the contrary, their olfactories are offended, they draw their tails between their legs, growl at each other, and may even fight, although both may show a lack of wisdom in so doing.

Our experience with the innovation has clearly demonstrated its ineffectiveness. It has repeatedly been shown that a frown or scowl on the countenance of the United States is not a cure for revolutions. If it were so, should we today have military forces, as indeed we long have had, in Haiti and Nicaragua? Nay more, would the various revolutionary governments in South America, which we have, with an alacrity suggestive of commercial and political competition, lately been hastening to recognize, have come into existence?

But this is not all. Not only does our recent departure keep us in an attitude of intervention in the domestic affairs of other countries, but it has indoctrinated our people in the preposterous and mischievous supposition that the recognition of a government implies approval of its constitution, its economic system, its attitude towards religion, and its general course of conduct. Not only is this supposition contrary to elementary principles of international law, which assure to each independent state the right to regulate its domestic affairs, but it is flagrantly at variance with the facts. It is, for instance, inconceivable that the government of the United States has at any time approved all the governments with which it held diplomatic relations. Even at the lowest ebb of our fortunes, I believe we should have resented such an imputation. As I speak, I hear, in the words of Ossian, "the voice of the days that are gone; they roll before me with their deeds." I hold in review the motley procession: governments liberal and governments illiberal; governments free and governments unfree; governments honest, and governments corrupt; governments pacific and governments even aggressively warlike; empires, monarchies, and oligarchies; despotisms decked out as democracies, and tyrannies masquerading as republics—all representative of the motley world in which we live and with which we must do business. Nor are these other people always given to admiring us as much as we admire ourselves. Even in the most recent times we cannot be unaware that we are often denounced as a nation of money grabbers; that our Uncle Sam is caricatured and spoken of as Uncle Shylock; and I have even seen our people depicted as a herd of swine. Misunderstanding is something of which no nation can have a monopoly, and the perception of this fact should induce us to be circumspect, deliberate and tolerant, even charitable, in our judgments.

But I will be more specific. The original and correct enunciation of principle by the United States on the subject of recognition, as heretofore quoted, related to the revolution in France. Not long afterwards there arrived at Philadelphia, then the capital of the United States, a new minister from France, Edmond Genêt. Genêt had first landed at Charleston, South Carolina, and, gurgling with the fermentation of the revolution, had on his way to Philadelphia made speeches and committed acts, not unauthorized by his government, which were disturbing to the United States and not in harmony with its foreign policy. Nevertheless, the government of the United States unanimously decided to receive him as minister. Who, one may ask, were the men who then composed the government of the United States? At the head of the government was George Washington, to whom we all may bow in reverence as the first and greatest of our Presidents—warrior, statesman and administrator, who stands before the world as one of its greatest exemplars of character and the very incarnation of common sense; Thomas Jefferson, author of the Declaration of Independence, masterly in his grasp of principles, distinguished for his broad intelligence, founder of the University of Virginia, and author of the Bill of Rights; Alexander Hamilton, soldier, statesman, profound lawyer, great administrator, and founder of the financial system of the United States, of whom it was aptly said that he struck the rock of credit and it gushed forth; General Knox, Secretary of War, who served his country with equal ardor and efficiency in peace and in war; and Edmund Randolph, Attorney General, in one of whose opinions we find the first clear enunciation of the legal principle underlying the doctrine of territorial jurisdiction over bays. Having passed through the long and arduous struggle for independence, these men may still have been somewhat lean of body, but their nerves were strong and steady; and I am prepared to pit them against any government we have ever had, no matter how numerous its members may be, for aggregate wisdom, sagacity, and common sense.

When Genêt was received as minister, the Reign of Terror in France was in full swing. The government of Louis XVI, our friend in our struggle for independence, had been overthrown, and Louis had himself been beheaded; the Goddess of Reason had been enthroned, and the streets echoed with hoarse cries for hanging at the lamp posts the prelates of the dethroned church; the guillotine had been installed, and heads were daily rolling into the basket; the Place de la Concorde was encrimsoned with blood, and the Jacobite government was conducting abroad what Edmund Burke called an anarchic propagandism. In these things there must have been much to offend the sensibilities of our sober rulers at Philadelphia and much to excite their strong disapprobation.

The rule the administration of Washington applied to France it applied to all other cases. They applied it even to the Barbary powers, popularly known, because of their lawless depredations on commerce, as the Barbary Pirates, with whom they established diplomatic relations and concluded treaties, one of which, the treaty with Tripoli, declared that, as the government of the United States was "not in any sense founded on the Christian Religion," and had "in itself no character of enmity against the laws, religion, or tranquillity of Mussulmen," no pretext arising from religious opinions should ever produce an interruption of the harmony existing between the two countries. With the omission of the introductory recital a similar declaration was inserted by the United States in the treaty with Tripoli of 1805, and in the treaties with Algiers of 1815 and 1816. This was but an enunciation of the principle of religious liberty.

The great Roman poet, Virgil, the two thousandth anniversary of whose birth has just been celebrated, has well said, *Facilis descensus Averno*—the descent to the nether world is easy. From the fallacious supposition that our recognition is conditioned on our approval it is easy to descend to the conclusion that our approval impliedly pledges our support; and at this point our legislation regarding the export of munitions of war comes to constitute a positive danger, probably not foreseen when the legislation was adopted.

By a joint resolution approved April 22, 1898,[7] the President

7. 30 Statutes at Large, 739.

was authorized to prohibit the export of coal or other material used in war from any seaport in the United-States until otherwise ordered by him or by Congress. This measure was simple, and its object was well understood. We were then entering into the war with Spain, and it was desired to guard against the shipment of war materials which might come into the possession, immediately or eventually, of the Spanish forces. On March 14, 1912, however, the act of 1898 was amended by a joint resolution of a very different kind.[8] At that time the civil disturbances which began with the fall of President Diaz were in progress in Mexico; and the so-called amendment empowered the President, whenever he should find that "in any American country" there existed "conditions of domestic violence" which were promoted by the use of arms or munitions of war procured from the United States, to prohibit the export of those articles to such country, "except under such limitations and exceptions" as he should prescribe, until otherwise ordered by himself or by Congress. By a joint resolution approved January 31, 1922, the terms of the joint resolution of March 14, 1912, were re-enacted, but broadened so as to include, in addition to any American country, "any country in which the United States exercises extraterritorial jurisdiction"; and the joint resolutions of 1898 and 1912 were repealed.

It seems evident that, if the strange notion that recognition of a government implies approval of it, and furthermore that approval carries a pledge or jurisdiction of material support against its enemies, is to be maintained, the joint resolution of 1922 should be either repealed or substantially amended. The war-making power under the Constitution of the United States is vested not in the President but in the Congress of the United States; and from this is would seem to follow that the war-making power should not be delegated to the President generally and indefinitely, over a vast part of the earth's surface embracing many peoples and many governments.

Yet another fallacy that has come to prevail is the supposition that recognition and the establishment of diplomatic relations imply the relinquishment of claims. Nothing could be more contrary to the truth, or, when coupled with the Kellogg pact, more nearly approach the limit of human incoherence; for, while the pact declares we will not fight over our differences, they cannot be peacefully settled without resort to diplomacy. While international law classes the severance of diplomatic relations among non-amicable methods of procedure, pointedly implying dissatisfaction and protest, it is equally

8. 37 Statutes at Large, part 1, p. 630.

true that the maintenance of such relations does not involve the abandonment of any claim or difference but only keeps open the channel of discussion. As for commercial non-intercourse, those who are acquainted with history know that this has often proved to be a prelude to war, of which, if war actually comes, it is an incident and characteristic.

We sometimes hear the question mooted as to the usefulness of establishing diplomatic and consular relations with this, that, or the other country, be it great or small. As one often and long connected with our foreign service, I am not predisposed to spend time in discussing a question which implies that the presence of our diplomatic and consular officers in a foreign country, with which we do business or wish to do business, is either worthless or worth less than it costs us. I shall be more disposed to discuss this rather foolish question when it is proposed to abolish the service altogether.

Finally, we hear it said that we must preserve our "ideals"; but we show little faith in them when we assume that they cannot stand contact or competition with different ideals. Washington and his cabinet certainly cherished their ideals, but they believed in propagating them in the modest and self-respecting way so well expressed in the Scriptural injunction: "Let your light so shine before men, that they, seeing your good works, may glorify your Father which is in heaven." We do little to propagate our ideals when we tell those who differ with us that because of this fact we cannot speak to them; but must, in the words of Kipling, regard them as "lesser breeds without the law." Moreover, the "idealistic" theory cannot be squared with the insistence of nations upon diplomatic intercourse, even at the cannon's mouth. It was not identity of ideals that induced the western powers to compel the nations of the Far East to establish diplomatic relations. In China the necessary force was used first by Great Britain, and then by France. In the case of Japan, the cannon were borne as a visiting card by the naval forces of the United States under Commodore Perry.

I will conclude this review of the subject of recognition by quoting from that immortal document, "Washington's Farewell Address," these wise and solemn injunctions:

Observe good faith and justice toward all nations. Cultivate peace and harmony with all . . . The nation which indulges toward another an habitual hatred or an habitual fondness is . . . a slave to its animosity or to its affection, either of which is sufficient to lead it astray from its duty and its interest. . . . Harmony, liberal intercourse with all nations are recommended by policy, humanity, and interest.

To these weighty words I will only add the famous apothegm

of Jefferson, in his first inaugural—"Peace, commerce and honest friendship with all nations, entangling alliances with none."

To those familiar with diplomatic history, and to those who know the story of the dark days through which we passed in the crisis of our own Civil War, it is needless to say that there is no nation, great or small, whose friendship, present or future, is to be reckoned as negligible or to be spurned with contumelious words.

There is yet another topic on which I desire to speak, and that is our profession—the profession of the law. My choice of this profession never was a subject of debate. From my early days I was drawn to the study of the law, and I have never ceased to be profoundly interested in it. In my humble sketch in *Who's Who in America,* there appears after my name the single word "lawyer," and this part of the sketch was, I confess, written by myself. I have been called a "publicist," a "professor," a "jurist," and an "internationalist," to say nothing of other things. But my highest ambition has been to be known as a student and expositor of the law; and, in order to realize this ambition, if for no other purpose, I have been to some extent a practitioner, quietly but not wholly without emolument.

As a boy I knew a very successful legal practitioner who began his career as a preacher, then turned to be a doctor, and finally gained admission to the bar. In referring to these transformations he was wont to say that he first tried the cure of men's souls, and found it very unremunerative; that he then tried the cure of their bodies, and found the results more encouraging but not wholly satisfactory; and that finally, he tried the cure of their passions, and had found this the most profitable of all, especially where the cure was not immediately effective. But the view he took of his various professions, although it tends to provoke a smile, just as the sayings of the villain may do on the stage, is not to be commended; for, while "the laborer is worthy of his hire," the man who practices his profession solely for the money that he can make out of it falls short of his duty and can hardly be reckoned a good citizen.

The noble building in which we are now assembled and its accumulated treasures stand as a monument to the lawyers whose love of their profession and sense of public duty led them to organize the Association of the Bar of the City of New York. The Call for Organization, issued in 1869, briefly recites as the motive of its signers the belief that the organized action and influence of the legal profession properly exerted not only would lead to more intimate relations between its members than existed, but would at the same time "sustain the profession in its proper position in the community" and thus enable it "in many ways to promote the interests of the public."

Among the signers of this call was Samuel J. Tilden, and I particularly mention him, not because he was more famous as a lawyer than were various other signers, but because, as appears by William Allen Butler's memorial of him, he was the leading figure in an incident of the meeting at which the call was issued. The hour was late, but, as Tilden was quitting the room, he was called back by general acclamation, and, standing near the door, made a stirring speech which, as Mr. Butler declares, struck the keynote which aroused and quickened public sentiment to the need of action. From this speech Mr. Butler quotes the following passage:

If the Bar is to become merely a mode of making money, making it in the most convenient way possible, but making it at all hazards, then the Bar is degraded. If the Bar is to be merely an institution that seeks to win causes, and win them by back door access to the judiciary, then it is not only degraded, but it is corrupt. . . .

The Bar, if it is to continue to exist, if it would restore itself to the dignity and honor which it once possessed, must be bold in aggression. If it will do its duty to itself, if it will do its duty to the profession which it follows, and to which it is devoted, the Bar can do everything else. It can have reformed constitutions, it can have a reformed judiciary, it can have the administration of justice made pure and honorable, and can restore both the Judiciary and the Bar, until it shall be once more, as it formerly was, an honorable and elevated calling.

Conceived and born in this spirit the Association of the Bar of the City of New York has continued to render, as it still does, great services to the legal profession and to the public. On the other hand, we must admit that the developments of the past half-century have not been favorable to the perpetuation of the dominant influence which the legal profession in early times exerted in our public life. Among these developments is the growth of what is popularly called "big business," and its concentration in large corporate organizations. It goes without saying that a lawyer who has many clients is in a more independent situation than a lawyer who has only one client and thus becomes dependent upon a single source of compensation.

Nor is the diminution of financial independence the only unfavorable development. There always has been and there always will be an impression that persons constantly employed to advocate a certain view will naturally tend to believe in it. That there is some truth in this impression we hardly can deny. Our attitude toward questions, no matter what they may be, is likely to be affected by our habitual modes of reasoning; nor is this by any means discreditable to us.

But, wholly apart from things of this kind, which may affect, often unduly, the attitude of the public, the cases of actual professional misconduct are numerous enough to indicate the need of an effort to elevate professional standards. The bar in the United States is now much preoccupied with this subject, and the first remedy usually suggested is the raising of the technical requirements for admission to practice. It appears, however, that the evils of which we complain have grown and flourished while those requirements were being raised. The capacity to pass our bar examinations is not exclusively found in honest men. The real problem, therefore, is that of excluding from admission to the bar those who lack the personal and intellectual integrity which our profession may rightly demand of those who seek to enter it.

As one who has had opportunities for observation and reflection, I would suggest for consideration the question whether our law schools, as well as some other departments of our educational institutions, should not deal more than they do with questions of personal conduct, and, besides teaching students how to analyze cases and apply technical rules, give instruction as to how the knowledge thus gained should be used, and as to the moral as well as the legal obligations which a man owes to his profession and to the public.

Most fully do I agree with my friend, Mr. Justice Stone, in the statement made by him several years ago, in an eloquent public address, that something more should be done by our law schools to teach lawyers "to clothe the bare skeleton of legalism with the grace and dignity and beauty which are rightly attributes of the most sacred aspiration of mankind, the aspiration for the realization of justice on earth." Instead of employing the methods of mass production to swell the ranks of our over-crowded professions, what we need to do is to raise professional ideals and the tone of professional conduct.

To this end I believe that the horizon of our law students should be broadened, that more instruction should be given in foreign law, ancient as well as modern, and in the history and development of law; and that this should be accompanied with instruction in the lives and achievements of the historic characters of our profession. "Lives of great men all remind us," sings Longfellow, "we can make our lives sublime." Most profoundly do I believe in this principle. A generation is short-sighted and labors under a serious handicap when it seeks to raise itself exclusively by its own boot-straps. We need the inspiration and guidance of the great examples that have gone before us. I cannot tell how often I have read the report of Calvin's Case—the case of the *Ante Nati*—as written three hundred years ago by old Coke, the great Chief Justice, prodigious in learning and steadfast in his support of the independence and integrity of the bench; and I have never read it without a renewed sense of the dignity, the grandeur and the majestic responsibilities of the legal profession. The case was, said Coke, the shortest in form and longest in substance ever decided by the English bench; for its decision involved consequences no less momentous than that of the title of the Crown to the allegiance of a vast number of those whom it claimed as its subjects. The cause was argued in the first instance in the King's Bench, and afterwards openly in the Exchequer Chamber, first by counsel and then by all the judges of England, including the Lord Chancellor and Coke himself; and in concluding his report Coke declares "that no commandment or message by word or writing was sent or delivered from any whatsoever to any of the judges, to cause them to incline to any opinion in this case"; and this, he said, he remembered, because it was "honorable for the State, and consonant to the Laws and Statutes of this Realm." [9]

The administration of the law by judges and by practitioners has its high and ennobling traditions; and, happily, exemplars of those traditions may be found in all times which we care to remember or to imitate. Let us hold aloft these inspiring examples, and cherish and defend them, not only for our own sake but for the sake of those who are to come after us.

9. Calvin's Case, 7 Reports, 1.

# BOOK REVIEW

EUROPEAN TREATIES BEARING ON THE HISTORY OF THE UNITED STATES AND ITS DEPENDENCIES. *Edited by* FRANCES GARDINER DAVENPORT. Vol. II. 1650–1697. Washington, Carnegie Institution, 1929. Pp. vi, 386. $3.00.

It fell to my lot to review the first volume of the present collection of treaties, but the task of reviewing the second is simplified, if not indeed rendered practically superfluous, by the just and understanding preface contributed by Dr. J. Franklin Jameson, who, having been in close touch with Miss Davenport's work up to the time of her lamented death two years ago, pays a well merited tribute to the exact and unostentatious learning, integrity of mind and character, and devotion to duty which united to give to whatever she did an exceptionally authentic and informative quality. The first volume, which appeared in 1917, extended to the treaty of Münster of 1648. The manuscript left behind by the editor, which brings the collection down to the treaties of Utrecht of 1713, will furnish material to fill two volumes of print, of which the present volume is the first. This volume includes the treaties covering the period from 1650 to 1697, ending with the treaty of Ryswick.

The treaty text is in each instance preceded by a copiously annotated introduction explaining the position of the treaty not only in the history of European diplomacy but also in its relation to the history of colonial America, and this is followed by bibliographic notes. Then comes the treaty text, which is also minutely annotated, so that the significance of each clause may be readily grasped and every obscurity as far as possible done away with. Every care, it may be needless to say, was taken in order to secure in every instance the most authoritative text.

The volume published in 1917 contained forty treaty texts. The present volume contains forty-four. Among the contracting parties we find the United Netherlands, Great Britain, Sweden, Denmark, Brandenburg, France, Savoy, Portugal, Spain, the United Colonies of New England, New Netherland, Virginia, and Nova Scotia; and among the subjects dealt with are lands and boundaries, the island of St. Thomas, partition, guaranty, peace, truce, commerce, alliance, the conduct of hostilities, and neutrality. It appears that Miss Davenport had intended to give in a general introduction a comprehensive survey of the course of European diplomacy respecting America during the second half of the seventeenth century, but was prevented by illness from so doing. From the special or particular introductions, however, the attentive and studious reader will be enabled to gain, in connection with the texts themselves, an intelligent view of the course of events and of the combinations, manoeuvres and contests by which it was influenced. The introduction to the peace of Ryswick gives, for instance, in the space of eight richly annotated pages, a strikingly detailed but equally compact account of the conflicts of interest, controversies, and contests that led up to that celebrated international act.

The designation of a work such as that now in question merely as a collection or compilation of treaties utterly fails to convey a correct or adequate conception of its character and contents. Rarely will a treatise or narrative of equal bulk bear the impress of so much painstaking investigation, or of an examination of sources so critical and complete. In reality it is in a true sense a scholar's manual and guide for the period it covers and the subject to which it relates.

Reprinted from *The American Historical Review*, XXXV (1930), 376–377.

# A FURTHER EXCEPTION[1]

## JUDGE MOORE DISPUTES STATEMENT IN WHITE BIOGRAPHY

To the Editor of *The New York Times:*

Having read in *The Times* of December 26 a letter from M. Jusserand, formerly French Ambassador at Washington, in relation to a letter he had read in the recent biography of the late Henry White, in which he is represented as having been "extremely prejudiced" against England, I venture to call attention to a misrepresentation concerning myself in the same volume.

Referring to the delegation of the United States to the Fourth International American Conference at Buenos Aires

1. Reprinted from *The New York Times*, January 3, 1931.

in 1910, the biography states that the delegation comprehended myself, General Crowder, Paul S. Reinsch and David Kinley, later president of the University of Illinois; and that the "wives of these four men accompanied them, a fact which caused White some justified uneasiness."

It is not an agreeable thing to read such a statement concerning either one's wife or one's self, but I have heretofore refrained from taking public notice of it. I wrote to the publishers and stated the facts, and they promptly answered that they would erase the statement and substitute another page. The other day, however, I received a letter from a friend in California, who said that he had just purchased a copy of the book and had noticed in it the slur to which I have referred. As it is thus evident that copies containing the offensive statement have not been withdrawn but are still on sale, I feel obliged publicly to state the facts.

The only one of the delegates above mentioned who was accompanied by his wife was Professor Reinsch, and as he is dead and no longer in a position to defend her, I will say that she was remarkably unobtrusive in her demeanor and unlikely to cause any disturbance. As concerns General Crowder, Dr. Kinley and myself, the facts are simply these: General Crowder never had a wife, Mrs. Kinley remained in the United States and my wife was in Europe with our children.

So far, therefore, as concerns General Crowder, Dr. Kinley and myself, the indecorous statement that the presence of our wives with the delegation caused the chairman of it "justified uneasiness" is simply false and destitute of any foundation whatever.

JOHN BASSETT MOORE.

New York, December 30, 1930.

# DWIGHT MORROW[1]

## A TRIBUTE TO THE LATE STATESMAN

To the *New York Herald Tribune:*

It is a just and touching tribute that is paid in your editorial page of today to Dwight Morrow. In intellectual and moral integrity he has no superior among our public men, present or past. With a mind singularly clear and a power of analysis at once acute and profound, he formed his own conclusions and, having formed them, was ready to take all the

1. Reprinted from the *New York Herald Tribune,* October 8, 1931.

consequences, political or personal, of acting upon them. It should not, however, be supposed that this did not often involve a sacrifice of feeling on his part. His attachments were strong and his sympathies warm; but he was ever moved and controlled by his sense of justice, which knew no bounds. Fully appreciating the fact that human differences largely spring from prejudice and misunderstanding and that neither party to a quarrel is likely to be wholly right, he sought to look at both sides and to give to each what was due. In this way he played the part of a conciliator of differences, abroad as well as at home.

His loss is, as you say, irreparable. At no time in our history have men of his type been needed more than now, with his statesmanlike grasp of public questions, his devotion to the public interest as a whole and his superiority to any influence other than that of the desire to serve, with all his power, his fellow men.

I speak as one who knew him as a man and cherished him as a friend.

JOHN BASSETT MOORE.

New York, October 6, 1931.

# BOOK REVIEW

POST-WAR TREATIES FOR THE PACIFIC SETTLE-
MENT OF INTERNATIONAL DISPUTES. *By* MAX
HABICHT. Cambridge, Harvard University Press, 1931.
Pp. xxvi, 1109.

The object of this volume is to bring together the original
texts of all the treaties of investigation, conciliation, arbitration, and compulsory adjudication concluded since the Armistice of November, 1918, so that the reader may gain a complete
view of what was accomplished in this field during the first
decade after the so-called World War. The work is divided into
two parts, the first of which gives the treaty texts, together
with an English translation, wherever English was not used
in any of the official acts. The second part is analytical. This
part contains four chapters, the first of which treats of the
extension of the application of pacific procedure, and also of
the different systems or methods employed, of which the author
exhibits eleven distinct examples. The second chapter deals
with the loopholes, commonly called "reservations," the ways
of escape, such as "vital interests," "independence," "national
honor," and "the interests of third powers"; the Monroe Doctrine, and the "regional understandings" of the Covenant of
the League of Nations; territorial integrity, constitutional
principles, "domestic" questions, and so on. The third chapter
is concerned with methods of investigation and conciliation,
and advisory procedure. The fourth chapter covers the wide,
difficult, and important domain of judicial pacific procedure,
the international adjudication of disputes, thus involving an
examination of the composition and setting up of tribunals,
the formulation of the terms of submission, the ascertainment
of the law applicable to the case, and other phases of the employment of the judicial method, whether immediately and
directly, or after conciliatory or mediatorial efforts. There are
also appendices containing (1) an alphabetical list of the signatories of the pacific agreements made during the decade in
question, and (2) a detail of the commissions of investigation
and conciliation, permanent and non-permanent, and an alphabetical list of the commissioners. There is also a bibliography
and an index.

I have thus described the contents of the volume in detail, for two reasons: First, because in no other way can an adequate conception be conveyed of its comprehensively informative character; secondly, because I feel that it is due to the author to take precautions against the hasty supposition that his work is an ordinary and perfunctory compilation of readily accessible texts. In the latter particular I may admit that there is an element of personal sentiment, not unconnected with the circumstance that years ago an eminent advocate of peace, more distinguished for oratory than for accuracy, habitually spoke of my *History and Digest of International Arbitrations* as a "collection of arbitration treaties."

No one who has not done work such as that which has produced the present volume can conceive of the unsparing, uncompromising labor and pains bestowed upon its preparation. That the mere gathering of the materials, to say nothing of their analysis, classification and discussion, was a task beyond ordinary patience and endurance, is shown by the rarity of such publications, in spite of the fact that the information they afford is essential to the intelligent conduct of the development of what may properly be called the international judicial system. In the prosecution of this great design the co-operation of scholars and statesmen is of the first importance. Two of the foremost practical exponents of international arbitration of whom we have any knowledge were Hamilton Fish, who, as Secretary of State of the United States, negotiated the great Treaty of Washington, under which the *Alabama* claims and other momentous and dangerous questions were determined by arbitration; and the late Baron Rio-Branco, of Brazil, one of the most profound scholars I have ever known, whose career was specially distinguished by the determination of boundary disputes by the judicial method. It may with substantial accuracy be said that neither of these statesmen ever made a public speech, in the commonly accepted sense; but, by their work, they builded foundations and set precedents that still hold out promise for the future. To statesmen of their type, works such as the volume now under review, filled with pertinent information carefully gathered, and intelligently classified and discussed, are of great value.

Reprinted from the *Columbia Law Review* XXXI (1931), 1223-1224.

# INTER-GOVERNMENTAL DEBTS[1]

To the *New York Herald Tribune:*

Although I have heretofore taken no part in the public discussion of the subject of international debts, whether public or private, I cannot help feeling that perhaps the most important phase of the matter has, by reason of a purely controversial treatment of the subject, been generally overlooked. There can be no doubt that the present situation exercises a most depressing influence on all kinds of markets. If private debts are not paid when due, and no assurance can be given of their eventual payment, the transaction of business, which cannot always be conducted on a cash basis, is necessarily hampered and the process of buying and selling is retarded and restricted, with perhaps disastrous results to all concerned.

But, at the present moment, there is the additional complication of inter-governmental debts, the full and actual significance of which, judging by most public utterances, seems to be little comprehended. Unfortunately, soon after the close of the war, a plea for cancellation was put forward in this country on the ground that we had been derelict in our duty in not going earlier to the aid of the allies, who had in reality been fighting our battles, and who, even before the war began, had, without our being conscious of the fact, been preserving the Monroe Doctrine for us, particularly in South America. This plea was as unfounded as it was offensive. It goes without saying that not a single power that tumbled into the war in Europe in 1914 was actuated by the desire to benefit the United States by preserving the Monroe Doctrine or otherwise. In reality, our people as a whole were unacquainted with the complex underlying causes of the war, as perhaps they still are, and the proposal that they pay a penalty for their inaction was not well received. I vividly recall the answer nightly displayed at the movies in the legend—"Love, Honor, and *Repay.*"

Among those who habitually address the public the answer also took another form, which we still daily hear, and that is that we, being peculiarly addicted to sacrifices to the cause of peace, will consider revision to the extent to which the debtor governments will reduce their armies and scrap their navies;

1. Unprinted letter to the *New York Herald Tribune,* January 6, 1932.

and it seems really to be expected that other peoples, who happen to know something of our history and of the numerous wars in which, not always under compulsion, we have enthusiastically engaged, will accept, on a gold basis, this self-profession of exceptionally peaceful propensities. It never seems to occur to those who profess such things to reflect on what we undoubtedly should say if, for instance, England or France should approach us with a similar proposition. Without undertaking to forecast the precise phraseology of our answer, what our government would do is indicated by the anouncement, in the newspapers of this morning, by the Secretary of the Navy, of a ten-year building programme which will assure us of a navy "up to the London treaty limitations," which means parity with Great Britain and superiority to any other single power. Might not such an answer be regarded by ourselves as a manifestation of self-respect, and by others as a measure of our exceptional devotion to the cause of disarmament?

In the confused babel now prevailing the great fundamental fact is overlooked that we have in this matter of reparations and inter-governmental debts, which is inextricably interwoven with the matter of private debts, a substantial and profound selfish interest. Just as the creditors of an individual have a common interest in the solvency of their debtor, so have the people of the United States a vital interest in the solvency of their foreign debtors, whether such debtors have a private or a public character. How can we defend our laws relating to bankruptcy, insolvency and receiverships, if the creditor has no interest in the solvency of his debtor and the ability of the latter to pay?

I have always thought that, if the subject of inter-governmental debts had originally been discussed on the basis of common sense and good business, the attitude of our people towards the discussion of the question would today be very different from what it is. By reason of the antecedents above mentioned, there exists today a propensity to suspect as a cancellationist anyone who hints at even a temporary suspension of payments. I should not myself think of proposing cancellation. The laws to which I have referred are not based on any such theory. The theory on which they rest is the necessity of a present sacrifice or forbearance for the sake of preserving an interest which otherwise might be wholly lost. Here at home, among ourselves, we daily and hourly recognize the necessity of considering the future as well as the present, of dealing practically with the question of eventual as well as with that of present ability to pay; and we do this in the interest of the creditor as well as in the interest of the debtor.

It is a sound general principle that a nation is not likely to profit by the impoverishment of other nations. If we have, in recent years, acted on the supposition that we could grow richer and richer by selling to peoples whose financial plight was obviously becoming more and more precarious, and who were paying us for what we sold to them largely by borrowing from us, there is ample justification in the present situation for considering the question whether we should not, in our own interest, co-operate in every possible measure to remedy and escape the injurious consequences of the mistake that evidently was made. In this connection we daily descant on the sins of our bankers. I hold no brief for bankers, international or national, or for any other class; but we surely all have a common interest in the fate of banks, on which we are ourselves even now loudly calling for an extension of credits beyond what many judicious authorities conceive to be safe or expedient. The ability of our banks to help our people in their present predicament is necessarily affected by the ability of the banks to collect what is due them abroad. Nor is it a question solely of the banks. Many of our great industrial companies doing business in foreign countries have a vital stake in the financial condition of the peoples of those countries. Immense sums are, I venture to say, at this moment due to such companies for what has been sold by them abroad, not only in their own interest but also in the interest of our commerce and industry as a whole. This is no time for crimination and recrimination. The situation demands a comprehensive consideration of all interests, with a view to a solution helpful to all, on the broad basis of enlightened self-interest.

During the past month the condition of things, in which national sentiment and susceptibilities inevitably play a part, has been much aggravated by peremptory declarations on this side of the water and retaliatory threats of repudiation on the other side. We thus approach the final stage of unreason and open conflict with the possible consequence of irreparable loss to both parties. Is it too late to secure a reconsideration of the subject on the basis of the interest which we ourselves have in the matter? We are told that Samson, when he pulled down the temple, himself perished with his victims, the Philistines. He incurred this fate because he thought only of his enemies; and, as we are generally reputed to be the Samson among modern nations, and feel not a little flattered by this view, may we not properly inquire whether he personally profited by what happened to him? While hard pressed debtors are proverbially prone to regard their creditors as enemies, it is by no means wise for creditors so far to resent this attitude as to close the door to discussion and co-operation in their own behalf. The ability to pay is not fixed and invariable. On the contrary, it daily fluctuates with the changing conditions of a changing world. Recognition of this fact is dictated by enlightened self-interest.

JOHN BASSETT MOORE.

New York, January 6, 1932.

## WAR AND ITS EFFECT ON DEBTS, PUBLIC AND PRIVATE

### OUR DEBTS TO ENGLAND[1]

To the Editor of *The New York Times:*

I have just read in *The Times* the statement that "our debt to England after the Revolution was due to the assumption by our government, in the treaty of peace, of the private debts of British subjects in this country." "The obligation," the statement continues, "was duly admitted, but the objection was made that the British put obstacles in the way of our discharging it." This statement, judging by the tenor of the article in which it appears, seems to have been based on something said in a recent debate in the British Parliament; but, however this may be, the statement is erroneous.

During the Revolution some of the States passed acts of sequestration and confiscation under which debts due by their citizens to British creditors prior to the war were paid into the State treasuries, and such payment was made a plea in bar to any future action for the recovery of the debt. The confiscation of debts being then considered a violation of established international practice and disreputable, the American negotiators of the treaty of peace, in spite of the weakness of the old Federal Government, incorporated in the treaty an article (Article 4) declaring that creditors on either side should meet with no lawful impediment to the recovery of the full value in sterling money of all bona fide debts previously contracted. When, however, the British creditors came to sue in the State courts, there being then no Federal tribunals in which they could bring their actions, the courts were inclined

1. Reprinted from *The New York Times*, February 16, 1932.

to hold that they were bound by the State statutes rather than by the treaty.

This condition continued until the adoption of the Constitution of the United States, in which, with a view to remove the obstacle that had stood in the way of British creditors, there was inserted the provision that all treaties made or which should be made under the authority of the United States should be "the supreme law of the land," and binding on the judges in every State, "anything in the Constitution or laws of any State to the contrary notwithstanding." But, while this provision removed the "lawful impediment" that had previously existed, many practical difficulties, largely due to the lapse of time, loss of proofs and insolvency of debtors, still remained.

In order to meet this situation, there was incorporated in Article 6 of the Jay treaty of 1794 a provision for the establishment of an international board to deal with the claims. This board duly met in Philadelphia in 1797, but in the course of its deliberations serious differences arose and in the Summer of 1799 its proceedings were suspended. Negotiations then ensued between the two governments for a direct settlement of the claims, with the result that there was concluded in London on January 8, 1802, a convention by which Article 6 of the Jay treaty was annulled, and the United States agreed to pay the sum of £600,000, at the rate of $4.44 to the pound, at Washington, in three annual instalments, in satisfaction of all liabilities under that article. This sum, amounting to $2,664,-000, was duly appropriated and paid to the British Government, which distributed the money among the claimants through a commission appointed under an act of Parliament.

I happen to be somewhat minutely acquainted with this transaction, the full record of which in all its phases is given in the third volume of my *International Adjudications*, which was published not long ago. The treaty of peace contained no clause by which either party assumed any debts, public or private. I write this letter because I think we have enough actual subjects of controversy with other countries without invoking imaginary ones from the past. I may further remark that the case for the British holders of defaulted bonds in this country is often weakened by combining all such bonds in a grand total, including even Confederate States bonds. A claim on account of these bonds was presented to the mixed commission under the twelfth article of the treaty of Washington of May 8, 1871, and was rejected.

Claims on account of certain other bonds were dismissed by the British and American mixed commission under the convention of February 8, 1853, of which Joshua Bates, who, although born in the United States, was then senior partner in Baring Brothers & Co., of London, was umpire. Some of the repudiations or defaults I would not undertake to defend, but they do not all fall into one category. Nor is it likely that bonds of our States or municipalities were ever sold or purchased on the supposition that the United States would, in case of default, pay or be under any obligation to pay either principal or interest. United States purchasers are in this respect in the same plight as foreign purchasers.

JOHN BASSETT MOORE.

New York, February 14, 1932.

## JEFFERSON'S REFERENCE WAS SOLELY TO INDIVIDUAL DEBTS [2]

To the Editor of *The New York Times:*

The day after the publication in *The New York Times,* on February 16, under the title "Our Debts to England," of my letter pointing out that the treaty of peace between Great Britain and the United States of 1783 contained no clause by which either government assumed the payment of debts, public or private, I received from two different sources evidence tending to show that the erroneous statements lately made on the subject were based on inferences drawn from a quotation made by J. Beaumont Pease, chairman of Lloyds Bank, Ltd., in his speech at its general meeting on February 5, from a paragraph in a note addressed by Thomas Jefferson, as Secretary of State, to Mr. Hammond, British Minister at Philadelphia, on May 29, 1792.[3] The paragraph, which is short, reads thus:

To the necessities for some delay in the payment of debts may be added the British commercial regulations, lessening our means of payment, by prohibiting us from carrying in our own bottoms our own produce to their dominions in our neighborhood, and excluding valuable branches of it from their home markets by prohibitory duties. The means of payment constitute one of the motives to purchase, at the moment of purchasing. If these means are taken away, by the creditor himself, he ought not in conscience to complain of a mere retardation of his debt, which is the effect of his own act, and the least injurious of those it is capable of producing. The instalment acts before enumerated have been much less general, and for a shorter term than what the chairman of the American merchants thought reasonable. Most of them required the debtor to give security, in the meantime, to his creditor, and provided complete indem-

2. Reprinted from *The New York Times,* February 28, 1932.
3. *American State Papers, Foreign Relations* (folio), I, 201, 208.

nification of the delay by the payment of interest, which was enjoined in every case.

## REFERRED TO PRIVATE DEBTS

Mr. Pease's quotation ends with the words "his own act," in the third sentence. The rest of the paragraph clearly shows that Jefferson referred to private debts owing by one individual to another. Mr. Pease was not bound to quote the whole. But, as he was speaking of "war debts and reparations," and had just declared that France and the United States had "to a great extent refused to take (in payment) any commodities but gold," his omission left open the way to the inference that Jefferson referred to debts the payment of which the United States had assumed.

In reality Jefferson was answering a complaint by Hammond that in some of the States the recovery of debts was legally impeded, in violation, as he claimed, of the fourth article of the treaty of peace, which is quoted and explained in my previous letter. While in Massachusetts justice had, said Hammond, "been liberally dispensed," and full interest allowed even during the war on debts due to British creditors, yet "in a more distant State (Georgia)" the Legislature had never confirmed the treaty. He also complained of other impediments, including the so-called "instalment laws," which impeded the full recovery of all private debts. It was to these laws that Jefferson, in the paragraph above quoted, particularly referred.

Nevertheless, reasoning by analogy, Jefferson's argument may as a whole be powerfully invoked against a policy that unduly restricts and hampers the exchange of commodities, a policy that has specially flourished since the "war to end war"—a glib phrase which, surveying the present state of the world, with its desperate rivalries, its national and racial hatreds, its vengeful pursuit of "the right of self-determination," its hostile tariffs, its boycotts and its wars, glaringly attests the unconscious hypocrisy and utter worthlessness of emotional professions of self-righteousness as a guarantee of peace. "By their fruits ye shall know them." Never were words more truly spoken.

## CO-OPERATION BADLY NEEDED

I am glad to see in Mr. Pease's speech the candid statement that "primarily, of course, the war is responsible," directly or indirectly, for the present industrial and financial depression, with its attendant unrest and its disturbances, actual or threatened, of political, economic and social order. But it is quite as important also to emphasize the fact that except for certain makeshifts such as the Dawes Plan and the Young Plan, designed to avert or to postpone a crisis, there is nothing to show that, until the crash not long ago suddenly resounded, there was any general realization in political, financial or industrial circles of the inevitable breakdown of the restrictive and retributive system to which the war, and the passions and interests engendered or inflamed by it, had given rise.

For the very reason that the present cry for international cooperation comes, as is usual with acts of repentance, somewhat late, there should be no delay in trying to give it practical effect. This cannot come all at once. But one important step would be the general comprehension of these elementary truths: (1) that impoverished nations do not make good customers or safe debtors; (2) that, while history furnishes abundant examples of national aggrandizement by acts of conquest and plunder, yet, if we contemplate national enrichment by peaceful processes, it is a sound general principle that each nation has an interest in promoting the prosperity of other nations.

JOHN BASSETT MOORE.

New York, February 23, 1932.

## WASHINGTON: TO WHOM THE AMERICAN PEOPLE OWE ETERNAL GRATITUDE[1]

To the *New York Herald Tribune:*

As we hear in these days of the "unknown" Washington, and thrifty writers, professing to wish to "humanize" him, do not balk at discredited gossip, it may be appropriate to point out that the people of the United States owe to Washington obligations such as they owe to no other man. First, they owe to him their independence, which he achieved under adversities through which no other American of his time could have successfully borne them. Secondly, they owe to him, more than to any other man, the carrying through of the national movement that resulted in the formation and ratification of their Constitution. Thirdly, they owe to him the firm establishment of the government under that Constitution, with the co-operation and support, which no one else could have commanded, of men of all parties and different, even antagonistic, political creeds.

1. Reprinted from the *New York Herald Tribune*, February 22, 1932.

This unparalleled achievement, or combination of achievements, was rendered possible only by the confidence felt in his statesmanship and the homage paid to his character. Of all testimonies on this subject the most remarkable is that of Thomas Jefferson, who, in a letter to a friend, on January 2, 1814, twenty years after he ceased to be Washington's Secretary of State, paid to him the most beautiful tribute I have ever read by one human being to another.

His integrity [says Jefferson] was most pure, his justice the most inflexible I have ever known, no motives of interest or consanguinity, of friendship or hatred, being able to bias his decision. He was, in every sense of the words, a wise, a good, and a great man. . . . On the whole, his character was, in its mass, perfect, in nothing bad, in few points indifferent; and it may truly be said, that never did nature and fortune combine more perfectly to make a man great, and to place him in the same constellation with whatever worthies have merited from man an everlasting remembrance. For his was the singular destiny and merit, of leading the armies of his country successfully through an arduous war, for the establishment of its independence; of conducting its councils through the birth of a government, new in its forms and principles, until it had settled down into a quiet and orderly train; and of scrupulously obeying the laws through the whole of his career, civil and military, of which the history of the world furnishes no other example.

Such is the man to whom we owe eternal gratitude.

JOHN BASSETT MOORE.

New York, February 20, 1932.


# COMMENT ON THE LECTURE SYSTEM IN AMERICAN AND EUROPEAN UNIVERSITIES [1]

My dear Dr. Duggan:

I have just read with much interest your comment on "The Lecture System in American and European Universities."

Personally, I always followed, as you know, the Socratic method, question and answer, *in free discussion,* supplemented by expositions of my own, except in diplomacy, in which I read a course of lectures carefully prepared beforehand. At the University of Virginia, when I was a student there (1877–80), the professors

1. The above letter was sent to the Director of the Institute of International Education by Judge John Bassett Moore in comment upon Professor Duggan's editorial regarding the lecture system in American and European universities, published in the February *News Bulletin.* Reprinted from the *News Bulletin,* VII (Institute of International Education, March, 1932), 4–5.

usually asked questions, which we answered if we could; but there was little discussion in the sense of a free interchange of views. A few of the professors delivered long oral and oratorical discourses, which were not strikingly effective for educational purposes. The majority now and then read well prepared lectures. In Greek and Latin we handed in careful translations of original texts into English, and also translations of English texts into Greek or Latin, as the case might be. Our work in Greek and Latin was serious and thorough, and was exceedingly valuable from every point of view.

Happily, we had no rules or regulations, beyond the requirement of attendance at lectures or recitations. The roll was always called, and repeated non-attendance was considered a ground for intimating to the student, or to his parents or guardians, that his continued residence was a waste of time.

The usual standard exacted on examinations was 80, applied in a very strict and rigid sense, so that rarely more than one-fourth in a particular subject received a certificate of graduation. Each subject was treated as a separate school—the School of Latin, the School of Greek, the School of Mathematics, etc. There were no regular courses, everything being elective. But a student might get an A.B. or an A.M. by accumulating the requisite number of certificates of graduation in specified schools. Because of the high standard exacted, failure on an examination was not considered a disgrace or a reproach. But I have always thought that the maintenance of the high standard had a stimulating effect, besides tending to develop a sense of manhood and of individual responsibility. The tendency to whine and beg for leniency is developed by low standards, so that the failure to get a degree is regarded as an evidence of special demerit. A system that tends to make supplicants for favor is, in my opinion, indefensible.

I abhor the promiscuous granting of degrees. It prostitutes education and degrades character. The correct system would be to give to each student, if he deserved it, a certificate of attendance and good conduct at lectures, and to award degrees only for exceptional merit. We are unfortunately wedded to the other plan, which does not tend to develop either manhood or scholarship. But on several occasions, when I have expressed my view to the heads of well known institutions, they have fully concurred in it. The great obstacle to its adoption is the difficulty of getting out of the present morass, in which our armies of recruits are seen floundering about, with arms outstretched for diplomas.

The great obstacle in the way of making changes either in the European system or in our system is, of course, the persistent and rather universal tendency to think and act along traditional lines.

Ever faithfully yours,

J. B. Moore.

# PAN AMERICAN DAY AND THE
## WASHINGTON BI-CENTENNIAL[1]

New York, N. Y.
April 12, 1932.

John L. Merrill, Esq.,
  President, The Pan American Society,
  New York, N. Y.

Dear Mr. Merrill:

A mere expression of regret over my absence from the celebration of Pan American Day would do injustice to my feelings. Ever since 1885, when my first service in the Department of State, at Washington, began, I have taken a deep interest and often an active part in the conduct of our relations with the American countries; and as the result of long and varied associations, official and personal, I entertain for the peoples of our sister States not only an abiding sentiment of respect and good will but also an ardent desire for the perpetuation and development of the ideal of Pan Americanism.

We live today in a world racked and torn by the passions inflamed by a great war and perpetuated by the peace by which the war was nominally ended. In consequence we have had new wars and rumors of wars, until we have at length reached the stage at which professed apostles of peace, aghast at the prospect, have nothing better to offer than the frantic proposal to avert armed conflicts by equipping our peace pacts with artificial teeth and claws, with which, under the euphemistic guise of "economic sanctions," they may bite and scratch their way to universal concord and brotherly love.

From this fantastic conception, indifferent alike to the teachings of history and the daily manifestations of human nature, we turn with grateful relief to the International Union of American Republics, formed more than forty years ago for the purpose of cementing relations of friendship between the independent nations of America and promoting the cause of peace with justice. As a human institution, it naturally has

1. *News Bulletin* of the Pan American Society, Inc., No. 4, May 1, 1932; reprinted, under the title "Judge Moore's Striking Statement," in *Cuba*, journal of the Cuban Chamber of Commerce in the United States, V, No. 7 (July, 1932), p. 18.

not achieved perfection. It has not prevented the occasional commission of acts which we could not unite in commending as exemplifications of the ideal which it raised in the western world. But there can be no doubt that through the conferences for which it provided, and its permanent official organ, the Pan American Union, it has accomplished results of the highest beneficence not only to the nations of America but to the world as a whole. Based upon the principle of conciliation combined with the mutual recognition of national rights and aspirations, it has repeatedly averted the calamities of war and brought about the peaceful settlement of serious disputes.

No infatuation can be greater than the supposition that war, which is itself simply a contention by force, can be prevented by a union of nations for the use of force. War, even though peace be its professed object, is waged for victory; and its consequences may bring disaster to victor and vanquished alike.

In the last analysis the preservation of peace must ever depend upon the propensities and desires of peoples and of those by whom their affairs are administered. We celebrate this year the bi-centennial of the birth of George Washington, one of the wisest men and greatest characters the world has ever known, who, although now often dubbed by peddlers of millennial devices an "isolationist," was, as a dispenser of justice and good will, an internationalist in the most practical and most exalted sense. When, in his immortal Farewell Address, he adjured his countrymen to observe good faith and justice toward all nations, to cultivate peace and harmony with all, and particularly to avoid the attachments and antipathies that tend to make a nation a slave to its partialities and its passions, he preached nothing that he had not practised in his conduct of foreign affairs. Conceding to all independent states equality before the law, he made to the improvement of international relations contributions of far-reaching and incalculable value, not the least of which was the revival of the practice of international arbitration, which recurrent wars in Europe had for two centuries caused to fall into disuse. Recalling today his precepts and his deeds, we do well to acclaim him as an apostle of the spirit and purpose of Pan Americanism.

Very faithfully yours,
JOHN BASSETT MOORE.

# BACK TO FUNDAMENTAL PRINCIPLES[1]

To the *New York Herald Tribune:*
The convincing statement by the Secretary of the Treasury, published in this morning's papers, on the necessity of balancing the budget clearly emphasizes the necessity of recurring to fundamental principles, which, in times like these, are so easily thrown to the winds, in spite of the fact that each day furnishes additional proof that the main cause of the prevalent distress is the violation of them during the last fifteen years.

The first of these principles is the obvious truth that the incapacity to pay one's living expenses and what one owes cannot be relieved by increasing his indebtedness unless the new borrowing and expenditure can show a productive return. But governments do not operate for profit. They live on taxes, and the taxes must be wrung from the people, to the diminution of their capacity to pay and of their working capital. Again and again Mr. Mellon was assailed for his insistence on reducing the national debt and for his use for that purpose of the installments paid on the international debts. It is manifest that our plight today would be even worse than it is but for the wise foresight then shown.

The second fundamental principle is the preservation of our constitutional system and, above all, the vital essence of local self-government. Today there is abroad in the land a determined demand, coming directly from the people, for economy in government. In some of our states it has already had a pronounced and practical effect. The people can directly get at their local governments and, being familiar with them close at hand, do not ascribe to them magical powers. But how about the national government? We hear a great deal about the telegraph, the telephone and the radio having made the whole world one. This is part of the twaddle of the time, and we must endure it; but it certainly is not true of government in the United States. In the glamour of its elevated and remote situation the national government is regarded as an inexhaustible source of bounty that can start the wheels of industry, end unemployment, regulate prices and, without regard to the needs of consumers, make production profitable by means of practically unbridled expenditures and an inflated or "managed"

1. Reprinted from the *New York Herald Tribune*, May 30, 1932.

currency. Confidence is to be created by destroying the basis of confidence, or, in plain words, by creating in the mind of every individual a state of uncertainty, in addition to that growing out of the question of supply and demand, as to what is involved, in a financial sense, in each of the myriads of transactions of all kinds that hourly take place between the millions of people by whom the country is inhabited.

No one would dream of attributing such magical powers to our local governments, state and municipal. What is there in our history, present or past, to show that the representatives of the people, when translated to Washington, are transformed into supermen, or that the operations of a central government are more immune than those of a local government to the workings of inexorable economic laws? What is there in the history of any other country to give color to such a supposition? And yet today, when our states, north and south, are heroically balancing their budgets, and the drought-stricken farmers of Arkansas are heroically repaying the national loans directly made to them, we see representatives even from states that once took up arms in assertion of their right to govern themselves in their own way, proposing enormous appropriations for loans even to states and municipalities which, if not thus encouraged to increase their expenditures and their debts, would contrive to live within their income.

We are thus inevitably brought, by the disregard of fundamental principles once believed to be inviolable, to the breakdown not only of our system of government but of government itself. By many this breakdown is imputed mainly, if not wholly, to prohibition; but it is better to look at the facts as they are. Undoubtedly a country is unfortunate in which it is popularly remarked that one of its most profitable industries enjoys freedom from taxation because of its criminal character, and that the place in which a person is safest from intrusion by agents of the law and by bandits is the speakeasy. This condition of things was, however, ushered in not by prohibition, but by national prohibition. In many law-abiding states prohibition had existed for generations, and, being sustained by public sentiment, it was, I believe, as well enforced as were the most of the laws, and with results often distinctly beneficial.

Nor do I share the view, so enthusiastically held by many, that the revocation of the Eighteenth Amendment would greatly alleviate our economic situation. My criticism of the amendment rests upon the broader, deeper and more permanent ground that, as an attempt to regulate the sumptuary habits of our people by a uniform rule and to supplant the control previously exercised by the individual states, it tended to subvert the very foundation of our system of government. The United States is too big, and the local differences in population, in habits and in sentiment are too pronounced, to admit of the application of a uniform national rule in matters of this kind. Perhaps it may be defended as a case of "bold experimentation," but we now know the result. Respect for law has been diminished; morality, public and private, has been debased, and government itself has been undermined.

But let us not flatter ourselves with the thought that this calamity has come upon us suddenly. National prohibition is merely time's latest and most glaring example of the inevitable effect of the decay of local self-government and the attribution of all powers, including that of magic, to a single and distant agency, constantly overwhelmed with its burdens, often harassed and in doubt, and sometimes incapable of action. What we now most need to do is again soberly to face the realities of life; to get back to law, to reason and to experience; in a word, to return to fundamental principles.

JOHN BASSETT MOORE.

New York, May 27, 1932.

# THE CONFEDERATE DEBT[1]

Passed Upon and Disposed Of by an International Arbitration.

To the Editor of *The New York Times:*

In some of the recent contributions to your columns on the subject of international debts, there has been much discussion of the unpaid Confederate debt, of which an interesting historical review was given in the letter of Mr. Wilbur Bates in your issue of July 17. It seems, however, a pity that the discussion of this subject should continue, as it evidently is carried on without knowledge of the fact that this debt was formally and authoritatively outlawed sixty years ago by the decisions of an international board of arbitration. It would thus appear that, although truth is eternal, its opposite also may be tenacious of life.

By the treaty between the United States and Great Britain signed at Washington on May 8, 1871, under which the *Alabama* claims were settled, provision was made (Art. XII) for the submission of all other claims of the citizens of either

1. Reprinted from the *New York Times*, July 25, 1932; *The Commercial and Financial Chronicle* (New York, August 16, 1932).

country against the government of the other, growing out of the Civil War, to three commissioners, one to be appointed by the United States, another by Great Britain, and the third by common agreement, or, this failing, by the diplomatic representative of Spain at Washington. The commission, as eventually constituted, consisted of the Hon. James Somerville Frazer, formerly a justice of the Supreme Court of Indiana; the Right Hon. Russell Gurney, M. P., a member of her Majesty's Privy Council and Recorder of London, and Count Louis Corti, Italian Minister at Washington, who was chosen by common agreement.

To this commission typical claims were presented on account of the non-payment of Confederate bonds. One of these claims was that of a British subject named Barrett, resident in England, who appeared as the owner of a "cotton-loan bond," of the denomination of £200, bearing interest at the rate of 7 per cent, and redeemable at par. It was contended that the United States was liable for the payment of the bond, principal and interest, because it had seized and appropriated in 1865 the public assets of the Confederacy, and particularly a large quantity of cotton that had been hypothecated by the Confederacy for the payment of the loan, and had thus prevented the Confederate States from paying the bondholders. The Secretary of State of the United States, when furnished by the agent of the United States with a copy of the memorial, protested to the British Government against the presentation of the claim and asked that it be withdrawn. With this request Great Britain refused to comply, and on Dec. 14, 1871, the commission, by a unanimous vote, dismissed the claim on the merits, on the following grounds:

The commission is of opinion that the United States is not liable for the payment of debts contracted by the rebel authorities.

The rebellion was a struggle against the United States for the establishment in a portion of the country belonging to the United States of a new State in the family of nations, and it failed. Persons contracting with the so-called Confederate States voluntarily assumed the risk of such failure, and accepted its obligations subject to the paramount right of the parent State by force to crush the rebel organization, and seize all its assets and property, whether hypothecated by it or not to its creditors.

Such belligerent right of the United States, to seize and hold, was not subordinate to the rights of creditors of the rebel organization, created by contract with the latter; and when such seizure was actually accomplished, it put an end to any claim of the property which the creditor otherwise might have had.

We are therefore of opinion that after such seizure the claimant had no interest in the property, and the claim is dismissed.

The same principle was applied by the commission in the rejection of another claim, brought by a British subject named Walker, who demanded damages for the loss of trust funds which were invested by order of a South Carolina court in Confederate bonds.

This ended the claims that were presented. But the treaty, besides making the decisions of the commission final and conclusive on all claims before it, further provided that every claim that might have been presented, whether actually presented or not, should, after the commission's work was closed, be considered, as "finally settled, barred, and henceforth inadmissible." This ended the claims as a whole; for, although the period for the presentation of claims did not expire until March 26, 1872, yet, in the face of the unanimous and sweeping condemnation of the claims of Barrett and Walker, no other claims on account of Confederate debts were presented.

Nothing is better settled in law than the principle that those who lend money to insurgents take the risk of their failure. This is also common sense. Such a loan, whether prompted by the hope of gain or by sympathy with the cause, is in the nature of a bet that the insurrection will succeed. If the cause is lost, equally so is the stake; and neither victor nor vanquished can be reproached. Had the purchasers of Confederate bonds bought bonds of the United States, which were then cheap, they would have made a handsome profit. They made a deliberate choice and must abide the consequences.

I have yet another reason for writing this letter. Whenever a general arbitration treaty is submitted to the Senate the objection is invariably raised that its ratification would expose the United States, among other things, to claims for the payment of the Confederate debt; and, although the facts I have here narrated are duly recorded in my *History and Digest of International Arbitrations,* which was published by the United States Government in 1898, I have yet to see a specific official refutation from any quarter of the erroneous supposition just mentioned. On this ground alone it is not out of place again to try to bring the facts to the notice of the public.

JOHN BASSETT MOORE.

Sagaponack, N. Y., July 21, 1932.

# BOOK REVIEWS

THE INTERNATIONAL JOINT COMMISSION BETWEEN THE UNITED STATES OF AMERICA AND THE DOMINION OF CANADA. *By* CHIRAKAIKARAN JOSEPH CHACKO. New York, Columbia University Press, 1932. Pp. 7, 431.

Swift tells us that he who makes two blades of grass to grow where only one grew before deserves well of mankind. The author of the present volume deserves a like encomium, as he has made a blade to grow where none grew before. In furnishing to the world for the first time a systematic and comprehensive exposition of the non-spectacular but effective work of an international board that has for twenty years adjusted differences that have arisen along the 3,000-mile stretch of "undefended boundary" between the United States and the British dominions to the north, he has performed a real service to all who are interested, as students or as administrators, in the development of processes for the application of principles of law, of equity, and of mutual convenience to the relations of neighboring nations.

The International Joint Commission now in question was organized under the treaty between the United States and Great Britain, signed by Elihu Root and James Bryce at Washington, on January 11, 1909, for the purpose of preventing disputes regarding the use of the boundary waters of the United States and Canada, and of settling all questions then pending or which might arise involving the rights, obligations or interests of either in relation to the other, or to the inhabitants of the other, along their common frontier. The commission is composed of six members, three appointed by the United States and three by Canada. In matters involving the use, obstruction, or diversion of waters, the commission may by a majority render a decision; but in other questions it has no arbitral power, and can only report its conclusions to the two governments. Where the commission in any case equally divides, each side makes a separate report to its own government, and it then remains for the two governments to endeavor to reach an adjustment. The commission is empowered to administer oaths and to take testimony, and is required to hear all parties interested in the proceedings before it.

Not only are the boundary waters of the United States and Canada, including the Great Lakes, the thoroughfare of an immense commerce, but they are also used for domestic and sanitary purposes, for irrigation, for industry, and for the development of light and power. The diversification and multiplication of uses eventually led, as the author points out, to the realization on both sides of the boundary of the need of a permanent administrative machinery, international in its constitution and operation. The jurisdiction of the joint commission is partly compulsory and partly voluntary. The compulsory jurisdiction comprises the effective supervision of the use, obstruction, or diversion, either by the governments or by private persons, of boundary waters or of waters flowing from and across the boundary, and the adoption of adequate safeguards against injury to interests on either side of the line. These aspects of the subject are presented by the author in full detail in a chapter on the commission's judicial powers; and, as an aid to the visualization of the problems involved, there is published at the beginning of the volume, with the permission of the secretary of the Canadian section of the commission, a map of the waterways in respect of which questions have arisen or are likely to arise. Chapters are also devoted to the administrative and the investigating powers of the commission, to its voluntary jurisdiction, and to its procedure. The cases with which the commission has dealt, and the decisions and adjustments reached, are carefully analyzed, explained, and summarized. The survey clearly demonstrates that the commission has made a substantial contribution to the cause of international justice and contentment, and given to the world another and highly instructive example of what may be accomplished not only for peace but for prosperity by applying judicial and conciliatory methods to the settlement of international differences that necessarily grow out of competitive national interests.

The reader cannot fail to perceive that the author has been animated in the performance of his laborious task by an enthusiasm for his subject. This circumstance enhances the pleasure with which the reviewer welcomes the author as a co-laborer in a field which he has himself so long tried to cultivate.

Reprinted from the *Columbia Law Review*, XXXII (1932), 925–926.

COMPULSORY ARBITRATION OF INTERNATIONAL
DISPUTES. *By* HELEN MAY CORY. New York, Columbia
University Press, 1932. Pp. xiii, 281.

This volume, which I am happy to commend as a thoughtful,
well written and useful contribution to the scientific literature
of international arbitration, is not a general study of the subject, but, as the introduction points out, deals exclusively with
"the system of obligations whereby states have undertaken, in
advance, to have recourse to arbitration for the settlement of
their disputes," as distinguished from specific and voluntary
submissions. This system, which obviously requires a distinctive title, has, as our author says, been known as compulsory
arbitration. But it is proposed now to limit the word "compulsory" to arbitration under agreements by which (1) the
jurisdiction of an existing tribunal with a definitely ascertained personnel may be invoked (2) by application of either
party to the dispute. The first condition is met by the Permanent Court of International Justice, but not by the Permanent Court of Arbitration, the members of which constitute
only an eligible list from which judges may be chosen for the
occasion.

On the merits of this proposal, to which the author does not
definitely commit herself, I venture some brief reflections; it
being one of the evils of our so-called science that, by the time
we have grown accustomed to one inaccurate term, we are confronted with several more. To the use of "compulsory" as a
comprehensive title, I never formally objected, although "obligatory" more accurately conveyed what really was meant; but,
before limiting "compulsory" to a part of the system, and thus
necessitating another name for the rest, we should feel satisfied that "compulsory" is not, in a proper legal sense, inapplicable to both. In fact, the term "compulsory," save in so far
as it denoted an obligation binding on the conscience, has
represented in this matter an aspiration rather than a reality.
So, an agreement between states that an existing tribunal may
take jurisdiction of their future disputes on a unilateral application does not evolve a power to compel either party to make
the application, or, if a judgment is given, to enforce it upon
both parties or either party. Such an agreement is an important practical gain; but I speak now of the nature of the
process and of proper terminology.

It is most gratifying to learn (p. 143) that the post-war
European treaties of general arbitration show "a distinct decline in the old-fashioned reservation of vital interests, inde-

pendence, honor and the interests of third states." For inveighing against treaties containing this reservation, and refusing to have anything to do with bringing them about, I of course was dubbed a "reactionary." I rather liked it, as I knew that "reactionaries," especially in the peace movement, often turned out to be prophets. On the other hand, we learn that more than half of the post-war treaties contain the stipulation that local remedies must be exhausted before the international arbitral jurisdiction is invoked. This is not only proper but also desirable. Peace is not promoted by claiming for aliens, in countries in which law and courts exist, extraterritorial privileges or exorbitant rights of diplomatic protection. Such claims make for anarchy, not for order; for oppression, not for justice.

It is interesting to find that, in the modern movement for general arbitral stipulations, the Spanish American countries appear as pioneers, having concluded among themselves from 1820 to 1890 about fifty such treaties. To none of these was Brazil a party. But this does not mean that Brazil was more warlike, or that her empire was less pacific, than were the neighboring Spanish republics. The latter's arbitral stipulations were only a phase of the aspiration after common action born of the ten years' struggle of the Spanish colonies for independence. Brazil, being Portuguese, not only bore no part in that struggle, but was for a time even the seat of the government of Portugal; a condition of things the European powers took steps to terminate, as unbecoming.

The questions which the present volume purports to include are so well covered by it that it is not practicable within the limits of a review to touch upon all of them, but I will mention one more. We are told that the meaning of the phrases "legal questions" and "claims of right," which have been used as marking the sphere of arbitration, has been "the battle ground of jurists." I do not challenge the accuracy of this statement; but I would benevolently advise the jurists to restrain their verbal militancy, and to pause for breath long enough to consider whether anything can be gained by attempting conjectural, hazardous and never-ending amplifications of terms that clearly define themselves. Whether a dispute that has actually arisen may be legal or non-legal, that is to say, determinable by the application of rules of law, may be a subject of legitimate debate; and there may also be a controversy as to what rules are applicable to the case and whether they are rules of law. But neither by learning, nor by logic, nor by imagination can these things be foretold; and, if discussed in advance, they should be debated only as suggestions of what the definition may properly be held to embrace, and not as forestalling what can be determined only when the occasion for authoritative decision arises. One of the great virtues of the remarkable Convention for the Pacific Settlement of International Disputes, concluded at The Hague in 1899, was that, while it did not purport to make arbitration compulsory, it essayed no exception beyond that which was implied by the word "law." The high-water mark of international arbitration is still represented by the adjudications of the disputes embraced in Article VII of the Jay Treaty, the *Alabama* claims, and the North Atlantic Fisheries dispute. The last was submitted under a special agreement by which (Art. IV) the tribunal was "chosen from the general list of members" of the Permanent Court of Arbitration. The advance and the recession of international arbitration will continue to be marked not so much by the number and the terms of general agreements, desirable as these, unless they consist chiefly of exclusions, may be, as by the actual submission of differences, showing that the professions of a desire for peace through justice are more than "sounding brass or a tinkling cymbal."

Reprinted from the *Columbia Review*, XXXII (1932), 1257–1258.

# THE UNITED STATES AND SAMOA[1]

TOWARDS the end of a long life Benjamin Franklin, one of the wisest observers of men and of things, sagely wrote: "Experience keeps a dear school." Entrance to it is free, and it is open day and night. Every man, woman, and child is matriculated in it; and, if the pupils would learn their lesson from books, the present volume would suffice for the purposes of graduation. But, unfortunately, the pupils are vain and obdurate. Refusing to profit by the mistakes of others, they insist on paying as tuition the cost of their own perverse or emotional experimentation.

During half a century the United States might have had the Samoan Islands for the asking. At times they were pressed upon it, and, had the proffered honor and responsibility been accepted, the government's action would not have been difficult rationally to justify; for, as sole proprietor, it would have been master of its fate, and not constantly in collision with other

1. Introduction to *The Foreign Policy of the United States in Relation to Samoa*, by George Herbert Ryden. (New Haven, Yale University Press, and London, Oxford University Press, 1933), pp. xi–xviii.

powers over an object of relatively slight importance. But, on a fateful date, the United States entered into a "consultative pact." Such things are innocent in appearance and alluring in sound, especially to those who do not stop to consider what the other parties have in mind. Towards the end of 1877 a Samoan chief, called La Mamea, visited Washington. He stood six feet four in his stockings, was good to look upon, and had learned English from missionaries. At White House receptions he towered above the multitude. The mighty men at Washington, few of whom could have told where Samoa was, were good-natured, and were human. They extended to the Big Chief, who had come a long way to see them, the right hand of fellowship; and on January 17, 1878, there was signed a treaty by which it was stipulated that, "if, unhappily, any differences" should have arisen, or should thereafter arise, "between the Samoan Government and any other Government in amity with the United States," the United States would "employ its good offices for the purpose of adjusting those differences upon a satisfactory and solid foundation." The phraseology was faultless, and it appealed to "all benevolent minds"; but it omitted to state the fact that there was no such thing as "the Samoan Government." The Big Chief knew this, but accepted the compliment.

What followed is clearly, faithfully, and impressively detailed in the present volume. The United States, after a succession of bewildering lessons in the school of experience, sought to raise things to a higher plane. Learned writers have argued that, because certain powers have, by contributing small amounts to a common fund, kept a lighthouse burning at Cape Spartel for a number of years, without creating serious international complications, international government is a perfect success. As a matter of fact, it is the worst of all kinds of government. Foreign interests, commercial and missionary, had sought to instil into the Samoan mind the idea that the islands must have a central government, preferably under a king; but, no sooner was a king chosen from among the native chiefs, than some other chief or chiefs rose in rebellion, and, taking to the bush, sallied forth in the cool of the day to fight.

It was in Samoa that Germany made one of her early essays at colonization. That German subjects constituted by far the largest element of bona fide foreign settlers, who occupied land and cultivated it, is clearly shown by the results of the international land commission eventually set up for the adjudication of titles. Out of 134,419 acres claimed by Germans, 75,000, or 56 per cent, were confirmed to them. The British claimed 1,250,-270 acres, and obtained confirmation of only 36,000, or 3 per cent; Americans claimed 302,746 acres, and obtained 21,000, or

7 per cent. The Germans, having a preponderant industrial and commercial interest in the group, not unnaturally sought a preponderant voice in local government, such as it was. This principle had been cordially conceded by Prince Bismarck to the United States in the Hawaiian Islands, where Germany had renounced her most-favored-nation clause in recognition of the preponderant interests of the United States. H. A. P. Carter, for many years the highly esteemed minister of Hawaii at Washington, more than once narrated to me the incidents of a night which, while on a special mission to Berlin, he spent by invitation at Friedrichsruhe, where Bismarck, as he smoked his big pipe, assured him that Germany would not stand in the way of the development of the closest relations between Hawaii and the United States. But, in Hawaii, there was a government, by no means perfect, but sole and supreme. In Samoa, there was just enough of a government to make a football for rival foreign groups. Out of this rivalry there grew turmoil and strife; and it was in an atmosphere of contention that the United States, in the exercise of "good offices" under the treaty of 1878, invited Germany and Great Britain to a conference at Washington. As a preliminary, agents were sent out to report on conditions in the islands. The conference took place in the summer of 1887.

In the pursuit of colonial aspirations, Germany had encountered British opposition; and Washington would not have been surprised if a continuance of this condition had been manifested in the conference. But it was not so. The United States presented a program based on the recognition of native rights. It was natural that Germany and Great Britain should, as actual colonial powers, view this proposal in a severely practical light. The United States has, since those simpler times, occasionally but not continuously, seen things in that light, and has now and then militarily occupied a country that was not its colony. But the Samoan conference had not gone far before it became evident that Germany and Great Britain had come to an understanding, the British representative consistently supporting the German claim that governmental control should follow the preponderance of commercial interests. As the exaltation of native rights and the dominance of preponderant commercial interests were not naturally harmonious, the conference more and more developed points of disagreement, and eventually an adjournment was taken until the autumn. This adjournment was hastened by the intense heat, from which the German minister, who was not physically robust, specially suffered. This I can personally attest. I was present at all the conferences and prepared all the protocols, writing the last and longest of all on July 21, 1887, with the mercury at 103 degrees in the shade.

Soon after the conference adjourned, action was taken by Germany which was regarded in the United States as summary and unjustified. Popular excitement rose to a high pitch. Congress voted money for the defense of American rights. But Prince Bismarck, taking a practical view of the matter, proposed a resumption of the conference at Berlin. This proposal was accepted, but it fell to the administration of President Harrison to carry it out. Commissioners were duly sent to Berlin. Their instructions were originally drafted by William Henry Trescot, an accomplished South Carolinian who had in earlier days seen service in the Department of State of the United States and then in that of the Confederacy, and who, after the installation of President Hayes, was employed by Republican administrations in various important diplomatic transactions.

The great Berlin Congress of 1878, under the presidency of Prince Bismarck, settled the affairs of Europe in a month. The Samoan conference opened on April 29, 1889, and lasted forty-five days; a treaty, pompously called the General Act of Berlin, was concluded on June 14. As thirty days are to forty-five, so were the affairs of Europe to those of Samoa. It would have been but poetic justice had La Mamea been present. Bismarck had hoped to end the business promptly. He was willing even to restore the unstable Malietoa to the throne. He agreed, in deference to the American delegates, to conduct the proceedings in English; and he presented, through his son Count Bismarck, then minister for foreign affairs, a simple proposal for the protection of the life, property, and commerce of the nationals of the treaty-powers by common action, leaving the matter of native government largely to the natives. The British representative concurred in this proposal. Mr. Kasson, who, although not designated as chairman of the American delegation, really acted in that capacity, seems to have been favorably impressed; but his government would not so have it. In spite of the lesson experience had taught, the United States, still bent on the "consultative pact" or "entangling alliance," insisted on setting up some kind of tripartite foreign authority for the nominal maintenance of a native government. Its prolonged and "vigorous" insistence was duly rewarded. The General Act, in the name of preserving native rights, becomingly set up among the simple islanders an elaborate and complicated foreign mechanism scientifically classified as a *condominium*. This contrivance was specially characterized by things transcending native conceptions and repugnant to native traditions.

But the United States insisted that tuition be paid in the school of experience. Chief Justice Ide, one of our own best temporary contributions to Samoa, was not far wrong in saying that the *condominium* substituted several foreign kings for the one native king whom the natives were never willing to have. Experience again repeated itself. No sooner was the native figurehead restored than the other chiefs went into rebellion. The chief rebel this time was Mataafa, in whose behalf the blood and treasure of the United States were on a former occasion ready to be freely and copiously expended. Our duties and responsibilities as a great and enlightened power were not, however, to be shirked. As the proponent of the *condominium*, we joined our copartners in deporting him and certain other recalcitrant chiefs to the Marshall Islands, without taking with them their families.

This transaction, as I can personally testify, peculiarly appealed to the sensibilities of Judge Gresham, a man of warm heart and strong human feelings, who became secretary of state in President Cleveland's second administration. Much that had occurred under the *condominium* was at variance with his views of right and justice as well as of policy; and on May 9, 1894, he made to President Cleveland a report in which he declared that, soberly surveying the history of the relations of the United States with Samoa, nothing had been gained by the departure from our established policy of avoiding entangling alliances beyond the expenses, the responsibilities, and the inconveniences that had so far been its only fruits. Remarking, then, upon the propensity of the imagination to free itself from restraint when contemplating distant objects, he averred that the present entangling alliance not only had failed to correct but had even exaggerated the very evils it was designed to prevent. This clear and unequivocal sentence of condemnation was the beginning of the end. The creaking machinery either refused to work or worked badly. Difficulties accumulated. The three governments virtually superseded the officials of the *condominium* by reversing their decisions and acting directly for themselves. Commissioners were eventually sent out to survey the evils that had been done and to suggest a remedy. They unanimously reported that the defects of the tripartite government were radical and irremediable. The only thing left was a division of the group. The accomplishment of this process is fully detailed in the present volume. It was complicated and prolonged by persistent bargaining by Great Britain, but not by the United States. Formal overtures for a partition were, as I happen to know, preceded by informal soundings which were not reduced to writing. When consulted on the subject, at

Paris, in the autumn of 1898, I communicated to Washington my unconditional approval of the principle of partition as the only feasible solution. A year elapsed before the treaty of partition was finally concluded.

A speaker at a peace meeting, when summoned to explain his demand for a big navy, ingenuously replied that he wished to be in the fashion. Combined with this all-pervasive desire is the innate tendency of man, as a reasonable being, to find, as Franklin once remarked, a reason for whatever he wishes to do, and also, as I venture to add, to ascribe to himself higher motives than he does to others for doing it. While the United States was contending for the right of native self-government in Samoa, there was consummated within its own borders the virtual legal disfranchisement of a native element in its own population at least as capable of self-government as were the Samoans. I mention these things not for reproach, but only for reflection. Will the people of the United States heed the lesson? Will they be less disposed than they were half-a-century ago, in the full flush of their first release from two decades of domestic entanglements, benevolently to embark on foreign adventures from which the best that can be hoped for is an escape from disaster? Or will they, scenting the distant aroma, speed o'er land and sea to the romantic rescue of the scorching chestnuts in order that others, having in them a near, definite, and permanent possessory interest, may at a convenient time divide and enjoy them? Should they take such a course, Dr. Ryden may justly exclaim—

> "Thou canst not say I did it; never shake
> Thy gory locks at me!"

New York, February 10, 1933.

# PROPOSED EMBARGO ON EXPORTATION OF ARMS AND MUNITIONS OF WAR[1]

New York, N. Y., March 27, 1933.

The Hon. HAMILTON FISH, Jr.,
    Member of Congress, Washington, D. C.

MY DEAR MR. FISH: Although I am unable to appear at the hearing on the so-called arms embargo resolution on March 28, I feel it to be my duty to write you a few lines on the subject. I

1. Letter to the Hon. Hamilton Fish, March 27, 1933; reprinted from *Hearings*, pp. 14–17; House Report No. 22, part 2, pp. 5–9; *Army Ordnance* XIII (May-June, 1933), 323–325.

will first state the objections to the proposed measure as it stands, and will then point out how it may readily be made to conform to international law.

It will soon be twenty years since the outbreak in Europe of what eventually became known as the "World War." Following that unfortunate event there developed, in the ordinary course of things, a war madness, manifested in the exaltation of force and the belittling of the enduring legal and moral obligations which lie at the foundation of civilized life. Peaceful processes fell into disrepute. We began to hear of the "war to end war"; and pacifists, enamored of this shibboleth, espoused the shallow creed that international peace could best be assured by the use of force or threats of force. We were told that preexisting international law had suddenly become obsolete and that the world had entered upon a new era in which the general tranquillity was to be maintained by "sanctions," by boycotts, and by war. But the final stage was reached in the spawning of the notion, now rampant, that peoples may with force and arms exterminate one another without breach of the peace so long as they do not call it war. This may appropriately be called the stage of bedlam. In all this, however, students of history will find nothing new. The development of such manias normally characterizes the progress of a great war, just as their decline marks the return to sanity.

To the final stage to which I have referred belongs the supposition that the law of neutrality no longer exists, and that in future there will be no more neutrals. It is on this theory that the proposed resolution is essentially based. It is true that the resolution does not in terms say so; and it is equally true that less is just now said about this phase of the subject than was said not long ago. But it is only on this theory that the sweeping terms of the resolution can be defended.

As a lifelong student and administrator of international law, I do not hesitate to declare the supposition that neutrality is a thing of the past to be unsound in theory and false in fact. There is not in the world today a single government that is acting upon such a supposition. Governments are acting upon the contrary supposition, and in so doing are merely recognizing the actual fact. In the winter of 1922–23, there was held at The Hague an international conference to make rules for the regulation of the activities of aircraft and radio in time of war. The parties to this conference were the United States, France, Great Britain, Italy, Japan, and the Netherlands.

I had the honor to represent the United States in the conference and to be chosen to preside over it. We were able in the end to reach a unanimous agreement, which was incorporated in a general report. An examination of this report will show that it was largely devoted to the definition of the rights and duties of belligerents and of neutrals in time of war, and that it treated as still existing the Land War Neutrality Convention, the Convention for the Adaptation of the Geneva Convention to Maritime Warfare, and the convention concerning Neutral Rights and Duties in Maritime Warfare, all made at The Hague in 1907. The conference by which the report was adopted took place more than two years after the making of the Versailles Treaty and the Covenant of the League of Nations; the various delegations, it should be needless to state, acted under the authority and instructions of their respective governments; and yet, the idea that the law of neutrality had become obsolete never was suggested. So far as I am aware, not a single party to the Versailles Treaty or a single member of the League of Nations has ever actually taken the position that the law of neutrality is a thing of the past. The principal powers in the League have on occasion taken precisely the opposite position.

The fact is notorious that, after the Greeks were egged on to make war on the Turks and war actually came, Great Britain decided to remain neutral in the conflict, into which Canada and perhaps some of the other self-governing dominions unequivocally announced that they would not be drawn without their consent. In other recent wars Great Britain has pursued a neutral course. Other governments have done the same thing. No government, so far as I am advised, has repealed its neutrality laws. Those of the United States still remain on the statute books; and, if they are to be repealed, it should be done directly and not by implication or by embarking on a lawless course in the name of peace.

We hear much today of the duties of the United States as a "world power," and the supposition seems widely to prevail that we have only lately reached that eminence. I am too good an American to think so poorly of my country and its achievements. The United States has always been a world power. It acted as a world power when, on the outbreak of the wars growing out of the French Revolution, its first President, George Washington, with Thomas Jefferson as his Secretary of State, proclaimed our neutrality. It acted as a world power when, some years later, it suppressed the activities of the Barbary pirates.

It acted as a world power when, in 1812, it went to war in defense of neutral rights. It acted as a world power when it proclaimed the Monroe Doctrine. It acted as a world power in extending its trade and opening up foreign countries to its commerce, as it so effectually did by peaceful processes during the presidency of Gen. Andrew Jackson. It acted as a world power when it refused to permit the intervention of foreign nations in our Civil War. It acted as a world power when it forbade the further maintenance of the European empire set up in Mexico by French arms during our Civil War. It acted as a world power when, in the administration of President Grant, with Hamilton Fish as his Secretary of State, it brought about, through the greatest of all international arbitrations, the amicable settlement of the *Alabama* claims, and in so doing made a signal contribution to the further development of the law of neutrality. It is useless to continue the specification of instances. Nations, like individuals, may increase their power by combining with a due attention to their own business the extension of their friendly offices to brethren in trouble, and by conserving their militant resources for occasions when their vital interests are at stake. A nation that undertakes to meddle with every foreign disturbance is bound to become an international nuisance, to its own detriment as well as to the annoyance of other countries. Power is neither gained nor kept by such methods.

It is obvious that certain recent agitations have been and still are carried on under radically erroneous impressions as to the legal significance of the supply of arms and munitions of war to the parties to armed conflicts. The statement is often made that the trade in contraband is lawful, and the statement is also often made that such trade is unlawful. These statements may seem to be conflicting; but, when properly understood, they are both correct. Because there is much dispute as to what the term "contraband" includes, and because it has so far been deemed proper to limit the burdens to which a neutral power is subject, international law has not up to the present time required neutral governments to prevent their citizens from manufacturing, selling, and shipping contraband, including arms and munitions of war, in the regular course of commerce. Hence, in the sense that a neutral government is not obliged to suppress such trade, the trade is lawful. On the other hand, however, international law recognizes the right of a party to a war to prevent such articles from reaching its adversary, and, if it seizes them, to confiscate them. In other words, international law, treating the trade as being, in an international sense, intrinsically unneutral and unlawful, permits the parties to the struggle to inflict the penalty, and to this the trader's government cannot object. The trader conducts the business at his peril.

But, while a neutral government is not obliged to suppress

the contraband trade of its citizens, it is forbidden itself to supply contraband to a belligerent, and particularly is forbidden itself either to sell or to give to him munitions of war. Neutrality, in the legal sense, embraces not only impartiality but also abstention from participation in the conflict.[2] The prohibition of the neutral government itself to supply arms and munitions of war is based upon the unquestionable fact that the supply of such articles to a fighting force is a direct contribution to its military resources, and as such is a participation in the war; and, if a government does this, it virtually commits an act of war. If it does this in behalf of one of the parties, it abandons its neutrality and is guilty of armed intervention; and if it does it for both parties, although it may be said to be impartial, it does what neither of the parties themselves can do, namely, fights for each against the other. It is not long since the United States became, through an inadvertent failure to observe these elementary principles, involved in an unfortunate incident affecting a great and friendly American country, the Republic of Brazil. Happily, the intervention quickly ended, as the government in behalf of which it was committed abruptly disappeared, and in a few days we duly recognized its successor, as fifteen other governments promptly did.

From the elementary principles of international law above set forth it necessarily follows that, if a government bans the shipment of arms and munitions of war to one of the parties to an armed conflict and permits it to the other, it intervenes in the conflict in a military sense and makes itself a party to the war, whether declared or undeclared.

The pending resolution is, I do not hesitate to affirm, opposed to the settled policy and the highest interests of the United States and also to the provisions of our Federal Constitution. If adopted, it would enable the President (1) to make international engagements of the most far-reaching kind at his will, without the advice and consent of the Senate, and (2) to carry us into war without the prerequisite constitutional declaration of war by Congress. Perhaps it may be answered that by the proposed resolution the Senate would voluntarily abdicate its constitutional powers regarding international engagements, and that the Congress would likewise abdicate its constitutional powers regarding the declaration of war. This argument might be accepted if the Senate and the Congress could constitutionally divest themselves of their constitutional powers and commit everything to the Executive. But, as they were unwilling to do this during the so-called World War, when

2. Moore, *Digest of International Law*, VII, sec. 1288, p. 863.

it was proposed to give the President complete dictatorial powers, I can only suppose that the present extraordinary agitation is due to the misleading and somewhat deafening clamor of those who, in the name of peace, would confer upon the President an unlimited right to engage in hostilities.

I refrain from saying an unlimited right to make war only out of deference to the profound and learned authorities who assure us that war can be abolished either by calling it peace or by refraining from calling it war. This is, I may remark, a favorite notion with those who demand that the Kellogg pact shall be equipped with "teeth" in order that it may masticate alleged "aggressors," and otherwise benignantly bite and gnaw its way to universal peace and concord. Unfortunately, there are many who appear to have been infected with these confused notions, which have been so industriously propagated in the United States. But, judged by the course of the principal members of the League of Nations during the past ten years, and by their attitude toward the hostilities lately in progress in the Far East and elsewhere, such notions appear never to have had any real charm for the responsible authorities of the countries which would have been required to make the chief sacrifices in blood, in treasure, and in tears. To say this is not to impeach their wisdom or their sincerity. It may merely indicate that, having had enough of war, they long for real peace and an opportunity to recuperate.

Should the proposed measure become a law, no gift of prophecy is required to foretell what will follow. Groups moved by interest or swayed, consciously or unconsciously, by propaganda will clamor at the White House and at the Department of State for the unneutral application of the ban in favor of those whom they like or approve and against those whom they dislike or disapprove. We are assured that we may trust our authorities to resist such importunities, and to refrain from doing things that would involve the country in trouble. In other words, we are told that our authorities may be relied upon to refuse to exercise the powers so sweepingly conferred upon them. This is indeed a singular argument. Couched in the language of irresponsibility, it is not only self-stultifying but also unjust. The burdens and cares resting, especially at the present juncture, upon those who administer our affairs, are already grave and harassing enough, without imposing upon them the pastime of playing with war. Within the terms of the pending resolution, our Government would be asked to set itself up in rash and arrogant judgment upon the acts of other nations and on the merits of their conflicts, with a view to give or to permit military aid to one as against another.

Before committing ourselves to this presumptuous program, spun of the wild and flimsy fantasy that, when nations fall out and fight, the question of the "aggressor," which still baffles students even of ancient wars, lies upon the surface of things, and may be readily, safely, and justly determined by outsiders, of whose freedom from individual interest or bias there is no guarantee, we should reflect upon the fact that, had such a notion heretofore prevailed, we might and in all probability should ourselves have been the victim of it. As a marshaling of all the incidents would unduly prolong this letter, I will call attention to only two.

During our Civil War we were more than once menaced with the possibility of intervention, and, had it taken place, no one can say how fateful would have been the consequences. But, as an American, I share with my fellow countrymen, as members of a great and united people, the universal sense that it is well that we were not permanently divided.

On April 6, 1898, there assembled at the White House the diplomatic representatives of six great European powers, who made in behalf of their governments what was called "a pressing appeal to the feelings of humanity and moderation of the President and of the American People in their existing differences with Spain." We need not question the motives of the governments by which this remonstrance against our armed intervention was made. The President of the United States did not question their motives in his answer; but, with the conscious dignity that became himself as well as his great office, he expressed the confident expectation that the remonstrating powers would equally appreciate the effort of the United States "to fulfill a duty to humanity by ending a situation the indefinite prolongation of which had become insufferable." Two weeks later the Congress of the United States adopted a resolution under which the Government intervened with arms. The governments that had remonstrated against this step evidently did not regard Spain as the aggressor in the unhappy controversy between that country and the United States. The implication was clearly and directly to the contrary; and, according to the theory on which the pending resolution rests, the remonstrants, when the United States forcibly intervened might appropriately have declared an embargo upon the shipment of arms and munitions to this country, while continuing to supply Spain with the implements of war.

All this might, on the new theory, have been done in the name of peace, and, if the United States had exhibited resentment, this might have been treated only as further proof of its malevolent and aggressive disposition. It is better to reflect on such things while the opportunity still exists. It would be inexcusably short-sighted to assume that what has happened before will never happen again. We might also remember that our war for independence was treated by the great majority of powers merely as an act of rebellion against lawful authority. We waged the War of 1812 in support of disputed claims of national right. Many of our own people, including General Grant, have condemned our war with Mexico as an unjust aggression; but I am not aware that any of them has taken the ground that the general interest or the cause of peace would have been advanced if the powers of the world, some of which were not then themselves above suspicion, had combined their forces to oppose or to crush us.

If the real purpose back of the pending resolution is simply to prevent the United States from furnishing implements of war to those who are engaged in armed strife, this may readily be done by providing for a comprehensive, non-partisan embargo on the shipment of arms to all countries engaged in armed strife, whether international or civil. Such an embargo would naturally be announced and imposed by public proclamation. Of this no foreign power could complain. There are already various countries which, in accordance with their laws, impose such a ban. This is entirely proper under international law. Whether such an inhibition would, without the cooperation of all other neutral nations, tend to limit the area, the destructiveness or the duration of wars is a conjectural matter on which I do not now undertake to pass. Nor do I intend to discuss the question how far such a policy may tend to render weaker nations, financially unable to maintain munitions factories of their own, incapable of asserting or of defending their rights against larger powers. Considerations such as these lie within the domain of policy. The general bans, where they exist, are based upon the belief that, as the supply of arms and munitions constitutes a military aid, it is better and safer to forbid it altogether. In imposing upon itself such a restriction a nation acts within its undoubted rights, and gives no just cause for reproach.

Sincerely yours,

JOHN BASSETT MOORE.

# A FEW SUGGESTIONS FOR WORLD PEACE[1]

I AM very sorry that your kind letter of February 28 has so long remained unanswered. Unfortunately, I find that I cannot be present at the meeting of "Forty-Niners" on the evening of March 17th. My recollections of the old days are very pleasant. The Forty-Niners of Columbia College share with the Forty-Niners of the Pacific coast the possibility of being regarded as long-bearded specimens of a bygone age; but I do not shrink from the association, as we were alike engaged in digging gold. I also reckon myself fortunate that we delved in times when it was believed that there was unity in human history, and that the more we studied the past the more we were likely to know and understand the present.

I once heard John Marshall, the great Chief Justice of the United States and the father of our constitutional law, belittled because he had never seen an electric light or used a telephone. As he had thus lived in a dark age, and had not been irritated into activity by a little tinkling bell, it was supposed that his mind was sluggish, and that he neither was forward-looking nor looked forward. New mechanical devices facilitating intercommunication seem now to have created the impression that the world is wholly new, that men and women do not think as they thought before, and that all nations, except those that we at the moment dislike, are altogether unselfish and benevolent, and inspired solely by the desire to do one another good. This was not the philosophy of the Forty-Niners. Some of them may have believed in war, and there were others who believed in peace; but none of them believed in the destructive philosophy of "the war to end war" which has landed us in our present chaos and depression.

Observing the programme of the evening, I trust that I may, as a Forty-Niner, be permitted to express the hope that no connection will be found to exist between the present international crisis and the recent advances in electrochemistry. The Forty-Niners, although occasionally skeptical of schemes of spiritual progress, interposed no obstacles, fundamentalist or otherwise, to the advance of the physical sciences; nor, while they little de-

1. Letter to Frank Hackett, Secretary of the "Forty-Niners," read at their annual meeting in 1933, the phrase "Forty-Niners" meaning those who were officially connected with Columbia University when it was on 49th Street. Reprinted from the *Columbia Alumni News*, April 7, 1933.

bated the supposed conflict between Religion and Science, do I believe that any of them would have ascribed the present international crisis to religious causes.

In the old days there was a work called the Bible, which has, I hear, lately been retranslated into current English and therefore not unnaturally reviewed as a new book. Many of the Forty-Niners had read the old version; some loved it, and, while there were differences as to details, all more or less acknowledged its homely truths. Among these was the propensity of men to go astray, and the need of repentance, of which sackcloth, perhaps even with ashes, was the symbol. As nations are but aggregations of human beings, their propensities and duties are not different from those of individual men. During the past twenty years nations have gone astray on a huge scale. They have manifested to the full the spirit of greed and the propensity to violence, together with a readiness, almost unprecedented, falsely to accuse one another and to find self-righteous excuses for whatever they wished to do. Consequently, their first and greatest duty today, collectively and individually, is to confess their sins, to repair as far as possible the wrongs they have done one another, to refrain from threats of war, whether open or disguised by specious phrases, and, recalling Mr. Kellogg's wise and reassuring declaration that, where two nations fall out and fight, both may plead self-defense, lend their impartial good offices to brethren in trouble and in a spirit of kindness co-operate in bringing about an amicable adjustment. Until this primary duty shall have been performed, disarmament conferences will continue to be essentially characterized by unwilling, irritating, insincere proposals, of which no one should be the dupe, and the spirit of peace will be stifled with plans for the use of force.

## PAN AMERICANISM: ITS MEANING AND SIGNIFICANCE[1]

NEARLY fifty years ago, on my first entrance into the Department of State, at Washington, I began to take a particular interest in the affairs of the independent countries of America, now represented in the Pan American Union. Since that time I have co-operated in every possible way, officially and unofficially, in efforts to cultivate among these countries friendly sentiments and good understanding;

1. Statement issued for Pan American Day, 1933.

and, in spite of any and all disappointments, I am not discouraged. On the contrary, taking the world as a whole, the nations of America have no reason to shrink from a comparison.

During the past hundred and forty years there have been two general wars, more or less worldwide in extent. These are (1) the wars growing out of the French Revolution and the Napoleonic Wars, running through more than twenty years, and (2) the recent so-called World War. Few will be found to deny that the unexampled depression now weighing upon the entire world is directly attributable to the so-called World War and to the infatuations that pervaded it and found expression in the treaties of peace by which it was only nominally ended. This war, like the general war that came to a close a hundred years before, was wholly European in its origin. No American nation did anything to bring it on, or in any way contributed to its causes. I say this not in a spirit of reproach, but only with a view to forestall the inclination hastily to impute any unfavorable conditions now existing in the Americas to causes purely local. They are largely attributable to the general dislocation and distress.

Several decades ago, there were writers who proposed to abolish what they called the "old doctrine" of the equality of Independent States and to put in its place the "new doctrine" that the Great Powers had, by their virtuous conduct and example, gained, under modern international law, a "Primacy" among their fellows which promised to develop into a central authority for the settlement of all disputes between the nations of Europe. In spite of the fact that this compound of dogma and prophecy was so completely discredited when the Great Powers fell out and went to war among themselves, we are still asked to accept shallow schemes for the maintenance of peace and concord among nations by paramount force. I observe, however, that in the recently proposed Non-aggression and Conciliation agreement between the Republics of America, it is expressly provided that in no case shall they resort to "intervention," that is, to measures looking immediately or eventually to the use of force, should the parties decline to accept what they recommended.

If to this proposal it should be objected that long experience has shown that such an expedient will fail permanently to preserve peace, we may at once convincingly answer that recent and current experience has glaringly demonstrated that threats of force not only will not preserve peace but that they may even tend to produce war rather than peace. The so-called World War was at one time much vaunted as a "war to end war"; but, in view of what has taken place, a person who should now assert that that boast was justified would be a fit subject for a psychologist.

In the future, just as in the past, the world must rely for the preservation of peace mainly upon the employment of peaceful methods, such as conciliation, mediation and arbitration, which, while tending to tranquillize the minds of the disputants, also afford to those who offer their services in the cause of peace an opportunity to reach just conclusions. Such has ever been the ideal of the Union of American Republics formed in the First International American Conference, which assembled at Washington in 1889. Among my most gratifying recollections is the circumstance that I was present at the opening of that great assemblage, and later took a humble part in the furtherance of its objects. Not only the nations of America, but all nations, have reason to be thankful for what was done on that occasion. To promote the harmony of a part of the world is to contribute to the harmony of all the world. In the prompt and cordial acceptance of the award just rendered by the special tribunal of arbitration on the vexed boundary dispute between Guatemala and Honduras, American nations have furnished a gratifying proof that the spirit of peace based on justice still survives. Let us hope that the promptings of reason heard in this instance may spread to other quarters; and to this end let each nation now at peace exert all its influence to limit existing areas of conflict, and to allay the chaos of the thought and passion in which the world has been too long engulfed.


# RECONCILIATION[1]


A YEAR ago I had the honor and the pleasure to be present at the celebration of Pan American Day under the auspices of the Pan American Society, and I am today happy again to enjoy that privilege. Meanwhile, the clouds that overhung the sky at the time of our last assembling have not passed away. We then met in the spirit of hope, and this spirit we must continue to cherish; but it has been well said that hope deferred maketh the heart sick, and it is idle to try to shut our eyes to what is actually before us.

In some remarks of mine, read and circulated on Pan American Day last year, I ventured to remonstrate against the sophism, which various supposed peace agencies, national and

1. Address before the Pan American Society, April 11, 1933.

international, have lately been trying to popularize, that the appropriate cure for war is more war. The prevalence just now of this strange notion may be traced to the so-called World War, which it was sought to glorify by calling it "the war to end war." Unfortunately, many became so infatuated with this alliteration that they thought it would be a good thing to perpetuate the principle in the provisions of the treaties of peace; and the happy effects are now perfectly exemplified in the frenzy that grips and affrights practically the entire world. During the past year this frenzy has not abated; it has, on the contrary, increased. The spirit of nationalism has become more and more proscriptive. Hatreds have been more and more inflamed. Restrictions upon commerce have been made more and more crushing. Such developments have inevitably increased the danger of war, and new wars have accordingly broken out. And yet, in the face of this glaring exposure of the fallacy that peace and good will among men may be created by violence, we still hear that the tranquillity of the world may be promoted and stabilized by boycotts, by playing fast and loose with the law of neutrality, and by the extension of the area of wars. As one who has had a long and intimate acquaintance and association with men of arms, with the men who will be called on to do the fighting if war breaks out, I may say that this is not the prevalent view among such persons. Wars are not brought about by the officers of our Army and our Navy. Not infrequently, however, they have been fomented by agitations recklessly conducted by persons who professed a special abhorrence of war.

Utterly rejecting the theory that the reign of peace is to be established on earth by violence, I take as my text today the sentiment of "Reconciliation."

The true and only foundation of peace among men is the concession to each of that which is justly his due. Perhaps in no period of history has this fundamental principle been more signally denied and more recklessly flouted than during the past twenty years. Through wars nations have been rent asunder; and peace has been made not in the spirit of justice, of mercy or of magnanimity, but in the spirit of vengeance. Such things have been done before; they have indeed been done habitually. But we profess to be better than our ancestors. There are many who maintain that we are living in a new world; that even human nature, or at any rate that part of it which is represented by themselves, has undergone a radical change; and that, being the heir of all the ages and in the foremost files of time, we have a will to peace such as never existed before. This frame of mind is, however, as old as the world. It may be correctly described as emotional hypocrisy. It is an emanation of that scourge of humanity, self-righteousness, which leads each group and each nation to regard whatsoever it does as right and whatsoever any other group or nation may do as wrong.

Let no people, let no nation claim that it is entirely free from this spirit. No doubt perfect justice is unattainable in this world. But there is an ideal of justice towards which every nation, every people, every individual should aspire. This ideal can be attained only through the reconciliation of our conflicting views and our conflicting interests. We are not all alike. No two men and no two women are alike. No two nations are alike. We differ in race, we differ in creed, we differ in color; and, as each group inclines to regard the things in which it differs from others as marks of its own superiority, all differences tend to provoke antagonism. This tendency is general and obdurate, but the fact that it is general and obdurate does not relieve us of the duty of contending against it.

The antithesis of reconciliation is war. The motives and objects of war have been various; but, as war is a contention by force, it is waged for victory. The struggle, as it progresses, becomes more and more intense. Each day brings its tale of death and of desolation. Griefs accumulate; the passions burn more fiercely; the hoarse cry of vengeance grows louder and more insistent, and the cases are rare in which the peace that is extorted does not by humiliating conditions sow the seeds of future wars. By no one has this tragic truth been more impressively stated than by a celebrated French soldier and diplomatist of the eighteenth century, to whose lot it fell both to make war and to make peace. I will quote his words:

A humiliating peace is but an outrageous affront which the vanquished tremblingly endure. It embitters their resentment; they will bear it only so long as may be necessary to recover from their wounds. Accepting it in fear, they will break it without remorse; and the gods whom they forswear will approve their efforts. Then, on both sides, a ruthless frenzy will make the war bloody and the hate everlasting; will bring exhaustion, terror, oppression, slavery, shame and destruction. These are the bitter fruits of every humiliating peace: the law forever prostrate, the truce forever a sham.

In the spirit of this solemn protest let us pledge ourselves today to strive for peace through reconciliation. We meet here as citizens and representatives of the nations of America. Each of us is supposed to love and certainly ought to love his own country, but this cannot excuse us for being on bad terms with our neighbors. The Pan American Union was organized as an agency of peace. In its constitution there is no provision for coercion. Its fundamental principle is the equal recognition of rights. Its motto is impartiality. Its processes are conference, conciliation, and arbitration. In a world rent with strife it has labored for concord, seeking to still the voice of passion and to stay the course of violence. In the cultivation of mutual understanding, it has the unofficial but efficient co-operation of the Pan American Society. Let us invoke upon both the blessings of Heaven, and pray that they may live long and prosper.

# AN APPEAL TO REASON[1]

## I. THE NEW PSYCHOLOGY

THE April number of *Foreign Affairs* was conspicuous for an exhibition of telepathy, given in its first and second articles. This was very appropriate, as international relations often depend not so much on knowledge, experience and wise maxims as on temporary psychological conditions caused by accident, by oratory, by confused impulses and by craft, against the effects of which statesmen should ever safeguard their countries by avoiding the nebulous commitments and legal uncertainties that so readily contribute to senseless and destructive wars.

The first article, written by Mr. Stimson, lately Secretary of State, says in substance that certain measures adopted since the so-called World War, chief among which are the Covenant of the League of Nations and the Kellogg Pact, prove the existence of a new psychology, a new will to peace such as the world has never known before; and this, in spite of the daily demonstration throughout the world of a frenzied state of mind rampantly manifested in armed hostilities and in a spirit of intolerance such as is rarely seen.

The second article, written by Professor Taussig, of Harvard, treats of changes which he deems to be necessary in our commercial policy in order that we may bear our proper part in promoting the peace and prosperity of the world as well as our own. This article tells us that our tariffs ever since 1909 have dealt with foreign countries "simply and solely on the penalty basis—the threat basis, or, if you please, the holding up of a club"; that they "offered nothing in the way of concession"; that the crowning demonstration of what may be called our emergence from "isolation" and our moral regeneration and will to peace—the Tariff Act of 1930—put into the hands of the President the still stronger weapon of the complete exclusion of the products of any country that was conceived to discriminate against us; and that, while flourishing the club with ever-increasing violence, we changed our traditional interpretation and application of the most-favored-

1. Published, in abridged form, in *Foreign Affairs*, XI (July, 1933), 547–588. Reprinted in *The Manchoukuo Question in Its Wider Aspects* by Seiji Hishida, Ph.D., Columbia University (Tokyo, 1934), pp. 45–88.

nation clause in such a manner as to breed "friction, animosity, commercial warfare," particularly among our allies in the late war, and especially with "our nearest neighbor, our best customer," Canada. This sentence of condemnation is the more impressive because it is accompanied with a confession by Professor Taussig of error and change of heart in certain particulars on his own part, and with the declaration that we should now "turn from economic threat and economic war to friendly offer and friendly intercourse." Accepting these statements just as they are made, I forbear to debate the question whether the maxim that the tariff is "purely a domestic question" has inspired recent efforts, by means of international conferences, to heal the wounds and mitigate the resentments that continue to characterize commercial competition, the tranquilizing influence of which so many professed advocates of peace would now, on high moral grounds, re-enforce by boycotts. Such inquiries are, however, relatively unimportant. What we are now concerned with is the nature of the proof of humanity's alleged rebirth.

Nothing could more convincingly betray the fustian texture of the new psychology and will to peace than the circumstance that among its postulates there is not one which is not contrary to palpable realities, to the teachings of history, and to the formulation, in universal legal principles, of the results of all human experience.

Fortunately, we are able to diagnose the supposedly new state of mind with unusual exactness. It is scientifically traced back to the radical change in human nature which, first manifested in calling the World War a "war to end war," led to the formation of the League of Nations. The League, it is said, has not only prevented war but has "developed, particularly among the nations of Europe, a community of spirit which can be evoked to prevent war." But this was only the first lurch. It was, we are assured, nine years later, in 1928, that there was taken the "still more sweeping step," the culminant leap, in the signing of the "Pact of Paris," vicariously known as the Kellogg or Kellogg-Briand Pact, to which sixty-two nations are now parties.

Before this Pact, we are told, international law had largely been "a development of principles based upon the existence of war" and its "legality;" while the law of neutrality imposed upon neutrals the duty not only "to maintain impartiality" between the belligerents but even to refrain from passing "moral judgment" on the rightfulness or wrongfulness of the cause of either party, "at least to the extent of translating such a judgment into action." Such is the scant presentment of that unlovely and suddenly obsolete thing known as international law, with its immoral element of neutrality that is now to be transmuted into war in the interest of peace.

But this is only a modest beginning. We are assured that the Kellogg Pact showed a change in "world public opinion toward former customs and doctrines" so revolutionary that many have not been able to grasp it; a "revolution in human thought born of the consciousness that unless some such step was taken modern civilization might be doomed"; a revolution so radical that "war has become illegal throughout practically the entire world." In consequence, war, it is said, is "no longer to be the source and subject of rights"; its very existence "makes one or both parties wrongdoers, to be denounced as lawbreakers"; and that so "many legal precedents" have in consequence been rendered "obsolete" as to impose "on the legal profession the task of reëxamining codes and treatises." The Kellogg Pact would, indeed, seem to have overturned almost everything except the Versailles Treaty, which, with the gyroscopic aid of the League of Nations, has continued to ride on an even keel. But, even this proud ship may be facing a compulsory change of course, as Signor Mussolini, holding aloft the Pact as his sextant, is demanding a reckoning. Under all the circumstances, it is no wonder that any cold analysis of what the Pact really is should be deprecated as an attempt to reduce it to a mere gesture and to destroy the faith of the world in efforts for peace. We are therefore properly expected to be content with the information that "the only limitation" to the Pact's "broad covenant" against war is "the right of self-defense"—a right, it is declared, "so inherent and universal that it was not deemed necessary even to insert it expressly in the treaty." But, lest some doubting Thomas might suggest that an "inherent and universal" limitation might prove to be troublesome if not nullifying, we are summarily assured that it "does not weaken the treaty," since the "limits" of the limitation "have been clearly defined by countless precedents." Unsatisfied readers of this assurance have been trying to conjecture what these precedents may be.

But of the exposition of the radical and revolutionary nature of the Kellogg Pact something more yet remains to be told. The Covenant of the League of Nations is associated in the public mind probably more with its proposed "sanctions" than with anything else; and this is, I venture to think, unfortunate. The Covenant provides for "arbitration," for "judicial settlement," for investigation, for mediatorial offices, and for a Permanent Court of International Justice, which was established more than ten years ago. But such processes are too insipid. They excite less interest and receive less attention than current local scandals. The "sanctions," which are both economic and military, bulk more largely, as they point towards war, unless war has just now become obsolete. But it is not treated as obsolete by the Covenant. The Covenant is redolent of it. By Article 16 any member of the League resorting to "war" in disregard of certain provisions is deemed to have committed an "act of war" against all the other members, which are then to sever and prohibit all intercourse, financial or commercial, with the Covenant-breaking state, and to unite in military measures on land, on sea and in the air against it. It may also be expelled from the League.

To these provisions, in which "war" is the dominant note, the Kellogg Pact does present a perfect contrast. The Pact, as we are told, "provides no sanctions." But we are invited to tread on highly controversial ground when we are asked to believe that the Pact "does not require any signatory to intervene with measures of force" in case it is "violated"; that, resting instead "upon the sanction of public opinion" and "the will . . . to make it effective," "it will be irresistible" if the people of the world "desire to make it effective"; that the "critics who scoff at it have not accurately appraised the evolution of world opinion since the World War"; and that the Hoover-MacDonald declaration at Rapidan in October, 1929, that their governments were resolved to accept the Pact not only as a declaration of good intentions but as a positive obligation to direct national policy in accordance with its pledge, "marked an epoch." How a declaration of the parties to a pledge that they mean to keep it can be said to mark an epoch, we need not inquire. But the intimation that those who regard the Pact alone as practically futile are unfriendly scoffers can by no means be accepted; for, among those who now insistently demand that it be furnished with "teeth," with which to affright and bite aggressors, the most conspicuous are those who, before it was signed, acclaimed it as a self-enforcing device. Nothing has caused so much scoffing or suspicion as this change of front.

In order to ensure entire precision, I have explained the new psychology in the very words used by Mr. Stimson, its authoritative exponent and sponsor, in two issues of *Foreign Affairs*.[2] Mr. Stimson, just as might have been expected, has not changed front on the Kellogg Pact. He still says that its efficacy must depend on public opinion and not on force. It is only when the sanctions of the Covenant and the alleged "decisions" of the League are invoked that he welcomes, as agencies of peace, the

2. *Foreign Affairs*, Supplement, October, 1932; and April, 1933.

menaces and measures of war which the Covenant prescribes. I have no quarrel with Mr. Stimson. He is present in my reflections only as the spokesman, and as a sincere spokesman, of a group identified with a certain type of mind and thought, and with a belief in methods and measures which I, who modestly pray for peace in my own time, profoundly distrust not only because they have no visible moorings on earth or in the sky, but also because they have infected many of my countrymen with confused notions of law and of conduct which, while they endanger our own most vital interests, hold out hopes of partisan intervention that encourage European governments to defer the readjustments which only they can make and which are essential to peace and tranquillity in that quarter. As long as we persist in our misguided rôle, so long will discussions of disarmament be dominated by thoughts of war rather than of peace.

## II. THE KELLOGG PACT

As the Kellogg Pact is invoked as the crowning proof of the world's recent regeneration, I will now state just what it is. I give it the name of its putative author, as M. Briand neither proposed nor formulated the multilateral agreement that was eventually signed. From time immemorial treaties of amity and commerce have contained a declaration that there shall be "perpetual amity," or a "perfect, firm and inviolable peace," between the contracting parties. The Kellogg Pact does not go so far. Resolved into its elements, it comprises two things: first, a general renunciation of war "as an instrument of national policy"; and secondly, a general pledge to settle all differences by peaceful negotiation. What M. Briand on June 20, 1927, proposed was an exclusive pact between France and the United States renouncing war "as an instrument of their policy towards each other," and pledging the two countries to settle their disputes by pacific means. There was also a florid preamble, very loosely drawn, in which the proposed contractants were spoken of as "two nations that no war has ever divided," the formal and serious maritime war of 1798, which actively continued until September 30, 1800, having been overlooked. But, for reasons of domestic and of foreign policy which may be surmised, M. Briand's proposal of an exclusive renunciation and pledge was not acceptable. There was delay; and six months had elapsed when on December 28, 1927, Mr. Kellogg suddenly fluttered the Eagles in the European dovecotes by proposing to France a renunciation and pledge in which all the principal governments of the world should unite. The Eagles anxiously exchanged notes, but soon found common ground in the discovery that they all had national policies, no matter how divergent they might be. They also remembered that the United States had its Monroe Doctrine. Then there was the Lansing-Ishii agreement, which recognized the "special relations" resulting from "territorial propinquity" and the consequent "special interests" of Japan in China; and which, although formally cancelled in 1923, left a visible trail of implications. Nevertheless, the phrase "national policy" had a dubious history. Even the United States had been charged with having asserted the Monroe Doctrine brusquely, if not aggressively, on occasions which some of the Eagles could hardly have forgotten. It was important that the phrase should be muffled, and this the Eagles proceeded to do.

We need not go into all the notes that were exchanged. It suffices to mention that which the British Government, speaking individually but with the loud acclaim of the Eagles, presented on May 19, 1928; a note which, after quoting "the renunciation of war as an instrument of national policy," declared that there were "certain regions of the world the welfare and integrity of which" constituted "a special and vital interest" for that government's "peace and safety," and that, as their protection against attack was "a measure of self-defense," no "interference" with them could be "suffered." The regions, it will be observed, were not named; and complete liberty as to their future designation was thus reserved. Then, in order effectually to preclude subsequent challenge or quibble, there was added this unequivocal condition: "It must be clearly understood that His Majesty's Government in Great Britain accept the new treaty upon the distinct understanding that it does not prejudice their freedom of action in this respect." The way for this addition had indeed been thoughtfully paved by Mr. Kellogg himself in a public address three weeks before, in which he declared that nothing in the proposed treaty in any way restricted or impaired "the right of self-defense"; that this right was "inherent in every sovereign state" and "implicit in every treaty"; and that each nation "alone is competent to decide whether circumstances require recourse to war in self-defense."

In thus assuring to belligerents, each of which decides that it acted in self-defense, the right to fight out their differences in peace, the new and regenerate psychology is for once superior to the old. Should it be said that this reduces the Pact to a bare expression of a sentiment and a moral obligation to act upon it, it is altogether to Mr. Kellogg's credit that he dealt with the matter with his usual candor and without evasion. I have always surmised that Senator Borah, as an advocate of the "outlawry of war," played in this transaction a larger part than is generally known, especially as I observed that in the national campaign of 1928 he did not abate his appeals for the maintenance of an effective navy—not, of course, for the purpose of providing the renunciation of war with "teeth," but for the purpose of enabling the United States to exercise the right of self-defense that had been so amply safeguarded.

The notes in which the interpretations and conditions of the signatories were expressed, including that of Great Britain of May 19, 1928, were mentioned in and annexed to the circular note which the United States addressed on June 23, 1928, to France, Germany, Great Britain, Italy, Japan, and certain other governments, formally inviting them to accept the Pact as thus explained. It was accordingly signed at Paris on August 27, 1928. As the signing of a contract with a mental reservation is both illegal and dishonest, so no government can be supposed to have signed the Pact with an intention to deny or to repudiate the recorded conditions on which it was accepted. By M. Briand those conditions were specially cherished because they embraced a concession to his demand that the later renunciation of war should never be asserted to interfere with the full application of the war-making provisions of the Covenant. Nor, so far as concerned the recognition of local special interests, whether claimed by Great Britain, by the United States, by Japan, or by any other power, can they be said to have introduced anything new. The only distinctive phases of the Monroe Doctrine were the vastness of the area to which it applied and the specification of the grounds on which it was to be invoked. Otherwise, it merely enunciated a principle as old as mankind: the natural and instinctive principle that peoples are more deeply concerned in what directly affects them and takes place at their doors than in what is remote.

On this principle every nation has from time to time acted. Nor could we do anything but wish the parties to the Kellogg Pact to observe their renunciation of war as an instrument of national policy and their promise peacefully to settle their differences. But when I am told that the making of the renunciation and the promise constitute an epoch in history, and denote on the part of the signatories, or even of any of them, a radical change in their attitude toward war and toward the use of the vast armaments which they continue to maintain and show so much reluctance to reduce, I can hardly be reproached for recalling the Law and the Prophets and the Sermon on the Mount. On these foundations great churches have been built, and untold millions still worship at their shrines. Fundamentally, they all teach brotherly kindness, justice, and peace; and yet, the most heavily armed and most warlike of modern nations have been those that profess the Christian faith. It is these that brought to the Far East the modern implements of war. I would not destroy the nimbus of the Kellogg Pact; but when I am asked to believe that the renunciation and the promise complete a moral revolution, said to have begun during the World War, more radical than the commands of the Almighty and the precepts of Christ, and all vows of obedience to them, had been able to effect, I am asked to exhibit a credulity beyond the capacity of common minds.

No wonder that, as M. Paul-Boncour, M. Briand's great friend, has authoritatively told us,[3] the Kellogg Pact was for M. Briand, before all else, a means to draw the United States, the decisive factor in Allied victory, into the League of Nations. For, asks the spokesman of M. Briand's thoughts, could it be imagined that when some "aggressor" had torn up the Covenant, and the sanctions of Article 16 were set in motion against him, the United States, the initiator of the Pact, would remain indifferent to its violation and would not "throw into the duel" for peace the weight of the power which, as France had not forgotten, nothing could resist? Evidently it never occurred to M. Briand that France could ever be voted an "aggressor," or that the United States could ever be so voted so long as she fought for France. This was both ingenuous and logical, and worthy of M. Briand's clear intelligence. But, when I reflect on his eagerness to draw permanently into the service of an organization which France and her political allies and sympathizers have so largely dominated the irresistible military power of the United States, I cannot limit my recollections of that great statesman to his efforts for several years before his untimely death to bring about a better understanding between France and Germany; nor does it detract from the merit of those efforts that they were no less in the interest of France than in that of Germany. M. Briand began his political career, as so many other French statesmen have done, as a Socialist; and, while Socialism in France is not just what the American people suppose Socialism to be, it is associated with the idea of benevolence. This quality M. Briand possessed. Nevertheless, I do not forget how, as a member of government in 1911, when diplomatic tension between France and another country suddenly developed, he emerged as a "man of iron," and, calling

3. *The New York Times*, April 10, 1932.

railway strikers to the colors, compelled them to man the trains. Nor is it conceivable that if called to choose between France, even though she might not be clearly in the right, and the rest of the world, he could for an instant have hesitated to follow the fortunes of his native land, which he loved and served so long and so well.

### III. TELLTALE ARMAMENTS

Let us further test the world's alleged rebirth. While I personally do not believe that the maintenance by a country of an effective army and navy denotes a desire, either general or specific, for war, a study of national armaments may furnish a conclusive answer to the question whether a new will to peace has really overcome us. For this purpose I will compare the military and naval preparations in 1914 with those in 1932 of the principal agents in the regeneration that began in Europe in 1914. In the Versailles Treaty the British Empire, France, Italy, Japan and the United States figure as the Principal Allied and Associated Powers, but Russia was originally among them; among the powers classed as minor, which include numerous American countries, we may mention Belgium, Poland, Roumania, Czechoslovakia and Yugoslavia. Of the minor group I give, for 1914, only the figures for Belgium, Roumania and Serbia. In all cases I will omit men available for unorganized services, and give only active forces and trained reserves.

The war strength of the Central Powers and of the Allied and Associated Powers, as given in *The World Almanac, 1914,* is shown by the following tables:[4]

### WAR STRENGTH OF THE CENTRAL POWERS, 1914

| Countries | Actives | Reserves | Total |
|---|---|---|---|
| Germany | 870,000 | 4,430,000 | 5,300,000 |
| Austria-Hungary | 390,000 | 1,610,000 | 2,000,000 |
| Bulgaria | 60,500 | 320,500 | 381,000 |
| Turkey | 400,000 | 300,000 | 700,000 |
| Totals | 1,720,500 | 6,660,500 | 8,381,000 |

4. I take the figures from *The World Almanac, 1914,* lest those given in the issue of 1915 may include increases in 1914 during which the war broke out. The figures in the *Statesman's Year-Book* for the same year are somewhat different, but they do not effect any substantial change.

## WAR STRENGTH OF THE ALLIED AND ASSOCIATED POWERS, 1914

| Countries | Active | Reserves | Total | |
|---|---|---|---|---|
| France | 720,000* | 3,280,000 | 4,000,000 | |
| Great Britain | 254,500 | 476,500 | 731,000 | Triple |
| Russia | 1,290,000 | 3,300,000 | 4,590,000 | Entente |
| Totals | 2,264,500 | 7,056,500 | 9,321,000 | |
| Belgium | 42,000 | 180,000 | 222,000 | |
| Servia | 32,000 | 208,000 | 240,000 | |
| Italy | 250,000 | 950,000 | 1,200,000 | |
| Roumania | 95,000 | 100,000 | 195,000 | |
| United States | 89,604† | | | |
| Japan | 250,000 | 950,000 | 1,200,000 | |
| Totals | 3,023,104 | 9,444,500 | 12,378,000 | |

* Including colonial troops.
† Exclusive of National Guard and Militia of the States.

Turning now to armaments in 1932, an examination of them startlingly suggests that the victors in the "war to end war" are, so far as concerns the new faith, unconvinced believers who are as skeptical of their own conversion as they are of the conversion of what they left of their former enemies. Germany, dismembered, reduced in population, deprived of colonies and financially doomed by reparations, was restricted by the Versailles Treaty to an active force of 100,500 men, with no trained reserves. We hear, however, charges of "bootleg" armaments, the value of which, were not full details strategically withheld for some useful occasion, we might be specially qualified to discuss, as the United States enjoys a monopoly of armed bootleggers. Austria, left by the peace with hardly enough territory to sustain Vienna, her historic capital, at whose gates the Turks centuries ago were twice hurled back and Western Europe saved from an Ottoman invasion, is restricted to an active force of 21,200. Hungary now has an active force of 35,000. Bulgaria is limited to 33,000. Banished Turkey comes off best, with 133,000 actives and 532,800 reserves, making a total of 665,800 men. Were these four powers now allied, their combined actives would number 322,700 and their reserves 532,800, making a total war strength of 855,500.

The appalling unbelief of the European victors is shown by the following totals of war strength:[5]

5. The following figures are taken from *The World Almanac, 1933.*

| Countries | Actives | Reserves | Total |
|-----------|---------|----------|-------|
| France | 607,000 | 6,328,000 | 6,935,000 |
| Great Britain | 206,811 | 295,313 | 502,124 |
| Italy | 457,189 | 6,017,500 | 6,474,689 |
| Poland | 332,100 | 1,645,000 | 1,977,100 |
| Belgium | 89,224 | 495,000 | 584,224 |
| Czechoslovakia | 138,000 | 1,489,000 | 1,627,000 |
| Roumania | 244,850 | 1,485,550 | 1,730,400 |
| Yugoslavia | 138,934 | 1,447,724 | 1,586,658 |
| Totals | 2,214,108 | 19,203,087 | 21,417,195 |

Battered Russia, who now flocks by herself, is credited with 848,600 actives and 18,000,000 reserves; but she has signed the Kellogg Pact, aggressively specializes in non-aggression agreements, and constantly exasperates regenerates by proposing more radical reductions of armaments than they consider safe. Japan upholds the faith of the Far East with 225,000 actives and 1,952,000 reserves, making a war total of 2,177,000 men. To China there is attributed a military strength of nearly 2,000,000, but they are disunited. The United States bobs up feebly with 132,069 actives and 307,120 reserves, making a total of 439,189. But no one can forget the demonstration of latent but irresistible power, and of aptitude for correct consultative leadership that filled M. Briand with confident expectations.

But this is not all. To the impressive totals of man-power just disclosed, and the increased effectiveness of the previously familiar implements of war, we must now add various new death-dealing agencies, including poison gases, which all the regenerates are now diligently manufacturing, and the terrorising air forces that swarm in the sky. In military air forces Great Britain is credited with 45,433 men; France, with 40,005; Italy, with 23,452; the United States with 13,369. The figures for 1929–1930 gave the United States 27,324 men, the British Empire 34,737, France 32,554, Italy 22,193, Japan 16,821.

Naval figures for 1914, because of the subsequent replacement of certain large types of ships with smaller and more effective types, the changes in the character and quality of armament, and the increased range of guns, do not of themselves furnish a basis for accurate comparisons of fighting power. Great Britain's 671 naval craft, with a personnel of 146,000 and a reserve of 50,077 seamen, included super-dreadnoughts, dreadnoughts, pre-dreadnought battleships, cruisers, light cruisers, torpedo gunboats, gunboats, 248 destroyers, 100 torpedo boats, and 85 submarines; France's 388 consisted of dreadnoughts, pre-dreadnoughts, armored cruisers, protected cruisers, torpedo gunboats, 159 torpedo boats, 87 destroyers and 76 submarines; with a total reserve of 114,000 men, of whom about 25,500 are serving with the fleet; Italy's 190 included dreadnoughts, pre-dreadnoughts, armored cruisers, protected cruisers, torpedo gunboats, 35 destroyers, 86 torpedo boats and 25 submarines, with a personnel of 39,927; Russia's 117 embraced dreadnoughts, pre-dreadnoughts, armored cruisers, protected cruisers, over 80 destroyers, some torpedo boats, and some submarines, the number not being given, with a personnel of 53,500; Japan's 152 included dreadnoughts, pre-dreadnoughts, armored cruisers, torpedo gunboats, 52 destroyers, 30 torpedo boats and 13 submarines, with a personnel of 51,730; the United States' 164 included dreadnoughts, pre-dreadnoughts, monitors, armored cruisers, protected cruisers, scouts, 50 destroyers, 19 torpedo boats, and 34 submarines, with a personnel of 64,780 and a naval militia of 7,526.

Turning now to the "enemy group," in 1914, Germany's 333 naval craft consisted of dreadnoughts, pre-dreadnoughts, old coast service battleships, armored cruisers, 38 protected cruisers, 152 destroyers, 47 old torpedo boats, and 37 "or more" submarines, with a personnel of 73,000 plus a reserve of about 110,000 men. Austria-Hungary's modest 122 contained dreadnoughts, pre-dreadnoughts, armored cruisers, cruisers, torpedo gunboats, 18 destroyers, 63 torpedo boats and 6 submarines, with a personnel of 17,920; Turkey's 27 consisted of dreadnoughts, old battleships, cruisers, torpedo gunboats, 8 destroyers and 9 torpedo boats, with a personnel of 30,929 and 9,000 marines.

In 1932, the "enemy group," reckoned as possibly unregenerate, does not bulk largely in naval statistics. Austria no longer figures at all as a naval power, nor does Hungary or Turkey. Germany has built some "pocket" battleships, which, as the sobriquet would suggest, seem to be classed, rather more than less, as concealed deadly weapons, on which the law looks with disfavor.

On the other hand, the reputable naval forces of the United States, the British Empire, Japan, France, and Italy are given in the following table of underage vessels, "underage" meaning vessels which, under the Washington and London treaties of 1922 and 1930, cannot as yet be replaced with other ships:[6]

6. Based on *The World Almanac, 1933*.

| Type | United States | | British Empire | | Japan | | France | | Italy | |
|------|-----|------|-----|------|-----|------|-----|------|-----|------|
| | No. | Tons | No. | Tons | No. | Tons | No. | Tons | No. | Tons |
| Capital ships | 14 | 429,300 | 15 | 473,650 | 10 | 298,400 | 6 | 133,134 | 4 | 86,532 |
| Aircraft carriers | 3 | 77,500 | 6 | 115,350 | 4 | 68,870 | 1 | 22,146 | .. | ..... |
| Cruisers "A" | 9 | 82,900 | 19 | 183,686 | 12 | 107,800 | 6 | 60,000 | 5 | 50,000 |
| Cruisers "B" | 10 | 70,500 | 24 | 112,020 | 17 | 81,455 | 5 | 33,016 | 4 | 19,584 |
| Destroyers | 14 | 16,560 | 40 | 52,849 | 72 | 93,205 | 44 | 75,499 | 52 | 60,697 |
| Submarines | 51 | 51,290 | 36 | 43,774 | 69 | 76,408 | 62 | 58,586 | 28 | 24,549 |
| Totals | 101 | 728,050 | 140 | 981,329 | 184 | 726,138 | 124 | 382,381 | 93 | 241,362 |

In surveying the foregoing table we particularly note the aircraft carriers, which did not exist in 1914, and the increased number of submarines. But the mere increase in numbers by no means fully measures the increase in actual power. The present submarine is far in advance of that of 1914. The range of guns also is much greater, while the employment of aircraft in naval warfare has substantially augmented a fleet's fighting and destructive efficiency.

As the former "enemy" powers no longer seriously complicate the naval equation, can it be possible that, in the nervous wrangling of the victors over every proposal to curtail their vast military and naval establishments, there is no consciousness of the conflicting interests and ambitions and the unsettled differences that actually divide them? In asking this question, I impute to them no evil. On the contrary, I incline to believe that the unworldly insistence of certain circles on assigning them, while they dispute at Geneva, a place among the angels, is as embarrassing to some as it is dangerous to others, and stands in the way of their united translation. An honest confession is good for the soul. Without candid self-examination, rational thinking, and frank facing of actual conditions, there is little chance for sound relations, international or otherwise. In 1823, George Canning, then British foreign secretary, gifted and sagacious, declared that, with the split at Verona, the open hating of England by the French ministry, and the cessation of "Areopagus"—a term elegantly suggestive of what is now vulgarly called "uplift"—things were "getting back to a wholesome state again." And so it proved to be. Somnambulistic fumblings and revolving complaisance often retard agreement. Moreover, the impression that international conferences always do good is as erroneous as would be the supposition that parliamentary intrigues and debates always promote the public welfare. For ten years before 1861, discussions in Congress helped the drift toward civil war. The proposals and manoeuvres, which have marked the ominously prolonged Disarmament Conference at Geneva, and particularly the persistent effort to create the impression that, should it fail, the responsibility will rest with the United States, give ample room for a basic examination of its real temper and tendencies.

## IV. THE LETHAL BLOW OF FACTS

There can be no higher or more convincing proof of the purely imaginary character of the supposed united "will to peace" than that which is furnished by the statement made in Parliament on March 23 last by Mr. Ramsay MacDonald, British Prime Minister, on the general European situation, his recent visit to Rome, and the persistent failure of the Disarmament Conference at Geneva. Mr. MacDonald cannot be charged with unfriendly bias. He believes in peace, and has made personal sacrifices to the cause. He therefore spoke as a friendly witness, and as one having authority, when he ascribed the slow progress and the unsatisfactory results of the Disarmament Conference to the "extraordinary difficulty" caused by the "diverse interests, diverse points of view, and diverse needs in disarmament" of the many nations concerned; to the "tremendous differences" that separated "delegation from delegation and nation from nation"; and above all to the fact that "the last word in these matters is the political word." It was for these reasons, said Mr. MacDonald, that the British Government had at last submitted a draft of an international convention containing as its essential features "figures regarding various armaments" and a provision for "security."

This plan, apart from details as to armament, suggests the allotment to each of various European countries of an average daily effective armed land force. For Germany it proposes 200,-000, for Bulgaria and for Hungary 60,000 each; if we add Austria's unmentioned 20,000 we have a total of 340,000 men for what is left of the former "enemy" countries. Among the victors France is allowed 200,000 home forces and 200,000 colonial, in all 400,000; Belgium, 60,000 home, and 15,000 colonial, in all 75,000; Italy, 200,000 home, 50,000 colonial, in all 250,-000; Poland, 200,000; Rumania, 150,000; Czechoslovakia, 100,-000; Jugoslavia, 100,000; Greece, 60,000. This would give to the victors, exclusive of Great Britain, for whom figures were not submitted, a comfortable total of 1,235,000 as against 340,-000 to the vanquished. To Russia, which now stands aloof, it was proposed to allow 500,000. From these figures it would seem that "security" presupposes not equality, but an overwhelming superiority for the victors, even without the persistently sought for "consultative" co-operation of the United States.

But, after all, the question is not so simple as this. There may still be persons who innocently suppose that the victorious Powers, in their common ardor for the good of humanity, completely and forever sank, while waging war together, all national ambitions and all selfish interests. This view could hardly have been shared by those who knew the contents of the treaties (the existence of which was by no means so "secret" as it is often alleged to have been) for the division of the spoils of war; nor should such a view have been entertained by any sensible man. Conflicts of interest, of ambition and of sentiment between nations must continue to exist as long as they exist among the human beings of which nations are composed. No one, therefore, should be surprised at Mr. MacDonald's candid confession that the inability of the Disarmament Conference to agree was due to the fact that the national delegations were kept widely apart by "diverse interests" and "tremendous differences" in regard to which the last word must be the "political word." Equally creditable to Mr. MacDonald was his admission that another and special complication was the fact that they were pledged by the Versailles Treaty, made thirteen years ago, "to give equality to Germany," and that the time had gone by when by a combination of Powers "any European people" could, permanently and without even a gradual mitigation, be kept down by obligations which it regarded "as being inconsistent with its self-respect and its honor." Day after day at Geneva, said Mr. MacDonald, he felt that he was "looking upon a stage with something moving immediately behind the footlights," something "of a different character from the movements and the lights— an ominous background full of shadows and uncertainties." Europe was, he declared, very unsettled, in a very nervous condition; and, unfortunately, "the one thing" that could "save us all," "well-founded confidence in each other," was "more lacking today" than it had been "for a very long time." Referring, then, to recent "events" and "speeches," and to the peace treaties of which that of Versailles was the first, he said that they all had for months and months been conscious that certain acts done some years ago were coming to flower and fruit, and that on those now living fell "the responsibility of dealing with the ripened event." He then narrated his visit to Rome, made on the invitation of Signor Mussolini. The Italian Premier, he said, felt that Article 19 of the Covenant, which provides for the consideration of international conditions the continuation of which may endanger the peace of the world, was not meant to become dormant; that, while the Covenant enforced respect for treaty obligations, it also contemplated the possibility of a revision of treaties when conditions arose which might lead to a conflict; that, after the lapse of ten years, they had entered on the first period when there should be coöperation in revision; and that, if this view were adopted as an immediate aid to peace and to the solution of Europe's difficulties and dangers, the friendship engendered would have further beneficial consequences.

Mr. MacDonald forbore to mention the well-known fact, to which it is proper here to refer, that, while Great Britain and Italy had no unsettled scores, there were outstanding differences and rivalries between France and Italy which no doubt influenced Signor Mussolini in insisting that any reductions of armaments, and particularly of naval armaments, made by Italy should be fully reciprocated by her strongest neighbor. This also has a bearing on his proposal of the Four Power Pact; and if, as some have suggested, such a Pact would constitute a rift in the League, the cause must be traced to the League's inability to bring about any substantial amelioration of the conditions of the peace treaties. President Wilson spoke of Article 10 of the Covenant, guaranteeing existing territorial boundaries, as its "heart"; and so it was. Perhaps Article 19 may be spoken of as the lungs; but, while one may live with only a part of a lung, he cannot live without his whole heart. As to the significance of his attitude, Signor Mussolini has spoken with his accustomed clarity. In an article published in Italy on May 22nd, the anniversary of Italy's entrance into the "World War," he declared that Italy had long regarded those against whom she had fought "not as enemies, or even as former enemies," but as friends, and had practiced with them "a policy of peace, justice and collaboration." He further declared that his article was "directed against those who sought to forget or diminish the sacrifice voluntarily assumed by Italy after Italy saved or at least powerfully aided them."

## V. THE PEACE TREATIES

Mr. Ramsay MacDonald in the statement heretofore mentioned quoted the saying of a well-known politician—"Every treaty is holy, but no treaty is eternal." He cited this saying with direct reference to the Versailles Treaty. The Comte de Ségur, a celebrated French soldier and diplomatist of the eighteenth century, when ambassador at the Russian court wrote a piece which Catherine the Great warmly applauded, and she particularly commended the following words:

A humiliating peace is but an outrageous affront which the vanquished tremblingly endure. It embitters their resentment; they will bear it only so long as may be necessary to recover from their wounds. Accepting it in fear, they will break it without remorse; and the gods whom they forswear will approve their efforts. Then, on both sides, a ruthless frenzy will make the war bloody and the hate everlasting; will bring exhaustion, terror, oppression, slavery, shame and destruction. These are the bitter fruits of every humiliating peace; the law forever prostrate, the truce forever a sham.

No contrast could be greater than that between the treatment of France under the peace treaties of 1814–15 and the treatment of Germany under the Versailles Treaty of 1919. The war of the coalition against France began in 1793. At the head of the coalition was Great Britain, then France's traditional rival and inveterate foe; and among Great Britain's allies were Austria and Prussia. The series of wars that followed, including the Napoleonic Wars, continued with little interruption until 1815; and, after all the mutations of the intervening years, there appeared with Great Britain, in the first line of the victors, Austria and Prussia, of whom Castlereagh spoke as "the two States which were to form the immediate bulwarks of Europe." The day after Waterloo there were, it was said, few families in England that were not in mourning. And yet, by the treaties of 1814–15, the boundaries of France were hardly diminished, no pecuniary burden was imposed that she could not readily bear, and she was subjected to no degrading conditions. Thus was exemplified the old peace psychology now out of fashion and deeply despised.

Let us now turn to the new and advanced psychology—the psychology of phrasemaking, of frenzied oratory and of vengeful retribution. A century later, at Versailles, the vanquished were summoned to accept, without negotiation, the doom pronounced upon them in their absence, with its rending of historic ties, its dispersal of peoples, its dismemberments, its extorted confession of guilt, its confiscations and its ruinous reparations. In a current volume on China, a Chinese sage is reported to have declared that the Versailles Treaty was "the most uncivilized paper written since men knew how to record thought," and to have prophesied that it would "not only upset the economic balance of the world but lead to more wars." In comparing the earlier treaties with the later, I have often thought of the contrast as being typified on the one hand, by the Duke of Wellington, a man of action—calm, sagacious, magnanimous; and, on the other hand, by President Wilson, Lloyd George and Clemenceau—by the Fourteen Points, to be duly ground into dust; by the cry for the crushing of Germany, the imposition on her of the entire cost of the war, and the hanging of the Kaiser as a crowning proof that the world had been "made safe for democracy." Such was the new "idealism" —the euphonious designation of whatever cannot be defended on grounds of reason, of human experience, or of common sense.

Let us now become backward-looking; let us turn our eyes back to 1815, toward the dark ages in which railways, steamships, telegraphs, telephones and the radio had not illuminated the human understanding, and knit men together in common brotherhood; to the days in which the "will to peace" did not clamor for economic sanctions, for boycotts, and for threats and acts of war as the appropriate means of assuring universal concord and permanent tranquillity. As we turn toward the past there looms out of the darkness the heroic figure of the Duke of Wellington, the Iron Duke, the man of deeds, who knew the agonies of war and the blessings of peace; the man who for years firmly bore on his Atlantean shoulders not only the fate of his own country but also in large measure the destiny of the world. He had in time of war governed alien populations under martial law—the will of the military commander. But, what was his will and what did he do? He has himself told us. He governed with such moderation that political servants and judges who at first had fled afterwards returned and acted under his direction, the judges sitting in the courts of law and administering justice according to the laws of the land. He exemplified the principles of justice and magnanimity, and never broke his faith to friend or to foe. Consulted in 1814 as to whether Great Britain should not demand, as a condition of peace with the United States, the retention of the territories she then occupied in the latter country, he answered in the negative. Abasing himself before no man, he boxed no compass by his tergiversations, nor courted popular favor by specious appeals. If the new ideal, of which the Duke of Wellington represents the antithesis, correctly interprets what is meant by making the world safe for democracy, it is obvious that something is needed either to make democracy safe for the world, or to save the world from it. Recent developments seem to indicate a preference for the latter alternative.

Nothing I say concerning President Wilson and his acts can be ascribed to personal feeling. On his urgent insistence I reentered the Department of State in April, 1913, as Counselor; but I expressly limited my obligation of service to a year, and no unfriendly relations either with him or with Mr. Bryan, his Secretary of State, hastened my resignation. I knew Mr. Wilson from the time when we were students together at the University of Virginia. In those days he was an interesting and good-tempered companion. His partner in the law during the brief period of his practice was to the end of his days my cherished friend. The reluctance later exhibited to thresh out the merits of questions face to face with persons who differed with him, even if latent, did not then emerge. In going to Paris he made a grievous mistake. There were friends who urged him not to go, and he would have done well to accept their advice. He said that he was urged to come. So he was—and he was welcomed, in a very real sense, to a hospitable grave. His predicament from the beginning was impossible. The head of a State, he lowered himself to the official level of his foreign competitors, while his own associates were his subordinates and subject to his command. Standing on an eminence and alone, he was a conspicuous and inviting target. Although at times singularly patient in the pursuit of his aims, his temperament was not that of a negotiator; nor was he conversant with foreign conditions. Of international law he knew little, and of diplomatic history scarcely more. His life interest was the study of politics, not international but domestic, and chiefly of Great Britain and the United States. Understanding the psychology of the American people and their sentimental addiction to grandiose schemes, he sedulously cultivated a captivating style of oratory the indulgence of which pleased and even deceived himself and enchanted his hearers more than it instructed them. As President he for a time played the game of domestic politics with marvelous skill. But his rare and special equipment for success in politics at home was worse than useless at Paris, from which he departed as a Samson shorn of his locks. It was a tragic fate from which, before he was worn with the cares of office and the harassing spectre and responsibilities of a war, a stronger and more realistic view of his predicament might have saved him.

## VI. INTERGOVERNMENTAL DEBTS

Of the intergovernmental debts I can speak only briefly. Had they all been wiped out, together with the fantastic reparations, the world would, I believe, have been spared most of its present financial ills. To such a comprehensive oblivion I usually found that men not classed as "cancellationists" were receptive. But, unfortunately, immediately after the war, the plea was heard in the United States that, without cancellation of the reparations which the Allies were to receive from Germany, their debts to the United States should be forgiven, on the ground that they had really been fighting our battles, and had even before the war been preserving for us the Monroe Doctrine, and that we had been derelict in the performance of our duty in not going earlier to their aid. As our people were then generally unacquainted, as perhaps they still are, with the complex underlying causes of the war, and were wholly unacquainted with the occasions on which the Monroe Doctrine was preserved for us, the plea was not unnaturally resented, and the popular response was nightly made in the cinema legend —"Love, Honor, and *Repay*."

By reason of these antecedents, there exists today a propensity to suspect as a "cancellationist" anyone who hints at any reconsideration of the debt settlements. Had the subject originally been discussed on the basis of common sense and good business the attitude of our people toward revision probably would today be different from what it is, especially in view of recent demonstrations of the variableness of the "ability to pay" on which the settlements were professedly based, to say nothing of questions of politics and of commerce.

On the other hand, equally unfortunate, I believe, was the suggestion, so often made and so sentimentally popular, to revise the debts to the extent to which the debtor governments would reduce their armies and navies. I have never thought that this association of debts and armaments was likely to have a beneficial result, especially as the connection between armaments and their cost is so variable, and may at times be wholly dominated by military needs, real or fancied.

From the first the position was taken in certain European quarters that the payments of debts due by Germany and by Germans to individuals must be subordinated to the payment of reparations. As this necessarily implied that debts due by government to government were superior to debts due to individuals, it tended to reinforce the feeling in the United States that the intergovernmental debts were of a superior order, and less subject to revision than were other debts. Moreover, the sound general principle that nations are not likely in the long run to profit by the impoverishment of other nations was flagrantly disregarded in the Versailles Treaty. But, for this error and its consequences the United States must bear a share of the responsibility, as President Wilson and his delegates signed the treaty as representatives of the United States. While it must have been fully understood at Versailles that this signatory commitment of the United States was subject to the approval of the United States Senate, the subsequent refusal of the Senate to approve the treaty could not efface the cooperation of the representatives of the United States in its formulation and conclusion. But changes in conditions often require a reconsideration of the question of ability to pay in the interest of creditor and debtor alike; and for this reason, and also for the reason that much ill feeling has been caused by allegations of fact in one country the accuracy of which is denied in another, it would, I believe, be in the interest of all concerned comprehensively and promptly to examine the present situation in all its bearings, financial, commercial and legal, by means of a small but well qualified international commission. The governments need to find common ground, and for this purpose they share with the public the need of enlightenment. In the proposed examination I would even include, but as a separate and less urgent matter, the facts and the law respecting the repudiated debts of various States of the United States, concerning which an authoritative and discriminating statement is much needed. In this suggestion I do not include the Confederate States debts, which were examined and outlawed sixty years ago by the unanimous decision of a mixed commission under the treaty between the United States and Great Britain, signed at Washington on May 8, 1871. But, in the report of the commission now proposed, I would have this fact formally recorded.

## VII. INTERNATIONAL LAW AND NEUTRALITY

But it is when we come to consider what is said by some of those who assume to administer or profess to teach international law that the utterances of the new psychology cause the gravest apprehension. International law is condemned for conceding to war "legality," while the part relating to neutrality is rejected as forbidding "moral judgments" and their translation into action. Neither of these assertions can be accepted. On the contrary, they betray not only a total lack of comprehension of the law of neutrality, but also a fundamental misconception of the nature and function of all law, whether national or international.

Law does not create human activities; it merely recognizes and regulates them. The law of husband and wife neither perpetuates nor increases the propensity to perpetuate the human race; it merely recognizes the fact that the failure legally to regulate such a relation would invite a demoralizing uncertainty and chaos, while a legal ban would be both futile and ridiculous.

The pert retort that war does not perpetuate human life but destroys it would cause me not the slightest embarrassment. Defining civilization as the development of human activities under the restraint of endurable conventions, we must admit that peoples called civilized have constantly sought to increase their own growth and prosperity by war on peoples called uncivilized. War is defined as a contention by force, and, whether it be waged with fists or with frigates, its existence is coeval with the history of man; and, whatever may be its merits and demerits, it has been believed to be to some extent inevitable. An individual who commits an act of violence can readily be subdued; but such is not the case with men in the mass. The teachings of Christ are pervasively peaceful; but those who profess to accept them have seldom exemplified the precept not to resist evil. The early Christian Church beyond all cavil effectively exerted a distinctly peaceful influence, and often prevented wars between the peoples over whose minds and hearts it held sway; but the so-called religious wars, by which the division of the Church was followed, are conspicuous for their fierce and relentless character. The ancient writers on international law and relations evidently were better acquainted with these things, or were more candid with themselves, than are the proponents of our latest philosophy.

Theodore Roosevelt once exclaimed that we must have "Utopia or Hell." But as a consistent advocate of preparedness he apparently remembered that the world had always had the second alternative but never the first. The fathers of ancient as well as of modern international law similarly recognized the preponderance of proof. More than three hundred years ago Grotius, treating as undesirable extremists those who would declare all bearing of arms unlawful and those who regarded all war as lawful, wisely observed that when men urged things too far their authority was apt to be slighted, and their capacity for good diminished or destroyed. Therefore, while denouncing the evils of war, he did not suppose that he "legalized" it when he enjoined observance of the distinction between combatants and non-combatants, the humane treatment of captives, the sparing of private property, the abolition of its confiscation, the enlargement of the bounds of commercial freedom, and the establishment of rules of decision by which grave disputes have in countless cases been determined and strife and passion allayed. He recognized conquest only so far as the re-establishment of peace made it inevitable. Not with the smallest foundation can he or his enlightened followers, who have formulated rules and treaties mitigating the practices of war, be held responsible for the late World War, or for the acts that have, in violation of their precepts, sown the seeds of future wars. Those who, holding international law in some measure responsible for the recurrence of international wars, would plunge the world into chaos by sanctions and outlawries, must in all charity be supposed to have overlooked the constant recurrence of civil wars, to whose appalling total, which recent years have greatly increased, the United States once made a contribution of the first magnitude. I have been wont to remark that international wars will cease when civil wars end. Within the state there is legal organization and sanction beyond anything yet proposed in the international sphere, while the very phrase "civil" implies that the war is outlawed. Nevertheless, when obliged to characterize the civil strife then raging in the United States, our Supreme Court, after observing that a civil war was "never solemnly declared," but became such "by its accidents—the number, power and organization of the persons who originate and carry it on," learnedly declared that "the laws of war, as established among nations, have their foundation in reason, and all tend to mitigate the cruelties and misery produced by the scourge of war," and that, in consequence, "the parties to a civil war usually concede to each other courtesies and rules common to public or national wars." And the Court then adopted from Vattel, renowned for his learning and humanity, this profoundly illuminating passage:

The common laws of war—those maxims of humanity, moderation, and honor—ought to be observed by both parties in every civil war. Should the sovereign conceive he has a right to hang up his prisoners as rebels, the opposite party will make reprisals; . . . should he burn and ravage, they will follow his example; the war will become cruel, horrible, and every day more destructive to the nation.[7]

The results of an attempt to deal with insurgents in arms solely on the theory that their conduct is "illegal," and that they must unconditionally submit to force, were perfectly exemplified in the chaos and destruction that took place in Cuba after 1895 and led to the intervention of the United States in 1898.

In reality, the current delusion that international law "legalizes" war, and therefore must now yield to the war-tending and warlike processes prescribed by the Covenant, comprising "sanctions," boycotts, and war itself, is merely the legitimate offspring of the new and consoling theory that peoples may with force and arms exterminate one another without breach of the peace, provided they do not call it war.

From the same anarchic womb springs the exultant cry that the law of neutrality, because it blocked the new channel to peace, has been torpedoed, and that the neutral owners gurgled approval as they drowned. This would be a sad tale, if it were

7. The Prize Cases, 2 Black, 635, 666, 667.

true. But it is false. There is not in the world today a single government that is acting upon such a supposition. Governments are acting upon the contrary supposition, and in so doing are merely recognizing the actual fact.

In the winter of 1922–23 there was held at The Hague an international conference to make rules for the regulation of the activities of aircraft and radio in time of war. The parties to this conference, over which I had the honor to preside, were the United States, France, Great Britain, Italy, Japan and the Netherlands. The delegates acted under the instructions of their respective governments. An examination of our unanimous report will show that it was largely devoted to the definition of the rights and duties of belligerents and of neutrals in time of war, and that it treated as still existing the Land War Neutrality Convention, the Convention for the Adaptation of the Geneva Convention to Maritime Warfare, and the Convention concerning Neutral Rights and Duties in Maritime Warfare, all made at The Hague in 1907. The idea that the law of neutrality had become obsolete never was broached.

So far as I am aware, not a single party to the Versailles Treaty or a single member of the League of Nations has ever taken the position that the law of neutrality is a thing of the past. The principal Powers in the League have on occasion taken precisely the opposite position. All the judges of the World Court, in the Kiel Canal case, unhesitatingly concurred in the view that the law of neutrality remained unmodified. None of them thought of doubting the continuing force of the international law of neutrality; none had, prior to my resignation from the Court in 1928, whispered such a doubt; nor am I aware that any doubt has since been suggested. In the war between Greece and Turkey in 1922, Great Britain decided to remain neutral in the conflict, into which Canada and perhaps some of the other self-governing dominions unequivocally announced that they would not be drawn without their consent. In a statement to the House of Commons on February 27, 1933, concerning the then existing embargo on the shipment of arms to China and Japan, Sir John Simon, then Secretary for Foreign Affairs, expressly spoke of Great Britain as a "neutral government," and of the necessity, for that reason, of making the embargo apply to China and Japan alike. In other recent wars Great Britain has pursued a neutral course. France and other governments have done the same thing. On the recent declaration of war by Paraguay against Bolivia, the governments of Argentina, Chile and Peru immediately issued declarations of neutrality, thus showing, as they intended to remain neutral, an intelligent respect for international law, to the literature of which some of their publicists have ably contributed.

Governments intending to remain neutral in a conflict do not, it is true, always issue proclamations. In the case of a small or distant conflict, a proclamation may seem to be needless; but the laws stand on the books and are enforced whenever the occasion may arise. Neutrality proclamations are only clarifying warnings. Neutrality always has had, as classical records show, the highly moral and expedient object of preventing the spread of war; and it furthermore prohibits the doing in time of peace of acts designed to contribute to the starting of wars abroad. In the days of the old psychology, before the crafty throat of war began to coo of peace, neutrality was chiefly offensive to war-mongers and war-profiteers. To-day, however, and very naturally, it is even more detested by the devotees of the war-gospel of peace through force. But even they should be willing to reflect on the fact that its abolition would make every war potentially a world war, and that its individual repudiation by the United States would, whenever war anywhere broke out, immediately expose us to attack, as well as to claims for damages and to forcible measures of redress for any specific unneutral acts. It would also enable any Power or combination of Powers having an interest so to do to proceed against us as an enemy. Should little Costa Rica or Salvador enter upon the course now urged upon the United States, how long would they be permitted to remain on the map? And might not the United States demand precedence as Lord High Executioner? It is not logical for those who clamor for peace to cry out for measures the adoption of which only a nation commanding overwhelming force could hope to survive.

It is argued that increased population, industrialism, and interdependence, and the increased variety and speed of communications, have made neutrality increasingly ineffective, and have also made it likely that war, when it starts in any part of the world, will envelop the whole. In reality, the better and speedier the means of communications the more effectively can a government enforce its neutrality. That the enforcement of neutrality by the United States became easier and more effective with improvement in communications is as notorious as it was natural. The supposition that the recent great war is entitled to pre-eminence as a world war, that improved means of communication caused it to become so, and that it shows that every local war is now likely to cover the earth, is remarkably unfounded. It did not begin as a local war, but embraced all the European Great Powers and some of the lesser. It did not exceed the belligerent spread of all previous wars, or equal that of some of them. Its extent in no sense resulted from improved means of communication. The numerous local wars that have since occurred, but have remained local, clearly demonstrate that the supposed greater likelihood of spread is fanciful. But, on the evidence before us, it must be admitted that the erroneous belief that every war is now likely to become a world war creates a passion to make it so.

The supposition that the law of neutrality imposes moral indifference to the merits of armed conflicts and makes any intervention in them unlawful, I can only call baseless. The law of neutrality does not require a neutral state to remain so. A neutral state may, should it so desire, enter the conflict; but it cannot be both in and out. The law of neutrality merely applies the rule of common honesty. Parties to an armed conflict are entitled to know who are in it and who are not. Members of the League of Nations, as I have already shown, by no means regard the law of neutrality as obsolete. No matter from what point it is viewed, the demand that the law of neutrality shall be considered as obsolete is so visionary, short-sighted and chaotic that no measure designed to give effect to it should ever be placed on the statute books.

## VIII. ARMS EMBARGOES

Repugnance to the law of neutrality is justified only on the part of those who, as shown by the original draft of the recent Arms Embargo Resolution before Congress, wish public authorities not legally invested with the power to declare war to be able at any moment, either alone or in association with others, to involve the country in war. This repugnance naturally distinguishes those who wish the United States to assist in enforcing the "decisions" of the League of Nations, pending the fulfillment of their desire that the United States become a member of the League. This object reverberates in the letter of Viscount Cecil, published in *The Times* of London, February 21, 1933, on the "very important pronouncements" made by the "Democratic President-elect of the United States" on January 11, and by the "Republican Secretary of State," Mr. Stimson, a month later; pronouncements which, he says, "make it clear that both parties in the United States stand for participation in an arms embargo against an aggressor State," while "the *Republican* Secretary of State declares that in this connection a decision by the League as to which is the aggressor is for practical purposes conclusive!" In still cherishing, as we have seen they do, the law of neutrality, members of the League no doubt regard it as an assurance against becoming involved in the untold wars to which, though neither desired by themselves nor approved by the League, the chaos resulting from the abolition of neutrality would expose them, as well as all other nations.

The Arms Embargo Resolution, as presented to Congress during the late Administration, proposed to authorize the President of the United States, either alone or in association with other Powers, discriminately to prohibit the shipment or sale of arms and munitions of war to one of the parties to a war, while leaving unrestrained the shipment and sale to the other. In this form the resolution, unless deliberately designed to disregard existing international law, evidently proceeded upon a complete misconception of the legal significance of the supply of arms and munitions of war to the parties to armed conflicts. The statement is often made that the trade in contraband is lawful, and the statement is also often made that such trade is unlawful. These statements may seem to be conflicting; but, when properly understood, they are both correct. Because there is much dispute as to what the term contraband includes, and because it has so far been deemed proper to limit the burdens to which a neutral Power is subject, international law has not up to the present time required neutral governments to prevent their citizens from manufacturing, selling and shipping contraband, including arms and munitions of war, in the regular course of commerce. Hence, in the sense that a neutral government is not obliged to suppress such trade, the trade is lawful. On the other hand, however, international law recognizes the right of a party to a war to prevent such articles from reaching its adversary, and, if it seizes them, to confiscate them. This essential right we have ourselves always exercised in our wars; and we never should, I suppose, dream of giving it up. The trader carries on the business at his peril, and his government is forbidden to protect him. But as the supply of arms and ammunition to a fighting force is a direct contribution to its military resources, a neutral government cannot itself supply such articles to the parties to an armed conflict, or permit its citizens to supply them to one party but not to the other, without abandoning its neutrality and making itself a party to the conflict, whether war has or has not been declared. It would therefore be altogether indefensible, whether the resolution be limited to America or extended to the whole world, to pass it in a form that would enable the Executive alone to expose the United States to reprisals and justifiable war by other nations by doing things that in their nature carry a country into war.

Had it from the beginning been agreed that every war was

to be treated as a universal war, the course of history might have been changed, but not for the better. Said Cromwell: "Put your trust in God; but mind to keep your powder dry." Napoleon, than whom there could be no higher authority on such a subject, said, "Providence is always on the side of the last reserve"; and the truth of this saying was as clearly demonstrated in his final defeat at Waterloo as it was in his previous victories. Moralists now proposing to regenerate the world by violence, without regard to the consequences to their own country or to any other, might also reflect on Lowell's line: "Truth forever on the scaffold, Wrong forever on the throne." Dryden spoke of "Worth on foot and rascals in the coach." As our advanced moralists of course expect to ride in the coach, they might do well to consider how they might themselves be classified when the country came to pay the cost of their reckless superiority to law and to the lessons of history.

It is said that our authorities may be relied upon to refuse to exercise the powers so sweepingly conferred upon them. This is indeed a singular argument. Couched in the language of irresponsibility, it is not only self-stultifying but also unjust. The burdens and cares resting, especially at the present juncture, upon those who administer our affairs are already grave and harassing enough without imposing upon them the pastime of playing with war.

It is also said that the resolution as originally drafted would merely confer on the President the same power as that conferred on other heads of states, including that of Great Britain. But this statement wholly overlooks our constitutional limitations. The British Crown possesses the power to declare war and to make alliances; the Constitution of the United States denies to the President the power to do either. On the contrary, the war-declaring power is vested in Congress, and the making of alliances requires the advice and consent of the Senate.

Should the United States desire to prohibit the furnishing of implements of war to those who are engaged in armed strife, this may readily be done by providing for a comprehensive, non-partisan embargo on the shipment of arms to all countries engaged in armed strife, whether international or civil. Such an embargo would naturally be announced and imposed by public proclamation. Of this no foreign Power could complain. There are already various countries which, in accordance with their laws, impose such a ban. This is entirely proper under international law. That such an inhibition, without the co-operation of all other neutral nations, tends to limit the area, destructiveness or duration of war I do not now undertake to affirm. Some notably humane writers, such as Westlake, have urged that a total ban might render weaker nations, financially unable to maintain munitions factories of their own, incapable of asserting or of defending their rights against larger Powers. Considerations such as these lie within the domain of policy. The general bans, where they exist, are based upon the belief that, as the supply of arms and munitions constitutes a military aid, it is better and safer to forbid it altogether. In imposing upon itself such a restriction a nation acts within its undoubted rights, and gives no just cause for reproach.

### IX. THE AGGRESSOR

It is dangerous to allow a fallacy to pass unchallenged because its refutation should seem to be superfluous. Especially is this so when it may easily be imposed on uninformed or unreflecting minds by appeals to the sentiment of benevolence. These truths are perfectly exemplified by the spread of the recent agitation for the punishment of "aggressors."

The word "aggressor" does not occur in the Covenant, but it has been used as the technical designation of the nation to which the warlike devices of the League of Nations were intended to apply. For this reason many attempts have been made at Geneva to define an aggressor, but never with any success. Among these may be included the delphic effort of M. Briand. "A cannon shot," said M. Briand, "is a cannon shot"; and "you can hear it, and it often leaves its traces." Then, conjectures M. Briand, the League says "Cease fire"; and, "if one of the adversaries refuses, we can surely say that he is not really very anxious about peace." I have great respect for M. Briand, and if this was the best so able a man could do, the case must indeed be desperate. Certainly a cannon shot is a cannon shot. But if the adversary who ceased fire on Geneva's command should then be killed or disabled, he neither could nor would feel grateful, nor would his example inspire enthusiasm. Besides, even if Geneva had large military forces of her own in Europe, and they were not already preoccupied with exerting a peaceful influence in that quarter, it is a long way, for example, to Singapore; and decisive wars have often been of brief duration.

M. Briand's delicate and fragmentary suggestions clearly indicate that he did not intend them to be taken seriously as a definition. More serious in tone but equally futile is the suggestion made on the part of the United States at Geneva on May 22, 1933, that "the simplest and most accurate definition of an aggressor is one whose armed forces are found on alien soil in violation of treaties." Whether the framer of this definition was or was not thinking of Manchuria, he immediately impaled the sudden seizure and occupation of Vera Cruz by the United States in April, 1914, in disregard of the treaty with Mexico of 1848, which expressly provided that neither party should resort to force before trying peaceful negotiation, and, if that should fail, arbitration. The excuse, should it be attempted, that there was no time for discussion, would merely puncture the definition. Moreover, were there no treaty, would an armed invasion cease to be an act of aggression? Might not such an invasion, even if a treaty were violated, be excused as an act of self-defense? In the celebrated case of McLeod, which nearly brought on a war, Great Britain excused her invasion of United States territory on that plea; but as the United States denied that the facts justified the plea, Great Britain made a soothing apology without admitting any wrong. Would, or would not, the new definition justify the landing of foreign troops to preserve order, as has often been done without the consent of the local government? Would it, for instance, make our military occupation of Nicaragua an act of aggression? Furthermore, will it be asserted that the answer to the question whether a treaty has been violated lies on the surface, and may not be a subject of honest difference of opinion, both on the facts and on the law, even among disinterested and impartial judges? I say "disinterested and impartial"; for it is obvious that, if the trial were left to interested and partial judges, the answer would necessarily reflect their interests and their prejudices. Evidently, the draftsman of the definition was less prudent than the knowing M. Briand. It has also been suggested that the aggressor is he who fires the first shot; but the law does not require a man who believes himself to be in danger to assume that his adversary is a bad shot.

Probably it would be unfair to surmise that the persistent effort, after a decade of ghost dancing, to define the "aggressor," always reflects the desire by means of some formula readily to obtain the military co-operation of the United States nominally in the righteous cause of peace. The thought of restraining aggressors is very ancient; but the attempt to define aggression for practical purposes has always failed, because, as has been well said,[8] it is impossible to specify beforehand the objective criteria on which the decision whether an act was overt would necessarily depend. Although nations when they go to war always profess to repel overt acts, yet they frequently do not go to war on account of them; but an assurance of associate force would necessarily increase their propensity to do so.

8. "The Slippery Aggressor," *The World Tomorrow*, June, 1930.

Moreover, it is notorious that overt acts are sometimes craftily provoked for the purpose of justifying aggression; and it may be significant that the definition of the "aggressor" peculiarly preoccupies the minds of those who are best prepared to commit aggression.

On the other hand, the taking of a forcible initiative may be the only means of safety; and the importance of this principle is necessarily enhanced by the insistence of nations or groups of nations on maintaining a preponderance of military power. Portugal acted on this principle when, in 1762, the combined forces of France and Spain were hovering on her frontier. In many instances the question of aggression remains indeterminate. The Hundred Years' War, which began in 1292, originated in a fist-fight between two sailors, the one Norman and the other English, in the port of Bayonne. In the battle of Navarino which, in 1827, resulted in the destruction of the Turkish fleet by the combined naval forces of England, France and Russia, the first actual shot was fired by the Turks; but English naval writers later candidly admitted that the Ottoman commander probably believed that he was repelling an attack. In the case of the destruction of the armed brig *General Armstrong* by a British squadron in the port of Fayal, Louis Napoleon, acting as arbitrator, held that the brig was the aggressor; but our Congress, believing this decision to be wrong, eventually compensated the brig's owners, officers and crew for their losses. When, in 1894, a Japanese cruiser, before war with China was declared, sank the British vessel *Kowshing,* carrying Chinese troops to Korea, an immediate outcry took place in England; but the excitement soon died down on the public justification of the cruiser's act by Holland and Westlake, two eminent English authorities on international law.

As experience has conclusively shown that the attempt to decide the question of the aggressor on first appearances is reckless of justice, we must, unless our purposes are unholy, rely on an impartial investigation of the facts. But this takes time. The Assembly of the League of Nations assumed jurisdiction of the Sino-Japanese conflict on September 21, 1931; the report of the Lytton Commission was signed at Peiping, China, on September 4, 1932; the Assembly adopted the report of its own committee on February 17, 1933. The actual time covered by the proceedings was seventeen months, and even then a final conclusion was not reached. Decisive wars have ended in less time. Napoleon escaped from Elba in February 1815, and the decisive battle of Waterloo took place in the following June. The war over Schleswig-Holstein of 1864 was brief; the war between Prussia and Austria of 1866 lasted six weeks; the

United States declared war against Spain in April, 1898, and the peace protocol, which ended the military conflict and defined the basis of peace, was signed in the following August. These are only a few examples.

That intimations that a party to a dispute may be penalized as an aggressor may not have a deterrent effect has just been shown by the course of Peru in her recent dispute with Colombia. The hostilities continued until the sudden death of Peru's Chief Executive brought to the presidency a statesman who happened to have been a diplomatic colleague, at London, of the leader of the Colombian Liberal party. An exchange of personal messages and a journey by aeroplane to Lima resulted in the conclusion of a pact of peace. The friendly human touch quickly obtained what official admonitions had been unable to secure.

Had the principle of preventing aggression been applied one cannot say what might have been the results to the United States. Our War of Independence was generally regarded in Europe as an act of rebellion against lawful authority. In the war of 1812 we appeared as aggressive assertors of the freedom of the seas. General Grant pronounced our war with Mexico of 1846 an act of unjust aggression. The Government of the United States dealt with secession as an act of rebellion. In April, 1898, the diplomatic representatives of six great European Powers assembled at the White House and in behalf of their governments made what was called "a pressing appeal to the feelings of humanity and moderation of the President and of the American people in their existing differences with Spain." They evidently did not regard Spain as the aggressor. President McKinley in his reply expressed the confident expectation that the remonstrating Powers would appreciate our offer "to fulfil the duty of humanity by ending a situation, the indefinite prolongation of which had become insufferable." Had they, when we forcibly intervened, declared an embargo upon the shipment of arms and ammunition to the United States, while continuing to supply Spain with the implements of war, we should have resented in appropriate ways their partisan action.

Should we attempt to apply retrospectively the principle of staying or punishing the aggressor we should be obliged to determine the question whether the forcible creation of that great agency of law and civilization, the Roman Empire, or the forcible progress of any other great historic movement, should not have been prevented; whether the formation of the British Empire or the extension of France and her colonial empire should not have been opposed; whether the establishment of the Russian Empire should not have been resisted; whether the world should not have prevented the United States from becoming what it is; also, whether the forcible association in earlier times of the vast aggregation of states now known as China did not result from a neglect by other states of their duties and, perchance, their opportunities.

The opposite of self-defense is aggression. We have been told that the limits of self-defense "have been clearly defined by countless precedents." Students of this subject have remarked that it would be "interesting to know" what these "countless precedents" are, but their curiosity has not been gratified. It will not be. The attempt so to define self-defense that its future application would be clear and practically automatic is just as futile as the attempt similarly to define aggression has been —and must continue to be.

### X. CONSULTATIVE PACTS

In our last presidential campaign the platforms of both the major parties covetously leered toward a consultative pact. Normally, each platform views the other with alarm, and when they agree a general alarm is justified. One can only wonder whether freakish impulse or some cunning Mephistopheles caused the recent amorous accord.

The obtaining of a "consultative pact" has long been on the program of the conference so persistently staged at Geneva in the name of disarmament. To the uninitiated the word "consultative" seems to imply a friendly or platonic communion. Who would refuse to consult? Who would be so unneighborly as to refuse what is daily done as a mere act of civility? But no one should be deceived by this. Agreements are interpreted according to the subject matter. A reduction of armaments in consideration of a "consultative pact" would necessarily indicate as the subject of consultation the number of men, of ships and of aircraft that should be contributed in order to supply the place of what had been given up. In the present state of Europe, this would tend to increase rather than to diminish the existing tension and danger. While it would please certain countries, it would inflame others. To-day Europe is divided into hostile camps. Why should we encourage any of them to strike while the iron is hot? A disinclination to strike might readily be converted into eagerness by reliance on our aid.

An innocent-looking clause in our treaty with the Samoan Islands of 1878 nearly got us into war, although it merely required the use of our "good offices" for the adjustment of differences between the Samoan and any other government. This

clause was accepted by the United States in a spirit of pure
benevolence, but there was no real Samoan government. One
day, when the shadowy government seemed to be menaced, our
consul at Apia ran up the American flag and declared a protectorate over the islands. This he was not authorized to do;
but it precipitated a quarrelsome consultation which ended in
the setting up of an international government that proved to
be so calamitous that the United States eventually agreed to
divide up the islands and have done with it.

The commitment of the United States to such a "consultative pact" as is desired at Geneva would, I believe, constitute
the gravest danger to which the country has ever been exposed,
a danger involving our very independence. It seems to be
thought that we are an easy mark, and I say this not in any
spirit of reproach. We all are human. Lambs are killed by men
as well as by lions, but lambs are specially appetizing to the
cultivated taste of the old and polished European nations.
Younger peoples may act wisely in modestly avoiding ban-
quets at which they may be obliged to consult others regarding what they shall eat or to take the risk of indiscriminate
indulgence. It has been intimated that France might pay the
overdue instalment on her debt to us if we would compensate
her by a "consultative pact." The proposal made by us some
weeks ago of a non-aggression agreement seemed to produce a
general sense of disappointment, if not of disgust. But, should
we enter into a consultative pact for the sake of a payment due
on an old account, we should remember that for every dollar
paid us for our amiability we might have to return a million
or two for war.

Of all conceivable devices the "consultative pact" is the most
pernicious. It operates both as an incentive and as a lure. While
it encourages the co-partner to do what he might otherwise refrain from doing, it fails, by reason of its indefiniteness, to
deter the co-partner's antagonist from doing what he might
not otherwise attempt. Numerous examples might be adduced
to show this.

Such an understanding between Great Britain and France,
called an *entente*, figures largely in the breaking out of the
general war in Europe in 1914. This is clearly set forth by
Lord Loreburn, formerly Lord Chancellor of England, in his
*How the War Came,* which was first published in London in
1919. In this volume Lord Loreburn shows how, as the result
of an agreement with France in the nature of a consultative
pact, by which armed support was implied, the British people
were brought into the war without previous knowledge of the
danger in which they really stood. Acting under the secret

understanding, Mr. Asquith, having obtained from Lord Lans-
downe and Mr. Bonar Law an undertaking to assist him in
Parliament, gave to France on August 2, 1914, a definite promise of armed naval support against Germany that irrevocably
pledged the country to war. Commenting on the settled policy
which had had the support of England's greatest statesmen,
Lord Loreburn well observes that if England was to abandon
her habitual aloofness from "continental alliances," whether
"formal or in the infinitely more dangerous guise of 'understandings,' " it was "clearly necessary" that the country also
should have had "if not compulsory service, at all events a
population trained to arms."

In the draft of a disarmament convention which the British
Government, with a view to meet the persistent demands of
France and other countries, submitted to the Disarmament
Conference at Geneva on March 16, 1933, the first part relates
to "security"; and it is highly significant that the proposed
parties to the convention are the parties to the Kellogg Pact.
It is also worthy of notice that the occasion on which the parties are to consult is a breach or threatened breach of the Pact.
But the British dominions, although parties to the Pact, are
not among the Powers to be consulted. Probably this may be
explained by the adverse and independent stand the dominions
took in 1922 when it was suggested that they should support
British intervention in the war between Greece and Turkey.
The object of the conference, when called, is to agree on action
respecting the threatened breach or, if a breach has occurred,
"to determine which party or parties to the dispute are to be
held responsible." The word "aggressor" is not here used. The
phrase "to be held responsible" denotes a purpose to hold
somebody responsible and to allow the greatest possible latitude in the determination of that question, no matter what its
nature may be, whether it involves considerations of fact, or
of law, or of politics, or of power. Such latitude, it must be
admitted, is essential where nations combine to regulate one
another's affairs, or to control one another's conduct, or to
penalize misconduct. The proposed convention, while candidly
recognizing these facts, wisely requires the concurrence of a
number of governments; but, while requiring unanimity on
the part of the Great Powers, unless one or more of them
should be parties to the dispute, it requires the concurrence of
only a majority of the smaller Powers. Although it is easy to
conceive of questions on which the judgment of the latter
would be more likely to be impartial, the proposal savors of
the hegemony of the Great Powers, of which so much was said
before 1914, when the Great Powers themselves tumbled into

an appalling Great War. Conferences may be useful and even necessary; but when nations come to determine, through their political authorities, questions of legality, morality and good faith raised by acts that have happened, or seem likely to happen, and to impose prohibitions or punishments, it is idle to conceal from ourselves the fact that they are moving and breathing in an atmosphere of force and of war, and probably without the benefit of that calmness of mind and impartiality which judicial proceedings are intended to assure among nations as well as among individual men.

A commitment more contrary to the vital interests of the United States as heretofore understood could not be conceived of. It would destroy the last vestige of the power to control our own destiny that has heretofore been the most cherished part of our birthright.

In this connection we should not fail to consider the psychology of our own people. Although not military in the sense of keeping large armaments and preparing for war, they are ingenuous, adventurous and militant. They rose and threw off the colonial yoke, although it was milder than that of other countries—the mildest of the time. President Madison, quiet and gentle in spirit, was pressed into the War of 1812. In the Greek war for independence some of our public men warmly advocated our participation. In 1846 Congress declared the existence of war with Mexico without awaiting the printing of the diplomatic correspondence. In 1852 it required all the sober sense and self-control of our statesmen to resist the popular movement for intervention in Hungary. We drifted into the Civil War in 1861 on disputed points of constitutional law. In our war with Spain in 1898, most of the European Powers regarded our action as aggressive. After the impulse to enter the World War got its stride, President Wilson denounced Senators who opposed it as "willful men." Our demonstrated readiness to go to war, in spite of our impression that we are the most peaceful people in the world, makes it specially dangerous that we should commit ourselves to interested appeals to impulses better understood by others than by ourselves. Nor should we forget how suddenly and unexpectedly wars often break out and the trivial incidents which sometimes precipitate them. I would not abandon my fellow-countrymen to consultative shambles.

## XI. MANCHURIA

Having read the entire Lytton report, I am impressed with its comprehensiveness. The sincerity of its effort to ascertain the truth is shown by this paragraph:

It must be apparent to every reader of the preceding chapters that the issues involved in this conflict are not as simple as they are often represented to be. They are, on the contrary, exceedingly complicated, and only an intimate knowledge of all the facts, as well as of their historical background, should entitle anyone to express a definite opinion upon them. This is not a case in which one country has declared war on another country without previously exhausting the opportunities for conciliation provided in the Covenant of the League of Nations. Neither is it a simple case of the violation of the frontier of one country by the armed forces of a neighboring country, because in Manchuria there are many features without an exact parallel in other parts of the world.

The report's chief defect is, I think, the importance which at the outset it assigns to "the improvement of modern communication" as having induced the flagrant acts of force which extorted from China the Treaty of Nanking and the cession of Hongkong. Long accustomed to reflect on the trade rivalries and struggles for empire of European Powers in the Far East during preceding centuries: on the gain and loss of vast colonies, and the truly world wars that were fought, when ships were small and slow; and on the fact that what was done in 1841 only chiseled the margin of China's seclusion and did not break its spirit, I cannot share the common habit of thinking of "isolation" as an antonym of speed, even though Japan, by a deliberate self-development that embraced the assimilation of all speedy devices, induced her exemplars in speed to renounce their earlier privileges. Only by taking all these things into account can the attitude of the East toward the West and of the West toward the East be so understood as to help the reader to perceive whether the word "nationalism," which the report so often uses, predominantly denotes, in a particular instance, an anti-foreign sentiment or an aspiration after national unity. The divisions in China largely account for her present plight. In treating of Manchuria, the report does not overlook the fact that it was Russia's progressive absorption not only of that province but also of Korea that caused Japan, in concern for her own national life, to risk war with Russia thirty years ago. But the measures suggested by the report for the adjustment of present conditions are exceedingly complicated and largely depend for their successful application on a co-operation between China and Japan such as the western nations have not shown respecting the limitation of armaments or the readjustment of the balance of power as between themselves, to say nothing of their continued refusal to relinquish their extraterritorial rights in China because their surrender would be premature. The "conditions of a satisfactory solution" suggested by the report embrace compatibility with the interests of China and Japan, consideration of the interests of Russia, conformity to the provisions of the Covenant, of the Kellogg Pact and of the Nine-Power Treaty, the recognition of Japan's rights and interests in Manchuria and of her historical associations with that country, a conventional restatement of the respective rights, interests and responsibilities of both China and Japan in that quarter, provision for the prompt settlement of minor disputes, the adoption, consistently with China's sovereignty and administrative integrity, of measures of government and autonomy so drawn and executed "as to satisfy the essential requirements of good government," the establishment of a local gendarmerie effective for the purposes of internal order and security against external aggression, the conventional improvement of commercial and political relations, and, as these various conditions can hardly be fulfilled without a strong central government in China, the establishment of a temporary international co-operation in the internal reconstruction of China. The report further says that, if an adequate *rapprochement* between China and Japan is not secured, no solution, no matter what its terms may be, can ever be fruitful. The suggestions also propose various declarations and treaties, the details of which are fully elaborated; but foreign co-operation and supervision largely figure in them.

The report of the Committee of the Assembly of the League, to which these suggestions were submitted, cannot be highly commended. Its tone is that of reproof. Japan is not called an "aggressor," but this is strongly hinted; and references to provisions of the Covenant that contemplate the use of force are rather plentiful. The Assembly adopted the report on February 17, 1933, together with recommendations some of which summarily stated definite conclusions; and acceptance of the recommendations as a whole was made a condition of representation of the parties on a special committee which it was proposed to appoint to assist them in their negotiations. Japan then protested and resigned from the League. Had the Assembly tendered friendly and impartial good offices, and, as a great Secretary of State of the United States once suggested to an offending government, used "some kind words," it might have contributed to the actual and amicable solution of the immense difficulties which the Lytton report so clearly explained. On February 27, 1933, Sir John Simon, speaking for the British Government to the House of Commons concerning the armed struggle in Manchuria, had declared: "Under no circumstances will this Government authorize this country to be a party to the conflict."

In view of Great Britain's vast interests in the Far East the

foregoing statement is impressive. Other European governments have spoken in a similar sense, and the arms embargo
by Great Britain, which was so soon revoked, stood alone.
Strangely, it was chiefly in the United States that cries for
boycotts, arms embargoes and other measures were heard.
These cries reverberated internationally; and there was used
in both countries, even in official statements, language that reflected the prevailing excitement. Diplomatic windows are
peculiar. They automatically open to bouquets, but never to
gravel. A single brick may shatter all the panes. Even a well-
intended admonition, if the surface is rough and hard, may
have a like effect. During the war between Russia and Japan
in 1904, when Theodore Roosevelt was President and John
Hay was Secretary of State, the United States specially enjoined on all its officials, civil, military and naval, the practice
of courtesy, moderation and self-restraint, lest resentment
might be aroused. The Nine-Power Treaty has constantly been
mentioned, and references to it are altogether proper. It enunciates an old principle intended to avoid danger in situations
which actual conditions complicate. The parties to it, besides
the United States, China and Japan, are Belgium, the British
Empire, France, Italy, the Netherlands and Portugal. In the
United States it has constantly been spoken of as having
special "sanctity." No doubt, a nation's faith should ever be
inviolable, whether pledged to other nations or to private individuals; nor should a pledge to the latter be less sacred because
its violation may be less dangerous. But the application of the
terms of treaties to actual cases is often disputed and uncertain, and nations are inclined, especially when they are under
pressure, to be tenacious of their own opinions. France, for
instance, in 1923 refused the proposal of Great Britain to refer
the question of the legality of the occupation of the Ruhr to
the Permanent Court of International Justice. On the other
hand, the many references to arbitral boards show how often
nations disagree on questions of interpretation.

The thought of armed intervention by the United States in
Manchuria, while glaringly inconsistent with the recent vote
to abandon the Philippines, inevitably suggests the possible
failure of its object as well as other serious consequences.
Should the attempt to occupy the territory be successful, the
perplexing questions whether to hold and administer it, or to
turn it over to China, as she would naturally wish, or to some
other Power, or to set up an international government, would
necessarily have to be determined. Article 35 of the General
Act of Berlin of February 26, 1885, relating to protectorates
on the coast of Africa, recognized "the obligation to insure the

establishment of authority in the regions occupied by them
. . . sufficient to protect existing rights, and, the case arising,
freedom of trade and of transit on the conditions that they
may have agreed upon," and this obligation was pronounced
by the highest authorities to be based also on "the nature of
the case." Where efficient local government does not exist, the
total failure of our trial some years ago of international government in little Samoa indicates that of all kinds of government the international is the worst.

The phrase "open door" is often used in a fighting sense, although war might necessitate the door's temporary closure.
The "open door" means trade, but, of course, not in the highly
obnoxious sense of "free trade," although a very moderate conventional tariff has long been imposed on China. For 1932 the
figures of United States trade with China and Japan are as
follows: exports to China $56,171,000, imports from China
$26,176,000; exports to Japan $134,537,384, imports from
Japan $134,011,311. Without undertaking now to suggest what
our final attitude towards the new state of Manchukuo should
be, I am bound to say that the proposal of permanent "non-
recognition" too vividly recalls the uncertainty and failure,
and the disorder, local and international, which attended the
recent trial of that futile and demoralizing process as a means
of preventing revolution or other unconstitutional acts in
other lands.

In 1919 President Wilson did not submit to the Senate a tripartite treaty he had signed at Paris to guarantee the eastern
frontier of France, although in the long run internal order is
maintained on both sides of the Rhine. Many examples, including the war of thirty years ago between Russia and Japan
and the unended conflicts that have since occurred, show what
a quagmire Manchuria offers for the swallowing up of blood
and treasure, without permanent and uncontested reward to
those who take their chances in it. The much vaunted annihila-
tion of space and time has not yet enabled a nation thousands
of miles away to exert its military power as effectively as it
may do at home or in its immediate environment. For a distant
nation to take the chances of armed intervention in Manchuria, unless in pursuit or defense of a vital interest, would
suggest a recklessness savoring of monomania.

### XII. OUR BIRTHRIGHT

Washington, in his farewell address, said:

Against the insidious wiles of foreign influence, I conjure you to
believe me, fellow-citizens, the jealousy of a free people ought to be
*constantly* awake, since history and experience prove that foreign

influence is one of the most baneful foes of republican government. . . . The great rule of conduct for us, in regard to foreign nations, is, in extending our commercial relations, to have with them as little *political* connexion as possible. . . . Europe has a set of primary interests which to us have none, or a very remote relation. Hence she must be engaged in frequent controversies, the causes of which are essentially foreign to our interests. . . . Why quit our own to stand upon foreign ground? Why, by interweaving our destiny with that of any part of Europe, entangle our peace and prosperity in the toils of European ambition, rivalship, interest, humor, or caprice?

The original draft of this admonition was made by Alexander Hamilton who, like Washington himself, was born a British subject; but their minds embraced the entire world.

Jefferson, not forgetting the Declaration of Independence which he drew, warned his countrymen that their form of government exposed them more than any other to "the insidious intrigues and pestilent influences of foreign nations," and that nothing but an inflexible neutrality could preserve us. Their mutual jealousies and their complicated alliances were, he said, all foreign to us. They were nations of eternal war. His motto therefore was: "Peace, commerce and honest friendship with all nations—entangling alliances with none."

Sagacious John Adams, who spent many years in Europe and signed our first treaty with Holland as well as the treaty with Great Britain acknowledging our independence, when a European diplomatist remarked that he seemed to be afraid of being made the tool of the Powers of Europe, exclaimed, "Indeed I am"; and when asked "What Powers?" replied "All of them." And he added:

It is obvious that all the Powers of Europe will be continually manœuvering with us to work us into their real or imaginary balances of power. They will all wish to make of us a make-weight candle, when they are weighing out their pounds. Indeed, it is not surprising; for we shall very often, if not always, be able to turn the scale. But I think it ought to be our rule not to meddle; and that of all the Powers of Europe, not to desire us, or, perhaps, even to permit us, to interfere, if they can help it.

Nothing more profoundly true was ever said; and this was fully recognized by all our national administrations and by our greatest statesmen down to twenty years ago, when, to the disturbance of our interests and our happiness, we began to swing on the trapeze at international political performances and even to pay for the privilege of so doing.

Not long ago a callow stripling, when I mentioned the name of George Washington, curtly remarked that his ideas were out of date and unsuited to the modern world. This is an essential postulate of the shallow dupes who, prating of our having lately become a "World Power," urge that we blindly don an imported livery of "world service," to be paid for, on demand, in unestimated instalments of blood and treasure. But it is a sad day when the children of a nation are taught to prattle ignorant and perverted slights of the men who, with steady and skilful hands, laid the foundations of its greatness and prosperity; men to whom, by reason of their exemplary valor, integrity and wisdom, an understanding world has awarded the highest place among the immortals. Thomas Jefferson, who spoke with the authority of an intimate official association, and with an intelligence that embraced all times and all climes, declared that in elevation of character, in sureness of judgment, in firmness of purpose, in inflexible justice and in scrupulous obedience to the laws, civil and military, throughout his whole career, Washington furnished an example unparalleled in history. Jefferson himself stands before the world as a great political genius, whose ideas still stir men's minds. Alexander Hamilton, soldier, jurist, great administrator, of whom Webster said that "he touched the dead corpse of Public Credit, and it sprung upon its feet," is still studied as a profound political theorist, at home and abroad. And what of Benjamin Franklin, discoverer, inventor, philosopher, consummate diplomatist, at home in all lands, of whom Charles Phillips eloquently said that his fame would revive the hopes of men in ages yet to come?

Such are the men whom our vaporers of current sublimities would shelve as fossils in our museums of natural history, on the hasty supposition that by various modern devices, by which men may more rapidly and more frequently communicate, and more quickly hurt or help one another, discordant races and peoples have been harmoniously united in thought and in action and in brotherly love. Where congeniality is lacking, propinquity does not tend to create affection; on the contrary, it tends to breed hatreds. Where are today the danger spots of the world? They are coterminous countries. The French and the Germans have for centuries lived side by side. No artificial device is needed to enable them quickly to come into contact. The thin line of their common frontier can instantly be strided. For ages they have crossed and re-crossed it in peace and in war; and yet, how much have they learned to love one another? Their recent fierce and desperate conflict, and the unappeased sorrows and resentments by which it was followed, will be accepted as a conclusive answer, except by those who would employ processes of peace that would cause the echoes of war daily to haunt the fireside. The times must be out of joint when a warlike ardor for peace depreciates the glory that was Greece and the grandeur that was Rome; when new and untried visions are held superior to the proved philosophies of Plato and Aristotle, of Cicero and Seneca, of Bacon and John Locke; and when the wisdom of great statesmen, heard with reverence only twenty years ago, is suddenly rejected as having no current value.

We hear much today of the duties of the United States as a "World Power," and the supposition seems widely to prevail that we have only lately reached that eminence. But the United States has always been a World Power. It acted as a World Power when, on the outbreak of the wars growing out of the French Revolution, its first President, George Washington, with Thomas Jefferson as his Secretary of State, proclaimed our neutrality. It acted as a World Power when, some years later, it suppressed the activities of the Barbary pirates. It acted as a World Power when, in 1812, it went to war in defense of neutral rights and the freedom of the seas. It acted as a World Power when it proclaimed the Monroe Doctrine. It acted as a World Power in extending its trade and opening up foreign countries to its commerce, as it so effectually did by peaceful processes during the presidency of General Andrew Jackson. It acted as a World Power when it refused to permit the intervention of foreign nations in our civil war. It acted as a World Power when it forbade the further maintenance of the European empire set up in Mexico by French arms during that war. It acted as a World Power when, in the administration of President Grant, with Hamilton Fish as his Secretary of State, it brought about, through the greatest of all international arbitrations, the amicable settlement of the *Alabama* claims, and in so doing made a signal contribution to the further development of the law of neutrality.

It is useless to continue the specification of instances. Nations, like individuals, may increase their power by combining with a due attention to their own business the extension of their friendly offices to brethren in trouble, and by conserving their militant resources for occasions when their vital interests are at stake. A nation that undertakes to meddle with every foreign disturbance is bound to become an international nuisance, to its own detriment as well as to the annoyance of other countries. Power is neither gained nor kept by such methods. Although megalomania may be sincere, it is noted for its mistakes.

In the French National Convention which met on September 21, 1792, the dominant factor was called the Mountain. This group, comprising the most radical Jacobin element, of which Marat and Robespierre were the chief spokesmen, was always in a state of more or less delirious eruption. During the Reign of Terror, with which the group is identified, the French Government instructed its minister in the United States to bring about "a national agreement, in which two great peoples shall suspend their commercial and political interests, and establish a mutual understanding to defend the empire of liberty, wherever it can be embraced." This appeal is similar to that which is constantly heard in the United States today, but it did not move the loyal statesmen who then guided our destinies.

Those who oppose our intermeddling with what does not properly concern us are dubbed "isolationists." We should not resent this; we have good ancestral justification. All through her history Great Britain has held aloof from continental alliances except so far as they might seem to be temporarily necessary for her safety. In the Thirty Years' War which convulsed the entire Continent she took no part. At the close of the wars of the Spanish Succession she dropped her alliances and made her own peace. As is pointed out by Lord Loreburn in the volume heretofore quoted, every single Great Power on the Continent was, during the sixty years preceding 1914, repeatedly engaged in continental war; France thrice, Germany thrice, Russia twice, Austria three times and Italy four times. During the same sixty years Great Britain was involved in continental war only once, when, in 1854, in alliance with France she backed Turkey against Russia and committed the mistake later described by Lord Salisbury as "putting her money on the wrong horse." One of Great Britain's reasons for abstention as declared by her statesmen was the prevalence of deadly animosities and conflicts of interest that still survived among the continental Powers. The British policy was to maintain good relations with all her continental neighbors not only with a view to exert a friendly influence in composing their differences but also to avoid commitments which might compel a participation in foreign wars and deprive the country of its independent control of its own policy. But there was yet another reason; all the great continental Powers had adopted universal compulsory service. Great Britain's cardinal principle was to rely upon an overwhelming superiority at sea. It was these things that led Lord Salisbury, when Secretary for Foreign Affairs at the close of the last century, to boast of England's "splendid isolation." When an inheritor of the name of Queen Elizabeth's great minister used this phrase it did not occur to Englishmen to reproach him for an abandonment of their "world leadership," or to wail over their neglect of their international duties. On the contrary, when Lord Salisbury spoke of "isolation," Great Britain was still tingling with memories of the Diamond Jubilee, when statesmen coming from the ends of the earth to pay homage to the Great Queen saw without dread the vast fleet that confidently rode the inviolate sea that washes England's shores. In the United States, the victims of the new psychology use the word "isolation" as a term of opprobrium. It would be as sensible to condemn as an "isolationist" a man who did not tie himself up with unnecessary contracts, and especially of the kind that were likely to impoverish or to ruin him, without benefit to himself and perhaps with injury to others. Such epithets serve only to exemplify the want of knowledge and of understanding of those who employ them.

Conspicuous in the lingo of the past decade is the plea for the continuance of the kind of "leadership" with which we began to bless the world less than twenty years ago. Some of our very eminent men have urged this plea. But I have often wished that those who use such language would reflect on how it may strike other peoples, in Europe and elsewhere. Why, for instance, should the British, the Dutch, the French, or the Italian people pant for our spiritual, our moral or our political guidance? Why should they regard as superior to them a people whom they benevolently associate with mass production, skyscrapers and prohibition? If they were to express their inmost thoughts would they not confess that such utterances sound to them somewhat boastful, somewhat neglectful of their great historic tradition? How should we ourselves now feel if the eminent foreign statesmen who lately responded to President Roosevelt's invitation to visit him, had, before leaving the United States, intimated that we needed their "leadership," and that any counsels or conditions they suggested should be accepted in that sense? Perhaps it is unfortunate for us that they did not say so. But, having had long experience in leadership, they can well afford to pay a polite deference to those who ingenuously profess to have usurped their ancient prerogative.

We also hear much of the "international mind." Would to God that we had more of it! But in devoutly expressing this wish I do not confine it to my own country, nor do I lack a definite conception of what an international mind ought to be. Having for many years been connected with the administration of foreign affairs, I can truthfully affirm that there is no nation towards which I cherish a feeling of enmity. I have always been a peacemaker; and, as an international judge, I am willing to stand on my record as one who strove to act without fear or favor. But I confess that of all countries I love my own the best. No international mind is, in my opinion, to be desired or to be trusted that is not built on a national foundation. The man who cannot sing his national anthem with a whole heart is not fit to be entrusted with negotiations with foreign Powers. No experienced diplomatist would trust out of his sight an adversary who did not seek to obtain for his own country a square deal. Only those who are disposed to maintain the rights and interests of their respective countries can treat with one another on the basis of mutual self-respect. The best diplomatists are those who are willing to give as well as to take; who can grasp and apply the equitable solution that assures to each that which is justly due; who, in leaving behind them no heartburnings and resentments, conserve the interests of all. It is a pleasure to remember the men of this type with whom I have dealt.

We are told that discovery and invention, trade and commerce, and industrial organization cannot be reversed. But nobody wishes or proposes to reverse them. We are told that the world has become too dependent on comforts to be willing to give them up; but, although dependence on comforts is not a sign of strength, either physical or mental, no one is specially advocating their abandonment. But the culmination is reached when we are told that we cannot "retire within our own borders" and lead a life of "isolation." When have we ever done such a thing, or proposed to do it? The late Grand Duke Alexander of Russia, on revisiting the United States in 1928 after an absence of thirteen years, said that on his return the impression he got was that what he had admired as the robustness of American life "had given place to the sickening self-consciousness of an hysterical idealism," and had been superseded by the "same hodgepodge of badly digested ideas" as had characterized the Guards Barracks in St. Petersburg thirty years back.

So this [he exclaimed] was the American share of the Versailles spoils! It seemed bewildering that any nation should send 2,000,000 men across the ocean, fight for something that did not concern it in the least, tear up the map of the world and lend billions of dollars to its competitors—all for the purpose of acquiring the worst traits of pre-war Europe.

And for what is our birthright to be thrown away? Among other things, for membership in an association which, although established in the name of peace, is in the present state of the popular mind chiefly characterized by warlike devices. I am not opposed to an association of nations for the purposes of peace, and would not disparage any useful work the League has done. But the League, in dealing with political matters, suffers from the radical defects of its charter, the Covenant, my first and consistent opinion of which fully accords with that so thoughtfully and prophetically expressed by Mr. Elihu Root as early as March 13, 1919, in these words: "The more I study it, the more satisfied I am that it has some very useful provisions, some very bad ones, some glaring deficiencies, and that if it is not very materially amended not merely in form but in substance, the world will before very long wake up to realize that a great opportunity has been wasted in the doing of a futile thing." Most fully has this profoundly prescient comment been justified by the recent and too frequent occasions on which loose, excited and unfulfilled threats of employing the warlike devices of the Covenant have exposed the League to reproach if not to contempt. Nor do I hesitate to mention as an example the unhappy conflict between China and Japan in which, while warlike words were heard from Geneva, the ministers for foreign affairs of powerful members of the League were disavowing in their capitals any intention to intervene in the armed strife in Manchuria.

In its very origin and constitution the League had the character of a political club which nations could enter only by invitation. To this phase Argentina at once intelligently objected. There was a list of original members and a list of states invited to accede. No then recent enemy state was on either list, although President Wilson, before going abroad, had declared that Germany would necessarily be admitted, for the purpose of controlling her if for nothing else. Mexico, although never an enemy state, was, because the United States did not then approve her, unbidden to the banquet of peace. Russia, in spite of her vast contribution in blood and in treasure to the Allied cause, was excluded because she had fallen from grace and entered upon courses that were not approved. With exclusions such as these, it was a travesty, even had the United States been present, to say that the voice of the world was heard at Geneva.

But the most fundamental defect of the plan was the creation of warlike devices on the fantastic assumption that the members of the League would, in making use of those devices, divest themselves of their individual interests and prepossessions, of their historic and instinctive antagonisms, and altruistically unite in enforcing the ideal of impartial justice. In the ordinary administration of the law, persons who have formed prejudgments are peremptorily excluded from the jury as being presumptively incapable of weighing the proofs and rendering a fair and just verdict. The members of the Council of the League of Nations are the delegates of governments; the members of the Assembly also represent governments. It cannot either justly or rationally be expected of such bodies to divest themselves of all prepossessions or consciousness of national interests, to say nothing of the fact that they must inevitably differ in opinion. It is for reasons such as these that where a conflict between nations occurs and the warlike devices of the Covenant are invoked they so readily excite apprehension and distrust. It is very significant that the professed friends of the League are the readiest to censure it for not hastening to employ the warlike devices. On the assumption that such persons accurately represent the spirit of Geneva and are influential in its deliberations, those who do not believe in war as the prime, or as the natural and appropriate, creator of peace cannot help reflecting upon the demonstrated fact that war may as readily be used for unjust as for just ends, for oppression as well as for liberty, for the crushing of some and the exaltation of others, and for evil as well as for good. No wonder that the League is visibly rocked and rent and the world disturbed and divided whenever an agitation arises for the use of the warlike devices which visionary men in an excited and unsettled time foisted upon those who were wiser and more modest in the estimation of what was practicable and desirable. It was on this rock that the great Confederation of Europe, based on the treaties that ended the Napoleonic Wars and the Holy Alliance, eventually was wrecked. Although it contained no elaboration of warlike devices for the preservation of peace, the attempt of subsequent conferences to employ united military action divided the Powers and brought to an end their association. Such a result may be regarded as inevitable.

Esau, thinking that he was about to die, sold his birthright for a mess of pottage; but the Bible censures him for having despised his birthright. What would have been the nature of the censure if he had thrown his birthright wantonly away, or had allowed himself to be cheated out of it? Europe is the victim of history, a seething mass of hereditary feuds. They exist in the western part as well as in the eastern, and they are peculiarly bitter in the southeastern, where the war in 1914 originated. The Balkan Peninsula may be likened to a Vesuvius, always in danger of an eruption. Once, when I asked an Albanian to meet a Serbian he did not know, he hissed in reply: "He i-s-s my en-ne-my!" The United States may, if it should unhappily see fit to do so, associate itself with these feuds and henceforth help to fight them out. It may embitter and help to perpetuate them, but it cannot end them.

In my early days I learned from great teachers the unity of

human history. Human nature has not changed. Human propensities, human appetites and human passions have not changed. We come into the world in the same way, and our necessities are the same. The struggle for existence still continues and it will go on. As one long and intimately acquainted with men of arms, I may say that they do not share the new view that peace and tranquillity on earth may be promoted and stabilized by boycotts, by playing fast and loose with the law of neutrality, and by the extension of the area of wars. Wars are not brought about by the officers of our Army and our Navy; but wars have often been fomented by agitations recklessly conducted by persons who professed a special abhorrence of war. The motives and objects of war have been various; but, as war is a contention by force, it is waged for victory. The struggle, as it progresses, becomes more and more intense. Each day brings its tale of death and of desolation. Griefs accumulate; the passions burn more fiercely; the hoarse cry of vengeance grows louder and more insistent; and the cases are rare in which the peace that is extorted does not by humiliating conditions sow the seeds of future wars.

The true and only foundation of peace among men is the concession to each of that which is due. No doubt perfect justice is unattainable in this world. But there is an ideal of justice towards which every nation, every people, every individual should aspire. This ideal can be attained only through the reconciliation of our conflicting views and our conflicting interests. We are not all alike. No two men and no two women are alike. No two nations are alike. We differ in race, we differ in creed, we differ in color; and all differences tend to provoke antagonism. If we would keep men and nations at peace, we must remove the causes of their discontent, elevate their moral sentiments, inculcate a spirit of justice and toleration, and compose and settle their differences.

Such is my message, on which I am prepared to stand before any future Seat of Judgment, in all confidence that no sudden reversal during the past twenty years of the ways of God to man will exclude me from the reward promised to good and faithful servants.

# THE NEW ISOLATION[1]

FOR some years it has been the fashion of certain co-operative groups and their organs, here and abroad, to dub as "isolationists" all persons in the United States who were unable impulsively to accept certain plans and modes of action, by no means so untried as their proponents assumed them to be, as the instrumentalities of a new and peaceful world order. But, as Grotius sagely observes, it is easy to push things too far, and, by losing sight of what is fundamental, to go to extremes and assume untenable positions. In this way those who would, in the speed of their desire, leave others behind, may perchance find themselves in a state of isolation, with injury to the cause which all may wish to serve. In the present instance, the cause I particularly have in mind is that of international law. There evidently are many who think and teach that this body of law has, by reason of the late so-called "World War" and what attended and followed it, become obsolete. But the vast majority of those who so think and teach are in the United States; and, judging by my own experience and observation, I am forced to conclude that, taking the world as a whole, they occupy an isolated position. It is in this sense that I have ventured to use the title "The New Isolation." In so doing, I do not refer to differences of opinion as to the efficiency of the League of Nations as an instrumentality for the enforcement of international law. On the contrary, I refer to the rejection of what have heretofore been regarded as fundamental parts of international law, such as the law of neutrality, and to the attribution of a peaceful character to processes of coercion that have heretofore been considered as savoring of war.

In a volume published nearly thirty years ago, I ventured to say that one of the most important events of all time was the advent of the United States of America into the family of nations. This did not purport to be a mere patriotic boast. Reasons were given for what was affirmed, and conspicuous among them was the fact that of the policy of the new-born nation the keynote was freedom founded on law. In its early days and for many years thereafter, the United States was distinguished for its adherence to the principle of legality and for its contribu-

1. Reprinted from *The American Journal of International Law*, Vol. XXVII, No. 4 (October, 1933).

tions to international law, the basal principle of which, as it was then understood, was the legal equality of states. It naturally never was supposed that all states were in fact equal. What was meant by equality was equality before the law. This principle is recognized in the Covenant of the League of Nations. The instrumentalities of the League are an Assembly, in which all the members of the League are represented, and a Council, in which only some of the members are represented; but, both in the Assembly and in the Council, a member has but one vote. The same principle is further assured by the provision that, except where the Covenant otherwise expressly provides, as it does in matters of procedure, decisions require the unanimous agreement of all the members represented at the meeting. From this principle of legal equality it necessarily results that it belongs to each state to organize itself in its own way, and to conduct its domestic political affairs without interference by other governments. Sir Robert Phillimore, celebrated both as a publicist and as a judge, ranged as "first in the rank of internal and domestic rights, the liberty incident to every independent state, of adopting whatever form of government, whatever political and civil institutions, and whatever rules it may please, without the interference or control of any foreign power." [2]

Proceeding upon these principles the United States made certain distinctive contributions to the development of international law, embracing the expansion of the system of neutrality, the assurance of the freedom of the seas, the abatement of national monopolies of commerce, the promotion of the free navigation of international waterways, and the settlement of international disputes by arbitration. Even of the Monroe Doctrine, which was proclaimed as a national policy, the avowed object was the confirmation to American nations of their right to freedom and independence.

International law means a law between states, and it obviously ceases to be international in proportion as certain states assume to assert and exercise superiority over other states. In proportion as the latter tendency develops, the relation between different governmental organizations becomes assimilated to that between sovereign and subject. Should a certain number of states combine to establish control over other states, the former would in effect assume the function of a superstate to which other states would be subject, and the principles of international law in the proper sense of that term would cease to be applicable to the relation, no matter whether the superiority was exercised solely by force or "with the consent of the gov-

2. *International Law* (3d ed.), p. 216.

erned." It must, however, be admitted that, except as regards certain inferior governmental entities, which are not regarded as being in a proper sense independent states, no such organization now exists in the international sphere. While there are provisions in the Covenant of the League of Nations which might be so applied as to establish in fact a superstate, League organs and individual members of the League have often denied that their association has that character. On the contrary, the members of the League of Nations regard their relations as being governed by international law, except so far as they may be regulated by specific provisions of the treaty or alliance solemnly called the Covenant.

When we consider this high tradition, it might seem surprising that the supposition that international law, as it existed prior to the so-called World War, has become obsolete, should now chiefly prevail in the United States. The tendency, however, to depart from fundamental principles did not wholly originate in that great conflict. Premonitions of it may be found in certain previous acts, among which the most notable is President Wilson's declaration of policy with regard to Latin America. This declaration, which was publicly made on March 11, 1913, and telegraphed the next day to all the diplomatic officers of the United States in the vast regions to which it applied, announced that the co-operation of the United States with other governments was possible only so far as it was supported by the observance in their own affairs of orderly processes free from the exercise of arbitrary or irregular force; that there could be "no lasting or stable peace" between the United States and those who sought to seize the power of government "to advance their own personal interests or ambition," and that we should "prefer" in our friendships those who acted in the interest of peace and honor, and who respected the restraints of constitutional provisions.

With the motives by which this declaration was inspired we are not now concerned. That it was made without consultation with anyone qualified to pass upon its legal significance and practical consequences we may safely assume. It was obviously prompted by a feeling of repugnance to the newly established government of Huerta in Mexico. But, in its indiscriminate announcement of an intention on the part of the United States to inspect and judge the conduct of all American governments from the Rio Grande to Cape Horn as regarded their observance of their constitutional law, and to visit with displeasure, by non-recognition or otherwise, the violation or neglect of constitutional prescriptions, it struck at the very roots of the legal equality of independent states. That such a measure should

tend to create abnormal situations, and should foster and prolong disorders rather than end them, was inevitable.[3]

For a hundred-and-twenty years the rule by which the
United States was guided in the recognition of foreign governments was that laid down by Jefferson, as Secretary of State,
in an instruction to Gouverneur Morris, Minister to France,
March 12, 1793, in these words:

We surely can not deny to any nation that right whereon our own
Government is founded—that every one may govern itself according
to whatever form it pleases, and change these forms at its own will;
and that it may transact its business with foreign nations through
whatever organ it thinks proper, whether king, convention, assembly,
committee, president, or anything else it may choose. The will of the
nation is the only thing essential to be regarded.

Ten years later, on receipt of the news that Napoleon had
proclaimed an Empire in France, Madison, as Secretary of
State, in order that recognition of the new *régime* might not be
unduly delayed, sent to our minister at Paris a blank form of
credence signed by the President, with instructions to fill it out
in the form and style required by the new government, and to
present it whenever he was satisfied that the Empire was in
possession and control of the governmental power and the territory of the nation—the usual conditions precedent in all cases
of recognition by the United States, whether the new *régime*
was republican or monarchical, popular or nonpopular, elective
or hereditary. From that time down to 1913, this was the rule
by which our government was guided. "We do not," said President Pierce, in 1856, "go behind the fact of a foreign government's exercising actual power to investigate questions of legitimacy." It is true that, while Seward was Secretary of State,
there were certain instances in which recognition was withheld
because the new government was of revolutionary origin; but
this was only a temporary and politic attitude suggested by our
own Civil War, and is to be classed with Seward's protests

3. In the *Foreign Relations of the United States*, 1913, p. 440, there is
a telegram sent on December 5, 1913, by Mr. James M. Sullivan, United
States Minister to the Dominican Republic, to Mr. Bryan, Secretary of
State, saying that he had told the Dominican cabinet "that President
Wilson's declaration of principles concerning Latin America reserved
the right to enter any Latin American country to see that the people's
rights were not lost by force or fraud." Although we may properly assume that Mr. Sullivan was not instructed to interpret the declaration in
these precise terms, yet, as his interpretation is published in the official
record without any accompanying expression of disapproval, it must be
accepted as proof that the declaration strongly stimulated new thoughts
on international order.

against the recognition by foreign governments of the belligerency of the Confederate States—protests in principle expressly abandoned by the United States in 1869, and not since revived.

The right asserted by the President of the United States in 1913 to inspect and judge the governments of all other American countries as regarded their observance of their constitutional law naturally remained unreciprocated; nor did European governments seek to imitate it. Indeed, even as regards the United States, there was a time when such a pretension on the part of other governments might have been attended with substantial inconvenience. I particularly refer to our four years' civil war and the calamitous era of "reconstruction" by which it was followed. During this long period constitutional limitations often received scant attention, and one senator of the United States went so far as to declare that he approved the action of the government in proportion as it violated the constitution. Half a century has since elapsed, and we now find ourselves in an era in which constitutionalism the world over seems to be in a somewhat precarious state. Apparently there are large numbers of persons who approve governmental action in proportion as it emancipates itself from the trammels to which previous constitutional interpretations would subject it. Few governments are now in a position to cast stones at sinners in other lands on the assumption that they are themselves without fault. The time therefore is ripe for a full return to international law and the practice of reciprocity.

The attempt of one government to interfere in the domestic politics of another government has always been attended with danger. When in 1848 Lord Palmerston, then British Foreign Secretary, recommended to the Spanish Government, through the British Minister at Madrid, "the adoption of a legal and constitutional course," and the enlargement of the basis of party representation in the administration, the Spanish Government indignantly returned the note in which the advice was given, and dismissed the British Minister. During the presidential campaign of 1888, President Cleveland dismissed the British Minister at Washington, because in a letter to a supposed citizen of the United States of British nativity, he advised the latter as to how he should vote. Nations, whether great or small, are proverbially sensitive as regards their independence, and intermeddling with one another's domestic affairs should be avoided as far as possible. It therefore is not strange that the United States has during the past four years been endeavoring to rid itself of the incubus of its past errors in this regard, and has on various occasions shown much alacrity in recognizing revolutionary governments upon their first appearance on the political horizon.[4]

But another and most unfortunate result of the "declaration of policy" of 1913 and of the attempt to apply it was the eventual and probably unforeseen involvement of the United States in a strange revival of the ancient and discredited distinction between governments *de facto* and governments *de jure* as regards their recognition and their competence, national and international. These terms were originally used to denote the distinction between governments ordained of men and governments ordained of God. An hereditary monarch, claiming to derive his powers from God and not from the nation, was said to rule by divine right—*jure divino*, and his government was called a government *de jure;* while the government ordained of men was called a government *de facto.* Thus the government of the Commonwealth in England, first by Parliament, and afterwards by Cromwell as Protector, was, by reason of its revolutionary, mundane origin, classed as a government *de facto;* but even in those times its acts were accepted as having legal validity, internally and externally. More than three centuries later, however, the government at Washington was at a particular juncture unable to find in Mexico any government to its liking. There were reciprocal intellectual and emotional repulsions. When, in April, 1914, Vera Cruz was seized, Carranza, the head of the Constitutionalists, though in arms against Huerta, sternly protested. The withdrawal of Huerta, through the friendly mediation of certain American Powers, did not solve the problem. No Mexican leader could accept the tutelage of a foreign government and survive. The skies continued to darken and the confusion to increase. As time wore on, the fallacy of the supposition that the United States might contribute to the restoration or preservation of public order in Mexico, or indeed in any other country, by refusing to recognize as having

4. Beginning with September, 1930, we may cite, as examples, the recognition of new governments in Argentina, Peru, Bolivia, Brazil, Guatemala, Spain, and again in Peru, as officially announced in the Press Releases of September 20, 1930, pp. 192–193; November 8, 1930, p. 322; January 10, 1931, p. 21; April 15, 1931, p. 341, and May 23, 1931, p. 410. Although in several of these cases, no mention whatever was made of the "*de facto*" character of the new government, it is specially gratifying to observe that, in the case of Brazil, the Secretary of State, after referring to the request of "the *de facto* Government of Brazil" for recognition, formally announced that our Ambassador at Rio de Janeiro had been instructed to reply that the United States would "be happy to continue with the new Government of Brazil the same friendly relations as with its predecessors." The term "*de facto*" was thus expressly made to run the entire gamut of legality. It was a welcome relief from the fitful but monotonous discords of "*de jure*" jazz.

authority any government which it did not consider "constitutional," especially in the sense of having been freely and fairly
elected by the whole people, became more and more glaring. Besides, expansive rights and responsibilities had been somewhat
loosely assumed in the name of the Monroe Doctrine. It was
also said that Mexican commanders would be held "personally
responsible" for what they did. All these things, implying a
total negation of local authority, naturally tended to spread
the expectation that the task of governing the country might or
even should be undertaken by the United States itself. In this
unwelcome predicament, political exigencies demanded that
somebody at length be recognized. But the embarrassments
arising from prolonged delay, from possible imputations of inconsistency and failure, and from the uncertainties of a turbu-
lent situation, suggested the need of a special formula; and a
consoling *modus vivendi* was found in the recognition of the
Carranza government late in 1915 as *de facto*, but not *de jure*.
It was not, however, then supposed either by the political or by
the judicial department of the Government of the United States
that this signified that the acts of the Carranza government
were to have no external legal force. This conception fitfully
and uncertainly emerged from another set of political and emotional "reactions."

It is said that international law does not impose upon governments an obligation to recognize other governments, without regard to how they are constituted or how they act. In a
limited sense this is true; but in a general sense it is untrue. In
a general sense international law does impose upon nations the
duty in time of peace to recognize one another's governments
and to practice commercial and diplomatic intercourse. The
fact is notorious that the nations of the West even used force
to compel the nations of the East to do this. It is not easy to
conjecture how international law and the amenities of international life could be preserved if the governments of the world
refused to recognize or to talk with one another.

The theory that courts cannot consider as having external
validity the acts of a government which has not been recognized
as a government *de jure* may be said to lack support either in
principle or in authority. The business of courts is to administer justice not only as between man and man but also as between men and governments, where private rights are involved.
It is true that in doubtful cases, such as that of the Sultan of
Johore, the testimony of foreign offices has been accepted as to
whether a party who claimed exemption from suit as a sovereign really bore that character. But it has not heretofore been
supposed that a foreign state or foreign sovereign might not

seek justice in the courts as regards a contract with an individual, unless diplomatic recognition had been accorded by the government of the country, in which the suit was brought. In a leading case in 1825, a great British judge declared that, if a foreign state was recognized by Great Britain, it was not necessary to prove that it was an existing state; but that, "if it was not so recognized, such proof becomes necessary." [5] Six years earlier a justice of the Supreme Court of the United States, sitting on circuit, declared that national independence might be deduced by the courts from history, and that "no official recognition is necessary." [6]

The soundness of these decisions is hardly open to question. The executive recognition of governments is a political act, and may be delayed for political reasons. Moreover, when once accorded, it may at any time be withdrawn; but, even though this be done as a mark of dissatisfaction or as an act of reprisal, it does not signify that the courts are to suspend their administration of justice. For the termination of relations out of which grow individual rights, there are appropriate means. Commercial intercourse may be legally severed or war may be declared; but, so long as business relations remain lawful, the courts may enforce the rights growing out of them, according to the law by which they are properly determinable.

It is a settled principle that the courts of one country will not undertake to judge the legality of acts of governmental power done in another country. In 1892 there took place in Venezuela a revolution by which the government of President Palacio was overthrown and a new government, under General Crespo, was installed in power. In their march toward Carácas the revolutionary forces under General Hernandez captured the city of Bolivar, where George F. Underhill, a citizen of the United States, was in charge of the waterworks. On entering the city General Hernandez, proclaiming himself as supreme civil and military chief, proceeded to conduct the government. Underhill sought to leave the country, but Hernandez compelled him to remain and run the waterworks. When, two years later, Hernandez visited the United States, Underhill sued him for damages for unlawful arrest and detention. The case came on for trial early in 1895, before Judge Wheeler, in the United States Circuit Court at Brooklyn. As a matter of unrecorded history, I may state that the case was submitted for decision on a brief hurriedly prepared by myself and presented in typewritten form, there being no opportunity to print it. I now have a copy before me, and would not alter anything in it. While it narrated the circumstance that the Crespo government had been diplo-

5. *Yrisarri* v. *Clement*, 2 C. & P., 223, 225 (1825).
6. *Consul of Spain* v. The *Concepción*, Fed. Cas. 3137 (1819).

matically recognized by the United States, it laid no stress on that point, but proceeded upon the fundamental principle that Hernandez was not judicially answerable in the United States for what he did in Venezuela in the exercise of actual governmental power. Judge Wheeler, fully accepting this view, directed a verdict for Hernandez on the ground that, because his acts "were those of a military commander, representing a *de facto* government in the prosecution of a war, he was not civilly responsible therefor."

This judgment was affirmed by the Circuit Court of Appeals and later by the Supreme Court of the United States. In the opinion of the Supreme Court, which was delivered by Chief Justice Fuller, the diplomatic recognition of the Crespo government was said to have a retroactive effect; but one may regard this observation as superfluous, in view of the authority given to the United States Minister at Carácas to recognize the new government, if it was "accepted by the people, in possession of the power of the nation, and fully established." A few days after receiving these instructions, the minister, as the official record states, "fulfilled the formalities of recognition." [7] It was not pretended that the recognition increased the power of the new government or had any creative force. The fundamental principle on which the decision rested, first and last, was thus stated in Chief Justice Fuller's opinion:

Every sovereign State is bound to respect the independence of every other sovereign State, and the courts of one country will not sit in judgment on the acts of the government of another done within its own territory. Redress of grievances by reason of such acts must be obtained through the means open to be availed of by sovereign powers as between themselves. Nor can the principle be confined to lawful *or recognized* governments, or to cases where redress can manifestly be had through public channels.[8]

The same principle was applied by the Supreme Court twenty years later in upholding the validity of titles required by citizens of the United States to property seized in Mexico by Villa in the exercise of military power.[9]

7. *Foreign Relations of the United States,* 1892, p. 635.
8. *Underhill* v. *Hernandez,* 65 F., 577; 26 U. S. App., 573; 168 U. S., 250, 18 S. Ct., 83.
9. *Oetjen* v. *Central Leather Co.,* 246 U. S., 297, 38 S. Ct., 309 (1918), this *Journal,* XII (1918), 421; cf. *Terrazas* v. *Holmes,* 115 Tex., 32, 275 S. W., 392 (1925); *Princess Paley Olga* v. *Weisz,* [1929] 1 K. B., 718.

I forbear to go more extensively into the analysis of judicial decisions on the point now under consideration because this task has been so well performed by Prof. Edwin M. Borchard in his article on "The Unrecognized Government in American Courts," published in this *Journal,* XXVI (1932), 261–271. I desire further to say that I fully concur in all the positions taken and all the comments made by Professor Borchard in that article.

No government could have been more destitute of any *de jure* authority which the United States could recognize than that of the Confederate States. Nevertheless, in *Thorington* v. *Smith* the Supreme Court held that a contract made during the Civil War, between persons residing within those states, for the payment of Confederate States treasury notes could be enforced in the United States courts, the contract having been made on a sale of property in the usual course of business, and not for the purpose of giving currency to the notes or otherwise aiding the Confederate cause.[10]

In deciding this case the Supreme Court observed that the Confederate Government never was recognized by other Powers; that no treaty ever was made with it; that no obligations of a national character were created by it, binding after its dissolution, on the states which it represented, or on the national government; that it was regarded simply as the military representative of the insurrection against the authority of the United States. But, said the court, the fact that it exercised the powers of government within the territory it controlled "made obedience to its authority, in civil and local matters, not only a necessity but a duty," and that "without such obedience, civil order was impossible." Therefore, in the case just cited, and in a series of subsequent cases, the Supreme Court upheld acts done under and in obedience to its authority as well as acts done under and in obedience to the authority of the states of which it was composed.[11]

The general propositions to be deduced from these cases are summed up in *Baldy* v. *Hunter,* and among them is the principle that "judicial and legislative acts in the respective States composing the so-called Confederate States should be respected by the courts if they were not 'hostile *in their purpose* or mode of enforcement to the authority of the National Government, and did not impair the rights of citizens under the Constitution.' " It will be observed that the limitation arising from the "purpose or mode of enforcement," was wholly based upon the constitutional law of the United States and in no respect upon international law.

The supposition that the power rests with the President of the United States or with the executive head of any other country to pronounce upon the *"de jure"* or constitutional status of the governments of other independent states has no basis in legal principles. It is also a practical absurdity. The extraconstitutional "Electoral Commission," composed of fifteen members, on whose report President Hayes was inaugurated in

10. 8 Wall. 1, 9–11 (1868).
11. 1 Moore, *Digest of International Law,* pp. 52–60.

1877, persistently voted 8 to 7. If a country's own statesmen and jurists so evenly divide on questions arising under their own laws, how strange it would be to concede the determination of such questions to foreign rulers. Unfortunately, however, by a kind of chance, the phrase *"de jure"* has lately served in the United States as a "conjure word," which has been defined as a word that betrays us, without thinking and in a superstitious way, into taking things "down in a gulp," without stopping to "pull them apart and see what they really stand for." [12] We therefore need to recur, as Jefferson said, to fundamental principles; and these principles, so far as concerns the present question, may be stated thus:

1. The President, as head of the Executive Department, is, by the Constitution, invested with power to appoint and receive public ministers and consuls, and thus, incidentally, with the power to recognize foreign governments.

2. If the President recognizes a foreign government, the courts, as the constitutional depositary of the judicial power, do not deny to such recognition its constitutional force; but they are not obliged to await it. Intercourse between nations has often gone on for generations without the exchange of acts of recognition by their executive heads. The courts, meanwhile, have enforced legal rights and, incidentally, taken cognizance of the existence of foreign governments as a matter of public notoriety, or on specific proof, as the circumstances might render proper. When accepting public notoriety as sufficient, the courts have instinctively assumed that judges are not forbidden to know what everybody else knows.

3. The President of the United States has no power, either under the Constitution or under international law, legally to decide the question whether a foreign government is *de jure*, or, in other words, established in conformity with the constitution and laws of the country over which it actually rules. While it is not possible to prescribe or to define the considerations or the influences that may actually play a part in the executive determination of the question of recognition, it is certain that the government of an independent state can neither be endowed with a constitutional character nor be deprived of it by the concession or the withholdment of foreign recognition. Such is the law in the United States under the Constitution.

4. The case is the same under international law. International law is enshrined in the Constitution of the United States, but the President is its constitutional interpreter only to a limited extent. He may assert his interpretations in diplomatic dis-

12. *Selected Writings of James Hardy Dillard:* John F. Slater Fund, Occasional Papers, No. 27, p. 57.

cussions or he may instruct the officials of the United States,
especially in time of war, as regards their conduct in international situations. But the power to pass laws binding upon the
courts in such matters is committed to the Congress of the
United States, just as the power to declare war is vested in the
Congress and not in the Executive. The Congress is expressly
invested with the power to define offenses against the law of
nations, and, incidentally, to give to that law an interpretation
legally binding on the courts.[13] But no power is conferred either
on the Congress or on the courts to pass upon the *"de jure"* or
constitutional character of a foreign government and to deny
to its acts "external" force because it was not constitutionally
established, while attributing to its acts internal force because
it is the actual government of the country. Nor can such power
be claimed under international law. The United States no doubt
would regard such an attitude on the part of any foreign authority, whether legislative, executive or judicial, as an affront;
but affronts sometimes may not be followed by extreme consequences. Confusion, however, is an inevitable consequence of
the infringement of fundamental principles, and confusion
should always be avoided.

It never can be out of place or out of date to recur to fundamental principles as declared by great judges whose fame is
associated with the assertion and enforcement of them. When
Chief Justice Marshall declared that "an act of Congress ought
never to be construed to violate the law of nations if any other
possible construction remains," [14] he anticipated by more than
ten years a similar declaration by one of the greatest of British
judges, Lord Stowell, who, in applying an act of Parliament
couched in general terms, limited its operation in such a way as
to avoid a violation of international law.[15] It is a remarkable co-
incidence that, contemporaneously with this utterance by Lord
Stowell, Chief Justice Marshall, in another great case, declared
that, if it were the will of the Government of the United States
to retaliate upon Spain a rule respecting captures which Spain
was said to apply to the United States, the United States would
"manifest that will by passing an act for the purpose," and that
until such an act was passed the court was "bound by the law
of nations," which was "a part of the law of the land." Eye had
not then seen nor ear heard, neither had it entered into the
mind of man, that the law-making, law-interpreting and law-
determining power in the United States was, as regards external matters, vested in the Executive; or that there had been

13. *United States* v. *Arjona* (1887), 120 U. S., 479.
14. *Murray* v. *Schooner Charming Betsey* (1804), 2 Cranch, 64.
15. *Le Louis*, 2 Dodson's Adm., 239.

vested in the United States, and pre-eminently in the President, by any law, national or international, the supreme power to regulate the establishment and observance of constitutional law in other countries, and to bottle up governments not deemed to be *"de jure"* by denying to their acts "external" force.

For the introduction of this novel legal incongruity I am, after a survey of our records, executive and judicial, constrained to award the chief credit to the ingenuity and eloquence of counsel, perhaps aided by the post-war impression that all international law, private as well as public, was obsolete, and by certain other sentiments that somewhat pervaded the circumambient air. According to the universal rule that previously prevailed, acts were interpreted and enforced in conformity with the law properly applicable to them, and this was the law of the place where they were performed or to be performed, or the law by which it was expressly agreed that they should be governed. This rule applied to all countries except those in which foreigners enjoyed a right of extraterritoriality. Recent departures from this rule in the United States may also partly be ascribed to the confusion that began to appear here in 1913 in regard to the meaning and effect of recognition. The mere acknowledgment of the fact that certain persons were actually exercising authority in certain territory began to be spoken of as the "recognition" of a *"de facto"* government." This was a misuse of terms, apparently due to the erroneous supposition that, if *de facto* authorities were not "recognized" as a "government," their acts would be invalid externally if not internally, while, if they were recognized as a government *"de jure,"* all their acts would be completely validated. Very remarkable language of this kind may be found in a dictum in the opinion of Mr. Justice Clarke in the case of Oetjen *v.* Central Leather Company, heretofore cited. The question at issue was whether the courts in the United States had jurisdiction to declare invalid the title to some hides purchased in Mexico by a Texas corporation, early in 1914, from a military commander acting under the authority of the "Constitutionalist" government of Carranza, which was recognized by President Wilson as the *"de facto"* government of Mexico on October 19, 1915, and as the *"de jure"* government on August 31, 1917. The hides, which were seized at Torreon under a general assessment levied in agreement with the local community, formerly belonged to a Mexican citizen, a Huertista, who fled the city on its capture by the Constitutionalist forces. On these facts the lack of jurisdiction was completely established by the well-reasoned decision in *Underhill* v. *Hernandez,* in which no *"de jure"* decoration figures. But, in the course of his opinion, Mr. Justice Clarke went out of his way to remark that, "when a government which originates in revolution or revolt is recognized by the political department of our government as the *de jure* government of the country in which it is established, such recognition is retroactive in effect and validates all the actions and conduct of the government so recognized from the commencement of its existence." By no law, national or international, can such a statement be justified; nor could any statement more vividly exemplify certain erroneous impressions lately prevailing. The supposition that recognition of any kind "validates all the actions and conduct" of the government recognized is as startling as it is novel. Recognition "validates" nothing. On the contrary, it opens the way to the diplomatic controversion of the validity of any and all "actions and conduct" that may be regarded as illegal. In the case of governments, just as in the case of men and women, the recognition of the existence of an individual entity does not imply, either retrospectively or prospectively, that its acts are legal.

No one could believe less than I do in the principle of communism, whether applied in the form of state capitalism in Russia or under any other guise elsewhere. But we are now dealing not with economic questions but with questions of international law. That the Government of the United States has in fact recognized the Soviet Government there can be no doubt. In saying this I do not specially rely upon the circumstance that both governments are with mutual knowledge, desire and satisfaction parties to certain multilateral treaties, including our own Kellogg Pact; but I do have in mind, among other things, the fact that the United States nearly four years ago, pending a controversy between Russia and China, called the attention of the Soviet Government to its obligations under that reciprocal engagement. We did this not indeed directly, but through the French Government; but our dignity would have been saved, and our self-respect would hardly have been lessened, had we made the representation directly, since the indirection of our procedure drew upon us a retort which it was by no means pleasant to read. While the Department of State, apparently using an esoteric formula, has said that it "does not regard the acts and decrees of the Soviet *régime*" as those of "a recognized government," it admits that this attitude "is not based on the ground that that *régime* does not exercise control and authority in territory of the former Russian Empire." From these statements what are we to deduce? Are we to regard the government of the Czar as still ruling over the territory of the former Russian Empire? Are we to regard the meteoric government of Kerensky, who years ago disappeared from Russia, as still ruling the country? Or are we to consider the country as being without a government? An affirmative answer to any of these questions would seem to be impossible on the part of a rational being. What really is meant is that, because there are some particulars in which we do not approve of the government that has for years been in the sole exercise of power in Russia, we have not as yet established diplomatic relations with it.

We are credibly advised that the Soviet Government has so far been recognized by twenty-four Powers in all parts of the world, including all the Great Powers of Europe and some of the highly orthodox lesser ones, such as Sweden, Norway and Denmark. Ten years ago the Permanent Court of International Justice, when consulted concerning a dispute between Finland and Russia, did not hesitate to treat the Soviet Government as the sole national authority and proper international spokesman of the independent Russian state.[16] But, when the Department of State calls the Soviet power a *régime* and not a government, I am not disposed to criticize it. It was said of George Bancroft, who was as shrewd as he was historical, that he often addressed American visitors in German and German visitors in English, thus saving his time and avoiding definite commitments. A Frenchman would not be insulted by calling his government a republican *régime*. Perhaps the Department is to be congratulated on the choice of this word, since, taken with its context, it correctly indicates that, although the Soviet Government exists, we cannot altogether approve it. But the establishment of diplomatic relations with a government never was formerly supposed to imply approval either of its form or of its acts. Our establishment of such relations with the Barbary "Pirates" probably was hastened by our disapproval of what they did, and by our desire to obtain redress.

Well has it been said by Chief Judge Pound, in delivering the opinion of the New York Court of Appeals in *M. Salimoff & Co.* v. *Standard Oil Co. of New York,* decided July 11, 1933 (262 N. Y., 220), that as, according to the view taken by some of our courts, only the acts of a *"de jure"* government, politically recognized as such by the United States, can have extraterritorial effect, corporations non-existent in Russia have been juridically vivified in the United States, and, like fugitive ghosts, endowed with extraterritorial immortality. It is true that the learned Chief Judge adds that the courts may not recognize the Soviet Government "as the *de jure* government until the State

16. Moore, *International Law and Some Current Illusions, and Other Essays* (1924), pp. 124–129, *supra,* pp. 99–103.

Department gives the word." But with all humility I venture to maintain that the supposition that it is the prerogative of the President of the United States to determine the *de jure* character of foreign governments, in the Americas or elsewhere, rests on nothing but an executive *ipse dixit,* which was contrary to our settled practice founded on international law; that this *ipse dixit,* which was not followed by any other government, has in various recent acts of recognition been discarded by our own; and that there is no reason to believe that it was, as our courts have sometimes unfortunately inferred, originally intended to operate as a legal restraint on the exercise by our judicial tribunals of their customary and appropriate powers. In other words, while governments and even sovereignties often have been and still may be described, according to their antecedents, as *de facto* or *de jure,* it is not by this classification that their powers are created and measured, either internally or externally. Moreover, on the doctrine of the *retroactivity* of recognition, as laid down both in *Underhill* v. *Hernandez* and *Oetjen* v. *Central Leather Company,* an anomalous situation would arise if, after "external" force had been judicially denied to the acts of a foreign government because it had not been politically recognized as *"de jure,"* it should be thus decorated. Would not an application for a reversal of judgment then be in order? No such question, however, could occur if heed were paid to the sound doctrine laid down in *Underhill* v. *Hernandez,* in which the court appropriately treated political recognition only as confirmatory proof of the actual existence of the foreign authority and not as a measure of its powers.

But the acts of recognition to which I have heretofore adverted have lately been superseded by a direct recognition of the highest validity. On May 16, 1933, the President of the United States addressed an official message individually and directly to the heads of the world's governments, including that of Russia. The message this time was addressed to the Soviet government, not indirectly through another government, but directly to "President Michail Kalinin, All Union Central Executive Committee, Moscow, Russia." The grand object of the message, as its text recites, was "the improvement of social conditions, the preservation of individual rights, and the furtherance of social justice." In view of the broad scope of this appeal, the message naturally was addressed to the head of each government, and through such head to "the people" of the nation. Each head so addressed was thus expressly recognized as the official organ of the people over whom his government ruled. Chief among the specific measures recommended was disarmament; but, in view of the slow progress that had been made with that difficult and thorny subject, it was proposed that all the nations should immediately "enter into a solemn and definite pact of non-aggression." If the head of the Soviet Government, which is well known to specialize in non-aggression pacts, had immediately and directly telegraphed to the President of the United States, in response to this direct and official appeal, a draft of such an agreement, it is hardly imaginable that, had the *de jure* specter risen from the limbo of a disordered past to counsel its rejection, the President would not instantly have commanded it to avaunt and quit his sight!

In this connection it may be useful to point out that, if recognition is given without specific qualification, it necessarily means full recognition. In other words, our diplomatic representatives are not accredited to the *"de jure* government," or to the *"de facto* and *de jure* government"* of Great Britain, of France, or of any other country. Such an address would savor of burlesque. Credentials addressed to the executive head of the titular government of a state constitute full recognition of his government. Nor can it be pretended that the accrediting of a diplomatic representative is necessary. Such a contention would involve the absurd supposition that the head of a state cannot perform diplomatic acts directly. The head of a state naturally needs no credentials. A diplomatic agent does not carry with him documentary proofs of the authority of the ruler by whom he is accredited. The heads of states take public notice of one another's official character; and when, acting in that character, one of them addresses to another, whether by telegraph, by post, or otherwise, a written communication invoking his official co-operation in a great international undertaking, it is farcical to say that the ruler by whom the communication was officially sent did not fully recognize the government to the head of which the communication was officially addressed.

I have heretofore observed that recognition and withholdment of recognition are often determined by considerations of politics or even of sentiment. In June, 1903, a military revolution took place in Serbia. King Alexander and his Queen were assassinated, and Peter Karageorgevitch was proclaimed as his successor. Shocked by the unusual and afflicting character of this transaction, the European Powers and also the United States delayed the recognition of the new government until May 9, 1904—nearly a whole year. But it never was suggested that the laws and other acts of the government meanwhile had no "external" force; nor was it then imagined that, in order that they might have such force, foreign governments must hide their blushes and glorify the new *régime* as *"de jure."*

During the past thirty or forty years, there has unfortunately crept into some of our judicial decisions the idea that it specially belongs to the Executive Department of the government to determine the questions of treaty interpretation. This impression probably is to be ascribed to the uncritical reading of certain cases in which acts of the "political department" of the government were held to be binding on the courts. This phrase is conspicuous in some of the opinions of Chief Justice Marshall relating to land claims within the territories ceded to the United States by Spain and by France. No one ever maintained the distinction between judicial functions and executive functions more clearly and firmly than did Chief Justice Marshall. But, in the cases I now have in mind, the acts of the "political department" were acts of Congress establishing government within the ceded territory and specifying the area within which they operated. Behind these legislative acts no court was authorized on constitutional or other grounds to go. But, except so far as the courts may be bound by acts of legislation, they are by the terms of the constitution itself interpreters and enforcers of treaties, and are not bound by executive utterances.

Congenitally connected with the supposition that the United States might recognize or refuse to recognize other governments in accordance with its judgment as to whether they were properly conducting their domestic affairs, was the notion evolved from the seizure of Vera Cruz that other countries might be invaded and occupied without the commission of an act of war or breach of the peace so long as the word war was not used in connection with the proceeding. But it can hardly be believed that this view would be taken if the case were reversed. The city of New York is not popular in all parts of the United States. It is the center of the "money power"; it levies toll on what passes through its gates; it is the seat of the great exchange which becomes unpopular when those who resort to it suffer losses. Nevertheless, if it were seized and occupied by a foreign Power as an act of reprisal for what the government at Washington had done, I cannot doubt that the country would unite in regarding it as an act of war. Isolated acts of war do not, I may remark, necessarily result in the creation of the legal condition of things called a state of war. If, however, they are forcibly repelled, there may result a state of war, even though it may not be formally proclaimed as such; and neutral nations may take such measures as the particular conditions seem to require.

The tendency to confuse war and peace and to magnify the part which force may play in international affairs not unnaturally followed the so-called World War. During that great conflict there developed, in the ordinary course of things, a war-madness, manifested in the exaltation of force, and the belittling of the enduring legal and moral obligations which lie at the foundation of civilized life. Peaceful processes fell into disrepute. We began to hear of the "war to end war"; and pacifists, enamored of this shibboleth, espoused the shallow creed that international peace could best be assured by the use of force or threats of force. We were told that pre-existing international law had suddenly become obsolete, and that the world had entered upon a new era in which the general tranquillity was to be maintained by "sanctions," by boycotts, and by war. But the final stage was reached in the spawning of the notion, now rampant, that peoples may with force and arms exterminate one another without breach of the peace, so long as they do not call it war. To this final stage belongs the supposition that the law of neutrality no longer exists, and that in future there will be no more neutrals. On this theory was framed the Arms Embargo Joint Resolution introduced in Congress at the last session, and couched in terms evidently designed to authorize the President of the United States, either alone or in association with other governments, to prohibit the shipment of arms either to both parties to an armed conflict, or to one and not to the other. Fortunately, the Senate Committee on Foreign Relations unanimously adopted an amendment to require the embargo, if proclaimed, to be applied impartially.

As a lifelong student and administrator of international law, I do not hesitate to declare the supposition that neutrality is a thing of the past to be unsound in theory and false in fact. There is not in the world today a single government that is acting upon such a supposition. Governments are acting upon the contrary supposition, and in so doing are merely recognizing the actual fact. In the winter of 1922–23, there was held at The Hague an international conference to make rules for the regulation of the activities of aircraft and radio in time of war. The parties to this conference were the United States, France, Great Britain, Italy, Japan and the Netherlands. I had the honor to represent the United States in the conference and to be chosen to preside over it. We were able in the end to reach a unanimous agreement, which was incorporated in a general report. An examination of this report will show that it was largely devoted to the definition of the rights and duties of belligerents and of neutrals in time of war, and that it treated as still existing the Land War Neutrality Convention, the Convention for the Adaptation of the Geneva Convention to Maritime Warfare, and the Convention concerning Neutral Rights and

Duties in Maritime Warfare, all made at The Hague in 1907. The conference by which the report was adopted took place more than two years after the making of the Versailles Treaty and the Covenant of the League of Nations; the various delegations, it should be needless to state, acted under the authority and instructions of their respective governments; and yet, the idea that the law of neutrality had become obsolete never was suggested. So far as I am aware, not a single party to the Versailles Treaty or a single member of the League of Nations has ever actually taken the position that the law of neutrality is a thing of the past. The principal Powers in the League have on occasion taken precisely the opposite position. The fact is notorious that, after the Greeks were egged on to make war on the Turks and war actually came, Great Britain decided to remain neutral in the conflict, into which Canada and perhaps some of the other self-governing dominions unequivocally announced that they would not be drawn without their consent. In other recent wars Great Britain has pursued a neutral course. Other governments have done the same thing. On February 27, 1933, Sir John Simon, discussing in the House of Commons the embargo, soon afterwards revoked, on the shipment of arms to China and Japan, spoke of Great Britain as a "neutral government," and of the consequent necessity of applying the embargo to China and Japan alike. On the recent declaration of war by Paraguay against Bolivia, Argentina, Chile, and Peru immediately declared their neutrality. No government, so far as I am advised, has repealed its neutrality laws. Those of the United States still remain on the statute books; and, if they are to be repealed, it should be done directly and not by implication or by embarking on a lawless course in the name of peace.

In view of the conclusive proof that the governments of the world, including those that are parties to the Covenant of the League of Nations, still treat the law of neutrality as a subsisting part of international law, it might at first blush seem strange that there should exist in the United States a special cult devoted to the dissemination of the notion, of which doctrinaire reverberations are occasionally heard elsewhere, that the law of neutrality is obsolete. But this phenomenon is easily explained. There are in the United States many persons who, deploring the fact that their government is not a party to the Covenant, ardently desire that it should co-operate with the League, and that it should to that end renounce its rights and escape its obligations under international law, so far as they may stand in the way of the enforcement by the League of any coercive measures, economic or military, which it may see fit to take. The notion that the law of neutrality is obsolete is merely a blindfolding device, spun by wishful or purposeful thinking, to attain that end. As regards the enforcement of the provisions of the "Covenant," the members of the League, and particularly the Great Powers, we may say without reproach, naturally and necessarily consult their interests and convenience as well as physical and other possibilities. So far, there is nothing in their conduct to justify the assumption that governments are now more willing or more able than they have been heretofore, without regard to conditions at home or abroad, to rush to the impartial punishment of friends and foes alike, in the name of justice, supposedly ascertained or actually unascertained. Nor do I believe that the cause of law and order in the world would be advanced by the creation of chaotic conditions in which coercive methods would be promiscuously and emotionally used for the attainment of fancied moral ends.

The law of neutrality is sometimes vehemently denounced as immoral, because, as is said, it obliges governments to refrain from judging the merits of quarrels and aiding those whom they may believe to be in the right. No supposition could be more erroneous. The law of neutrality does not preclude any government from taking part in a war if it sees fit to do so. It merely requires the observance of candor and decency in international dealings, by inhibiting acts of war under the guise of neutrality.

It is obvious that certain recent agitations have been and still are carried on under radically erroneous impressions as to the legal significance of the supply of arms and munitions of war to the parties to armed conflicts. The statement is often made that the trade in contraband is lawful, and the statement is also often made that such trade is unlawful. These statements may seem to be conflicting; but, when properly understood, they are both correct. Because there is much dispute as to what the term contraband includes, and because it has so far been deemed proper to limit the burdens to which a neutral Power is subject, international law has not up to the present time required neutral governments to prevent their citizens from manufacturing, selling and shipping contraband, including arms and munitions of war, in the regular course of commerce. Hence, in the sense that a neutral government is not obliged to suppress such trade, the trade is lawful. On the other hand, however, international law recognizes the right of a party to a war to prevent such articles from reaching its adversary, and, if it seizes them, to confiscate them. In other words, international law, treating the trade as being, in an international sense, intrinsically unneutral and unlawful, permits the parties to the struggle to inflict the penalty, and to this the trader's government cannot object. The trader conducts the business at his peril.

But, while a neutral government is not obliged to suppress the contraband trade of its citizens, it is forbidden itself to supply contraband to a belligerent, and particularly is forbidden itself either to sell or to give to him munitions of war. Neutrality, in the legal sense, embraces not only impartiality, but also abstention from participation in the conflict.[17] The prohibition of the neutral government itself to supply arms and munitions of war is based upon the unquestionable fact that the supply of such articles to a fighting force is a direct contribution to its military resources, and as such is a participation in the war; and, if a government does this, it virtually commits an act of war. If it does this in behalf of one of the parties, it abandons its neutrality and is guilty of armed intervention; and if it does it for both parties, although it may be said to be impartial, it does what neither of the parties themselves can do, namely, fights for each against the other. It is not long since the United States became, through an inadvertent failure to observe these elementary principles, involved in an unfortunate incident affecting a great and friendly American country, the Republic of Brazil. Happily, the intervention quickly ended, as the government in behalf of which it was committed abruptly disappeared, and in a few days we duly recognized its successor, as fifteen other governments promptly did.

From the elementary principles of international law above set forth it necessarily follows that, if a government bans the shipment of arms and munitions of war to one of the parties to an armed conflict and permits it to the other, it intervenes in the conflict in a military sense and makes itself a party to the war, whether declared or undeclared.

Among those who, as I am compelled to believe, would, if they had their way, most effectually isolate us from peace, the most popular method of abolishing war appears to be the boycott. It fell to my lot to live through the days when the word "boycott" had its origin, and I can personally assure those who are now enamored of it that it never was then supposed to have a peaceful import. On the contrary, it was used to denote a type of irregular warfare so exceptionally vicious that the only way adequately to describe it was to bestow on it the name of Captain Boycott, its central figure and victim. Captain Boycott was a land agent in Ireland in the era of the Land League, of "agrarian crime," of the imprisonment of Parnell, and of the Phœnix Park murders. He evicted many tenants, and in re-

17. Moore, *Digest of International Law*, VII, §1288, 863.

taliation his neighbors refused all intercourse with him and his family, would not work for him or trade with him, and would not allow others to do so. In self-defense, which is allowable even under the Kellogg Pact, he asked for and obtained military protection; and with the growth of passion on both sides Ireland came to wear the aspect of a seething cauldron of war-like activities. The world did not then regard this as a step towards peace.

No better exposition of the nature of the boycott can be found than that which is made by my former colleague, Mr. Garrard Glenn, now a member of the law faculty of the University of Virginia, in a recent article entitled "War Without Guns." [18] Setting out with Dr. Johnson's famous injunction, "Let us clear our minds of cant," and himself happily defining cant as the utterance of "an idealist who has ceased to analyze his own processes," he explains the meaning of the boycott with a dialectic force and wealth of illustration that demonstrate his comprehensive acquaintance with the records of human experience and expose the poverty of the "new thought." Recognizing the fact that trade itself may be and often is predatory, he reaches the conclusion that, by reason of employing methods of coercion which war itself employs, and by seeking the ends which war is designed to attain, "the national boycott, in and of itself, *is* war." He admits that this suggestion may be disagreeable if not offensive to some well-meaning persons; but he supports his thesis with reasons that have not been answered. From time immemorial commercial non-intercourse has been regarded as a measure incompatible with friendly relations and provocative of war, and it consequently has often been adopted as an appropriate preliminary to a declaration of war. Nothing could be more inadvertent or more incongruous than the contemplation of it as a peaceful measure.

Equally devoid of a peaceful character are the non-national or non-governmental boycotts enforced by popular or concerted action, as was that in which the term originated. While their avowed object is coercive, no forecast can be made of the methods they may employ, of the extent to which they may be carried, or of the pitch to which popular passions may be raised. In a community thus divided against itself, no one could undertake to be answerable for the consequences. In the general loosening of salutary restraints, honest but reckless resentment and unscrupulous malevolence or greed might be found to unite in the overthrow of justice and order and the suppression of individual liberty. Where unregulated popular action is invoked to accomplish ends which the law either forbids or sanc-

18. *The Virginia Quarterly Review* (July, 1932), p. 388.

tions, no one who retains his balance is safe from the lynching which chartered spite and emotional virtue may administer. By such conditions governments have been and may yet again be put in peril in their external as well as in their internal relations. Some time ago, when a sudden excitement arose over the conflict between China and Japan, and eminent champions of the boycott as a peaceful measure publicly advised its application to the latter country, an active movement was conducted through the mails by a group of individuals for the institution of such a campaign. While this agitation was in progress a person whom I know went to a well-known shop to buy a small piece of silk, with no thought of what its possible origin might be. But, as this highly important transaction was about to be concluded, the cry reverberated, "What! buying a piece of Japanese silk?" and there was suddenly staged a near-riot, from which the innocent victim could only withdraw. Considering the antecedents, nothing could be more logical than such a scene; but it was moblike, disorderly, irresponsible and oppressive, and such as even the laws of war do not tolerate.

But this process, with its infinite capacity to isolate us from the contamination of peace and especially from that of neutrality, is to be sanctified and ennobled by employing it against "aggressors." This is another dulcet and delusive term which has exceptional charm for those who, imagining that the continuity of history has been finally ended, believe that no useful lesson for the future can be gained from the study of wars and their origin. Many efforts have been made to define the aggressor. But I will not examine them in detail on the present occasion, as I have lately discussed them, as well as their intimate connection with proposals for "consultative pacts," in another place.[19] I will, however, remark that there is nothing more easy than to scribble definitions of things that are undefinable, and that, after twelve years of debate, the results of the attempts to define "the aggressor" are chaotic. Some of the proposed definitions are short, and others are long. The Soviet Government has elaborated the longest, but it is lexicographic rather than lucid. The French have perhaps produced the shortest, by defining aggression as "the presence of troops on territory not their own." Nothing could be more sweeping, or leave more to interpretation. The United States has toyed with this definition, with a short amendment that by no means clarifies it. The British Government has absolutely and prudently refused to be trapped by any definition.

The French definition was accompanied with a plan for the

19. "An Appeal to Reason," *Foreign Affairs* (July, 1933), pp. 566–574.

ascertainment of the fact of aggression. Major General Fuller, an eminent British authority on questions of war and of diplomacy, has declared that whoever thought out the French proposal "must have been either a lunatic or a humorist." [20] I cannot wholly concur in this view. I am inclined to think that the author combined with a sense of humor enough of cynicism and craft to know what he was about. The reason of the British Government for refusing to agree to any definition was that, while no one could foresee the elements that a particular situation would present, a Power desirous of committing aggression would be advised as to how it might safely proceed. No term is more elastic or more susceptible of interested interpretation, whether by individuals or by groups, than "aggression." While self-defense is allowed under all systems of law, it is common knowledge that aggression may be the only means of defense. What may be aggression in one instance may by no means be aggression in another instance. Each case must be tried on its merits, and in cases between governments one never can be sure that the production of essential evidence can be obtained. Little by little, year by year, have the documents relating to the antecedents of the war that began in Europe in 1914 dribbled out; and the disclosures have rendered necessary the revision of many impressions previously entertained. The fact is also to be borne in mind that the most vital communications are not always put in writing. When war occurs the parties always denounce one another as aggressors. It is a fundamental principle even of French military strategy, as exemplified by Napoleon and by Foch, that the only chance of victory or of safety may lie in taking the aggressive. Even the people of the United States, who regard themselves as the most peace-loving and long-suffering on the earth, have on numerous occasions been charged with aggression. This was notably the case in our wars with Mexico and Spain.

But a special danger, especially as regards the United States, is the connecting of the determination of "aggression" with a "consultative pact." There are, I believe, few persons who realize the extent to which propaganda has been used in connection with international relations; and there prevails not only in Europe but elsewhere the impression that there is no country so susceptible to propaganda as is the United States. It therefore is not strange that we have been systematically influenced by it to an extent that would be inconceivable in the case of Great Britain, of France, or of Italy. Only this year a

20. "Aggression and Aggressive Weapons," *Army Ordnance* (July-August, 1933), pp. 7–11.

leading English periodical has said: "During the war the astonishingly efficient British propaganda service convinced the Americans of some of the most bizarre fairy tales that have ever been devised. To this day most of the population has not recovered from the alleged information which it then swallowed whole." [21]

The very frankness with which this avowal is made evidently denotes a cheerful confidence that we have not changed; and that, the more we are persuaded to isolate ourselves from international law, the easier it will be to guide us in the special paths which others would provide for us.

In saying this, I am fully conscious that I expose myself to the charge of failing to keep step with the movements of the "new thought," as it is daily manifested, with kaleidoscopic coruscation, at conventions, lectures, dinners, and other public gatherings pervaded by the sentiment that whatever was was wrong, and that, if we would be right, we must break with the past, discard the lamp of experience, and accept the latest emotional illumination. It was in this spirit of exaltation that we adopted the Eighteenth Amendment, which our states are now tumbling over one another to repeal, because it ushered in a reign of lawlessness and corruption so unparalleled in our history as to require additions to the popular nomenclature of criminal activities. In vain was it urged, when the measure was under discussion, that it struck a blow at the very foundations of our constitutional system, and that it would prove to be unenforceable. Such arguments were raucously derided as the reactionary utterances of persons blind to the possibilities of the new era.

With similar incredulity have been treated the utterances of those, no doubt constituting a vocal minority, who, believing that international law still survived and that human nature had not suddenly changed, were unable to accept the supposition that a desirable "world order" could be achieved by the habitual use of the processes of war as agencies of peace. The course of events has afforded to this conception repeated and inviting opportunities to demonstrate its feasibility; and the results, though morally inevitable, have been to some of its special devotees so disappointing as to induce them, in a spirit of exasperation, to offer the United States, with its propensity to youthful adventure, as a possible and blundering sacrifice on the altar of their faith.

What the world most needs today is a return to law, and to the orderly modes of action which the observance of law as-

21. "Anglo-American Friendship," by Herbert Agar in *The Nineteenth Century* (London, January, 1933), pp. 62–69.

sures. In the national sphere, the alternative to law is despotism; in the international sphere, the alternative is anarchy. With law, let us have liberty; and with law and liberty, let us have peace.

## JOHN HAY: AN ESTIMATE[1]

THE present biography of John Hay embodies the results of a candid and conscientious use of the materials in the author's possession. In view of what it reveals, even an enemy of Dr. Dennett, to say nothing of his friends, could hardly suspect him of having suppressed anything. Nor has he set down aught in malice. He feels, as I did, that Hay's previous biographer, Thayer, had sacrificed him to his hero, Theodore Roosevelt, solely on the latter's recounting of his own deeds, as, for instance, in the case of the Venezuelan blockade, which was eventually dramatized as a critical and momentous incident. But Hay was not the only person who thus suffered at Thayer's hands. Taking the Alleghenies as a dividing line, western men in general, including President Mc-Kinley, to whom Dr. Dennett does discerning justice, were, in the words of the Hon. Bardwell Slote, committed to posterity "unhonored," if "unhung."

The actual facts in the case of the Venezuelan blockade are matters of public record; they may be found in the sixth volume of my *Digest of International Law*. The truth, and I know it at first hand, is that, so long as there was no attempt permanently to occupy Venezuelan territory—and on this point the written utterances of the three European blockading powers, and particularly those of Germany, were frankly and publicly accepted—Washington, which had troubles of its own with President Castro, was not specially sorry to see him weaned from his persistent refusal to admit diplomatic interposition in the matters in controversy. As late as November 13, 1902, Hay told the British ambassador at Washington that the United States "could not object" to European powers taking steps to obtain redress from Central and South American countries "provided that no acquisition of territory was contemplated," and this was quoted by President Roosevelt himself in a speech at Chicago on April 2, 1903. These public,

1. Review of *John Hay: From Poetry to Politics*, by Tyler Dennett. Reprinted from *The Saturday Review of Literature*, X, No. 17 (November 11, 1933), 249–251.

notorious facts, to say nothing of others that might be detailed, are altogether incompatible with the day-dream of crisis that later sprang up and flourished in new and favorable soil.

As Dr. Dennett's volume is fresh from the press, I have seen only the review of it in the *New York Herald Tribune*. This review, which is printed as a framework about Alexander's "sketch" portrait of Hay of 1886, bears the headline "A True Gentleman and Scholar in Politics," and opens with the statement that Hay "is remembered today as the author of the 'Pike County Ballads,' of which he was ashamed, and of the 'Bread-Winners,' which he denied, and of the Open-Door Policy, which was his by adoption." This summary is later mitigated by the statement: "Yet his achievements, both in the field of letters and of diplomacy, had substance as well as atmosphere." Although the reviewer probably did not write the headline, it really reflects the emphasis here and there solicitously placed by Hay himself on the word "gentleman."

There are various conceptions of what constitutes a gentleman. The ideal was supposed to be represented by the Chevalier Bayard, who was said to be "without fear and without reproach." But, when President Grant was charged with excessive drinking, the answer that he "drank no more than a gentleman should" was deemed sufficient; and it was once said to the credit of a man of fashion, who became involved in a scandal, that he "perjured himself like a gentleman." While these tests tend to confuse the mind, it is certain that, beginning with Livingston and Jay, under the Articles of Confederation, and with Jefferson, Randolph, Madison, and Monroe, under the Constitution, it can hardly be considered a mark of distinction among our secretaries for foreign affairs to be classed simply as a "gentleman," or, superlatively, as a "true gentleman." Hay in the closing sentence of his eulogy of McKinley said that McKinley "taught us how a gentleman should die." This was in 1902. In 1903 he expressed to Roosevelt in a personal letter the comfort he found in working for a President "who, besides being a lot of other things, happened to be born a gentleman." Here a certain emphasis evidently was laid on the accident of birth. And yet, no contrast could be greater than the patient, even tender, consideration invariably shown to Hay by McKinley, and the jolts which, as Dr. Dennett shows, he often endured from Roosevelt. There is nothing to indicate that Hay ever felt slighted or wounded by anything Abraham Lincoln either said or did; but I am not aware that he ever called Lincoln a "gentleman." Indeed, Dr. Dennett remarks that in Lincoln he "had to overlook many standards upon which he himself set great store." In reality, was not this one of the "mysterious reasons," which Dr. Dennett is at a loss to supply, for Hay's having ended his service at the White House before Lincoln's "great responsibilities," growing out of the war, "were over"? Personally, I consider the last sentence of Hay's otherwise admirable address on McKinley to be the weakest in it. William McKinley, by grace of God, did not need to be catalogued as a gentleman, either living or dying.

Dr. Dennett introduces his narration of Hay's career as Secretary of State by a summary of his achievements. The advantage of this method may be open to doubt. We are told that Hay "obtained the security of an unbroken Alaskan coastline"; "a clear title to the exclusive possession of Tutuila, one of the best harbors in the South Pacific"; "the right by treaty for the United States to build and defend the Panama Canal"; "the acquiescence of England to [sic] American paramountcy in the Caribbean sea"; and "in China, substantial support, until the formation of the Anglo-Japanese alliance in 1902, of the doctrine of the integrity of the Chinese Empire." We are assured that these concessions were accompanied by the hearty good will of England in the transfer of the Philippines to American sovereignty, and that for the whole the United States "conceded a couple of islands on the Alaskan coast; yielded equality of rates through the proposed canal, and surrendered in Samoa a tripartite agreement which had already proved unworkable."

We may consider these claims in the order in which they are stated. Hay no doubt loyally defended the cause of the United States respecting Alaska. As Third Assistant Secretary of State, in the first administration of Cleveland, it fell to my lot to take part in the early informal conferences with Canada on the Alaskan boundary; and, before publishing in the *North American Review,* in October, 1899, my article on that subject, I conferred with Hay and found that he entertained no doubt as to the rights of the United States. The Canadian claim was, in my opinion, peculiarly groundless, even though some of those who urged it may have believed in it. The dispute was submitted, in 1903, not to an arbitral board, but to a joint commission, composed of three citizens of the United States and three British subjects, who were to decide by a majority vote. Hence, no decision could be made unless an appointee of one party should cast his vote in favor of the other. The treaty provided that the appointees should be "impartial jurists of repute," who should "consider judicially the questions submitted to them." Great Britain appointed Lord Alverstone, Chief Justice of England; the Lieutenant-Governor of Quebec, and a British Queen's Counsel. President Roosevelt appointed Elihu Root, Secretary of War; Henry Cabot Lodge, a senator from

Massachusetts, and George Turner, a former senator from the State of Washington. Of Root's eminence as a jurist there could be no question. It does not reflect on Turner to say that he had, in his political career, been a last-ditch upholder of the claim of the United States. Hay, in a private letter to Henry White, expressed special regret over the appointment of Lodge, who, he said, "as if the devil were inspiring him, took occasion last week to make a speech in Boston, one-half of it filled with abuse of the Canadians, and the other half with attacks on the State Department." He further stated that Lodge had insisted on being appointed to the tribunal. A decision favorable to the United States was reached by the casting vote of Lord Alverstone. While the case was pending, a report became current that Roosevelt had declared that, if the tribunal evenly divided, he would at once militarily occupy the territory in dispute. Hay did not approve such manoeuvres; but it was whispered that they influenced Lord Alverstone's vote. Lord Alverstone immediately denounced this insinuation, and the denunciation is repeated in his autobiography. But evil reports have a special capacity for self-perpetuation.

Dr. Dennett, referring to Hay's appointment as Secretary of State, remarks that "Sherman and Day, like Bayard, were easy men to follow," meaning that it was easy to shine by contrast with them. Sherman had been a statesman of great power; but it is true that, when he became the head of the cabinet, his memory had begun to fail. Day, some time after serving as Secretary of State, became a justice of the Supreme Court of the United States; and the record of his competency, independence, and sound judgment in that high station does not need to be supplemented by personal testimony. My associations with him, first in the Department of State and then at Paris, where I had the official title of secretary and counsel to the Peace Commission and fully discharged both functions, were of the closest character; and I feel justified in saying that, during the period of our co-operation in Washington, President McKinley was not troubled with the task, with which Dr. Dennett shows that he was later burdened, of revising diplomatic drafts. As for Bayard, had he never been Secretary of State, there is small likelihood that there would ever have fallen to Hay the perfunctory part of accepting the allotment of Tutuila, of which Dr. Dennett speaks as "one of the best harbors in the South Pacific." Strictly speaking, the harbor in question is the bay of Pago-Pago, in the island of Tutuila.

As I was officially connected with the Samoan controversy in its early stages and afterwards, I could narrate its entire history from personal recollection. But this would be superfluous, as there has just been published an authentic and exhaustive history of the subject by Dr. G. H. Ryden, of the University of Delaware. Both Germany and Great Britain recognized the ancient rights of the United States in the harbor of Pago-Pago, and the partition of the group, under which Tutuila fell to the United States, was desired by both, in their own interest as well as in that of the natives. Nor was there any opposition by Germany or by Great Britain to our acquisition of the Philippines. Great Britain earnestly desired it. No American had anything to do with the creation of this sentiment. The great engineering strike in England having resulted in the transfer to Germany of a profitable market in the Philippines, Great Britain dreaded that, unless the United States took over the islands, Germany might obtain from Spain preferential rights in them, if not their actual cession. Did space permit, I might enlarge on this subject. But I have yet one thing more to say concerning Bayard. With an aggressive courage and constructive force such as Hay had no occasion to exhibit either under McKinley or under Roosevelt, Bayard initiated and fought for the amicable and final settlement of the age-long dispute as to the North Atlantic fisheries that was incorporated in the Bayard-Chamberlain treaty of February 15, 1888. The treaty was debated by the Senate in open session, in the midst of a presidential campaign, with great partisan rancor. It was not ratified; but, with the *modus vivendi* that accompanied it, it brought tranquillity. On January 27, 1909, Elihu Root and James Bryce signed, at Washington, an agreement under which all the questions at issue were referred to the Permanent Court of Arbitration at The Hague. Not only did the award sustain Bayard's contentions, but it incorporated, in important particulars, the very terms of the unratified treaty. Bayard also made the first proposal, which was eventually carried out, for the protection of the fur seals in Bering Sea by joint international action.

The first Hay-Pauncefote Treaty was signed at Washington on February 5, 1900. It was based upon and sought to perpetuate the great principle of neutralization or, as some say, internationalization, that was enshrined in the Clayton-Bulwer Treaty of April 19, 1850. The only material departure was the concession to the United States of the right directly to construct and manage the canal, and to protect it by military police against lawlessness and disorder. In 1850 it was not believed that the federal government could constitutionally engage in such an enterprise on foreign soil. But constitutional views had changed. On the other hand, the opening of the Suez Canal, which the British Government substantially owned and actually controlled, modified the attitude of that government towards the ownership, if not the control, of the transisthmian canal by the United States. The Hay-Pauncefote Treaty was negotiated as well as signed at Washington. It seems that some kind of a draft was discussed in London, but Dr. Dennett has been unable to discover by whom the draft as signed was presented.

Immediately after my return from Paris, towards the end of December, 1899, Hay confidentially handed to me a draft of the treaty. Only one or two verbal changes were afterwards made in it. The draft was written on the paper of the British embassy. Pauncefote was a master of the subject. He had conducted in Europe, as the representative of his government, the negotiations relating to the Suez Canal convention of 1888. He needed no instructions. In saying this I do not intend to disparage Hay. As Dr. Dennett points out, I publicly defended the treaty, and my defense was reprinted as a pamphlet by the Department of State. Unfortunately, Hay had not conferred with senators and other persons of political importance, and taken them into his confidence. He assumed that the treaty would be approved by the Senate. Among the first to denounce it was a member of his particular coterie in Washington-Theodore Roosevelt. Public feeling rose high. The treaty was radically amended by the Senate, and the changes were substantially accepted by the British government. The treaty, as thus altered, was signed at Washington on November 18, 1901. In yielding to the requirements of the Senate, the British Government probably was influenced by the fact that the terms of the convention of 1888, by which the Suez Canal was ostensibly neutralized, had, as the British Foreign Office in 1898 publicly informed the House of Commons, "not been brought into practical operation."

The account given of Hay's conduct during the Boer War can scarcely enhance his fame. The intimation, even without accompanying particulars, that his espousal of the British cause was "probably" no inconsiderable factor in his success in obtaining concessions from England in matters of more immediate interest to the United States might be more impressive, were it not followed by the further interpretations that he was never an "underdog" man; that his associations in America were with those who had, rather than with those who had not; that his friends in England were chiefly Tories and always among the ruling classes; that he believed in the British Empire, and had great regard for its wealth and power; that the harrowing details of the Cuban concentration camps had not disturbed him, any more than had the evils of slavery thirty-five years before—and more to the same effect. Most significant of all is the letter he wrote to the United States minister at The Hague, urging him discreetly and indirectly to have the impression conveyed to ex-President Kruger, then an exile in Holland, that it would not be to his advantage to visit America, especially as he would be most warmly welcomed by assailants of the administration. No wonder that McKinley, on learning what had been done, directed that the minister be requested to consider the letter "as not written," and to return it, together with the letter conveying the request.

Naturally and, we may say, inevitably a chapter in the present biography is devoted to the recognition of Panama, and the events that preceded and followed it. The impression is expressly conveyed that the transaction was not altogether honorable. It is said to be "doubtful whether Roosevelt and Hay, without the Senators, could have saved the honor of the American Government," and that the United States "never had a Secretary of State who would have been able to do it alone." No doubt there were senators who preferred the Panama to the Nicaragua route, and the Senate necessarily had to act on the treaty with the Republic of Panama that was substituted for the treaty which the Colombian Congress had refused to ratify; but there is nothing to show that any senator was consulted concerning the recognition of the Republic of Panama, authorized by Hay's telegram of November 6, 1903, after what Dr. Dennett calls the "opera bouffe revolution staged" in the cities of Panama and Colon on November 3 and 4. It is intimated that Hay did not himself fully approve of what was done, and that he "had for months been merely a chip driven on the waves of a 'cosmic tendency.'" Certain passages are cited to prove this. Nevertheless, there is quoted a letter to James Ford Rhodes of December 8, 1903, in which Hay said: "I had no hesitation as to the proper course to take, and have had no doubt of the propriety of it since." Moreover, seven months later, in the address delivered on July 6, 1904, at Jackson, Michigan, in celebration of the founding of the Republican party, Hay declared that Roosevelt "struck while the iron was hot on the anvil of opportunity, and forged as perfect a bit of honest statesmanship as this generation has seen."

Perhaps these expressions of entire and even enthusiastic approval may to some extent be reconciled with mental dissent by accepting Dr. Dennett's view that Hay was "never a very ardent fighter for his opinions." Perhaps a further reconciliation may be found in Hay's private description of the Colombian politicians as "greedy little anthropoids." But, this was not the language of statesmanship. While disputes over money have often impelled governments to go to war, claims of national right are not established by opprobrious epithets. Dr. Dennett exposes as an imposture on the part of the Administration the celebrated telegram, sent to the American consul-general at Tangier in 1904, for the delectation of the Republican national convention then sitting at Chicago, demanding "Perdicaris alive or Raisuli dead." This was at best a cheap bit of political clap-trap of an uncommonly low order. Hay signed the telegram, but left it to Roosevelt to decide whether it should be sent. I venture to believe that, if Hay had taken a firm stand, his refusal to send such a message would not have produced a cabinet crisis. A profound change in our attitude towards Latin America took place when Root became Secretary of State. That he pursued his own counsels no one has ever doubted.

On the exchange of notes concerning China in 1900–1901, and the acquiescence of England in American paramountcy in the Caribbean, it is not possible on this occasion to speak at length. But it is plain that, apart from the Hay-Pauncefote Treaty, as amended by the Senate, nothing decisive in either matter was done by the United States from 1900 to 1904. The phrase "open door," as applied to the Far East, had long been in use, and was only a later designation of a commercial policy applied by Great Britain when, on acquiring Hong Kong, nearly sixty years before, she made it a free port. It was the basis on which the European powers afterwards co-operated in using force to open China to trade. Later came the spheres of interest, the threatened break-up of China, and the precautionary, if not preliminary, acquisition of European strongholds. When, at length, Japan in 1904 declared war on Russia, the latter had established her power over Manchuria, and was reaching out for Korea. No American, no European, power stayed the Russian advance, although Japan in resorting to arms was soothed and sustained by her British alliance. It is certain that, as regards the Far East, there has lately been a tendency in the United States to accept fictitious phrases at imaginary values. A similar tendency has been exhibited even as regards Europe. To this process of mental inflation I do not intend to intimate that Dr. Dennett has contributed or succumbed. I mention it chiefly as a caution to those who would unadvisedly gamble on the great diplomatic bourse.

On one point I venture to expostulate. Dr. Dennett represents the Department of State, when Hay became its head, as "an antiquated, feeble organization, enslaved by precedents" and inherited "routine," abhorring the typewriter as "a necessary evil" and the telephone as "an instrument of last resort," and "hardly adequate to the new responsibilities of the United

States as a world power." For what I deem to be good and sufficient reasons, I have consisently maintained that the United States has always been in the highest sense a world power. But I am not just now concerned with that question, or with the question whether the use of typewriters and telephones in diplomacy has contributed to the present happy state of international relations. What I have in mind is the old Department, as I knew it by personal contact, by personal study of its records, and by personal testimonies not preserved in books.

Dr. Dennett speaks of Hunter and Adee as the incorporation of whatever was continuous in American foreign relations for about three-quarters of a century. I knew them both. My first year in the Department was spent in Adee's office, though I worked for the most part directly with the Secretary of State and with the solicitor, Dr. Wharton. The next year Hunter died. Adee was appointed to succeed him, and I was made Third Assistant Secretary. Adee and Hunter were remarkably unlike. Dr. Dennett says that Adee was "a good imitator, and could so merge his personality with that of his superior that no one could tell in the final draft where Adee's red-inked interlineations had been inserted." In this there is much truth, but the quality of imitation does not determine policies. Adee probably most influenced decisions when he served with Hay, his former associate at Madrid, whose literary instincts he shared. Hunter served the Department fifty-seven years, and from time to time held most of the important positions in it. In his stalwart frame there was an element of iron, and his mind was similarly tenacious. For many years he was the only and indispensable guide to the Department's records, as well as the repository of its traditions and a responsible draftsman of its instructions and notes. Bancroft Davis, a great Assistant Secretary, and John H. Haswell, founder of the Bureau of Archives and Indexes, often recounted to me his invaluable services, which were on occasion publicly attested by Secretaries of State, such as Seward, Fish, and Evarts. His career may fitly be likened to that of old Hammond, of the British Foreign Office, who retired, however, after he had served for fifty years. In efficiency, I feel at liberty to affirm that the standard reached by the Department in the years 1886–89, when Bayard was its laborious head, Francis Wharton its solicitor, George L. Rives its Assistant Secretary, Adee its Second Assistant Secretary, and myself its Third, has never been surpassed. In my own behalf I would plead only twelve to fourteen hours a day of strenuous work. Wharton, a prodigy in industry, was world-renowned for his knowledge of law and of history, while

Rives, who had exceptional capacity for business, deserves to be ranked with Bancroft Davis among the great Assistant Secretaries.

In closing my review of Thayer's book, I remarked that, although I did not have with Hay a long, continuous, and intimate association, I happened to be thrown with him at times when he was under much stress, as in the summer of 1900; and that I had formed of him an impression more serious and more favorable than that which Thayer's account, which was perverted by his own attitude towards later events and by his preference for other individuals, would justify. Dr. Dennett has distorted nothing and omitted nothing. We cannot censure his sympathetic attitude towards a man not of robust physique, with a highly delicate and sensitive mental organization, given to moods of effervescence as well as of depression, who, in positions of public responsibility, strove to achieve worthy ends. On the record as presented, he can hardly rank with the Secretaries of State who, being masters in their own household, have originated policies and carried through specific measures, such as the great Treaty of Washington of May 8, 1871, that mark the turning points in our diplomatic history. For such achievements definite conceptions, fixity of purpose, constancy in action, and a determination to conciliate as well as to bear down opposition, are indispensable.

# BOOK REVIEWS

THE MISSION TO SPAIN OF PIERRE SOULÉ, 1853–1855:
A STUDY IN THE CUBAN DIPLOMACY OF THE
UNITED STATES. *By* AMOS ASCHBACH ETTINGER, *Some-
time Instructor in History, Yale University, Fellow of the
Royal Historical Society, London.* New Haven, Yale Uni-
versity Press, 1932. Pp. xi, 559. $4.00.

The Cuban diplomacy of the United States may be divided
into two parts, that which preceded our Civil War, and that
which has followed it. Such a division is by no means to be confined to our Cuban diplomacy; but this is a subject which limitations of space forbid me now to discuss, as it would involve
a consideration of the associations, professions, and shib-
boleths by which certain underlying and persistent tendencies
may at present be disguised. It is, however, a fact that, as regards our diplomacy prior to the Civil War, Soulé's brief diplomatic adventure at Madrid, although it has a strong personal
flavor, most vividly illustrates certain prewar trends of our
diplomacy, and of contemporaneous European diplomacy as
related to American diplomacy.

It is for this reason that the present work, which embraces
the results of an intelligent, indefatigable, exhaustive examination of both European and American sources, official and
unofficial, published and unpublished, has, as an illuminant,
an importance wider than its titular description would convey.
A Frenchman transplanted by chance to the United States by
way of Haiti, where he was suddenly and radically converted
to the view that the Negro race was outside the conception of
human liberty which he had before so valiantly championed,
Soulé found in Louisiana a congenial atmosphere and full opportunity for the display of his exceptional gifts. As an immi-
grant without pecuniary means, he naturally had at first a
hard struggle; but he was one of those aggressive and restless
personalities who, wherever they go, inevitably figure in sensa-
tions, gaining friends and making enemies, but on the whole
winning popularity as one of the resounding players in the
drama of the day. With these qualities he fought his way to the
top; and in the space of eight years, from 1847 to 1855, was
twice elected to the United States Senate, and achieved at

Madrid, as minister and duelist, a career unexampled in the diplomacy of the United States.

Soulé's appointment to Madrid Dr. Ettinger correctly attributes, as I think, to the expansionists who wanted Cuba, among whom Caleb Cushing influentially figured, and the "Young America" group, who demanded diplomatic appointments as a solace for the loss of cabinet positions. In reality, Dr. Ettinger, following Schouler, says "slave-holding" expansionists; but I cannot unreservedly accept this limitation. No slaveholder ever sang the beneficent effects of the expansion of the United States over "vast regions" to the south and the west, including the "purchased conquests," as the Supreme Court called them, of Mexican territory in 1848, with a sweeter or more sonorous eloquence than did the conservative Whig, Edward Everett, in declining in 1852 the invitation to the United States to sign the self-denying tripartite treaty. At an earlier day John Jay, an antislavery man, sang in similar strain the past performances and future prospects of "our western sons of liberty." Twenty years ago, in my *Four Phases of American Development*, I ventured (p. 174) the opinion that, but for the controversy concerning slavery, there would have been no appreciable opposition in the United States to the acquisition of Texas or of California and New Mexico, the general sentiment in favor of continental expansion being sufficient, as it was in the case of Louisiana, to overwhelm any local antagonism to the disturbance of the balance of power in the Union. The late Judge Gresham, antislavery man and Union soldier, who had a brother in the Mexican War, more than once remarked to me that the war spirit swept down the valley of the Ohio like a fire across the prairies. Lincoln suffered a political eclipse in Illinois because of his criticisms of the war, although he voted for the appropriations to carry it on. Von Holst has familiarized us with "slavocracy" and "slavocrats" as forces in our constitutional development; but, while they undoubtedly bore a definite relation to the Civil War, which hung on constitutional questions, they only shared, with some objective distortion, the expansionist spirit that accounts for modern as well as for ancient empires; the spirit that, for instance, impelled France, during the Civil War in the United States, to endeavor to subjugate Mexico. Perhaps one may, in the light of that significant episode, conjecture that the Monroe Doctrine, though now and then perverted, has tended to limit the disturbance of the peace of the western hemisphere.

Of the conduct of William L. Marcy, Pierce's Secretary of State, in the matter of the dismissal of Horatio J. Perry, secretary of the legation at Madrid, Dr. Ettinger takes a very unfavorable view, intimating, as I understand him, that Marcy's plea that the private exhibition of Perry's confidential letters was due to a "leak" elsewhere than in the Department of State was not well founded. But, even though my interpretation on this point may be wrong, I may say that there was such a "leak." On investigating this question forty years ago I learned from the late Dr. James C. Welling, the last editor of the *National Intelligencer,* and, at the time of the Soulé mission, assistant editor of that journal, that the disclosure was made through Perry's personal friend, Severn Teackle Wallis, a member of the Baltimore bar and author of two works on Spain, published in 1850 and 1853, to whom Perry, apprehensive lest his letter to Pierce, which duly appeared in the *National Intelligencer,* might lead to his sudden dismissal, sent copies of the confidential papers to be used, publicly or privately, in his justification. It was done privately, but unsuccessfully. What Dr. Welling told me was afterward confirmed by Mr. Wallis himself, who, indeed, gave me the papers!

On certain questions, including that of the extension of slavery, Marcy was more than suspected by dominant members of his party. Treading warily, he was sometimes obliged to subordinate strong personal sentiments to broad considerations of the general interest, as he did by remaining in office after Pierce, against his earnest remonstrance, recognized the Rivas-Walker government in Nicaragua. Cabinet members, as the final decision rests with the President, are peculiarly exposed to such a predicament. They must also consider the attitude of the Senate and of senators. Surveying Marcy's unusual record of varied and important achievements, we may feel thankful that, while quietly puncturing the Ostend Manifesto, peacefully adjusting disputes with Spain, and otherwise outmaneuvering his enemies, he avoided a final breach with his chief.

Reprinted from *The American Historical Review,* XXXVIII (1933), 343–345.

BOYCOTTS AND PEACE. *A Report by the Committee on Economic Sanctions. Edited by* EVANS CLARK. New York, Harper & Brothers, 1932. Pp. xx, 381. $4.

FORCE IN PEACE. *By* ALBERT E. HINDMARSH. Cambridge, Harvard University Press, 1933. Pp. xii, 249. $2.50.

PEACE PATROL. *By* LT.-COL. STEWARD RODDIE, C.V.O., *with an Introduction by* SIR ALMERIC FITZROY. New York, G. P. Putnam's Sons, 1933. 327 pp. $3.50.

It is fortunate, or unfortunate, according to the spirit of the times in which one lives, to have a memory. In my youth a man who remembered what he had seen or what he had read, especially if he had reflected upon it and grown wise, was highly esteemed. But—just now—such a person is in the same predicament as Caesar, Hannibal, Cato and other ancient worthies, who, as one of Congreve's characters declared, "would, if now alive, be nothing in the world, Sir; nothing in the world!" Unfortunately—just now—I happen personally to recall the times of Captain Boycott and the amiable activities of which he was the exemplar and also the victim; activities so exceptionally peaceful and productive of harmony that it was thought that the best way to identify them for future generations was to bestow upon them his name. It was the era of the Land League, of "agrarian crime," of the imprisonment of Parnell, of the Phoenix Park murders. Captain Boycott was a land agent. He evicted many tenants. Reciprocating his gentleness, they and their neighbors refused all intercourse with him and his family, would not work for him or trade with him, and would not allow others to do so. But the obstinate man, instead of receiving these attentions in a friendly spirit, asked for and actually obtained military protection; and, with the growth of passion on both sides, conditions got worse instead of better.

With a vision narrowed by these personal recollections, when I read the title *Boycotts and Peace,* I at first thought that this unusual association of names was a flash of Celtic humor; but, on examining the text, I found that it was a revelation of the new psychology, of the new "will to peace," which, in a world distracted by recent wars from the effects of which it is still acutely suffering, demands more war for its cure. I say more war, for war is nothing but a contention by force, and may as such be limited in its methods and in its extent. But the new psychology disdains these refinements, and would abolish war by calling it peace.

The contents of the volume are not of the same handiwork. They differ in texture and in quality. There is information concerning international loans, imports and exports, military equipment and capacity, foreign investments, the dependence or independence of various countries as regards military supplies, the war resources of various nations and their petroleum resources and requirements, all of which is useful in estimating their power to inflict injury as well as to repel it. Nothing could be more useful to nations, or at any rate to some of them, as a guide in making such military preparations as might presumptively enable them to survive the attempt to carry out the new peace programme.

This programme may now be presented. In a foreword called a "Note," by the editor, Mr. Clark, we are told that the word "boycotts," as used in the title, "refers to joint and simultaneous official embargoes against an offending nation by the other leading powers of the world, enforced under mutual agreements of each of them through their own customs and port authorities," as distinguished from measures undertaken by unofficial individuals or groups "or by single governments acting independently," and does not "imply the use of armed forces through military or naval blockades or otherwise"; that the word "sanctions" means "penalties prescribed by international treaties and agreements for their violation"; and that the phrase "economic sanctions" means "penalties which involve an economic loss or disadvantage to the nation which breaks a treaty." It should be obvious even to a casual reader that these supposed definitions furnish not the slightest help to the determination of what should be done in a particular instance. They speak of embargoes against "an offending nation by the other leading powers of the world." But, suppose there should be two or more "offending" nations; and suppose they should form a majority of the "leading powers." These powers are not enumerated. We are left to conjecture whether they include, for instance, Russia, which certainly shows no disposition to be led. But they assuredly embrace the "Great Powers"; and there is nothing more notorious than the fact that the Great Powers, although accustomed to act in combination, are prone to split into groups, just as they are now, on questions fundamentally affecting their particular interests. In consequence, the barest suggestion of coercion as among themselves necessarily excites the gravest apprehension. It is only against weak powers that irritating measures can be employed with a moral assurance of impunity. Stronger powers resent, resist, and retaliate. Would the United States change front and confess itself a sinner on the threat of a

boycott or an embargo? I say "confess," and I say it deliberately. For a capital defect of the present volume is the
assumption, which vitiates its whole thesis, of the possibility
of a unanimity of opinion such as never has existed or ever
will exist until human nature shall have undergone a radical
change.

Nor is it conceivable that boycotts could be effectively applied without the use of armed force through military or naval
blockades "or otherwise." There is nothing stronger than the
propensity to trade, and the attempt to prohibit its indulgence
inevitably gives rise to smuggling. With our melancholy experience with prohibition staring us in the face, how can anyone in the United States be blind to this fact? Our government
frankly recognized it in persuading various other governments
to consent to the extension of the right of search for the purpose of catching "rum runners." And how was this done, or
attempted to be done? By armed forces. The notion that official
"boycotts," official trade embargoes, can be made effective
without the use of armed force, on land and on sea, is altogether visionary. There would also arise questions of destination, of "continuous voyage," and, as a last resort, of ration-
ing, all involving visit and search on the high seas, the intelligent abolition of which in time of peace proved to be a great
step towards the establishment of international order and
tranquillity. Measures of war cannot be converted into measures of peace by giving them pacific titles. This is shown by
experience with "pacific" blockade, which has resulted in war
when tried against large powers and sometimes even when
tried against feeble ones. History furnishes numerous instances in which small states have heroically asserted what
they believed to be their rights against attempts at coercion
by larger states. I would suggest, as the proper title of the
present volume, "Boycotting Peace."

*Force in Peace* is a less pretentious volume, but is thoughtful and soberly reasoned, is compact with pertinent information, and clearly analyses the difficult problems which the new
psychology deftly evades with unjustified assumptions and
mystic phrases. Treating self-defense as the opposite of "aggression," the author quotes Mr. Stimson's statement that the
limits of self-defense "have been clearly defined by countless
precedents"; and then, instead of giving way to emotion,
calmly remarks that it would be "interesting to know" what
these "countless precedents" are, as "a clear definition of self-
defense has been the object of an immense amount of endeavor
by the League of Nations in its futile attempt to define aggression." There once was a popular ballad, which, as I recall

it, told of a man who went up in a balloon to visit the stars and sail around the moon; but not, I believe, in search of statistics. Statistics are of the earth, earthy; and, in spite of the fact that, if and when obtained, they are not always exhilerating, the author is justified in asking for them. He cites M. Briand in a delphic effort to define aggression, for the delectation of an audience at Geneva. "A cannon shot," said M. Briand, "is a cannon shot"; and "you can hear it, and it often leaves its traces." Then, conjectures M. Briand, the League says "Cease fire"; and, "if one of the adversaries refuses, we can surely say that he is not really very anxious about peace." I have great respect for M. Briand, and if this was the best so able a man could do, the case must indeed be desperate. No doubt a cannon shot is a cannon shot. But, if the adversary who ceased fire on Geneva's command should then get killed or disabled, he neither could nor would feel grateful, nor would his example inspire enthusiasm. Besides, even if Geneva had large military forces of her own in Europe, and they were not already preoccupied with exerting a peaceful influence in that quarter, it is a long way, I will not say to Tipperary, but, for instance, to Singapore; and decisive wars have often been of brief duration.

I associate *Peace Patrol* with the two foregoing volumes because it so aptly illustrates the peace-creating effects of force exerted in the idealistic sense of "war to end war." The author, who rendered gallant service and received wounds in the war, was sent by the British War Office to Germany immediately after the war to aid in supervising that country's disarmament, and he later was chief of one of the sections of the Inter-Allied Commission of Control. In his first report to England, he advised the raising of the "blockade," declaring that "the policy of continuing the starvation of Germany" appeared "not only senseless, but harmful to ourselves." Nowhere, he says, were he and his associates "treated with anything but tolerance and courtesy." Had the spirit of this soldier animated the politicians and praters of peace who the next year, at Versailles and elsewhere, proclaimed and exemplified the gospel, not of magnanimity and reconciliation, but of vengeance in forms sometimes even grotesque, the world would have been spared most of the agonies it has since suffered, and the principal perils to which it is now exposed.

Reprinted from the *Yale Law Journal*, XLII (1933), 1294–1296.